IN PURSUIT OF PRIVILEGE

To four teachers who made a difference:

William Westfall

Glen E. Holt

Joel A. Tarr

Kenneth T. Jackson

CONTENTS

....

INTRODUCTION

....

The Upper Class Is
a Foreign Country

L ike many other historians, I quote the adage "The past is a foreign country: they do things differently there" to let audiences
know that they should not expect the people we are discussing
to think and feel in the same ways we do.[1] That line is the first sentence
of a novel L. P. Hartley wrote about the British upper class in 1953. It is
the history of the upper class, Hartley was really saying, that is a foreign
country.

This book explores the foreign country that is the New York City upper
class. A notable example of its customs and practices was the Bradley
Martin costume ball of February 1897. Every year in New York City during
the 1890s, dozens of upper-class families spent from $50,000 to $100,000
apiece throwing parties, receptions, and other entertainments, and a handful, including the Bradley Martins, laid out more than $150,000 (equal to
$4.4 million today).[2] For their 1897 gala, the Bradley Martins ordered so
many orchids, lilies, violets, and other flowers to decorate the ballroom
of the Waldorf Hotel, at Fifth Avenue and Thirty-Fourth Street, that
greenhouses in New York City could not meet the demand and carloads
of blossoms had to be brought in from elsewhere. Intended to replicate
the glamour of the French royal court at Versailles, the ball was attended

by more than eight hundred men and women from high society, most of them dressed as European royals, nobles, knights, and courtiers from the sixteenth to eighteenth centuries. Bradley Martin went as Louis XV of France; his wife, Cornelia, went as Mary, Queen of Scots; John Jacob Astor IV, as Henry IV of France; and Ava Astor, as Marie Antoinette.

However, because the affair happened during a severe industrial depression and because the Bradley Martins insouciantly declared that their lavish expenditures would aid the poor by invigorating the urban economy, a backlash occurred: newspapers condemned the ball; clergymen criticized it from their pulpits; and some of those who had been invited, such as Theodore Roosevelt, then president of the New York City Board of Police Commissioners, stayed away rather than court public censure. The Bradley Martins, who received death threats and had to hire body-guards for protection, eventually left New York and moved to London.[3]

"What can explain," asked the *New York World*, "the extraordinary attention attracted to the Bradley Martin ball and the excitement created by it not only in this country but across the ocean as well?" According to the *World*, "this foolish and costly fancy-dress ball" showed "that we have in this young country, this democratic-Republic, a firmly established aristocracy—one as exclusive and as intolerant and as extensive as any in Europe, with no basis except wealth and a generation or two away from a plebian parent or grandfather." The outpouring of popular anger confirmed that many other Americans reviled the emergence of this new "tyranny of fashion, of wealth, of snobbery, and a recognized 'society'" and the concomitant weakening of democratic and egalitarian values.[4]

Upper-class New Yorkers like the Bradley Martins tried hard to create a separate and exclusive world for themselves, but they kept being assailed by the forces of economic growth and democracy and compelled to alter course. Their relentless pursuit of privilege was what made them different, and it is why the life they created for themselves can be considered a "foreign country." They had their own culture, their own practices, norms, and aspirations, and they were different not just from other New Yorkers but from other urban upper classes in other cities. Compared to other elites in the United States and Europe, upper-class New Yorkers have been more receptive to new people and ideas and much bolder in their quest for wealth, prestige, and power.

An initial colonial upper class that modeled itself on European norms started to run headlong into American capitalism and democracy by the 1790s and then spent the next two centuries trying to figure out how to handle that whipsaw. In the process it became more complex and more malleable while at the same time working feverishly to preserve its exclusivity, especially from the middle class that began to gain in numbers and status in the mid-nineteenth century. The tension between the pressures of American economic dynamism and democratic culture, on the one hand, and the enticements of exclusivity and superiority, on the other, is the focal point of this book.

What distinguished the New York upper class from the outset is that its members were comparatively dynamic, open, and aggressive (much like New York City) as opposed to the stuffy, family- and pedigree-oriented upper classes found elsewhere in America and Europe.[5] Members of the New York City upper class behave like this not so much because they are civic-minded (though at times they are) but because they pursue wealth, prestige, and power; in other words, they seek personal gain. Throughout their history, their salient trait has been that they keep their eyes on the "main chance," however it may present itself. And when they do strive for social pedigree, when they do comport themselves as if they were true aristocrats, they do so not so much because they believe in a true aristocracy but because it helps legitimate and thus strengthen their pursuit of wealth, prestige, and power. In the process, they help to shape the distinctive character of their city, just as they are reciprocally shaped by it.

Throughout its history the upper class has employed a number of strategies to distinguish itself from different social groups (including others of high status) and to build community and create meaning for its members. I concentrate on two particular categories, the "upper class" and "economic elites." The upper class consists of individuals who are tied together by family, friendship, and business bonds; are self-conscious in their possession of prestigious goods; and lead a distinctive way of life. The economic elite comprises people who make key economic decisions and those who provide support for the decision makers and who are connected by their pursuit of wealth and income.[6] In New York City, both the upper class and economic elites formed communities and possessed their own values, practices, and aspirations. The two groups interacted in complicated ways: sometimes they overlapped, cooperated, and shared; sometimes they separated and clashed.[7]

At heart, the mode of classification employed in this book involves a cultural phenomenon because it hinges on the judgments and perceptions of contemporary elites and nonelites. Even after New York City began growing in the nineteenth century, there would be no American equivalent to publications like *Debrett's Peerage* and *Burke's Peerage, Baronetage, and Knightage* that order and rank the hierarchies of titled European families with precision and authority. Assessments of the bona fides of American elites are inherently subjective, and nowhere is that more true than in demographically complex and economically vibrant New York City, where upper-class people long have been preoccupied with differentiating themselves and defining their prerogatives.

Rapid economic growth first began to enlarge and enrich New York City's upper class in the 1820s. The expansion of the urban economy gave enormous weight to business success and the accumulation of wealth, elevating uncouth newcomers like John Jacob Astor, who defied the association between high status and the titled nobility that was made by the established upper class, and dividing the upper class into separate economic and social factions. As more people from the middle and working classes began to make their fortunes, the upper class countered this blurring of class boundaries and social credentials by reasserting its traditional moral and political leadership, making use of the Civil War crisis to classify workers and immigrants as dangerous threats to the social order. The national and city economies kept booming after the Civil War. The upper class of New York City was at the peak of its wealth and prestige in the late nineteenth century and tried to foster a social world that valued exclusivity and refinement, yet centrifugal forces unleashed by the powerful urban economy destabilized it and thwarted its attempts to mark and preserve its boundaries.

From the corporate headquarters complex that started taking shape in lower Manhattan in the late nineteenth century and then dramatically expanded throughout the twentieth century arose a corporate elite of business executives, bankers, brokers, lawyers, and others. They were an economic elite that ultimately became a rising new upper class. Corporate elites owed their wealth and status to their training in college and graduate school and to their careers, and their ideas about work, education, and hierarchy conflicted sharply with those of the social elites. By the 1940s, looking to distance themselves from the Gilded Age upper class, corporate elites had formed their own communities and way of life. In the 1970s corporate executives and others solidified their beliefs into an antielitist ideology that they applied against the social elites, using the memory of the Gilded Age upper class to highlight their own more democratic values. They had an unusual, hybridized relationship with the middle class. Able to adopt a middle-class outlook as their basic identity now that the European aristocracy had lost most of its previous allure, corporate elites became adept at moving back and forth between upper- and middle-class orbits and at championing both professional achievement and social justice. They were being public-spirited when they espoused egalitarian principles and reviled past haughtiness and bigotry, when they sought to redress the shortfall of African Americans and other minorities in prominent universities and businesses, and when they advocated meritocracy that rewarded individual achievement and ability as measured through fair competition, but they championed those ideals then as they do so now largely because being civic-minded and democratic helped legitimate and therefore bolster the pursuit of privilege. The strain that city elites have long experienced juggling American economic vibrancy and democratic culture has been camouflaged rather than resolved.

This book covers the New York upper class from the 1750s to the present. This long history brings into greater relief shifts in the history of the urban economy that the upper class both drove and benefited from, including the rise of New York City as the dominant metropolis in North America in the first half of the nineteenth century, the emergence of Wall Street as a corporate complex and an international financial center in the late nineteenth and early twentieth centuries, and the enlargement of its financial and services sectors starting in the 1980s. This long history also encompasses events that were crucial to the experiences and understanding of upper-class New Yorkers, such as their uneven responses to the demands for more equal treatment that people in the lower orders made in the wake of the American Revolution and their reactions to the tumultuous New York City draft riots of July 1863. The upper class is vital to the histories of New York City and the United States precisely because of the friction that many of its members have experienced with democratic culture and egalitarianism. Members of the upper class are not villains simply because their ambitions and ways of life are different from those of other Americans, but the foreign land they inhabit coexists uneasily with the rest of the United States.

Unlike the extended time frame that this book adopts, most scholarly studies of the American upper class concentrate on the so-called Gilded Age of the late nineteenth century.[8] Historians are drawn to the Gilded Age because that is when the upper class was at the summit of its wealth and power and was unequivocal about flexing its muscle, with some of its members, like the guests at the Bradley Martin ball, even conceiving of themselves as a European-style aristocracy. The late nineteenth century was indeed significant and will be treated in depth here. However, these focused works of scholarship exclude important events and issues that occurred in other periods. Although there have been excellent studies of the upper class during the Gilded Age, their concentration on the era of maximum domination has led historians to discount the significance of the upper class's relations with other social groups and to miss its responsiveness to economic and social shifts.

Upper-class men and women unapologetically viewed themselves as indispensable leaders of their city and assumed that New York City would have fallen apart without them. Arrogance and hyperbole aside, is there any truth to these claims? Were upper-class New Yorkers social parasites and predatory capitalists, or did they accomplish things that made the city a significantly better place? The answer, obviously, is that they were both. It is a mixed bag, with the upper class acting as freeloaders and bloodsuckers in some ways and making positive contributions in other ways. Certainly, they could be snobbish and self-important, indulge in empty revelries, and exploit workers.

Yet without them New York City would be a smaller and less remarkable place. They spawned business enterprises that sparked massive economic growth; inaugurated public works projects such as Central Park and the original subway that became emblematic of the city; founded cultural institutions such as Columbia University, the Metropolitan Museum of Art, and the New York Public Library that helped elevate New York above the level of the great European metropolises; and provided skilled political leadership at vital moments such as the American Revolution, the Progressive Era, and after the terrorist attacks of September 11, 2001. Upper-class people, of course, are far from being the only New Yorkers who built this city, but their wealth and power afforded them an outsized role and disproportionate influence, and they used their resources to give decisive shape to the extraordinary city that New York has become.

This book takes an essayistic approach, exploring a series of related topics and ideas analytically rather than providing encyclopedic coverage. It investigates particular decades as slices or layers of the overall history of New York City. This method is an exploratory device and a convenience; in typical essay fashion, the analysis roams freely in time and is not confined strictly to the decennial calendar. I scrutinize seven periods: the 1750s/1760s, the 1780s/1790s, the 1820s, the 1860s, the 1890s, the 1940s, and the 1970s. These seven times witnessed important changes in the city's political economy that had a profound effect on the upper class and its relationship to New York City. In responding to these challenges, upper-class individuals made choices that revealed their priorities and reset their direction. I conclude the book by bringing the analysis into the present and speaking to how this history fits with contemporary developments.

We begin with the 1750s/1760s, when New York City first became internationally important as a headquarters for the British military during the Seven Years' War. Other wartime experiences—the Revolutionary War (1780s/1790s), the Civil War (1860s), and World War II (1940s)—also transformed the city's political and economic affairs and altered how elites organized their lives. Two other decades (the 1820s and the 1970s) marked fundamental shifts in the urban economic base that had far-reaching effects on the upper class, with the 1820s representing the beginning of the city's takeoff as a national metropolis and the 1970s encompassing its near bankruptcy during the fiscal crisis along with its transition to a finance and service economy. The Gilded Age, of course, was at its height during the 1890s.

These seven periods were pivotal in the history of New York City and its upper class. Even so, there are others that could have been studied, particularly in the twentieth century. An example is the Progressive Era, with its business and social reforms and its leadership by upper-class New Yorkers such as Theodore Roosevelt and Charles Evans Hughes. However, the Gilded Age remains so central to both the historical study and popular understanding of the upper class of New York City that no book that dispenses with it can claim to control this subject matter, and I devote two chapters to it. The Great Depression and the New Deal make the 1930s a critical time in American history, but the reactions that businessmen and others had to the New Deal during the late 1930s and the 1940s decisively shaped the actions of corporate elites from that point forward, and this book accordingly concentrates on the 1940s.

For the last half century, historians and other social scientists have been studying groups that previous scholars ignored or downplayed, including workers, immigrants, women, African Americans, and gays and lesbians. Although I write about a highly privileged population, I see this project as a sympathetic continuation of that body of work. I incorporate many of its substantive findings and conceptual schemes. Moreover, because of the tremendous social complexity of New York City, writing the history of any of its social groups, even one as rich and powerful as the upper class, necessarily involves taking the measure of its connections with other New Yorkers. Throughout its history, the population of the city has contained so many different types of people that no single group has ever constituted the majority. Everyone is in the numerical minority and is decisively affected by the actions of other people.

In this book, I thus view the history of the upper class in terms of its relationships with other social groups. Upper-class New Yorkers interacted with a wide range of people and had the wherewithal to alter many lives for the better by stimulating the economy, founding major cultural institutions, and improving the condition of workers and immigrants. However, at the same time, upper-class New Yorkers also acted selfishly and myopically. Time and again, they used their distorted depictions of other groups to justify their own tastes and circumstances and to advance their own agenda. After the Civil War, upper-class individuals portrayed workers and immigrants as a social menace, and in the 1960s and 1970s, elites romanticized minorities as paradigms of social justice and authenticity. As I show, in this sense a history of the upper class contributes to our understanding of larger struggles over power and prestige in American history. The record of the upper class is conducive to a tragic view of American history, wherein the promise that this country has held for greater equality and democracy and for a higher standard of living for everyone has been repeatedly undermined by the antagonism that members of different groups harbor toward one another and by the narrowness of their social vision.

I draw on the scholarship of the sociologist Pierre Bourdieu to explore how members of the upper class created their communities, marked their boundaries, and interacted with other groups, especially members of the city's lower social orders. In his work Pierre Bourdieu investigates social arenas in which struggles take place over access to and possession of specific resources or stakes: intellectual distinction, employment, housing, social class, prestige, and so forth. He is interested in the uses to which culture is put, the manner in which cultural categories are defined and defended, and the ways in which tastes originate and are mobilized as weapons in competitions for status. Borrowing his terminology from economics, Bourdieu calls the goods and resources that are up for grabs "capital" and identifies four main types: economic capital (wealth and income), social capital (valued relationships with others), cultural capital (knowledge of some sort), and symbolic capital (prestige and social honor). This analytical framework lets us make sense of the struggles of upper-class

New Yorkers over wealth, prestige, and power and allows us to comprehend that their efforts to achieve distinction and legitimacy strengthened their pursuit of privilege. It helps us interpret the masses of letters, diaries, articles, and other textual materials of upper-class New Yorkers that have been deposited in archives and libraries and made available on the Web.

I follow Bourdieu in viewing cultural tastes and social measures as tools that people wield in their efforts to possess these goods, with the definition and boundary marking of high-status categories (such as "upper class") among the most precious stakes up for grabs.[9]

We start in the 1750s, when New York City was a lesser seaport and provincial capital in the British Empire and when its upper class consisted of royal officials, merchants, planters, and leading professionals.

IN PURSUIT OF PRIVILEGE

∽ 1 ∾

"THE BEST MART ON THE CONTINENT"

The 1750s and 1760s

AN APPRAISAL OF NEW YORK CITY IN 1753

In 1753 William Livingston wrote a pamphlet entitled *A Brief Consideration of New York* that proclaimed the superiority of his native province and its major city over other colonies. The scion of one of the richest families in British North America, he grew up on Livingston Manor, a landed estate that occupied more than 150,000 acres near Albany. He moved to New York City after college and began writing pamphlets that earned him a reputation for trenchant social criticism. In *A Brief Consideration*, Livingston surveyed conditions in the colony with an eye to persuading its leaders to improve its prospects for social progress.[1]

Livingston attributed much of the economic success of the province to the mild climate and fertile soils of the Hudson Valley and Long Island that constituted "the inexhaustible Source of a profuse Abundance" of wheat, vegetables, and cattle.[2] Yet he maintained that trade, not agriculture, had made New York City "the best Mart on the Continent" and would eventually allow it to overtake Boston and Philadelphia to become the principal colonial seaport.

New York's promise, he believed, lay in its waterborne transportation. While the agricultural hinterlands of Boston and Philadelphia, situated in the interior and largely inaccessible by river, had necessitated that roads be built at great expense to take crops to market, New York farmers could traverse the Hudson River or Long Island Sound, an easier and cheaper means of transportation that gave them a competitive advantage.[3]

He also praised the superiority of New York harbor. Manhattan's landings were only sixteen or eighteen miles from the Atlantic Ocean, at the end of a broad and deep channel that protected shipping from stormy seas and was unobstructed by shallows or rocks. A royal official later called the harbor "a kind of Amphitheatre" that was "constantly Covered with Boats Sloops & every kind of Shipping passing & repassing through it & across it in all directions [which] seems alive with bustle & business."[4] Livingston exulted that the main anchorage of the city, off lower Manhattan in the East River, "is good, free from Bars, and not incommoded by Rocks, the Water of an equal and convenient Depth."[5] By contrast, the port of Philadelphia was located one hundred miles up a winding river on which vessels frequently ran aground, while Boston harbor was strewn with rocky islands that imperiled shipping.

Although Livingston proclaimed that New York would eventually outstrip its colonial rivals, even he had to acknowledge that it was a small and unimpressive city. He admitted that its economy and population were smaller than Philadelphia's and its upper class poorer and less elegant than Boston's. He tried to claim that its compact size enhanced its prospects for trade by saving labor and money in the loading and unloading of ships, but that argument seemed weak and defensive.[6]

As with many other descriptions of New York City that were made in the eighteenth and early nineteenth centuries when it was still a small place that did not yet signify in national or international affairs, Livingston's *A Brief Consideration* has sometimes been interpreted as foretelling metropolitan greatness. But that is a naïve and anachronistic reading that overlooks his true objective in writing this pamphlet.[7] His aim was not colossal growth—for that would have seemed unthinkable to residents of eighteenth-century New York—but rather the quality of leadership.

Operating in the Whig tradition of condemning luxury and frivolity as the root of moral corruption, Livingston had been conditioned to think that virtue was a prerequisite for modernization. And since he also believed that a society could achieve civic virtue only through the actions of enlightened leaders who manifested wisdom and reason, Livingston addressed his pamphlet to the colony's foremost merchants, lawyers, and planters, the brightest lights of a provincial upper class that was notorious for its political fragmentation and disputatiousness. Afraid that elites would let their selfish desire for wealth and leisure divert them from their civic responsibility, Livingston implored these men to join together to implement development projects that would stimulate the economy, such as the construction of a new market house, better drainage of the wharves, and the founding of an ironworks.

Livingston was less a prophet than a critic and a booster: he emphasized New York's promise because he feared it would continue to lag behind Philadelphia and Boston unless elites recognized its potential and acted on behalf of the general welfare, and he contended that growth would benefit all political factions and economic interests because he believed that its leadership must promote a common good separate from the struggle of private interests. His claim that New York was "the best Mart on the Continent," then, was sheer embroidery.

Ironically, however, Livingston's prediction that New York would realize its potential started to come true much faster than he could have anticipated. This chapter concentrates on the 1750s and early 1760s when New York City first began to gain international significance during the Seven Years' War. As the nucleus of British military operations in North America, the city served as the principal command and control center, troop quarters, supply depot, and naval base in the Western Hemisphere. As a communications hub, it was the chief source of North American war news published in the British press.

Until then, New York—much like Philadelphia and Boston—had been a minor seaport and provincial capital within an Atlantic economy of empires and trading. In terms of the size of their populations and the structure of their economies, the three northern seaports were not markedly dissimilar. Their main difference was cultural rather than economic. While New York had been founded as a trading post, the Massachusetts and Pennsylvania cities had been created as religious and political utopias, and the sense of religious mission remained paramount and modulated the pursuit of wealth there well into the eighteenth century. New Yorkers did not exhibit a similar aversion to moneymaking. To the contrary, the centrality of moneymaking in New York had been reinforced and legitimated by a series of events and accidents in the seventeenth and eighteenth centuries, including its role in the Seven Years' War itself. The New York City of the 1750s was not the New York City of today, but the cultural values that would eventually facilitate its rise as the dominant metropolis in North America were already apparent by the mid-eighteenth century.

In a colonial seaport whose lifeblood was commerce, merchants were the people who made the principal economic decisions and accordingly are the center of analysis here. From around 1700, a few wealthy merchants—known as "great merchants"—existed alongside the lesser merchants, with the bigger players garnering handsome returns through their control of transatlantic imports and their retailing of textiles and other wares. A consumer revolution in the middle of the eighteenth century further expanded the volume of the city's commerce, enabling the great merchants to accumulate even bigger fortunes that supplied a material basis for a luxurious way of life.[8]

New York's merchants did not yet constitute a distinct social group. Rather, merchants conceived of themselves and were seen by others as being part of a larger provincial upper class that also incorporated royal officials, planters, doctors, lawyers, and other professionals. This upper class had taken shape between the 1680s and the 1720s, driven by the expansion of the transatlantic trade. It was characterized by its relative openness and its preoccupation with individual economic advancement. Compared to the stuffy and backward-looking elites found elsewhere in the colonies, the New York upper class was relatively dynamic, adaptable, and aggressive. However, the standing of merchants within this New York upper class was compromised by the code of gentility and by the place of royal officials atop the status hierarchy. The incompatibility of gentility with overly aggressive moneymaking and the privileged status of royal administrators relegated merchants to a secondary position in that upper class.

In the end, what did not change in the 1750s and 1760s proved more important than what did change. Despite New York's newfound centrality in the British Empire, the Seven Years' War represents a false dawn in the history of the city. The war did not expand New York's economy or its population, alter the social composition or the status hierarchy of the upper class, or stimulate new ways of acting and thinking on the part of its merchants. Those transformations would begin later, during the nation-building efforts of the 1780s and 1790s, and would accelerate with the economic growth of the nineteenth century.

ON THE EDGE OF THE ATLANTIC WORLD

The primacy of empire and market in mid-eighteenth-century New York was reflected in the urban landscape. Its largest structure was Fort George, which stood on a small rise at the southwestern tip of Manhattan to protect against sea attack. Inside the fort's walls were the governor's palace, which was the largest residential building in the city, and a barracks. The next largest government building was the City Hall on Wall Street, the meeting place of the provincial council, assembly, and general courts. The structure associated most closely with commerce was the Merchants' Exchange, on Broad Street, where traders came to buy and sell goods and share news.[9]

When William Livingston published his pamphlet in 1753, New York possessed a flourishing commercial economy whose major imports were linen, silk, and manufactured goods from Great Britain; sugar, molasses, and rum from the West Indies; and wine from Madeira. Traders also hawked newly arrived enslaved Africans at the foot of Wall Street.[10] While Charleston, South Carolina, and Savannah, Georgia, exported staple crops such as indigo and rice, for which great demand existed in Europe, New York paid for its imports by conducting a general trade, primarily in agricultural goods and natural resources. Grains were its leading export, but the city shipped a remarkable number of materials overseas, as Governor George Clinton detailed in a 1749 report to officials in London:

And the Outward [trade] is to London and its Outposts, the latter more seldom, Naval Stores, Copper ore, Furs, and other the enumerated Species . . . To Ireland Flax Seed, Rum, Sugar, being Prise effects, and Staves. To Sev'l Parts in Europe, Grain, Hides, Deer & Elk Skins, Ox Horns, Sarsaperila, Indico, Logwood, Cocoa Nutts &c. And [the re-export of] Foreign Produce & Lumber, Moreover Argent Vivum, Coffee, Anato, Elephant's Teeth, Beeswax, Leather, Sarsafrax, Casia-fistula, Wines, and Other Goods as Prise Effects hitherto brought [into British territory from foreign nations] and in the Vice-Admiralty Courts here and elsewhere adjudicated upon proper certifying. To Madeira & the Azores, Grain and other Provisions, Bee Wax, and Staves. To English Districts North and South of this Continent & West Indies, Provisions, Chocolate, Lumber[,] European and India Goods with those Enumerated in the Plantation Acts, and [the re-export of] such other Imported here for conveyance home regularly[.] To neutral [Caribbean] Ports such as Coracoa, Souronhaim, & Saint Thomas; Provisions, Lumber, Horses, sheep & other live Stock with their Provender.[11]

Clinton revealed that New Yorkers also carried on a large coastal trade with other British colonies in fish, sealskins, whale products, turpentine, hops, cider, bricks, iron, and furniture. Many of the exports on Clinton's inventory—notably sarsaparilla, indigo, cocoa, chocolate, coffee, and wine—had not originated in the city's hinterland but rather had been produced elsewhere and become part of its vigorous re-export trade. The elephants' teeth probably entered the continent through Rhode Island, the colony with the largest slave trade at the time.

Clinton's report showed that the cargo that passed through New York harbor was extraordinarily varied and had multiple points of origin and destination around the Atlantic basin.[12] In recent decades historians have utilized the idea of an "Atlantic world" to comprehend the linkages that began to connect geographical areas in Europe, Africa, and the Americas in the premodern era and that tightened during the seventeenth and eighteenth centuries. Scholars generally agree that by 1700 a coherent economy dominated by Europeans and their American colonists had evolved in the Atlantic basin that was organized around production complexes, state-building institutions, commercial practices, and transportation and communication facilities. While it had become more integrated and cohesive over time, this Atlantic world was fluid, decentralized, variegated, and conflict-ridden, and it put a premium on access to trading networks and capital and on entrepreneurial judgment, risk taking, and flexibility. Merchants helped pull this Atlantic world together.[13]

The transatlantic, international perspective shows us that the important relationships that New York City had with distant locales largely determined the scale and structure of its economy, the composition of its population, and the sources of the wealth of its upper class. Much like Philadelphia, Boston, and Charleston, New York sat on the rim of the Atlantic world, a bustling seaport that was the entrepôt for New York, Connecticut, and East Jersey.

Reliable population data did not become available until the first federal decennial census was taken in 1790, and the exact sizes of American cities and towns cannot be determined for earlier periods. Probably the best estimate is that New York City had 11,000 inhabitants in 1743, fewer than either Boston (already beginning to stagnate, but still the biggest colonial town, with 16,380 residents) or Philadelphia (the second largest, with 13,000).[14] Except for Boston, American cities grew rapidly in the eighteenth century. By the 1760s Philadelphia had become the largest city in the colonies, New York occupied second place, and Boston languished in third. Even then the three ports remained roughly the same size: in 1760 Philadelphia had an estimated population of 23,750; New York, 18,000; and Boston, 15,630.[15]

The three seaports were regional centers whose economic hinterlands did not overlap appreciably or envelop the entire Eastern Seaboard.

Instead, each supplied goods and services (agricultural marketplaces, public administration, and information) for its own hinterland. The economic functions of the three cities corresponded closely enough for them to have similar occupational structures. According to Gary Nash, their social hierarchies had seven tiers, consisting, from top to bottom, of educated, highly prestigious professionals such as government officials, doctors, clergymen, and lawyers; merchants and shopkeepers; artisans and mechanics, a group that included craftsmen such as coopers, silversmiths, and sailmakers; free unskilled laborers; apprentices and hired servants; indentured servants; and enslaved Africans.[16]

There were some notable economic differences among the three cities. Boston, settled in 1630 by a group of Puritans to provide the Massachusetts Bay Colony with a port, had one of the best harbors in New England. Its initial economic success relied on the plentiful fishing grounds that lay just off the coast, and what started as a small industry—with fishermen bringing in catches of cod and merchants exporting most of it to the West Indies—eventually transformed into a very lucrative economic activity. With fishing and shipbuilding as its economic base, Boston quickly became the leading settlement in Massachusetts Bay and, by 1700, the largest English town in North America. Commerce emerged as the primary activity early in the eighteenth century, as merchants such as the Hutchinsons, Lloyds, and Hancocks created a flourishing coastal trade and built a profitable exchange with the sugar islands in the West Indies. Draft animals became another major source of earnings; horses, cows, and oxen raised in New England pastures were sent to the West Indies for use on sugar plantations.

But Boston did not have the rich agricultural economy the other provincial ports did, and the thin soils and short growing season of its hinterland prevented it from producing a staple export, like wheat, that could sustain further prosperity. In the eighteenth century, when the main exports of New York and Philadelphia were wheat, flour, and provisions, Boston still primarily traded in fish and draft animals. Boston also came under added pressure as a result of the growth of secondary New England towns like Salem, Portsmouth, Marblehead, and Newport that cut into its shipbuilding and fishing business. By midcentury, Philadelphia had surpassed Boston as the largest city and busiest port in the colonies.

The English Quaker William Penn had planted Philadelphia in 1682 to give his coreligionists and political dissenters who were being persecuted in Europe a place of safety and to create a model city of enlightenment and reason. Because the Delaware River valley was the main wheat-growing area in the British colonies, Philadelphia merchants carried on an extensive traffic in staples such as wheat, flour, corn, butter, pork, and beef, which they marketed in the West Indies and throughout Europe and exchanged for manufactured goods and valuable commodities like sugar, rum, molasses, salt, wine, and mahogany that could be sold up and down the Atlantic coast. Philadelphia thus enjoyed a much greater direct trade with Great Britain and southern Europe than any other provincial town. Although Philadelphians also engaged in the coastal trade with other continental colonies and in the West Indies trades, transatlantic commerce was the major source of the wealth of their city. Philadelphia also seems to have equaled or even passed Boston as an industrial center around midcentury; its leading manufacturing occupations were the leather and fur trades, followed by shipbuilding and ship-fitting crafts and then by metal trades. By the 1760s the signs of Philadelphia's prosperity were apparent everywhere from the erection of new homes and the arrival of thousands of immigrants to the construction of new wharves along the Delaware.

New York's commerce was more diverse and complex than Philadelphia's. While wheat and provisions had become its principal exports in the eighteenth century, New York City sent large quantities of furs overseas longer than any other northern colony did, due to its lucrative trade with the Native Americans in the upper Hudson River valley. New Yorkers traded with the other continental colonies, with British possessions in the West Indies, and with England. They exported flaxseed to Ireland. The West Indies and coastal trades remained the city's most important ones in the 1750s and 1760s, as merchants sought to overcome the limitations of their hinterland by exploiting their contacts with merchants in the Dutch—and later the Danish—West Indies and by performing an array of entrepôt services, like underwriting marine insurance, that allowed them to obtain sugar from the Caribbean, rice and naval stores from the Carolinas, mahogany from Honduras, and so forth. In short, the absence of sufficient quantities of homegrown wheat, flaxseed, and other commodities forced traders in New York (like those in Boston) to be adroit in order to penetrate European markets. They were phenomenally successful in this endeavor: the New York colony managed to send more goods to Britain and Ireland than Pennsylvania did and to maintain a favorable balance of trade with the mother country, something no other northern colony achieved.

Even so, a significant improvement in its transatlantic commerce took place after 1750. As the production of cereal agriculture declined in the Iberian Peninsula and Mediterranean Europe, New York merchants exploited the open market created by the Navigation Acts to construct a growing wheat, flour, and bread trade to southern Europe. While this commodity flow did not match Philadelphia's, it produced direct linkages with Europe and brought in substantial earnings that helped foster urban economic development and led to population increases.[17]

All the same, the total volume of New York's commerce remained smaller than that of Philadelphia, Boston, and even Charleston. That raises an obvious question: How could a seaport that would become a commercial giant in the nineteenth century have been so inconsequential a century earlier? The answer is that its geographical advantages were latent rather than immediate. Despite Livingston's boast that the Hudson River afforded an unparalleled trade route into the interior, the Hudson River valley and the regions to the west of it (which the Iroquois League controlled) were more sparsely populated and produced less than did the hinterlands of Boston and Philadelphia. The Hudson River was indeed a promising commercial route, and the regions it tapped were very promising, but the current reality was modest. New York was not yet what it would be.[18]

Despite their comparable population sizes and economic structures, substantial cultural differences set New York apart from Boston and Philadelphia. Certainly European travelers thought that New York seemed odd. Many remarked on the presence of both Dutch and English architectural styles, with tall older houses that turned their gable ends to the streets in the Dutch manner, reflecting the origins of the city more than a century earlier as New Amsterdam and standing out against the newer and shorter buildings that followed the English custom of fronting the street.[19] One British administrator who was familiar with the other colonial cities made a point of calling New York "a Dutch-town" to indicate how different it looked and felt.[20]

Visitors who commented on the idiosyncratic architecture of New York City or who expressed surprise at the number and variety of its churches were identifying the most conspicuous element of its distinctiveness: the remarkable social diversity of its inhabitants. Although all the American seaports were catchment reservoirs for an assortment of people from around the Atlantic basin, none was as polyglot as New York. Even Philadelphia, with its increasing immigrant population, was less diverse than New York, where no single ethnonational or religious group had a majority. By 1750 the chief ethnonational groups in New York City comprised the English, Dutch, Irish, French, Scots, Africans, Germans, and Sephardic Jews, and the main religious groups included Anglicans, Dutch Reformed, and Presbyterians, along with smaller congregations of Jews, Lutherans, and Quakers.[21] "The outstanding sociological feature of colonial New York City," Joyce D. Goodfriend writes, was "its melange of peoples," a situation that had persuaded "the English to endorse a policy of [cultural] toleration in New York and to rely . . . on strategies of cooption and conversion" rather than coercion when it came to dealing with other ethnoreligious groups.[22]

This openness was one element in a larger pattern of cultural disparities differentiating New York from Boston and Philadelphia that can be traced to their origins and to the widely disparate ideals and objectives of their founders. From the outset, the leaders of New York City put a higher, more unqualified value on materialism than did their counterparts in Boston and Philadelphia, where powerful religious ideologies framed understandings of the social order and restrained or redefined the pursuit of monetary gain. While the Dutch West India Company had started New Amsterdam in 1624 as a profit-making outpost of the fur trade,

Boston's Puritan creators had come to the New World to construct a model society that would be free of the corruption of England, and Philadelphia's William Penn had sought to implement his Quaker-inspired vision of social and religious toleration.

Pauline Maier argues that these founding ideologies were maintained, adapted, and strengthened by the responses to subsequent events and circumstances. The Puritan sense of mission and commitment to living in close-knit communities helped Bostonians survive the ordeals of initial settlement, according to Maier, while they interpreted its eighteenth-century economic decline in accordance with the stern ideology of the founders, by recognizing it as test of their virtue.[23] Much the same held true during the Revolutionary crises of the 1760s and 1770s, which Bostonians answered with a commitment to moral responsibility and a willingness to make sacrifices on behalf of the entire community. Maier says, "The ideals of the fathers provided . . . a way of understanding and of organizing experience, of ordering history, and so continued to influence the life of the region and of its major city."[24]

Maier wrote about Boston and New York, but her findings can be extrapolated to Philadelphia. Even though utopian religious ideologies were central to the founding ideologies of both Boston and Philadelphia, E. Digby Baltzell concludes that the pronounced disparities between Puritanism and Quakerism had lasting effects on the upper classes and leadership traditions of the two cities. According to Baltzell, the Puritan stress on devotion to one's calling instilled a tradition of authority and hierarchy that spawned distinguished Boston families like the Adamses, Cabots, Peabodys, and Lowells. Trained to carry on the ideals of their forefathers and to conceive of themselves as aristocrats who had the responsibility to shepherd the other social ranks, members of these families became political, intellectual, and educational leaders of great note, with the Adamses, for instance, producing two presidents of the United States, an ambassador to Great Britain, the chief executive of a railroad, and a preeminent writer-philosopher. By contrast, Baltzell tells us, the democratic and egalitarian ethos of Quakerism encouraged upper-class Philadelphians to rest on their privileges or retreat into private pursuits rather than taking leadership positions where they would have to exert their authority on the rest of society.[25]

New York City was altogether different. Over time, instead of being modified or attenuated by utopian considerations, the pursuit of monetary gain was strengthened and legitimated by a series of unexpected and accidental events that its opinion makers interpreted as confirming the centrality of moneymaking. In fact, the social diversity of New York City—the attribute that registered so strongly with the eighteenth-century observers cited earlier—itself involved a response to economic failure. In the 1630s and 1640s, after failing to attract enough Dutch settlers to develop New Netherland and afraid that neighboring English colonies were becoming strong enough to overpower it, the West India Company gave economic stimulus precedence over the transplantation of Dutch society, adopting a policy of admitting almost all foreigners, including French Huguenots and Sephardic Jews fleeing religious persecution, and immigrants from England, Scotland, Ireland, and Germany.[26] The priority that the West India Company assigned to profit making with its immigration policy further reinforced the original understanding that economic gain had a fundamental importance, an emphasis that William Livingston himself sustained in writing *A Brief Consideration*, a document that belongs to the New York tradition of focusing on development and that was alien to the commitment to mission that had become entrenched in Philadelphia and Boston. Livingston was urging elites to display greater civic-mindedness, but he did that because, in typical New York fashion, he wanted them to align their individual material pursuits with strategies for improving the urban economy.

Although *A Brief Consideration* puts New York in a larger colonial context through the insightful contrasts it draws with Boston and Philadelphia, Livingston restricted his comparisons to these two northern ports instead of bringing in other North American cities and towns. He was clearly employing Boston and Philadelphia as a backdrop that would allow New York to stand out in sharper relief and prove his argument that the city needed better leadership if it was to prosper, but the insularity of his urban vision is arresting all the same. He made no mention, for instance, of Charleston, even though the South Carolina capital was the fourth-largest city in the colonies, with a population of about 8,000 in 1760. Most likely, he omitted Charleston because it seemed geographically remote from the Middle Atlantic and New England colonies and because its trade in staple crops differed from the more general commerce of the three northern ports.[27]

Livingston also avoided possible comparisons with London, Paris, Amsterdam, and Lisbon. These great European metropolises—large, powerful, and wealthy—probably lay beyond the scope of his imagination, for few contemporaries conceived of the small American cities and the European giants in the same terms. Two decades later, a Swedish traveler observed that New York City vied with Boston and Philadelphia for urban supremacy in the colonies but added in a dismissive afterthought that "at present it is about half again as large as Gothenburg in Sweden."[28] According to the best calculations of their populations, in 1750 the five largest European cities were, in rank order, London (with 676,000 residents), Paris (560,000), Naples (324,000), Amsterdam (219,000), and Lisbon (213,000). There were sixteen European cities that had more than 100,000 inhabitants and twenty-four cities that had between 50,000 and 100,000 residents (figure 1.1).[29]

Colonial American cities and towns were secondary and tertiary centers in an Atlantic urban system that centered on those European metropolises. According to Brian J. L. Berry, "America's oldest cities were mercantile outposts of a resource area whose exploitation was organized by the developing metropolitan system of Western Europe."[30] Through their coordination of worldwide commercial and military enterprises, the European metropolises had sustained rapid population and economic growth. London, for instance, surpassed Paris as the largest city in Europe as its population tripled in size between 1600 and 1750. By the mid-eighteenth century, London dominated the English economy; it was the country's principal port for foreign commerce, the hub of its domestic trade, its leading manufacturing base, and a financial center.[31]

From the viewpoint of metropolitan Europe, late seventeenth-century New York was fairly unimportant. Two or three years could pass without

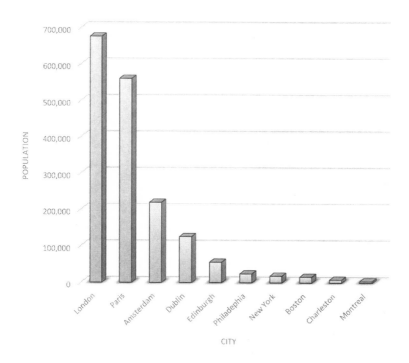

FIGURE 1.1 Population of Selected Atlantic Basin Cities, 1750/1760. *Source*: Paul M. Hohenberg and Lynn Hollen Lees, *The Making of Urban Europe, 1000–1950* (Cambridge: Harvard University Press, 1985): 227; Carl Bridenbaugh, *Cities in Revolt: Urban Life in America, 1743–1776* (New York: Knopf, 1955): 5.

a single reference to New York City appearing in England's premier newspaper, the *London Gazette*.[32] After the Netherlands recaptured the city during the Third Anglo-Dutch War of 1672–1674, the States General of the Netherlands agreed in the Treaty of Westminster to return it to England in exchange for the South American colony of Surinam. New York was merely a bargaining chip for these great powers, and the account of the treaty signing that ran in the *London Gazette* did not mention the restoration of New York City.[33]

New York continued to benefit by way of its "Dutch connection" with places in the West Indies like Curaçao, where the Dutch trade remained important, but England was a rising power that was beginning to exercise economic and political authority abroad and to organize an empire, and the city prospered as part of the British Empire. Its merchants thus became avid participants in a cultural and economic system called "gentlemanly capitalism."[34] British historians such as P. J. Cain and A. G. Hopkins attribute the origins of the British Empire to the effects of this gentlemanly capitalism, which they identify as a set of cultural, political, and economic forces that was propelled by a group of merchants and financiers who used overseas trade as a means to acquire the wealth, prestige, and connections they needed to reach a higher social level. "The English gentleman was made as well as born," Cain and Hopkins assert.[35] For the founders of the Bank of England, Lloyd's insurance company, and the East India and South Sea companies, a thick pocketbook was a vehicle for attaining the gentlemanly ideal of graciousness, refined speech, polished manners, and elegant houses.

Many of these men on the make came from marginal backgrounds in England and Scotland. Active across the Atlantic world building ships, constituting business networks, extending credit and insurance, supplying armies, and moving people forced and free, they employed their commercial networks and the government's policy-making apparatus to form a military-fiscal state that facilitated the rise of the British Empire.[36]

MERCHANTS AND THE CITY

There were roughly five hundred merchants who conducted overseas or coastal trade in New York City in the 1750s, including about one hundred great merchants renowned for their wealth and prestige who specialized in trading directly with English and Dutch mercantile houses for textiles, household luxuries, and pharmaceuticals. Most of the approximately four hundred lesser merchants concentrated on the coastal and West Indies commerce and mounted fewer voyages and handled less tonnage than did the great merchants. Some of these lesser merchants, working on the edge of insolvency and hard-pressed to organize even a single voyage per year, could not be easily differentiated from shopkeepers and artisans.

Jews like Jacob Franks, Hayman Levy, and Isaac Mendes Seixas made up a third group of merchants who were either descendants of Sephardic refugees or migrants from Germany. While the small scale and fluidity of the commercial economy led its Jewish and Gentile dealers to cooperate on some business matters, New York's Jewish merchants traded chiefly with their coreligionists or conationalists in other continental colonial cities and overseas in places like Curaçao. These Jewish merchants and their families remained separate from the rest of urban society, including the upper class; indeed, their lives demonstrate that wealth alone did not confer status and was not enough for them to join or socialize with that upper class.[37]

A series of letters that Abigaill Levy Franks wrote to her son in London in the 1730s and 1740s illuminate these social patterns. A lively, opinionated woman whose extended family had prospered from transatlantic trade, Franks took an intense interest in local politics and contemporary literature and enjoyed gossip about the doings of upper-class New Yorkers like the De Lanceys. Yet she socialized almost entirely with other Jews who also belonged to Congregation Shearith Israel. Although she was not especially observant, Franks worked hard to raise her children as practicing Jews and experienced an emotional crisis akin to mourning each time one of them married a Christian and passed out of the orbit of the small New York City Jewish community. The upper class of New York City may have been relatively more open than its equivalents in Boston and Philadelphia were, but it was far from being entirely open.[38]

Compared with the upper classes of other American colonies, New York's upper class also was unusual for including separate groups of merchants and planters that were commensurate in size, wealth, and prestige. Tensions between these mercantile and landed interests were a fixture of the political sphere in the New York colony. Upper-class New Yorkers may have monopolized politics and asserted a paternalistic ethic of civic leadership that justified their stewardship of the province, but they clashed with each other, too. Enriched by the recent expansion of transatlantic commerce, the merchants obtained an edge over the planters and held most of the province's elected offices as members of a court party that bore the name of Lieutenant Governor James De Lancey. The De Lanceys were opposed by a party called the Livingstons (for the family of William Livingston) that was composed largely of planters and lawyers. The angry disputes that erupted between the De Lancey and Livingston parties made politics so contentious that New Yorkers became known for being—in the phrase of Patricia H. Bonomi—"a factious people."[39]

Politically divided, socially disparate, and geographically dispersed, the people who belonged to this upper class nonetheless conceived of and organized themselves as a collective entity that was distinct from the two other core groups that constituted the social order, the loose collection of lesser merchants, shopkeepers, clerks, and auctioneers who were called "people of middling rank" and the artisans, tenant-farmers, laborers, sailors, and manual laborers known as "farmers and mechanics." While people of the middling sort and farmers and mechanics had recognizable places in this hierarchical society, scholars by and large believe they did not have the internal cohesion, uniformity, and self-awareness that would enable us to regard them as social classes.[40]

The upper class, on the other hand, clearly *was* a class, one that Frederic Cople Jaher says comprised "an intimately connected group of manorial grandees, overseas merchants, and leading lawyers" whose lifestyle produced shared meanings, experiences, and identities along with wealth and symbols of rank and prestige.[41] Its members knew each other very well and had strong personal networks that were fortified through intermarriage. Most came from families that had been moneyed for at least a generation, and some for long enough to have bloodlines that passed for being aristocratic in the colonies. John Van Cortlandt, a sugar refiner who was the grandson of the first lord of Cortlandt Manor, married a daughter of merchant Nicholas Bayard, while Gerard Beekman, another great merchant, was descended from the Van Hornes and Abeels and related by marriage to the De Lanceys, De Peysters, Duyckincks, and

Van Dycks. Birth counted for a lot, but talented outsiders or their off-spring could enter the upper class provided they were white, Protestant, and appropriately affluent and refined. Jacob and William Walton had achieved such social mobility: they owed their wealth to their father's accomplishments as a shipbuilder and merchant and their social prominence to their judicious marriages into good families. Hugh Wallace, who emigrated from Ireland in the early 1750s and became a successful merchant, entered the ambit of the Low, Gouverneur, and Cuyler families by wedding a Low daughter.[42]

Many in New York's upper classes lacked intense religious feeling. A degree of religious belief and practice, such as regular church attendance, was expected, and membership in the Church of England conferred prestige, but strong religious belief was not fundamental to the worldviews of most merchants. They (and others in the upper class) did not use religion to smooth over or explain the frictions that arose in their daily lives, nor did they experience feelings of guilt from indulging in luxuries, committing sexual peccadilloes, or participating in shady business dealings. This does not appear to have been the case in Philadelphia and Boston.[43]

In other ways, however, New York's upper classes had much in common with their counterparts elsewhere. The framework that the upper class used to order their social relationships involved a series of small, overlapping circles of family members, friends, business associates, and acquaintances. Upper-class provincials organized their social lives into small groups of relatives, friends, neighbors, and other intimates that became sites of intense personal experience and feeling and from which outsiders could be readily excluded.

Contemporaries took an expansive view of family and friendship ties that extended beyond relationships of blood and marriage. In a study of England that appears to be germane to the colonies, Naomi Tadmore argues that the boundaries between family and nonfamily were more porous in the eighteenth century than they are today and that people in early modern society applied the notion of "family" to a variety of contexts and voluntary associations. Family forms, Tadmore says, took root "within rich webs of kinship, friendship, patronage, economic ties, neighbourhood ties, and, not least, political ties."[44]

Such deeply meaningful relationships made upper-class New York a kind of cousins' world in which people felt connected because of similar ancestry, background, and experiences. Clusters of these intimate circles intersected and formed interlocking chains, enabling members of the upper class to enter other sets while courting, traveling, or conducting business or to introduce suitable newcomers into their own circles. Since the boundaries separating the handful of gentlefolk from the mass of commoners and distinguishing genteel conduct from uncouth behavior were sharp, people could be reasonably confident that intruders would be detected.

STATUS HIERARCHY

Despite this encouragement of intragroup integration, the upper class was socially stratified. Wealth, birth, and religion all mattered, but perhaps no social category had greater significance for merchants' life chances than status. According to Max Weber, status consists of non-economic qualities such as prestige and honor and can be a significant component of stratification, even in settings in which the market thrives. In colonial New York City, the social and economic orders coexisted in dynamic tension.[45]

The great merchants were wealthy, but royal governors, lieutenant governors, judges, councilors, and other imperial officials had more prestige than traders and other members of the provincial upper class did, thanks to the spread of a new national political culture that accompanied the expansion of the British Empire. The authority of the monarchy and administrators as the embodiment of the empire swelled in the eighteenth century and gave rise to acts of ritual grandeur meant to foster an aura of national greatness that would legitimate the empire and unite the populace in support of it.[46] This ceremonial splendor was expressed through commemorations of the monarchy; celebrations of military victories; and an outpouring of patriotic songs, plays, and portraiture.

Inevitably, these rituals spilled over to British North America. That the royal government, not the private sector, was the ultimate source of power and prestige in a colonial capital like New York was conveyed through rites such as the artillery salutes that were fired from Fort George to mark the arrivals and departures of governors, lieutenant governors, and high-ranking military officers and the festivities that honored the birthdays of the king and queen and special occasions like the coronation of King George III in 1761.[47]

The gulf in status between royal officials and the rest of the upper class was particularly pronounced when it came to merchants. Lawyers, doctors, and clergymen were in an anomalous position since their educational attainments and professional standing warranted respect. Merchants possessed no such mitigating factors and, like lawyers but unlike medical doctors and clergymen, were tainted by the marketplace. Although we have seen that the pursuit of material gain had priority in New York City, moneymaking could paradoxically hurt or endanger the place individuals occupied in the status hierarchy, especially if carried out too nakedly or forcefully.

The standard of quality was set by a code of gentility that required people to seek a refined inner life and to adhere to polite modes of speech, body, etiquette, dress, and conduct. Gentility was incompatible with the marketplace, and traders in the colonies and Great Britain who aspired to gentlemanly standing learned to distance themselves from the hard-nosed quest for the main chance. A case in point is Benjamin Franklin, who, as the youngest son of a poor Boston artisan, had humble origins. After becoming wealthy as a printer and tradesman in Philadelphia, Franklin retired from active business and devoted himself to scientific experiments and public service, shrewdly using these intellectual and civil pursuits to win acceptance as a complete gentleman.[48]

The privileged station of royal officials is evident in newspaper death notices. In 1760 the *Gazette* mourned the passing of Lieutenant Governor James De Lancey, the colony's most powerful political figure, in an unusually lengthy tribute that expressed the values and achievements prized by social arbiters of the day:

He was descended of an honourable Family in this City, and had his education at Cambridge, under the Tuition of Mr. Herring, afterwards the celebrated Arch-Bishop of Canterbury. Here he laid the solid Foundation of his future importance. His early accomplishments soon after his Return, introduced him into His Majesty's Council and the second Seat in the Supreme Court of Judicature.

In the Year 1733, he took the first Seat on the Bench, and having for Twenty years discharged that important Trust with the greatest Applause, His Majesty was pleased to confer on him the Honours of the dignified Station in which he died.

To do ample Justice to this eminent Character in so contracted a Compass, and on so sudden and alarming an Occasion, is what the World will hardly expect, or his distinguished Accomplishments, indeed, permit. He enjoyed a quick Conception, a deep Penetration, a clear Judgment, and a retentive Memory. These natural Talents heightened and improved by his Attainments in Literature, and an intimate Acquaintance with Mankind, made him an agreeable and instructive Companion to those who were honoured with his Conversation; and qualified him to fill the most important Offices with uncommon Dignity and Lustre.

His Genius provident, active, fertile in Expedients, and capable of averting or improving the most unexpected Occurrences, joined to a perfect Knowledge and Esteem of our happy Constitution, and a zealous Attachment to His Majesty's illustrious House, rendered him a most able and faithfull Counsellor to the Crown; and to the Rights, and Liberties of the People, a Cordial and unshaken Friend.

In the chief Seat of Justice, he was for Capacity and integrity equaled by few; excelled by none. Patient in hearing, ready in distinguishing, and in his Decisions sound and impartial. He gave such universal satisfaction, that even the vanquished confessed the Justice of the Sentence. To form him, in short, a shining Ornament of the Law, Nature, and his own Industry had united their utmost Efforts.

His promotion to the Government at a Season the most momentous to the Colonies, was signally advancive of his Majesty's Service, and the public Emolument. And by the Confidence the People reposed in his superior Abilities, they were induced to exert themselves in the Common Cause [against France in the Seven Years' War], with the greatest Vigour and Alacrity.[49]

Much like a modern résumé, this death notice methodically put forward James De Lancey's personal history: his family heritage and his education; the trajectory of his career in public service; his character traits and intellectual talents; his faithfulness to the royal government; and his record of accomplishment in his two highest offices, as chief justice and lieutenant governor. There was, however, one conspicuous omission. Neither the *Gazette* nor the *Mercury*—which printed the same article verbatim—saw fit to mention that De Lancey came from a leading mercantile family or that his father, Stephen De Lancey, had made his fortune in commerce.

The deaths of less distinguished royal officials, such as judges, councilors, assemblymen, and administrators, were announced in similarly polite notices that complimented their service to His Majesty's government, their gentlemanly standing, and their contributions to the public welfare.[50] Of James Alexander, a councilor and lawyer who died in 1756, the *Mercury* declared: "He had the Honour to serve the King in several important offices, and was a wise and faithful Councilor to his Majesty for the Provinces of New-York and New-Jersey." The same paper commended Archibald Kennedy, a former councilor who had become receiver general and collector of customs, as a "Gentleman" who had an "amiable Character."[51]

These men had been well-off, but the papers stressed their public positions over their occupations and did not give the extent or sources of their wealth. The handful of references that were made to moneymaking invariably sounded a cautionary note that diverged sharply from the sycophantic treatment accorded royal officers. This was especially true of lawyers and merchants. For instance, in 1756 the *Mercury* lamented the demise of Joseph Murray, a lawyer and councilor, by declaring:

> As a Counsellor he gave his Opinion and Advice according to the Dictates of his own Reason, without Favour or Affection; it was the Cause and not the Person that directed his Judgment; and neither Threats nor Frowns could make him deviate from what he thought right: His Purse was always open to the true Objects of Charity: He was an excellent Husband, a kind Master, and a true Friend; a most regular Man in all his Conduct.[52]

The *Mercury* praised Murray for obtaining his wealth honorably and fairly, adding, in a comment that revealed its qualms about material acquisitiveness and, in particular, the legal profession, that he had been "the most considerable Lawyer here in his Time; by which Profession he acquired a large fortune, in such a Manner as justly intitled [*sic*] him to the Character of an honest, upright, judicious Man."[53] No matter how exemplary Murray may have been in his path to riches, the *Mercury's* aversion to the market led it to stress that his eminent reputation derived not from his legal career but rather from his gentlemanly standing and his tenure as a councilor. Similar reservations prompted the *Gazette* to extol another lawyer for possessing "a Character unblemished, even by that licentious Malice of the World, which takes a particular Pleasure indiscriminately to vilify the whole Profession."[54]

Merchants were treated the same way. In 1756 the *Mercury* lauded the late Paul Richards for the "great Integrity and Merit" he had shown as mayor and assemblyman, all but ignoring his activities as a trader, and two years later it reassured its readers that Jasper Farmer's "Honesty in Trade, his affable, humane and generous disposition" and his "noble Spirit of Patriotism" confirmed his gentlemanliness.[55]

THE GENTEEL LIFESTYLE

One Sunday night in October 1760, a thief broke into Nicholas Burger's home in Queen Street and stole a silver teapot, a cream pot, six silver table-spoons, a pair of silver sugar tongs, and six silver teaspoons, all stamped with makers' marks showing that a prominent silversmith had manufac-tured them. This silver reveals as much about the meaning a refined life-style had for the Burgers as it does about the extent of their material assets.[56] Like other upper-class people, the Burgers employed their wealth to advance their claims to gentility and high status. In Pierre Bourdieu's model, these elegant possessions amount to symbolic capital.

By the mid-eighteenth century, economic growth had given affluent colonists like the Burgers the means to emulate the fashionable Georgian mansions being constructed in England that signaled the advent of a new kind of upper-class life, one that centered on the display of consumer items that evidenced the gentility of their owners. A study of newspaper advertisements shows that a spectacular increase in the marketing of con-sumer goods took place between the 1730s and the 1750s. In the 1730s the *New York Weekly Journal* published more ads for real estate and for slave sales than for consumer goods. Of the consumer products that were listed, notices for plain foodstuffs such as orange butter, mackerel, cheshire cheese, and oatmeal greatly outnumbered those for fancy nondurables, like olive oil and capers imported from the Mediterranean, or durables, such as draperies and books. By the early 1750s, however, the *New York Evening Post* carried ads for a multiplicity of consumer merchandise, including wines and spirits; coffee, tea, molasses, honey, sugar, and flour; knives, spoons, kettles, pots, dishes, and drinking glasses; medicines; jew-elry; spectacles; snuffboxes, pipes, and tobacco; paints and window glass; lamps and mirrors; almanacs, histories, arithmetic manuals, and Bibles; and a variety of cloths and clothing.[57]

Upper-class New Yorkers like the Burgers made use of this mid-eigh-teenth-century consumer revolution to create a lifestyle patterned on European aristocracies and landed gentries, whom they deeply admired.

However, they copied the European aristocracy not because they thought of themselves in those terms, but because it helped strengthen and legitimate their own pursuit of wealth, status, and power.

Houses were their focal point. Large, costly residences went up that had superior building materials such as brick and glass, which had been previously unavailable in the colonies in either quantity or quality, and their interiors boasted fine carpets, candles, cabinetry, silverware, and furniture that imparted a smooth and pleasant surface. These mansions contained enough rooms for families to devote separate spaces to cooking, eating, sleeping, and entertaining, thus concealing or segregating base activities like food preparation and consumption that were inimical to refined manners. If upper-class people could habituate themselves to standards of delicacy and graciousness, however, this politeness was not a possibility for artisans and mechanics, most of whom lived in one- and two-cell dwellings where rooms had multiple uses and privacy was an alien concept. Commoners accordingly became associated in the eyes of polite society with grossness of body, dress, mind, and taste.[58]

One example of an upper-class New York City home was the six-room, two-story brick house where Abraham Lodge, a prosperous attorney, and his family resided during the 1750s. On its first floor there was a hallway that had four high-backed Windsor chairs and two lanterns; a parlor that had mahogany furniture, a large gilt-framed painting, several smaller paintings, china, cut glass, mirrors, silverware, a casket for the family jewelry, a large fireplace with brass andirons; and a dining room that had a mahogany table and chairs, another fireplace with brass andirons, a clock, sconces, glass candlesticks, paintings, and china. The three upstairs bedrooms also had elaborate appointments, and the basement contained a wine cellar, a storeroom, and the kitchen. The family's four slaves lived above the kitchen.

Like the English gentry they mimicked, upper-class New Yorkers valued sociability for nurturing refined manners and sentiments and strengthening personal bonds. Elaborate formal balls and dinners took place in private spaces, preferably in someone's residence, or else in public places such as taverns and coffeehouses that were transformed into privileged terrain for the duration of the event. When the British army returned to New York after conquering Quebec City in 1759, for instance, William Walton honored General Jeffrey Amherst by holding a magnificent reception at the Walton mansion.

More intimate gatherings also occurred in private houses. In 1754, Ezra Styles, a New Haven lawyer who would later become president of Yale College, made a two-day trip to New York City during which he was almost always in the company of gentlemen and gentlewomen and their retainers. Apart from visiting major public buildings, Styles spent nearly all his time in the residences of friends and relatives who facilitated his entry into their circles. He stayed with Peter Keteltas, a wealthy merchant, and took tea and supper with Keteltas and his friends. He listened to Keteltas and a musician play the violin, organ, and spinet in the musician's quarters; dined at the home of a Mr. Biars in the company of three ladies from Philadelphia; called on a prominent lawyer at his dwelling; and accompanied Keteltas to William Livingston's house, where five or six young men shared a light meal and discussed politics "over a bottle."[59]

MICROSEGREGATION IN URBAN SPACE

By the 1750s, residential neighborhoods in New York City were already differentiated according to wealth and occupation. The laboring poor, including free African Americans, made their homes on the northern outskirts of the city, which were also the site of noxious businesses like slaughterhouses, stables, and cow pens. People of middling rank and prosperous artisans resided in the middle part of town. A Jewish neighborhood that included Jewish merchants had formed along the East River north of Wall Street.

Most great merchants and professionals lived at the southern end of Manhattan, in either of two residential enclaves, Hanover Square and Bowling Green. Hanover Square was a combined business and residential area that was located within a block of the waterfront, where the

FIGURE 1.2 Bowling Green was the premier upper-class neighborhood in New York City from the 1730s until the 1830s. This view of it appeared in the *New York Mirror* newspaper in 1830. (Library of Congress.)

dwellings of well-to-do merchant families such as the Waltons and the Debrosses shared space with countinghouses, retail shops, taverns, and public markets. Close by were shipyards, ropewalks, and warehouses, as well as the Customs House, the Exchange, and the coffeehouses where traders met. The single most fashionable residential quarter was Bowling Green (figure 1.2), which had developed on lower Broadway near where the city's first park, also called Bowling Green, had been laid out opposite Fort George in 1733.[60] By the 1750s, this enclave was home to the Livingstons, Van Cortlandts, De Peysters, Morrisses, De Lanceys, and Bayards. Neither Hanover Square nor Bowling Green constituted a separate urban environment where the well-heeled could secrete themselves away. Both were very small areas—just a few blocks long—that were not isolated from the rest of the city and that contained modest houses as well as mansions.

Like the other colonial cities, New York City was geographically compact and socially dense. That meant that upper-class New Yorkers constantly interacted with people from the lower orders who felt and behaved very differently. An example of elites' and commoners' contrasting uses of urban space is provided by the celebration of the repeal of the Stamp Act in May and June 1766. Many reports of upper-class amusements are available for the early- and mid-eighteenth century, but newspapers, letters, diaries, and travelers' narratives usually ignored more popular festivities.[61] The Stamp Act repeal is a rare occasion for which observers left detailed written descriptions of the carousing of common folk. This happened for political reasons: opponents of the Stamp Act wanted to paint the resistance to the British government as a united effort that incorporated all ranks and to demonstrate the loyalty of His Majesty's subjects following repeal, while its advocates drew on the revels of commoners to discredit the protests with stories of out-of-control, mob-like rowdiness.

News of the repeal reached New York around May 20 and immediately triggered great rejoicing. Hundreds of boys ran excitedly through the streets, the militia fired artillery pieces, church bells rang, and bonfires were lit. A British army officer who had favored the enforcement of the Stamp Act disparaged this merriment as an "imitation of the late Mob" that involved "Drunkeness" and the "firing of muskets and pistols, breaking some windows and forcing some Knockers off the Doors."[62]

In the wake of these spontaneous activities, the Sons of Liberty and others decided to organize an official celebration a few weeks later, scheduling it to coincide with the anniversary of the birthday of King George III on June 4 to create an aura of patriotism and harmony. Some aspects of the gaiety involved sensations of light and sound that were accessible to everyone—the illumination of buildings, the ringing of church bells, a fireworks display, and discharges of cannon from the fort and warships. Most of the pageantry, however, followed two separate tracks that reflected the bifurcation between polite people and commoners. At noon, the councilors, top military officers, and leading citizens made a formal procession to Fort George, where they waited on the governor and toasted the health of the king. In the evening, the governor, the commanding general, military officers, and members of the provincial elite attended an elegant dinner and ball that featured more toasts and cannon salutes and stately and graceful formal dancing. These upper-class fêtes were ceremonial and decorous in tone, paid close attention to rank and hierarchy, occurred mostly indoors, and required precise bodily movements with respect to the dancing.

Apart from a similarly heavy consumption of alcohol, commoners celebrated otherwise. Their festivities happened on the Commons, where a huge bonfire was built on one end and artillery pieces, the top of a ship's mast, and a flagstaff that displayed the colors were positioned on the other end. Two oxen were roasted. The meat was served starting around 4 p.m., along with bread, biscuits, strong beer, and rum punch. Swarms of people ate, drank, visited, moved about, and yelled their thanks for the repeal of the Stamp Act until midnight. Unlike the upper-class gatherings, commoners socialized in an informal manner that neither reified hierarchy nor entailed control of the emotions and the body: their revels occurred out of doors and satisfied earthy appetites for food and drink. Even the patterns of noise were dissimilar: while the loudest sounds audible at the events of the upper class (the dance music and the artillery salutes) were cadenced and orderly and were generated by musicians and soldiers rather than by upper-class individuals themselves, commoners produced a cacophony of shouting and talking. Just the sensation of hearing alone revealed the chasm that divided the social orders.[63]

And yet, as map 1 shows, elites and commoners lived close together and were always interacting. The built-up areas of colonial cities extended only three or five miles from their centers, the distance an average person could walk in an hour, a crucial limiting factor, because walking was how most urban residents moved around prior to the introduction of mass transit in the early nineteenth century. But although the high population densities produced by this structuring of spaces made for constant social exchanges, most inhabitants had a degree of choice in their interactions and the face-to-face society of colonial New York hardly implied equality:

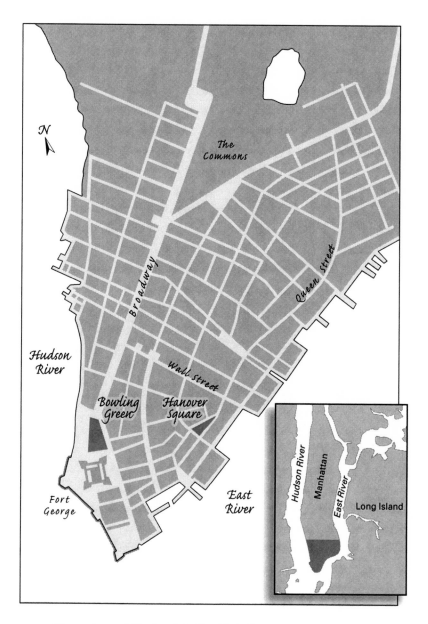

MAP 1 Upper-class neighborhoods in New York City, c. 1760.

physical proximity does not lead to parity in a society that is hierarchically ordered.[64] Nobody had more locational choices than the upper class, but upper-class New Yorkers did not try to eliminate physical and social exchanges with other groups or to remove their residences or workplaces into separate zones. Certainly that sort of segregation would have been difficult: they cohabited with servants, slaves, employees, and other retainers in highly stratified households. Yet physical proximity was not the only reason why upper-class New Yorkers did not distance themselves spatially from commoners. For one thing, examples of the uncouth, coarse, and ill-bred helped them demonstrate their own refinement. Gentility established a dual standard that required elites to not only monitor their own conduct and feelings but also to judge themselves in contradistinction to commoners. In addition, the upper classes expected to provide guidance for the lower classes. In a hierarchal society that associated restraint, moderation, and wisdom with the upper class and that respected patriarchy, elites needed to be in close contact with the rest of the population if they were to offer moral instruction.[65]

SOCIAL BLINDNESS

But the upper class could not completely control the social interactions that occurred in public spaces. The small geographical scale of eighteenth-century New York City lay it open to dubious people and situations, which posed a dilemma for the upper class.

One shield was offered by the practice of socializing in private homes. Similarly, on weekends and in the summer, many withdrew from the coarseness of the city to the shelter of country houses that were located farther up Manhattan Island, on Long Island, or in New Jersey. Another defense was provided by the voluntary societies that proliferated after midcentury, such as the New York Harmonic Society, which staged concerts featuring the works of Bach, Handel, and Haydn, and the New York Society Library, a subscription library established in 1754 that numbered

Robert R. Livingston, Philip Livingston, and William Walton on its membership rolls. Early social libraries were a space apart from both work and home—semiprivate, membership-only institutions that one historian says served as "a place to converse as well as read, to debate publicly as well as study quietly."[66] These voluntary societies were "third places," Ray Oldenburg's phrase for "a great variety of public places that host the regular, voluntary, informal and happily anticipated gatherings of individuals beyond the realms of home and work."[67] In the eighteenth century, third places validated the sophisticated tastes of their upper-class patrons and preserved their exclusivity by recruiting members through friendship and family networks.

Yet the genteel code stressed that the threat of rudeness and coarseness was ever present, and even in some third places the lines between polite and rude society were not always clear. Some voluntary associations, like the Hungarian Club and the Old Church eating and drinking society, became known for the prodigious amount of alcohol their members consumed, the raunchy jokes they told, and the poor table manners they displayed. Others, such as St. Andrew's Society and St. George's Society, both organized on the basis of ethnicity, were not identified with high standards of decorum, no matter how well their adherents conducted themselves, because they enrolled people from a broad social spectrum.[68]

In any case, this effort to move socializing onto more genteel terrain could not completely succeed in the microlandscape of eighteenth-century New York, and many polite men and women wound up being discomfited by the uncontrolled mixing with strangers that took place in the open. How upper-class individuals imagined and moved through their environments and related to other inhabitants involved a series of actions and choices that sprang from their perceptions, values, and apprehensions. As Kevin Lynch showed in his classic *Image of the City*, people who are confronted with a complicated urban landscape select some of its most distinctive features and organize them into mental representations, or maps. Lynch demonstrated that these maps vary considerably among individuals and social groups.[69]

Some eighteenth-century upper-class New Yorkers responded to their predicament of uncontrolled mixing through a process of mentally mapping the city that let them exclude impolite people and places from their versions of reality. "Space perception," anthropologist Edward T. Hall observes, "is not only a matter of what can be perceived but what can be screened out."[70] This screening can be discerned in the diaries, letters, and travel accounts in which individuals registered their experiences and impressions. In these texts, the upper class did not so much describe their surroundings and interactions as rework the urban environment in their minds and reposition themselves within the matrix of urban social relationships.

Many studiously ignored crowds and the street, neither mentioning nor depicting particular strangers or the mass of people, concentrating instead on their friends and relatives, as if they were among their intimate circles with nobody else present. They rarely made anything like the references to the collective "mood of the crowd" that became conventional in the nineteenth century. It was the existence of a social sphere, neither wholly public nor private, exposed to coarse experiences that contravened genteel conventions and did not allow for the exercise of patriarchy, that made them uneasy. They consequently rendered themselves oblivious to the strangers who surrounded them in the public space. In such narratives, these excluded outsiders are not so much invisible as they are shadows that call attention to the primacy that the upper classes put on their social circles and on gentility.[71]

Consider again Ezra Styles's 1754 trip to New York. Styles spent much of his two days there in public or semipublic spaces: on Sunday he attended services at the New English and Old Dutch churches and, the following day, strolled through a public market, entered a few shops, paid a visit to the New English Church and inspected the tombstones in its churchyard, toured a synagogue, went to Fort George and saw the governor's mansion and the barracks inside the fort's walls, stepped into the Exchange, promenaded on the Commons, and climbed the steeple of the New Dutch Church to catch a panorama of the city. Time and again he passed through the streets, probably on foot, to reach the various homes where he lodged, dined, drank tea, listened to music, or shared a few bottles.

But when Styles sat down and recounted his experiences in his diary, he reimagined New York as a genteel landscape by concentrating almost entirely on his small group of friends and acquaintances who belonged to polite society—ignoring uncouth people and encounters. He made a point of listing the names of most of the refined people he met, as if drawing a ring around his intimates and marking their environment as genteel terrain. For instance, in his entry for Monday, Styles wrote: "Waited on Mr. Smith, &c., & in evening a most elegant collation at Mr. Wm. Livingston's with Mr. Scott, & Mr Smith, & Hillhouse, & Wickham, & Ketteltas; supped, & settled politics over a generous bottle."[72] In the two brief paragraphs he devoted to his stay in New York, Styles supplied the personal names of ten gentlemen whom he met and mentioned interactions with six other polite people (a dinner enjoyed with "three Philada. ladies"; a ferry ride shared with "three other Dutch gent.") whom he did not identify by name.[73] Styles made no reference to any strangers or crowds he had encountered on the street, in church, or on the ferries. Impolite people and sites were, of course, omnipresent, and Styles's purposeful and conspicuous omission of nearly all of them from his diary was evidence of his ability to control his feelings and actions and to create a sanctuary for himself and his friends.

Indeed, Styles cited only two men who did not belong to refined society, a shopkeeper named Mr. Noels who sold curiosities in the market and a musician who played the violin, spinet, and organ with Peter Keteltas at the musician's home. This musician posed a dilemma for Styles's technique for sorting the polite from the impolite: although he had opened his home to Styles and Keteltas for a private entertainment that resembled the other intimate gatherings that occurred during his visit and appears to have been a cultivated person who was on good terms with Styles's companions, this musician lacked the independence, dignity, and refinement of a true gentleman since he was, in all probability, paid for his performances and classes. Styles resolved this quandary by effacing the musician's personal identity and individuality, referring to him as "Mr. ____, musician."[74] Yet Styles had no qualms about naming the shopkeeper—"Mr. Noels"—since his status was not in doubt.

This social blindness had its limits and was neither absolute nor unconditional. Some people were simply more personable or observant than others. Travelers, enjoying a release from social conventions or wanting to spice their accounts with colorful particulars, often detailed interactions with tavern keepers, landladies, stagecoach drivers, ferry masters, and others who were outside the boundaries of polite society.

Sexuality could be a factor. Alexander Hamilton, a Philadelphia doctor of high status whose account of his 1744 journey through the colonies was later published as *Gentleman's Progress*, was always on the lookout for liaisons with attractive women of any station. According to his biographer, Hamilton struggled with his erotic urges, pulled between his physical desire for women and an ethic of restraint he had internalized in his native Scotland that reviled sexual relations outside of marriage and compelled respect for genteel women. Hamilton sometimes resolved this internal conflict by frolicking with lower-class women, whose baseness allowed him to suspend his self-denial and give rein to his animal desires and emotions.[75] He thus remarked that one "beauty" who was accompanying her husband on a ferry ride to New York "had an amorous look, and her eyes, methought, spoke a language which is universally understood."[76] After Hamilton had been in New York for several days, an acquaintance confided that taking a walk along the main battery of the fort after sunset would be "a good way for a stranger to fit himself with a courtesan" and have "a good choice of pretty lasses among them, both Dutch and English."[77]

Not everyone was so rakish. Frances Goelet, a New York merchant who made a number of trips to London in the 1740s and 1750s, wrote lengthy journal entries about his experiences in the capital that related his conversations with fellow traders at coffeehouses, outings to theaters and churches, sightseeing excursions, introductions to the aristocracy, and invitations to fine homes, almost all praising the charm and refinement of his companions and their environs. Only a few ugly incidents, like his references to the robberies committed by highwaymen, marred his depiction of a polite London.[78] That meant that Goelet had turned a blind eye to London's lower classes and to unemployment, poverty, and disease. His journals thus provide a better guide to his mind-set than to the British metropolis.[79]

THE SEVEN YEARS' WAR

War became a catalyst for social change in New York City. During the Seven Years' War, the city became the primary British military base in North America, a command and supply center, and a troop encampment. This boosted its economy and intensified its ceremonial splendor.

Great Britain fared poorly for the first three years of the conflict. The turning point came in December 1757 when war minister William Pitt made North America, not Europe, the main theater of operations. Pitt recognized that the French were at their strongest in Europe and determined to hold the line there while striking at France's weakest point, its North American empire. Pitt wanted to use Britain's powerful navy to stop France from sending supplies and reinforcements to North America, giving his nation's relatively small regular army and its colonial militias the leeway to assault New France. Isolated from the mother country and lacking a large population from which to recruit their own territorial forces, New France could then be dismembered.[80]

Pitt's strategy put a premium on supply systems: siege campaigns required extensive lines of communication to move troops, food, clothing, and munitions to the point of attack.[81] Already the site of one of Britain's three storehouses in North America, New York was selected as a command center for geographical reasons. It had a harbor that could accommodate ships bringing troops and supplies from Great Britain and a central location that was astride both of the principal avenues of attack: first, up the Hudson River, Lake George, Lake Champlain, and the Richelieu River toward Montreal; and second, along the eastern seacoast and then down the Saint Lawrence River to Quebec City.[82]

Some administrative units, like the adjutant general's office, were permanently stationed in New York, but the city was more of a staging ground than a headquarters. The army typically went into the field in the spring and campaigned until retiring to its winter quarters, with enlisted men bivouacking in huts and barracks on Staten Island and Manhattan. Senior officers lived in style: during the winter of 1760–61, for instance, Major General Jeffrey Amherst, the commander-in-chief of the British Army in North America, resided on Nassau Street, and Brigadier General Robert Monckton had lodgings on Beaver Street, both fashionable addresses.[83]

Gary Nash writes that the Seven Years' War "brought the greatest infusion of English capital in their history" for the northern seaports and "drove forward the commercialization of life in the port towns," and New York especially benefited from this wartime stimulus.[84] It became the assembly area for major expeditions, the distribution point for funds used to pay for supplies and wages, and the base of operations for several dozen "gentlemanly capitalist" merchants who obtained contracts to provision the armed forces.[85] Labor shortages compelled the adjutant general's office to advertise for ox-team drivers and wagoners to accompany the army on its campaigns and led to the recruitment of ship's carpenters, seamen, and laborers from neighboring provinces.[86]

The ritual splendor that surrounded the imperial government reached new heights in New York City during the war and reinforced the superior position that royal officials enjoyed in its status hierarchy. Frequent military reviews and the speeches that the governor and lieutenant governor delivered about the war effort ratcheted up the ceremony. Not only that, important military officials became a daily presence in the city. Even when they were not in residence, Amherst, Monckton, Brigadier General John Forbes, and other commanders regularly passed through on their way to destinations like Albany, the West Indies, and London. Their arrivals and departures were honored with artillery salutes, the illumination of homes and shops, and respectful notices in the newspapers. Following the surrender of New France, Amherst returned to a hero's welcome that featured songs of praise at Trinity Church, a proclamation of thanks from the city government, and special honors during commencement exercises at King's College (the forerunner of Columbia University).[87]

"HIS MAJESTY'S PROCLAMATION
FOR A GENERAL PEACE"

Soon after a ship reached port carrying a copy of the proclamation of King George III of the peace treaty with France, a ceremony took place on July 25, 1763, exalting the glorious British success. Similar to the commemorations that occurred in other colonial capitals and, like them, echoing the ritual magnificence that increasingly suffused the activities of the royal family and the central government in London, this New York observance affirmed the authority of the British Empire and the prestige of its officials.

The event began when a group of eminent citizens who included leaders of the provincial council and the city government, clergymen, and "other Gentlemen in Town" went to Fort George to pay their respects to Lieutenant Governor Cadwallader Colden, General Jeffrey Amherst, and other generals. Newspaper accounts indicated that this rite reproduced the composition of the provincial status hierarchy. Royal officials were in the superior position of representing the imperial government and receiving town leaders. Merchants, doctors, lawyers, and others were no doubt among the "other Gentlemen in Town" and the "principal Gentlemen of the Place" who were noted as having participated, but the papers did not bother to list their names or occupations. All eyes were instead on Colden and Amherst; and only they were named in the newspaper accounts. Commoners probably celebrated this triumph much as they would hail the repeal of the Stamp Act three years later, but on this occasion the newspapers ignored them.[88]

It was fitting that the signing of the peace treaty should be proclaimed in the presence of Amherst and other senior officers, for the critical role that New York had performed in the Seven Years' War gave the city more international prominence than it had known at any time in its previous 140-year history. As a command center and supply base and a staging ground for major offensives, New York had become a source of war news published in London. To be sure, many of the dispatches that ran in the *London Gazette* were written at the front and made no mention of the city at all. The readers of London newspapers were interested in the war rather than in New York, and the handful of notices that did refer to the city used it as a dateline to describe the movement of armies and navies, the outcome of battles, or the presence of Amherst and other military leaders. "Yesterday," the *London Gazette* reported in 1759, "a Mail arrived from New York, which brings an Account of the Success of His Majesty's Arms on the River Ohio."[89] And again in 1763: "This Day, arrived an Express from Sir Jeffrey Amherst, Commander in Chief of His Majesty's Forces in North America, dated New York, September 3, with the following Advices."[90]

These notices paid little attention to the city itself or its inhabitants and conveyed no sense that it was an important or even a distinctive place. There was nothing like the cluster of meanings attached to the name "New York" that would begin to emerge in the early nineteenth century as urban growth created associations with wealth, power, modernity, and immigration. And no wonder: New York remained negligible in European terms, with a population that was less than 3 percent that of London. It was the war, not New York City, that mattered here.

New York had finally become a central place, due to imperial policy decisions that gave it a vital wartime role, but this centrality lasted only as long as the hostilities did.[91] Once the war ended, the British government withdrew most of its forces from North America and terminated its supply contracts, throwing New York and the other American ports into a depression. Prices collapsed, unemployment soared, and bankruptcies mounted.

In effect, the Seven Years' War amounted to another of the boom-and-bust cycles that afflicted colonial American cities It did not expand the city's economic base or increase the size of its population. It did not transform any of the cultural and social arrangements of the provincial upper class, including its status hierarchy, its members' disdain for the marketplace, and their construction of an imagined urban landscape that was devoid of the lower ranks. These upper-class relationships and understandings would change later—beginning fitfully during the American Revolution, gaining speed in the 1780s and 1790s, and finally reaching fruition in the early nineteenth century.

All that lay in the future. For the moment, the end of the war meant that New York reverted to being a lesser provincial entrepôt. Certainly nobody could have imagined that, less than a quarter century after that magnificent commemoration of the imperial victory in the Seven Years' War, another ceremony would mark the liberation of New York City from the British Empire.[92]

2

UNCERTAIN ADJUSTMENTS

....

The 1780s and 1790s

"THE EXTRAORDINARY WORTH OF THE GREAT OFFICERS BOTH CIVIL AND MILITARY"

Early on November 25, 1783, some eight hundred American soldiers under the command of General Henry Knox fell into formation at their camp in northern Manhattan and began marching south. They had been detailed to take control of New York City once the British troops that had captured it early in the Revolutionary War withdrew.

Knox's men halted north of the built-up area for several hours, until a cannon signaled that the last British soldiers were boarding their transports. The detachment then entered the city and raised an American flag, the first one to ever fly over New York City. Meanwhile, General George Washington and New York State governor George Clinton had been waiting at a tavern on the Bowery. Once Knox gave the all-clear, Washington and Clinton began a grand entrance march designed to proclaim the wartime victory and sovereignty of the United States (figure 2.1). For many patriots, the liberation of New York City—the last piece of the country still under enemy control, apart from

FIGURE 2.1 The triumphal entrance of General George Washington into New York City following the evacuation of the British military on November 25, 1783, as depicted in *Harper's Weekly* in 1866. (Author's collection.)

some frontier areas—meant nothing less than the final achievement of national independence.

The procession reproduced the prevailing status hierarchy: Washington and Clinton were in the lead, mounted on horses, attended by their aides, and escorted by light cavalry; then came the lieutenant governor and other state officials; next were General Knox and fellow army officers; then a group of distinguished citizens; and finally a knot of less renowned citizens. The parade ended at a tavern in lower Manhattan, where dignitaries greeted Washington and Clinton and toasted national independence.[1]

The celebration that unfolded in November and December 1783 was organized much as the commemoration of the Seven Years' War had been twenty years earlier. Both remembrances featured grand parades of prominent public officials, artillery salutes, patriotic toasts, and exclusive balls and dinners. Military and government leaders took center stage in each, while merchants, lawyers, and other members of the local upper class who did not have positions in the empire were relegated to the back.

At first glance it may seem odd that the revolutionaries should use the rites and symbols of the British Empire to legitimate the new nation and their leadership of it, but those traditions were what they had known and absorbed almost all their lives. Even though these American patriots were utilizing the cultural tools that were available to them, however, they employed them for their own purposes. Having concluded a long war that had left the economy damaged and their new nation divided and lacking an effective central government, these leaders hoped that paying homage to hierarchy, stability, and tradition would help integrate all the country's citizens, from the most exalted to the humblest, in a society that they would dominate and a government they would guide.

Ceremony was unusually important to these upper-class Americans because ceremony was about all they had. And they had reason to feel uneasy: the old configuration of rank and hierarchy would slowly give way to demands for greater pluralism and equality, patriarchal leaders would have to share the political sphere with representatives from other social groups, and an invigorated market economy would create new fears and uncertainties.[2] Even as they unflinchingly asserted their right to governance, upper-class New Yorkers were being forced to acknowledge in new ways the presence of the less privileged. That was a legacy of the Revolution and its immediate aftermath. For elites, the challenge of organizing new relationships with commoners was the main development of this time period. The greatest conflicts occurred in state and local politics; politics allowed for a new kind of social interaction that other public venues did not.

This desire for order and stability accounts for the one divergence from the ceremonies of 1763, the special attention that upper-class observers paid to commoners. Except for unusual circumstances like the Stamp Act repeal, city newspapers previously had ignored the presence of ordinary people. In 1783, by contrast, New York's newspapers made a point of depicting the raucous merrymaking that occurred in public spaces as artisans and farmers raised liberty poles and enlisted men fired thirteen-gun salutes with their muskets. Wanting to demonstrate that all Americans supported the cause, the newspapers now took note of the popular celebrations, although they concentrated on the upper class.[3]

In reality, these observances reflected the city's social divisions even as they proclaimed its unity. Of all the events that were held, only a gala fireworks exhibition that the Continental Army staged near Bowling Green on December 2 was open without regard to social class or status group.[4] Every other activity was confined to members of particular groups, and there was little sense of a public realm where all the people could associate.

The existence of these social gulfs made elites apprehensive about the lower orders. As upper-class onlookers weighed the significance of the evacuation, most reassured themselves by stressing its orderliness. On November 29, Robert R. Livingston could write that "we have been five days in town without the smallest disturbance."[5] The *New York Packet* contrasted the city's current tranquility with the civil disruptions that had characterized the occupation: "no mobs—no riots—no disorders . . . everything is quietness and safety"; while the *Independent Journal* praised American troops for entering New York with "an inviolable regard to order and discipline, as Tyranny could have never enforced."[6]

The papers attributed the city's harmony to the high quality of the patriot leadership. "Nothing," the *Journal* commented, "but an unremitting and exalted sense of the extraordinary worth of the great officers both civil and military they had the honor to attend, naturally prompted the troops and inhabitants to rigidly observe [discipline and order]."[7] The message was obvious: the presence of commoners demonstrated American unity, while their fealty to their betters ensured social stability.

New York's elites (and others) faced significant challenges during the era of the American Revolution. While the Revolutionary War caused hardships for people in many parts of the country, it was nothing short of a calamity for residents of New York City, which British forces occupied for seven years, longer than any other American city. A fire that destroyed a quarter of the city's dwellings in September 1776 created a severe housing shortage that was not remedied until after the war.

The fighting severed the British-controlled city from its largely patriot-controlled hinterland, disrupting the commodity flows essential to the functioning of the regional economy and leading to scarcities of bread, meat, and firewood, price gouging, and smuggling. Far worse, American prisoners of war were held captive on ships anchored in the East River in conditions so wretched that some 11,000 of them perished, far more than the 6,800 Americans who died in combat during the Revolutionary War.[8]

The Revolution split the city's upper class between Loyalists and patriots and forced many elites to make hard choices about their allegiances. Several major population exoduses occurred in the course of the war, including the evacuation itself, when thousands of upper-class (and other) loyalists fled to Canada, Great Britain, and other destinations.

The postwar period was no less turbulent. Upper-class New Yorkers clung to their old beliefs about rank, hierarchy, and gentility even as they responded haltingly to demands for greater pluralism and equality. They decided to reintegrate loyalists into their circles and civil society and to let talented newcomers who had gained wealth and position during wartime enter the upper class.

The reviving economy was also a source of distress; some upper-class New Yorkers saw unbridled speculation and the spread of banks and corporations as dangers to social and economic stability. All the same, the emphasis that elites put on enterprise through their support of the construction of roads and canals, land speculation, reopening trade with Great Britain, and voyages to China and other novel destinations helped the urban economy recover from the war. Their leadership and civic-mindedness enabled New York to weather these difficult years, a signal contribution that reflected the priority that some members of the city's upper class had traditionally attached to openness, dynamism, and acquisitiveness.

They had to be adaptable if they were to keep their eye on the main chance, and so they were. They made slow, almost unconscious modifications of their individual and social actions to adjust to the new cultural surroundings that enabled them to retain their status and authority.

THE TRANSFORMATION OF POLITICS

After the Revolution, the most direct challenge to upper-class New Yorkers' continuing rule involved state and local politics. Elites remained ascendant but lost their monopoly on politics when members of the two other social orders—farmers and mechanics and people of middling rank—contested elections and policy decisions.

This new reality was brought home by the city elections of 1783, the first to be held following the evacuation, when a slate of radical candidates selected by a committee of mechanics decisively defeated rival parties of moderate Whigs and former Tories. The winning ticket included two small traders, Isaac Sears and Marinus Willett, who had been part of the coalition of artisans and small merchants that had organized popular resistance to Great Britain before the Revolution. Sears, Willett, and their allies took antielite positions in the 1783 elections, seeking to prohibit former Tories from voting and to confiscate Tory property and advocating the restructuring or eradication of royalist institutions such as the Anglican Church and King's College. A group of upper-class conservatives led by Alexander Hamilton and Philip Schuyler eventually dislodged them from office, but state and city politics had been wholly transformed into an arena that was at once contested and shared. Upper-class leaders would sometimes act of their own volition, sometimes form alliances with moderates from the lower orders, and sometimes be defeated by the radicals and others.[9]

The heightened presence of artisans and mechanics was made apparent in the Grand Federal Procession of July 23, 1788.[10] Organized by Federalists as part of their campaign for New York State to ratify the Constitution, the Grand Federal Procession consisted of five thousand men and boys who wore colorful costumes and carried signs and banners as they marched in clearly defined ranks through the streets of lower Manhattan and passed in review before delegates of the Confederation Congress and prominent citizens. Merchants, lawyers, physicians, the president and students of Columbia College, militia officers, and leaders of the Society of the Cincinnati had conspicuous positions in the order of march, and the parade was managed by a contingent of thirteen "gentlemen" that included members of the prominent Livingston, Le Roy, and Bleecker families.

While elites had controlled prior ceremonies, what was new about the Grand Procession was the participation of thousands of mechanics, who arrayed themselves according to their crafts, with more than sixty different trades represented.[11] Their involvement made the Grand Procession a vital moment in urban politics, "an event of almost transcendent significance in New York's post-Revolutionary history," according to Edwin G. Burrows and Mike Wallace.[12] The massed presence of the trades, Burrows and Wallace continue, "gave tangible expression to the organized artisanal presence that was already altering the course of municipal affairs" and demonstrated that these mechanics "had come to see themselves as equal citizens, actively engaged in the life of the community."[13]

Still, the procession was simultaneously political theater meant to reify social hierarchies. Each of the trades had selected officers, adjutants, and orderlies who were to maintain order in the ranks, and who in turn were supposed to take directions from the parade's superintendent and its thirteen marshals. Appraising these elaborate preparations, the *New York Packet* concluded that the representation of "the various classes of citizens which are to compose the Procession" corroborated the primacy of elites over other social ranks and affirmed the stability of urban society.[14]

Now that they had lost their political monopoly, upper-class New Yorkers were attempting to write a new script that permitted and acknowledged the participation of the lower orders in politics and other spheres—provided they accepted the benign leadership of their betters. Elites saw themselves as trustees who would act in the best interests of commoners and, in turn, receive the deference due their wisdom and their elevated station. They obviously could not picture themselves being obligated to carry out the wishes of their constituents.

Yet as the political arena became more inclusive, some upper-class New Yorkers also modified their perceptions of commoners. John Anderson Jr., a lawyer, and his brother, Alexander Anderson, a medical student, both enjoyed holidays like Independence Day and wrote about the festivities in depth in their journals. Yet the brothers often rendered themselves oblivious to the other spectators. They described the military parades, artillery salutes, fireworks displays, and other events that happened on these patriotic anniversaries and recorded their exchanges with friends and family members. However, they made little mention of the masses of strangers present in the streets.[15] The same was true of their accounts of events in their everyday lives.[16]

Like other upper-class people, John Anderson generally concentrated on his intimates—literally placing himself inside their orbit by naming them or their retainers individually—and acted as if nobody else was present. Anderson expressed no apprehension of menace or danger and was not manifesting any fear of the crowd. Instead, he felt discomfited by uncontrolled mixing in public space with strangers who were lower in rank, because it threatened to erase boundaries and veil credentials. He was unwilling to acknowledge or enter a social sphere that seemed neither entirely public nor private and that violated polite expectations of sociability.[17]

Yet John Anderson gradually began to register the presence of others at public ceremonies, commenting, for example, on "the procession of Tammany's—Democrats—mechanicks &c &c" who marched in the Independence Day parade in 1795 and on the participation of "different societies" another year.[18] He became more aware of the crowd, observing at one point that "the concourse of people [watching fireworks on the Battery] was very great."[19] These references were to groups and organizations that had social meaning for him rather than to particular individuals, and they were brief, fleeting, and unspecific, but that they happened at all is noteworthy. It shows that Anderson was retreating from social blindness and adjusting to the new cultural conditions.

John and Alexander Anderson patronized coffeehouses and taverns; went to the circus, museums, and the theater; and promenaded on the Battery.[20] Although these venues were social spaces where people of different backgrounds mixed, most of the encounters with people from other social orders that the brothers recorded in their diaries occurred in the political realm, particularly as the outbreak of the Napoleonic Wars heightened partisan rivalries between Republicans and Federalists.

John, a fervent Republican, described "a number of people, english & french" who rejoiced at France's recapture of Toulon by dancing around French and American flags at the Tontine Coffee House and, several days later, a group of "citizens, & Frenchmen" who paraded through the streets for the same purpose.[21] His brother detailed a scrap that broke out between "Aristocrat[s] & Democrat[s]" at the Tontine and a public meeting "where a multitude had assembled" to advocate that the United States remain neutral in the fighting. [22]

A COUSINS' WORLD: NEW YORK'S UPPER CLASS AND THE REVOLUTIONARY WAR

These political tensions and conflicts were real enough. Class conflict was a key factor in many postwar disputes in city and state politics, including plans by some representatives of small artisans and farmers and mechanics in the state legislature to confiscate the property of wealthy loyalists, levy punitive taxes on them, and expel their families from the state. Similarly, the legislature passed laws to de-Anglicize royalist institutions like the Anglican Church, King's College, and the Chamber of Commerce. It abolished primogeniture and entail to open the great landed estates to division by inheritance and, the radicals hoped, break them up. To permit more ordinary people to acquire farmsteads, the state government drastically reduced its fees for surveying and purchasing land.[23]

However, state and local politics were the only stage where upper-class New Yorkers encountered direct challenges to their power and status. Unlike the French and Russian Revolutions, there was no concerted effort to overthrow the upper class during the American Revolution or in the immediate years afterward. Indeed, the toppling of the empire and the achievement of independence enhanced the prestige of the upper class and gave its members national governing authority for the first time.

In many respects, the persistence of New York's upper class is surprising. No social group was affected by the American Revolution in terms of the disruption of their daily lives more than the upper class, and nowhere were they more affected than in New York State. New York City's three major population shifts—the exodus of patriots who took flight following the British invasion of 1776, the subsequent influx of loyalists from elsewhere in the country who found safe haven in British-occupied New York and made it a center of the Loyalist population, and the evacuation of 1783—disrupted upper-class networks and caused financial hardships.

The most significant occurrence was that the war split New York's upper class between loyalists and patriots. Most scholars concur that the primary determinant of whether the province's upper-class leaders became loyalists or patriots was the political party to which they had belonged prior to the conflict, with members of the ascendant De Lancey party tending to remain loyal to the Crown. Dealing with the British ministries in London on administrative and patronage matters had enmeshed De Lanceyites like New York City's mayor David Mathews and chamberlain J. H. Cruger with the imperial regime. Moreover, the De Lanceyites were dominated by great merchants whose transatlantic commerce with partners in the British Isles and the British West Indies gave them a stake in the empire.[24] Merchants in the other colonial cities were similarly predisposed, but according to Gary Nash, a higher percentage of New York's top merchants sided with the imperial government and opposed the resistance movement than did their brethren in Philadelphia and Boston.[25] One reason was that De Lanceyites were overwhelmingly Anglican, an affiliation that embedded them in a heritage of hierarchy, tradition, and ritual. Another was that the many De Lanceyites who had come from elsewhere in the empire, such as Ireland, Bermuda, Scotland, and England, felt little connection to the thirteen colonies.

By contrast, members of the minority Livingston party tended to become rebels. Composed mainly of planters and lawyers who had less of a stake in the empire than merchants, and associated with the Presbyterian Church and its clashes with the Anglican establishment, the Livingstons thought of themselves in terms of Britain's Whig opposition.[26] Robert R. Livingston served as a delegate to the Continental Congress and was elected chancellor of New York State in 1777, and William represented New Jersey in the Continental Congress and became that state's first governor in 1776. While Peter Van Brugh and Philip were moderate Whigs who were active in the resistance, the fifth brother, John, was a Tory who stayed in New York City during the war.

John Livingston's choice tells us that the pattern of De Lanceyites becoming Tories and Livingstons Whigs should be seen as a central tendency rather than a hard-and-fast rule. The Revolution caused many members of the provincial upper class to feel less certain of alliances based on class, for the first time ever. Upper-class people typically enjoyed a large degree of freedom in their life circumstances, mastery of their social environments, and prestige and wealth, but now events beyond their control interrupted their way of life and ruptured their family and friendship circles. Individuals had to make difficult decisions that reflected their values, temperaments, and relationships.

Consider the divergent paths taken by Maria De Peyster Bancker Ogden's three sons. While Johannes fought in the Continental Army and Gerard became treasurer of the Provincial Congress, her oldest son, Evert, was an ardent Loyalist who remained in New York City, joined the city militia, and served as city surveyor. Another example is James Duane, a lawyer who was drawn to the Tories by his close friendships with several influential De Lanceyites and by his respect for hierarchy and tradition. However, Duane's marriage to Maria Livingston brought him into the Livingston orbit and led him to become a patriot. Strong personal relationships often trumped values and material interests.[27]

Tight family and friendship networks that helped the upper class cope with wartime exigencies and personal bonds often proved to be stronger than political affiliations and national allegiances. The experiences of William Smith Jr., the colony's chief justice and a member of its provincial council, exemplifies the importance of these networks. As fighting broke out in 1775 and 1776, Smith's position in the provincial government and his lawyerly insistence that the conflict be resolved by negotiation rather than by arms predisposed him toward the Loyalist camp. But instead of irrevocably committing himself to the Crown by staying in occupied New York, Smith, his wife, and their daughters took refuge for the next two years at Livingston Manor. Even though Robert R. Livingston, the lord of the manor, and three brothers were supporters of national independence, the Livingstons embraced the Smiths, because the wives of William Smith Jr. and Robert R. Livingston were sisters.

Other relatives who were in residence at the manor included Maria Livingston, the wife of James Duane, a member of the Continental Congress; Sarah and Janet Livingston, both married to American generals; and Catherine Livingston Patterson and her Loyalist husband. It was less that family trumped politics than that upper-class family relationships were so interwoven with political, business, and the military matters that people continually juggled an array of potentially conflicting beliefs and loyalties. In the cousins' world of the New York upper class, the tug of family ties and the code of gentility encouraged cooperation and group harmony. As governor of New Jersey, William Livingston refused to let Whig and Loyalist relatives cross the lines into British-controlled areas, yet he nonetheless intervened with Governor George Clinton of New York to ask that his sister receive a pass to enter Manhattan so that she could recover house rents there.

But upper-class networks could not completely forestall harsh treatment. In 1778, William Smith Jr.'s friends and allies in the revolutionary government of New York State were unable to squelch demands from opponents like John Jay (himself married to a Livingston) that Smith swear an oath of allegiance, and Smith finally had to declare his loyalties. Leaving his Livingston Manor sanctuary, he went to New York City and became an adviser to the occupation government. He sailed to England during the evacuation of 1783, returning to North America several years later with a Crown appointment as chief justice of Quebec. Smith was reviled in postrevolutionary America as a high-ranking imperial official who had typified Toryism, but that was not enough for the close-knit eighteenth-century upper class to expel him. After the war, his Livingston and Schuyler relatives sheltered his wife and daughters in New York City and maintained a warm correspondence and business ties with him, while friends in the state government kept his property from being confiscated and lifted his order of banishment in 1790. Smith, however, died in Canada in 1793, never having set foot in his native land again.[28]

The experience of William Smith Jr. suggests that the war altered the membership of the upper class even if it did not transform its structure. At first, it was loyalists who benefited from the population turnover, with many of them using the war to make money and attain higher status. Some merchants who had obtained military provisioning contracts during the Seven Years' War did so again during the Revolutionary War. Loyalists filled cynosures in the occupation government; for instance, William Waddell, a Tory merchant who had narrowly escaped being tarred and feathered by the patriots in June 1776, received an officer's commission and appointments in the occupation government as rewards for his fidelity.[29] Hundreds of upper-class loyalists arrived from parts of the country that had fallen under rebel control, including Robert Alexander, a Maryland lawyer who resigned from the Continental Congress rather than support national independence, and John Mawdsely, a Rhode Island merchant.[30]

But loyalists soon found themselves in trouble. In August 1782, *Rivington's Royal Gazette* reported that British and American diplomats in Paris were negotiating a peace treaty that would end the war and secure British recognition of the United States. Loyalists who feared being the targets of popular violence when rebels returned home became further alarmed when the revolutionary state government passed legislation authorizing that loyalists be deprived of the right to vote and hold office, that their property be confiscated, and that anyone convicted of treason be executed.[31]

By November 1783, more than thirty-two thousand loyalists and sympathizers had fled to Canada, Great Britain, the West Indies, and other destinations. Along with commoners who had sided with or fought for Great Britain and African American slaves who freed themselves from their masters by escaping to Canada, this migration also included hundreds upon hundreds of upper-class New Yorkers. It is the largest exodus of upper-class people in American history.[32] Among the evacuees were grandees like Andrew Eliot, a Scottish native who was the province's last royal governor; William Bayard, a wealthy merchant from a distinguished old family; and Vincent Ashfield, a merchant who had owned estates in New Jersey. Prominent Anglicans such as Charles Inglis, who became Nova Scotia's first bishop of the Church of England, and Mary Auchmuty, the widow of the Reverend Samuel Auchmuty, also left, as did less distinguished members of the upper class, such as timber merchant Benjamin Garrison and auctioneer Patrick McDavitt.[33]

For all the misery that these refugees endured, the state's upper class emerged from the Revolution relatively unaltered as a collective entity. Its social structure and its wealth and power remained intact. What changed was its membership. In place of the loyalists who had left came an influx of newcomers who used the reputations and connections they had made during the war to enter the upper stratum. While the departing loyalists included patricians who belonged to old families that stood for hierarchy, rank, and dignity and high officials of the Church of England who personified tradition and stability, the newcomers were strivers who were intent on clawing their way upward. The net effect of this subtraction of Loyalist insiders and addition of patriot outsiders was to make the upper class less aristocratic and more aggressively materialistic. As in the past, events had made New York's upper class more open to outsiders and more money oriented than its counterparts in Philadelphia and Boston.

Alexander Hamilton and William Duer are cases in point. Born poor and illegitimate in the West Indies, Hamilton showed youthful promise as a writer and a clerk, and local merchants sent him to be educated at King's College in New York City. A brilliant war record and a close relationship with George Washington helped him overcome the stigma of his birth and become an outstanding political leader and lawyer in postwar New York. In 1780 he entered the cousins' world through his astute marriage to Elizabeth Schuyler, the daughter of Major General Philip Schuyler, who had extensive landholdings in the upper Hudson Valley and was a major figure in New York politics and society. Through intermarriages and friendships, the Schuylers had become close to the Van Cortlandt, De Peyster, and Van Rensselaer families.

Unlike Hamilton, William Duer was a gentleman from birth. A native of Devon, England, Duer came from a family in the English landed gentry that owned plantations on Dominica and Antigua in the West Indies.

Following his education at Eton College and service as aide-de-camp to the governor general of the East India Company, Duer went to Dominica to take over a family estate that he had inherited. While on a trip to the New York colony to buy lumber in 1768, Duer met Philip Schuyler, who lived north of Albany on an estate that overlooked the Hudson River. Schuyler persuaded Duer to settle in the colony, and on his advice, Duer purchased a tract of land ten miles away from Schuylerville and built a house, a sawmill, warehouses, and a store. Through their friendship, Duer became a member of the province's landed gentry and habituated himself to its relationships and ideals.

His English background disposed Duer to loyalism, but his associations with the upriver gentry exerted a countervailing influence. Most of the people he knew—Philip Schuyler, James Duane, and the Livingstons—were moderate Whigs who had gradually come around to supporting independence, so Duer moved in that direction too. He proclaimed his sympathies by taking a seat in the New York Provincial Congress in 1775 and later helping to draft the state's first constitution. He later served in the New York State Senate and the Continental Congress.

Late in 1778 Duer began to concentrate on restoring his depleted finances. Through his ties with congressional delegates and military officers, he obtained contracts to provision the Continental Army with grain, flour, and timber. He also bought confiscated Loyalist farms in New York State. Through his connections with the diplomatic corps, he supplied masts and spars to the Spanish navy and wheat to the French forces. He also wed Kitty Alexander, the daughter of William Alexander, a wealthy New Jersey landowner and a major general in the Continental Army who called himself "Lord Stirling."

After the war the Duers moved to New York City, where William added to his fortune through army supply contracts, foreign trade, and land speculation. William and Kitty Duer threw themselves into the social whirl of the New York upper class, but neither had grown up inside the upper class or married into it, and having much weaker attachments to it than Alexander and particularly Elizabeth Hamilton did, they could not fully penetrate its family and friendship circles.[34]

Ultimately, Duer did not exchange the hierarchy, gentility, tradition, and stability that had been his birthright as an English gentleman for new values such as social or political equality; rather, his success in entering the American squirearchy meant that he had seamlessly transferred the meanings he had imbibed at home to his adopted land.

A study of the memberships of eight elite organizations confirms that the New York City's postwar upper class was highly integrated. The eight groups ranged from the alumni of King's College from its first graduating class in 1758 through 1800 and the pew holders of Trinity Church in the 1790s to the trustees and members of the New York Society Library in 1793 and the officers, governors, senior staff, and members of the New York Hospital Society in 1803.[35]

Their memberships overlapped significantly.[36] Sixty-eight percent of the Manufacturing Society's directors belonged to one or more of the other seven groups. The same was true for half of the American Academy, 48 percent of the Hospital Society, 40 percent of the Free School Society, and 21 percent of the New York Society Library. Generally speaking, the more institutions a man belonged to, the more prominent he was likely to be.[37] The pattern of the most prominent men having the highest number of associations confirms that late-eighteenth-century urban elites were generalists who threw themselves into many realms of city life rather than specializing in a particular sphere, like the economy or politics. They considered public office and good works to be their civic responsibility and believed they had a far-reaching right to governance and everyone was subject to their stewardship. They concerned themselves both locally and nationally and conceived of themselves as leaders of the nation, the state, and the city. Most of those with multiple affiliations belonged to at least one humanitarian society, and several had leadership positions in the New York Hospital or the Free School Society.[38]

These upper-class linkages extended to prestigious institutions besides the eight that were surveyed. Those with multiple memberships were also leaders of associations like the Society of the Cincinnati, established by Continental Army officers to foster brotherhood among veteran officers, confer distinction for their patriotic sacrifices, and lobby for pensions for the society's members and their dependents. There was also substantial overlap with ethnocultural organizations like the Saint Andrew's Society and the Saint George's Society and with other humanitarian groups like the Society for the Prevention of Pauperism.[39]

The groups that these upper-class New Yorkers did *not* join is equally telling. The foremost artisans' organization in the city was the General Society of Mechanics and Tradesmen, a trade association founded in 1786 on behalf of skilled craftsmen. New York City's postrevolutionary upper class was truly self-contained and inclusive; the threads that bound elites together stopped short of the General Society, and there was little intersection between the memberships of the eight institutions and that of the General Society. Of the 613 men and women who joined the General Society through 1799, only five belonged to two or more of the eight institutions.[40]

Immediately after the Revolutionary War, members of this highly interconnected upper class faced two main challenges: deciding whether loyalists should be integrated into civil society and determining what steps should be taken to revive the urban economy. The responses that upper-class New Yorkers made to these two interrelated problems reflected the value they put on class cohesiveness and the priority they attached to profit making.

POSTWAR NEW YORK: A SPIRIT OF ENTERPRISE AND COMMUNITIES OF TRUST

In 1788 Jacques Pierre Brissot De Warville, a French journalist and political activist who had stopped in New York City during a tour of the United States, expressed incredulity at the restoration of the urban economy from its wartime devastation. He marveled that "everywhere streets are being widened and extended . . . On all sides houses are going up and streets are being laid out; everywhere I see workers filling in land, excavating, building, laying pavements, erecting public pumps."[41] A committed republican who would help lead the Girondist faction during the French Revolution, De Warville interpreted New York's renewal as proof that representative government brought economic prosperity and social happiness. Several years later, the bustling urban economy made a similar impression on William Strickland, a stolid Yorkshire country gentleman and future baronet. Strickland later recalled that his first view of the United States had come as his ship made landfall on the East River and he caught sight of docks "coverd with workmen, merchandize and carriages, . . . a scene breaking out upon us of the utmost activity [that left us] in silent astonishment."[42]

De Warville and Strickland were right to conclude that New York had recovered quickly from the war. Shipping grew rapidly after 1783 and drove economic growth. New York City started to increase its share of foreign and coastal trade in the 1790s and in 1797 overtook Philadelphia as the nation's leading port with respect to the value of both imports and exports. In 1800, New York was still the second-largest city in the United States but had almost drawn even with Philadelphia. Ten years later, New York City had pulled ahead.[43]

Signs of a new vitality were evident across the United States in the 1780s and 1790s, from the land speculators who acquired huge swaths of the backcountry to the federal and state governments' construction of more postal offices and turnpikes to the New York and Philadelphia investors who pooled their resources to underwrite the voyage of the *Empress of China* to Guangzhou, which pioneered American trade with China. The creation of more profit-seeking corporations, such as the Bank of New York, permitted larger amounts of capital to be amassed. All this activity contributed to the spread of a new culture of economic dynamism that one scholar calls "a vigorous spirit of enterprise."[44]

The phoenix-like rise of New York City from its wartime ruin was the single most notable outcome of this economic vigor. The key to the city's growth was the enlargement of its hinterland. Following the defeat of their British allies during the Revolutionary War, the Iroquois nations in the central and western regions of what became New York State could no longer defend their homelands, allowing American and European speculators to snap up tracts across upstate and settlers to establish farms in its lake and river valleys. As more wheat and other farm products moved down the Hudson River and out through New York harbor, New York State nearly tripled in population between 1790 and 1820, rising from the fifth-largest state in the union to the largest.[45]

The foundations of this speedy postwar renewal were laid by city residents who put their personal welfare and urban prosperity ahead of national allegiances. During the occupation, many civilians had coped with their predicament by passing through the lines to pay social calls, aid relatives, share news, and transact illicit business, a strategy of accommodation that built on the older tradition of toleration of urban social diversity.[46] Thus, rather than support the radical Whig program of denying citizenship to and expelling Tories, war-weary New Yorkers heeded Alexander Hamilton's pleas for toleration. In coming to the aid of their friends, relatives, and business partners, these leaders also had the best interests of their city at heart, forging a climate of acceptance that aided the rebuilding of the urban economy.[47]

A similar willingness to gloss over past sins for the sake of social harmony and economic recovery enabled several hundred Loyalists and people with family or business connections with Great Britain to remain in the city following the evacuation. Initially, Tories did encounter hostility. In December 1783 the *Independent Journal* delivered a warning on behalf of "a great number of injured and enraged Whigs" to "those Tories who sold goods at vendue, under the authority of the British government, [and who now] have the audacity still to continue that business."[48] Collin McGregor, a Scottish resident, described notorious Loyalist newspaper printer "J. Rivington's being once or twice kick'd & cuffed & prevented from Printing."[49] But wartime memories eventually faded and loyalists won grudging acceptance. "There is still & will be a perpetual coolness betwixt numerous families & their new neighbours," McGregor said, "however, they associate now & then, & there is a possibility of its wearing off."[50]

This spirit of tolerance enabled New York traders, even former Loyalists like chinaware dealer Frederick Rhinelander, to resume business contacts with British merchants free of social condemnation. In 1774 Rhinelander's coldness to resistance had caused radicals to accuse him of being "unfriendly to Liberty" and "an Enemy to my Country" and prompted New England merchants who handled much of his trade to refuse to pay their bills or handle his crockery.[51] Rhinelander and his family exited New York City to avoid this Whig pressure. He returned during the British occupation and not only resumed his regular trade but augmented his income by transporting gunpowder and provisions for the British military and by outfitting privateers who attacked rebel shipping.[52] As peace negotiations gained momentum in February 1783, Rhinelander assured his British correspondents "that we intend to continue in the same line of business as formerly."[53] He stopped recording orders eight days before the evacuation but was back in business within a month.

At first Rhinelander used surrogate firms in his transactions with merchants in places like Massachusetts and Rhode Island where he anticipated trouble. Significantly, he encountered almost no friction in New York City itself. Supplementing his chinaware business by trading in provisions and speculating in land, Rhinelander became the progenitor of one of nineteenth-century New York's leading families, a testament to his nimbleness as a merchant as well as to the tolerant urban environment that protected him.[54]

Even Loyalists who abandoned New York retained ties with relatives, friends, and business partners there. Some Tory traders who went into exile in London signed powers of attorney that put their merchandise, vessels, and real estate under the authority of Theophylact Bache, a Yorkshire-born merchant and ex-Loyalist who stayed put after the war and remained ensconced in the upper class.[55]

A prominent mercantile house during the 1760s and 1770s was Phynn, Ellice and Inglis, two of whose three Scottish founders had come to New York with supply contracts during the Seven Years' War. James Phynn and Alexander Ellice remained in the city after the end of the conflict, starting families with American women and entering its upper class. Along with transatlantic commerce, Phynn and Ellice operated flour mills, speculated in property, and traded furs in northern portions of the New York colony. Archetypal gentlemanly capitalists, Phynn, Ellice, and John Inglis never wavered in their allegiance to the Crown. Early in the Revolutionary

War, Phynn and Ellice left occupied New York for London, where they reestablished their partnership and resumed their lavish standard of living.

Phynn and Ellice were enraged at the revolutionaries who had driven them from their homes and confiscated their property, and neither returned to America. Yet as specialists who depended on the Anglo-American connection for much of their business, they could not afford to cut their link with New York City, especially since it was rooted in a close family relationship, with Phynn's brother-in-law, fellow merchant William Constable.[56] Born in Dublin in 1752, Constable was the son of a British army surgeon who had served in North America during the Seven Years' War and then stayed. The Constables settled in Schenectady, where William's older sister married James Phynn and William became a clerk for Phynn, Ellice and Inglis.

Constable was employed as the partners' agent in London when hostilities began in 1775 and immediately recognized new moneymaking possibilities. After relocating to occupied New York and becoming a partner in a Tory mercantile house, Constable sailed with the British invasion fleet that captured Philadelphia in 1777 and opened a branch store there. The failure of his store put him in debt to his investors in New York and Great Britain, but Constable hit upon a simple expedient for eluding his creditors: he switched sides, remaining behind after the British evacuation of Philadelphia in June 1778 and swearing allegiance to the revolutionary government. This espousal of American liberties did not stop him from bribing officials and moving his goods across enemy lines when he could obtain a better price; according to his biographer, Constable was "one of those business-as-usual merchants who traded wherever and however profit took them and who drove the Pennsylvania radicals and likeminded men from other states to peaks of patriotic anger."[57]

After the war, Constable moved to New York City and established the new firm of Constable, Rucker & Company. He negotiated the repayment of his debts to his British creditors, renewed his relationship with his brother-in-law, and resumed his dealings with Phynn, Ellice and Inglis. He ingratiated himself into New York's upper-class society by joining the Chamber of Commerce and the New York Society Library.[58]

In 1786 St. George Tucker, a delegate to the Confederation Congress from Virginia, penned a scathing portrayal of a fictive ex-Tory named Mr. Spee who resembled William Constable. Tucker called Spee "that plodding fellow" and related how he had made a low bow to a "Gentleman in a pea Green silk" who belonged to Congress and had had a distinguished record as a Revolutionary War officer.[59] By demonstrating this opposition between the polite and the impolite, Tucker showed that Spee was no gentleman.

> When the British Army took possession of this place Mr. Spee remained here. To shew his Loyalty to his sovereign and at the same time gratify his own private propensities, Mr. Spee became one of the contractors for the Army. Thus he served his King and his God Mammon at once. When Continental Currency was first emitted Mr. Spee was one of the first to advise the counterfieting [*sic*] and dispersing it through the rebel colonies. Here too he served two different Ends, by enriching himself and depreciating the rebel Currency. The royal cause began to decline. Mr. Spee was still ambidexter. His agents buy up Continental Certificates of every Denomination—officers rights to Land, etc. N. York is evacuated. Mr. Spee had by a well-timed accommodation of small sums of money, gained the friendship of some officer prisoners during the war. Relying on their countenance, he determines to brave danger and stay in N. York while his Brother Tories were embarking for Nova Scotia. Here was a new field for making money—Houses, Land, Goods, etc., belonging to those timid Souls, went abegging for purchasers. Mr. Spee had money and availed himself of the Occasion. Let what will turn up, Spee is sure to be the first to gain advantage by it. He now cringes and bows to every man in power whom he meets, and anticipates the joy of pillaging both countries.[60]

Yet collaborators like Constable and loyalists such as Frederick Rhinelander had to be reabsorbed into civil society if the urban economy was to be restored. While lesser merchants such as Isaac Sears, Alexander McDougall, and Jacobus Van Zandt had become revolutionaries, the preponderance of New York City's great merchants had been Loy-alists, including such notables as James and Oliver De Lancey, James Jauncey, Miles Sherbrooke, Hugh and Alexander Wallace, and Isaac Low. A measure of their prominence in the postwar mercantile community is that several of them obtained high offices in the Chamber of Com-merce, with John Alsop becoming its first president after the war and Theophylact Bache serving as vice president. The Chamber readmitted other ex-loyalists, like Henry Remsen, Peter Keteltas, and Robert Lennox. Whatever qualms patriot traders may have felt, the reintegration of these former Tories was crucial, because their connections to British merchants facilitated economic revival.[61]

Even apart from this willingness to accommodate ex-Loyalists, the res-toration of Anglo-American trading was no simple matter. British mer-chants demanded full and immediate repayment of debts owed to them since the beginning of the war, with interest. When New York merchant James Beekman cited the city's wartime devastation in pleading with the London firm of Fludyn Maitland for more time to repay his obligations, he received the tart reply that "the general Distress of your country [is something] which we are too well acquainted with and too sensibly feel from all quarters."[62] It was, Fludyn Maitland insisted with an insult that impugned Beekman's character, no reason for his "not being quite so reg-ular to Engagements as a Man of Integrity must ever wish to be."[63] British merchants were dismayed by the military defeat, sensitive to American nationalism, and furious that their property had been confiscated, while American traders were in the unenviable position of being junior partners in unequal transatlantic trading relationships who desperately needed access to British capital and markets.

But for Constable, Phynn, and many others, the benefits of coop-eration outweighed the discomforts. American and British merchants formed communities of mutual trust that expanded their trading net-works and provided access to capital and markets and information about the trustworthiness of business partners. By the mid-1780s, Constable, Rucker had established a co-partnership with Phynn, Ellice and Inglis that would last for more than two decades and entail collaboration on

Anglo-American trade; American efforts to penetrate markets in India, the West Indies, and China; and land speculation on U.S. frontiers.[64] Constable caught the conflicted nature of this relationship when he wrote in 1794 that "Mr Ellice hates the country tho' he is now buying lands in every corner of it."[65]

Such communities of trust did not develop in patriotic hotbeds like Boston, where the prolongation of wartime anti-British sentiment intimidated merchants and impeded the restoration of commerce, as the *Mercury* incident of 1785 illustrates. HMS *Mercury* became the first British warship to visit Boston after the Revolutionary War when it entered harbor in August 1785, escorting merchantmen that were there to load sheep, cattle, and provisions for transport to the British West Indies. Because the arrival of this flotilla coincided with a severe depression, the *Mercury* became a flashpoint for popular anger against the British prohibition of American vessels from carrying American exports to British possessions. Continuing their prewar activism, the Bostonians passed a series of resolves protesting the British ban. In yet another instance in which Boston's economic distress encouraged its leaders to evoke the severe ideals of its founders in summoning the populace to endure trials and sacrifices, radicals who interpreted this episode as a national affront compelled merchants to impose a policy of nonimportation of British goods, with traders who resisted the popular will to be roundly denounced.[66]

In its account of this fracas, New York's *Daily Advertiser* derided the self-righteousness of the Bostonians. "The violent patriots of New-England" had supposed that there was "nothing competent to contend with their decrees" but "now begin to see and *feel* the folly of their proceedings in prohibiting the English from their coasts."[67] In a final twist of the screw, the paper accused Bostonians of being enthralled by their own virtue, a luxury that sound, businesslike New Yorkers eschewed.

Unlike the straitlaced and tradition-bound elites in Boston and other American cities, New York elites were relatively dynamic, open, and aggressive. They made a vital contribution to their city's postwar recovery and growth. The aura of toleration and the spirit of enterprise they helped foster were central to New York's civic identity, but their support of these activities was really meant to legitimate and thus reinforce their own pursuit of wealth, prestige, and status. They helped mold the singular character of their city, even as they were molded by it.

The enlargement of the urban hinterland, the revitalization of the economy, the accommodation of former Tories, and the ascent of ambitious newcomers such as Hamilton and Duer fueled New York City's economic advances and showed that materialism was becoming more acceptable to members of the upper class in this emerging commercial city. Yet New York City also became the seat of the national government following the Revolutionary War, and an intensification of ritual grandeur and the creation of new patterns of upper-class socializing threatened to blunt the pursuit of moneymaking.

THE MAKING OF "THE REPUBLICAN COURT"

New York City became the capital of the United States in January 1785 and, following the ratification of the Constitution three years later, the seat of the new federal government. On April 30, 1789, George Washington took the oath of office as the first president of the United States at Federal Hall, at the corner of Wall and Broad Streets. While George and Martha Washington made their home nearby, the executive and legislative branches were housed in Federal Hall, where fundamental decisions were made about the creation of the president's cabinet and the executive departments, the establishment of the Bill of Rights, and the organization of the Supreme Court.[68]

In the eighteenth century, the capital city of a country was the place where the best and the brightest from all realms intersected and gave expression to a nation's civilization. London, Paris, Madrid, and Rome were not only political centers but also economic and cultural nuclei where the elites of government, finance and trade, and the intelligentsia came together.[69] Although the new United States paled in comparison with the great European powers, New York City had some of the rudiments of this model of a capital city. Not only was the political power of the new nation concentrated in lower Manhattan, but travelers were awestruck by the luminaries who brightened daily life there. George Washington, John Adams, Thomas Jefferson, James Madison, and John Hancock could be glimpsed attending church, walking in the streets, or riding horseback. Merchants and financiers went there to press for the passage of special legislation or to lobby for contracts; military officers to attain promotions or plum assignments; and engineers, architects, and surveyors to make deals with the land commissioners. One evening in 1786, St. George Tucker dined at the home of James Duane in the company of Nathaniel Gorham, the president of the Confederation Congress; Baron Friedrich von Steuben; and Henry Knox. The next month he shared a meal with the Spanish minister and went shooting with the son of the Dutch minister.[70]

Some observers, however, contended that the national government had a harmful effect on upper-class New Yorkers. A staunch Republican who loathed displays of what he termed "English luxury," De Warville concluded that the presence of the capital made the New York City upper class more extravagant and ostentatious than that of any other American city.[71]

> The women wear silk and gauze dresses, hats, and even elaborate hairdos. Carriages are rare, but the few that exist are elegant. The men dress more simply than the women . . . but they compensate for this simplicity when they sit down at table, where the most expensive wines make their appearance.[72]

De Warville thought that this wealth and opulence had seduced city residents:

> The presence of Congress and of the diplomatic corps and the influx of foreigners have greatly contributed to increase the corruption of the city by the evils of luxury. The citizens are far from complaining about this; they prefer the splendor of wealth and worldly pleasures to the simple life and the innocent delight it affords.[73]

In 1787, the Reverend Manasseh Cutler journeyed to New York from rural Massachusetts to negotiate a land deal with the Confederation Congress. A Congregationalist minister, a physician, a botanist, an entrepreneur, and later a U.S. congressman, Cutler was hardly a naïf, yet the extravagance he encountered in lower Manhattan stunned him. Because the conduct of governmental affairs was interlaced with patterns of upper-class amiability, his visit became a social whirlwind. He lodged at the home of a wealthy merchant, ate dinner with the British consul-general, took tea with two college presidents, and toured Columbia College. In the process, Cutler met Benjamin Franklin, several French aristocrats, and a member of the British Parliament.

Since many events took place in the homes of important officials, Cutler saw at firsthand the national leadership's taste for luxury and its interactions with the urban upper class at dinners and balls, the theater, and church.[74] Cutler mocked a pretentious dinner that Secretary of War Henry Knox threw in the "high style—much in the French taste" for the benefit of a French nobleman.[75]

Nothing astounded him more than a sumptuous feast given by William Duer, then the secretary of the Board of the Treasury. Cutler marveled that Duer "lives in the style of a nobleman" and exhibited his wealth and taste by serving "not less than fifteen different sorts of wine at dinner."[76] Aware that these aristocratic trappings spoke to the Duers' social ambitions, Cutler observed that Colonel Duer's wife was known as "Lady Kitty," having inherited that made-up title upon the death of her father, the self-styled Lord Stirling of New Jersey.[77]

The ritual grandeur that had suffused New York when it was a provincial capital and a military base in the British Empire was magnified by its designation as the capital of the United States. The arrivals and departures of presidents of the Confederation Congress and other officials became occasions for celebration that recalled the respect accorded royal governors and military commanders in colonial New York. In January 1785 the *Independent Journal* reported that the Confederation Congress president Richard Henry Lee, its secretary Charles Thompson, and several congressmen had received "every mark of deference and satisfaction" upon landing in Manhattan, with the governor, the mayor, and leading citizens meeting their barge and with cannons firing a thirteen-gun salute from the battery.[78]

The installation of the new federal government in 1789 ratcheted up this spectacle. There was public elation that spring when Vice President John Adams and leading senators and representatives arrived in town and again when Congress convened for the first time under the auspices of the Constitution. Federal Hall, where the Congress met, had been enlarged and improved at great expense and embellished with nationalistic iconography, like the sculpture of an eagle that adorned its pediment, and it became a major attraction for New Yorkers and visitors alike. While the Senate held closed sessions, the House of Representatives was open to the public, attracting a motley collection of the unemployed, pickpockets, and the wellborn, who attended its meetings as a form of entertainment.[79]

All this pomp centered on George Washington, who entered New York on April 23 and was inaugurated as president seven days later. Traveling from Mount Vernon, Washington was met in Elizabethtown, New Jersey, by a deputation of senators and representatives and transported across the bay on a barge that was rowed by thirteen sailors, to the roar of U.S. and allied warships firing thirteen-gun salvos. Several thousand spectators watched from the shoreline as the general landed in lower Manhattan and was welcomed by Governor Clinton and a host of state and national leaders. A formal procession of public officials, military units, foreign ambassadors, troops, and ordinary citizens then escorted Washington to a reception in his honor. The hoopla lasted for several more weeks.[80]

In the year and a half before the federal government left New York City, almost every step that Washington took was closely watched and acquired totemic importance. He became the focal point of the Independence Day celebrations; his arrivals in and departures from the city were solemnized by the presence of the governor, the mayor, and large bodies of troops and by the firing of artillery salutes; the celebrations of his birthday were grander than those of the birthdays of the British king and queen had ever been; and he worshiped in a special pew at the front of Saint Paul's Chapel.[81] All that splendor prompted one republican

New Yorker to object that the townspeople had caught "an itching to copy the pomposity of the Europeans."[82]

Washington's impact on the upper class is of special interest here.[83] Washington became the new sun around which the upper-class solar system realigned itself; lesser notables without ties to national politics or political figures who fell out of favor with the administration found themselves in deep space, while high federal officials and people in Washington's social circle were inner planets warmed by their nearness to the great man. According to some accounts, the number of upper-class social activities that took place in the city—receptions, balls, concerts, dinners, teas—more than doubled following the establishment of the federal government.

George and Martha Washington hosted many social events. Of a banquet that the Washingtons gave at their Cherry Street residence in August 1789, William Maclay, a U.S. Senator from Pennsylvania, pronounced, "It was a great dinner & the best of the kind ever I was at."[84] The menu featured a soup course, "Fish roasted & boiled meats, Gammon Fowls" and "Apple pies puddings &ca.," and the guests included Vice President John and Abigail Adams, Chief Justice John and Sarah Jay, New York governor George and Cornelia Clinton, and New Hampshire senator John and Elizabeth Langdon.[85] Washington also instituted the levee, a type of formal reception where rulers were attended by members of their courts and other gentlepeople. Levees had become ultrafashionable in the French and English royal courts of the late seventeenth and the eighteenth centuries, and by the mid-eighteenth century this custom had been adopted by royal governors in the British colonies. Washington maintained it in the early republic. He usually held his presidential levees on Tuesday and Friday afternoons, receiving congressmen, federal administrators, upper-class New Yorkers, and prominent visitors to the city.[86]

Socializing acquired a new scale and refinement following the installation of the federal government and became the fulcrum around which a distinct new social circle formed. In his 1855 book about high society in New York City during "the days of Washington," journalist Rufus

Wilmot Griswold coined a term to describe this circle: "the republican court." Griswold appears to have invented this phrase himself, but contemporary observers used very similar language in representing the new social universe taking shape in the capital. In June 1789, a visitor from Maryland declared that "the American Court . . . is as gay as any Court in Christendom," while a Massachusetts inhabitant caustically wrote: "Our great folks at NY seem to be adopting manners & style of a Court and I expect soon to hear that such a person kissed his Majesty [Washington]'s hand—Glorious Privilege! Amazing Glory!"[87]

People had been mentioning the existence of an aristocratic court in New York City since at least the Seven Years' War. In doing so, the New York upper class were aping a European fashion. In European capitals such as London and Saint Petersburg, the vicinity of the monarch's palace, the barracks of the guards regiments, the mansions of the nobility, and sometimes the cathedral church was known as "the court end of the city." By the 1760s, some upper-class New Yorkers were calling lower Broadway near Bowling Green the "court end" of town, an application that made sense because this locale was the site of Fort George, the governor's mansion, and the homes of the Bayards, De Peysters, De Lanceys, and Livingstons.[88] This usage survived the American Revolution. As late as August 1787, a New York City newspaper printed an advertisement for the rent of a "genteel" room in a house that was "not unpleasantly situated, in the court end of the city."[89]

Some commentators became alarmed that this courtly style had taken root around the new federal government. In June 1789 an Albany newspaper printer spoke disparagingly of the rise of an "American court" and the danger it posed to republicanism and denounced the newfound elegance and exclusivity of socializing in federal New York:[90]

We also find *Levees, Drawing-rooms,* &c. that are not such distant, incomprehensible things as we have imagined, and I suppose, that in a few years, we shall have all the paraphernalia yet wanting to give the superb finish to the grandeur of our AMERICAN COURT! the purity of republican principle seems daily to be losing ground.[91]

Inside the federal government Senator Maclay came to object to its social atmosphere as well. After attending a presidential levee in June 1789, he wrote in his diary: "Indeed from these small beginnings I fear we shall follow on, nor cease till we have reached the summit of Court Etiquette, and all the frivolities fopperies and Expence practiced in european Governments."[92] A staunch republican, Maclay registered this concern again and again in 1789 and early 1790.[93]

Rufus Wilmot Griswold's expression "the republican court" is an oxymoron. Critics like Barber and Maclay understood "the court" and "republicanism" to be in direct opposition, since they thought that courts were *royal* courts, the hated European monarchical assemblages of nobles, officials, artists, and retainers. Now, if these warnings were to be credited, a royal court had formed in the United States. Although these sightings of an "American court" were made through a republican lens that magnified and distorted social reality, they were not chimerical. An exclusive circle had developed around the highest government officials and their families who set trends in fashion and socializing for the rest of the upper class and were the object of gossip and envy. This circle was larger and more prestigious than anything that had existed during the Confederation Congress and had its own social events, protocol, and hierarchy as well as an awareness of its own importance. It was becoming a community that partly overlapped with the urban upper class and was partly separate from it. George and Martha Washington occupied its nucleus; the Adamses, the Jays, the Knoxes, the Duers, and the Livingstons were near the center. Altogether, it appears to have contained somewhere from two to three hundred people. The makeup of this court epitomized its imperial inheritance: its emphasis was on high government officials, while merchants and others were excluded or marginalized.[94]

By the second session of Congress, a social calendar that featured a different event every weekday had come into being, controlled by upper-class women who became the gatekeepers and monitors of the court and whose place in its hierarchy was determined by the eminence of their husbands. The president's Friday afternoon levee had evolved into a Friday evening reception, with Martha Washington being "at home" and acting as the hostess for "respectable" visitors and "gentlemen and ladies." Abigail Adams, wife of the vice president, gave a reception on Mondays; Lady Elizabeth Temple, married to the British consul, entertained on Tuesdays; and Lucy Knox, wife of the secretary of war, did so on Wednesdays. In charge on Thursdays was Sara Livingston Jay, a lively, inquisitive woman who was the daughter of William Livingston and the wife of Chief Justice John Jay.

Like other members of the court, Sarah Jay calculated her own prestige on the basis of her proximity to and knowledge about the Washingtons and other highfliers. In her letters to her husband, she scrutinized the president's illnesses and tracked his physical movements, expressing joy when Vice President John Adams called on her and regret when his wife declined a dinner invitation due to ill health. Nothing, however, matched the delight that Sarah Jay felt upon receiving a call from Martha Washington while staying on Long Island in 1790, and she excitedly told her husband that she and Martha Washington had taken breakfast, dinner, and coffee together and visited a mutual friend.[95]

Abigail Adams put things more straightforwardly. In July 1789 she sent her sister a detailed account of a conversation she had had with the president in his bed chamber while he was recovering from an abscess. "I found myself," Adams admitted, "much more deeply impressed than I ever did before their Majesties of Britain."[96] In just a few short years the tremendous amount of social capital accrued by the republican court had altered upper-class socializing in New York City, creating a new circle that stressed protocol, ritual, fashion, entertainment, and proximity to rulers.

But New York City was unpopular with congressmen, who objected to the poor quality of its housing and its high cost of living. Even more important were the complaints of southerners that the geographical remoteness of the city required excessive periods of travel.[97] In addition, Thomas Jefferson, James Madison, and others felt that a capital located in an agrarian setting would exert a better moral influence on the country than one situated in a commercial city like New York or Philadelphia, where republicanism might be tainted by moneymaking and by associations with monarchical Europe. For all these reasons, the federal government in July 1790 approved a residence bill calling for a new capital city to be built on the banks of the Potomac River and for Philadelphia to be the temporary seat of government until the new site was ready. On August 12, 1790, Congress met for the last time at Federal Hall and adjourned after agreeing to convene in Philadelphia later that year. Two weeks later, Washington left New York City, never to return.[98]

Following the departure of the federal government, the *Cumberland Gazette* commented that "this city looks very dull" and "there is nothing new stirring."[99] National leaders were no longer a fixture on the local scene, and the ritual grandeur that had suffused New York City since the Seven Years' War and increasingly since the Revolutionary War abruptly ceased. The republican court went to Philadelphia with the government and stopped interacting regularly with New York elites.[100]

It seems almost certain that New York City would have evolved differently had it retained the national government. It would not have become the mostly business-oriented city that it is today, a place primarily dedicated to the accumulation of wealth. Business doubtless would have been important but not paramount. Taking a longer view, the transfer of the federal government should be understood in the context of the series of events and incidents that since the city's establishment as a Dutch trading post accidentally legitimated and strengthened its emphasis on profit making.

The removal of the national capital had profound implications for New York City's upper class as well. It meant that business would be the main source of wealth and prestige for urban elites and that businessmen would gain precedence over the great officers both civil and military and eventually rise to the summit of the urban status hierarchy.

Yet it also meant that conflicts over the limits and extent of materialism would be a constant refrain.[101]

THE JUDGES AND THE JUDGED

In December 1791, William Duer assembled a syndicate of New York financiers to speculate in bank stocks and bonds. Active stock trading had commenced in the city just a year earlier, and Duer did not want to miss the speculative frenzy that had ballooned around stocks, bonds, and bank shares. However, the following spring the market fell, Duer's securities lost almost all their value, and he could not raise the money needed to pay the interest on his notes. He was ruined. Several of his creditors had him committed to the city prison in March 1792.

Duer's collapse triggered a financial panic, the first in city history, that depressed the urban economy and shook what little public faith there was in the nascent securities market. Stock trading was poorly understood and had a low reputation in the eighteenth century, with its many critics equating it with gambling, indebtedness, and theft. Angry denunciations of securities brokers and speculators filled city newspapers following the crash of the 1792 bull market. In this bleak environment Duer became a scapegoat for fears about the economy, with the fury against him inciting a crowd to stone the jail where he was being held in protest of his failure to repay his debtors.[102] Duer languished in debtors' prison until he was released on parole in 1799, due to failing health. He soon died.[103]

His punishment had been near total social ostracism. William Duer was a gentleman by birth and entered the state's upper class by dint of his wealth and political connections, but his roots in that upper class proved to be shallow. A few stalwarts like Alexander Hamilton (himself a recent addition to its ranks) and Robert R. Livingston stuck with Duer to the end, but most of his erstwhile friends and companions quickly washed their hands of him.

Duer's saga was fundamentally different from that of William Smith Jr., most of whose friends and acquaintances stood by him despite his notoriety as a Loyalist and refused to oust him from the circles into which he had been born. The social intimacy that militated against Smith's expulsion from the cousins' world suggests that upper-class boundaries were not as porous as they appear to be when the focus is on the likelihood of newcomers entering the group. The probability of entry into the elite is significant, of course, but Duer's experience reveals that exiting it can be quick and decisive. While Duer's antecedents could be considered superior to those of most upper-class New Yorkers, he lacked the robust personal attachments that cemented their close-knit community. An outsider by birth, marriage, and temperament, Duer had made matters worse by gravitating to the republican court and keeping his distance from local elites. He was not one of them, and they let him have it when he got into trouble.[104]

One sign of Duer's disgrace was that the newspapers ridiculed him. In March 1792 the *New York Journal & Patriotic Register* quoted a "gentleman" as quipping that "it would be against [Duer's] *interest* to pay the *principal*, and against his *principle* to pay the *interest*."[105] The *Journal & Patriotic Register* blamed "the spirit of speculation and the desire of amassing fortunes" for producing "evil consequences" and said that Duer's financial predicament should have been anticipated since "a thirst for rank and distinction" inevitably gave birth to "the child of speculation."[106] Dismissing speculators like Duer as "the imaginary *noblesse* of yesterday," the newspaper concluded that "insolence is almost peculiar to sudden acquisition, and the man of exorbitant wealth, generally proportions his importance to the size of his strong box."[107] In fact, Duer was not a villain; instead, he was an unlucky and, perhaps, an unwise investor.

Along with revealing Duer's tenuous position in the upper class, these attacks exposed deeper concerns about the relationship between polite standards of conduct and the marketplace. The papers contended that Duer's failure demonstrated the hollowness of his claims to polite standing (when in reality his credentials were stronger than most others in the upper class) and that his fall confirmed the dangers of letting wealth and ambition replace birth and character as criteria for membership in the upper class.

The financial panic prompted upper-class New Yorkers to engage in a debate in the pages of the *Daily Advertiser* in the spring of 1792 about the morality of an economy increasingly predicated on securities, speculative investments, banks, and corporations. This debate gained added force because the panic coincided with a controversial plan to open a New York City branch of the Philadelphia-based Bank of the United States, a project that seemed especially ominous because one of its proposed directors had been a partner in Duer's botched speculation.

A few of the correspondents who participated in this exchange argued that capitalistic institutions like the new bank branch would promote regional economic development and provide a modern financial structure. Most, however, expressed uneasiness that the new economy was elevating miscreants like Duer who seemingly lacked the moral character and leadership skills that had been instilled in members of the established upper class from birth. The country had managed to escape social disorder after the Revolution, but the speculative economy seemed to be blowing the lid off. For if greed and envy caused ordinary people to spurn the guidance of the upper class and try to rise above their station, the result would be a heightening of the chaos and uncertainty that the financial panic had instigated and an intensification of social instability.[108]

Philip Livingston told the *Daily Advertiser* that speculation amounted to gambling and yielded "the cheats, the quarrels, the oaths, and the blasphemics amongst the men; and amongst the women, the neglect of household affairs, the unlimited freedoms, the indecent passions, and lastly, the known inlet to all lewdness."[109] Another letter writer warned that speculation fed the "insatiable and boundless appetites" of ordinary people whose thirst for wealth and rank would tempt them to take out loans that they could never repay.[110] Their outcome would be financial bankruptcy and moral depravity akin to Duer's. Not only that, but the boundaries between the social classes would erode and trust in the benevolent leadership of the upper class would be undermined.

This debate reveals that prominent New Yorkers were nervous about the new economic arrangements. As much as the upper class had adapted to the political transformations of the revolutionary period and for all the priority it put on enterprise by admitting ex-Tories back into the fold, its acceptance of materialism was limited, ambiguous, and contradictory. Elite New Yorkers did not harbor the profound moral qualms about the pursuit of material gain that their counterparts in Boston and Philadelphia did, but they should not be mistaken for prototypes of modern businesspeople.

Upper-class New Yorkers could eagerly pursue internal improvements and land deals to make a profit and develop the city's economy and then,

in almost the same breath, express anxiety that enterprise fostered speculative manias, encouraged luxury, and let sharps like William Duer infil-
trate and degrade the upper class and undermine the social order. They
at once embraced free enterprise and condemned it morally; they were
promoters and skeptics, the judgers and the judged. All that would make
for terrific social and cultural conflicts when New York City experienced rapid economic growth and generated vast personal wealth in the
nineteenth century.

⌒ 3 ⌒

WEALTH

. . . .

The 1820s and Beyond

"THE RICHEST MAN IN THIS REPUBLIC"

All through the morning and early afternoon of April 1, 1848, several thousand people went to the exclusive Lafayette Place–Bond Street neighborhood to see the body of the wealthiest man in America, John Jacob Astor, lying in a coffin in the hallway of his son's home. A newspaper reported that "crowd after crowd" gathered there and that "thousands rushed in [to the house], until the hall was crowded almost to suffocation."[1]

Following this public viewing, a procession took the coffin several blocks to Saint Thomas's Episcopal Church for the funeral. An undertaker headed the line of march, followed by a cluster of Episcopalian priests, some family physicians, and the coffin and its pallbearers. Relatives and family friends came next, then several thousand onlookers, and in the rear, wearing livery and with napkins pinned to their sleeves, the Astor family's waiters.[2]

Organized to honor Astor for his successes and help his progeny consolidate their positions in the upper class, this funeral service was a response to an exotic new phenomenon in American life, the emergence of colossal individual wealth. When John Jacob Astor died in March 1848, the existence of huge personal fortunes was sufficiently novel for newspapers to italicize the word "millionaire" in their death notices.[3] People also resorted to the familiar lexicon of the hereditary nobility to make sense of this new source of distinction, with a register of the richest New Yorkers—ranking Astor first and his son William seventh—entitled *The Aristocracy of New York* (1848).[4]

Astor's funeral was as strange as his wealth. The Astor family had cobbled together a public funeral for a private citizen who had never held public office by employing the trappings of the prestigious Episcopalian Church and by borrowing ritualistic elements from official funerals, such as the public viewing of a corpse lying in state and the procession through the streets. At heart the funeral was about legitimacy, and the role that the Astor family had assigned to the general public was paramount to realizing that aim. Ordinary people who filed past his coffin in the home of his son or who watched the procession became a democratic audience whose spectating could be represented as confirming the greatness of "the richest man in the country."[5] Their presence was all the more crucial, since almost nobody from the established upper class attended, other than pallbearers like Philip Hone.

The death of John Jacob Astor gave Americans occasion to try to come to terms with the emergence of these immense fortunes. Some observers praised the tycoon for confirming the superiority of American society to Europe. That a "poor youth without knowledge of our language or our people" could accomplish so much meant that "the United States held forth an inviting promise," the *New York Herald* said.[6] Others, though, feared that personal riches would erode American democracy, a tack that the *New York Tribune* adopted in calling Astor "the richest man (as far as earthy possessions can be called wealth) in this Republic," drawing on the eighteenth-century Whig ideology to counterpoise "wealth" with "Republic" and to denigrate material success.[7]

A poor butcher's son who had been born in the German Palatine in 1763, Astor (figure 3.1) migrated to New York City in 1784 with limited resources and then went on to earn millions from his ownership of the

FIGURE 3.1 John Jacob Astor. (Author's collection.)

American Fur Trading Company and investments in Manhattan real estate, becoming the richest person in the United States by 1840.[8] He made a concerted effort to enter the upper class of the city by, for instance, renting a pew at fashionable Trinity Church in the 1790s. Although he had been raised a Lutheran and worshipped at the German Reformed Church at the time of his death, he and his family nonetheless arranged for his funeral to occur in a prestigious Episcopalian church.[9]

But Astor had to travel too great a social distance to enter that upper class, and his aggressive business practices, uncouth manners, and lowly origins gave its members cause to exclude him. In 1815, for instance, he offered to take Albert Gallatin, a former secretary of the Treasury and U.S. senator, into a business partnership on generous terms. In his diary, James Gallatin recounted his father's reasons for refusing this gesture:

Although he respected Mr. Astor, he never could place himself on the same level with him. I am not surprised, as Astor was a butcher's son at Waldorf—came as an emigrant to this country with a pack on his back. He peddled furs, was very clever, and is, I believe one of the kings of the fur trade.[10]

For James Gallatin, the signs of Astor's social inferiority were palpable: "He dined here and ate his ice-cream and peas with a knife."[11] When Astor visited them in Paris five years later, Gallatin had this snobbish reaction:

> Really Mr. Astor is dreadful. Father has to be civil to him, as in 1812–13 he rendered great services to the Treasury. He came to *déjeuner* to-day; we were simply *en famille*, he sitting next to Frances. He actually wiped his fingers on the sleeves of her fresh white spencer. Mama in discreet tones said, "Oh, Mr. Astor, I must apologize; they have forgotten to give you a serviette." I think he felt foolish.[12]

With his single-minded devotion to moneymaking, Astor had immersed himself in the marketplace, earning a reputation as a sharp dealer and becoming embroiled in a number of legal disputes over his business transactions. Unfortunately for his social aspirations, these actions clashed with the refined inner life and the politeness in manners and sentiment that gentility esteemed and with the visible disdain for moneymaking that being upper class demanded. You were supposed to accumulate a lot of wealth, but you had to act as if you were not making any effort to do so.[13]

Astor was no more successful at improving his public standing than he was at infiltrating the upper class. In 1836, Washington Irving published *Astoria, or Anecdotes of an Enterprise Beyond the Rocky Mountains*, lionizing his friend and patron as a visionary leader whose resolute pursuit of profits had furthered the national welfare. The volume examined the millionaire's 1811 founding of Fort Astoria, at the mouth of the Columbia River, as a fur trading outpost. As the first permanent U.S. settlement on the Pacific Ocean, Fort Astoria was extremely important in promoting

American commerce, securing U.S. claims to the region, and supporting explorations of the West Coast. However, according to Irving, the failure of the administration of President James Madison to adequately defend Fort Astoria provided an opening for the British navy to seize it during the War of 1812, impeding the American push into the Pacific Northwest for years to come. As Irving saw it, federal officials had been shortsighted and ineffectual, while Astor, the businessman, had been statesmanlike.[14]

Irving's book merits a place in American cultural history as an early portrayal of the businessman as national hero, but it did not change anyone's mind about John Jacob Astor. Works by far less accomplished rhetoricians would succeed in glorifying their tycoon subjects later in the nineteenth century, but great wealth was too new and outlandish and conflicted too sharply with the prevailing democratic and egalitarian ethos for Washington Irving to pull that trick off in the 1830s. Irving could not get his readers to square their understanding of Astor with the prevailing view of statesmen as selfless and dignified gentlemen who performed valuable public services.

In the end it was money that colored popular perceptions of Astor. Newspaper death notices agreed that his chief flaw had been his stinginess. "If Mr. Astor was industrious in the accumulation of his riches, he was likewise very penurious and niggardly in money matters," the *Herald* said. "What he saved he kept and locked up to the day of his death."[15] The *Tribune* called Astor "a hard man" who was stingy and calculating and a dullard who "rose early and went soon to bed" and lacked social graces.[16]

Soon the publication of his will sparked complaints about his charitable contributions. Astor left $400,000 to construct a public library that would become a forerunner of the New York Public Library, $25,000 apiece to Columbia College and to the German Society of New York, $20,000 to the Association for the Relief of Respectable Aged Indigent Females in the City of New York, and smaller amounts to other benevolent organizations in New York City and Germany.[17] These gifts were substantial, varied, and well considered, and compared favorably with the bequests of other wealthy New Yorkers in this pre–income tax era. But instead of recognizing his charitableness and civic leadership, the newspapers disparaged Astor as a tightfisted businessman whose preoccupation with the bottom line had drained his human compassion.[18]

This discussion of the meaning of the Astor fortune, together with misgivings about the California gold strike a year later, precipitated an exchange about the place of enormous wealth in American society. In 1850, Horace Mann, a moral reformer and educator in the New England tradition of liberal Protestantism, delivered a lecture at the Boston Mercantile Library warning about the vices of moneygrubbing. Mann declared: "Men are rapidly coming to the worship of one deity;—the only misfortune is that it is neither the living nor the true one. They deify wealth . . . [they] love it with all their heart and soul and mind and strength."[19] Americans, he said, had become gold worshippers rather than God worshippers. "Great wealth is a misfortune, because it makes generosity impossible. There can be no generosity without sacrifice."[20] Mann warned that on judgment day God would decide whether the man of vast wealth had given almost everything he owned to charity in an effort to relieve human suffering, or whether,

> like John Jacob Astor, he was hoarding wealth for the base love of wealth, hugging to his breast, in his dying hour, the memory of his gold, and not of his Redeemer; gripping his riches till the scythe of death cut off his hands, and he was changed, in the twinkling of an eye, from being one of the richest men that had ever lived in this world, to being one of the poorest souls that ever went out of it.[21]

A few months later, Charles Astor Bristed, a socialite and journalist who was the favorite grandson of John Jacob Astor, wrote a reply to the prim and pedantic Mann defending his grandfather and addressing the peculiar position of the wealthy man in democratic America. Bristed insisted that far from treating others unfairly, the rich man was liable be treated unfairly himself, in a paroxysm of antielitism and antimat alism. Anywhere else Astor would have been a source of national p but in the United States he became "an object of suspicion and ha to people who envied him and "denounced [him] as a *millionaire* an *aristocrat*" for having moved up in the world.[22] "As soon as a man does anything, or has anything done to him, to put him above others," Bristed charged, "he violates the first article of the democratic creed, 'Every man's as good as another.'"[23]

John Jacob Astor represented a significant departure in U.S. history, the rise of businessmen who concentrated on the pursuit of wealth, accumulated vast fortunes, and rejected the importance that the eighteenth-century upper class had attached to political leadership. A review of Freeman Hunt's celebrated *Lives of American Merchants* (1856) shows that many of Astor's contemporaries fit this profile. Compiled from the pages of Hunt's monthly *Merchant's Magazine and Commercial Review*, the first edition of *Lives of American Merchants* contained biographical sketches of thirty-four prominent businessmen. Nineteen had never held elective or appointive political office and had largely devoted themselves to business. That pattern was more typical of younger men than it was of older men, an indication that a new breed was evolving.[24]

The problem for public perception in this era was that the reality of great wealth continued to be tied directly to the status of the aristocrat and that expectations for rich men were still those associated with the attributes of a hereditary aristocracy—ancestry, public service, gentility, and so on. This link would have to be broken before the self-made man of wealth could be accepted in American society, and that did not happen until the second half of nineteenth century. This was the underlying dynamic that shaped responses to Astor and his kind.

For members of the established upper class, this disturbing new way of obtaining wealth and power posed two problems: How would its members accommodate men like Astor, and how would men like Astor distinguish and legitimate themselves? James Harper, a founder of Harper & Brothers publishing house and a mayor of New York City, was born in a farm village on Long Island in 1795 and originally went to Manhattan to apprentice in a printing shop. Cornelius Vanderbilt grew up on Staten Island and initiated the ferry service from there to Manhattan that became the foundation of his shipping and railroad empire. William Colgate, once an apprentice soap maker, owned the largest soap company in the world by the 1840s. With all these parvenus on the scene, there would be increasing differentiation of status and wealth within the upper class, and the difficulty of achieving distinction and legitimacy would be all the more vexed.[25]

The context of the reactions to Astor and the other strivers who became extremely wealthy is the phenomenal economic advance that New York City experienced between 1820 and 1860.[26] One ramification of this growth was that the upper class was now an *urban* upper class and no longer encompassed the entire state as it had in the eighteenth century. As the city and the rest of the state expanded economically and demographically, their elites grew apart.[27] A second consequence was that rapid economic development enlarged and enriched this urban upper class, bringing in newcomers like John Jacob Astor, introducing new sources of merit, and putting enormous weight on the pursuit of business success and the accumulation of wealth. And a third and final result was that merchants became a distinct, coherent, and self-conscious group that was now on top of the urban status hierarchy. The increased emphasis on wealth and enterprise in this booming city had weakened much of the old opposition to materialism, but while profit making was no longer reviled in and of itself, antimaterialism did not so much disappear as take on new and more complex forms and became reactive to business dominance. Antimaterialism, for example, let members of the existing upper class react to nouveaux riches by stressing their own refinement, learning, family history, and so forth.

As a result of its greater wealth, heightened social fluidity, and weaker group cohesion, New York City's upper class increasingly diverged from those of other big U.S. cities such as Philadelphia and Boston. The entry of so many wealthy newcomers compounded elite New Yorkers' preoccupation with the main chance and their promotion of urban economic development. These traits had long distinguished New York's upper class from those of Boston and Philadelphia, but now they became magnified.

Two key characteristics of the New York City upper class surfaced in this period. One was internal complexity. As the upper class became larger and wealthier, multiple and partially competing ways of belonging to it arose, and by the 1850s it had split into different economic and social factions.

The development of these separate elites confused and worried upper-class New Yorkers, who could no longer be entirely sure of their bona fides, especially because this splintering coincided with the advent of a coherent middle class that further blurred upper-class boundaries. Elites struggled to establish their credentials and assert their leadership. A primary response of members of the established upper class was to emphasize their ties to Europe and especially the European aristocracy. They emulated the peerage not so much because they wanted to be aristocrats but rather to distance themselves from the Astors of their own city.

The second characteristic was a permanent malleability. The dynamic urban economy would cause the upper class to experience recurring social and cultural changes, with its different factions constituting distinct faces that it would present to the world. That malleability meant that the relationship that the upper class had with the city and with other social groups would repeatedly shift.

"THE METROPOLITAN CITY OF THE NEW WORLD"

Imagine going to Trinity Church, at the corner of Broadway and Wall Street, in the 1850s and climbing its steeple to have a panoramic view of the metropolis.[28] The urban landscape would look completely different than it had forty or fifty years earlier. In the far north, one would see that the hills and valleys were still wooded. Yet the edge of the built-up district now reached as far as Forty-Second Street—"It *daily* extends northward," an English visitor exclaimed in 1854—and much of the land there had already been divided into lots and streets had been built.[29]

West, east, and south of Trinity Church, Manhattan was thickly crowded with people and buildings. Looking to the west, one would behold wharves that extended up the New York side of the Hudson River to Greenwich Village. On the Jersey side of the river stood Hoboken, a bucolic pleasure resort, and Jersey City, a port and manufacturing town. Turning eastward, directly below Trinity Church, one would spot Wall

Street, with the landmark Treasury Building, the Custom House, and the Mercantile Exchange attesting to its commercial clout. Another locale that could be glimpsed in the east was Five Points, the worst slum in the Western Hemisphere, where Irish Americans were the principal inhabitants and large numbers of Germans and African Americans also lived.[30]

Farther east one would observe docks and shipyards lining both sides of the East River for two and a half miles and a swarm of ferries, merchantmen, and warships out on the water. Across the East River stood Brooklyn, an independent municipality that would be the third-largest city in the United States in 1860. Turning southward, one would catch sight of the upper bay and of Staten Island, where many upper-class families owned summer houses. From the southern tip of Manhattan to just above City Hall lay a mile-long stretch of Broadway that was reminiscent of Bond Street in London. The site of stylish hotels and shops and a promenade for elites, this part of Broadway was renowned for its fast pace, its social extremes, and the spectacle of its everyday life.[31]

The transformation of this urban landscape was a result of the phenomenal economic growth that had occurred during the first half of the nineteenth century, when a transportation revolution integrated markets all across North America into a coherent national economy. After the War of 1812, the construction of extensive networks of turnpikes, canals, steamboats, and railroads accelerated the movement of people and goods; stimulated trade, manufacturing, and finance; fostered a more highly articulated distribution system; and encouraged regional specialization.[32] This transportation revolution also altered where Americans lived. In 1800 the geographic center of the United States had been located close to the Atlantic coast, just eighteen miles west of Baltimore. By 1860 it had crossed the Ohio River to a point near Chillicothe, Ohio.[33]

The integration of this national economy reconfigured American urban places into webs of primary, secondary, and tertiary centers. At its pinnacle stood New York City, which went from being a regional center that more or less corresponded to Philadelphia and Boston to become the trade, manufacturing, financial, and communications center of the United States. Its population jumped from 123,706 in 1820 to 813,669 in 1860. Even more significant than its absolute population growth, however, was its growth relative to rival cities. New York had barely edged past Philadelphia to become the largest city in the United States in 1810, but fifty years later it was 30 percent larger than Philadelphia and four times bigger than Boston.[34]

Two-thirds of all U.S. imports, one-third of its exports, and 70 percent of its immigrants passed through New York harbor on the eve of the Civil War. The transportation revolution gave merchants and planters linkages that tied New York City more closely to other cities and regions in the United States and overseas. That happened because enterprising New Yorkers, aided by public and private investments and by new transportation technologies, proved adept at supplying those linkages.

The cultural orientation of New York City to the pursuit of material gain and the geographical superiority of its harbor had acquired overwhelming importance following the expulsion of the Iroquois from western and central New York State during and after the Revolutionary War. Merchants and political officials initiated transportation projects—ferries, turnpikes, bridges, canals—that expanded its hinterland and captured an ever growing share of domestic and, later, international traffic. New York State not only invested more money in transportation than other states did during the early republic, but its investments were also more productive, since many of them supplemented the natural advantages of the Hudson River. After the War of 1812, increased government and business spending and the technological breakthrough of the steam engine made for larger and more robust networks, to the immense benefit of New York City.

Two improvements were especially crucial. New Yorkers built the Erie Canal across upstate New York, providing a water-level route from the Hudson River to the Great Lakes that redirected midwestern commerce through New York City. The city also benefited from the triangular cotton trade. In the 1820s New York shipping lines began carrying cotton bales from the southern United States to European ports, where the cotton was exchanged for manufactured goods, which were transported to New York and then taken by coastal packet to southern ports. The enormous importance of cotton meant that the growth of New York City hinged on the labor of enslaved persons. Together, the Erie Canal and the triangular cotton trade gave the city control of the two leading commodity flows of the mid-nineteenth century.[35]

Guidebooks had begun to label New York City "the Metropolitan City of the New World" and "the first city on the American continent," but some Europeans could not stomach the idea that it was on a par with the great European metropolises, an attitude that led the English writer Frederick Marryat to sneer, "New York is not equal to London, nor Broadway to Regent Street although Americans would compare them."[36] Other Europeans perceived the frenetic energy and commercial orientation of the American colossus and concluded that it was nothing like the European capitals. An Austrian composer called New York "that human ant-hill" and remarked that the city "seemed to me to be like a huge fair, so great was the amount of merchandise on the docks and so brisk the activity in the commercial districts."[37] This inclination to contrast New York with sophisticated European capitals that exemplified urban grandeur flowed from the notion that a cultural dichotomy separated western Europe from the United States.

The problem with this dichotomy was that it obscured the close resemblance that New York City bore to a set of less prepossessing European cities, the North Atlantic ports of Hamburg, Amsterdam, Glasgow, and Liverpool. Like New York, these four European cities were associated with the marketplace because their social structures were dominated by merchants. Like New York, they sustained rapid economic development and population growth in the nineteenth century and had the polyglot populations typical of large ports.[38] New York City was not yet as singular as either its boosters or its detractors imagined.

A METROPOLITAN ECONOMY

Antebellum New York City had the complex economy typical of big metropolises. The three main sectors of that economy—in order of the number of their employees—were commerce, manufacturing, and finance.

Although commerce had long been the leading sector and the primary source of upper-class wealth, a remarkable expansion of the volume of trade and the range of goods that had occurred since the 1790s enriched merchants and encouraged them to think of themselves in new ways. By the mid-nineteenth century merchants saw themselves as a distinct social group. Although the term "businessman" (originally "business man") did not enter into widespread usage until later in the century, these merchants were increasingly feeling and acting like businessmen, engaging self-consciously and on a full-time basis in particular specialized activities in order to generate revenue.[39]

The production, marketing, and distribution functions had become more specialized.[40] The all-purpose, general merchant of the eighteenth century was becoming obsolete, and merchants now functioned as wholesalers or jobbers, importers or exporters, and auctioneers or forwarders and concentrated on a single line of goods, such as hardware or produce. With greater specialization came the formation of a hierarchy of mercantile occupations. The two most prestigious categories of merchants listed in an 1837 business register were the 120 commission merchants who, like Grinnell, Minturn & Company, bought and sold commodities on consignment, and the twenty-five shipping merchants, such as Howland & Aspinwall and Schermerhorn, Willis & Company, who organized international commerce like the cotton and China trades.[41]

Manufacturing, the second most important economic sector and growing, employed 11 percent of the total population of New York City on the eve of the Civil War. Unlike factory towns such as Manchester, Great Britain, or Lowell, Massachusetts, that concentrated on a single product, New York was dominated by no single industry. In 1855, the city's largest industry (in terms of the size of its workforce) was the clothing trade, with 14,960 employees; yet clothing manufacture accounted for only a third of the city's industrial workers, and there were nine other industries that had at least 1,500 workers apiece. Manufacturing also had a distinctive geography in Manhattan, where the large, capital-intensive factories that characterized Chicago and Pittsburgh after the Civil War were absent. High land costs, the availability of cheap immigrant labor, and the proximity of a large regional market favored small-scale, labor-intensive industry, such as the garment trade and tobacco making.[42]

Financial services consisted of intermediaries who connected the suppliers of capital with its users, coordinated transactions, and arranged for payments to be made. As early as the 1790s every large American city had a physical space where various kinds of financial services clustered together, but at the time this sector had little occupational or institutional specialization. Bankers were generalists who did not concentrate on either investment or commercial operations; merchants and auctioneers bought and sold securities as well as merchandise; and securities brokers traded in gold and currency along with stocks and bonds.

During the 1820s and 1830s New York surpassed Philadelphia to become the financial center of the nation. This shift from Chestnut Street to Wall Street started with the securities industry. Founded in 1817, the New York Stock and Exchange Board (later renamed the New York Stock Exchange) was initially a local market that handled only a few securities on a regular basis. After it floated New York State bonds for the construction of the Erie Canal, however, the board eclipsed the Philadelphia exchange with respect to the volume of trading, and around 1820 became the foremost securities market in the United States.

Because increased commerce brought increased bank deposits, the opening of the Erie Canal allowed New York City to also challenge Philadelphia's supremacy in banking. Philadelphia remained the nation's banking center through the mid-1830s, largely because it was the site of the Second Bank of the United States, which served as the central bank and main clearinghouse for the country. However, after President Andrew Jackson withdrew federal funds from the Second Bank in 1833, causing it to dwindle in size, and then let its charter lapse in 1836, Wall Street pulled ahead in this sphere, too. Banking operations in New York grew rapidly in the 1840s and 1850s.[43]

All the same, the United States continued to be a capital-importing nation—and the source of that capital was Europe. Financiers in New York City functioned primarily as agents for European merchant banks, funneling European capital into burgeoning American enterprises.

The relationships that developed between New York firms and their European partners were often highly personal. The New York mercantile house of Prime Ward and King had strong connections with Baring Brothers, a powerful London merchant bank that auctioned federal and state government bonds and insurance company securities to European customers, while the Rothschilds used two New York City firms as their American correspondents, Prime Ward and King and Le Roy Bayard. Boston merchant Junius S. Morgan moved to London in the early 1850s and became a partner in a banking house there, and his son, J. Pierpont Morgan, relocated to New York in 1857 to act as a representative for his father's bank and other London firms.[44]

"THE DANGERS OF WALL STREET"

As it gained wealth and power, the New York City business district acquired a place in the national imagination for the first time, when, in the 1830s and 1840s, a new literary genre responded to rapid economic growth by warning of the moral and social dangers of excessive materialism.

Most books in this genre were set in lower Manhattan and had businessmen for their protagonists. Strongly influenced by the stress that the Second Great Awakening put on personal salvation and social reform, this genre comprised cautionary tales that had an evangelical cast, purportedly written by merchants and brokers who had sinned and then experienced redemption. Actually, they were almost entirely the work of journalists who tapped a popular new outlet for sensationalist literature through the contrivance of posing as businessmen ensnared by an uncontrollable desire for wealth. According to the standard narrative, the malefactors committed serious transgressions that ruined themselves and others financially and morally, before eventually reforming and then writing their books to atone for their blunders and alert the public to this menace.

An early example of the genre is *The Perils of Pearl Street, including a taste of the dangers of Wall Street* (1834), which relates the story of Billy

Hazard, an innocent boy from a rural village who repeatedly tried and failed to make his fortune in New York City. A first-person account told from Hazard's perspective and published anonymously, *The Perils of Pearl Street* was penned by a New York City bookseller and author named Asa Greene, who portrayed Hazard as the son of honest and industrious tradespeople. Eager to make his fortune as a merchant and enter high society, Hazard ignored the example of his respectable parents and set off for New York City, where he experienced a series of misfortunes in the business district, an immoral landscape ruled by knavish merchants and brokers who cheated their customers, creditors, and employees. Greene shows Hazard becoming a clerk for a dry goods merchant, only to lose his salary when the firm failed; taking a job as a drummer for another company, only to see it become insolvent; becoming a partner in a dry goods store, only to have it go bankrupt; and finally, squandering the rest of his savings in a stock speculation. Despite repeated fiascos over ten years, Hazard's hunger for wealth was all-consuming, to the point that he postponed his marriage to the lovely and virtuous young woman waiting for him back home. Only when she gave up and married someone else did Hazard comprehend that he had destroyed himself through his greed and selfishness—and that materialism was undermining the social order:

> I hate a purse-proud man . . . Give me any sort of aristocracy before a monied one. An aristocracy of learning; an aristocracy of wit; an aristocracy of virtue; in short, an aristocracy of talents, or good qualities of any kind, is the only one which is endurable—is the only one which is rational proper.[45]

These were standard eighteenth-century virtues, and Hazard paid a steep price for flouting them. Heavily in debt and alone in the world, he abandoned mercantile pursuits and resolved to take up honest work (as a writer, no less) and repay his creditors.

Most of Billy Hazard's misfortunes occurred in the commercial sector, and the book paid little attention to the nascent financial industry, supplying, in the words of its subtitle, merely "*a taste of the dangers of Wall Street.*"

However, after the collapse of a speculative bubble triggered the Panic of 1837 and a five-year-long economic depression, writers operating in this genre turned their attention to financial services. The commercial and manufacturing sectors employed more people and generated more revenue, yet the financial industry came in for inordinate condemnation following the panic. In a producer economy that valued thrift and probity, financial services seemed mysterious and intangible and were associated with gambling, theft, and duplicity. Long before the financial industry dominated the physical space of Wall Street or employed much of its workforce, the name "Wall Street" had acquired a decidedly negative meaning in the American imagination.

Two books exemplify this new outlook. In *A Week in Wall Street* (1841), Frederick Jackson (presenting himself as a victim of stock swindling during the Panic of 1837) portrayed the securities market as a comic stage where the folly of the multitude intersected with the wicked designs of the few. The two protagonists, Mr. Friendly and Mr. Bottomley, were stockbrokers who were conspiring to drive up the price of securities in Morrison Kennel, a company that had been formed for the dubious purpose of digging a shallow ditch across New Jersey, a reference to that state's troubled Morris & Essex Canal.[46] Friendly and Bottomley approach Mr. Spriggins, a gentleman who unwisely prides himself on being a shrewd businessman, con him into buying hundreds of shares of Morrison Kennel, and then unload their holdings once the market peaks, clearing a $100,000 profit. Then the price of the stock plummets and Spriggins is ruined. While Asa Greene had characterized poor Billy Hazard as an innocent, Frederick Jackson believed that Spriggins had his own cupidity to blame for his fall.

William Armstrong's *Stocks and Stock-Jobbing in Wall Street* (1848) appeared seven years later. Pitched as the work of a "reformed stock gambler" eager to expose the "peculiar, mysterious, keen, spicy, and rascally transactions" that brokers and speculators used to fleece the innocent and unwary, *Stocks and Stock-Jobbing* belonged to this tradition of cautionary tales that simultaneously warned and entertained the reading public with accounts of Wall Street greed.[47] Yet even as it borrowed from older tropes in damning Wall Street, the book was also a primer that aimed to help beginners traverse the stock market. Thus, *Stocks and Stock-Jobbing* was written not as a narrative, as earlier books in this genre had been, but as a manual that readers could consult for practical investing tips or to look up unfamiliar terms like "bulls" and "bears" in its glossary.

Stocks and Stock-Jobbing embodied a schizoid response to Wall Street, morally condemning its intrigues while also celebrating its individual enterprises. Slowly and fitfully, moneymaking was coming into new favor and success was being redefined to include acquisitiveness.[48]

URBAN GROWTH AND THE TRANSFORMATION OF THE NEW YORK CITY UPPER CLASS

Think of the urban economy as a hot-air balloon and the upper class as the wicker passenger basket suspended below it. When the leading American cities had been more or less the same size in the late eighteenth century, their hot-air balloons and wicker baskets had similar dimensions. As New York City took off between 1820 and 1860, however, its balloon became much bigger and more buoyant than those of its rivals and could reach higher altitudes and make longer flights. Its basket also became correspondingly more complex, with internal panels that compartmentalized the crew and passengers into different cabins. Spectacular economic development enriched the upper class, augmented its power, expanded its size, added new members to it, and altered its social structure.[49] It was on its way to the stratosphere.[50]

The question of how large and rich this upper class had grown became a matter of great public interest in the first half of the nineteenth century, leading journalists to prepare compendiums of its richest citizens. The best-known of these works was *Wealth and Biography of the Wealthy Citizens of New York City*, which was created by Moses Y. Beach, the publisher and editor of the *New York Sun* newspaper. It first appeared in 1842 and sold so well that Beach turned out eleven more editions by the end of the 1850s. He listed every New Yorker believed to be worth at least

$100,000, the equivalent of $2.5 million in today's terms. The sixth edition (issued in 1845) has 963 names; the tenth edition, 1,025 names; and the twelfth, 1,061. By this measure, a tiny group of perhaps one thousand New Yorkers had achieved immense wealth.

Today we know that Beach did not have access to tax rolls or census records and that he was sloppy and made careless factual errors. Also, his overemphasis on great individual fortunes and his unsophisticated equation of wealth with social status precludes our using his publications to determine the precise size and structure of the upper class.[51] However, the real significance of *Wealth and Biography of the Wealthy Citizens of New York City* lies in providing insight into another noteworthy development, the growing popular enthrallment with material abundance. His compendiums should be seen as forerunners of *Forbes Magazine*'s celebrated annual rankings of the four hundred wealthiest Americans. Between the 1830s and the 1850s, Americans became mesmerized by the vast riches being accumulated and started to consider the social effects of that wealth. For example, *Harper's Weekly* published numerous articles assessing the vices and virtues of wealth, usually upholding the moral example of the rich while also imploring them to use their money to aid the poor or patronize literature and the arts. A representative article defended wealth as "a proof of the superior capacity, industry, and economy of its possessor" and contended that its stimulation of the economy made "all of us better off."[52] The proliferation of this literature suggests that ordinary Americans were beginning to regard great personal wealth as an indication of upper-class status and that popular and upper-class appraisals of whether particular individuals belonged in the elite category were diverging.

Obituaries in New York City began applying wealth as a yardstick of personal meaning. When tobacco manufacturer George Lorillard died in 1836, the papers calculated that he had been worth $3 million.[53] When his brother Peter died seven years later, the *Journal of Commerce* called him "among the most wealthy men of our country, his estates being estimated at four millions of dollars."[54] This bald equation of Peter Lorillard's value as a human with the size of his fortune discomfited the *Commercial Advertiser*, which noted that Lorillard's benevolence to the poor had led "the whole Christian community" to mourn his death.[55] In short, his charity demonstrated his moral superiority and legitimated his wealth.[56]

How large was this upper class? One estimate was made by Charles Astor Bristed in his *The Upper Ten Thousand* (1852), a compilation of sketches about New York high society. Bristed and Beach were interested in entirely different kinds of people: while Beach concentrated on the rich, Bristed had his eye on blue bloods like himself who possessed the cumulative advantages of good birth, inherited wealth, impeccable manners, wide acquaintanceship, and travel. Beach and Bristed also disagreed about the basis of the upper-class distinction—Beach stressed wealth, while Bristed admired social refinement and disdained materialism. Almost everyone in his "upper ten thousand" was prosperous, but Bristed viewed money as a means to enjoy a special way of life. Bristed described the ideal New York gentleman as a person of birth, wealth, refinement, and wide experience who "speaks half-a-dozen languages, dabbles in literature . . . talks metaphysics one minute, and dances the polka the next—in short, [who] knows a little bit of every thing, with a knack for reproducing it effectively."[57] Money might open the door to this exclusive world, but money could not buy the sophistication and close personal relationships that typified the upper class. Indeed, mere wealth could be problematical, and Bristed excluded the social element that another writer derided as "the shoddy society": nouveaux riches who were "rude, ignorant, uncouth in their manners" and whose every action betrayed "how little accustomed they are" to fashionable society—people, in other words, like his own grandfather.[58]

It is not clear how Charles Astor Bristed arrived at his calculation that the social elite comprised ten thousand people. Since he was writing for a popular audience and wanted to make a splash, he may have picked a large round number out of thin air. But the figure made sense to him in light of his own experiences as a member of the fashionable set, and it also rang true with other authors who adopted it themselves.[59] Because Bristed excluded parvenus as well as people on the social and economic edges of the upper class, a higher estimate may be in order—perhaps as much as fifteen thousand (equal to 2.9 percent of the total city population in 1850) or twenty thousand (3.8 percent). In any event, the upper class was now almost as large as the entire city had been a century earlier.[60] In its large size and its great wealth, that upper class was entirely unprecedented in American history.

Bristed's *The Upper Ten Thousand* and Beach's *Wealth and Biography of the Wealthy Citizens of New York City* demonstrate the leading role that American journalists had begun to play in defining the boundaries and establishing the legitimacy of the upper class. Because the United States lacked the hereditary aristocracies of European nations, Americans had ample latitude in deciding who belonged to the upper class. A European aristocrat's pedigree and his place in the peerage could be fixed precisely, but the social rank of an American was subject to interpretation. There has never been any hard-and-fast, objective delineation of a member of the American upper class: every calculation is inherently subjective. These interpretations have usually depended on two separate and sometimes conflicting determinations—first, whether other members of the upper class accepted someone, and second, whether the general public recognized someone as being upper class. Popular journalists usually delivered the public judgment. The decisions could be at odds: the Gallatins and other upper-class New Yorkers had deemed John Jacob Astor to be beyond the pale, but reporters had considered him to be part of the upper class by virtue of his wealth.

New York was not the only big American city to sustain drastic economic and social changes in this period, and other urban upper classes also became larger and wealthier.[61] But there were more rich people in New York City than anywhere else, and the wealthiest New Yorkers had more money than their counterparts elsewhere. When John Jacob Astor died in 1848, almost three hundred residents of New York City were worth more than $100,000 in assessed real and personal property, far more than in any other U.S. city. Two New Yorkers—Astor and Peter G. Stuyvesant—had more than $1 million apiece, and nine had more than $500,000. Compared with the other upper classes, the upper class in New York received larger infusions of fresh blood and was more heterogeneous, as outsiders from its own middle and lower classes, from New England and the Middle Atlantic states, and from Germany tried to enter its ranks. These influences, in turn, made for an even greater focus on the part of the upper class on the pursuit of wealth and status and on the promotion of economic development.

This reciprocal relationship between urban economic growth and the fixation of economic elites on the main chance meant that members of the established upper class would have to find ways of responding to these new realities.

RESPONDING TO WEALTH

New York's existing upper class was now under great social and psychological pressure. The sort of eminent old families that commanded hegemonic authority elsewhere—the Cabots, Perkinses, and Peabodys in Boston and the Cadwaladers, Biddles, and Whartons in Philadelphia—faced stiff competition in New York City. Old New Yorkers could not monopolize their social and economic terrain and had to worry about preserving their social distinctiveness even as they lost their financial superiority.[62]

Some of them responded to the advent of nouveaux riches like Astor, Vanderbilt, and Colgate by accentuating their possession of credentials and tastes that money presumably could not buy. Asked by census takers in 1850 and 1860 to identify their profession or occupation, blue bloods Joseph Stuyvesant, William Rhinelander, George P. Rogers, William Barclay Parsons, William Butler, and H. P. Scoles described themselves as "gentlemen." Many more did so in 1860 than in 1850, a sign that a trend was underway. Some of these men were more than sixty years old and may have thought of themselves as having retired from work, but others were in the prime of life: Butler was twenty-six years old, Scoles, thirty-three, and Stuyvesant, forty. They had consciously chosen to disassociate themselves from the workplace in a city that was increasingly preoccupied with moneymaking.[63]

Yet nineteenth-century gentlemen inhabited a much different social and cultural milieu than their eighteenth-century predecessors had, and one way or another, they needed to adjust to the realities of the market. Taking a packet boat to Liverpool in 1830, Cornelius Rapelye Suydam, an upper-class resident of Newtown, on Long Island, who was the descendant of an old Dutch family, jotted down in his diary the names of his seven fellow passengers. Tellingly, Suydam listed them in precise order of their social rank: first came a Dr. Shey, whom Suydam identified as "a gentleman" and praised for being a "very agreeable, pleasant companion, abstemious in his habits of eating and drinking"; next came four merchants who all had "agreeable manners"; and then a Mr. Canning of Birmingham, an "agreeable young fellow" who apparently did not have a profession or an occupation and whose social status was uncertain.[64] The last person on his list was a Mr. Clarke who owned coal mines in Virginia, in Suydam's telling, a vulgar and irreligious man who used profane language, told crude stories, and drank cocktails before breakfast. Suydam despised Clarke—and feared that the social mobility of people like him was eroding proper values and standards.

Suydam reproduced this social hierarchy automatically, so deeply ingrained was it in his perception of the world. But whether polite society liked it or not, the market could not be avoided, and Cornelius Rapelye Suydam himself exemplified the inroads that materialism had made: he was a merchant and he was traveling to Manchester to buy textiles. He had one foot in the more competitive economic order that was coming into existence and the other in the older moral universe of the eighteenth-century upper class.

Other upper-class New Yorkers internalized the new meanings and associations, as can be seen in one of the most extraordinary documents to be created by any upper-class New Yorker in the nineteenth century, a spiritual diary that James Ferguson De Peyster kept between 1841 and 1852. Spiritual diaries were daily examinations of the self and the outside world that were written to monitor the quality of one's soul and to heighten one's religious devotion. As places where people wrestled with their greatest fears, spiritual diaries were characterized by expressions of anguish and confessions of shame and unworthiness, yet it is equally significant that diarists' understandings of their dilemmas changed markedly over time.

Spiritual diaries made in seventeenth-century America and Europe typically viewed piety in opposition to worldliness and interpreted an excessive concern about material success as proof of a departure from a godly path. To the seventeenth-century spiritual diarist, vanity, self-approbation, and acquisitiveness must be fought. By the eighteenth century, though, spiritual diarists had come to think that business success in moderation was a token of salvation.

James Ferguson De Peyster took a different posture toward materialism. The scion of a prominent Old New York family, De Peyster was a South Street merchant who specialized in the cotton trade, lived on fashionable Bond Street, and socialized with other members of the upper class, particularly the Livingstons, Beekmans, and Van Cortlandts, to whom the De Peysters were related. The De Peysters had originally belonged to the Dutch Reformed Church, but the paternal grandfather of James Ferguson De Peyster had converted to the Church of England in the mid-eighteenth century as a way to anglicize the family, and De Peyster was thus an Episcopalian. Except for the newfound respectability of Methodism, the religious hierarchy of the urban upper class had remained unchanged since the late eighteenth century, with Episcopalians on the top rung and Presbyterians, Dutch Reformed, Congregationalists, Lutherans, and Methodists just below it.

His diary shows that De Peyster was in a state of almost constant emotional distress. He continually wrestled with feelings of unworthiness and condemned himself for his spiritual and worldly inadequacies. He compartmentalized his moral life and expressed no qualms about his participation in the cotton trade, took no interest in colonization or abolitionism, and expressed no concern about the welfare of workers and immigrants. He took no part in the revivals of the Second Great Awakening. Instead he focused almost entirely on his business. Holding onto a more traditional form of piety and falling under the influence of his own daily spiritual examinations in his diary while functioning as an entrepreneur, De Peyster put terrible pressure on himself. The interaction of piety and commerce, reinforced by daily diary entries, led him to suffer a great deal of agony.

Strikingly, however, and unlike spiritual diarists of the seventeenth and the eighteenth centuries, rather than trying to keep the different elements of his life in balance and being on the alert for an excessive devotion to business, De Peyster perceived his business troubles (and his anxieties over them) as a sign of spiritual troubles. In short, he interpreted his *lack* of material success as proof of his moral failings and as the chief impediment to his spiritual improvement. In the more unabashedly commercial New York City of the mid-nineteenth century, excess materialism had lost its stigma.[65]

De Peyster voiced his trepidations in an unmistakably Calvinist idiom that he may have inherited from his Dutch Reformed forebears.[66] Of his fears and anxieties, however, there can be no doubt. Throughout the 11 years that he kept this diary, De Peyster expressed apprehension about fluctuations in the market, his ability to navigate its ebbs and flows, the outcome of specific transactions, the bankruptcy of other mercantile houses, and his own reputation as a merchant. Yet his greatest dread was that he would no longer be able to support his family in its accustomed style. Sadly, De Peyster had reason to worry. He suffered severe losses in 1846 and 1847 that he could not cover and had to move his wife and children into a smaller and less expensive house outside the most exclusive upper-class neighborhood.[67]

To a modern reader, James Ferguson De Peyster seems to have been mildly depressed, a condition that his economic marginalization almost certainly aggravated. Fifty years earlier, the De Peysters had been part of a cohesive upper class that exercised leadership across the business, political, religious, and charitable arenas. Now, however, his neighbors in Lafayette Place–Bond Street included newcomers like William B. Astor and Cornelius Vanderbilt, whose extraordinary riches eclipsed his material assets and diminished the value of his social distinction.

De Peyster was probably not in any danger of falling out of the upper class, and his diary does not indicate that he was worried about that prospect. Yet his relative position had slipped, and he was plainly uneasy about being adrift in an urban environment in which merchants concentrated more totally on business than before, people increasingly measured themselves by their pocketbooks, and a position at the apex of the upper class required a lot more money. His extreme religiosity may have been atypical of upper-class New Yorkers, even during the Second Great Awakening, but in his own idiosyncratic fashion, De Peyster was grappling with problems of social distinction and business achievement that confounded others in his set.

A rift had clearly opened between business and social orientations. But had discrete social and economic elite *communities* formed? Two organizations that can provide us with proxies of economic and social elites are the Chamber of Commerce of the State of New York, the oldest and most prominent business group in the city, and the Union Club, its oldest and most exclusive private men's club.[68] Thirty-eight men belonged to both associations, amounting to 8 percent of the membership of the Union Club and 9 percent of that of the Chamber. These thirty-eight individuals had achieved eminence in both the social and economic realms, and included the likes of leading merchants James De Peyster Ogden, Moses H. Grinnell, Moses Taylor, and Edward Minturn.

However, these men were not representative of the midcentury elite; taken as a whole, the memberships of the two bodies diverged. Unlike the Chamber of Commerce, the Union Club contained a number of representatives of old families: eight Livingstons, six Ogdens, four Suydams and Hoyts, three Delanos, and two Hamersleys and Costers. Among the 274 Union Club members whose occupations could be identified, merchants made up the largest category, with eighty-seven, including twenty-nine commission merchants and one shipping merchant.[69] Edward Cunard, a principal in the renowned British shipping company of that same name, and Cornelius Vanderbilt, the self-made steamship magnate, also belonged. There were sixty-two lawyers, sixteen bankers, ten insurance company executives, and two publishers.

Yet many Union Club members had little or no direct connection to business. Seventeen members had occupations that conferred social honor or that involved specialized professional training that detached them from the market, including five physicians, four judges, three engineers, two professors of surgery, two foreign consuls, and a painter. Twenty-eight identified themselves as "gentlemen," such as patrician historian George Bancroft and Old New Yorkers Goold Hoyt and William E. Laight. In addition, the club admitted a handful of U.S. Army and Navy officers to membership at a reduced cost. Ten officers, including Major General Winfield Scott, a hero of the Mexican-American War, were on its roll in 1854.[70] Since the officer corps was generally regarded as a natural aristocracy that subscribed to its own code of honor, the presence of military officers contributed to the aura that the Union Club wanted to project of manly fellowship and social prestige uncontaminated by crass commercialism.[71]

By the 1850s, the upper class was larger, more fluid, and more heterogeneous than ever before. There were now multiple ways of being part of that upper class, from the gentlemen who took pains to distance themselves from the marketplace, to men like James Ferguson De Peyster who were prominent both socially and economically, to the newly moneyed like William B. Astor and Cornelius Vanderbilt. Separate social and economic communities that had somewhat different populations and that adhered to disparate cultural values had arisen. These two groups were not fully coherent or completely separate; individuals both shared and competed with one another.[72] Most attended the same churches, supported the same civic institutions, and resided in the same neighborhoods.[73]

Another development that significantly affected the upper class was the formation of a distinct middle class. The reorganization of the American economy in the early nineteenth century created an occupational base that let men become managers, professionals, and clerks in hierarchical enterprises, separated the workplace from the home, and encouraged an ethic of domesticity that sentimentalized the family and situated women as keepers of the conscience. At the same time, new forms of sociability like evangelical and temperance associations extended the role of the family further into the community and fostered a vision of classless fellowship.[74] Out of these common experiences and values, the newly formed middle class fashioned themselves into a relatively coherent and self-conscious social group that inhabited the central rungs of the occupational and wealth ladders.

The emergence of this middle class eliminated the clear-cut distinction between polite and impolite society that eighteenth-century upper-class men and women had used to confirm their superiority to commoners and to detect interlopers. To be sure, the wealth and the life experiences of the foremost merchants and professionals were poles apart from those of clerks and salesmen, but divisions between the upper and the middle classes were not always straightforward or obvious in a commercial city where top businessmen and middle-class clerks alike embraced the same early Victorian values of industriousness, probity, and self-discipline. Boundaries between the upper class and the middle class were subjective and prone to interpretation.[75]

The upper class lost control over the definition of manners and feeling as a result of the emergence by the 1830s of a new literary genre that commercialized and broadened gentility—the etiquette book. Appealing to middle-class men and women who wanted to improve their characters and life situations but lacked relatives and friends to impart the mysteries of taste and manners, etiquette manuals resolved this social dilemma by turning gentility into a commodity that could be acquired.[76] They offered exhaustive lessons about how to bow, dress, make calls, hold oneself, dance, and speak intended to reassure their anxious middle-class readers that anyone who mastered these teachings would be "welcome in all society" and could "not be a failure."[77] According to the best-selling *American Chesterfield* (1828), middle-class people who displayed merit and good breeding could readily enter high society.[78]

That, of course, was preposterous. Poring over etiquette manuals could not enable a person from the middle class to acquire the cultivation and refinement that Charles Astor Bristed esteemed or penetrate the tight web of personal relationships that bound the upper class together. Significantly, rather than fall into this trap of emulating the upper class, some handbooks contested the very premises of high society, redefining politeness to stress practices and mores that typified middle-class sociability. Thus, *The Habits of Good Society* (1860) accused members of the upper class of being snobbish and dull, insisting that "good society" counted for more than "high society." People in good society, it explained, came from

upright families and possessed strong moral characters, restrained temperaments, and sensible tastes. In short, they were respectable, the core virtue of the early Victorian cultural system.

The Habits of Good Society emphasized that good society comprised individuals who were on a relatively equal footing and populated the same social terrain. Here the middle class had the immense advantage of being in tune with the American democratic ethos, even if that is precisely what the upper class ultimately held against them—they were not European enough.[79] Knowing about Europe and having European tastes and connecting to the European aristocracy was a mark of upper-class status, a crucial attribute that they used to identify themselves. Although upper-class New Yorkers in this period were genuinely enthralled with European aristocrats, it would be a mistake to conclude that they aspired to that lofty station. Rather, they used the signs and meanings of the aristocracy to legitimate themselves and to break away from parvenus and the middle class.

Faced with this flood of nouveaux riches and with the emergence of a coherent middle class, upper-class New Yorkers had to find the means to tighten their communities and set themselves apart.

One way they did so was through their choice of places of residence. With their current neighborhoods in lower Manhattan being consumed by the expansion of the business district, upper-class New Yorkers had to settle elsewhere. Their leading alternatives were an exclusive residential area situated farther uptown in Manhattan and a commuter suburb that was emerging in Brooklyn.

NEW UPPER-CLASS NEIGHBORHOODS:
THE BROADWAY ARC

Brooklyn Heights sits on the western end of Long Island, directly across the East River from lower Manhattan. In 1814, when it was still a rural area occupied by farms, Robert Fulton inaugurated the use of steamboats on the ferry route to Manhattan, and crossings of the half-mile-wide channel soon took just four to six minutes and cost a mere two cents. Thirty-five years later, a guidebook could report that ferry traffic had grown "so great as to strike a stranger with astonishment," with two lines running around the clock and a third going from 4:30 a.m. to 12:30 a.m.[80]

Land speculators, aware that merchants who worked in Manhattan could now commute to their offices from the Heights, initiated a building boom that turned Brooklyn Heights into an affluent commuter suburb.[81] In 1842, a Massachusetts merchant praised the neighborhood for its "very pleasant" wide and clean streets, shade trees, and handsome brownstone and brick dwellings, and declared, "I think if I were doing business in New York I should make this my residence."[82] Many people did just that: Brooklyn Heights attracted prosperous inhabitants who subscribed to the newly emerging domestic ideologies that idealized women as the keepers of moral purity, prized the home as a haven for the family, and cherished the countryside as a refuge from urban tumult. This early manifestation of the mounting American commitment to achieving *rus in urbe* has led Kenneth T. Jackson to call Brooklyn Heights "the premier suburb of the first half of the nineteenth century."[83]

A house in Brooklyn Heights was thus a real option for upper-class New Yorkers, who were being crowded out of their old neighborhoods in lower Manhattan. Hanover Square and Bowling Green were losing their gloss as economic development intensified the demand for commercial land and led to the construction of warehouses, merchants' offices, shops, and rooming houses in what used to be upper-class enclaves.

This rearrangement of elite residential space was part of a larger transformation of urban geography, a shift that began with the inauguration of horse railways in 1832. By enabling passengers to travel greater distances between their homes and workplaces without having to spend more time in transit, horse railways permitted upper- and middle-class men to commute from neighborhoods on the outskirts to their offices downtown. That, in turn, helped move the boundary of settlement farther north and changed the urban morphology. Instead of the dense, compact, and jumbled landscape of the past, the built-up area now covered a larger geographical area and featured separate locations for retailing, manufacturing, and residence. Instead of living cheek by jowl in a micro-landscape, the affluent increasingly resided on the periphery and the poor were relegated to the center, a spatial pattern that gradually expanded the social and physical distance between these groups.[84]

Upper-class New Yorkers needed to move somewhere. In choosing where to relocate, upper-class individuals had to make basic decisions about the course of their lives and their civic commitments. Staying in New York would have meant remaining in a city that urban economic development had transformed almost beyond recognition. And the compact social geography of the antebellum city ensured that elites would reside in close proximity to workers and immigrants and could not isolate themselves from social turbulence. Yet relocating to Brooklyn Heights had its own disadvantages. People who moved there would have distanced themselves from friends and relatives who had stayed behind, their churches, their voluntary societies, and their children's schools. Moreover, since Brooklyn was an independent municipality, anyone who settled there could no longer vote in local elections, hold municipal office, or serve on juries in New York City, no small matter for an upper class accustomed to thinking of New York as *its* city and to exercising patriarchal authority over the lower orders.[85]

Many of those who abandoned Hanover Square and Bowling Green migrated north along Broadway to an extensive new upper-class residential district that coalesced in the first half of the nineteenth century. It took the form of a shallow arc that centered on Broadway and extended northward about a mile from Houston Street to around Twenty-Second Street on the east side. Because the extent of land-use specialization and social segregation in antebellum cities was limited, the Broadway arc was not exclusively or continuously upper class, as later upper-class neighborhoods such as Murray Hill and the Upper East Side would be. Instead, it was a patchwork. Working- and middle-class homes, shops, and factories were interspersed throughout it, and upper-class homes—like banker August Belmont's mansion on Fifth Avenue and lawyer Robert B. Roosevelt's home on Broadway—were nearby. However, the Broadway arc did contain several pockets in which the upper class predominated. These pockets were physically larger and socially more exclusive than Hanover Square and Bowling Green had been, but, even there, upper-class residents could not avoid uncontrolled interactions with members of the lower classes.

One such pocket was Gramercy Park, a planned neighborhood on the east side of Manhattan, between Eighteenth and Twenty-Third Streets and between Third and Fourth Avenues (see map 2). Gramercy Park lay at the northern end of the Broadway arc and was considered far uptown at the time it was built in the 1830s and 1840s. To foster an elegant metropolitan atmosphere that would attract upscale home buyers and be secluded from the commotion of the business district and the squalor of Five Points, Samuel P. Ruggles, its developer, modeled it on London's famous Russell and Bloomsbury Squares, creating a private garden that was enclosed by an iron railing and a thick hedge and that was owned and maintained by the title-holders of the adjoining lots. Among the notables who resided in the row houses fronting this beautiful little park were former mayor James Harper, merchant Peter Cooper, and iron manufacturer Abram S. Hewitt.[86]

The single most exclusive pocket was located at the base of this arc, where it spilled across Lafayette Place, Bond Street, Great Jones Street, and Bleecker Street. This was the Lafayette Place–Bond Street neighborhood, which extended west to embrace Washington Square, an elegant residential square that a contemporary observer said "contains 9¾ acres, handsomely laid out, and shaded by thrifty trees. It is surrounded by a wealthy population, and in summer is much resorted to as a place for promenading."[87] Lafayette Place, which Charles Astor Bristed called "a short, wide street, with a marble colonnade on one side and large brick and granite mansions on the other," was home to William B. Astor and merchants Franklin and Warren Delano and Jacob Le Roy; Bond Street to General Winfield Scott and Albert Gallatin; Great Jones Street to former mayor Philip Hone and merchant Peter Schermerhorn; and University Place to Frederick De Peyster.[88]

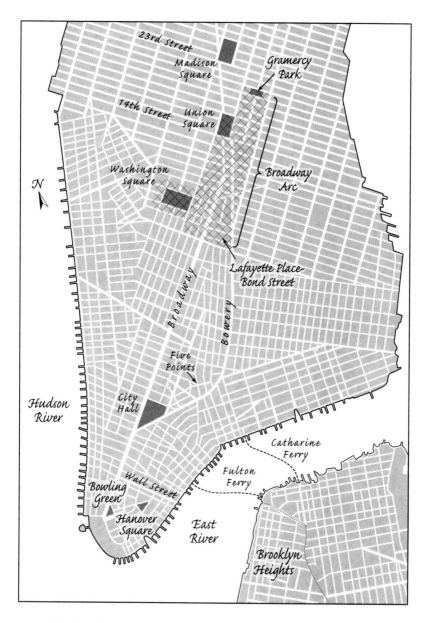

MAP 2 The Broadway arc, c. 1850.

Unlike the commuter suburb of Brooklyn Heights, Gramercy Park and Lafayette Place–Bond Street were neither self-contained nor disconnected spatially or socially from the rest of the city. Lafayette Place, for instance, was only a block from the Bowery, a wide thoroughfare whose butcher's stalls, secondhand furniture shops, and taverns imparted a raucous, down-at-the-heels atmosphere. Indeed, the proximity of these two streets led journalists to dramatize the extremes of wealth and poverty that typified antebellum New York City by contrasting "aristocratic" Lafayette Place with the "democratic" Bowery.

Nevertheless, Gramercy Park and Lafayette Place–Bond Street possessed fashionable housing stock, social exclusivity, nearness to family and friends, an easy commute, and separation from the business district. And, for elite New Yorkers who were highly conscious of their status and prerogatives, moving to the Broadway arc had one other incalculable advantage: while Brooklyn Heights had strong associations with the middle class, the upper-class identities of Gramercy Park and Lafayette Place–Bond Street were irrefutable.

An inspection of the 1850 manuscript census can reveal whether or not members of the established upper class moved to Brooklyn Heights. Because the vagaries of the census data and the fuzziness of the social divisions between the upper and middle classes makes it difficult to be sure which residents belonged to the elite, I employed three separate categories as proxies for elites: first, any man in an occupation or profession that could reasonably be regarded as "elite," such as merchants, lawyers, doctors, brokers, bankers, manufacturers, publishers, clergymen in prestigious denominations, and flag officers; second, anyone who claimed $3,000 or more in real estate; and third, anyone who had $20,000 or more in real estate.

The findings are unambiguous. In all three cases, people who were born in New England significantly outnumbered those who were born elsewhere, including New York State. Of the 542 men living in Brooklyn's First Ward who held elite occupations, 216 (39.8 percent) had been born in New England, compared with 155 (28.5 percent) born in New York State. Yankees also topped New Yorkers with respect to the value of real estate: 45

(41.6 percent) of the 108 residents who claimed $3,000 or more in real property were from New England, compared with 38 New Yorkers (35.1 percent), while 17 Yankees (43.5 percent) and 12 New Yorkers (30.7 percent) were among the 39 people who owned at least $20,000 worth of real estate.[89]

The residents of a comparable section of Manhattan, the Gramercy Park area, had different regional origins. In 1850, there were twice as many New Yorkers as Yankees in elite occupations in Gramercy Park, while native-born New Yorkers outnumbered New Englanders by at least two-to-one in both the $3,000 and the $20,000 categories.[90] These results put the preponderance of New Englanders in Brooklyn Heights into sharp relief. Yankees left New York City but Knickerbockers stayed.

This New England presence was the product of an internal migration that took place in the first half of the nineteenth century as booming New York City eclipsed seaports in New England. Thousands of merchants, sea captains, and other New Englanders moved to the city on the Hudson in search of opportunity: members of the Griswold family from Old Lyme, Connecticut, and the Grinnells from New Bedford, Massachusetts, came as agents of New England firms; the Lows had been merchants in Salem, Massachusetts; Anson G. Phelps of Connecticut became a metal and cotton importer; and Rowland H. Macy, the son of a Nantucket sea captain, opened a dry goods store in New York City that evolved into the famous department store.[91]

Brooklyn Heights became a destination point for many of these migrants and an outpost of their distinctive New England culture of evangelical, reform-minded Protestantism, similar to the Western Reserve in Ohio and the Willamette valley in Oregon. In the 1840s émigrés organized two Congregational houses of worship, the Church of the Pilgrims and Plymouth Church, that reinforced its reputation as "a city of New Englanders."[92] The first pastor of Plymouth Church was the brilliant Henry Ward Beecher, a member of a celebrated New England family who, using its pulpit to advocate social reforms and public morality, made it a center of abolitionism, with a congregation that included renowned abolitionists like Lewis Tappan, a native of Northampton, Massachusetts, and a retired New York City merchant.[93]

Very few upper-class New Yorkers joined this trek to Brooklyn Heights: members of neither the economic nor the social faction relocated there in any numbers. In 1850, nouveaux riches Morris Ketchum, Moses Taylor, James H. Constable, and James and Philip Harper continued to reside in Manhattan, as did almost every member of old families such as the De Peysters, Stuyvesants, Beekmans, Roosevelts, and Schuylers.[94] Of the 265 members of the Union Club in 1854 whose home addresses could be identified, 236 (89.0 percent) lived in Manhattan, including 187 (70.5 percent) within the Broadway arc. By contrast, only five members (1.8 percent) were Brooklyn residents.[95]

The comforts that drew New Englanders to Brooklyn Heights were not potent enough to lure many upper-class New Yorkers.[96] Robert Fulton's steamboat had made it possible for the New Yorkers to move away, too, but they were committed to their city and they stayed.[97]

UPPER-CLASS HOUSEHOLDS

In 1832 Joseph Brewster, a hatter and a speculative builder, constructed a house in the 344–393 block of Fourth Street as an investment. After he and his wife lived in it for three years, Brewster sold it for $18,000 (which is equal to $460,000 today) to Seabury Tredwell, a prosperous hardware importer from an Old New York family, and his wife Eliza.

There was nothing to set the Tredwells' red brick and marble row house apart from the many similar dwellings that went up in this vicinity before the Civil War. Yet while the rest of these structures were subsequently demolished or transformed beyond recognition, this house and its furnishings have been preserved almost completely intact because the youngest Tredwell daughter, Gertrude, born five years after the family moved to Fourth Street, never married and continued to live there until her death at age 93 in 1933. Three years later, the building became the site of what is now the Merchant's House Museum and began its mission of opening a window onto the lives of upper-class families in antebellum New York.

The Tredwells belonged to the upper class by dint of their family background and upbringing, their personal networks, and their money. They could afford to live well and made use of this house to corroborate their wealth, prestige, and taste.[98] The front and rear parlors that occupied most of its first floor had wooden Ionic columns and plaster moldings inspired by the fashionable Greek Revival design. These parlors (figure 3.2) were filled with the kind of expensive, overstuffed chairs and sofas that led a satirist to remark of another upper-class New York City residence that "the inside . . . looks like an upholsterer's shop."[99] The Tredwells received guests who were making social calls in the front parlor, which as the most important room in the house, was richly outfitted with furnishings made of mahogany, red silk, gold-veined Italian marble, and black Belgian marble. The rear parlor was separated from the front parlor by a set of doors

FIGURE 3.2 A view of a parlor in an upper-class New York City residence, from *Gleason's Pictorial Drawing-Room Companion*, c. 1854. (Author's collection.)

and served mostly as a family sitting room and dining room; its best feature were the dining chairs that came from the workshop of celebrated New York City furniture maker Duncan Phyfe. The house also boasted recent innovations such as a bell system that summoned servants to a particular part of the house by giving a different ring for each room and a coal-burning cast-iron cookstove, an advance in cleanliness and convenience over the earlier practice of preparing food by putting heavy kettles and spits of meat over an open-hearth fire.[100]

The 344–393 block of Fourth Street was in the heart of the city's most stylish neighborhood, and most of its inhabitants enjoyed a social rank and a level of wealth on a par with or even superior to those of the Tredwells. In the early 1850s, the Tredwells' neighbors included the families of two commission merchants, a Wall Street attorney, an insurance company president, a physician and professor of medicine, and a self-described gentleman.

Tremendous wealth was nearby: the Tredwells lived so close to the Lafayette Place mansion of John Jacob Astor that their property abutted his stables. In 1862, when Seabury Tredwell reported having an income of $6,900 to federal tax officials, Cornelius Vanderbilt, over on Washington Place, earned $500,000, and William B. Astor, on Lafayette Place, took home $600,000.

Yet the patchwork urban landscape meant that the upper class did not control the social terrain of this block. In addition to the domestic servants who resided with its upper- and middle-class families, this block had a number of lower-middle-class and working-class households. A bootmaker lived seven doors down from the Tredwell family in 1851, and a widow who would soon move into cheaper lodgings in a working-class neighborhood farther uptown boarded across the street from them. Another widow who ran a school out of her house appears to have been middle class.

Their block was integrated physically and socially with the rest of the city, and the surrounding area had a variety of land uses and wide social gradations. In 1851, a cabinetmaking shop stood at one end of the block, at the corner of Lafayette Place, and a coal yard occupied much of the next block to the east, between Lafayette Place and Broadway, within sight and smell of Seabury and Eliza Tredwell's front stoop. At its other end ran the Bowery, which divided upper-class Lafayette Place–Bond Street from an adjacent working-class neighborhood. Many of the butchers, porters, laundresses, and seamstresses who lived on Fourth Street east of the Bowery doubtless had occasion to traverse the Tredwell's 344–393 block, going to work or doing household errands. The presence of these middle- and working-class people and the proximity of commercial and industrial land uses does not mean that Lafayette Place–Bond Street was any less of an upper-class district. Rather, because the emerging urban spatial structure was still in its infancy and because land uses were just starting to become specialized, it was an upper-class area whose inhabitants were accustomed to social mixing and were adept at managing their interactions with strangers from the lower classes.[101]

In this varied landscape, homes like the Tredwells' were important instruments of social filtering and network building. Although balls and dinners were increasingly held in commercial venues such as Delmonico's Restaurant, the Astor House, and the Fifth Avenue Hotel, most upper-class socializing remained centered on private houses. Friends and relatives often gathered informally in the Tredwells' rear parlor for supper parties or card games, but the front parlor was the scene of a more formal custom that lay at the heart of upper-class sociability, known as "calling." A woman or man who wished to call on the Tredwells would arrive via carriage at a set time, usually in the late morning, the early afternoon, or the evening, and be met at the front door by a servant. The visitor would then be admitted into the vestibule, which served as a channel between the public space of the street and the private space of the home as well as a reception area where guests could be scrutinized. The visitor would present her or his engraved calling card to the servant and ask for a particular member of the household. If the person was "not at home" (either physically absent or wanting to avoid the visitor), the genteel caller would depart. Should Mrs. Tredwell choose to be "at home," the visitor would be admitted to the front parlor and, following a short interval that let her admire its furnishings and prepare for the encounter, the host would make her entrance. Calls lasted anywhere from 10 minutes to a half hour, after which the visitor went on to her next call.

An indication of the intricacies of the calling protocol is that one mid-nineteenth-century etiquette book devoted twenty pages to the subject. This complexity is a clue to its cultural significance: calling was precise, orchestrated, and ritualized, demanding a polished performance that obliged participants to acquire emotional discipline and adhere to an exacting social code. Visitors communicated particular messages by the way they folded their cards: in some locales, turning down the upper right-hand corner signaled a personal visit; the upper left corner, congratulations; the lower right, the caller's imminent departure from the community; the lower left, condolences; and the entire left-hand side of the card, a visit to the whole family. There were rules that governed the correct times of day to call, how long callers should stay if other visitors were present, suitable topics of conversation, and the conduct of servants.

Calling enmeshed people in social networks and built community. For example, calling was de rigueur for upper-class men on New Year's Day. Every January 1, Eliza Tredwell and her daughters prepared a buffet table and a punch bowl for the benefit of the young men who dropped by. An upper-class importer who lived on another block of Fourth Street usually started his rounds of relatives and family friends about noon and then spent the entire afternoon going from house to house. One year, he visited more than forty-five households, hurrying so much that he barely had time to greet the male friends he passed on the street as they rushed to complete the same task.[102]

For more formal affairs like the parties, balls, and dinners that represented the peak of upper-class socializing, the Tredwells opened the pocket doors between the front and rear parlors to create a single big room that could accommodate larger numbers of people. In the early 1840s, John A. Hadden, a young merchant who lived on Lafayette Place, filled his diary with accounts of these social engagements—accompanying his sisters to a party at a neighbor's house, attending a dance cotillion in another private home, and going to a ball that his militia regiment held at a public hall. These entertainments were sumptuous. For an 1860 ball honoring the Prince of Wales, about $10,000 was spent to ornament the Academy of Music with special chandeliers and extra gas jets, thick carpets, muslin wall coverings, and flower arrangements. Even routine balls featured elegant trappings intended to transport the guests to a heightened realm of the senses, an effect that could also be achieved by adopting special themes, like an 1854 affair on Great Jones Street devoted to the epoch of Louis XV where guests came costumed as French nobles. Also popular were masquerade balls where people could take on new identities, often borrowed from European aristocracy.

Preparing for these parties and balls demanded a level of wealth, knowledge, and personal contacts that only the established upper class possessed. Consider the experience of Julia Kean, a young woman from a Bond Street family who was staying with the Biddles in Philadelphia in 1832 when she received an invitation to a ball in that city. Ordinarily, Julia's mother would have helped her get ready—but on this occasion she was back in New York City. So an older woman from the Biddles' circle stepped in and told Kean that the pink crepe that she wanted to wear to the ball was pretty only when it was put on over a dress that was made of satin in the same hue. This unnamed woman took Kean to a shop where they found the right shade of satin and bought a pink satin flower for Kean's hair (at a cost of $3.50) and silk for her underdress (at $1 per yard). The woman then had her own dressmaker sew the outfit. To complete the ensemble, Kean asked her mother to purchase long kid gloves, silk stockings, and blue and silver flowers in New York and ship them, along with a muslin skirt she had recently acquired, to the Biddles' Chestnut Street address. Julia Kean also ordered new calling cards for herself. On the day of the ball, a hairdresser came to fix her hair and a family retainer helped her to dress and put on her emeralds. The Biddles also arranged for a young woman from a proper Philadelphian family to accompany Julia Kean to the ball.

The author of a 1930 family history denigrated these elaborate arrangements for having been "pleasantly frivolous," but that reading is wrongheaded. In fact, this effort took planning and coordination, marshaled considerable human and material resources, and showed great social sophistication, all so that an eligible young woman could seamlessly and comfortably enter a new set. In a letter she wrote her mother the next morning, Julia Kean could boast, "We of course carried a great many beaux in our train and I had plenty of partners. I have never seen so great a display of beauty, the room was crowded with beautiful girls and just enough men to fill up the corners and screen us from the heat of the fire."[103] She added, "Everyone is so hospitable and attentive to strangers here, that I feel quite at my ease and as if I had known all the young ladies for years."[104] Because Julia Kean had the appropriate personal relationships, family pedigree, and tastes, the social membranes that would have stopped arrivistes or middle-class people let her pass.

A salient trait of these balls was that their hours conspicuously departed from the everyday rhythms of commercial New York. Even on weekdays, guests did not start to arrive until 9:00 or 9:30 p.m. and the dancing began no earlier than 10:00 p.m. and often continued until dawn.[105] Some observers saw these late hours as evidence of the aristocratic pretentions and slothfulness of social elites. In the 1820s writer James Kirke Paulding described attending a dinner party that broke up at 9 p.m. and then accompanying several of the guests to a tea party that started around 10 p.m. The most high-status guests—Paulding called them "the real fashionables"—did not reach the tea party until 11:30 p.m., when the room filled with people who spent the next several hours drinking champagne, eating oysters, and gossiping. Some continued until daybreak, at which time, Paulding said, "Many of the young ladies looked sleepy, and the elderly ones did certainly yawn most unmercifully."[106] Many had been going to parties five nights a week for the past two or three months, staying out all night and then spending much of the following day in bed, a regimen that Paulding blamed for their poor health: "Their persons are jaded, their eyes sunk, their chests flattened out, their sprightliness repressed by midnight revels, night after night."[107]

Critics disapproved of these late-night affairs for being undemocratic and inimical to sound business values, a position that the *New York Commercial Advertiser* took in ridiculing the "absurdity of copying English hours for gayety without copying the compensating English hour for repose."[108]

Disgusted that upper-class New Yorkers should adopt "such habits as distinguish aristocrats from the working classes," the *Commercial Advertiser* condemned these would-be "lords and ladies [who] please themselvs [*sic*] with going home to sleep when the clowns are getting up to toil" and then lying "abed like a lord until noon."[109] It advocated that balls commence at 7 o'clock instead of 11 so that the "man of business" could attend and still discharge his responsibilities the next morning.[110]

In actuality, there was a larger purpose to these balls and parties than the dissoluteness and lassitude that incensed Paulding and the other detractors: these tastes and practices constituted cultural and social capital that social elites used to mark themselves. Supposed "frivolities" like the elaborate costumes and the late nights let the fashionable set distance itself from the workaday world of merchants and professionals and demonstrate its capacity for beauty and pleasure. The message was that truly upper-class New Yorkers did not need to be respectable but could stay up all night and enjoy themselves.

When John A. Hadden attended such affairs, he expected the guest lists to be confined to the social elite so that he would only encounter people of quality. Hadden relished adding to his networks of acquaintanceships suitable men and women whom he had not yet met, but he was not at ease unless he could be confident of their bona fides. The difficulty was that the mid-nineteenth-century urban upper class was so much larger and less intimate than the eighteenth-century upper class had been that he could not possibly know everyone who belonged to it.[111] After "a large and brilliant party" in December 1841, Hadden recorded the names of almost everyone he spoke with, including close friends from the Howland and Aspinwall families who were part of his set, along with people he knew only by reputation and to whom he had not yet been formally introduced. Their names—"*Mr. Hy Robinson Mr. Gaillard Mr. Augustus Clausson*"—he underscored, adding, "I do not recollect ever to have met at once so many persons that I know by sight as I did on this occasion."[112] The tension that Hadden felt between preserving the customary closeness of his circle and extending his networks was aggravated by the expansion of the upper class.

While Hadden felt apprehensive about mixing with strangers, particularly with attractive young women, he mainly worried about the quality of the people who were present. The significance of recognizing Messrs. Robinson, Gaillard, and Clausson on sight, of being acquainted with Miss Abbott, and of being able to "speak to" members of the Lee family was that he felt confident that they were part of his social universe. Although he usually recovered from his social discomfort—at Mrs. Lee's party, he wound up being introduced to six ladies and dancing with each of them—he always wanted to know whether unfamiliar people were suitable or not.

In a study of Buffalo, New York at the turn of the twentieth century, Mary Rockwell argues that social rituals like calling, parties, and balls should be understood as gateways that controlled access to the upper class—and that woman were the gatekeepers. Rockwell tells us that upper-class women in Buffalo used their supervision of debutante balls, parties, social clubs, and charities to shape the identity of their class, enforce its social codes, and monitor its membership and boundaries.[113] Her conclusions are applicable to antebellum New York City, where women organized most upper-class social activities. John A. Hadden, whose diary entries almost always identify the matron responsible for a particular party, understood the power that older women exercised in regulating society. For Hadden and others, the best assurance that the men he met were gentlemen and that the young women he danced with were marriageable was that upper-class matriarchs had vetted them. The antebellum practice of holding weddings and funerals as well as parties and dinners within the female sphere of private homes heightened the authority of these women.[114]

Upper-class social networks centered on the family, which tended to be large and complex, containing three or more generations of lineal descendants along with collateral relatives such as in-laws, aunts and uncles, and sometimes cousins, nephews, and nieces. A young clerk would occasionally be present, too, and subject to family oversight, even if he was not a blood relative. In 1855, one of the married Tredwell daughters resided at 377 Fourth Street with her husband, a 34-year-old physician, and their

8-month-old daughter. Seabury Tredwell's widowed sister lived there, too. Counting the eight children and the usual complement of four servants, the Tredwell household often numbered sixteen or seventeen people.

This pattern was commonplace. In 1850, Benjamin De Forest, a 78-year-old merchant and his 60-year-old wife Mary who made their home on Bond Street, cohabited with their 40-year-old son, his 30-year-old wife, and their three children. Thomas and Roxanne Bench shared domestic space with an unmarried 28-year-old daughter and a married 24-year-old daughter, her 27-year-old husband, and their two young children. Unmarried adult children usually remained at home: the four Tredwell daughters who never married spent their entire adult lives at 377 Fourth Street. This was also often true of sons. In 1850 the De Witts, a 70-year-old lawyer and his 60-year-old wife, lived in the Gramercy Park area with their six unmarried sons, who included two merchants and two lawyers with established careers who ranged in age from 38 to 28, a 20-year-old clerk, and a 14-year-old student.

Families also encompassed multiple households in the same neighborhood. Brothers Charles and William Macy lived in adjacent dwellings on East Twenty-First Street, while Catherine, Gerald, and Helen Stuyvesant resided within three blocks of one another near Stuyvesant Street on Second Avenue. The Macys and the Stuyvesants had broken down the physical barriers between house and street, extending the purview of family into the neighborhood, like a protective cocoon.[115]

Just as close family relationships made for tight networks that were virtually impenetrable to outsiders, the presence of several generations of a single family and their servants under the same roof recapitulated a patriarchic system for ordering human relations.[116] Domestic servants were essential to the upper-class construction of social reality. By midcentury, domestic servants who lived with upper- and middle-class families to do their cleaning, cooking, sewing, shopping, washing, and ironing had become ubiquitous in American cities. In performing this hard and dirty work, the servants kept the household functioning and, equally important, enabled elites to preserve their aura of refinement by avoiding the coarse and vulgar side of daily life.

Servants were overwhelmingly female, mostly Irish immigrants or, less commonly, African Americans or German immigrants. In 1855, the Tredwells employed four live-in servants: Ann Clark, a 24-year-old English immigrant, and three Irish women, Bridget Murphy, 19 years of age, Mary James, 31, and Mary Smith, 18. The four women spent most of their time in the ground-floor kitchen, tending the fire, pumping and boiling water, baking, plucking chickens, making preserves, chopping ice, and so forth. They slept in two small rooms (one of which is shown in figure 3.3) on the top story, the only floor in the house that did not have a fireplace. There was also a large workplace on this floor where they sewed and mended and put the laundry on a drying rack.

Wealthier families had more elaborate retinues. William B. Astor, his wife, Margaret, and their three children had six servants, all natives of Ireland, including a coachman, a waiter, and four maids. Tobacco

FIGURE 3.3 In 1855, the four immigrant women who worked as servants for the Tredwell family shared two bedrooms on the fourth floor of the house. This photograph shows one of those bedrooms, which the Merchant's House Museum has restored to its 1855 appearance. (Courtesy of Merchant's House Museum.)

merchant Peter Leareatac and his five children required the services of eight domestics: a laundress, a seamstress, a cook, a servant, a waiter, and three coachmen; while shipping merchant Meredith Howland employed two coachmen, a waiter, a cook, a housekeeper, a porter, and six other servants. By 1860, some Lafayette Place residents were employing butlers and footmen, reminiscent of the households of European aristocrats.[117]

Domestic servants constituted upper-class New Yorkers' principal contact with the working class and with immigrants. Servants, of course, had minds and agendas of their own, and Irishwomen were famously recalcitrant. Nevertheless, the presence of servants gave elites a means of organizing their interactions with the lower classes and of confirming their understandings of these groups within the context of patriarchic relationships that they could dominate. Living together under the same roof with their employers, economically dependent on them, and subject to constant monitoring and correction, live-in servants seemed to upper-class people to embody the possibilities and pitfalls of large-scale immigration and of the working class in general.

Convinced that wayward servants required benevolent guidance if they were to become obedient and responsible, leading New Yorkers founded the Society for Improving the Character and Usefullness [sic] of Domestic Servants in 1825. As the demand for domestics exceeded its supply and as servants manipulated market scarcity to secure jobs that paid better or required less grueling toil, the society complained about the decline of "faithful and respectable servants in our City."[118] The society claimed that servants who moved from position to position unwittingly put themselves in moral danger: "They become impatient of control, or of advice, negligent of their duty, and, after wandering from place to place, deteriorating at every change, they not unfrequently [sic] end their days in the miserable haunts of vice."[119] The society published a registry that contained the names of faithful servants and implored prospective employers to hire only from it and on the recommendation of past masters.

Other contemporaries, less confident that servants who came from the dregs of Europe could be reformed, believed that they should be managed sympathetically nevertheless. An 1838 etiquette manual instructed upper- and middle-class women that:

> much has been said respecting bad servants and there are a great many bad ones amongst the numerous class; but it is more their misfortune than their fault: they are for the most part taken from a class of society who do not attend properly to the training of their children, and are placed too frequently with those who pay no attention to their comfort.[120]

The advice that this manual gave for handling servants amounted to a prescription for dealing with the lower classes as a whole: treat them with kindness and steadfastness yet without familiarity, offer corrections "in a calm, dignified, and firm manner" rather than out of anger, "and you will have at least a chance of sometimes making them attentive, zealous, and grateful and of having your services performed with order and electricity [sic]."[121] As Harper's Weekly told its readers, the interactions between mistress and servant involved "reciprocal and mutual obligations": "If the servant owes obedience, faithfulness, and zeal, the mistress as plainly owes kindness, watchfulness, and a judicious superintendence."[122]

The upper-class outlook on workers and immigrants remained fluid and had not yet hardened into an unyielding conviction that these social groups were dangerous and had to be constrained. That solidification of attitudes would begin during the Civil War.

UPPER-CLASS MILITIAS

By the 1830s and 1840s, volunteer militia regiments and companies that drew on the military heritage of the American Revolution and the War of 1812 and afforded opportunities for masculine camaraderie and display had blossomed in cities and towns across the country. Philadelphia had its Washington Greys; Boston, its City Grays and its Tigers; Brooklyn, its Columbian Riflemen and its Washington Horse Guard;

and New York City, its Washington Greys, its Jefferson Guard, and its Lafayette Horse Guards.[123]

These militia units were part of a multitude of elite and quasi-elite voluntary associations, such as literary and historical societies and sporting clubs, that proliferated between the 1820s and 1860s. As institutional expressions of the interlocking circles of relatives, friends, and acquaintances that formed the core of upper-class society, these associations fostered fellowship and affirmed the social station of their members. Some of these societies had upper-class adherents, others a mélange of middle-class business and professional men who sought social mobility and are best considered "would-be gentlemen."[124]

Elite militias afforded upper-class men (and others) opportunities to form communities, establish social hierarchies, and express values. They also provided a counterpoint to homes. The activities that took place within the home were gendered female, entailed women as the major actors, and occurred in private space, while the militias enrolled men and boys and promoted masculine ideals. Soldiers had more difficulty controlling their relationships than did female gatekeepers, since the military units operated in public as well as private space and competed openly with one another. A few New York City regiments, like the splendid Washington Greys, became celebrated for their military élan and social exclusivity and displayed the breeding and authority of the upper class. But middle- and working-class men formed their own companies and vied with the upper class for glory in public settings like parades and reviews.

Militias were subject to the authority of the governor and the state legislature and were part of a military chain of command that issued regulations and orders. In practice, however, institutional arrangements were loose, and regiments and companies had wide latitude in recruiting members, selecting their commissioned and noncommissioned officers, scheduling training exercises and social activities, designing uniforms, and setting dues. This autonomy made for social stratification, and by the 1830s and 1840s militia units reproduced much of the social complexity of New York City. Many companies were largely working or middle class and constituted extensions of neighborhoods and ethnoreligious communities, just as volunteer fire companies and local political clubs did, while regiments like the Washington Greys recruited largely from the upper class and prided themselves on their social prominence.[125]

In 1845 Alfred G. Jones, a prosperous lawyer, and two of his friends went to the rooms of a military society that specialized in the study of military law to decide if they wanted to join. Jones weighed the costs and benefits of membership, noting that members paid annual dues of $12 (the equivalent of $357 today), plus an additional fee for the purchase of their uniforms. He knew that membership in the society would entitle him to enroll in a militia unit called the City's Brigade, which appealed to him because he wanted to attend its dinners and parties. Jones justified the cost of the uniforms by deciding he would need them to look his best at these soirées, so he applied for membership, was accepted, and was soon drilling with the City Guard and enjoying soldiery comradeship. In 1852, Edward N. Tailer, a twenty-two-year-old resident of Lafayette Place–Bond Street, enrolled in a trainee unit of the Twelfth Regiment and began drilling and marching in parades.[126] Training exercises were monotonous and time-consuming, but Tailer stuck it out because he loved "attracting [the] attention of the people" in his neighborhood during maneuvers, repairing with his mates to a tavern or restaurant after their drills, and attending regimental balls in his dress uniform.[127]

If financial considerations did not deter Jones and Tailer, other men found the outlays for dues, uniforms, and firearms to be prohibitive. An 1820 announcement that the Second Company of New York State Rifleman was seeking new members offered reassurances that its uniforms were "by no means expensive"—yet the $30 price tag for uniforms and a rifle (which is equivalent to $575 today) was out of reach for many working- and middle-class New Yorkers.[128] The proviso that recruits apply for admission to a company and be approved or rejected by vote of its officers or its members was another filter that resulted in the members of particular companies having similar backgrounds.[129]

A hierarchy of New York City's military companies and regiments had formed by the 1830s and 1840s. The place that a corps inhabited on this hierarchy corresponded to the status and wealth of its soldiery, the splendor of its uniforms and its military maneuvers, and its arm of the service, with the cavalry being the most prestigious branch, the artillery next so, and the infantry last. At the top of the ladder were the Washington Greys, celebrated for their social exclusivity, brilliant uniforms, and military prowess. At the bottom were units composed of poor workers, like the company an elite observer derided as "a motley crowd . . . [of] some with coats, some without, some with rifles, some with muskets, some with a fowling piece, some with brooms, rakes, pitchforks, or the handles of them."[130] Most of the rest were somewhere in between, jostling with one another for an edge.

The military system of ranks meant that units were also stratified internally.[131] Because New York State let companies and regiments choose their own commissioned and noncommissioned officers via elections, decisions about ranks and promotions had a social dimension that turned on the friendship networks, wealth and status, reputation for manly fellowship, and military prowess of the candidates. Most elections were not openly contested. Rather, the crucial moment involved the nomination of the candidates, a step that occurred behind the scenes and was not detailed in official records. A candidate could usually expect to receive no opposition. Militia companies and regiments normally picked "natural" leaders—men from prominent families who were sociable, proficient at military matters, and whose fathers or older brothers or cousins had served as officers in the same outfit.

Units took pains to exclude undesirables. In 1864, one company became embroiled in an election controversy when a newly minted officer was discovered to be a Catholic. The rest of the officers concluded that there had been a technical flaw in his election and decided that a new contest would have to be held, which had the desired outcome. Elections reified social hierarchies, confirmed cultural values, and checked abuses of authority and poor decisions. This system was strikingly reminiscent of the predemocratic elections that were common in the eighteenth century, in which positions were almost never contested and nominations always went to the local elite. At a time when a new political culture of universal manhood suffrage, mass electioneering, and increased voter turnout was emerging, the militia companies represented a preserve in which members of the upper class retained that older system now that elections for public office had gone democratic.[132]

Militias occasionally performed substantive duties, often directed against workers and immigrants. In 1849 they helped suppress the Astor Place riots, killing more than thirty people, and eight years later they put down riots involving two Irish gangs. Yet their focus was on social and ceremonial events. Entire regiments assembled at encampments in the Hudson valley and on Long Island for training exercises (figure 3.4) that involved sport and camaraderie above all else, while individual companies made day excursions to Staten Island, Hoboken, and Flushing for shooting competitions. These affairs usually concluded with dinners at local hotels or pavilions that involved much drinking and carousing. Another bright spot on the social calendar were the visits that militia companies from different cities exchanged with one another, with the New Yorkers

FIGURE 3.4 In this image from *Harper's Weekly* of March 1860, New York City's vaunted Seventh Regiment is seen marching up Pennsylvania Avenue in Washington, D.C., a year before the outbreak of the Civil War. (Author's collection.)

regularly traveling to Boston, Albany, Newark, and Philadelphia, where they paraded and were fêted by the militia units of the host city.[133]

Elite companies constantly marched through the streets of Manhattan—en route to out-of-town excursions, to honor corps visiting from other cities, or as part of ceremonies like the opening of the Croton Aqueduct or on the Fourth of July. Holiday parades were extravaganzas that lasted for hours and drew thousands of onlookers, with upper-class infantry companies, cavalry troops, and regimental bands taking prominent positions in the line of march and receiving extensive newspaper coverage.[134] Still more important were the balls and parties that were a staple of the winter social season. Just about every unit staged balls, dinners, or other affairs where their citizen-soldiers wore their finest uniforms and socialized with one another and their friends and relatives. In February 1837, the Washington Greys held a ball at Niblo's Saloon for eight hundred people, and four years later the Twenty-Seventh Regiment threw one at the Washington Hotel where guests danced to the music of a military brass band past 3:30 a.m.[135]

These young men competed fiercely over the elegance of their uniforms and the precision of their marching, in a rivalry that did not involve military prowess so much as its image, at the service of social prestige. As we saw with the preparations of upper-class women for balls, the apprehension of upper-class men about status and hierarchy caused them to pay close attention to the seemingly frivolous. Since dress provided a visual mark of social merit, regiments and companies drawn from the upper class became preoccupied with the design of their uniforms and chose attire that let them outshine the horde. On a trip with his Sixth Company to Washington, D.C., in 1841, John A. Hadden developed an admiration for the marching and drilling of that city's Independent Blues. What he liked most about the Blues, though, were their uniforms, which, he carefully noted in his diary, consisted of blue pants, coats trimmed with yellow and white fabric, and caps that had yellow and black pompoms.

Hadden was not alone in his fashion consciousness. Newspaper stories of parades and reviews almost always described the uniforms of the elite units that had participated, as when the *Commercial Advertiser* commented that the visiting Charleston Northern Volunteers wore plumed hats and blue uniforms turned up with buff and trimmed with gold, and that the Third Regiment of the Washington Greys had switched from blue cloth to gray. Company meetings were sometimes consumed with debates about uniforms. In 1853, one corps established a committee to recommend a new cap design and charged it with determining whether the cap should have pompoms and what size and color it should be. A decade earlier, the Twenty-Seventh Regiment had been convulsed with quarrels over the style of cap and the color of pants it should adopt, a dispute that went on for months, leading to allegations of voting irregularities and to the passage of new election rules.[136]

Militia soldiers relentlessly critiqued the marching and drilling of rival units. Hadden praised the "full & regular" marching of the Independent Blues and their ability to execute the manual of arms soundlessly, although he disdained their failure to pay "sufficient attention to pointing the toe toward the ground."[137] By contrast, he felt that the Hancock Light Infantry of Boston "marched with a very unnatural stiffness" because they took very short steps of eighteen inches rather than the standard twenty-eight-inch stride.[138] Newspaper accounts dwelled on these matters.[139] At heart these rivalries involved the struggles of gentlemen and would-be gentlemen to attain prestige and to consolidate their boundaries.

For young men who spent most of their time and energy on business matters, the militia service supplied friendship, physicality, and excitement. It also provided a respite from the city's incessant materialism, or so it seemed. In 1857, *Harper's Weekly* mocked a fictive Knickerbocker merchant named Smith who "in his latter days realized that his parents did him a grievous wrong in apprenticing him in the bootjack business, and that he ought to have gone to West Point and served in the U.S. Army."[140] Disappointed, Smith becomes a lieutenant colonel in the militia, in effect playing soldier in his spare time. At the core of this derisory article was the awareness that elite militias promoted distinctions that were grounded in material success rather than in social honor or military proficiency.

Indeed, New York City's upper-class militias did not subscribe to the honor culture that was central to the moral outlook that white Southerners took during the antebellum period. According to Bertram Wyatt-Brown, white Southern men embraced a code of honor that sanctioned raw, belligerent behaviors and attitudes, including violence, bravery, glory, and revenge. These values were alien to elite militias in New York City: violence and heroism simply did not figure in their worldview. Their conception of "honor" was more akin to early Victorian respectability and constituted another belief system that the upper class shared with the middle class. Perhaps the best indication of the indifference of upper-class New Yorkers to honor culture is that few of them sent their sons to West Point or Annapolis to become career military officers. The Knickerbocker merchant Smith might enjoy ordering around his militia company or hobnobbing with General Winfield Scott at the Union Club, but he went no further than that. By contrast, white Southerners (elites and nonelites) were disproportionately represented among West Point graduates.[141]

Even so, many observers believed that militia service made a significant contribution to the welfare of the upper class by teaching upper-class men self-control and orderliness, prime Victorian values that were highly esteemed in this commercial metropolis. Men typically joined in their early twenties or late teens, so that, as they were embarking on their business and professional careers near the beginning of their adult lives, they could rehearse basic cultural values and social practices such as respect for hierarchy, reliance on friendship and family networks, and mastery of elaborate behavioral codes. Militias fostered the same habits of mind and feeling that calling did.

These elite volunteer units are best understood as making a cultural performance aimed principally at the upper class itself. Their extraordinary emphasis on appearing in public space through their parades and drills—not to mention the extensive newspaper coverage of their activities—represents a drastic change from the aversion of the late eighteenth-century upper class to public space and to uncontrolled mixing with other social groups. An explanation for the exuberant public performances of the mid-nineteenth-century upper class is provided by anthropologist Alessandro Falassi, who observes that festival competitions can create hierarchy out of equality by validating the form and rules of a contest, the selection of its participants, and the designation of its winners and losers.[142] In effect, these young would-be aristocrats sought to transform parade spectators into an audience and engross them in a rite of competition that confirmed upper-class authority.

Hierarchy and order were all-important in the confused terrain of fast-growing New York City, and it was not lost on anyone that the volunteer companies were military organizations whose enlisted men obeyed the commands of their superior officers. As the *New-York Gazette* remarked in commending an "exceedingly neat and soldier-like" company of Washington Greys that conducted maneuvers in 1834, "The marching and whole deportment of the men reflected credit upon the officers."[143] These companies provided a model of leadership and order for the rest of society, employing wealth, military prowess, masculinity, and patriotic symbols to legitimate the city's changing upper class and demarcate its boundaries. That members of the volunteer regiments withdrew to exclusive banquets and dinners held in private and semiprivate space after participating in the parades only underlined their assertion of authority and identity.[144]

It is unlikely that many people in other social groups were won over to this viewpoint, and upper-class New Yorkers did not fully succeed in establishing their legitimacy in the chaotic social terrain of mid-nineteenth-century New York. That would come later, during and after the Civil War. But social control was not the point; rather, the upper class itself was the prime audience. In these turbulent times, when the status of the upper class was put into question by various forces, New York City's elite needed to affirm itself as a community of feeling and heritage and to assert its leadership. As most did not care about the poor and were oblivious of their living conditions, regimental displays provided the reassuring illusion of seeming to contour a society that was becoming dangerously boundless. As the *New York Times* exulted in 1859, the splendor and discipline of the volunteer units who took part in the Evacuation Day parade demonstrated that their blue-blood members came from better "raw material" than the "demoralized mob."[145]

The militias would soon confront a true test of arms in the Civil War. They would find themselves in the midst of real battles and would have to decide what was more important—their military hobby or their elite existence back home.

$\sim 4 \sim$

ALL FOR THE UNION

· ·

The 1860s

A CRITICAL MEMORY

In July 1863, upper-class New Yorkers lived through the worst urban disorder in American history, the New York City draft riots. As Irish and other workers revolted to block the enforcement of a conscription law and to take retribution for their grievances, the city's compact social geography made it impossible for elites to insulate themselves from the violence.

Caroline Woolsey remarked that the doorsteps on her street near Washington Square were covered with black ashes from buildings that were burning elsewhere in the city.[1] George Templeton Strong, a Wall Street lawyer, witnessed a throng of perhaps five hundred "of the lowest Irish day laborers" wreck two dwellings on Lexington Avenue, and then returned to his own home in Gramercy Park and filled its bathtubs, pots, and pails with water to protect it from arson.[2] A few days after the riots ended, an upper-class woman named Julia Lay wrote: "I have tried to feel tranquil but I have not been able. I cannot eat, I am so afraid of every unusual noise. I'll trust in the Lord and be of good courage."[3] She had seen dead bodies carried past her door, watched a regiment form on her street, and heard it fire volleys into a group of rioters three blocks away. She had not slept for several days. Although the city was peaceful again, Lay remained terrified that the riot "is likely at any moment to break out like a wild beast."[4] This fear and the meanings that people like her gave these disturbances would help alter attitudes about the lower classes in the decades to come.

The 1863 draft riots proved to be a critical memory for the upper class. For all the social chaos that phenomenal economic growth and heavy immigration had produced earlier in the century, upper-class New Yorkers had generally been optimistic that hoi polloi possessed enough self-control and independence to take direction from their betters and accept their proper place in the body politic. But the draft riots revealed that entire communities lacked the self-discipline and orderliness required of the citizenry of a democratic nation and instead were prone to a savagery that had ripped the city apart. Adopting a metaphor that Julia Lay and others had used in 1863, the preeminent nineteenth-century historian of the draft riots likened the mob to a vicious animal that crouched "grind[ing] its teeth in its den" before it sprang on its prey.[5] This point of view accorded with the imperative of Victorian culture to safeguard the innocence of the upper and middle classes against external dangers and corruption.

Tied to the draft riots, two major developments in the 1860s profoundly shaped the history of the upper class in New York City and its relationship to the city. First, the establishment by the federal government of a stronger national financial infrastructure through its creation of a standard currency and a national banking system would enable New York City to tighten its control of the economy in the coming decades. Still more important was the federal war-financing program of loans and bonds, which spurred the expansion of the city's fledgling financial sector even as it funded the war effort. The many merchants and financiers who participated in this project contributed significantly to the Northern victory.

Second, the upper class utilized the Civil War to counter the blurring of class boundaries and social credentials caused by the urban growth that had occurred in the first half of the century. At its core this response involved the upper class's definition of itself as a community of heritage and feeling that provided leadership in government, the economy, and society, a definition that elites could readily manipulate because it was subjective. Drawing on their memories of the draft riots and on Victorian cultural values, upper-class New Yorkers came to classify many workers and immigrants as dangerous classes that threatened the social order. While the attitudes and impressions that undergirded this view of a dichotomous urban society and of the upper class as its stewards had been present in inchoate form in the antebellum period, during the Civil War they began to coalesce into an authoritative worldview that most upper-class and middle-class New Yorkers would embrace as an accurate description of reality. This representation helped harden class lines and gave the members of the upper-class an understanding of themselves and the rest of urban society that was coherent and compelling.

The institution that served as the incubator for this social perspective was the Union League Club, a private men's club formed in 1863 by a group of upper-class New Yorkers affiliated with the U.S. Sanitary Commission who wanted to counteract the opposition to the war that prevailed in their social set and in the city as a whole. The primary contribution of the Union League Club was ideological: it became a seedbed wherein the upper class began to articulate this new sense of legitimacy for itself and voice the need for patriarchal leadership of the lower classes. This ideology gave upper-class New Yorkers reason to imagine they all had been for the Union and a heightened (and wildly exaggerated) sense of their own responsibility for the Union victory. And because wartime nationalism and the draft riots confirmed these messages in the eyes of New York's elites, the Union League Club's representation of itself and of the upper class generally as guardians of the social order and its portrayal of immigrants and workers as beasts proved highly influential.

In establishing a version of the Union victory in the Civil War that underscored their own indispensability as leaders who guided the urban economy and restrained the lower classes, upper-class New Yorkers were mainly interested in confirming their legitimacy and thus enhancing their pursuit of privilege. Their success in these endeavors added to their power in the last half of the nineteenth century.

A SPECTATOR'S WAR: UPPER-CLASS NEW YORKERS' RESPONSES TO COMBAT

Like other upper- and middle-class individuals of his day, John H. Ward Jr. kept a diary where he registered his feelings and experiences. Ward was a sociable young man from an upper-class family in Lafayette Place–Bond Street who had graduated from Columbia College in 1858 and had become a lawyer. Most of his diary entries revolved around the interactions of his small circle of relatives and friends at dinners and the theater and on country outings.

On January 19, 1864, however, Ward wrote about a personal tragedy, the death of his best friend, Will Meade. The trouble had begun in late July or early August 1863 when Alexander "Andy" Stewart Webb, a family friend who was a West Point graduate and a brigadier general in the Army of the Potomac, asked Meade to become his aide-de-camp. Descended on his mother's side from the Lispenards, an Old New York family, Andy Webb was that rare member of the urban upper class to come from a martial lineage. His paternal grandfather, Samuel B. Webb, had been a distinguished Continental Army officer. His father, James Watson Webb, owner and editor of the *New York Courier and Enquirer*, had also been an army officer. At the Battle of Gettysburg, Andy Webb commanded a brigade in the center of the Union line that repulsed Pickett's Charge, thanks in large measure to his own bravery in rallying his men after several companies had broken, an act for which he received the Congressional Medal of Honor.

Andy Webb must have cut a romantic figure to young Will Meade. In his diary, Ward wrote that a mutual friend had persuaded Meade that becoming an officer and seeing combat was "a big thing," and so "Will found himself committed" to complying with Webb's request.[6] But even though Meade dutifully went to Albany to obtain his commission, Webb evidently had not provided him with the information or contacts to succeed there, and after floundering around for a while, Meade decided that he was being "impolitic" and returned home empty-handed.[7] Meade next tried to gain his lieutenancy in a cavalry regiment being raised in a county to the north of New York City, but he did not know anyone there and the appointment went to someone else. Webb kept pressing Meade to join him. After relinquishing his law practice and borrowing money from his grandfather, Meade traveled to Washington in mid-August and spent two weeks looking for someone who could effect his appointment. Failing yet again, Meade resigned himself to not becoming an officer and, according to Ward, "took the fatal resolution" of joining Webb as a civilian volunteer, reporting to the general's headquarters in Virginia that September.[8] Meade immediately made himself useful by resolving disputes among the staff officers, but he soon contracted malaria and had to be evacuated to a hospital in Washington. His parents rushed to his sickbed and used their connections to obtain the best possible medical attention, but he died anyway.[9]

Our interest in this tragedy lies in the insight it provides into upper-class New Yorkers' beliefs about their obligations to one another and about their proper role in the war. For while his friend's untimely and needless death obviously distressed John Ward Jr., he was also disturbed by the sense that important cultural values and social practices had been breached. Ward faulted Andy Webb for failing in his duty to Willy Meade as a fellow member of an upper-class community held together by a web of mutual obligations and relationships. Ward probably knew that Andy Webb had been seriously wounded at Gettysburg and that six weeks later he had been elevated to divisional commander and given weighty new responsibilities. Nevertheless, Ward thought that the general owed Meade loyalty and compassion in his capacity as Meade's mentor and patron. For Ward, personal relationships counted for more than Webb's burden as a wartime commander and even Meade's questionable fitness to become an officer. (Meade's sole qualification appears to have been his blue blood.) Second, Ward blamed Meade for allowing himself to be seduced into embarking on a quixotic adventure in pursuit of military glory or out of a misguided sense of civic duty, instead of remembering that he should have stayed home practicing law and nurturing his relatives and friends.

Ward did not use these words, but he and many other upper-class New Yorkers appear to have regarded themselves as capital and the common horde as labor. Members of the upper class would provide the leadership and set a moral example, ideally from a safe distance that protected their lives and sensitivities, while the grotesque physical business of warfare fell to labor. Third, and most importantly, Ward believed that if Meade had to fight, he should have done so as an officer. As he saw it, Meade's critical mistake had been to forgo his lieutenancy and become a volunteer aide, relinquishing the status and authority that were his due. For Ward, the real tragedy was that Willy Meade had not valued himself highly enough. That he threw his life away without accomplishing anything followed almost inextricably from that blunder.

John Ward Jr. himself was no stranger to military hardship, having enrolled in the state militia in 1857, becoming, like his older brother, William Greene Ward, an officer in the Seventh Regiment's select Sixth Company. In April 1861 the two brothers transferred to the Twelfth Regiment, with William becoming its executive officer and John a company commander. When Robert E. Lee's Army of Northern Virginia invaded Maryland in September 1862, the Twelfth was guarding strategic Harpers Ferry, Virginia, and the Wards were among the twelve thousand Union soldiers taken prisoner when Confederate forces captured the town. John Ward Jr. was paroled from military prison a month later, on the condition that he not take up arms against the Confederacy again. He was in a position to know, as Willy Meade could not, that war was no boyish game. Ward spent the rest of the conflict in New York, his social life a continuous round of balls and dinners, calls on family and friends, and trips to the theater, the opera, and his clubs. He remained active in the militia and won election as colonel of the Twelfth Regiment. For Ward, the militia provided valorization of his social and professional standing, a respite from business pressures, and male companionship, not the opportunity for glory and public service that military service had meant for poor Willy Meade. Ward, in short, stayed true to the upper-class New York ethos and did not attach personal value to combat service.[10]

Unlike Ward, who had fought and become a prisoner, most upper-class New Yorkers detached themselves physically and emotionally from the fighting. Take Edward N. Tailer Jr., at the start of the war a thirty-one-year-old importer who resided in Lafayette Place–Bond Street.[11] Even though he was a member of an elite militia company before the war, Tailer chose not to go on active duty. Once, however, he went to the front in another capacity, as a tourist at the Gettysburg battlefield. As a result of the development of railroads in recent decades, Tailer could make his excursion to Gettysburg and come face-to-face with the blood-letting in a way that had not been possible in previous American wars.[12]

Less than three weeks after the end of the battle, Tailer took a train to Harrisburg. That evening he visited fortifications that had been thrown together to defend the state capital against the invading Confederates.[13] En route to Gettysburg the next morning, he met three New York City merchants who were apparently going there in the hope of securing government contracts to clear the battlefield of the dead and debris. Tailer, in contrast, was not on a business trip or a humanitarian mission; he was a sightseer who wanted to explore the battle site. Hundreds of other people were doing the same thing, either out of curiosity, to scavenge for valuables and souvenirs, or to search for the bodies of their loved ones.[14] The four men reached Gettysburg that afternoon and then took a carriage to the summit of Big Round Top, where they surveyed the field. Tailer had not bargained for the sights and smells of the misery that surrounded him:

> Over 3000 horses were killed, and hundreds are still unburied, filling the air with a most horrible stench. The graves of the poor soldiers are many of them unmarked, and the rain has already uncovered many a poor fellow—in fact, I accidentally knocked off a rebel's hand.[15]

It was too much for him. "The atmosphere of Gettysburg was of such an offensive nature that I concluded to leave early this A.M. [on July 24th, the day after his arrival], being afraid of falling sick here."[16] Tailer hopped an early morning government train that "was full of wounded—prisoners & bodies of the dead," made his connections, and reached New York City that evening.[17]

Few upper-class Northern civilians, other than doctors and nurses, encountered mass death more closely than Tailer had. Few could have beheld those hideous scenes without quaking, but they had a particularly strong effect on someone with Tailer's genteel disposition. Like Willy Meade, Tailer had unwittingly contravened upper-class mores and practices, in his case the need to impose barriers that would shield polite society against people and encounters deemed vulgar, offensive, animalistic, or barbaric. Breaching that code by voluntarily subjecting himself to Gettysburg's horrors had discombobulated Tailer, and a few days later he decided to recover his equilibrium by going to Saratoga Springs, an upper-class summer resort near Albany where many of his friends and relatives were staying. Arriving without a reservation, Tailer found that the village was packed with other society people and had to settle for second-rate lodgings. For these upper-class New Yorkers, there might not have been a war going on. After several days of frolicking had restored his spirits, Tailer tired of "the follies of Saratoga life" and returned to New York City and the "quiet comforts" of his home.[18]

Ward and Tailer embody different upper-class male responses to the fighting.[19] Ward, who was on active duty for six months and a prisoner of war for another month, was atypical, while Tailer's disengagement was more representative of upper-class New Yorkers. Generally speaking, upper-class New York men avoided risking their lives in the war.[20] Yet there was one Northern city from which large numbers of upper-class men went to fight and die in the war. In Boston, blue bloods such as Oliver Wendell Holmes Jr., James Jackson Lowell, and Paul J. Revere answered the call to arms, many of them serving in the Twentieth Massachusetts Volunteer Infantry, nicknamed the Harvard Regiment because the preponderance of its officers who had attended that college.[21] In contrast, Robert A. McCaughey, the historian of Columbia University, reports that the record of Columbia College alumni and students was one of "relative uninvolvement in the Civil War."[22]

This high rate of participation of Boston Brahmins was an expression of the New England tradition of social mission and personal sacrifice. An enduring tribute to this legacy is the Shaw Memorial, a spectacular bronze sculpture designed by Augustus Saint-Gaudens that sits across from the State House in Boston. Dedicated in 1897, this monument honors Colonel

Robert Gould Shaw and the African American soldiers of the Fifty-Fourth Massachusetts Infantry who died with him in combat. Shaw and his parents were upper-class Unitarians and committed abolitionists who moved in the literary and intellectual circles of New England, and Shaw enlisted three days after shots were fired on Fort Sumter. He proved to be a skilled leader who was courageous under fire. In July 1863, he and at least thirty-eight of his men died during an assault on a Confederate fortification outside Charleston, South Carolina.

There is no New York City analogue to the Shaw Memorial and its personification of upper-class Boston's religious mission and its stern commitment to social justice. New York City has no shortage of Civil War memorials that venerate famous statesmen and officers, yet nearly all of them celebrate people from other places, including the statues of President Abraham Lincoln, Secretary of State William H. Seward, Admiral David G. Farragut, and Generals Ulysses S. Grant, William Tecumseh Sherman, Philip H. Sheridan, and Winfield Scott Hancock. (Here I am referring to New York City according to its Civil War–era boundaries, when it was confined to Manhattan Island.) While the presence of this statuary is in keeping with the function of New York City as a national metropolis, it is telling that only two Civil War memorials of any note are dedicated to members of its social or economic elites, Daniel Butterfield, a Utica-born merchant who served as chief of staff for the Army of the Potomac, and Andy Webb, who was honored as much for his tenure as president of City College as for his battlefield heroics.[23]

Upper-class New Yorkers did not, in the main, compile a particularly distinguished record during the Civil War. Most members of the social and business elites did not feel compelled to make contributions to the war effort that involved personal sacrifice or inconvenience, such as entering the military or the civil administration. As we saw in the last chapter, values such as bravery, glory, violence, sacrifice, and duty were not part of the ethos of elite militia units in the 1840s and 1850s. Leadership instead denoted business and social prominence, moral respectability, and the attendant obligation to governance, a conception that remained unaltered with the coming of the Civil War and that would later be reformulated in the Union League Club's assertion of its right to rule. Most upper-class men had regarded their antebellum militia involvement as no more than a romantic gloss on their pursuit of material plenty, and felt no reason to join now.

When the nation was on the brink of civil war in 1861, nearly all of the social and economic elites in the city were hostile or indifferent to the commitment of the Lincoln administration to stopping the expansion of slavery and demolishing the "slave power." Once the fighting started, most remained true to the city's tradition of private enterprise and continued to pursue their own interests, just like Edward N. Tailer Jr. And after the war had ended, they saw no need to memorialize the actions of the few among their peers who, like Webb, had enlisted and fought heroically.

Notwithstanding the presence in the front lines of aristocratic Southerners and Boston Brahmins, upper-class Americans have often avoided doing much fighting in our wars.[24] And yet, paradoxically, the Civil War would ultimately expand the urban elite's wealth and power and enhance its reputation and tighten its boundaries. In a deft sleight-of-hand trick, elites managed to persuade themselves—and others—that they had been primarily responsible for the Northern triumph and that workers and immigrants had been its chief obstacles. In truth, during the Civil War, their actions were exceptionally small-minded and mean. They advanced a distorted vision of public service and an ideology that demonized poor New Yorkers instead of aiding them.

"THE THEATRE OF FINANCIAL OPERATIONS"

In February 1861, Abraham Lincoln stopped in New York on his way from his home in Springfield, Illinois, to his inauguration in Washington, D.C. Lincoln had received only about a third of the city's votes in the 1860 election, and the intensifying secession crisis had not improved his footing there. At a reception at City Hall, Mayor Fernando Wood demanded that the president-elect abandon his antislavery platform and permit the nation to return to "its former harmonious, consolidated and prosperous condition."[25] Scolding Lincoln that the dismemberment of the country would wreck New York City, Wood declared:

> All her material interests are paralyzed. Her commercial greatness is endangered. She is the child of the American Union. She has grown up under its maternal care and been fostered by its paternal bounty, and we fear that if the Union dies the present supremacy of New-York may perish with it.[26]

Although nobody could have anticipated the magnitude or the duration of the conflict that lay ahead, Wood's conviction that war would ravage the metropolitan economy expressed the conventional wisdom in the city. The fear was that war would block its two main streams of commerce: the flow of grains from the Midwest and, especially, that of cotton from the South. The *New York Herald*, a Democratic organ, lamented that the sectional crisis had "brought this great community to a lively appreciation of the value of our late relations with the south and brotherhood with the people of the south" and predicted that the impending war would be "particularly destructive of the material interests of this great city."[27]

In this view, it was cotton that had built New York City. As South Carolina's U.S. Senator James Henry Hammond notoriously declared in 1858 in his "Cotton Is King" speech, rapacious Northern merchants had enriched New York and other Yankee cities by seizing control of a trade in cotton that rightly belonged to the South. One New York City newspaper restated the Hammond argument this way:

> The vast trade of this city is declared to be the creation of Cotton—that Cotton builds our ships, erects our palaces, enriches our merchants, supports our foreign commerce, and causes this city to grow while Southern cities remain stationery. As we have seized the Cotton trade, so we flourish.[28]

From this perspective it was easy to imagine that, without the cotton, South Street mercantile houses and Wall Street banks would collapse.

For cotton was indeed vital. In his diary entries for the 1850s, for instance, merchant Frederick H. Wolcott routinely noted the fluctuations in the price of cotton. Wolcott did not deal in cotton; rather, he was using its price as a yardstick to measure the ups and downs of the overall economy.[29]

These projections that warfare would devastate the cotton trade came true. Before the war, cotton and rice grown in the South had comprised a major portion of the business of Brown Brothers & Company, a trading firm. When Lincoln was elected in November 1860, Brown Brothers had a surplus of nearly $480,000 in its accounts with Southern planters and traders, but by the following June, that balance had fallen to $1,209. The conflict disrupted the movement of other commodities. Moses Taylor specialized in sugar and had extensive dealings with traders and planters in Louisiana, and the outbreak of hostilities prevented him from recovering debts owed him by merchants in New Orleans.[30] Although he shifted his operations to the Caribbean, the nucleus of North American sugar production, he nonetheless complained that the market remained "very dull & depressed" through 1861 and 1862.[31] Severe price fluctuations in the New York market had led sugar planters in the Caribbean to favor the more stable European exchanges.[32]

True to these predictions, the start of the war forced hundreds of city mercantile houses, banks, and insurance companies into bankruptcy and compelled retail businesses to reduce their hours and trim their staffs. But the urban economy proved resilient, and by the end of 1862 a boom was underway that would continue for the duration. By the 1860s that economy had grown so large and complex that it could compensate for downturns in one area, such as cotton, by expanding its activities in other sectors, like manufacturing and finance.[33] A more important factor in the recovery is that the massive government spending stimulated economic activity in New York City. In the four years of the Civil War, the federal government paid out $1.8 billion (in 1860s dollars), more than all previous U.S. government expenditures in the country's history combined. Two-thirds of these outlays went for goods and services needed to support the forces in the field, with many of the disbursements occurring in New York and other Northern cities.[34]

Six of the ten largest contractors for the quartermaster and ordinance departments of the U.S. Army were based in New York City.[35] Private shipyards in the East River employed more than five thousand men and built dozens of warships for the Navy Department, including the celebrated *Monitor*, laid down in the Greenpoint section of Brooklyn, while the Brooklyn Navy Yard expanded the size of its labor force nearly tenfold. City garment factories delivered uniforms, underwear, sheets, blankets, tents, and flags, while other suppliers furnished everything from gunpowder and cannons to horses, hay, and straw. By 1864, this boom had led to a chronic shortage of rooms in city hotels.[36]

The war economy had a particularly profound effect on the financial sector. As the single largest economic project that the national government had ever carried out, the Civil War overwhelmed the capabilities of the small federal bureaucracy, which had limited responsibilities in managing the economy and meager sources of revenue. Accordingly, the U.S. government approved measures that facilitated the imposition of a uniform national currency, created a network of national banks, and established higher sales taxes. These reforms created a more centralized and robust national financial system, making it easier for Wall Street to tighten its grip on the economy in the years ahead.

Wartime funding arrangements had a lasting impact on the financial industry in New York City. The federal government met its fiscal challenges in three ways during the Civil War: it increased taxes; it printed inflationary currency; and it borrowed money through the sale of interest-bearing bonds. Bonds became its primary instrument, accounting for roughly two-thirds of the total $1.8 billion raised. This heavy reliance on securities benefited New York's financiers. The *Shipping and Commercial News* captured the scope and importance of this funding program by calling it "the theatre of financial operations," thus equating war finance with the military theaters where the actual fighting occurred.[37]

New York's position as the national financial center ensured that Wall Street was the center of the action and New York firms such as Fisk & Hatch, H. Clews & Company, Livermore, Clews and Company, and Vermilye and Company handled the bulk of the transactions.[38] According to one scholar, the Civil War "greatly accelerated" the expansion of investment banking in America by increasing the size and improving the organization of its investment banking community, encouraging the formation of new firms, and concentrating money in the hands of private bankers and stockbrokers who became more specialized. In short, the war hastened the evolution of investment banking into a distinct financial sphere separate from trade and from commercial banking.[39]

Trading and membership records for the New York Stock Exchange are scattered prior to the 1870s and 1880s, but there is no question that the volume of securities transactions grew during the Civil War. Government bonds drove the market, but transactions in industrial and bank issues also swelled as the inflation of the money supply made more funds available for speculation and as stocks became a safe haven for houses that had experienced disruptions with commodities trading. For instance, by shifting some of its capital from the cotton trade into railroad, mining, telegraph, banking, and insurance securities, Brown Brothers hastened its transition into an investment bank. A new exchange that concentrated in railroad and mining issues, the Open Board of Stock Brokers, was formed in 1864, and the following year the New York Stock Exchange (which had adopted this name in 1863) unveiled a new $600,000 building that had separate rooms for stock and bond trading. Just a decade earlier, the Stock Exchange had not been able to afford a building of its own and had had to rent space in the Merchants' Exchange and the Corn Exchange Bank.[40]

The Lincoln administration, wanting to raise as much money as possible to avoid becoming dependent on foreign governments and financiers, staged a series of popular campaigns that succeeded in persuading one Northern family in four, on average, to purchase war bonds.[41] But the United States remained a net importer of capital, and the federal government's need to place its notes with investors in Europe created opportunities for New York investment houses. Established firms such as Barings & Company, George Peabody and Company, the Speyer Brothers, and the Rothschilds handled many of these loans, with August Belmont, for example, purchasing millions of dollars of Treasury notes for the Rothschilds. The war also provided openings for newcomers like

Levi P. Morton, a dry goods merchant who launched banks in New York and London.

Some German Jews also turned to investment banking, notably the Seligman brothers. Joseph Seligman, the oldest of eight brothers, had arrived in the United States from Bavaria in 1837, becoming a pack peddler and using his earnings to bring his relatives to America and to move into dry goods. By 1861, the Seligmans ran an import house and a retail store in New York City and an outlet in San Francisco. When the U.S. government began to market its securities, Joseph Seligman founded a private bank, J. & W. Seligman, that placed $200 million in U.S. securities in Germany before Appomattox.[42]

THE UNION LEAGUE CLUB AND MORAL LEADERSHIP

The primary significance of the Civil War to the history of upper-class New York is that elites used it to assert their right to govern the nation and the city. The Union League Club initiated these claims to leadership.

After the Republican Party endured a resounding defeat in the 1862 midterm elections, a group of upper-class New Yorkers who were serving together on the executive board of the U.S. Sanitary Commission began discussing ways to marshal support for the administration and its war program. This group included George Templeton Strong; Reverend Henry W. Bellows, a Unitarian clergyman; Wolcott Gibbs, a professor of chemistry at what is now City College of New York; and Cornelius R. Agnew, an ophthalmologist. In late November or early December 1862 Gibbs hit on the idea of creating a men's club that would bring together leading unionists, and then refined his scheme in conversations with his friends and with Frederick Law Olmsted, the secretary of the Sanitary Commission. They invited fourteen or fifteen other men from their family and friendship circles to join them. This decision to found a men's club as their chief response to the predicament of the Union demonstrated astonishing faith in the potency of their social networks.[43]

On February 6, 1863, Gibbs and the others inaugurated the Union League Club of New York, with sixty-six charter members. Of the fifty-four whose occupations can be identified, there were fifteen lawyers, nine physicians, seven merchants, five bankers, and four college professors. Three were self-described gentlemen.[44]

Sven Beckert calls the founding of the Union League Club a milestone in the emergence of a reform wing of upper-class businessmen. The creation of the club meshed with other efforts such as those of a small group of eminent merchants, manufacturers, and financiers, including Cornelius Vanderbilt and William E. Dodge, who objected to the conservatism of the majority of the economic elite and who had joined forces early in the conflict to sponsor prowar rallies, buy arms and ammunition for the military, fund volunteer regiments, and assist the families of soldiers. As the prolongation of the war made the restoration of the status quo antebellum seem less and less appealing, Peter Cooper and others broadened the scope of the reform program by advocating the abolition of slavery.[45]

The Union League Club gave these reformers an institutional base. Like other private men's clubs, the Union League Club adopted a rigid admissions policy intended to ensure its social exclusivity.[46] It set its annual dues at $25, an amount that restricted membership to the upper and upper-middle classes at a time when department store clerks received a starting annual salary of $400 and government clerks began at $600.[47] But while the Union League Club would be a space for upper-class male socializing, it was also a benevolent association that raised funds for the war effort and a political society that defended the Lincoln administration and sought to transform urban politics. Aspiring to be an instrument of civic reform nationally and locally, the Union League Club pledged to "strengthen love of and respect for the Union," back policies that would fortify the U.S. political economy, and raise the moral character of public affairs. Members had to be Republicans and had to support the Lincoln administration.[48]

To promote the war effort, the club urged New Yorkers to fly the Stars and Stripes, scheduled lectures by military heroes like Rear Admiral David G. Farragut, and paid cash bounties to recruits. It also championed the welfare of African Americans by sponsoring African American regiments, lobbying for equal pay and bounties, and favoring a constitutional amendment to abolish slavery and the creation of the Freedmen's Bureau.[49]

From the outset, however, the Union League Club was equally interested in local affairs. The political authority of the upper class within New York City had eroded in recent decades, due to electoral reforms such as the institution of universal white male suffrage and social changes such as the creation of a coherent working class and the mass migration of Irish and Germans. The Tammany Society, a local affiliate of the national Democratic Party that spoke for ethnic and working-class constituencies, and similar organizations had gained muscle, and representatives of ethnic and working-class interests had attained power in the Common Council, the legislative branch of the municipal government. A decisive moment came in 1854 when Fernando Wood, a Tammany member and a former congressman, secured the mayoralty over the opposition of many in the upper class. Despite being pilloried in the mainstream press for governing dictatorially and politicizing the police force, Wood won reelection two years later and was elected again in 1859.[50]

Without direct ties to the working class and powerless to control or form alliances with it, members of the Union League Club wanted to return to the good days when genteel men held the top offices and politics seemed less sordid. According to club leaders, "the intelligent and educated classes" who had stood aloof from public affairs had inadvertently created a vacuum that had been filled by the lowest and most degraded elements of American society.[51] The *Tribune* expressed these resentments in imploring the Union League Club to become "the nursery of public virtue" and supplant the working-class grog shop that constituted "the fruitful source of political and private vice."[52]

By July 1864, the Union League Club had 680 members, a tenfold increase from its founding a year and a half earlier, and incorporated a broader range of the many-sided urban elite. Members of Old New York families like the Beekmans, Roosevelts, and Suydams had joined, as had men with new money like Charles Astor Bristed, John Jacob Astor Jr., and George Lorillard. Merchants Peter Cooper, Herman R. LeRoy, and Moses H. Grinnell, department store owners Alexander T. Stewart and James M. Constable, and financiers Henry Clews and Washington R. Vermilye also belonged.[53] It was becoming a force in city affairs and an important upper-class institution.

By the time that it moved into a new clubhouse at the corner of Madison Avenue and Twenty-Sixth Street in 1868, the Union League Club had more than a thousand members and had almost as much social cachet as the Union and the Century, the most select men's clubs in the city.[54] It had also redoubled its efforts to provide moral and political leadership, with club president John Jay, the grandson and namesake of the Revolutionary War patriot, evoking its supposed influence on wartime policy making to justify its postwar efforts. As Jay saw it, "the country was in great part indebted" to the Union League for the Northern victory and the "illustrious part borne by the Club throughout the war justifies the country in expecting them to assist in solving the problems the war has left us" by guiding Americans through postwar reconstruction and political scandals.[55] Losing sight of its prior espousal of African American causes and increasingly preoccupied with its antipathy to Tammany Hall and other Democratic groups that spoke for immigrant and working-class constituencies, club leaders emphasized the threats posed by the falsified naturalization of immigrants, state aid for religious schools that were primarily Catholic and served immigrants, and voting fraud.[56]

The Union League Club had little discernible effect on national policy.[57] Instead, its achievements were ideological. Elites were its principal audience, and its message was that upper-class New Yorkers needed to govern to keep the lid on the lower classes and ensure continued economic growth. It urged the upper class to gain a stronger sense of identity, take pride in its accomplishments, and tighten its boundaries. Its contention that its leadership and policy making deserved much of the credit for the Northern victory substituted myth for reality and disregarded the unimpressive military record that upper-class New Yorkers had compiled, yet its adherents were conditioned to thinking of themselves in lofty terms and they accepted its claims uncritically.

Ironically, Jay and the others ignored the elites who really did contribute to the struggle, the manufacturers who produced ships, munitions, and other goods and the bankers who sold federal bonds. An argument can be made that the "theatre of financial operations" was decisive to military success because these profit-oriented businessmen brought the industrial and financial advantages of the North to bear in a war of attrition that eventually exhausted the Confederacy. But that line of thinking would have seemed crass and ignoble and would have smacked of wartime profiteering, while policy making seemed statesmanlike and dignified. In fact, the officers of the Union League Club were less interested in public policy than in using their claims to governance to produce cultural capital. They conceived of themselves in heroic terms, as a ruling class that was proficient at national leadership. Naturally they were above mere moneymaking and superior to grubby politicians and the common herd. This was a fantasy all right, but it was a fantasy that elites used for the down-to-earth purpose of legitimizing themselves and thus validating their authority. They wanted to set themselves apart, and they did.

Upper-class New Yorkers had been hearing similar messages about the importance of their leadership and the depravity of the lower orders from other sources, including popular histories of the city.[58] As members of communities that stressed their heritage, upper-class New Yorkers frequently turned to historical memory to proclaim their identities and communicate their vision of the social order. The subjectivity of memory gave the upper class wide latitude in determining who belonged to the elite, what their sources of legitimacy were, and what they had accomplished. Some upper-class leaders became memory keepers who interpreted the past and defined its meaning, shaping popular understandings of history.[59]

General narrative histories of New York City, such as David T. Valentine's *History of the City of New York* (1853) and Mary L. Booth's *History of the City of New York from Its Earliest Settlement to the Present Time*

(1859), had recently become a popular new literary genre.[60] Written by social and economic elites or their retainers for a readership that consisted largely of people of upper- and middle-class backgrounds, patrician history made the case that the upper class was a fixed and unchanging group whose prudent and farsighted leadership was responsible for urban growth and social harmony and whose patriarchal authority had generally gone unchallenged by other groups. Patrician historians used the past to assert the greatness of New York City and underscore its age and stability, proclaiming the indispensability of the upper class to its progress and confirming the superiority of its elites to the unwashed masses. These historians gave merchants most of the credit for the city's progress, portraying them as wise and socially conservative leaders who were adept at managing change and preserving order.[61]

These histories downplayed the importance of other social groups and omitted or distorted the class, racial, and ethnic dimensions of its history. Fairly typical was the view of Mary L. Booth of city history as a spirited march forward and of New Yorkers as a seamless whole who followed upper-class guidance. More or less ignoring labor disturbances, slave revolts, and other troublesome elements of the urban past, Booth kept her eye squarely fixed on the upper class. Patrician historians came from the same social stratum and had a similar outlook as the members of the Union League Club. George Bancroft, the country's foremost patrician historian, spoke at the opening of the first clubhouse of the Union League Club and later became a member.[62]

Leaders of the Union League Club took the message of the patrician historians, politicized it, tied it to the war, and disseminated it to the club's upper-class membership. In so doing, the Union League Club acted like a radio transmitter in modulating and broadcasting the message of the historians. Yet this transmission was unlikely to have reached a very large audience if it had not happened to coincide with the draft riots of 1863 that galvanized upper-class New Yorkers and corroborated this new understanding of their leadership role. The draft riots disposed a variety of New Yorkers to pick up the signals that the Union League Club was sending.

THE SOCIAL USES OF DRAFT RIOTS

The troubles started on July 13, 1863, when U.S. Army provost marshals trying to administer the new federal draft law held a lottery at an office at Third Avenue and Forty-Seventh Street to draw the names of men who were to be conscripted into the army. An angry crowd of five hundred people, led by a core group of Irish American firemen, attacked and destroyed the building, initiating four days of rioting by Irish immigrant and other white working-class New Yorkers (figure 4.1). Appalled by this violence, a young boatman from upstate New York exclaimed: "Last night [July 14th] was an awful night a great many men was shot you could hear the shots just like a 4th of july [*sic*] in some village."[63]

Irish immigrants lived in appalling poverty and endured ethnic and religious discrimination from the Protestant majority. In the six months since President Lincoln had made the abolition of slavery an official war aim by issuing the Emancipation Proclamation, speeches by Fernando Wood and other Peace Democrats had stoked Irish fears that the freed slaves would compete for jobs and drive down wages. And now, with the passage of a conscription law designed to rectify the manpower shortages caused by the wartime slaughter, the federal government proposed to tear working-class men from their families and send them to the butcher's yard, all, it seemed, to elevate African Americans above white workers. Worse yet was a provision of the conscription law permitting anyone who had been drafted to secure an exemption by paying a $300 waiver fee, a stipulation that put the burden of combat on the poor. The draft riots were carried out by desperate people who had serious grievances against the established order yet who lacked access to political and social channels for seeking redress for their grievances. Resorting to force because they had few alternatives, the rioters conducted reprisals against members of social groups and institutions whom they blamed for their suffering.

Mobs assaulted sites associated with the Republican Party, such as the offices of the *New York Tribune* and the home of its editor, Horace Greeley, and symbols of police and military authority, like police stations and draft offices. Yet their prime targets were African Americans. A large crowd attacked the Colored Orphan Asylum on Fifth Avenue, clubbing to death a nine-year-old girl who was discovered hiding under a bed. African American men were beaten and sometimes killed and mutilated. The bodies of African American men were hung from trees and lamp-posts. Their homes were destroyed.[64] By the time that five regiments dispatched from the Gettysburg battlefield could restore calm, at least 105 people died and another 2,000 were injured.[65]

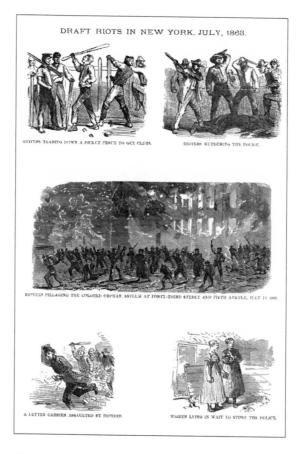

FIGURE 4.1 Illustrations of the New York City draft riots of July 1863 stressing the viciousness and inhumanity of the predominantly working-class and immigrant rioters, from Benjamin La Bree's *The Pictorial Battles of the Civil War* (1885). (Author's collection.)

A crucial determinant of the upper- and middle-class experiences of the draft riots was the spatial structure of midcentury New York. The recent introduction of mass transit had begun to foster a new social geography that featured the separation of home and work; the emergence of specialized locations for manufacturing, retailing, and finance; and the division of residential areas on the basis of wealth, race, and ethnicity. Yet this transformation was in its infancy, and the New York City of 1863 remained fairly compact and spatially undifferentiated. In Chapter 3 we saw that Lafayette Place–Bond Street bordered a working-class neighborhood that lay across the Bowery from it. This kind of propinquity has vanished now that American metropolises cover vast areas and physical distance reinforces social barriers. When a riot erupts in a big city today, its upper- and middle-class inhabitants generally encounter it at a physical and emotional remove and their lives are almost never at risk.

By contrast, the mid-nineteenth-century spatial pattern meant that the draft riots occurred in close proximity: terrible things happened down the street or next door. The mobs had specific targets and the violence was not indiscriminate. In fact, rioters did not attack upper-class people or buildings in Lafayette Place–Bond Street (although they did enter it), and the damage done to other upper- and middle-class areas was isolated and patchy. Provided they were wearing civilian clothes rather than military or police uniforms, upper-class New Yorkers were not objects of violence. Accounts of the riots abound with incidents in which upper- or middle-class people momentarily found themselves in great danger yet managed to get away unscathed. The narrators of these stories usually attributed their narrow escapes to some combination of their own manly character, good luck, or the providential arrival of soldiers or police, but a better explanation is that the rioters did not choose to brutalize members of the middle and upper classes. For there is no question that upper-class New Yorkers could have been readily detected in light of their distinctive clothing, deportment, and pronunciation and lack of calloused hands and other bodily signs of physical labor. Crowds that murdered African Americans let upper- and middle-class whites alone, so long as they could not be linked with abolitionism or the Republican Party and were not in uniform.

But even though upper-class New Yorkers were not targets, the urban social geography made it impossible for them to segregate themselves from the rioters, and many of them had terrifying experiences. On the first day of the riots, James Parton, the biographer of Andrew Jackson, and his wife, Sara, were walking on Fourteenth Street when they saw "streaming down Fifth Avenue a crowd of ill-dressed and ill-favored men and boys, each carrying a long stick or piece of board and one or two of them a rusty musket."[66] The rioters were pursuing an African American man who was on horseback and ignored the Partons and the other bystanders. A column of policemen dispersed this crowd before it did any damage. Nevertheless, several dozen rioters had breached the premier upper-class neighborhood. John Torrey, a botanist and chemist working for the U.S. Assay Office on Wall Street, had a close call returning to his home on the campus of Columbia College, which was then located at Madison Avenue and Forty-Ninth Street in what is now Midtown. "I found the whole road way & sidewalks filled with rough fellows (& some equally rough women) who were tearing up rails, cutting down telegraph poles, & setting fire to buildings," Torrey said. "I walked quietly along through the midst of them, without being molested."[67]

Upper- and middle-class New Yorkers who left accounts of their experiences stressed the outrages against African Americans as well as the assaults on soldiers and policemen. Similarly, merchants and manufacturers accentuated their dread that mobs would plunder their places of business. William Steinway, a partner in the Steinway & Sons piano-making company, agonized about the safety of his factory, on what is now Park Avenue between Fifty-Second and Fifty-Third Streets. After staying in the shop almost around the clock to protect it, Steinway wrote in his diary that, "I have been unable to eat for the last 3 days except bread & drinking water for excitement."[68]

But the incidents that feature most prominently in these portrayals involved acts of violence against private homes.[69] Torrey watched "an attack upon one of a row of new houses in our street" near the Columbia campus and found that "the mob had been in the College Grounds, & came to our house—wishing to know if a republican lived there, &

what the College building was used for."[70] He heard a rumor that rioters "were going to burn Pres[ident Charles] King's house, as he was rich and a decided republican."[71] No harm came to either Torrey's or King's house, but others were less fortunate. John Ward Jr. told the story of a doctor who resided at Broadway and Twenty-Ninth Street:

> The rioters burnt & gutted the next house & a whole row of buildings beyond, hung two negroes, etc. When it broke out his mother was alone in the house. He came home & saved his house by threatening the rioters if they dared come in. He was unarmed. The next day he had friends to assist him. The firemen stole a few shirts etc. & that was all he lost.[72]

Elizabeth Cady Stanton, the women's rights and abolitionist leader, was living with her family off Fifth Avenue on West Forty-Fifth Street, close to where several thousand men, women, and children sacked the Colored Orphan Asylum. As the asylum burned, a group of rioters charged down the Stantons' street, and, yelling "Here's one of those three-hundred-dollar fellows," seized her son Neil, who had been standing in front of their house.[73] Stanton expected her son to be killed, but Neil showed presence of mind by offering to stand his captors to a round of drinks in a saloon, and, after he treated them and joined them in giving three cheers for Jefferson Davis, they released him. Meanwhile, Stanton believed that, after murdering Neil, the rioters would return, break down her front door, and annihilate everyone inside. She sent her children and the servants to the top floor with instructions to run onto the roof and escape to a neighboring house in the event of an attack, but just then a squad of policemen and two militia companies turned onto their street, averting this imagined disaster.

Lucy Gibbons Morse, an accomplished novelist, had often discussed the riots in talks to women's groups and in letters to friends, but she did not organize her memories into a formal reminiscence until 1927. In it Morse wrote that she and her family were living on West Twenty-Ninth Street, between Eighth and Ninth Avenues, in a row of houses where their neighbors included the Sinclair family, who were related to Horace Greeley. As Quakers, the Gibbonses had heralded the publication of the Emancipation Proclamation by illuminating their house and hanging red, white, and blue bunting from it. Evidently this celebration had been noticed.

On July 14, a servant who had been dispatched to buy a loaf of bread from a bakery around the corner returned in tears, and reported that while she was in the shop a man had come in and announced, "We are going to burn Gibbonses and Sinclair's tonight."[74] It rained that night and nothing happened. As their cook swept their walk the next morning, however, a passerby warned her, "We are coming tonight."[75] Morse recalls that her older sister Julia immediately sent the cook away with her trunk because she and the rioters were Irish and the Gibbonses did not feel responsible for her. That seems like a cruel stroke, being cast out in the midst of an insurrection, but Morse supplied a significantly different account in a private letter that she wrote the day after the riots ended. Unlike her 1927 remembrance, this contemporaneous version of events makes no reference to the servants' volunteering information or sympathizing with their predicament. Instead, it has the Gibbonses overhearing "a faint rumor among the servant girls" that their and the Sinclairs' houses were to be fired.[76] And the next day, when the family sought to move its valuables to the nearby home of their uncle and aunt, Morse's July 1863 letter has an Irish servant named Bridget insisting on continuing with her washing and refusing to help them pack. Morse resorted to anti-Irish stereotypes in attributing Bridget's conduct to her stolidity and lack of common sense ("it was impossible to alarm her"), unable to bring herself to openly question Bridget's trustworthiness. Needless to say, one wonders about the loyalties of the servants and whether Bridget knew exactly what she was doing.[77] In any case, by the time that she composed her reminiscence sixty-four years later, Morse had squelched her doubts and could remember her household as having been a place of mutual affection and their servants as having been faithful.

Lucy and Julia did the packing themselves and transferred many of their belongings to the home of their relatives. Then, under their father's tutelage, they practiced firing pistols in their backyard. That night, as the two sisters watched from a neighbor's dwelling, two men on horseback galloped down the sidewalk and shouted: "Greeley, Greeley," attracting a crowd of several hundred people who began roaring, "Greeley! Gibbons, Greeley, Gibbons, Gibbons."[78] After wrecking the Sinclair place, the rioters invaded and ransacked the Gibbons's house. Foolishly or courageously, her father returned to look for his pistol, pushing through the rioters who had piled into the house. Nobody recognized him and he safely rejoined his daughters.[79]

In putting so much weight on the destruction of private houses, these narrators established the disregard of the rioters for human decency as well as the peril that existed to respectable New Yorkers, even to innocents like women and children who were in their own homes. In these depictions, the lower classes amounted to a missile hurled at the tender heart of upper- and middle-class New York. That women such as Elizabeth Cady Stanton and Lucy Gibbons Morse should have identified this threat to home and family gave this version of events all the more credence given nineteenth-century assumptions that females were inherently refined, nurturing, and compassionate. The guardians of domesticity had sounded the alarm.[80]

Some observers concluded that the draft riots must be the work of Confederate agents attempting to sow chaos on the home front by turning the city against the federal government.[81] "It was not simply a riot," the *Tribune* fulminated, "but the commencement of a revolution, organized by the sympathizers in the North with the Southern Rebellion."[82] For fear that the Confederates might strike again, the Union League Club stockpiled weapons and hung heavy wooden shutters on its ground-floor windows to deflect bullets.[83]

Yet even commentators who suspected a Southern link pointed to the wickedness of workingmen who, with no discernible provocation, had metamorphosed into a mob hell-bent on destruction. That understanding raised disturbing questions about political legitimacy and social stratification in the American republic, a subject that the editors of *Harper's Weekly* broached by asking whether the escalating revulsion that respectable citizens felt against the lower classes could be reconciled with the democratic principles of majority rule and egalitarianism. *Harper's* insisted that wretches who beat helpless African Americans to death and ravaged defenseless homes should not be considered "the people" and that the riots must not be regarded as a "popular uprising" or a "movement of the people."[84] Phraseology that presupposed a gulf between government and citizenry might explain mob violence in Europe but had no place in the one nation that exemplified democracy. In the United States, according to the magazine, it was the great mass of the population that constituted the people, including the soldiers and the policemen who enforced the laws and the citizens who obeyed them.[85]

For *Harper's*, the draft riots amounted not to a clash between the government and the people or between democracy and aristocracy but rather one between "barbarism and civilization" that pitted the unruly, vicious, and slothful against the law abiding, orderly, and industrious.[86] The tyranny of the low and ignorant over the rich and the respectable obliged the educated classes to lead. That was the same tattoo that the Union League Club had been beating out, but the draft riots gave it special force. Gone was the old notion that the lower classes possessed the self-discipline and moral fiber to accept elite direction and enter the body politic. Now, upper-class leaders must impose order.[87]

Some eminent New Yorkers who conceded that abysmal housing and health conditions in neighborhoods like Five Points had contributed to the uprising sought to improve the lives of the poor by passing reforms like the municipal tenement laws of 1867 and 1879. But most leaders reacted by damning the rioters and the working-class and immigrant communities from which they had sprung, as *Harper's Weekly* did in characterizing the rioters as "fierce and cruel" beasts who had a "fiendish spirit" and "mad passions."[88] These responses soon crystallized into a stable and coherent representation that many upper- and middle-class and "decent" working-class Americans would come to accept as the truth. Moving beyond the initial belief that the disturbances had been an isolated phenomenon, this new construct portrayed them as a spectacular manifestation of a general peril that the lower classes posed in every big American city.

In 1863, a Protestant minister named B. Peters wrote a pamphlet that told respectable New Yorkers to be grateful that the riots "have given us a glimpse of the moral condition of a formidable proportion of the population of our larger cities."[89] "Perhaps," Peters said, "most of us have had some idea of the moral corruption that lay festering beneath the wealth and poverty of our great cities, but who among us dreamt of such a gross condition of depravity, barbarism, and sin?"[90] Once demagoguery from "the worst political influences" inflamed the "aboriginal savages," Peters wrote, the "vilest, wickedest depravity" accumulated like floodwater behind a dam and then "burst upon us through an outbreak against law and order, in the short space of twenty-four hours."[91] Other commentators reached similar conclusions.[92]

This point of view was best articulated by William Osborn Stoddard, a prolific journalist who in 1887 published *The Volcano Under the City*, which would become the standard nineteenth-century account of the draft riots. Influenced by the resurgence of nativism and the rise of industrial violence in the 1880s, Stoddard played down the rumors that Confederate sympathizers had triggered the unrest, stressing instead the fiendishness of the "whooping, yelling, blaspheming, howling, demoniac" crowds that had poured from immigrant neighborhoods.[93] As the title of his book indicates, Stoddard supposed that immigrant laborers constituted a menace that lay seething below the surface of every major American city, liable to explode at any moment and threaten the educated classes.

Stoddard counseled that mob outbursts could not be prevented. Periodic eruptions were inevitable, and if respectable citizens were to survive them, their political leaders must control the lower orders. As he put it, "men now or hereafter intrusted with the guardianship of the public peace" must remain vigilant.[94] The lessons of the draft riots had now fused seamlessly with the plea of the Union League Club for elites to shoulder their civic responsibilities and govern rather than leave it in the hands of Tammany politicians.

"THE DANGEROUS CLASSES"

The day after the draft riots ceased, Edward N. Tailer Jr. wrote in his diary, "The riot has been composed of the lower classes of Catholic Irish and their doings will long be remembered by an outraged community."[95] Tailer's angry words proved to be more prescient than he could have imagined.

The memory of the draft riots became an instance of cultural hegemony, which the upper class capitalized on to legitimate and consolidate their power without resorting to force. According to Antonio Gramsci, the creator of the notion of cultural hegemony, people in the working class would, in many instances, identify their welfare with the welfare of the ruling class and maintain the status quo instead of rebelling against it.[96]

A vital tenet of the cultural system that arose following the Civil War was the conviction that immigrants and workers comprised what was called the "dangerous classes" of modern industrial society. This belief became conventional wisdom not only in New York City but throughout the United States and in Europe.

Even though antebellum references to the dangerous classes had identified workers and immigrants as the source of pauperism, crime, and political corruption, these expressions were often made compassionately and were couched and qualified. For example, reformers drew on this conception to support the efforts of the Children's Aid Society to improve the plight of workers. Warnings about unsavory elements were typically accompanied by avowals that *most* workers and immigrants were law-abiding and sometimes by reminders that immigration was essential to the economy.[97]

The idea of the dangerous classes fit perfectly with the now-dominant Victorian penchant for comprehending social experience in terms of dichotomies that separated the civilized from the savage, the human from the animal, the rational from the irrational, and the refined from the vulgar.[98] The draft riots powerfully reinforced and crystallized this idea, upending the earlier optimism that the majority of honest and self-controlled poor coexisted alongside a vicious minority. The draft riots and the subsequent calamities that memory keepers pointed to as proof of their construction of urban pathology—such as the Orange Riots of 1870 and 1871, the Tweed Ring scandals, the Paris Commune of 1871, and the Haymarket Affair of 1886—kept the memory of the draft riots fresh in New Yorkers' minds.

The effect that the draft riots had in galvanizing upper- and middle-class New Yorkers approaches the shock that the Haitian Revolution and Nat Turner's rebellion gave white Southerners before the Civil War. Even as late as the 1890s, leading New York City newspapers and popular magazines like *McClure's* and *Outlook* regularly published harrowing stories of the military officials, police officers, and ordinary citizens who had braved the mobs, and histories of the regiments that had ended the rioting. Similarly, experts interested in explaining the origins of criminality cited the draft riots as evidence that immigrants and workers were inclined to acts of violence and thievery due to their inbred natures. This formulation was archetypal Victorianism.[99]

As fears about pauperism, crime, crowd violence, and municipal corruption intensified, opinion makers used the idea of the dangerous classes to describe the lower echelons in their entirety. An ideology took hold that social unrest and even violent revolution threatened from below. This narrative became authoritative: elites convinced themselves that it was true and believed in its authenticity unreservedly. As part of a highly successful Victorian culture, belief in the existence of the dangerous classes extended beyond the United States to Great Britain, France, Germany, and other northern European countries during the second half of the century.[100] In an 1883 article in the *North American Review* entitled "The Dangerous Classes," the Reverend Howard Crosby summed up this new worldview this way:

> It has been our habit to look for national disaster from the lower strata of society. We fear the ignorance and vice of the masses. We see the appalling instances of recklessness and brutal violence in the haunts of infamy, as they are recorded in the daily press, and naturally conclude that this element of evil only needs growth—such growth as the rum-shop and a bribed police will promote—in order to overthrow the existing order and

carry desolation through the land. The reasoning is just. We have seen in our own country what a power for evil these debased classes are, in the riots of 1877. New York city saw these wild forces at work in 1863.[101]

Crosby's alarmist rhetoric is especially arresting because his article was an instance of social reversal, written to admonish upright citizens who neglected their responsibilities to the poor that *they* constituted the *real* dangerous classes. The notion of the dangerous classes had become so firmly embedded that it gave Crosby a hook to buttress his demand that restraints be placed on the "money power" that in his view had sullied American life.[102]

While this idea was still expansive enough for Crosby to convey a compassionate reformism, by now most references were contemptuous and fearful. Commentators agreed that the menace caused by the dangerous classes stemmed from an amalgamation of crime, pauperism, and vagrancy, brought to the boiling point of violent rebellion by the militant rhetoric of demagogic politicians like Tammany hacks and radical agitators like populists, socialists, and anarchists. The peril thus arose in groups that operated beyond the edges of decent society and threatened political and social stability.[103]

For instance, in 1886 the *Army and Navy Journal*, a trade publication for U.S. military officers, employed *The Volcano Under the City* in reinterpreting the draft riots in the light of the contemporary industrial violence and radicalism. Misremembering them as a radical plot to overthrow the established order, the *Army and Navy Journal* claimed, "The red flag floated aloft, and in various tongues arose the cry: 'Down with the rich men!' 'Down with property!' 'Down with the police!'"[104] That was a complete fabrication, but that was how the magazine recalled it. According to the *Journal*, the draft riots and recent labor strikes indicated that another attack on New York City was imminent and that the armed forces would have to meet it. Although the U.S. Army probably could not keep mobs of revolutionaries, convicts, and ruffians from seizing the rest of the city, the *Journal* was sure that the troops could defend Wall Street.

The great buildings of the lower part of the city, such as the sub-treasury, custom-house, stock and other exchanges, and trust companies, are most of them made of stone, brick and iron, and practically forts impregnable to everything except artillery. They could be held by a small garrison occupying each one, unless, indeed, the mob should take possession of them by strategy in advance of their military occupation. The real protection of this district, therefore, as of the entire city, depends upon providing every such banditti with an abiding assurance that in case of their temporary success the artillery would be there within an hour.[105]

Fears of this nightmare scenario led to the construction of armories in New York and other big cities to serve as bases where the military could repulse revolutionaries.[106]

At the core of Gramsci's formulation of cultural hegemony is the idea of consent. Consent, he believed, could not be imposed from above by a dominant class through force or coercion but instead had to be freely given from below. How did these transactions occur? Gramsci concluded that a dominant class gained the consent of subordinate classes by creating and maintaining a system of alliances with some members of those subordinate classes.[107] That is what happened with the dangerous classes construct.

Recall Stoddard's account of the draft riots. For all his denunciations of working-class barbarity, Stoddard was careful to identify law-abiding nonelite men and women who had rejected demagoguery and resisted the mob. *The Volcano Under the City* is full of stories of ordinary people who armed themselves and guarded important buildings; government clerks who stayed on the job to collect information about the violence and coordinate relief and rescue efforts; and rank-and-file soldiers and policemen who heroically repelled rioters. A disproportionate number of these exemplary individuals were workers. Stoddard and other proponents of the dangerous classes narrative did not worry overmuch about the allegiance of the middle class, who were considered by Victorian culture to exemplify respectability. The community of feeling and heritage promulgated by upper-class New Yorkers was subjective and flexible and could readily absorb people from the middle class. Precisely because Stoddard could not be confident about the working class, he highlighted paradigmatic "honest laboring men" who opposed the mob: such as the Brooklyn Navy Yard workmen who remained steadfast, even as a mob raid on that strategic facility was rumored to be underway, and the construction workers who left their job site in Central Park to parade through the streets in a demonstration of their support of the Lincoln administration.[108]

If respectable workers were to do the right thing, Stoddard realized, they must be protected from mob reprisals and they must know that their fidelity to the established order would improve their own lives. In his book Stoddard wrote:

> The intelligent American working-man more or less clearly understands that all existing property is in some sense or other his own and performs important uses for him. He knows that, whether it be nominally and legally in his individual possession or not, property in such a country as this cannot exist without him, nor can it be created without paying him tribute and doing something to better his condition.[109]

"Doing something to better his condition": this was the Gramscian bargain that would earn "the rich men of America . . . the agreement and consent of the working-men."[110]

Although upper-class Democrats such as August Belmont and Samuel J. Tilden had a direct line to the urban laborers and immigrants who formed an important part of their party's constituency, other members of the upper class had to devise their own appeals to the working class. Drawing on the concept of free labor that had become central to the ideology of the Republican Party before the Civil War, many of them came to advocate economic growth as a way to save the industrializing United States from the social chaos and radical politics that afflicted Europe and to ensure that respectable workers experienced social mobility. Economic development would inoculate honest workingmen against the radical ideas and political demagoguery that spawned the dangerous classes.[111] "It is not easy," Stoddard maintained, "for a European revolutionist transported to America to understand that human prosperity does not here, as in some other place known to him, stand for social oppression, or for caste privilege, or any kind of legalized robbery."[112]

Stoddard argued that in America prosperity led to individual opportunity. Starting in the 1880s and 1890s, a commitment to economic growth that stemmed in large measure from a paternalistic effort to reduce the threat of the lower orders became an article of faith for powerful New York City business groups, notably the Chamber of Commerce of the State of New York, and spurred major undertakings like the original subway and the main branch of the New York Public Library.[113]

These projects significantly improved the general quality of urban life and helped New York City equal the grandeur of the big European metropolises. Yet these advances derived partly from the upper class's pursuit of privilege at its most narrow-minded, selfish, and intolerant. During and after the Civil War, elites legitimated themselves by their patriotism and defined themselves more sharply in contrast to the lower classes by putting new emphasis on their cultivation and respectability. In so doing, they restored a bipolar and hierarchical opposition between the haves and have-nots that had not existed since the eighteenth-century dichotomy between polite and impolite society had eroded earlier in the nineteenth century under pressure of rapid urban growth, the expansion of the wealth and size of the upper class, and the appearance of a middle class. Together with a set of ideas about urban leadership, economic development, poverty, and immigration that had been around for several decades but that until now had never coalesced into a coherent worldview, the memory of the draft riots cemented the emergence of a moral community that was led by the upper class but encompassed the middle class and respectable workers.

The upper class emerged from the Civil War with two intertwined roles: as the bulwark against the social volcano and as agents of a paternalistic society that would give the lower orders enough of the rudiments of civilization to defang them. Both roles involved social control. In these ways, the memory of the draft riots contributed to the power of the city's upper class. By the end of the nineteenth century, that upper class would command additional wealth, cultivate new sources of prestige, and be at the pinnacle of its cohesiveness and power.

∼ 5 ∼

A DYNAMIC BUSINESSMAN'S ARISTOCRACY

....

The 1890s

BROKEN BARRIERS

The Union Club was caught in a dilemma. In the 1870s and 1880s it had a membership ceiling of 1,000, with a waiting list that usually had several hundred names on it. Starting in 1885, a small group of members tried to raise the limit to 1,100 or 1,200, but their proposals kept being voted down, in order, insiders revealed, to block the rising "income men" from gaining admission.

As the population of the city grew, the club's 1,000 members represented a smaller and smaller proportion of the upper class, and even of the social elite, but men's clubs that had tight membership restrictions were viewed as being more exclusive and prestigious, and the Union Club was proud of its preeminence as the oldest in the city. Its members worried that becoming too big and impersonal would undermine its standing as an "association of gentlemen." Their emphasis on status and exclusivity also meant excluding nouveaux riches who had made fortunes in the booming Gilded Age economy. Having come out of nowhere, without family antecedents, close relationships with others in the upper class, or social graces, the income men had only their wealth. An etiquette manual said scornfully of "our newer millionaires and plutocrats" that "it is undeniable that many of these captains of industry—however strong and virile their natures—become utterly helpless and panic-stricken at the mere sight of a gold finger bowl, an alabaster bath, a pronged oyster fork, or the business end of an asparagus."[1]

But the Union Club had to abruptly change its policy in 1891, when J. Pierpont Morgan and some others became disgusted by the blackballing of several of their acquaintances and decided to form their own club. Morgan, a member of the Union Club since 1865, was apparently also irked that he had never been elected to its ruling body, the august Governing Committee. Morgan's new Metropolitan Club became known as the "millionaires' club" for its openness to new money and its sumptuous clubhouse on upper Fifth Avenue and threatened to overshadow the Union Club. Confronted with this unexpected challenge, and needing more revenue to replace the obsolete building it had occupied since 1855 with a modern structure that could restore its competitive position, the Union Club increased its membership limit by 30 percent, to 1,300, later in 1891 and eventually to 1,500 by 1894. Although some of the men who filled these extra slots were the relatives of established members who had been on the waiting list for years, the club also made room for "income men" like Samuel L. Rea of the Pennsylvania Railroad. In accommodating the social changes caused by the supercharged urban economy, the Union Club absorbed the kind of members it had tried to exclude earlier and became a larger and less intimate place than some of its leaders had wanted it to be.[2]

A similar powerlessness to control the boundaries of polite society beset the preeminent arbiter of social exclusivity, the *Social Register*. When first published as the definitive "record of society" in 1887, the *Social Register* consisted almost entirely of the names of descendants of seventeenth- and eighteenth-century Dutch and English merchants. The *Social Register* sought to create a space that would be theirs alone, one that would enclose them behind walls that newly rich and middle-class people could not breach. The 1904 edition accordingly contained the expected complement of Old New Yorkers from distinguished families such as the Beekmans,

De Peysters, and Stuyvesants, along with a smattering of members from the second generation of families of newer wealth, like the Vanderbilts. Yet it also included Andrew Carnegie and John D. Rockefeller, the embodiment of rags-to-riches social mobility. Carnegie and Rockefeller clearly fell outside the *Social Register*'s conventional definition of "society," but excluding them would have seemed peculiar to many established upper-class New Yorkers who sat on charitable boards, socialized, did business with, or lived near the two multimillionaires, and it would have seemed outlandish to ordinary Americans who by now equated wealth with upper-class status. Like the Union Club, the Social Register Association had been forced to adjust to the realities of economically dynamic New York City, and it had become more open, more accommodating of diversity, and larger than it had initially intended.[3]

The combined enlargement and enrichment of the city's elites represented the single most momentous change facing the upper class during the Gilded Age. These pressures had existed to a degree before the Civil War, but rapid economic growth heightened their intensity and made them the central feature of upper-class life in the second half of the nineteenth century. Families like the Vanderbilts and Rockefellers accumulated fortunes that dwarfed those of the Astors and Lorillards from earlier in the century, widening the income gap within the upper class as well as between it and middle- and lower-class New Yorkers. As a result of the structural instabilities caused by the dynamic urban economy and the lack of a titled American ruling class, along with the cultural strains caused by the nation's democratic ethos, the upper class of New York City has throughout its existence been prone to thoroughgoing social and cultural changes.[4] Since rapid urban development began in the early nineteenth century, it has re-formed and then re-formed again as it gained new sources of wealth, grew larger and more powerful, and became infused with outsiders. The intensification of these demographic and economic pressures in the second half of the nineteenth century raised concerns within that upper class about the sources of its legitimacy and the need for more coherent and restrictive social and cultural codes.

The Gilded Age is the single most important period in the history of the New York City upper class; upper-class New Yorkers were at their maximum in terms of wealth, power, and showiness during the Gilded Age, and afterward this era would serve a yardstick for measuring other American urban upper classes. This is why historians and biographers who have studied the upper class of New York City have concentrated on the late nineteenth century.[5] However, by viewing the upper class in the context of the entirety of the city's history as this book does, we can comprehend that it was subject to the reciprocal tug of economic pressures and of cultural values.

The banks, exchanges, and corporate headquarters that went up in lower Manhattan as Wall Street became a financial center of world significance in the late nineteenth century were the primary symbol of elite wealth and influence. In fact, elites in New York City were at the peak of their wealth, prestige, and authority in this period. Yet urban economic growth had also let loose centrifugal forces that unsettled and destabilized the upper class by expanding its size, infusing it with fresh blood, and normalizing the possession of immense wealth. These developments alarmed upper-class New Yorkers who had absorbed lessons from Victorian culture about the necessity of defending genteel society against outsiders who were uncivilized, crude, unsophisticated, and materialistic.

The reality is that the reciprocal relationship between economic development and the preoccupations of the upper class was never more evident than in the Gilded Age. As the urban economy produced more and more people with wealth, members of the established upper class and newcomers alike became increasingly aware of their identities as elites. Compared to its counterparts in other big American cities, the upper class in New York was larger, more open to outsiders, quicker to pursue the main chance, and less constrained by stuffy tradition. These traits in and of themselves raised concerns within that upper class about the degradation of its social standards and the porousness of its boundaries. Upper-class New Yorkers thus went in pursuit of privilege to separate themselves from the middle-class and new-money swarms. They identified with Europe and with European social institutions, art forms, and aristocracies for similar reasons. They did not want to be aristocrats but wanted to use associations with the aristocracy and similar markers of taste to distinguish themselves.

This chapter and the next one both focus on the Gilded Age. They will examine the efforts of upper-class New Yorkers to affirm their credentials and build their communities through private men's clubs, women's networks, the Murray Hill neighborhood, genealogy, and European aristocracy. For a time, these practices succeeded in creating a social world that produced exclusivity and cultivation. Indeed, members of the upper class inhabited their social roles so completely that they wound up transforming themselves in the process.

In the end, however, upper-class attempts to draw boundaries around their businessman's aristocracy and to confirm its elegance and refinement broke down under the erosive effects of the city's own economic dynamism, in a process of abrasion that we will explore in the following chapter through an investigation of the famous Four Hundred, a project of Ward McAllister and Caroline Astor to lift the fashionable set closer to the level of the European aristocracy. The Four Hundred could not overcome the volatility of the Gilded Age upper class and was remarkably short-lived.

These two chapters also investigate the double pull that the upper class experienced between its self-aggrandizement and the genuine contributions it made to the growth and welfare of the city. Even though this upper class was becoming much more conscious of itself as an elite, it was not entirely self-focused. In unprecedented ways, upper-class New Yorkers supplied the crucial leadership that allowed New York City to reach for greatness. They played a decisive role in launching economic projects like the Grand Central Terminal and the IRT subway and in founding cultural institutions such as the Metropolitan Opera, the Metropolitan Museum of Art, and the New York Public Library, enhancements that helped New York become a metropolis of the first rank and improved the lives of its residents. Ironically, an upper class that embraced aristocratic forms and disdained ordinary people wound up ennobling the public sphere.

NEW YORK ASCENDANT

By 1900, New York City ranked as the second-largest city in the world, surpassed only by London. Fifty years earlier, New York had been comparable to four other major North Atlantic ports in terms of the size of its population and the structure and functions of its economy. But its population had continued to surge between 1850 and 1900, almost quintupling with the arrival of hundreds of thousands of Irish, Germans, Eastern European Jews, and Italians. It had reached a new level of urban complexity, finally becoming the equal of the great European capitals.

Commerce remained the chief economic sector in this period, but manufacturing and, in particular, finance were strengthened. As the commercial, manufacturing, and financial nucleus of a nation that sustained phenomenal economic growth after the Civil War and would soon succeed Great Britain as the world's preeminent industrial nation, New York served as a principal node in the urban network that bound Europe and North America.[6]

Sinews of this urban network threaded the metropolis. After the Civil War, the core of the port shifted from the East River to the Hudson River to accommodate the freight and passenger traffic moving through the rail and ferry terminals being constructed on the New Jersey side of the harbor. New York became the busiest port in the world shortly after 1900 and retained that position for more than fifty years. Wharves and docks lined the shores of the East and Hudson Rivers and much of the cavernous Upper Bay.[7]

In the early 1890s, the headquarters building of the Western Union Company on Broadway in lower Manhattan was the single busiest telegraph station in the world.[8] In 1891, journalist Richard Harding Davis captured the significance of that communications activity for the financial district it served:

> I never pass Wall Street but that I am filled with wonder that it should be such a narrow, insignificant street. One would think it would need more room for all that goes on there, and it is almost a surprise that there is no

visible sign of the fortunes rising and falling, and of the great manœuvres and attacks which emanate in that two hundred yards, and which are felt from Turkey to Oregon. But it seems just like any other street, except for the [telegraph and telephone] wires that almost roof it over.[9]

"Wherever the electric wires have penetrated," an investment banker marveled, "the Wall Street broker has followed."[10] The telecommunications revolution embodied in the telegraph and later the telephone allowed financiers to enormously expand their reach and tighten their control of remote business operations (figure 5.1).

"Information makes money in Wall street," the *Wall Street Journal* declared in 1896 in promoting subscriptions to the news bulletins of its parent Dow Jones & Company. "People who trade in Wall street naturally seek those offices which have the best information and the most of it."[11] A prime source of that knowledge was the Dow Jones Industrial Average of leading industrial stocks, inaugurated in 1884. Similarly, by introducing the telegraph in the mid-1840s, the stock ticker in 1867, and the telephone in 1878, the New York Stock Exchange enabled brokerage offices anywhere in the country to immediately learn the price and volume of shares being traded and to participate in these transactions. For the first time, the New York Stock Exchange became a genuinely national financial market.[12]

With improved transportation and communications facilities better integrating its North American hinterland and strengthening its linkages to Europe, South America, and other zones of a globalizing world economy, New York acquired added importance as a relay station for the movement of trade, capital, ideas, and people and as a business headquarters where decisions were made. That gave it unparalleled wealth and influence; it was the sole American national metropolis at a time when the small size and limited portfolio of the federal government afforded the private sector a relatively free hand in the economy. As a center of unbridled finance capitalism, New York benefited from the weaknesses of federal regulation, which meant that there were no countervailing institutions to prevent its businessmen from exercising their muscle nationwide. Relatively speaking, New York City was probably at the zenith of its

"As my bankers
in New York said to me"

IN every city, no matter how small, there are some manufacturers
and business men who make it a point to be in New York once
or oftener during the year.

The Equitable has the privilege of serving hundreds of them.
They arrive, register at the hotel, make their business calls, and
then drop in at the Equitable.

Sometimes they have banking business to transact; sometimes
they want merely to check up their own business observations
and forecasts with those of men at the heart of the financial
district. In either case their welcome is equally cordial and sincere.

We will be glad to have you numbered in this company of The
Equitable's friends from out of town. Come in on your next visit
to New York. You will bring us information from your section
that will be of value to us; and we will find important ways to
make our service valuable to you. Our Uptown Office, on Madison
Avenue at 45th Street, is convenient to your hotel.

THE EQUITABLE
TRUST COMPANY
OF NEW YORK

Banking Trusts & Investments · Safe Deposit Vaults
Total Resources over $300,000,000

37 WALL STREET

UPTOWN OFFICE: *Madison Ave. at 45th St.*   COLONIAL OFFICE: *222 Broadway*
London—3 King William St., E. C. 4   Paris—23 Rue de la Paix

FIGURE 5.1 As New York City rose to become a world-class
financial center on a par with London, Paris, and Berlin in
the late nineteenth and early twentieth centuries, financiers
in Wall Street gained greater control of the U.S. economy,
as this 1921 advertisement for the Equitable Trust Company
reveals. (Author's collection.)

wealth and power around the turn of the century, causing many people to
express fear and resentment about its clout.

Complaints about the "money power" radiated from virtually everywhere, including New York City itself. Daniel T. Rogers has shown that
the epithet "robber baron" that journalist Mathew Josephson popularized

in his 1930s exposé of Gilded Age financiers and industrialists had not originated with midwestern populists in the 1880s, as Josephson had supposed. Instead, the phrase was already being employed several decades earlier (and may have been coined) by Boston-born patricians Charles Francis Adams Jr. and Josiah Quincy Jr. and then came into widespread use in the critiques that New Yorkers and other easterners made of the takeover that Jay Gould engineered of the Western Union Company in 1881. As Richard R. John concludes, Josephson's error of attribution fostered the mistaken impression that the antimonopoly movement began in the countryside rather than in the urban east and that it appealed chiefly to farmers rather than the urban middle class or, for that matter, the social elite.[13] From its eastern urban origins, antimonopoly had spread quickly to the small towns and rural areas in the hinterland where there was anxiety about being crushed by larger forces and left behind. Many critics conceived of Wall Street in terms of conspiracies. In 1900 the *Adair County News* in central Kentucky blasted Standard Oil, the City National Bank, the United Trust Company, and other Wall Street companies for colluding with the McKinley administration and taking the nation to the brink of financial panic, a state of affairs that it characterized as "this gigantic and almost inconceivable assault upon the country's prosperity."[14] Newer sources of concern had also arisen, with stories about the villainy of J. Pierpont Morgan and about trusts becoming staples.[15]

From this perspective, New York City was like a giant oak tree whose extensive root system robbed other plants of moisture they needed to thrive and whose outsized canopy kept them in a perpetual shade.

"BUSINESS IS KING"

"Business is king."[16] That was the conclusion that British statesman and historian James Bryce reached in an article he wrote for *Outlook* magazine in 1905, surveying the changes that had occurred in the United States since the publication of his *The American Commonwealth* (1888).

In the tradition of works like Fanny Trollope's *Domestic Manners of the Americans* (1832) and Alexis De Tocqueville's *Democracy in America* (1835) that offered magisterial examinations of the United States from a respected European standpoint, *The American Commonwealth* had become a classic. In his 1905 piece, Bryce said that what most struck him about the American society of the day was "its prodigious material development" with the growth of commerce, industry, and finance.[17] According to Bryce, businessmen had gained prestige and power from that economic expansion and had begun "to overshadow and dwarf all other interests, all other occupations."[18] He thought that financiers and manufacturers were becoming more important and landowners, professional men, and men of letters less so.[19]

Cultural values had shifted profoundly from the time earlier in the century when John Jacob Astor had been pilloried for his wealth and business methods and when Washington Irving had been unable to burnish Astor's tarnished reputation. Now popular magazines like *McClure's* and *Outlook* ran fawning portraits of industrialists like Cornelius Vanderbilt and Philip Armour, and *Harper's Bazaar* and *Century* published reverential descriptions of the New York Produce Exchange, the Chamber of Commerce, and the New York Stock Exchange. This journalism echoed the famous defense of great wealth and business competition as a source of social progress that Andrew Carnegie made in his 1889 essay *The Gospel of Wealth*.[20] In 1899, for instance, *Outlook* informed its readers that Cornelius Vanderbilt II was not just a millionaire railroad king: no, he was "a Christian philanthropist who gave liberally of his wealth and of what was more valuable, his time and energy, to a great variety of philanthropic and Christian enterprises."[21] *Outlook* extolled Vanderbilt as "a man of great simplicity of character, easily approached, but strong, even to sternness, when necessary, and yet withal as gentle as a woman."[22] The magazine emphasized that Vanderbilt possessed his money not for himself but for others: he regarded his wealth "not simply as something personal, but as a great and sacred trust, which it was his duty to administer . . . with a wise and discriminating conscientiousness, for the benefit of his fellow-man."[23] Now the *Wall Street Journal* could respect even the reptilian Jay Gould for having built railroads, telegraphs, and elevated railways that had improved the country, even as it acknowledged his unethical business conduct and indifference to charity.[24]

New York City exemplified (and drove) many of the changes in economic productivity and the status hierarchy that James Bryce spoke of in his article. At the end of the century, commerce remained an important sector of the urban economy and a key source of upper-class wealth. Yet manufacturing, in keeping with its meteoric growth nationwide, had become far more significant than it had been at midcentury and now supplied more jobs than commerce did.[25] In 1900 New York City ranked as the nation's top manufacturing city. Unlike archetypal industrial cities like Pittsburgh or Lowell that specialized in a single product, manufacturing in New York City was highly diversified. And while factories in prototypical manufacturing cities were good sized and capital intensive, the extraordinarily high cost of land, the availability of cheap immigrant labor, and the proximity of large consumer markets discouraged concentration in New York. Instead, its factories generally occupied relatively little space, had small workforces, and were labor intensive. In 1900, its top three industries were women's clothing; men's clothing; and tobacco, cigars, and cigarettes.[26]

The distinctive structure of manufacturing had consequences for urban elites. The kinds of great industrialists who arose and exerted so much power in other U.S. cities—for instance, Philip D. Armour, Gustavus F. Swift, and George Pullman in Chicago; Andrew Carnegie, Henry Clay Frick, and H. J. Heinz in Pittsburgh; and the Pillsbury and Washburn families in Minneapolis—were uncharacteristic of New York City. There were, to be sure, exceptions: the Lorillard family made its fortune from manufacturing tobacco, the Havemeyers from refining sugar, and the Steinways from building pianos. In New York City, however, the main sources of great wealth have been commerce, real estate, finance, and business services, not manufacturing. And while many wealthy industrialists lived in New York City, most of them had relocated there after having made their money elsewhere, as with Carnegie and Frick from Pittsburgh and John D. Rockefeller from Cleveland.

A second consequence was that the strikes and industrial violence that broke out in New York City typically did not directly involve upper-class New Yorkers. It was the Homestead strike outside of Pittsburgh that ensnared Carnegie and Frick and the Ludlow massacre in Colorado that besmirched Rockefeller's reputation, not anything that took place in Manhattan or Brooklyn. By contrast, the worst labor incident of this period in New York City, the Triangle Shirtwaist fire of 1911, involved a small company owned by a pair of Russian Jews (Max Blanck and Isaac Harris) that had subcontracted much of the work to other immigrants. They were decidedly not part of the upper class. A similar ownership pattern typified the garment companies that were caught up in the massive strikes led by the International Ladies' Garment Workers Union before World War I. In New York, upper-class people could stay aloof from the most unsavory elements of American industrialization and affirm their elegance and their affinity for the European aristocracy all the more naturally. They were several cuts above those grubby manufacturers, or so they could believe.[27]

The single most important aspect of this urban economic growth is that between 1880 and 1914, New York City took its place with London, Paris, and Berlin on the top shelf of international financial centers. Although London remained the world's financial capital and Paris was a strong second, New York City, according to one scholar, had become "the rising star."[28] That occurred because phenomenal industrial development enlarged the capital needs of the United States in the late nineteenth century and made Wall Street the gateway for the pounds, marks, and francs that bankrolled American manufacturing.[29]

Investment banking became the nucleus of the financial sector. The investment banks that proved to be most successful either had offices in Europe or cultivated alliances with European banks that helped them place American stocks and bonds overseas. Two clusters of paired institutions arose, both along family and ethnoreligious lines. One was Anglo-American and Protestant and included firms like Bliss & Company (which worked closely with Morton, Rose & Company, of London), Henry Clews & Company (connected to Clews, Habicht & Company,

London), and J. P. Morgan & Company (long an agent for London's J. S. Morgan & Company). By the 1890s J. Pierpont Morgan was the most powerful investment banker in the United States, restructuring and refinancing railroads such as the New York Central and directing mergers for U.S. Steel and General Electric. The second cluster of investment banks was German Jewish. August Belmont & Company was the American agent for the Rothschilds; J. & W. Seligman & Company had houses in London, Paris, and Frankfurt; Kuhn, Loeb & Company, formed in New York in 1867, cultivated a relationship with M. M. Warburg of Hamburg; and Speyer & Company joined forces with Deutsche Bank. Two other notable German-Jewish investment banks were Goldman Sachs, founded in New York in 1869, and Lehman Brothers, a former cotton brokerage in Montgomery, Alabama, that moved its headquarters to New York City after the Civil War and entered the railroad securities market.

Large financial institutions that could procure domestic capital for the investment banks also emerged in New York after the Civil War. Trust companies and insurance companies grew tremendously, as did commodity exchanges such as the New York Produce Exchange. Even more important were the national banks. From the passage of the National Banking Act of 1863 until the creation of the Federal Reserve System in 1913, commercial banks in New York City functioned as the nation's central reserve and assumed special responsibilities for managing the money supply, particularly during the panics of 1873 and 1907. By 1910, six big banks in New York accounted for three-fifths of the capital and surpluses of all U.S. national banks. Their throttlehold on the national credit structure led the Pujo Commission of 1912 to crusade against the "money trust" and contributed to the formation of the more decentralized Federal Reserve System.[30]

The New York Stock Exchange (NYSE) ballooned in the late nineteenth century, with the number of its listed stocks and bonds more than tripling and with the volume of shares traded annually increasing by a factor of five from 1871 to 1900. Securities trading had lost its previous grubby reputation, and the sale of securities became central to a burgeoning corporate capitalism. By 1900 the membership list included titans such as

John D. Rockefeller, J. Pierpont Morgan Jr., George J. Gould, Edward H. Harriman, Collis P. Huntington, and Russell Sage. A seat on the exchange could now bestow or at least denote social status, and the scions of Old New York families such as the Beekmans, Delafields, Haights, and Suydams joined it.[31]

New York City also became a corporate center in the 1880s and 1890s, a development that initially stemmed from business efforts to curb competition via tighter combination and centralization. Trying to control the ruthless competition that made the price of a barrel of crude oil alternately spiral downward and upward, John D. Rockefeller resorted to the "trust," a legal mechanism that allowed rival operators to come together in a cartel that could force hundreds of small-fry producers to stabilize prices. This device also enabled Rockefeller's Standard Oil to absorb some of its adversaries. To give this huge endeavor a legal and administrative framework, a New York City attorney named Samuel C. T. Dodd created the Standard Oil Trust in 1883, whereby shareholders of its forty separate companies exchanged their stock for shares in the trust, which thereupon gained supervisory control over the enterprise from a centralized office in New York City. After moving the home offices of Standard Oil from Cleveland to New York, Rockefeller began to assemble properties in lower Manhattan for the site of a new headquarters, a ten-story building at 26 Broadway that became the most famous business address in the world when it opened in 1885.

Impressed by this achievement, ten other processing industries adopted trusts, with eight of them situating their home offices in New York City. Henry O. Havemeyer consolidated seventeen metropolitan sugar refining companies into a "Sugar Trust" that ultimately controlled 97 percent of national sugar production, and tobacco maker James B. Duke relocated his head office from North Carolina to New York City and formed the American Tobacco Company. Trusts proved to be unwieldy and unstable, however, and soon gave way to forms of combination that were tighter and more permanent. During the great merger movement of 1895 to 1904, more than 1,800 firms disappeared into consolidations, many of which—like American Can, Crucible Steel, and International Paper—controlled more than 70 percent of the markets in which they operated. In 1917, of the 500 largest corporations (in terms of gross revenues) in the United States, 150 were headquartered in metropolitan New York; the second leading corporate center, Chicago, housed only 32. This high degree of concentration persisted well into the twentieth century. In 1957, of the Fortune 500 firms, 144 were based in the New York region, a net loss of only six from 1917.[32]

As the availability of capital and financial expertise from Wall Street banks and exchanges made New York City an attractive corporate location, firms that provided corporations with professional and business services also sprang up in lower Manhattan: law firms, such as Cravath, Swaine & Moore, Cadawalader, Wickersham & Taft, and Sullivan & Cromwell (to use their current names), became proficient in antitrust, mergers and acquisitions, bankruptcy, and real estate law; advertising agencies, like J. Walter Thompson, devised national campaigns to promote the consumer products being introduced by Colgate-Palmolive and Nabisco; and accounting firms, such as Haskins & Sells (now Deloitte Touche Tohmatsu), devised auditing procedures that made it possible to evaluate complex transactions. By increasing the number of office jobs and by further separating administrative work from factory employment, this corporate headquarters complex fostered a distinctive white-collar world. Increasingly, it became a place where economic elites made their careers and fortunes.[33]

Major Wall Street institutions turned to architecture to celebrate their new prominence—and to signal that they had important civic missions beyond moneymaking. In 1901 the Chamber of Commerce of the State of New York opened a monumental new headquarters on Liberty Street, between Broadway and Nassau Street in the heart of the financial district. Just four stories high, the building had been designed in the Beaux-Arts style, and its façade consisted of marble on a rusticated base, capped by a terrace and a mansard roof. Its front, on Liberty Street, had six broad columns that framed three groups of statuary, each of which centered on one of three eminent New York statesmen: De Witt Clinton, Alexander Hamilton, and John Jay.

The Chamber of Commerce had developed into a pivotal institution in the new political economy that came into being with the expansion of heavy industry and finance after the Civil War. The most powerful nonprofit body in New York City, it was the driving force behind the consolidation of Manhattan, Brooklyn, the Bronx, Queens, and Staten Island into Greater New York in 1898 and the impetus for the planning and construction of the city's first subway, the 1904 line of the Interborough Rapid Transit Company. The heart of this new political economy was the interdependence of government and business leaders on all levels who acted together in using state intervention to promote national expansion.[34]

The New York Stock Exchange unveiled its own landmark classical revival building in 1903. To handle the expanding volume of trading and to integrate new communications technologies that were revolutionizing securities transactions, the Stock Exchange had enlarged and modernized its space on three separate occasions between 1869 and 1887. In 1901, needing still more room, the Exchange decided to erect a heroic new structure on its existing site near the corner of Broad and Wall Streets that would herald its coming of age as an important—and trustworthy— national institution. A broker had once lauded its old headquarters as "a fine, solid structure, devoid of anything showy, pretentious or decorative."[35] That could not be said of the new Stock Exchange, which matched the architectural grandiosity and imperial ambition of the Chamber of Commerce and suggested age and stability and importance.[36] During its dedication, Rudolph Keppler, the president of the Stock Exchange, extolled the national significance and solidity of the financial sector, quoting the observation of an unnamed New York City clergyman that "the great things for which Wall Street exists are not gambling: they are legitimate and in every way necessary to carry on the processes of modern civilization."[37]

Thanks in large measure to the peculiar structure of manufacturing in New York City, it was Wall Street that was the chief source of the city's expanded national influence. A Presbyterian minister put it this way in 1901: "Wall Street is one of the longest streets in the world. It does not begin at the foot of Trinity Church . . . and end at the East River, as many suppose. It reaches through all our American cities and across the sea."[38] This was clearly true: when J. Pierpont Morgan conferred in his office at 23 Wall Street about the Federal Steel Company, the Lake Shore Railway, or the Mexican Telephone Company, the reverberations from his decisions could affect jobs, wages, and prices in distant locations.[39] Wall Street accordingly became a flashpoint for conflicts over the pursuit of wealth, monopoly power, the limits of democracy, and business ethics. Industrialization had created a social crisis, and the newfound capacity of financiers and industrialists to utterly transform the lives of people in remote places, for good or for ill, gave rise to opposed positions about the role of Wall Street, with some applauding it for rewarding the talented and enterprising and contributing mightily to national progress, and others seeing the financial district as rapacious and socially divisive.

WALL STREET: OUR FATHERS' TRUE HEIRS

This period of U.S. history was thus replete with protests against the financial center. This opposition elicited responses from apologists who drew on American nationalism to uphold the financial district's integrity, and it would be their ideas that eventually became embedded in popular understandings of Wall Street. Moreover, as the financial sector became more and more important as a source of wealth and prestige for the high-status population in New York City, representations of Wall Street would increasingly shape the meanings that they and others gave their work and lives.

Political radicals were one source of censure. *John Swinton's Paper*, a labor organ, rebuked "our ruling swashbucklers" for trying to subdue workers by brandishing the raw military power available to the upper classes.[40] Socialist leader Eugene V. Debs railed against the corporate plutocracy and prayed for the arrival of "the final hour of capitalism and wage slavery."[41]

Another assault came from within the two-party political system, in the form of the crusade that William Jennings Bryan made against the gold standard during the 1896 presidential election. At the National Democratic Convention that July, Bryan secured the presidential nomination by delivering a spellbinding speech condemning the business interests in the great cities on the East Coast as "the few financial magnates who in a backroom corner the money of the world."[42] He staged the acceptance of the nomination in New York City—venturing, he told his supporters, "in[to] the heart of what now seems to be the enemy's country but which we hope to occupy before the campaign is over."[43] In his acceptance speech at Madison Square Garden, Bryan rebuked "the money changers" who ruled the nation from New York City and declared that the biblical commandment "Thou shall not steal" must apply to the strong as well as the weak.[44]

Bryan's nomination sent Wall Street into a frenzy. Business leaders resented his demagoguery and insisted that his policies would wreck the financial system. More than that, they saw Bryan as a harbinger of social revolution, with some fearing a violent working-class uprising on the order of the New York City draft riots or the Paris Commune. Inside the Stock Exchange, traders reacted to news of the nomination of the Great Commoner with a display of nationalism. A half hour before the close of trading, a broker held up a large American flag and paraded it around the boardroom, as cheering traders denounced secessionists, revolutionists, populists, and anarchists. NYSE governors later claimed that they had planned on closing the Exchange indefinitely had Bryan won the general election.[45]

Protestant clergy joined the attack against the elite financiers of Wall Street. The Protestant clerical opponent of Wall Street special privilege who had the broadest social impact was Reverend T. De Witt Talmage, pastor of the Central Presbyterian Church in Brooklyn, widely regarded in his day as the best preacher in America. Talmage was a social conservative, and while deeply suspicious of the working class, his concern that mounting labor violence threatened to exacerbate social divisions led him to take aim at business. For the next decade, he berated Chicago "grain gamblers" for driving up the price of bread and compounding the desperation of the urban poor; reprimanded Wall Street stock speculators for being in league with Satan; and censured bankers and trust officers for enriching themselves with other people's money. For Talmage, the danger of business practices that promised instant wealth lay in their encouragement of luck, impulsiveness, and desire that would undermine the Victorian virtues of industry, self-discipline, and perseverance.[46]

Wall Street's defenders were quick to reply to these assaults. A particularly influential response came from Henry Clews, a prominent investment banker and civic leader later dubbed the "dean of Wall Street." In 1887, Clews published a rebuttal to Talmage in the *North American Review* expressing his dismay that the Presbyterian minister had employed "his flashy wit and mountebank eloquence" to equate the financial district with brothels and gaming dens and to defile the reputations of Wall Street men who for the most part were "paragons of personal honor."[47] What made Talmage dangerous, Clews wrote, was his sure grasp of middle-class Victorian culture. Clews was concerned about respectability, the core Victorian virtue, not about religiosity per se. According to Clews, Talmage mistook constructive entrepreneurialism for mindless destruction and greed and did not comprehend that the financial center served as a "great distributor" by supplying money to start-up ventures and allowing industries to grow and the nation to prosper.[48] For Clews, who had been an agent for the sale of Treasury bonds during the Civil War and an early member of the Union League Club, the strongest evidence of the importance of Wall Street was that its financiers had raised the funds that let Union armies defeat the Confederacy. He acknowledged that swindlers and confidence men occasionally fleeced investors and injured the reputation of the Street, but these malefactors were the exception, and the great mass of Wall Street bankers and brokers were continuing the work of Washington, Jefferson, Madison, Franklin, and Hamilton.[49]

This powerful idea had received tangible expression four years earlier, when the Chamber of Commerce arranged for a statue of George Washington to be erected on the front steps of the U.S. Sub-Treasury, at the corner of Wall and Broad Streets, where Washington had taken the oath of office as the first president of the United States in 1789.[50] By 1883 this street corner had become the axis of the financial district, with the renowned investment house of Drexel, Morgan & Company located across from the Sub-Treasury on one side of Broad Street and the U.S. Custom House and the New York Stock Exchange on the other. If the accident of this spatial proximity was not enough for people to link the founding of the nation to the operation of the financial district, then the myriad centennials that were held between 1875 and 1889 of events from the American Revolution conditioned them to think in terms of historical memory. Covering themselves in patriotism, business apologists used this history to deflect battering from the likes of Talmage.

In wider popular memory the notion that there was a relationship between the nation's first capital city and its modern financial center was still sufficiently novel and unfixed in 1883 for the detractors of Wall Street to offer their own interpretations of J. Q. A. Ward's monument, as one skeptic did in concluding that the colossal bronze figure of "the Father of his Country . . . dwarfs and belittles its surroundings."[51] His point was obvious: children do not always meet the expectations of their parents, some fathers are more demanding than others, and perhaps the "Father of his Country" could be counted on to be the sternest taskmaster of all. This cynic swore that Washington looked "morose and disdainful" and that his countenance bore "a singularly disagreeable grimace": "The immortal George appears to look across at the Stock Exchange and raise his right hand in horror at the financial performances that obtain there, while his face betokens the most vivid disgust."[52]

By repeatedly driving these patriotic associations home, however, Wall Street supporters ultimately gave this new understanding the stability and continuity of meaning to resist further redefinitions and to be experienced as part of the normal scheme of things. In 1889, the Chamber of Commerce, the New-York Historical Society, and the Sons of the Revolution, a leading patriotic hereditary association, orchestrated a jubilee to memorialize the centennial of Washington's inauguration as president. The members of these organizations came from the city's social and economic elites, and the committee that planned the fête included Wall Street titans J. Pierpont Morgan, Cornelius Vanderbilt, and Jesse Seligman and wealthy Old New Yorkers Theodore Roosevelt, S. Van Rensselaer Cruger, and Rutherford Stuyvesant. In celebrating the enormous progress that the United States had made in its first century, these organizers emphasized that a line of descent ran from Washington, who had launched the new nation by taking the oath of office on Wall Street, to the heads of the financial institutions that now occupied the area.[53]

This link between the nation's origins and the financial district was reinforced by the plethora of New York City guidebooks produced in the late nineteenth and early twentieth centuries. Guidebooks typically put the financial district high on the list of locations that tourists had to visit while they were in New York, often devoting fifteen or more pages to its places of interest. Their portrayal of the neighborhood blurred the line between past and present and used history to exalt the financial center— reminding readers, in the words of *Pictorial New York and Brooklyn* (1892), that Wall Street "retains something descriptive of its ancient character or use in its modern designation."[54]

THE WORLD OF ELITES

The new order was synonymous with colossal personal wealth. In 1892 greater New York had 1,265 millionaires, nearly one-third of the total for the entire United States and a number that would have been inconceivable before the Civil War. John D. Rockefeller, the richest man in the world, was worth $1 billion in 1913, the equivalent of $22.3 billion today. Andrew Carnegie had a personal fortune of $150 million—about $3.2 billion today.

High salaries for elite businessmen were commonplace. In the early 1900s, when laborers on a major New York City construction project earned $600 to $675 a year if unskilled and $750 if skilled, the president of the Delaware & Hudson Railroad made $75,000 per year and the presidents of other large railroads between $35,000 and $60,000. At New York Life, the president received a salary of $100,000, and three senior vice presidents, $75,000, $40,000, and $25,000, respectively. Charles M. Schwab, head of U.S. Steel, reportedly took home $100,000. These salary figures underestimate total compensation, because they exclude stock options and bonuses. According to the *Wall Street Journal*, Schwab was entitled to buy a sum of U.S. Steel stock equal to 5 percent of his salary at a guaranteed price every year. For many years, the president of a leading New York City commercial bank collected a bonus of $50,000 that duplicated his annual salary, while J. P. Morgan & Company gave its employees bonuses that ranged from 20 to 100 percent of their salaries, depending on how profitable the firm had been in a given year.[55]

With the thriving economy enriching many people, the urban elite grew much larger. Although the category "elite" is too imprecise in American society (and the social structure of New York City too complex) to permit anything like an exact count, it seems reasonable to estimate that by 1900 somewhere between seventy thousand and one hundred thousand people had achieved the social or economic standing to be considered part of the elite. (Both figures amount to less than 4 percent of the total city population.) By this rough estimation, the elite was four or five times larger in 1900 than it had been in the 1850s. No organization was more affected by the tensions caused by the enlargement of the high status population than the Social Register Association. But the economy and population of New York City continued to boom, and in 1904 the *Social Register* contained the names of more than twenty-five thousand individuals.[56] It was simply impossible to know everyone or maintain real exclusivity anymore. Exclusivity had become an ideal; it was part of a story that elite New Yorkers told about their lives and tried to make come true.

In the face of this relentless growth, and bolstered by the Victorian penchant for erecting barriers that sought to preserve the pure and exemplary by excluding the unworthy and degraded, upper-class New Yorkers tried to tighten the boundaries and screen out the ordinariness of the middle class and the baseness of the newly moneyed. There was a new awareness about the need to bolster upper-class privilege.

"CLUB WORLD"

In the 1880s and 1890s, a distinctive social space called "Club World" or "Clubdom" took shape in New York City.[57] The site of most of the city's exclusive men's clubs, Club World centered on Fifth Avenue from about Twenty-First Street to Thirty-Ninth Street but also spilled over onto nearby streets and avenues. A few institutions, like the Metropolitan Club at Fifth Avenue and East Sixtieth Street, were situated beyond it.

The area merited its special name because private clubs reached their zenith in the late nineteenth and early twentieth centuries, when they became essential to how upper- and upper-middle-class New York men organized their lives. There were many different kinds of clubs: social clubs like the venerable Union Club and the Knickerbocker Club, politically oriented social clubs such as Union League Club and the Manhattan Club, special-purpose clubs (the New York Yacht Club and the American Jockey Club), clubs devoted to a single profession or occupation (the Lawyers', the Grolier, and the Lotos), ones with a cultural slant (the Authors' Club and the Century Association), athletic clubs (the Racquet Club and the New York Athletic Club), college alumni clubs (the University Club and the Harvard Club), and ethnonational clubs (the Progress Club, for German Jews, and the Caledonian Club, for Scots). This proliferation indicates the importance these clubs had for elite male New Yorkers.

In 1890 the *New York Times* estimated that there were 350 private men's clubs in New York City that had their own quarters, but that only 25 to 30 of them could be considered socially prestigious. The paper calculated that these first-rank institutions—such as the Union, the Union League, the Knickerbocker, the Calumet, and the New York Yacht—had an aggregate membership of about twenty-five thousand. Since men usually belonged to multiple organizations, the number of individuals who comprised Club World was probably no more than fifteen thousand.

Initiation fees and annual dues varied widely as well. For instance, the Nassau Boat Club, a New York City–based rowing association with modest facilities that did not profess to be socially exclusive, charged an initiation fee of $10 and annual dues of $25. By contrast, membership in top-flight clubs involved substantial costs that were beyond the means of middle-class New Yorkers and—since multiple memberships were the norm—also put a crimp in the budgets of upper-class people with more social than economic capital. The New York Athletic Club, the St. Nicholas Club, and the Century Association set their initiation fees at between $100 and $150; the University, Lotus, Calumet, and Manhattan Clubs at $200; and the Metropolitan, Union, Union League, and Knickerbocker at $300. The Union Club charged annual dues of $75 and the Metropolitan Club of $100.[58]

The most salient attribute of Club World was that it was entirely male. This gender exclusivity became a source of complaint on the part of some members and their families, and a few people urged the creation of mixed clubs where men and women would join as equal members. They were ignored. Instead of granting membership to females, club leaders expanded their hours and areas of access. The Lawyers' Club and the Commercial Club regularly opened their reading, dining, and dressing rooms to the wives and daughters of members, while the Manhattan Club and the Authors' Club instituted ladies' days and held ladies' receptions in the evening or late afternoon hours for wives and daughters.[59] These were obviously trifling measures, and in fact these clubs did not and could not admit women because the male-only policy was central to their very being. In explaining why women should be excluded, club defenders cited the supposed differences between male and female temperament. *Harper's Bazaar* maintained that women were "too exclusive, too eclectic, not sufficiently impersonal in their relations to one another, too much affected by each other's 'sphere' to meet in the club-room, discuss business, eat at a common set of club tables, and lead the life that men do."[60] As a result of their emotional makeup, women could not do what men did: "seek a refuge where they can enjoy the benefits of a club, read the papers and magazines daily laid out for them, eat an easily ordered meal, find a place to write their letters, in fact, enjoy all the comforts of a clubhouse."[61]

But if men's clubs were a refuge, what exactly were they a refuge from? The supporters of the clubs were not entirely clear on this point. Some wanted to escape the undifferentiated social mixing that made public space in New York City discomfiting by establishing semiprivate places where like-minded men of the same social station could congregate, while others prized the clubs for offering a respite from the demands of the marketplace. Most of all, however, the clubs provided a retreat from the place that dominated late Victorian culture, the home. Upper- and middle-class Americans regarded the home as a primary site to nurture families and children, teach morals and religion, entertain friends and relatives, enjoy fine music and literature, and conduct courtships. These activities were considered to be the purview of women, and in terms of its design and furnishings and social functions, the Victorian home was a feminized environment. The cultural ideals associated with the home also inspired a number of social reforms in the late nineteenth century, as tens of thousands of women sought to apply the moral virtues of the domestic sphere to the larger society by campaigning for the prohibition of alcoholic beverages, the elimination of prostitution, and the passage of mandatory school attendance laws.

All that could be suffocating—and men's clubs provided an asylum from the womanly home. It was easier for men to smoke (particularly cigars) and drink alcohol in the clubs. In offering a manly haven, however, they unwittingly confirmed the centrality of the home to late Victorian culture. By the 1890s the memberships of most New York City clubs had grown so large that their clubhouses no longer bore any resemblance to single-family dwellings, as they once had. With their massive bulks and imposing façades, these buildings evoked semipublic and public institutions such as hotels, banks, department stores, and libraries (figure 5.2). It was another story, though, with their interiors, which of necessity were given over to the same everyday activities—eating, reading, socializing, and sleeping—that took place inside private houses. To be sure, the interiors featured oversized fireplaces, stairways, and great rooms, had heavy tables, chairs, and sofas, and were adorned in dark hues that imparted a masculine atmosphere. They also had special rooms for manly pastimes like billiards. But the greatest part of the interior spaces open to members consisted of dining rooms, libraries, and bedrooms that were not so different from their counterparts in private houses and that were identified by the same names, with their main reception rooms, for instance, generally known as "parlors." Men's clubs were less an alternative to the home than a continuation of it. As a third place that provided venues for informal and voluntary gatherings beyond the realms of home and business, men's clubs could not admit women without crossing the line and becoming entirely too homelike.[62]

FIGURE 5.2 A formal reception held for the delegates to the Pan-American Congress at the Union League Club of New York in 1889. This illustration, taken from *Harper's Weekly*, shows the Union League Club's third clubhouse, located at Fifth Avenue and East Thirty-Ninth Street in the Murray Hill section of New York City. (Author's collection.)

Upper-class men made the clubs a significant part of their lives. Take Harper S. Mott, a graduate of Columbia College and Columbia Law School who had received a sizable inheritance of money and Manhattan real estate that enabled him to lead a leisurely existence. In the mid-1880s, Mott regularly took the 8:25 a.m. train from his home in upper Manhattan to his office in Wall Street, where he managed his properties, and returned home on the 3:35 or the 4:35, in plenty of time to take his carriage out for a drive or pursue his interest in local history. Mott usually went to the New York Athletic Club or the Lawyers' Club in the early afternoon to eat lunch, see friends, and conduct business. Club World was even more important to James N. De R. Whitehouse, the head of a family-owned stockbrokerage house. He and his wife, Vera, were socialites who went to Newport for the season in July and August and then spent late August in the Adirondacks. In New York City, James Whitehouse took his meals at the Union Club, the New York Athletic Club, or Delmonico's Restaurant on workdays; went to the Whist Club many weekday nights; and spent his Saturdays at the Badminton Club and the Players Club. The Whitehouses also patronized the Westchester Country Club and the Morris Park Cricket Club.[63] Altogether, James N. De R. Whitehouse belonged to about ten clubs.

The clubs were a priority for the very rich and powerful, too. J. Pierpont Morgan regularly dined at the Union Club and frequented the Century Association, the New York Yacht Club, the Union League Club, the Whist Club, and the New York Jockey Club, among others. Morgan also made time for club business: in his annual engagement diaries, appointments to plan the new headquarters of the New York Yacht Club or to review the Union League Club balance sheet share space with corporate and nonprofit board meetings and sessions to organize mergers and acquisitions. Morgan navigated urban public space by treating his clubs, home, and office, the meeting rooms at Grand Central Depot and the Chamber of Commerce, and Delmonico's Restaurant as private and semiprivate preserves. Like other upper-class individuals, he was constantly hopping from one of these islands to the next.[64]

For Mott, Whitehouse, and Morgan, these clubs were important for imposing a protective wall around men of financial and social position and allowing them to interact freely and informally, while excluding outsiders. Especially for newcomers, membership was a way to demonstrate one's bona fides and learn how to conduct and value oneself in rarefied company. All that raised the caliber of the elite category and made the clubs critical elite institutions. The *New York Times* defined the club ideal this way in 1891:

> A club is presumably an association of gentlemen, in which there can be no distinctions as to wealth, social standing, or anything else. The members of any given club meet on a common footing in their clubhouse, however different may be their several positions in the world outside. Anything which elevates one member above his fellow-members or procures for him superior advantages in the clubhouse is clearly antagonistic to the ground principles of club life, and must be prevented.[65]

To succeed as an "association of gentlemen," a club had to have a sociable environment that fostered strong bonds and open intercourse, and achieving that goal, longtime clubmen knew, depended entirely on the character and commitment of its members. They had to be "clubbable." "Clubbability" was an ambiguous term that could be stretched and manipulated as need be, but most members knew what it meant. The creation of a brotherhood required that the men be willing and able to *be* brothers: they had to get to know one another individually and develop loyalty to each other and the group. If they hoped to bring out the best in themselves and the other members, they could not drop in for a meal every few weeks and then nonchalantly go on their way. Nor should they be preoccupied with moneymaking, either. Top-notch clubs banned or limited business activities to ensure a sociable atmosphere; without a doubt these restrictions were impossible to enforce, and clubs were places to make business connections and meet clients, but the ideal remained.[66]

An 1896 obituary of one John L. Lawrence defined the model clubman. The son of a carriage maker who had made a fortune, Lawrence had closed the business after the death of his father and pursued a leisurely life. He belonged to the Riding Club and the Larchmont Yacht Club, but was proudest of his almost twenty-five-year association with the Union Club. According to the *Times*, Lawrence made the Union Club "virtually his home during the daylight hours for most of the year," daily occupying a window seat that looked onto Fifth Avenue.[67] He not only knew every member of the Union Club, but his engaging personality, ability to converse on a range of subjects, knack for putting other people at ease, handsome looks, and success at games perfectly suited this "association of gentlemen." The *Times* conceded that Lawrence's temper and quickness to resent an affront kept him entangled in personal squabbles, including a spat that had ended in a fistfight one summer in Newport, but a little eccentricity could be forgiven, and perhaps even esteemed as a mark of the value that a man put on himself. At any rate, the *Times* felt that Lawrence "probably was better known in the club world of New-York than any other man of his age."[68]

But sentimental portrayals of men's clubs as intimate gathering places were misleading. The continued economic development of New York City put even the most prestigious clubs under pressure to expand their memberships in the late nineteenth century. As the size of the economic elite grew, there was a corresponding increase in the number of men with the financial resources to be admitted to these clubs and the inclination to think about their identities and their relationships in a new light. While clubs could have chosen to remain small and exclusive by retaining low membership ceilings, they competed with one another for status and were forever jockeying to maintain or improve their position with respect to their rivals, another indication of the importance of social and business networking in the club system. Top-flight clubs, cherishing their lofty ranking, felt this strain acutely. Significantly, in the 1880s, the Union League Club began to consider dispensing with its guiding principle of screening applicants for their political views, and by the 1890s had become an exclusively social club that paid lip service to its previous stress on national and municipal policy making.

An added complication was that a club's standing depended as much on its reputation with the general public as it did on its reputation with upper-class New Yorkers. That was not the case in Boston and Philadelphia, where the upper classes were small and relatively self-contained and elites could ignore popular reputation, but the rapid growth of New York made for greater social instability and competitiveness within the upper class and led many to seek affirmation outside their circles. Beyond that, there was also a difference in social ethos. A belief that status depended on celebrity prevailed in New York City but not in Boston and Philadelphia, where members of the social elite went out of their way to dress and live inconspicuously. New Yorkers were showier and more ostentatious. Since popular status reflected the extensive coverage that mainstream newspapers and leading magazines devoted to Club World, the concern was that a club might be too small to attract public notice. A further peril was that a club that barred the newest tycoon might appear to be odd to ordinary people or might risk having a rival club admit him—and gain the benefit of his resources to build a new clubhouse or improve its facilities. In dynamic New York City, public reputation conflicted with selectivity, and prestige was ambiguous and unstable.[69]

The evidence, while fragmentary, suggests that elite men's clubs in other American cities were not under the same pressures. By the 1890s men's clubs had become a critical institution for urban business and social elites and existed in virtually every U.S. city. However, cities such as Philadelphia, Boston, and Baltimore that had well-entrenched social elites were not growing fast enough or generating hordes of income men for their clubs to accommodate, while an instant city such as Chicago that was developing rapidly did not have an old social elite that was being crowded out. Compared with other U.S. cities, the upper class in New York City was singular in its openness to newcomers, its readiness to shed traditions, and its aggressive approach to moneymaking.

The proclivity of the Victorian cultural system for social partition and hierarchy exerted its influence everywhere, but the large size and the quick expansion of the New York City elite made it a special case. We have seen how these strains led the Union League to expand its membership in the early 1890s. Nearly all of the city's other leading clubs experienced the same tensions and took the same course of action. By 1891 the Union League Club had about 1,700 members; the Manhattan

Club, 1,500; and the New York Athletic Club, 2,300. However, two prominent clubs, the Knickerbocker and the Calumet, chose to buck this trend, maintaining their small sizes and confining their membership to "men of good name and position." In 1891 the Knickerbocker had 500 members and the Calumet 400. The small size of the Calumet Club may have been a sign of weakness: it was beginning to lose members to the Metropolitan Club and would soon experience serious financial troubles.[70] That was not the case with the Knickerbocker Club, which had a long waiting list and was thought to stand first among all New York City clubs "in terms of exclusiveness and social standing."[71] Thus, *Town Topics*, the gossip sheet of the upper class, complained that too many governing officers of the Union Club lacked the quality of birth and family to warrant their eminent positions, yet praised the leaders of the Knickerbocker Club for combining wealth and social position and being "representative fashionable men of New York."[72] But even though the Knickerbocker was highly selective, almost nobody outside the upper class had ever heard of it, whereas the Union Club had a *public* reputation for being exclusive, and from an institutional perspective, that was what counted.

Clubs had similar admissions procedures. These rules required that a prospective member be proposed and seconded by established members, sometimes with written testimonials, and that the names of the candidate and the members who had proposed and seconded him be posted in the club's rooms for as long as three weeks, so that other members could review them. The candidate then had to be approved by the ruling body of the club or by an admissions committee. The Union Club gave its Governing Committee sole authority to admit new members, and the Down-Town Club entrusted decisions to its twenty-man board of trustees, with one adverse vote in five being grounds for exclusion. The Union League Club and the Harvard Club put candidates who passed an initial screening to a secret vote of the entire membership. Unsurprisingly, these gateways had the intended effect of reproducing the ethnoreligious character and the personal relationships of the social elite.[73]

Even for the wellborn, though, gaining admission could be nerve-racking. In February 1888, Harper S. Mott embarked on an elaborate campaign to join the Union League Club. He started by asking Frederick Law Olmstead, one of its founders, to sponsor him. After Olmstead agreed to help, he and Mott met on at least seven occasions to plot strategy, with the key step being the selection of the other members who would second his candidacy and write letters on his behalf. As soon as his name was posted, Mott lunched at the Union League Club to meet more members and let them take his measure. Meanwhile, he provided the same assistance to friends and acquaintances who wanted to join two of his clubs, the Lawyers' Club and the New York Athletic Club. This system of mutual obligations created strong bonds among upper-class men, helping to tie together and give shape to an upper class that was becoming large and formless.

Not only were admissions procedures labyrinthine, but rejections became common knowledge and, at times, public sensations. In 1893 the Union League Club blackballed Theodore Seligman, a son of longtime club member Jesse Seligman, because he was Jewish. If Jesse Seligman's prominence in the Republican Party had aided his own admission to the Union League Club in 1868, the club's deemphasis of political considerations in the late nineteenth century, coupled with the intensification of anti-Semitism, contributed to its rejection of his son. Jesse Seligman angrily resigned from his old club, leaving it with only one Jewish member, who also eventually quit in protest.

This "housecleaning" brought the Union League Club into line with the other top men's clubs. *Town Topics* reported approvingly that leading clubs had a tacit understanding that Jews were not to be proposed as members. As justification for this anti-Semitic policy, *Town Topics* cited the case of an unnamed Jewish publisher who had somehow slipped through the screening procedures of the Century Association, to the point that he was actually certified as being a Gentile.[74] With "the peculiar effrontery of his race," this newcomer then offended the sensibilities of regular members by inviting other Jews to the club as his guests and acting as if he had the same rights and privileges as anyone else, conduct so brazen that *Town Topics* demanded that this "undesirable incursion" of clubdom must be stopped in its tracks.[75] An upper-class New Yorker later recalled the casual anti-Semitism of his set: "It simply seemed to be accepted that [Jews] were to be avoided at all costs in terms of social mixing. It was as if they carried some easily contractible and unattractive, though not necessarily dangerous, ailment."[76]

Applicants could be blackballed for other reasons than "the Jew question." In 1891 the governing committee of the Union Club turned down Austin Corbin, the president of the Long Island Rail Road; John King, the president of the Erie Railroad; and W. Seward Webb, the president of several rail companies. While it is not possible to discern the reasons for decisions that were made in secret, contemporaries believed that these snubs were driven by the resentments that some old-guard New Yorkers felt toward the new wealth. Webb came from an Old New York family, but his marriage to a daughter of William K. Vanderbilt had catapulted him into the presidency of a number of companies in the Vanderbilt system—and made him a punching bag for the family's detractors. Corbin and King had been proposed by J. Pierpont Morgan, and their rebuffs may have been calculated to cut the investment banker down to size.[77]

More than any other Gilded Age institution, Club World was used by upper-class men to regulate their relationships with one another and define suitable conduct. Club World reified a masculine version of social hierarchy, promoted upper-class networking, and punished nonconformity. It stood for stability and tradition and upheld gentlemanly standards. It became a place where upper-class men pursued privilege by policing their boundaries and celebrating their prerogatives. However, the struggles that club leaders experienced when trying to restrict the size of memberships and exclude inappropriate outsiders points to the powerful effect that economic vitality had in encroaching on upper-class life in New York City.

Upper-class women faced their own social pressures and developed their own networks.

UPPER-CLASS WOMEN'S NETWORKS

Among the subscribers who contributed large gifts of money in the 1890s to create the New York Botanical Garden were three upper-class women: Helen M. Gould, a daughter of robber baron Jay Gould and a leading philanthropist in her own right; Esther Herrman, a Jewish philanthropist and suffragist; and Melissa P. Dodge, widow of the president of Phelps Dodge. Yet neither they nor any other women served on its board of managers or in other leadership positions. This was the norm: in this period, the governing bodies of major New York City cultural institutions did not include women.[78]

Upper-class women found other means to network and exercise power. One way they did so was by patrolling the gateways of high society. This role acquired greater importance as the growth of the upper class in the late nineteenth century intensified social competition. Upper-class social affairs in this period included weddings, teas, receptions, holiday musicals, charity balls, young people's dances, and children's parties, and upper-class women organized virtually all of them—selecting the dates and venues; creating the guest lists; sending invitations; deciding on decorations, refreshments, and seating plans; handling newspaper and magazine announcements; and supervising the attendants. By restricting access to these activities, New York society women "brought control to the exceedingly fluid social situation of the post-Civil War period."[79] They also monitored the guests to ensure that conversation flowed and adhered to appropriate topics and that bachelors and children stayed in check.[80] According to the author of an 1896 etiquette manual, "The graces and courtesies of life are in [women's] hands. It is women who create society."[81]

A scrapbook that an upper-class New York City woman named Pauline Robinson kept from 1894 to 1912 reveals the significance of these female-arranged events in creating social spaces where upper-class people could come together. For instance, Robinson stayed with friends on Jekyll Island, Georgia, for three weeks in February and March 1904; then visited another set of friends in Latrobe, Pennsylvania; traveled to Boston at the end of April; spent time in June on the Main Line of Philadelphia;

celebrated the Fourth of July in Shelburne, Vermont; went to Newport later that month; and stopped in Lenox, Massachusetts, and then in Winterthur, Delaware, in the fall. Almost everywhere, Robinson resided with friends or relatives rather than in hotels or inns and thus depended for her hospitality on other women (and their servants). Similarly, a young woman of marriageable age from an upper-class New York City family used dances, dinners, and parties to open a window of freedom for herself. Florence Adele Sloane was extremely frustrated by the restrictions of the respectable existence that she led, but on these special occasions she could meet new people and have lively conversations.[82]

In the late nineteenth and early twentieth centuries many women's clubs, societies, and associations sprang up in the United States. Because men participated minimally or not at all in organizations that dealt with "women's issues," these organizations became places where upper- and upper-middle-class women interacted. This was their Club World. In New York City, there were alumni groups such as the Emma Willard and Mount Holyoke Associations, literary societies like Minerva, local chapters of patriotic hereditary associations such as the National Society of Daughters of Founders and Patriots, and political organizations like the Woman's Republican Club and the Elizabeth Cady Stanton Political Equality League.

The most prestigious and influential groups were nonprofits that aided working-class and immigrant families and children, notably the Young Women's Christian Association (YWCA) and the Junior League. With an entirely female board of directors and administration, the YWCA was a complex enterprise that had ten thousand members and that operated nine branch offices and a girl's camp, all racially segregated. It offered classes in the Bible, home economics, foreign languages, and art; ran an employment bureau; and provided a residence for nurses.

Far more stylish was the Junior League, which Mary Harriman, the daughter of railroad executive Edward H. Harriman, founded in 1901 so that young New York City socialites could address the problems of urban poverty. Harriman also had a secondary objective of transforming society women's own lives, hoping that these young women would gain a serious purpose and become more independent and self-aware. Within a few years, the Junior League numbered some twenty-five to thirty young women "well-known to society" such as Gladys Vanderbilt, Beatrice Morgan, and Janet Dana, who volunteered at settlement houses and staged annual theatrical performances to raise money for their programs. The Junior League later opened a residential hotel on the East River at Seventy-Eighth Street that had rooms for 350 working-class girls.

From the start, the Junior League had a mixed reputation. The spectacle of debutantes dirtying their white gloves doing charity work in settlement houses, health clinics, and playgrounds exposed it to ridicule, and in actuality many of its volunteers dripped noblesse oblige and treated their assignments as a lark. At its best, though, the Junior League articulated an ideal of service and conscience that provided a moral corrective to the hard-nosed orientation of elite businessmen and that improved the lives of underprivileged New Yorkers.[83]

～ 6 ～

THE WAYS OF MILLIONAIREVILLE

....

The 1890s

"MILLIONAIREVILLE"

I n the late 1860s and the 1870s, upper-class residences resumed
their progression up the east side of Manhattan. Upper-class New
Yorkers continued to inhabit Washington Square and Gramercy
Park, but they abandoned the rest of the Broadway arc to retail shops,
stables, and warehouses and to middle- and working-class inhabitants.

In the 1880s, the finest upper-class neighborhood in the city was
Murray Hill, which occupied a corridor that ran along Fifth Avenue and
Madison Avenue from around Twenty-Third Street to Fiftieth Street. The
development of Murray Hill should be remembered as a major shift in the
residential patterns of upper-class New Yorkers. Here, for the first time,
elites carved out residential terrain that was large and exclusive enough to
be their own and that was separated from the living places of other New
Yorkers (except for servants and retainers). As part of an ongoing transformation of metropolitan space that had begun in the early nineteenth
century, Murray Hill also lacked the patchwork of commercial and industrial land uses that had characterized the Broadway arc. Murray Hill was
to physical space what Club World was to social space.

The northern and southern boundaries of Murray Hill were indefinite and unstable. In the early 1890s, John Jacob Astor IV, George J. Gould, August Belmont II, and others began to leapfrog northward, constructing mansions on upper Fifth Avenue that overlooked Central Park, pulling the entire district farther up the island even as commercial land uses gradually encroached on its southern locales. By contrast, elevated railways precisely fixed its eastern and western boundaries. To the west, the Sixth Avenue elevated railway imposed an iron barrier that was hardened by the presence on that avenue of mass-market department stores. To the east, Park Avenue (then called Fourth Avenue) and Lexington Avenue had a mixture of land uses and acted as a buffer zone. The Third Avenue elevated railway formed the eastern border of Murray Hill. Few upper-class New Yorkers cared to venture beyond this point, into the belt of tenement buildings, breweries, silk factories, gasworks, and slaughterhouses that lay between Third Avenue and the East River (see map 3).[1]

An indelible and scathing portrait of Murray Hill and its residents was made by William Dean Howells in *A Hazard of New Fortunes* (1890). Viewing this neighborhood as the fullest expression of the "great material civilization" of New York City, Howells has a character named Basil March who has recently moved to Manhattan from Boston marvel at the "well-dressed, well-satisfied, well-fed looking crowd [that] poured down the broad sidewalks before the handsome, stupid houses" during a Sunday afternoon promenade down Madison Avenue.[2] According to March, these promenaders were immediately identifiable as bourgeois New Yorkers.

> The men's faces were shrewd and alert, and yet they looked dull; the women's were pretty and knowing, and yet dull. It was probably the holiday expression of the vast, prosperous, commercial class, with unlimited money and no ideals that money could not realize; fashion and comfort were all that they desired to compass, and the culture that furnishes showily, that decorates, and that tells; the culture, say, of plays and operas, rather than of books.[3]

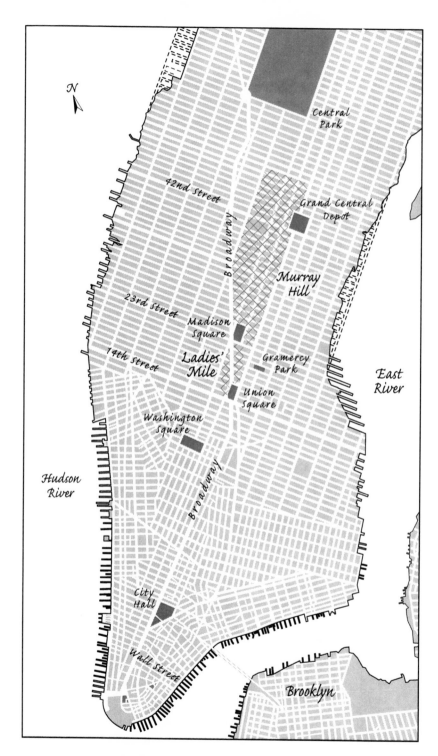

MAP 3 Murray Hill and Ladies' Mile, 1890.

A critic of the business orientation and economic dominance of New York City, Howells almost instinctively assumed that upper-class New Yorkers were spiritually and culturally bankrupt. He projected his antagonisms onto the mass of inhabitants who lived in this district and made disparaging linkages between affluence and dullness.

Howells, a longtime resident of Boston, also expressed the disdain of upper-class Bostonians for the ostentation of their New York City counterparts. In Boston, people of lineage and money prided themselves on being inconspicuous and enhanced their status by avoiding display. New York was just the opposite: its upper class put enormous emphasis on performance and self-presentation through their clothing, mansions, carriages, and yachts, the places where they were seen, and the personal relationships they cultivated. This difference reflected the intense social competition being generated by the large and unstable New York City upper class. Upper-class New Yorkers saw Boston as small and provincial and viewed their own city as the equivalent of the great European capitals like Paris and Vienna and coveted that European polish and sophistication. They were aggressive in signaling their importance and had high ambitions for themselves and their city.[4]

Howells was correct about the generally high level of prosperity in Murray Hill. In 1900, Cornelius Vanderbilt III lived at 21 West Forty-Ninth Street, on a block where a banker, a stockbroker, an insurance executive, a merchant, a manufacturer, a contractor, and four physicians also resided. Among the people who made their homes on the side streets adjoining the Fifth Avenue mansion of Caroline Astor were two merchants, two lawyers, a banker, and a civil engineer. While such upper-class residences had large retinues of servants, the paucity of middle- and working-class households was noteworthy and differentiated Murray Hill from the old Broadway arc. A schoolteacher who lived four doors down from the family of John D. Rockefeller on East Fifty-Fourth Street was a rarity in this neighborhood.[5]

Murray Hill also housed a remarkable concentration of elite institutions, including commercial establishments such as Delmonico's Restaurant and the Fifth Avenue Hotel; fashionable houses of worship such as

Saint Thomas's Church and Madison Square Presbyterian; the campus of Columbia College; and most elite men's clubs. Three other philanthropic organizations favored by upper-class New Yorkers—the Society for the Prevention of Cruelty to Children, the Charity Organization Society, and the Children's Aid Society—had their headquarters at Park Avenue and Twenty-Second Street. This institutional presence stamped the neighborhood as upper-class terrain. Indeed, Murray Hill gave upper-class New Yorkers a controlled and insular environment where they could pursue their own way of life.[6] Earlier in the nineteenth century, in the patchwork space of the Broadway arc, the city's upper class had refused to isolate itself. That they were now intent on carving out their own residential space was a sign that they had become more intensely conscious of their elite status.

While Murray Hill was reserved almost entirely for members of the elite, there was a lot of diversity within the Gilded Age elite. In New York City, post–Civil War economic development both widened and blurred the gaps between social and economic elites. The keenest observer of this gulf between economic and social elites in New York City was Edith Wharton, herself the product of a distinguished Old New York family. Much of Wharton's fiction explores the declension of an Old New York of impeccable lineage, exemplary manners, and closed social circles that had been shunted aside by the newly rich and unscrupulous businessmen of the modern city. Wharton described these enfeebled blue bloods as "museum specimens" in one short story and was fascinated by the futile and self-defeating responses that she believed Old New Yorkers made to new money.[7] Wharton also understood that the borders between social and economic elites and within the upper class itself were murky. A character in another of her short stories says: "It would take an arbitration committee a good many sittings to define the boundaries of society nowadays."[8]

The sharpest social divisions involved Jews. A distinct Jewish economic elite had crystallized in the 1870s and 1880s, and by the 1890s comprised several thousand people, almost entirely German Jewish in their national origins. As Howells himself noted, Jews constituted the only sizable minority group in an urban upper class that was otherwise almost entirely Protestant and largely native born.[9] The core of this Jewish community consisted of the families of wealthy investment bankers such as the Seligman brothers, Jacob H. Schiff, Mayer H. Lehman, and Abraham Kuhn; retailers like Isidor and Nathan Straus, co-owners of R. H. Macy & Company; and corporate lawyers Randolph Guggenheimer and Samuel Untermyer. Many of them—Jesse Seligman, Jacob H. Schiff, and Solomon Loeb, for instance—resided in Murray Hill. Major German-Jewish institutions such as Temple Emanu-El, the wealthiest and most prestigious synagogue in the United States, were also located there.

German Jews had limited interactions with upper-class Gentiles in the economic and political spheres and led separate social lives. They summered in the Catskills, the Adirondacks, and the Jersey Shore rather than in Saratoga Springs or Newport. Upper-class Jews also put a far higher value on charity than people in the dominant upper class. As a means of maintaining their autonomy and of expressing pride in their accomplishments, German Jews sustained an intricate web of Jewish social welfare institutions, organizing their social seasons around affairs that raised money for institutions such as Mount Sinai Hospital.[10]

To the south of Murray Hill, extending along Broadway from Twenty-Third to Fourteenth Streets, was Ladies' Mile, the most exclusive retail-shopping district in the country. As the site of elegant department stores such as Lord & Taylor (figure 6.1) and Arnold, Constable & Company and specialty stores like W. and J. Sloane, Brentano's, and Tiffany & Company, Ladies' Mile added panache and opulence to Murray Hill. It also divided upper-class customers who routinely patronized its stores from middle- and working-class people who went there to gaze at luxurious items and perhaps buy a special treat. Sophie C. Holt, a middle-class woman from Wilmington, Delaware, who traveled to New York in 1879 to purchase fabric and clothing, delighted in going there to window-shop and crowd-watch. But Holt was acutely sensitive to prices, and when she wanted to buy she went to bargain stores in lower Manhattan or to mass-market emporiums like Macy's on Sixth Avenue.

FIGURE 6.1 Shoppers using the elevator on the opening day of Lord &
Taylor's department store, at Broadway and Twentieth Street, in Ladies'
Mile, 1872. (Author's collection.)

An upper-class woman named Helen F. Newel had a far different experience during a buying trip she made to Manhattan two decades later. The wife of a prosperous Minnesota lawyer and state Republican leader who had recently become U.S. ambassador to the Netherlands, Newel was intent on assembling a wardrobe that would suit her new social station in The Hague. While the wide-eyed Sophie Holt wrote detailed descriptions in her diary about the sights of Manhattan, Newel had grown up in great comfort and affluence in New York City and was accustomed to a sophisticated lifestyle. In her diary entries she merely jotted down barebones references to daily events. Newel stayed at a hotel in Murray Hill and often dined and attended church with friends and relatives, but she concentrated on shopping.[11]

Newel spent the bulk of her time with a private dressmaker. Discriminating shoppers who could afford to patronize skilled artisans benefited from individual fittings, the use of outstanding materials, expert workmanship, and personal service. A Ladies' Mile furrier touted "the artistic, exclusive and novel effects produced by our designers" and guaranteed that "each article has its individual elegance, grace and daintiness"; while a French corset maker promised to reduce the hips, waist, and bust and provide a "Perfect form."[12] Prices could be prohibitive: at a time in 1892 when Lord & Taylor sold ready-made shirtwaists for between fifty cents and $7 apiece, I. Magnin peddled custom shirtwaists for up to $150.[13] The quality and selection of ready-to-wear clothing had improved markedly in recent decades, and stylish and well-made off-the-rack garments were widely available in the city. In sorting the Sophie Holts from the Helen Newels, however, Ladies' Mile made the association between wealth and taste seem all the more natural.[14] While the finest commodities were doubtless expensive, the message was that money alone could not impart the elegance and sophistication that Helen Newel demonstrated in selecting them.

Murray Hill was also known for the extravagant mansions that occupied its corner lots—like Alexander T. Stewart's at Fifth Avenue and Broadway, Leonard Jerome's at Madison and Twenty-Sixth Street, and Collis P. Huntington's at Fifty-Seventh and Fifth Avenue. Many of the architects who built these mansions had trained at the Ecole des Beaux-Arts in

Paris, and their designs mimicked Georgian town houses, Venetian palaz-
zos, and French chateaus. Richard Morris Hunt, for instance, created the
mansion of William K. and Alva Vanderbilt at Fifth Avenue and Fifty-
Second Street in the style of a French Renaissance chateau. It was largely
built by craftsmen brought over from Europe and was decorated with
stone and wood carvings, stained glass, and embroidered textiles imported
from the Continent. This mansion featured a ballroom that could hold
more than 1,200 people, while the 130-room palace of Cornelius Vanderbilt II at Fifth Avenue and West Fifty-Ninth Street (figure 6.2) was
the largest single-family private home ever built in New York City.[15] One
scholar has remarked that these "aristocratic houses were more than just
large; they were presentation stages for the spectacular trappings of the
ruling class."[16]

Murray Hill was central to Gilded Age representations of New York
City and contributed not only to how upper-class New Yorkers organized

FIGURE 6.2 A postcard of the residence of Cornelius Vanderbilt II and Alice Claypoole
Gwynne Vanderbilt, at Fifth Avenue and West Fifty-Ninth Street, postmarked 1912.
(Author's collection.)

their lives but also to how others perceived them and the city. By the end of the century travel books were lavishing as many as ten or fifteen pages apiece on Murray Hill, a locale that one handbook labeled "Millionaireville" and another called "Fashionable New York."[17] The guidebooks depicted the stylish homes, clubs, and hotels of Millionaireville as equally emblematic of New York City as sights like Wall Street, the Statue of Liberty, and Central Park. Some guidebooks laid out stagecoach or pedestrian tours of Murray Hill that let tourists "pass miles of the most magnificent and costly residences in America."[18] They supplied the home addresses of grandees such as John Jacob Astor IV, John D. Rockefeller, J. Pierpont Morgan, and Jay Gould, along with capsule descriptions of their mansions that estimated their construction costs. Like tourist maps that show the locations of the homes of celebrities in Los Angeles today, these travel books encouraged visitors to gawk at the fairy-tale mansions in Murray Hill. The disparity between the grandiose mansions of the new breed and the more modest homes of the Old New Yorkers was about wealth, but it was also about differing notions about the uses of wealth. In their preference for restraint and modesty the Old New Yorkers recalled the ethic of Boston Brahmins and proper Philadelphians, and they were thus doubly eclipsed by the showmanship and ostentation and money of the Vanderbilts and Huntingtons.[19]

Murray Hill helped make New York City famous for its brilliant high society and cultural refinement. Indeed, some of the multimillionaires who moved to New York from the industrial centers where they had made their fortunes were drawn by its social and cultural amenities as much as by business considerations. In 1870, thirty-five-year-old Andrew Carnegie took up permanent residence in New York City, renting a suite in a fashionable hotel and plunging into its Club World and its literary life. For Carnegie, David Nasaw tells us, the problem was that Pittsburgh "was just too small, too provincial, too uncultured and uncultivated."[20] "There were no fine hotels, no first-class opera company, no symphony society, no respectable theater, and no men's social club until the Duquesne Club was founded in 1873," Nasaw writes.[21] Before long Carnegie would withdraw from his full-time business pursuits to cultivate gentlemanly pastimes such as travel, writing, sport, and philanthropy in a quest for refinement that he could not have readily undertaken in Pittsburgh. Three decades later, coke and steel baron Henry Clay Frick relocated to New York City out of a concern that the polluted atmosphere of Pittsburgh was ruining his paintings and sculptures, eventually erecting a mansion at Fifth Avenue and Seventieth Street that is the current site of the Frick Collection.

Yet Carnegie and Frick could not persuade another Pittsburgh millionaire, Andrew Mellon, to join them in Manhattan. A dour Presbyterian who engrossed himself in his work and who sought wealth with astonishing single-mindedness even after he had become wealthy, Mellon disliked cultivated activities like the opera and the symphony. Although Mellon often traveled to New York City on business or en route to Europe, he detested the vulgarity and self-indulgence of high society in Murray Hill and refused to move to Manhattan.[22]

ARISTOCRACY

In 1896, eleven-year-old Grace Eulalie Matthews, the daughter of prominent Madison Avenue socialites, embarked on a yearlong grand tour of Europe with her family and their servants. The Matthews family had had money for three generations—Grace's great-grandfather had made a fortune in the soda water industry—and had become ensconced in the city's upper class. For the upper class, the grand tour was a way to become familiar with classical antiquities and Renaissance art and to mingle with fashionable European society and the aristocracy. Judging from Grace's diary, it was their brushes with European royalty that most excited the Matthews during their trek through France, Italy, Germany, and Great Britain, including catching sight of the Russian tsar and tsarina in Paris.[23]

Despite Americans' identification with and admiration of egalitarianism and individual social mobility, by the end of the nineteenth century many upper-class Americans openly venerated European aristocrats, and a handful wished to become aristocrats in their own right.[24] While a few of them achieved this goal, the vast majority had no such inclination: they were content to assert a blood relationship through membership in an ancestral society like the Sovereign Colonial Society of Americans of Royal Descent (founded in 1867), the Colonial Order of the Crown (1890), and the National Society of Americans of Royal Descent (1908); socialize with European royals or aristocrats; or simply view them from a distance. For the Matthews and other upper-class Americans who had accumulated great wealth and power, the aristocracy supplied a model for how they could conceive of themselves and express their own superiority. Stable, deep-rooted, decorous, and powerful, European aristocracies were imbued with a legitimacy that many wealthy Americans envied and wished to emulate. And while European royals and aristocrats frequently lived more opulently than American millionaires did, they did so with a sense of tradition that distanced them from the marketplace. Upper-class Americans drew on their associations with the aristocracy to separate themselves from the middle class and the nouveaux riches and to fortify their own pursuit of wealth, prestige, and power.[25]

The improvement of steamship and railroad transportation in the late nineteenth century made European aristocracies more accessible by facilitating transatlantic travel. In 1892, the *Social Register* reported that seven hundred prominent New York families had crossed the ocean in the past year.[26] After her husband became U.S. ambassador to the Netherlands in 1897, Helen Newel was delighted to be able to mix with the Dutch nobility, with their first social triumph coming when the Baroness De Grovestin "received us most cordially."[27] Later, during their presentation to Queen Wilhelmenia, Newel scrutinized the dress and comportment of the Dutch queen and the livery of her attendants. Newel was determined to enter this dazzling new world, and her diary entries are the study notes of a vigilant student. That ambition is what led Newel to return to New York City to go on her buying spree in Ladies' Mile, to make further social conquests in The Hague with a new wardrobe. Helen Newel feared that the chief impediment to realizing this objective of mixing with the aristocracy were the "dreadful" manners and social obtuseness of her provincial, Minnesota-raised husband, who in her view failed to live up to "the punctilious requirements of court & diplomatic life."[28]

Wealthy Americans who summered in Europe often socialized with the nobility. Robert W. and Harriet Goelet used their yacht, the *Nahma*, to entertain the Prince of Wales and to invite Kaiser Wilhelm II for luncheon and dinner. Similarly, Anthony J. and Margarita Drexel of Philadelphia gave dinner parties for the British Duke of Cambridge and Russian Grand Duke Michael and Grand Duke Boris and hobnobbed with King Edward VII and Kaiser Wilhelm II. Noblemen touring the United States became prized guests at upper-class dinner parties, as happened with the Prince of Wales (in 1872) and Prince Henry of Prussia (in 1902) in New York City. When the Duke of Marlborough stopped in Newport in 1887, socialites competed to snag him as a dinner guest and impress him with their elegance.[29]

Even more arresting were the marriages of American upper-class daughters to titled European men. One of the earliest of these unions, the 1874 marriage between Lord Randolph Churchill and Jennie Jerome, a daughter of New York City stock speculator and sportsman Leonard Jerome, is famous for producing a child, Winston, who would become the wartime prime minister of the United Kingdom in 1940. An estimated 454 American heiresses wed European aristocrats in the late nineteenth century, with 136 marrying earls or counts, 42 princes, and 17 dukes, and the rest baronets, knights, and barons. Cornelia Roosevelt married a Prussian baron. Consuelo Vanderbilt, the daughter of William K. and Alva Vanderbilt, wed the Duke of Marlborough. Anna Gould, the daughter of Jay and Helen Gould, took the comte De Castellane as her first husband and the duc de Talleyrand as her second.

These marriages allowed European aristocrats to replenish their family coffers and keep pace with the standard of living of the new industrial and commercial magnates. For American families that had a lot of money but modest social standing, having a daughter marry into the aristocracy meant vaulting domestic status hierarchies that had spurned or disdained them.

For immensely wealthy families like the Vanderbilts, marriage into the aristocracy meant the affirmation of their place within a transnational upper class that seamlessly meshed its American and European branches. It was one thing for William K. Vanderbilt to own mansions on Fifth Avenue and Long Island and in Newport and France and to operate a successful thoroughbred racing stable, but something else again for his daughter Consuelo to wed the ninth Duke of Marlborough and become mistress of Blenheim Palace.[30]

In her memoir *The Glitter and the Gold*, Consuelo Vanderbilt recalls learning a new level of class-consciousness when she married into the Marlboroughs and being surprised at the pervasiveness of pomp and ritual and the demands of protocol in the British peerage. Vanderbilt also observed that most American women who married titled Englishmen were quick to abandon the social practices and values of their homeland. As young females who were adhering to conventional gender norms by conforming to the ways of their husbands, their discarding of their American-ness did not provoke anything like the nationalistic fury that William Waldorf Astor triggered in 1899 by surrendering his United States citizenship.[31]

The great-grandson of John Jacob Astor, William Waldorf Astor had never achieved the public success in politics or literature that he thought was his due, despite setting the bar high for himself. At one point, Astor commissioned a family history that determined that the Astors were descended from an eleventh-century Castilian aristocrat named Pedro D'Astorga, a fortuitous discovery that put the embarrassing fact that John Jacob Astor had been the son of a butcher in a new light. The implication of this genealogical finding was that while the Astors might have fallen upon hard times and been reduced to menial labor by the eighteenth century, John Jacob Astor had restored the family to its rightful position atop society.[32]

Yet William Waldorf Astor himself fell short of this level of fictive family distinction. After serving one term in the New York State Assembly and another in the New York State Senate, Astor was defeated in two runs for Congress. Appointed U.S. ambassador to Italy, Astor used his three years in Rome to write a pair of historical novels, neither of which sold well or made much of a literary mark. In 1892, apparently because he was tired of having American newspapers invade his privacy and afraid that his children might be kidnapped, Astor decamped to England and set about trying to enter British society. He bought a town house in London and a country estate that overlooked the Thames, entertained lavishly, joined an exclusive London club, and used two newspapers and a magazine that he purchased to disseminate his ideas and his name.

Other upper-class Americans such as Andrew Carnegie and Anthony J. Drexel spent all or much of their time in Europe, but very few of them renounced their American citizenship, as Astor did in 1899. His decision to become a British subject prompted an angry crowd to burn him in effigy in what is now Times Square and led newspapers across the country to denounce him as a turncoat and a snob, with the *New York World* likening him to Benedict Arnold and another paper ridiculing his claims to be descended from "the immemorial Astorgas."[33]

An unnamed Londoner offered a calmer and more astute analysis in a letter to the *New York Times*. This correspondent pointed out that naturalization alone would not turn Astor into an Englishman and that he was certain to remain a hybrid "American-Englishman" who would never be accepted into English high society.[34] The letter writer also called attention to Astor's slender achievements. Even if Astor did succeed in buying his way into London society and in purchasing a title, this correspondent expected Astor to command no more political or cultural authority than he had in the United States, simply because "W. W. Astor . . . has never done anything more remarkable in America than to draw his rents" and was unlikely to have any substantive accomplishments in Britain.[35] "A man of this caliber," the Londoner concluded, "will neither be missed in America nor noticed as a worthy addition to Great Britain."[36]

His prediction that Astor would stick out awkwardly in London came true. Curiously, the experiences of William Waldorf Astor parallel those of his great-grandfather John Jacob Astor, insofar as both men could never manage to adapt to wrenching changes in their personal lives and social environments. Both had the misfortune to be mocked for their supposed social clumsiness in the popular press and to be derided by members of the social sets that they yearned to join, with John Jacob Astor remaining an outsider in New York City because of his rags-to-riches mobility and William Waldorf Astor in London because of the change in his citizenship. Yet both men also founded family dynasties. William Waldorf Astor finally realized his social ambitions when King George V rewarded his contributions to war relief by making him a baron in 1916 and then a viscount the following year. His branch of the Astor line thus became members of the British nobility.[37]

From this familial vantage point, William Waldorf Astor was scarcely the fool that his detractors made him out to be. He had concluded that the only way for him to become a true aristocrat was to move to a country that had a hereditary peerage and buy his way into it, and it turned out that he was right.[38]

GENEALOGY

In the late nineteenth century, upper-class New Yorkers also used genealogy to affirm their high standing. Because it was a hobby that could be pursued privately, genealogy was easier to control than relationships with aristocracy were, but it involved similar cultural dynamics. Although the first published genealogies made in North America date to the eighteenth century, most people who were interested in their ancestral linkages went about this task informally, consulting family bibles, letters, and diaries that had been passed down from their parents or grandparents or asking older relatives to share their memories. After accumulating a fortune in the 1840s and 1850s, Ezra Cornell wrote his relatives for information about other family members and the whereabouts of relics such as his grandfather's bible. His initial inquiries were casual, and he mainly wanted to create an emotional bond with distant family members and expand his family network now that he had risen in the world. Eventually, as he pushed his investigation into the early colonial period, his search became more standardized and involved sending codified questions about birth, marriage, and death dates to ever more remote relatives. He became interested less in tightening his family relationships and more in documenting its history.[39]

This earlier informal approach to genealogy did not disappear, but after the Civil War, the search for family antecedents became better organized and more systematic, evolving into a respectable hobby for middle- and upper-class Americans. The New York Genealogical and Biographical Society, founded in 1869, popularized the pastime in New York City by building an extensive library of family histories and providing a platform for genealogists to present their research. Companies appeared that published customized family histories and encyclopedias and handbooks of heraldry and genealogy. They also produced manuals that instructed people how to trace their own family trees.[40] By the 1890s there was so much public interest in the subject that works on genealogy and heraldry were among the most heavily requested materials at three New York City libraries.

These efforts to lift genealogy onto a higher literary and scientific plane carried a strong ideological message. At the inaugural meeting of the New York Genealogical and Biographical Society, one speaker displayed his family coat of arms and related that his ancestors included a Pilgrim who had come over on the Mayflower and a Protestant who had witnessed the execution of Mary, Queen of Scots, while another lecturer traced his lineage to a founder of Hartford, Connecticut. The emphasis here was on tracking the colonial American and European antecedents of present-day families, identifying forebears who had achieved distinction, and learning the origins of surnames. As anxieties grew over increased immigration, this exploration of the colonial heritages and English and Dutch antecedents of middle- and upper-class New Yorkers suffused genealogy with nativism and scientific racism and strengthened its capacity to legitimate social relations.[41]

Genealogy had close links to other social practices that expanded its cultural appeal. A new kind of social organization that venerated family heritage and colonial history, the patriotic hereditary society, came into vogue in the 1880s. Patriotic hereditary societies such as the Sons of the

Revolution, the Holland Society, and the Daughters of the American Revolution popularized genealogy by requiring proof of family lineage or ancestral accomplishment (like service in the Revolutionary War) for membership and by linking individual family history to nationalism.[42]

More broadly, popular historians used family origins to make sense of the past and elucidate individual success. Newspapers and magazines accordingly attributed Shakespeare's brilliance as a playwright, Washington's achievements as a general and a president, and Queen Victoria's influence as a monarch to their genealogies. *McClure's Magazine* ran character sketches of American statesmen Ulysses S. Grant, William McKinley, and General Leonard Wood crediting their greatness to their family lineages. *McClure's* allowed that these self-made men had prepared themselves with unremitting personal dedication but insisted that they had not come out of nowhere and that their seemingly sudden ascents were actually the product of generations of high breeding that had equipped them to break through and make their individual marks. Indeed, while the rags-to-riches myth of social mobility embodied in the Horatio Alger stories was employed in this period as part of the bargain to persuade working-class Americans that they could advance by toiling diligently and behaving well, many people who *had* risen from the depths did not embrace that myth. Since it was their success that set them apart, they had no reason to suppose that everybody was as good as everyone else. Since they wanted to feel at home in their new environment, they did not care to advertise their lowly origins.[43]

From the point of view of elites, genealogy was an ideal forum for expressing social distinctions, because its basis on the historical record and its systematic methodology made its findings appear to be irrefutable, and because its focus on individual families lent it a private cast that masked its ideological character. This combination of authority and flexibility appealed to middle- and upper-class people alike. The Todds were an upper-middle-class family of well-educated professionals who included the founder of a boy's school, the president of a national bank, a Presbyterian minister, and a real estate broker. Two of them had strong ties to New York City: Henry A. Todd became a professor of romance languages at Columbia College in 1893, and George B. Todd was an artist who specialized in heraldry, with an office on Madison Avenue and a studio in Yonkers. But the family was not concentrated in any single place, and genealogy helped them build solid personal relationships that could survive their geographical dispersal.

The Todds were thorough and painstaking amateur genealogists who brought to their hobby the same meticulousness that distinguished their professional lives. They searched colonial records in Connecticut, wrote town clerks across New England, asked the Bureau of Pensions about ancestors who had served in the military, and consulted the American College of Heraldry about lines of descent. Henry A. Todd traveled to England in 1886 to do genealogical work, and seventeen years later hired a researcher to look for more family records in London. Even so, their genealogy was very much a work of the imagination. The exhibition catalog for a recent survey of genealogy at the Newberry Library in Chicago concedes that although American genealogies of the nineteenth century were often well-researched and accurate, "when confronted with the question of European antecedents, critical standards could evaporate" and flights of fancy be taken.[44] According to this catalog, "probable" linkages to coveted European origins were sometimes manufactured based on flimsy etymologies and other dubious research practices. That was the case with the Todds. As a college professor who had a doctorate from Johns Hopkins University, Henry A. Todd shouldered most of the responsibility for writing the family history and insisted on adhering to strict research standards, but a desire to compile a complete narrative led him and the others to cut corners. Sometimes they incorporated Englishmen who happened to be named Todd even if they could find no evidence of a direct family relationship.[45] For example, F. W. Todd once decided that a seventeenth-century Englishman named John Todd must be the Yorkshire ancestor of that name for whom he and Henry A. Todd were searching, even though he admitted, "I have no 'proof positive' that John came from Yorkshire."[46]

Nevertheless, genealogy fulfilled emotional needs and furthered social aspirations. The Todds had modest ambitions: to uncover their English origins and confirm what they liked to call "the Todd pedigree."[47] They took pride in being descended from Protestants who had settled New England in the seventeenth century, but mostly they wanted to connect themselves to English culture and history by uncovering their English parentage. Their search for a proper English ancestry was a fantasy, but it had a serious side. The Todds were expanding their cultural capital by rejecting the racial and ethnic diversity of the country and by laying claim to a racially pure Anglo-Saxon background as a basis for their elevated social position. They came upon one nobleman whom they enthusiastically inserted in the family tree and were always on the lookout for knights and high sheriffs. If they unearthed any highwaymen or peasants or prostitutes they kept that dismaying news to themselves. For the most part, however, the historical predecessors who most pleased the Todds were prominent members of the gentry such as merchants, doctors, and lawyers.[48] It was enough for Henry A. Todd and his contemporaries to find ancestors from the gentry who resembled themselves: respectable people who were sturdy, reliable, and successful.

Many upper-class people aimed much higher, though. Levi P. Morton commissioned a genealogy that traced his immediate family lineage back to a Pilgrim ancestor who had arrived in Plymouth, Massachusetts, two years after the *Mayflower*. Morton's genealogy narrated the notable accomplishments that his forebears had made in North America, as founders of New England towns, Revolutionary War soldiers, Congregational ministers, and public officials. But, without providing any evidence of *biological* descent, it also asserted that the Morton family *name* had begun with Robert, comte de Mortain, a half-brother of William the Conquerer who had helped plan his invasion of England in 1066 and fought at his side at the Battle of Hastings. As spoils of that great victory, William the Conqueror had granted de Mortain vast landed estates that enabled him to become the progenitor of an aristocratic family that included earls and bishops and, these researches implied, an equally distinguished American branch.

Still more ambitious was the genealogical study that Joel Andrew Delano published in 1899. It duly noted that the "American House of Delano" had been founded by one Philippe de Lannoy, a nineteen-year-old

Pilgrim migrant of Flemish refugee parents who had landed in Plymouth in 1621. Yet by pushing his investigation even further, Joel Andrew Delano learned that the Delanos were descended from two old European royal families, one that he tracked to the eleventh century and the other to the fifth century. The monograph interspersed photographs of prosperous American Delanos with images of their ancestral homes in France and Holland and their French coat of arms. Its message was clear: with all that royal blood, no wonder the Delanos had done great things in America. They had no pretensions of actually being royals, but they were using their royal lineage to separate themselves from ordinary Americans. Like other upper-class New Yorkers, they were literally a breed apart.[49]

THE FOUR HUNDRED

The single most famous chapter in the history of the New York City upper class was the Four Hundred. As the primary tool of the turn-of-the-century upper class for creating exclusivity and displaying refinement, the Four Hundred became, in the words of Eric Homberger, "perhaps the greatest single American contribution to the idea of aristocracy."[50] It was remarkable for its brilliant social milieus, its internal power struggles, and its incongruence with conventional American notions about democracy and egalitarianism.

Ward McAllister, the self-designated arbiter of New York City's high society, coined the phrase "the Four Hundred" in March 1888, when he exclaimed during an interview with the *New York Tribune*, "Why, there are only about four hundred people in fashionable New York society."[51] (This attitude was satirized on the front cover of *Judge* magazine, figure 6.3.) McAllister came from a socially distinguished family in Savannah that was proud of its French and Scottish antecedents and its kinship ties to the upper classes in New York, Boston, and London. Trained as a lawyer, McAllister made a small fortune from his legal work in California during the gold rush, which he used to travel around Europe for a few years, visiting its capital cities and resorts and becoming captivated by the aristocracy.

FIGURE 6.3 The front cover of the November 8, 1890, issue of *Judge* magazine portrayed Ward McAllister as an aristocratic English dandy who functioned as "Snobbish Society's Schoolmaster," to the amusement of the more down-to-earth Uncle Sam. *Judge* was a satirical weekly magazine that was popular in the Gilded Age. (Author's collection.)

Settling in New York City following his return to the United States, McAllister married a rich socialite and embarked on his life's mission of refining its fashionable set to the purity of the European aristocracy. To create a leadership coterie that would assist him in raising the social standards of the upper class, he founded the Society of the Patriarchs, a group of fifty socially prominent men who staged balls for the likes of the Astors, Vanderbilts, Goelets, Cushings, Cuttings, and Beekmans. As president of the Patriarchs from its formation in 1872 until his death in 1895, McAllister planned the invitation lists, organized the dinners, and selected the decorations. Fascinated with genealogy and able to speak in depth about the ancestries of principal upper-class families in New York and other eastern cities, McAllister lamented that Old New Yorkers like the Patriarchs were being overshadowed by nouveaux riches who lacked their pedigree and quality.[52] Although he believed that newcomers who passed muster should be let into high society, McAllister was adamant that the old families remain in charge, and he created the Society of the Patriarchs to ensure their continued domination. He once said: "We wanted the money power, but not in any way to be controlled by it."[53] The term "money power" is usually associated with midwestern farmers, but here we see it being employed by a socialite who had his own reasons for detesting industrial capitalists.

McAllister enlarged his control over polite society by establishing an alliance with Caroline Schermerhorn Astor, who by common assent had become the ruling matriarch of the upper set. Astor represented an extraordinary amalgamation of economic, social, and cultural capital. As the daughter of merchant William Schermerhorn, she proudly traced her lineage in New York City to the 1630s, when the founder of her paternal family in North America had arrived from the Netherlands, shortly after the establishment of New Amsterdam. As the wife of William B. Astor Jr., she belonged to one of the wealthiest and most socially prominent families in late nineteenth-century New York City. Astor shared Ward McAllister's enthrallment with European aristocracy and his reverence for tradition, family lineage, and refinement. Together they set out to reform an upper class that was veering toward instability and incoherence as a result of urban economic vitality, attempting to make it more socially exclusive and culturally refined.[54]

In his 1890 autobiography, McAllister put forward his argument for the social and cultural significance of the "fashionable life":

> The mistake made by the world at large is that fashionable people are selfish, frivolous, and indifferent to the welfare of their fellow-creatures; all of which is a popular error, arising simply from a want of knowledge of the true state of things. The elegancies of fashionable life nourish and benefit art and artists; they cause the expenditure of money and its distribution; and they really prevent our own people and country from settling down into humdrum rut and becoming merely a money-making and money-saving people, with nothing to brighten up and enliven life; they foster the fine arts; but for fashion what would become of them? They bring to the front merit of every kind; seek it in the remotest corners, where it modestly shrinks from observation, and force into notice; adorn their houses with works of art, and themselves with all the taste and novelty they can find in any quarter of the globe, calling forth talent and ingenuity. Fashionable people cultivate and refine themselves, for fashion demands this of them. Progress is fashion's watchword; it never stands still; it always advances.[55]

The antimaterialist thread of this apologia is evident, and his contention that high society supplied a counterweight to moneymaking in a city known for its devotion to the almighty dollar had some merit.

The Four Hundred emanated from a class level that typically prided itself on its governance of American society, and yet one of the most conspicuous attributes of this would-be American aristocracy was its refusal to provide that sort of leadership. Indeed, the irony of the admiration of upper-class Americans of the ceremony and pomp of European aristocracies is that nobles still took part in governance in many places on the Continent in the late nineteenth century. However, Americans such as Ward McAllister, Caroline Astor, and Helen Newel who revered the titled aristocracy disregarded its political functions and concentrated instead on its glamour and exclusivity. They took from the European aristocratic model what they coveted and ignored the rest. They wanted to be just aristocratic enough to visibly reject the verities of the middle class and the flash of nouveaux riches.

This orientation was evident in other ways. Like the prose of *Town Topics*, Ward McAllister spoke in a distinctive idiom that was coy, mischievous, and sometimes malicious. This style of language signaled McAllister's rejection of the feelings of sentimentality and sincerity that middle-class Americans esteemed in this period. The Four Hundred derived meaning from their opposition to late Victorian respectability, and they were preoccupied with their own exceptionality, disdaining the multitude. While McAllister made much of the commitment of high society to charity and the arts, its contributions fell well short of those of the Jewish upper class and amounted to a conspicuous display of social capital.[56]

As Homberger observes, there is no mystery to McAllister's choice of the number four hundred. Many New York City ballrooms of this period had space for about 400 people, and the society pages of the early- and mid-1880s were filled with accounts of entertainments that drew between 400 and 450 people. Four hundred was thus a figure that was familiar enough to become lodged in the memories of other elite New Yorkers and was also small enough to ensure exclusivity.[57] The impression took hold that McAllister had proclaimed that there were precisely 400 people who mattered—no more, no less, and every one of them readily identifiable.[58] The use of such a small number, and its specificity, explains much of its appeal. If the uppermost set contained exactly 400 people, how could anyone suppose that New York's upper class had grown large, formless, and commonplace? Looked at from an economist's perspective, McAllister and Astor sought to reallocate social and symbolic resources to create scarcity and raise the value of their goods.

In any event, the numeral "400" quickly caught on and acquired a totemic stature. Less than a month after the publication of the McAllister interview, the *New York Times* lamented that "none of 'the 400'" was present for the opening night of a Verdi opera at the Academy of Music.[59] By the time that the Newport season ended in August 1888, socially elite

New Yorkers were speaking about a picnic of "McAllister's 400" and saying that "over 400 of the Summer guests" had attended a polo match; and by November and December of that year, there were accounts of some of the Four Hundred attending a wedding at Grace Church and of the Christmas exodus of "the four hundred" to Tuxedo and Hempstead.[60] Within the upper class of the city, the phrase soon became ubiquitous. A Murray Hill family used nearly four hundred roses to adorn its house for a reception for a daughter who was being presented to society, and guest lists of fashionable weddings were limited to around four hundred even if the ceremonies were being held in churches that could accommodate many more.[61] The idea soon spread to less elegant social circles and locations, and by the early 1890s German Americans in the city and residents of Harlem (then an upper-middle-class white area) boasted their own Four Hundreds, as did people in Newark, Baltimore, Philadelphia, Boston, and Chicago.[62]

Still this fundamental question remained: Who belonged to the Four Hundred? Three and a half years passed before Ward McAllister got around to releasing a list of names, a delay that was symptomatic of the arbitrariness of the enterprise. Unlike hereditary peerages, this would-be American aristocracy amounted to someone's opinion. In reality, the legitimacy of the Four Hundred rested on its acceptance by the general public, and it is noteworthy that the concept was reinforced by coverage in the popular press, much of it due to McAllister's operating as a masterful public relations agent and his adroitness at feeding stories to reporters.

The credibility of this project also depended on its endorsement by the socially powerful Caroline Astor, and not surprisingly, the final inventory was heavy on Old New Yorkers and omitted such industrialists and financiers as Collis P. Huntington, Jay Gould, Andrew Carnegie, John D. Rockefeller, Edward H. Harriman, and J. Pierpont Morgan.

Members of the social elite reacted to the release of this list with backbiting and antagonism that demonstrated their competitiveness. These responses, in turn, received a thorough public airing and were tantamount to performances of aristocracy. In 1892, an upper-class New Yorker published a satirical booklet entitled *The Greatest Show on Earth* that compared high society to a circus and that lampooned the Four Hundred as "400

Living Wonders! A Menagerie of Rare and Trained Animals!," complete with illustrations that showed identifiable individuals (including McAllister himself) as clowns, lion tamers, acrobats, and other performers.[63] *Town Topics* had always reveled in running salacious articles about the out-of-wedlock births, adulteries, gambling losses, and morphine addictions of blue bloods, rarely identifying the people who committed these indiscretions by name but usually supplying enough details for readers to put two and two together. It occasionally published unflattering and thinly disguised profiles of society figures who had an exaggerated sense of their own importance.[64] Predictably, the magazine had a field day with the publication of McAllister's list, relishing the anguish of the high and mighty who found themselves omitted.

Noting that some in the Four Hundred were apparently seeking to form an inner circle of 150 or 200 ultrafashionables, *Town Topics* delighted in the quandary of those who would be left out of that set: "The idea of any division of the 400 being shut out and pleading for admission instead of sternly refusing it as they have done for years, presents an exceedingly diverting social spectacle."[65] Hadn't the worthies who were now protesting their exclusion from the "swells" and the "howling swells" once cold-shouldered the outer 4,000 and the 40,000? *Town Topics* urged high society to formalize this policy of contraction by reducing the inner circle by half every year, so that the top 100 people would eliminate the bottom 100 one year, the top 50 would drop the lower 50 the next year, in a game of musical chairs that would end only when the original Four Hundred had been distilled to four individuals.[66]

In actuality, it was impossible to preserve tight boundaries in vibrant New York City, and greater pressure was exerted to enlarge the Four Hundred than to reduce it. A number of "sore-heads and left-outs" sniped at McAllister for omitting them, causing hostesses who adopted firm standards of eligibility to worry that they risked being disliked by "nine out of ten people in society."[67] Yet again, the subjectivity of the rankings created disagreement about how far the Four Hundred should be expanded—to 800? To 1,000? To 1,500? Caroline Astor eventually relented and added 200 slots to her version of the Four Hundred.[68]

Applying the work of Bourdieu, the Four Hundred can be understood not as an aristocracy but as a cartel. In New York City, "aristocracy" was a metaphor and a performance and sometimes an aspiration rather than a political or social reality, and the idea of a cartel, taken from economics and understood in terms of social stratification, best explains its operations. At heart the Four Hundred constituted an attempt on the part of major players to control the production and distribution of social prestige and to raise the value of their cultural capital by creating a scarcity of the goods available in the market. This emphasis on exclusivity was yet another response to the expansion of the city's upper class in the Gilded Age. Cartels arise to stabilize and structure economic sectors that are unstable and unstructured, and that is just what the vigorous urban economy had done to the upper class. Economists recognize that cartels work best in oligopolistic industries where there are a small number of firms and where the products are homogenous, factors that contribute to the success of anticompetitive measures such as price-fixing, the allocation of territorial monopolies, and bid rigging. These conditions obviously did not exist in the social realm of the upper class of *fin de siècle* New York, where the surging economy made for tremendous volatility and the Four Hundred was inherently unstable.

Like many other cartels, the Four Hundred could not survive the centrifugal forces of its dynamic industry and ultimately it collapsed. Indeed, the Four Hundred is most significant for its short life span. Deciding exactly when it ended is not a simple matter, given its unofficial status and its structural instability. A conservative assessment might put its demise at 1896 or 1897, using McAllister's death in 1895 and the disbanding of the Patriarch Society two years later as benchmarks. The *New York Tribune* took this position in 1900 by remarking that New York society had "broken up . . . into various sets" and "the original Four Hundred . . . has become almost Four Thousand."[69] A more expansive estimate would be that the Four Hundred survived until Caroline Astor suffered a nervous breakdown and went into seclusion in 1906. By then, fashionable society had become so large and diverse that no single person emerged to replace Astor as its consensus head, and equally important, nobody tried to replicate the Astor-McAllister strategy of cartelization. Even by the more generous calculation, the Four Hundred had lasted only two decades.[70]

HIGH CULTURE

From our contemporary standpoint, there is much about the Gilded Age upper class that is unappealing if not downright repellent. Except for the women's service organizations that helped the poor, the expressions of exclusivity and superiority that upper-class New Yorkers made in the arenas of men's clubs, women's networks, Murray Hill, genealogy, aristocracy, and the Four Hundred were almost entirely self-aggrandizing. They had become preoccupied with their credentials when rapid economic growth had expanded and enriched the urban elite, inundated it with newcomers, and ratcheted up the leverage of vast wealth in allotting rank and prestige and shaping life trajectories. They had become engrossed with bonding with others in their set and with accruing the social and political capital they needed to assure themselves of their status as an elite. They had grown so powerful that their efforts at achieving legitimacy met little public resistance and were taken to be normal and unexceptional.[71]

However, these upper-class New Yorkers were also pulled in a more public-spirited direction and provided vital leadership that improved urban economic and cultural infrastructures. A commitment to economic development and cultural enrichment that was part of their determination to match the great European capitals led elites to spearhead a remarkable series of public works and cultural projects, including the first subway, the massive Pennsylvania Railroad improvement, Grand Central Terminal, the New York Botanical Garden, the Bronx Zoo, and the New York Public Library.[72] Without these major advances New York could not have become a world city.

In all these instances, upper-class New Yorkers undertook significant leadership responsibilities. August Belmont II was indispensable to the subway and the Vanderbilts to Grand Central Terminal. Cornelius Vanderbilt II, Andrew Carnegie, J. Pierpont Morgan, John D. Rockefeller, D. O. Mills, and Addison Brown started the New York Botanical Garden in the 1890s with donations of $25,000 apiece. Beyond opening their checkbooks, they also gave their time and expertise, with Vanderbilt serving as president of the inaugural board of managers of the Botanical Garden, Carnegie as its vice president, and Morgan as its treasurer. That same decade, Carnegie, Vanderbilt, Morgan, William C. Whitney, Jacob H. Schiff, Helen M. Gould, and others contributed to the founding of the Bronx Zoo. Existing institutions such as the American Museum of Natural History and the Metropolitan Museum of Art expanded significantly in the late nineteenth century, due in large measure to the money, leadership, and networks of the upper class. Needless to say, this support had significant costs. As scholars who have examined the links between leaders of the Bronx Zoo and the Museum of Natural History and the ideologies of scientific racism and nativism have shown, major cultural organizations amply reflected the apprehensions and ambitions of upper-class and upper-middle-class New Yorkers.[73] A study of two key institutions—the Metropolitan Opera and the Metropolitan Museum of Art—will help us understand how elites imagined New York as a great city, worked out their inner conflicts, and related to the public.

The founding of the Metropolitan Opera in 1880 is commonly ascribed to a rebellion of new elites against old elites. Opera represented a pinnacle of nineteenth-century high culture, and well-off Americans entertained themselves and demonstrated their wealth and refinement by attending productions of celebrated operas. But even though the Academy of Music on Fourteenth Street had been the premier opera house in the United States from its opening in 1854, it had only nine opera boxes, the small spaces where the well-to-do could watch a performance in semiprivacy while displaying themselves to those in the other boxes and the rest of the auditorium. Post–Civil War economic growth put pressure on the Academy of Music to accommodate the social aspirations of nouveaux riches by adding more boxes, producing, according to the standard account, a dispute between old elites such as August Belmont I, the chairman of its board of directors, and Pierre Lorillard, who wanted to preserve the exclusivity of their inner circle, and new elites such as the Vanderbilts, who demanded a place for themselves. The story goes that when the old guard refused to build more boxes, the dissidents used their fortunes to establish the rival Metropolitan Opera House and eclipse the Academy of Music.

A shortage of boxes did lie at the heart of this conflict, and the stalwarts of the Academy of Music did come from the Knickerbocker elite, but in two respects the clash was more complicated than the standard interpretation allows.[74] First, the founders of the Metropolitan Opera did not represent a monolithic new elite, and second, they tied their desire to obtain boxes for themselves to an important civic objective. While titans of the new industrial economy such as William H. Vanderbilt, his son William K. Vanderbilt, William C. Whitney, and Levi P. Morton were organizers of the Metropolitan Opera, so were patricians James A. Roosevelt, Robert Goelet, William Rhinelander, and Adrian Iselin and scions of the second and third generations of wealth like Edward Cooper and John Jacob Astor III.

There was no simple split between old and new elites. Instead, the differences between the two camps involved a clash between those in the old guard who sought to preserve existing upper-class boundaries by excluding newcomers and those in the old and new elites who took a big tent approach. Like the men's clubs that admitted nouveaux riches in order to steal an advantage over rival clubs, supporters of the Metropolitan Opera favored inclusivity for a reason. With the revenues from more box rentals, they intended to create a facility that would be not merely the finest in the United States, as the Academy of Music was, but that would match or exceed the greatest European opera houses.[75] Reporting to the board of directors in May 1880 about the planning of a new opera house, Egisto P. Fabbri, an investment banker who chaired its building committee, said, "There is no Theatre or Opera House in this country that can be taken as a model for what we intend to have."[76] Rather, Fabbri urged the board to set its sights higher:

The Opera Houses in Europe, especially those lately built, are noted for the perfection of their interior arrangements, and of everything affecting acoustics, stage property, comfort, ventilation, and safety, and before any plans should be adopted by us they should be carefully examined, and reported upon.[77]

Agreeing with Fabbri, the directors resolved to build an opera house that would put opera in New York City on the plateau of the great European metropolises that in their view exemplified high culture. They wanted New York City to take its place with London, Paris, and Rome, and giving it a splendid opera house was a major step in that direction.

Pooling the resources of the large and diverse upper class was critical to the success of this project—and that is where the boxes came in. When Fabbri delivered his report, the board had already raised $600,000, more than 40 percent of the total construction cost. Everyone who contributed $10,000 to the Metropolitan Opera-house Company was entitled to the use of a box in the new building, and the $600,000 had been contributed by fifty-five "gentlemen of wealth and influence" who had subscribed for sixty boxes at $10,000 apiece.[78] The directors raised the remainder over the next three years.

Their policy of inclusivity had its limits: there were no Jews among the original incorporators or stockholders and very few if any appear to have become stockholders in subsequent years. Indeed, the social profile of the stockholders resembled that of the top men's clubs. Even so, tensions arose between patrons who were more moneyed and those who were less moneyed, especially over a provision of the bylaws that required that stockholders be assessed on a pro-rated basis to cover their share of any deficits. When cost overruns led several directors to propose in March 1882 that the deficit be erased by compelling each box holder to contribute an additional $5,000 (the equivalent of $108,000 today), three of the less wealthy directors objected that "it was a very large sum for the privilege [of being] a stockholder" and offered a countersuggestion that the design of the opera house be scaled down or its completion delayed.[79] That, of course, would have meant compromising or even abandoning the intention to erect a first-rate structure. Ignoring their protest, the full board approved the assessment and the project went ahead as originally conceived.[80]

When it opened a year and a half later, newspapers saluted the Metropolitan Opera House for upgrading "the primitive surroundings in which New-Yorkers have listened to opera" and for being on a par with La Scala in Milan, the New Opera in Paris, and Covent Garden in London.[81] Located at Broadway and West Thirty-Ninth Street, the new building was outstanding. Among other amenities, it had 122 boxes. Along with providing many more boxes, the architects had made them equal in status. A review of the new opera house that appeared in *Harper's New Monthly Magazine* saw that "any box is as desirable as any other box."[82] A hierarchy of boxes had existed at the Academy of Music, with some having more luxurious appointments, more space, and better views of the stage than others. By contrast, to prevent squabbling among the box holders at the Metropolitan from undermining the effort to enlist different elements of the multifaceted upper class in raising the money, the architects had devised a standard design. Every box was about fifteen feet deep, had a small dressing room, and could hold six people. At six people apiece, the 122 boxes had a total intended capacity of 732 people, or nearly twice the size of the Four Hundred. Other than twelve baignoir boxes on the ground floor that were somewhat less desirable, the rest of the boxes were similar in their acoustical properties, distance from the stage, and accessibility to stairways.[83] This layout of the boxes (figure 6.4) clearly demonstrates how the upper class changed in the late nineteenth century as it became much larger and more diverse and came to put enormous stress on its cohesiveness and its prerogatives.

One official of the Metropolitan Opera House boasted of the company's "having produced an important and necessary public building in New York, answering a great public requirement . . . [and acquiring] public popularity."[84] That did not come cheaply, however. In his 1880 report, Fabbri had warned the directors about an obstacle they were likely to encounter as they pushed forward, the absence in America of the government subsidies for high art that were commonplace in Europe. Opera is

FIGURE 6.4 The interior of the Metropolitan Opera House, showing its boxes, during a performance of Richard Wagner's *Siegfried*, c. 1888. (Library of Congress.)

among the costliest and most labor-intensive of the performing arts, with big outlays required for sets, costumes, singers, conductors, musicians, and backstage workers. Starting from scratch, the Metropolitan Opera had to supply, at fantastic expense, new costumes and sets for each of the sixteen productions that it staged during its inaugural winter season of 1883–84. A bidding war that broke out that year between the Metropolitan Opera House and the Academy of Music for the services of conductors and singers further strained the finances of the two institutions. As it happened, the Academy of Music was in crisis and would abandon opera after the 1886 season, but that did not help the Metropolitan Opera in the short run. Its deficits were much higher than anticipated, with, for instance, the scenery, costumes, and props for that first winter season running $60,000 over budget.

The Metropolitan Opera House's most significant response to this crisis involved switching from French and Italian to German opera. For the next seven years, the Metropolitan Opera House became a veritable German opera house: the composers whose works were performed were primarily Germans like Wagner and Beethoven; most of the managers, conductors, and singers were German-born and German-trained; and operas were sung only in German. Although German singers and conductors were cheaper to employ than their French and Italian counterparts, the rationale for this strategy was not to reduce costs but instead to enlarge audiences. Expanding on the big tent formula that had been their guide from the start, Metropolitan Opera leaders sought to broaden their subscription pool by appealing to the 370,000 German Americans who lived in Manhattan in the 1880s, a large and comparatively affluent community with many upper-class and upper-middle-class members who took pride in German culture and could afford opera tickets. The directors knew their city and were willing to tap its resources. There was another alternative. They could have stuck to "high artistic standards" and kept performing mainly French and Italian works. They could have shunned the new audiences. But they were New York centered and were willing to make use of what their city offered. Other stockholders disliked heavy Wagnerian opera and resented the accommodation of German Americans, many of whom were Jewish, and the Metropolitan Opera ended this experiment as soon as it could, in 1891. By then, it had succeeded in helping the company stabilize itself.[85]

The Metropolitan Opera is a good example of upper-class New Yorkers using their resources to establish a top-notch cultural institution that fostered their ambitious vision of the city. Their willingness to define their social boundaries broadly was essential to the success of the new institution, both during the initial split from the Academy of Music when its directors amassed the funds for their original capital campaign by overcoming some of their internal class divisions, and later when they responded to financial emergency by incorporating German Americans. The creation of the Metropolitan Opera House indicates that in comparison with other American upper classes, New York's was relatively open to newcomers, ready to dispense with customs and institutions that had come to seem behind the times, and ambitious in its aspirations for itself and its city. While the directors had embraced perhaps the highest of the high arts in founding the opera house, they had to be innovative to get there.

However, as a private corporation that served a prosperous audience and did not receive government subsidies, the Metropolitan Opera was relatively insulated from external politics. That was not true of the Metropolitan Museum of Art, which in the 1880s and early 1890s was caught up in a political dispute over its refusal to provide free public access to its collections on Sundays. Housed on public land and a recipient of municipal funding, the Metropolitan Museum of Art had less control over its political environment and was more susceptible to external coercion than the Metropolitan Opera was, and eventually it relented.

The Metropolitan Museum of Art was founded in 1870 by prominent members of the Union League Club, who wanted to endow New York City with a national art museum that would make available to the American people the caliber of art and art education that existed in Paris, Madrid, and Saint Petersburg.[86] By the 1880s the museum had attained modest size and quality, with a mission that chiefly revolved around its educational programs on site and in the schools. Yet its art collections were mediocre. Its most prominent collection was a group of 174 Old Masters paintings that a trustee had donated, but many of its other pieces were copies, like its casts of Egyptian sculptures and reliefs.

The museum was a private organization largely controlled and financed by the upper-class New Yorkers on its board of trustees. Yet its first permanent structure had been constructed on public land in Central Park and at municipal expense. Furthermore, the municipal government contributed $15,000 to its annual operating budget, as forgiveness of its rent and as compensation for providing free admission on several weekdays. In recognition of this arrangement, the city comptroller and the president of the parks department served ex officio on its board of trustees. However, the municipal subvention constituted a fraction of its total operating budget, and even including revenue from bequests, gifts, and ticket sales, the museum usually ran a budget deficit that the trustees covered out of pocket. Perhaps its highest institutional priority was the acquisition of new works of art. But the museum had a tiny acquisitions budget and largely depended on gifts of art from the private holdings of its trustees and other rich people to develop its collections.

The situation was ambiguous: the municipal government could exert some influence on the institution but had little control, while the museum was always hard-pressed for funds and needed to retain, if not increase, its government subsidy. And yet, with the museum relying so heavily on them, the trustees and their families did not conceive of it as a public entity and instead acted as if it were their private club. The trustees expected Louis P. di Cesnola, the director, to open the museum at their convenience to accommodate friends or relatives who could not go there during regular hours. Emily J. De Forest, the daughter of a former president of the board of trustees and the wife of its current president, used the museum as her personal repair shop, routinely sending her tapestries and sculptures there to be cleaned and repaired and then throwing a fit if they were not returned to her quickly enough. Dissatisfied with the skills of her dressmaker, De Forest asked di Cesnola to find a museum employee who could train the woman. These favors were part of a reciprocal relationship that museum administrators understood and cultivated, in order to obtain donations. Over the years, Emily and Robert De Forest gave the Metropolitan Museum of Art her collections of lace, pottery, and stoneware and more than $400,000 in cash.[87]

This view of the museum as an essentially private institution shaped the responses that its trustees and administrators made to calls to open its galleries free of charge on Sunday afternoons. This plea was first raised in 1880, the same year that the museum inaugurated its new building in Central Park. At the dedication, John Taylor Johnston, a railroad executive and art collector who was president of the board of trustees, acknowledged the civic dimension of the museum's institutional mission by expressing thanks for "the gift of this beautiful building" from the City of New York and pledging that the board "would spare no pains to make this museum worthy of the great City which it is intended to adorn."[88]

However, while the trustees conceived of the museum as a showcase that would demonstrate that their city was on a plane with Europe, they had a narrow understanding of the public and did not believe it should be universally accessible to all New Yorkers.

At the time, the Metropolitan Museum of Art was open on Mondays and Tuesdays for a 25 cent entrance charge and for free Wednesdays through Saturdays and was closed on Sundays for religious reasons. This admissions policy discriminated against the majority of the urban population: the entry fee was an impossibility for workingmen, most of whom earned less than $2 a day, and the Sunday closings had a similar effect, since laborers and clerks generally worked six days a week. Labor unions and anti-Sabbatarian associations in the United States and Great Britain had recently begun a movement to open cultural institutions to "honest workingmen" free of charge on Sundays so that they and their families could better themselves.[89]

Accordingly, the public works board approved a resolution in April 1885 asking the Metropolitan Museum of Art (and the American Museum of Natural History, which was also situated on public land and tax supported) to institute free Sundays.[90] The board of aldermen passed a similar resolution, and Mayor William R. Grace signed it into law. Noting that the municipality had financed the construction of their buildings and subsidized their operations, this resolution censured the two organizations for depriving "thousands of people of this city who have no other time for visiting said museums . . . of the recreation and intellectual development these museums were instituted to afford to all people" and asked them to do "justice to this worthy class of our citizens."[91]

Some trustees thought that the Metropolitan Museum of Art had a moral obligation to provide popular access and wished to comply with the resolution. Attorney Joseph H. Choate argued that the dependence of the museum on the public purse compelled it to accommodate the public, if only in its own self-interest. "Nothing can in my opinion be more shortsighted than to ignore them, to defy their wishes, and to deny to them the full enjoyment of the Museums which they can never have if they are closed all day Sunday," he said. "It would serve us exactly right, if our stupid obstinacy in this matter resulted in the forfeiture of our annual public grants."[92] The museum was too hard-pressed to afford to lose any major revenue stream.

But Choate was in the minority, and the rest of the board harbored a privatist conception of their duties. A strict Sabbatarian, board president Johnston threatened to resign from the board and withhold his financial support if Sunday openings became a reality.[93] Morris K. Jesup resented this outside interference with the prerogatives of the board. Questioning whether popular support actually existed for Sunday openings, Jesup blamed demagogic politicians who had concocted the scheme for trying to gain favor with the masses and the daily newspapers that had promoted it for attempting to boost their circulations.[94] Other trustees feared alienating important museum donors; as one said, "There are some of our best contributors who do not like the Sunday idea and may withdraw their offerings if we yield to the popular clamor."[95]

Choate rejected this thinking:

> The argument that we should continue to keep [the two museums] closed in deference to the prejudices of certain wealthy people who, we hope, may leave us something in their wills, is in my judgment contemptible. We have done that before and the very men on whose account our Trustees muzzled themselves died without leaving the Museum a dollar. Besides I don't think we ought to take the money of such people on any understanding or expectation that the public demand for Sunday openings be neglected.[96]

As Choate understood, the class prejudice of the rich was the issue. A year earlier, the *Boston Traveller* had reported that during five or six years of free Sunday hours at the Museum of Fine Arts in that city, "anywhere from five to ten times more visitors attended on Sundays than on other days, and . . . they were chiefly people from the poorer classes—artisans, mechanics, and laborers—who were exceedingly orderly."[97] A majority of the trustees of the Metropolitan Museum of Art regarded the museum as their space and wanted to keep the rabble out.

Citing the opposition on religious grounds of the Roman Catholic archdiocese, the Presbytery of New York, and Sunday school associations, the board of trustees rejected the proposal in 1885.[98] However, the supporters renewed their efforts six years later, and this time, because the departure of Johnston from the board for health reasons had removed its most fervent Sabbatarian, they succeeded. Leading the drive to overturn the old policy was Robert De Forest, the new president of the board (and Johnston's son-in-law), who linked Sunday openings to the effort to make the museum a world-class organization. For the Metropolitan Museum to reach the level of the Prado and the Louvre, De Forest asserted, it must raise a lot of money, and the municipal government was a very promising source. In short, De Forest urged the trustees to approve Sunday openings not for the sake of poor New Yorkers but rather to cultivate local politicians who were in a position to help the museum. Although De Forest asked the board to condition its acceptance of Sunday hours on a commitment from the municipal government to raise the annual subsidy by as much as $30,000, other trustees were leery of a quid pro quo that would give elected officials greater leverage over their decisions and rejected this recommendation. They accepted the core of his proposal, however, and on May 27, 1891, di Cesnola notified the board of public works that the trustees had agreed to the Sunday hours.[99]

More than eleven thousand people showed up four days later for the first free Sunday, the largest single-day crowd to that point in the history of the museum.[100] Newspapers characterized the visitors as respectable clerks, salesmen, and workingmen who, despite being longtime city residents, were visiting the museum for the first time. According to the papers, most were neatly dressed and many seemed knowledgeable about art. The *Brooklyn Eagle* praised the Sunday opening for brightening the lives of the poor and pronounced it "a good thing for humanity and not an injurious thing for Christianity," while the *New York Times* remarked that the orderliness of the museum-goers confounded the worries of "those who expected to see Essex Street Polish Jews and Thirty-Ninth Street and Eleventh Avenue hod carriers, in ragged clothing and dilapidated hats."[101]

But the director of the museum saw it differently. In a report that he made in November 1891 to the board about the first four months of Sunday operations, di Cesnola disparaged the Sunday visitors as "both very undesirable and objectionable."[102] In his eyes, they were not respectable workers, but rather hooligans. Having learned their tastes in "the specimen of dime museums on the Bowery," they "had come here fully expecting to see freaks and monstrosities" and "brought with them personal habits which were repulsive and entirely peculiar to themselves."[103] According to di Cesnola, they smoked cigars, chewed tobacco, and spat on the floor. They sat down in the middle of galleries or on stairwells and then pulled out their lunch baskets and ate. They touched the art and stole porcelain and someone had broken the claws off a sculpture of a lion. They became irate anytime the attendants tried to stop their misbehavior or eject troublemakers. For di Cesnola, the folly of breaching the walls that shielded high from low culture and protected reputable from disreputable people had brought about "a real abomination."[104]

Art museums were respected repositories of high art, and the ability to appreciate fine art enabled elites to know that their tastes had not been acquired through education or imitation but were innate.[105] Sunday openings compromised this production of rank and authority, causing, di Cesnola informed the board, great offense to loyal supporters of the museum and leading more than four hundred people to cancel their memberships. One patron had rescinded her pledge to donate a collection of paintings valued at $150,000 and $50,000 in cash.[106]

This report said more about the upper-class discomforts and fears than it did about the comportment of working-class visitors. No doubt some problems like the damage to the artworks had occurred, but di Cesnola was blaming an entire social group for the actions of a handful of people. He also seems to have ignored the failure of the museum to handle the unparalleled large size of the Sunday crowds. Moreover, despite his acknowledgment that the "objectionable element" of lower-class guests had disappeared in late August or early September and that "now the majority of those who visit it on Sunday is composed of the quiet, respectable, intelligent artisan class," di Cesnola still wanted to eliminate free

Sundays, because he thought the program was too expensive to manage and also because he did not believe that universal access should be an institutional priority.[107] Some trustees privately agreed with him. Not wanting to hurt the institution by incurring the wrath of the press or municipal officeholders, however, they gritted their teeth and let public access continue.

While upper-class New Yorkers had enhanced the quality of urban life by founding and nurturing the Metropolitan Museum of Art, they had envisioned the institution as a precious jewel that would embellish their class and their city while remaining off limits to hoi polloi. It had taken a struggle, but now people of all stripes could use their creation. Their legacy is no less valuable for being conflicted.

ECHOES

While an upper class has been in existence in New York City for more than three centuries, it is the Gilded Age upper class that has captivated the scholarly community and the general public alike. For many people, the Gilded Age upper class *is* the upper class.

One sign of this enduring interest are the landmark studies that have been made of it, starting with Thorstein Veblen's famous *The Theory of the Leisure Class* (1899). In portraying earlier leisure classes as arising from "barbarism" and in criticizing their "predatory habits," Veblen gave voice to the awe and revulsion with which he and many of his contemporaries reacted to the lavish expenditures and economic muscle of the nouveaux riches of their day.[108] *The Theory of the Leisure Class* is a sweeping work that begins in the feudal period and investigates the development of conspicuous consumption and conspicuous leisure on a national and even a global scale, but there was significant overlap between his American leisure class and the New York City upper class of this period. Two later inspections of the Gilded Age upper class that became milestones in Americans' understandings of wealth and power are Gustavus Myers's

The History of Great American Fortunes (1909) and Matthew Josephson's *The Robber Barons* (1934).[109]

Similarly, the bulk of scholarship on New York elites has concentrated on the late nineteenth century, with historians analyzing the creation of a new capitalist order, the political and social decisions of the wealthy industrialists and merchants who dominated public affairs, and the cultural landscape of nonprofit institutions. The epic stories of titans like Andrew Carnegie, John D. Rockefeller, and J. Pierpont Morgan have been catnip for biographers.[110]

The Gilded Age upper class has also remained alive in popular memory. As the quintessence of that upper class, the Four Hundred continues to reverberate, especially with New Yorkers. Observers have regularly applied the term to contemporary high society, with one echo being heard in a 1959 newspaper headline about the funeral of W. Vincent Astor, the last direct descendant of John Jacob Astor to be a major presence in the city: "Rites for Astor Attended by 400."[111]

At times the Four Hundred has been an object of emulation. A 1974 article in *Town & Country* about the best society parties of the past one hundred years settled on Gilded Age New York as the place where the most glamorous romps occurred, thanks to "new-rich tycoons with untouched, untaxed millions [who] competed to see who could give the most outrageous, outlandish parties."[112] In the early 1990s, a society columnist named David Patrick Columbia began publishing an annual list of four hundred socially prominent New Yorkers, at first in a magazine and later on his own website. Consisting of publicists, club owners, screenwriters, representatives of old and new money, and titled Europeans, Columbia's four hundred is a bland version of the original Four Hundred but shows that the idea has survived into our day.[113]

Some people who loathe the elitism of the Four Hundred have reworked the formula to stress business and professional merit and to ensure greater social diversity. For instance, a "New Four Hundred Ball" that aspired to be at once elegant and nonelitist took place in the 1980s.[114] On the quadricentennial of the voyage of Henry Hudson into New York harbor in 1609, the Museum of the City of New York compiled a list of four hundred "movers and shakers" who in one way or another had shaped the history of the city, a democratic assemblage that included Alexander Hamilton, Al Smith, Berenice Abbott, and Grandmaster Flash.[115]

All in all, upper-class New Yorkers themselves have also conceived of the Gilded Age upper class as archetypal. But while some lamented its demise or even sought to imitate it, others reacted to its extravagances and injustices and used it as a foil to draw attention to their own sources of distinction.

7

MAKING SPACES OF THEIR OWN

The 1940s

THE ROCKEFELLERS

Rockefeller Center is a monument to the possibilities of enlightened corporate capitalism. The project began in the mid-1920s as a plan of John D. Rockefeller Jr. to provide new accommodations for the Metropolitan Opera Company. When that scheme unraveled early in the Great Depression, the Rockefellers transformed their initial cultural venture into a commercial enterprise. The original complex consisted of fourteen coordinated buildings that were erected on three blocks in Midtown, featuring the seventy-story RCA Building; Radio City Music Hall, a massive Art Deco amphitheater; underground pedestrian concourses; and open spaces like the promenade and the sunken plaza.[1] In 1941, Rockefeller Center had five million square feet of office and retail space and a daytime population of around 150,000 people who went there for business or pleasure.[2] The 1985 designation report of the New York City Landmarks Preservation Commission praised it for being "unprecedented in scope, near visionary in its urban planning, and unequaled for its harmonious integration of architecture, art, and landscaping."[3]

The Rockefeller family has made many other contributions to New York City—Riverside Church on Morningside Heights in Manhattan; the Museum of Modern Art in Midtown; the Cloisters, a medieval art and architecture branch of the Metropolitan Museum of Art that is housed in parts of five European abbeys that were disassembled and transported to northern Manhattan; Rockefeller University, a leading biomedical research center; and major donations to Lincoln Center for the Performing Arts on the Upper West Side. The Rockefellers helped bring the headquarters of the United Nations to New York City. No family has had a greater impact on the physical landscape and cultural infrastructure of New York City than the Rockefellers. Their gifts have helped make New York City the spectacular metropolis it has become; take them away, and New York would be a more ordinary place.[4]

Besides their huge fortune and their commitment to civic missions that would justify their wealth and atone for past business ruthlessness and for notorious incidents like the Ludlow Massacre of 1914, their penchant for organization is also a legacy of the Rockefellers. Starting with the innovation of the Standard Oil Trust in 1883, the Rockefellers have been adept at using organizations to achieve their ends, from the family office in Room 5600 of the RCA Building that handled their investments, to foundations like the Rockefeller Foundation and the Rockefeller Brothers' Fund that have directed their philanthropic endeavors, to auxiliaries like the Rockefeller Archive Center that generate knowledge about the family and its activities. They have also retained public relations consultants, lawyers, scientists, architects, and art historians who used their expertise to refine and perpetuate the mission of the family. As extensions of the family, these retainers helped the Rockefellers become perhaps the most powerful family dynasty in modern America.[5]

However, as crucial as the Rockefellers have been to New York City, the most significant result of the twentieth-century organizational transformation was the rise of the corporate executive.

FROM PROPRIETORS TO MANAGERS

In 1955 *Fortune* magazine compiled a profile of senior corporate managers based on a survey it had made of the roughly thirty thousand corporate executives in America who earned $50,000 or more a year, equal to $420,000 today. According to the magazine, its findings showed that "there is visible a kind of composite way of executive life" and that the contemporary businessman "lives on an economic scale not too different from that of the man on the next-lower income rung."[6] That had not been true a quarter-century earlier in 1930, when despite the inroads that the Great Depression made on their incomes, senior executives enjoyed the use of "expensive adjuncts that other men could not begin to afford" such as commuting to the office in chauffeur-driven Pierce-Arrows and wearing costly made-to-order suits and shoes. However, *Fortune* said, now that executives had to surrender around 40 percent of their salaries in federal income tax, they could no longer afford such luxuries and led a more middle-class existence.

Thus, their homes were relatively small and unpretentious—"perhaps seven rooms and two and a half baths," *Fortune* disclosed—and their families made do with part-time help rather than live-in servants.[7] They entertained by hosting small dinner parties at home or by inviting a few guests to their country clubs instead of by holding the elaborate dinner dances that had been the rule in the 1920s.[8]

If a single person personified the New York executive of 1955, *Fortune* decided that it was Don G. Mitchell, the fifty-year-old president and chairman of the board of Sylvania Electric Products, a leading electronics and lighting manufacturer. With forty-seven plants and nineteen laboratories, Sylvania was a vast, intricate organization that Mitchell had run for the past nine years. Mitchell was certainly not a product of the upper class. The son of a dentist, he had been born in Bayonne, New Jersey, and graduated from the University of Florida. He worked in sales for several corporations before being hired in 1942 as vice president of sales at Sylvania and then being promoted to president four years later. In 1955 he earned a base salary of $120,000, the equivalent of around $1 million today.

Mitchell and his wife Constance were not ostentatious people. They raised their three children in an eleven-room brick house in Summit, New Jersey, that they had bought for $17,000 in 1938, or $217,000 in current dollars. While that sum was far more than most other Americans could afford during the Depression, by the living standards of chief executives during the Gilded Age or the 1920s it was decidedly modest. And like many suburbanites, Mitchell commuted to his office in Midtown by taking the train and the subway. To be sure, Mitchell had access to resources and perquisites that no ordinary white-collar worker could command. Two or three times a week when he stayed in the city for a late dinner or meeting he booked a room at the swank Savoy-Plaza Hotel, and he belonged to the Union League and Brooks Clubs in New York City and the Baltusrol Golf Club in New Jersey, three of the most prestigious clubs in the New York region.[9] Even so, the Mitchells thought of and carried themselves as middle class or perhaps upper-middle class. They were not listed in the *Social Register*, and their way of life had little in common with that of social elites. Mitchell relaxed by reading biographies and gardening, and he described their social life as "limited."[10] With his demanding job, he did not have time for much else besides his family.

We have seen that many nineteenth-century businessmen came from similarly modest roots. Where Mitchell differed from them was not in his origins but rather in his indifference to concealing those origins behind a false front of high status. He felt no need to pretend that he had been born somewhere other than Bayonne, or to feel defensive that his father was a dentist, or to apologize for going to the University of Florida instead of an Ivy League school. His prominence in business was his credential.

The middle-class sensibility that corporate executives like Mitchell exhibited in this period was not the consequence of higher income taxes that *Fortune* imagined it to be. Instead, it was due to two other actions that were being taken by corporate elites: first, their response to the tainting of big business during the Great Depression by emphasizing their commonality with other Americans, and second, their efforts to create social spaces of their own separate from those of the social elites. For the first time, the path to achieving business distinction and to legitimating and reinforcing their quest for wealth, power, and status did not necessitate replicating the ways and values of the upper class. As a result, many corporate elites came to inhabit the fuzzy edges between the upper class and the middle class.

The executives in this *Fortune* survey were symptomatic of a major shift in the American economy, the advent of salaried managers as the cornerstone of modern business enterprises. Control of most large businesses had passed from proprietors who owned and operated their own companies to managers who administered enterprises in which they had a negligible ownership stake; in short, ownership and management diverged. Salaried managers first became an identifiable occupational category in the 1870s. The number of proprietors, officials, managers, and inspectors then rose more than 500 percent from 12,501 in 1870 to 67,706 in 1900, and by the early 1920s, when the U.S. occupational census counted 2.6 million executive and managerial positions in business, "manager" had become a large and universally recognized job classification.[11]

Except in a few industries like railroads, the large and complex bureaucracies that are commonplace today had not existed at the turn of the twentieth century. In 1903, J. P. Morgan & Company, the most powerful investment bank in the United States if not the world, had fewer than 150 employees on its entire payroll. With just seven partners and less than a half-dozen salaried associates, J. P. Morgan & Company occupied only the ground floor and part of the basement of its seven-floor building at the corner of Wall and Broad Streets (see figure 7.1).[12]

However, corporations soon began to grow in size and complexity, generating a demand for salaried managers. Speaking before the American Management Association in 1953, Don G. Mitchell called the training of senior executives "the most important issue" facing American corporations.[13] He explained:

There are highly trained men in the typical company who can handle an assignment in their fields extremely well but the vital need is for the executive who can inspire, lead, coordinate, and direct these specialists and

10749   OFFICES OF J. P. MORGAN AND CO., NEW YORK.

FIGURE 7.1 In 1903 J. P. Morgan & Company was housed in the ground floor and part of the basement of the Drexel Building, at the corner of Wall and Broad Streets. This postcard of the Drexel Building dates from around 1915. (Author's collection.)

give a sense of direction to an organization that would otherwise follow a very devious route to its objectives.[14]

Mitchell could have cited any number of modern corporations as proof of his point that "the tremendous physical expansion of existing industries and the rapid development and growth of many new ones . . . and the growing complexity of business operation" required better managerial training.[15] In 1947 the American Express Company had 4,370 employees worldwide, dispersed across approximately 150 offices in 28 different countries, while his own Sylvania Electric had twenty-seven thousand people on its payroll.

To control and coordinate these huge organizations, corporate headquarters had grown correspondingly large and elaborate. Headquarters evolved into labyrinths. In 1947 Equitable Life had seventeen functional divisions (such as auditing, group insurance, and underwriting), most of them headed by a vice president and each reporting to the company president.[16] Two decades earlier, *The Eastern Underwriter*, an industry trade journal, had pronounced the newly opened home office of Equitable Life, near Pennsylvania Station in Midtown, a "factory of insurance."[17] The capability of this twenty-two-story building to systematically carry out a series of complicated operations reminded the trade journal of the assembly lines used by the Ford Motor Company to manufacture its Model Ts, but from our perspective it better resembles a laptop computer that processes reams of information.[18]

The internal configuration of this skyscraper was part of a fundamental restructuring of the urban economy. Nineteenth-century New York City had been given over to commerce and manufacturing, but in the twentieth century the movement and processing of goods was succeeded by the movement and processing of information. Increasingly, it was knowledge, not commodities and manufactured products, that flowed through its communication and transportation networks, and white-collar workers like managers, professionals, and clerks, not blue-collar workers, who produced that knowledge. And in 1955, for the first time white-collar workers accounted for a majority of jobs in the New York region.

To accommodate this shift, a surge in the construction of office buildings took place inside the central business districts of Manhattan, with
gross floor space in private office buildings in Manhattan increasing four-
fold from 30 million square feet in 1900 to 126 million by 1936. By 1941
there were more than 1,100 office buildings in Manhattan. Famous skyscrapers like the Woolworth and Chrysler Buildings became the trade-
marks of this boom, but it was the sheer mass of this new office space
that was significant for the remaking of the urban economy.[19] The new
structures were concentrated in the downtown financial district, which
spread west and north of Wall Street in those years, and Midtown, which
emerged as a second central business district. Many of these buildings
housed corporate home offices, law firms, advertising agencies, accounting
companies, and other professional and business services.[20] As New York
City unseated London as the prime international financial center by the
1940s, investment banks, brokerages, and insurance companies proliferated as well. The corporate headquarters complex that had originated in
the Gilded Age had come of age.[21]

Senior executives and their families and close associates formed the
corporate elite. It had first arisen with the beginnings of the corporate
headquarters complex in the late nineteenth century, but its growth and
maturation in the first half of the twentieth century constitutes the most
important change to affect the New York City upper class during this
period. The burgeoning corporate complex enabled new kinds of people
to achieve upward mobility and create their own way of life.

Because the transition to managerial control and to finance and professional and business services were national phenomena, corporate sectors
took shape in many American cities. Yet the New York City corporate
complex was easily the largest and the most powerful, and its corporate
elite was similarly large and powerful. When writers like novelist Sloan
Wilson (in *The Man in the Gray Flannel Suit*, 1955) or journalist William
H. Whyte (in *The Organization Man*, 1956) wanted to take the measure
of American corporate culture, they grounded their observations on New
York City.[22] By this time New York had become—in the phrase of Kenneth T. Jackson—"the capital of capitalism."[23]

The dominance of its corporate sector was irrefutable. In 1954 the New York region tallied 20 percent of all jobs in business headquarters in the United States. By contrast, the Chicago region, in second place, accounted for 10 percent of the total and Detroit, in third position, for 8 percent.[24] In 1955 New York City had 174 million square feet of office space, more than the rest of the top ten office centers in the country combined.[25] When *Fortune* magazine published its inaugural list of the five hundred largest industrial corporations in the nation in 1955, almost a third of them were headquartered in the New York region, compared with 10 percent in Chicago, the second-leading site, and 5 percent in third-place Pittsburgh.[26] In a further continuation of trends that began in the early nineteenth century, the rise of this corporate elite also meant that the New York City upper class would become still more internally diverse and open and would face new challenges from within to its values and practices.

Tangible social gradations existed within this New York corporate elite. There was a bottom zone that consisted of businessmen and professionals who made a decent living as middle managers but who clearly belonged to the middle class. Nor was there any uncertainty about the status of those in the top zone: individuals in this bracket made huge salaries and commanded great power. Some lived on a palatial scale, with stylish homes in choice Manhattan neighborhoods and multiple country houses that bolstered their claims to legitimacy, while others, like Don G. Mitchell, had more modest lifestyles. Those in the top zone were in a position to choose.

Yet there was also an intermediate zone of corporate elites who were mostly upper-middle class. They are the main topic in this chapter, because the mode of life they constructed and the ideology they and their successors formulated became the basis of a new upper class that in time would challenge the prerogatives and meanings of the Gilded Age upper class. People in this intermediate zone had good jobs as corporate presidents, vice presidents, lawyers, bankers, and the like. They were not part of the *Social Register* crowd and most did not want to be. They cared more about managing these gigantic organizations than about social pedigree, and they took pride in their educational and career successes. Their attention to career and their work ethic gave them a middle-class orientation, yet they also wanted to separate themselves from those in the broader middle class who had not reached their level of wealth and status.

They were hybrids who combined some characteristics of the Gilded Age upper class and some of the twentieth-century middle class. With economic and social forces acting to cloud class lines, the problem for individuals in this zone was how to distinguish themselves from that broad middle class, while simultaneously avoiding being mistaken for the nouveaux riches and arrivistes whose showiness and posturing betrayed their lack of belonging. To achieve this separation, they used social markers like the suburbs where they lived, the country clubs that they joined, and the private schools where they sent their children.

Wealthy suburbs like Rye and Scarsdale in New York and Summit in New Jersey became crucial landscapes. Corporate elites who moved to the suburbs retained strong ties with the city: they socialized, attended cultural events, and shopped in Manhattan, and through the 1940s almost all of their workplaces were still located there. What changed was that they could now choose to be part of the city and its upper-class world when they wanted to and yet withdraw from it at other times. That let them congregate with people like themselves and pursue distinction on their own terms.

In mounting the corporate ladder, moving to the suburbs, joining country clubs, and dispatching their children to prep schools, corporate elites did not directly contest the values, practices, or prestige of the blue bloods who had achieved ascendancy in the Gilded Age, but by the 1940s they had created their own communities. Instead of a single upper class that incorporated every one of status and wealth under a single canopy and assigned places to individuals according to a vertical hierarchy that valorized the exceptionality of the social elite, the high-status population came to comprise a number of subgroups that were arrayed more horizontally. In constructing their own social spaces, corporate elites helped shift the social structure of the upper class from the vertical toward the horizontal, further muddying the boundaries between it and the middle class.[27]

Those in the intermediate zone did not fully resolve their dilemma between appearing overly middle class, on the one hand, and distancing themselves from the upper class and nouveaux riches, on the other. They had their own ideas about work, education, and social hierarchy that conflicted with those of social elites, but they lived in the shadow of that Gilded Age upper class, and to detach themselves from the middle class, they adopted or mimicked upper-class institutions and practices like country clubs and private schools. The problem was that these institutions conveyed disdain for the very dedication to work and moneymaking that lay at the core of their own identity. To resolve this dilemma, corporate elites needed to crystallize their values into a coherent ideology, but that did not happen until the 1970s.

Another noteworthy development took place in this period, the emergence of a stronger federal government during the 1930s and 1940s that transformed the political economy of New York City and thus the lives of its corporate elites via regulation of the stock market and control over the war economy during World War II.

"A NARROW, CROOKED STREET"

Between 1932 and 1934, the U.S. Senate Banking Committee, led by its chief counsel Ferdinand Pecora, conducted an inquiry into the causes of the stock market crash of 1929 that corroborated popular fears and anger about Wall Street. According to Pecora, its examinations of "demi-gods of Wall Street" such as Richard Whitney, president of the New York Stock Exchange, and investment bankers J. P. Morgan Jr. and Thomas W. Lamont forced "men whose names were household words, but whose personalities and affairs were frequently shrouded in deep, aristocratic mystery" to render a public accounting virtually unprecedented in American history.[28] In exposing duplicitous practices that had benefited the wealthy at the expense of ordinary investors and in blaming Wall Street for destabilizing the financial system and sparking the depression, the Pecora Commission demolished the claims of financiers to high-mindedness, integrity, and civic leadership. It took years for corporate America to recover from that self-inflicted wound.

Around the country and in New York City itself, convictions of prominent businessmen and professionals for offenses like securities fraud and bank embezzlement increased. In 1932–1933, an ex–Wall Street publicity agent admitted that for almost a decade he had manipulated security prices by bribing financial reporters for the *Wall Street Journal*, the *New York Times*, and the *New York Herald Tribune* to slant their coverage in favor of his clients. The president of a large industrial company, the publisher of a Philadelphia newspaper, and several stockbrokers and lawyers were convicted of a scheme that fleeced $5 million in its securities.[29] The pervasiveness of these scams prompted the author of one exposé to revile the New York Stock Exchange as "The Great American Swindle, Incorporated" and to accuse its "Jesse James financiers" of enriching themselves by emptying "the pockets of American stock owners."[30] These revelations caused late nineteenth-century suspicions about New York City to return to the boil. One travel guide conceded that other Americans thought of New York "as a city of greed and glitter," and another conveyed an obvious double meaning in depicting Wall Street "a narrow, crooked street."[31] This profound loss of faith in American capitalism led novelist John Marquand to marvel, "It is difficult to realize, in light of the present, that Bankers and Business Executives once were heroes, in the Twenties."[32]

How did elite New York City businessmen handle this reversal? Aside from lessening their prestige and power, these disclosures of business misconduct encouraged the passage of federal regulations that most of them abhorred and fought to limit. Their responses also shaped their understandings of themselves by further predisposing them to conceive of themselves in middle-class and professional terms. Identifying with the middle class let them situate themselves in the American mainstream, while highlighting their professional credentials and skills let them attribute their career successes to their individual abilities rather than to anything deceitful or underhanded. They were proclaiming themselves to be true products of American social and economic democracy. Because their incomes and lifestyles were closer to those of the middle class, it was easier for businessmen in the intermediate zone than for those in the top zone to recalibrate their identities in this manner.

In his memoir Pecora recalled that Wall Street leaders maintained that "they had nothing to do with the misfortunes that overtook the country in 1929–1933" and "were simply scapegoats sacrificed on the altar of unreasoning public opinion to satisfy the wrath of a howling mob blindly seeking victims."[33] That stance hardened business resistance to President Franklin D. Roosevelt's New Deal reforms, particularly of the stock exchange. "Bitterly hostile" to federal regulation of the securities market, Pecora observed, Wall Streeters saw overturning the New Deal laws as a first step to restoring their lost autonomy and reputations.[34]

Executives and their apologists reacted by trying to recycle the past heroic imagery of businessmen. Early on in the Depression, *Fortune* magazine replied to the growing disenchantment with business by publishing fawning profiles of financiers like J. P. Morgan Jr., W. Averell Harriman, and the senior partners of Kuhn, Loeb & Company and of white-shoe lawyers like John Foster Dulles of Sullivan & Cromwell. These articles contended that stewardship of the national economy was best entrusted to the heirs of great fortunes who were experts at managing complicated business organizations and could be counted on to be serious-minded, responsible, and honorable.[35]

These profiles misfired because they drew on representations of the upper class that were widespread during the 1920s but were rendered archaic by the Great Depression.[36] In the 1920s, upper-class New Yorkers had reprised the Gilded Age by reveling in their wealth, exclusivity, and elegance.[37] They also took up the nightlife in the 1920s. With a new-found sophistication and worldliness, upper-class trendsetters relished flouting the Victorian proscription of behaviors and feelings perceived as being carnal, instinctual, and uncontrolled. They frequented saloons, cabarets, and speakeasies; drank alcohol in open violation of the Eighteenth Amendment; and mixed with celebrity movie stars and professional athletes. Some experimented with jazz, and a similar desire for personal liberation and transgression inspired a vogue in upper-class circles for the fast tempo, bodily contact, and sensuality of the tango.[38]

This was the dazzling social milieu that F. Scott Fitzgerald captured in novels like *This Side of Paradise* and *The Great Gatsby*, but it vanished during the Depression when many upper-class people could no longer afford excessive spending.[39] In the 1930s, the stark juxtaposition of recent glamour and the present-day hardship deepened popular ire at upper-class social frivolity and business wrongdoing, as the story of Richard Whitney suggests.

A Boston Brahmin descended from Puritans who had landed with John Winthrop in 1630, Richard Whitney was an important figure in both the social and economic elites in New York City as well as in business resistance to the New Deal. After his education at the Groton School, where he captained the baseball team and was school prefect, and at Harvard College, where he belonged to the storied Porcellian Club, Whitney followed his older brother to Wall Street, founding his own bond brokerage firm and buying a seat on the New York Stock Exchange. Through his brother and his uncle, both partners at J. P. Morgan & Company, Whitney became the principal bond brokerage agent for that bank. Through his wife, daughter of a president of the Union League Club and widow of a descendant of Cornelius Vanderbilt, he cemented his position in the city's social elite.[40]

This patrician's patrician gained national renown from his efforts to halt the stock market crash on Black Thursday—October 24, 1929. The president of the New York Stock Exchange happened to be away that day, and Richard Whitney, its vice president, was in charge. Working to prop up prices and end the hysteria, he boldly stepped onto the trading floor and made generous bids for U.S. Steel and other blue chips.[41] That halted the panic selling—temporarily.

Elected president of the exchange the following year, Whitney sought to repair its frayed reputation and safeguard its prerogatives by speaking on national radio and to business groups around the country.[42] He vigorously fought the securities legislation that the New Deal proposed in 1933 and 1934, arguing that a cumbersome government bureaucracy would impede economic recovery by interfering with broker-client relationships and by disrupting capital flows, a stand that caused the *Wall Street Journal* to praise his "stubborn, unbending" fight on behalf of an institution that was "a victim of popular wrath and misunderstanding."[43] However, Whitney's implacable hostility to the Roosevelt administration led to his being passed over for a sixth term as NYSE president in 1935 in favor of a member of a liberal faction that advocated cooperating with the new regulatory regime rather than fruitlessly trying to topple it.[44]

Two years later, a New York County grand jury indicted Whitney for embezzling tens of thousands of dollars from the New York Yacht Club, the estate of his father-in-law, and other accounts after his brokerage firm had filed for bankruptcy. He pled guilty and served three years in Sing Sing Correctional Facility. This scandal became a sensation, and news of it demolished the fantasy that personal status and honor alone could guarantee responsible business conduct. It also prodded corporate elites to find positive means of restoring their legitimacy and protecting their prestige and power.[45]

Corporate public relations had originated shortly after the turn of the century as part of an attempt to block the enactment of Progressive reforms. The industry reached new heights in the 1930s and 1940s by facilitating corporate resistance to the imposition of new business regulations. Cleveland-based Hill and Knowlton opened a branch office in the Empire State Building in 1933 to coordinate a steel industry campaign to sway New Deal policy making, eventually relocating most of its operations to its New York City bureau and becoming the preeminent corporate public relations concern in the United States. Other PR firms aided public utility and chain store corporations in their disputes with the federal and state governments. Corporate advertising also appealed directly to the public; for instance, General Motors, General Electric, and Westinghouse created exhibits at the 1939–1940 New York World's Fair that showed how their products improved the lives of ordinary Americans.[46]

Business leaders also reacted by stressing their professionalism. Seeking to lure wary investors back to the stock market, investment guides depicted stockbrokers as disinterested professionals who adhered to strict ethical codes.[47] "The successful manipulation of money, in and out of the security markets, is truly a great profession," a 1939 manual asserted.[48] According to these books, the best way for investors to avoid undue risks and to make money in the stock market was to receive guidance from Wall Street professionals who had the knowledge of economics to analyze corporate financial statements and the command of social psychology to forecast market trends. Brokers were trained professionals who could be trusted to put the interests of their clients first, not the fly-by-night crooks of recent memory.[49]

Graduate business schools took a similar tack. Top business schools revised their curricula to incorporate professional ethics and corporate responsibility to employees, customers, suppliers, and the general public. The notion was that aspiring CEOs should learn to manage big corporations and to anticipate and solve the modern economic problems that had triggered the Great Depression in the first place.[50]

In addition, business leaders responded by conceiving of and presenting themselves as more middle class. In the late 1940s *Forbes* magazine published a series of biographical profiles that played up the common touch of corporate leaders. One article revealed that the first job that Walter S. Gifford, the president of AT&T, ever had with the phone company was as a $10-a-week factory worker. It also mentioned that Gifford listed his home address and phone number in the Manhattan telephone directory and would field calls from customers complaining about their telephone service.[51] Given the rekindling of popular animosity toward New York City and Wall Street, *Forbes* emphasized the rural beginnings of some of these senior managers, like the president of a major oil company, originally a "Missouri farm boy" who had risen at 5 a.m. to do his chores and made extra money by serving as the janitor of his school.[52]

This same impulse to demonstrate that business executives were no longer acting godlike had impelled *Fortune* to spotlight the middle-class lifestyles of executives like Don G. Mitchell in its 1955 survey. Some businessmen still fabricated upper-class backgrounds for themselves, but there were more and more like Mitchell who felt no need to mask or apologize for their beginnings. At no other time in American history have economic elites been so inclined to conceive of themselves in terms of the Horatio Alger myth of upward mobility.

A HEIGHTENED FEDERAL PRESENCE

Tightened federal regulation of business during the 1930s and 1940s altered the political economy of New York. Another sign of this heightened federal presence was the many public improvements paid for by the New Deal that were built in this period, such as the Triborough and Bronx-Whitestone Bridges, the Brooklyn-Battery Tunnel, LaGuardia Airport, and public housing projects.[53]

The mobilization for World War II also changed the relationship between the federal government and New York City. The Brooklyn Navy Yard was the largest naval construction facility in the United States during the war, operating around the clock to launch vessels like the battleships *Iowa* and *Missouri*, while private shipbuilders in the region constructed hundreds more, including John F. Kennedy's famous *PT-109*, which was laid down in Bayonne, New Jersey. In the 1940s New York City was still the busiest port in the country, and its transport facilities were equally vital to the war effort.[54]

Whereas Wall Street firms had been preeminent in organizing war finance during the Civil War, the development of an active federal government relegated Wall Street businesses to the backseat during World War II. In addition, New York City received a smaller share of the total value of war contracts for manufacturing than Detroit, Los Angeles, and northern New Jersey.[55] The difficulty for New York was that military procurement agencies preferred dealing with big corporations that had large production capacities and robust supply networks—and companies in New York were typically small in scale and capitalization. And while manufacturers in New York specialized in consumer nondurables like garments, the war economy required intermediate goods (like steel from Pittsburgh) and durables (aircraft from Los Angeles, tanks from Detroit). There was a mismatch between the dictates of the war effort and the structure of New York's urban economy.[56]

CORPORATE ELITES

Descendants of socially prominent families could still be found in the upper corporate ranks in the 1940s. Robert Clarkson, the chairman of the board of the American Express Company from 1935 to 1960 and the son of a previous AmEx chairman, traced his lineage to the Livingstons and Clarksons of Old New York, while Cornelius Vanderbilt III, W. Vincent Astor, F. Higginson Cabot, and Theodore Roosevelt Jr. served on the AmEx board of directors in the first half of the twentieth century. There were Vanderbilts active in the management of the New York Central Railroad through the 1940s and Morgans involved with the successor firms to J. P. Morgan & Company. David Rockefeller did not retire as chairman of Chase Manhattan until 1981.[57]

But inherited wealth was the exception, and relatively few of the men who achieved high corporate positions came from the social elite or old money. Corporate capitalism enabled new kinds of people to rise in the world. Consider the eighteen top executives of the Equitable Life Assurance Society in 1949—its president and the heads of its seventeen operating divisions. Ray D. Murphy was its chief actuary, a vice president, and a member of the board of directors and later became its president and chairman of the board. His 1964 obituary in the *New York Times* and his company biography took note of his descent from Governor William Bradford of the Plymouth Colony and his graduation Phi Beta Kappa from Harvard College. Yet this was not the whole story: in reality, Murphy hailed from a lower-middle-class background in Springfield, Massachusetts, where his father, an English immigrant, had been a bookkeeper for a shoe store. The rest was embellishment, selectively employed to create a false impression of high status. Murphy came from an older generation than Don G. Mitchell, and the old sources of social prominence appear to have had a greater appeal for him.

None of these eighteen Equitable executives were listed in the *Social Register*, and the only one to come from an affluent New York City family was the head of the law department, Warner H. Mandel. A German Jew who was more prosperous than wealthy, Mandel was decidedly outside the established upper class and even the German-Jewish elite. Thomas I. Parkinson, the longtime president, and Joseph R. Boldt, vice president for policy claims, were both Catholic. Most of the rest belonged to mainstream Protestant denominations, but in one way or another, they were also outsiders who had used the corporation to achieve social mobility. Henry Greaves had immigrated to Brooklyn from Barbados in 1892 at about age 14, became an office boy at Equitable Life two years later, and over the course of the next sixty years slowly moved up the corporate ladder, to vice president in 1952. Alvin B. Dalager came from a Norwegian American family of grocers in Austin, Minnesota, where he joined Equitable as a salesman. When he performed well in that capacity, the company transferred him to its agency in Saint Paul and promoted him to supervisor. Later he moved to Wilmington, Delaware, and became an agency manager. After two decades in the field, Dalager entered the home office in 1937 as a second vice president in the agency department, retiring as a senior vice president seventeen years later.[58]

These Equitable executives may not have come from inherited wealth or social prominence, but they had good corporate jobs that paid well and let them live well. However, the extent to which they were elites—that is, the extent to which they exercised great wealth and power—was in question.

By contrast, those clearly in the highest zone of the corporate elite had immense power and prestige. Members of the top echelon of the corporate elite belonged to the boards of directors of nine major nonprofit groups in 1948: the American Museum of Natural History, Columbia University, the Metropolitan Museum of Art, the Metropolitan Opera, the Museum of Modern Art, the New York Botanical Garden, the New York Philharmonic, the New York Public Library, and New York University. To be a member of these boards was to be a heavyweight; it represented the epitome of elite status in the city.

It is not possible to draw a hard-and-fast line between board members who owed their rank to their socially prominent families and their inherited wealth and those who owed it to their corporate positions, since some board members from socially elite families were also capable businessmen (like Cornelius Vanderbilt Whitney, a founder of Pan American Airways and of a Canadian mining concern, and bankers Junius S. Morgan and Robert Lehman). Nevertheless, it is possible to identify individuals who would have been considered "income men" in the previous generation—in other words, those who owed their wealth and prominence entirely to their career success. These were the members of the top zone of the corporate elite.

Among their ranks were magazine publisher Henry Luce (who sat on the board of the Museum of Modern Art), CBS chairman William S. Paley (the Museum of Modern Art and the New York Philharmonic), RCA president David Sarnoff (the Metropolitan Opera and New York University), IBM's Thomas H. Watson Sr. (Columbia University and the Metropolitan Museum), Samuel H. Kress, the founder of a chain of five-and-ten stores (the Metropolitan Museum of Art), and corporate attorneys John W. Davis (the Metropolitan Museum of Art) and Frederic Coudert (Columbia University). These boards allowed corporate and social elites to interact and share authority.[59]

Some corporate elites in this zone used the national security arena to strengthen their claims to prestige and power. As the federal government enlarged its security and fiscal apparatus in the first half of the twentieth century, crucial leadership positions went to outstanding New York City lawyers, financiers, and executives who could apply their professional expertise and understanding of large organizations to policy making. Some of the most renowned names in the midcentury American foreign policy establishment came from Wall Street: John Foster Dulles, a partner with Sullivan & Cromwell, became secretary of state during the Eisenhower administration; James V. Forrestal, an investment banker for thirty-four years at Dillon, Read, & Company, became secretary of the navy during

World War II and was the first secretary of defense from 1947 to 1949; and John J. McCloy, a banker and lawyer with Cravath, Swaine & Moore and later chairman of the Chase Manhattan Bank, was assistant secretary of war during World War II, president of the World Bank from 1947 to 1949, and U.S. high commissioner for Germany from 1949 to 1952.[60]

The axis of this "New York foreign policy elite" was the Council on Foreign Relations, which had been founded in 1921 to facilitate exchanges among government officials, businessmen, journalists, and academics who sought to bolster American power overseas.[61] Based in New York City and funded by Wall Street firms, the Council on Foreign Relations derived from two clusters of investment bankers and lawyers, one led by Thomas W. Lamont, a partner at J. P. Morgan & Company, and the other by former secretary of state (and onetime white-shoe lawyer) Elihu Root.[62]

One way people in the top zone displayed their wealth and legitimated their claims to power and prestige was through their ownership of extravagant houses that no middle-class person could possibly afford. In the early 1930s, James V. Forrestal, then a vice president at Dillon, Read & Company, built a five-story Georgian-style marble and brick town house on Beekman Place on the Upper East Side that had bay windows and brick terraces that overlooked the East River. It had an oval foyer made of marble, and the rooms on its main floor were paneled in old English wood and trimmed with solid gold leaf. Forrestal and his wife also had a thirty-acre estate on Long Island.[63]

RCA's David Sarnoff owned a six-story, thirty-room mansion off Fifth Avenue on East Seventy-First Street. On East Seventy-Fifth Street near Fifth Avenue, Thomas H. Watson Sr. lived in a town house that had a marble winding staircase in its entryway and a living room adorned with paneled walls, Persian rugs, and photographs showing him with luminaries like Franklin D. Roosevelt and Winston Churchill. Watson also had a farm in Indiana, a summer house on the Maine coast, and later a country home in New Canaan, Connecticut. Financier Bernard M. Baruch had a residence on Fifth Avenue that was staffed by a cook and four maids, along with a seventeen thousand–acre plantation in South Carolina where he raised rice and cotton, went quail and duck shooting, and entertained world leaders. William Paley, the chief executive of CBS, had a winter retreat in the Bahamas and a succession of homes in Manhattan, including a triplex at Park Avenue and Fifty-Eighth Street, a six-story town house on Beekman Place, and an apartment in the St. Regis Hotel. His pride and joy was Kiluna Farm, an eighty-five-acre estate on the north shore of Long Island that boasted a main house that overlooked Long Island Sound, along with guest cottages, an indoor tennis court, two swimming pools, barns, greenhouses, and gardens.[64]

Corporate elites who had reached this level did not need to worry about their credentials: even if they had new money, their wealth and power made their rank incontestable. It was a different story for those in the intermediate zone who had the prestige and more importantly the salaries from their corporate positions to lead comfortable lives. However, their lesser degree of wealth, prestige, and power combined with their commitment to work and their origins outside the upper class stamped them as middle class.

Many corporate elites in this intermediate zone were suburbanites. In moving to the suburbs, they distanced themselves from the established upper class, while blurring their boundaries with the middle class.

COMMUTERS

The New York Central Railroad station in Rye, a wealthy suburb that lies north of New York City in Westchester County, was about a mile from the wooded street where a Wall Street stockbroker named Arthur C. Gwynne lived with his family. Even though Gwynne had gone to college and worked in Manhattan, he was completely immersed in Rye. He had grown up there, he belonged to its Apawamis Club, a country club, and he served as a vestryman of its Episcopalian church and as a member of its school board. For more than sixty years, Gwynne caught the 8:09 a.m. train for Grand Central Terminal and returned on the 5:23 p.m., reading the newspaper or chatting with one of his neighbors in the morning and napping on the trip home.[65] "Lots of people hate it, but I like commuting," he said in 1948.[66]

The following year, the Lackawanna Railroad honored eighty-seven--year-old Henry B. Twombly for completing sixty years of commuting between his home in Summit, New Jersey, and his office in lower Manhattan. Before becoming a named partner in a Wall Street law firm and overseeing the incorporation of about a half-dozen blue chips like General Electric and Otis Elevator, Twombly had quarterbacked the Yale football squads that went undefeated from 1882 to 1884 and had been tapped for Skull and Bones, the most prestigious secret society of that college. He and his family put down roots in Summit: he served on its board of health for almost a quarter-century, his wife helped establish a settlement house there, and their son became its mayor. Twombly daily boarded the 8:07 a.m. train and from the railroad terminal in Hoboken would have taken a ferry or what is now the PATH subway across the Hudson River.[67]

If not for their third child, Barbara, marrying a young man from nearby Greenwich, Connecticut, George H. W. Bush, who went on to be the forty-first president of the United States, the Pierces of 31 Onondaga Street in Rye would have been a fairly typical affluent suburban family of the 1940s. Marvin and Pauline Pierce were both Ohioans: his father was an insurance agent, while her father was a prosecuting attorney and later a justice of the Ohio Supreme Court. They met as undergraduates at Miami University of Ohio, marrying in 1918. Three years later Marvin Pierce landed a job as assistant to the publisher with the McCall Corporation, which produced magazines such as *McCall's* and later *Redbook* from its headquarters on Park Avenue in New York City. In the Depression year of 1934, Pierce received $22,500 in salary and bonuses, which comes to $357,000 today. He was promoted to vice president in 1935 and to president in 1946.[68]

Marvin and Pauline Pierce had a comfortable way of life that rested squarely on his considerable business success. The couple did not belong to the Manhattan social elite and, apart from his job, had few strong attachments to New York City. They lived in the city initially, but shortly before Barbara was born in 1925, they moved to Rye, a town of some six thousand residents that resembled the small Ohio cities of their child-hoods in that everyone seemed to know everyone else.

Marvin Pierce walked fifteen or twenty minutes to the train station for the commute to Manhattan. He read the paper in the morning and sat in the club car and had a drink and played bridge on the return. The family—with four children and two live-in servants—owned a three-story, five-bedroom house that occupied a quarter-acre lot in the Indian Village section of Rye.[69] "The houses [in Indian Village] were modest by Rye stan-dards," Barbara Bush recalled, and theirs was certainly no mansion.[70]

It was, she went on to say, nonetheless "a life of privilege."[71] In New York City the Pierces probably would have ranked as upper-middle class, but here they were something more, not exactly upper class but, by virtue of their income and their social standing, not middle class, either. The Pierces belonged to the Rye Presbyterian Church, of which Marvin was a trustee, and to the Apawamis and American Yacht Clubs. Pauline Pierce was an ardent gardener who won prizes from the local garden club for her flower arrangements, and she hosted teas, luncheons, dinner parties, and debutante dances for their set. They sent their children to good prep schools and colleges. In moving to Rye, the Pierces entered a social space where they associated with people like themselves whose way of life also revolved around the success that the men had in the corporate world and the relationships that their families forged in the privileged suburbs where they resided.[72]

Pierce, Gwynne, and Twombly were well-to-do and profession-ally prominent, but the centrality of commuting and career to their lives branded them and their families as middle class.[73] In the early and mid-twentieth century, popular culture representations strengthened that identification between work and middle-class status. Starting around the time when Pennsylvania Station and Grand Central Terminal were built, linkages among corporate employment, commuting, and middle-class status were reinforced by a genre of comedic novels, plays, and eventually movies like *Mr. Blandings Builds His Dream House* (1948) that poked fun at the misadventures of harried junior executives who moved their families from the city to the "wilds" of Connecticut and New Jersey in the hope of attaining the good life. These lampoons depicted their protagonists—ruled by the iron discipline of railroad timetables, made anxious by their sky-high home repair bills, failing at pastoral pursuits like ice-skating and vegetable gardening, and watching their children turn into uncontrollable rural bumpkins—as ordinary middle-class Americans whose unseemly ambition to become country squires was the source of their troubles.[74] They should have known their place and stayed put.

Pierce, Gwynne, Twombly, and other corporate elites in this intermediate zone may have been gentry, not nobility, but the gentry still formed part of the elite and were in the top quadrant of American society.[75] Certainly they were someplace beyond the broad, ill-defined middle of American society to which these popular culture expressions relegated them. With economic and social forces working to obscure class lines, the problem for people in this intermediate zone was how to detach themselves from the broad middle class, while at the same time taking pains not to be confused for the nouveaux riches and arrivistes whose exhibitionism lay bare their true ordinariness.

To achieve this separation, people in the intermediate zone devised social markers that would identify themselves to one another and confirm their status: elite suburbs, country clubs, and private schools.

UPPER-CLASS SUBURBS

In 1908 George Howe became a salesman for a real estate company that was building Park Hill-on-Hudson, a planned suburban community of stylish mansions and bungalows located in Yonkers, a city in southern Westchester County that borders the Bronx. Sited on a wooded plateau that gave sweeping views of the Hudson River and conceived with winding roads, parks, and a country club, Park Hill had become a desirable place of residence for industrialists, lawyers, publishers, and advertising executives who worked in downtown Manhattan. It was a prototypical upper-middle-class suburb.[76]

Most of these men were railroad commuters, and at this time their trains were drawn by coal-powered locomotives that were dirty, smelly, noisy, and prone to frequent delays. These impediments help explain why Westchester County was predominantly rural past Yonkers and why much of it seemed distant from lower Manhattan. In 1913, however, the New York Central Railroad electrified its suburban lines and inaugurated Grand Central Terminal, causing commuter traffic to soar. By 1930 a total of twenty-six million people commuted in and out of Grand Central Terminal annually, an increase of almost 300 percent from 1906. The construction of limited-access highways such as the Bronx River Parkway further accelerated commuting.[77]

Alert to these new business possibilities, George Howe became a real estate broker in Westchester County and nearby Fairfield County in Connecticut, maintaining, at the peak of a career that spanned more than a half century, six offices in Westchester County, three in Fairfield County, and another in the Fieldston section of the Bronx.[78] In 1959 Howe wrote of having watched "at firsthand the wonderful development of this beautiful suburban area north of New York City":[79]

> As I ride around and see the splendid boulevards and highways, the charming residential districts, the very active cities and villages with their numerous new public buildings, schools, parks, and their commercial and industrial districts, I can hardly believe my eyes.[80]

Howe was a community builder who actively shaped suburban physical and social environments. To promote various real estate endeavors, for instance, he became a founder of the Briar Hills Country Club in Briarcliff Manor and Bonnie Briar Country Club in Larchmont and aided in the formation of the Whippoorwill in Armonk, Saxon Woods in Scarsdale, and beach clubs in Larchmont and Mamaroneck.[81]

He specialized in high-end residential transactions, sometimes selling unbroken tracts to wealthy home buyers—as in 1951, when he helped the president of a major chemical company purchase a three-acre waterfront estate on Manursing Island in Rye that featured a swimming pool overlooking Long Island Sound. Other times he found country estates and farmland that could be subdivided into building lots and developed with detached houses, as he did in the early 1950s with the two hundred–acre Mount Kisco estate of tire magnate David A. Goodrich.

Many of Howe's clients were very rich, including Alfred Rhett DuPont; Albert Warner, a founder of Warner Brothers Studios; John S. Burke, chief executive of the B. Altman & Company department store chain; and Archibald R. Graustein and F. B. Hufnagel, presidents of International Paper and Crucible Steel, respectively. Yet he also sold countless less costly residences and relatively modest one- and two-acre building sites to upper-middle-class professionals and business executives.[82]

Suburban development happened elsewhere in the region. In the decade before Grand Central Terminal opened, the Pennsylvania Railroad undertook its own massive improvement project by building tunnels that carried its electric-powered trains under the Hudson River from New Jersey and under the East River from Long Island to a magnificent new railroad station it erected in midtown Manhattan. Together with the vehicular highways and river crossings completed in subsequent decades, this Pennsylvania Railroad project meant that residential construction surged east and west as well as north of New York City.[83]

In the 1920s the Regional Plan Association defined the New York metropolitan region to consist of thirty-one counties in New York State, Connecticut, and New Jersey, an area of almost thirteen thousand square miles, or about the size of Maryland. In 1940 this vast region contained thirteen million residents, one-tenth of the population of the entire United States. Its core remained New York City, but almost half of its inhabitants lived outside the five boroughs—in industrial centers such as Newark, New Jersey, and Bridgeport, Connecticut; in working- and middle-class suburbs; and in rural villages.[84]

Among its most important places (in terms of the wealth and influence of their residents) were the elite suburbs that boomed following the completion of Grand Central Terminal and Pennsylvania Station. Between 1910 and 1940, the populations of suburbs such as Rye and Bronxville in Westchester County, Greenwich in Connecticut, and Westfield and Ridgewood in New Jersey more than doubled or tripled.[85] Tens of thousands of upper- and upper-middle-class people took advantage of the new rail and highway improvements to decamp to outlying areas. The primary attraction, particularly for members of the corporate elite, was the opportunity to create spaces where they could separate themselves from the established upper class, while also shielding themselves from the poor.[86]

Insight into this elite suburbanization can be obtained from a statistical analysis of almost 2,500 elites in the New York region that is based on a 1947 biographical dictionary. Most of those in the study group were economic elites, with many working in the corporate complex in Manhattan.[87] Virtually everyone in the study group continued to work in New York City, but almost half of the people in the survey lived within the metropolitan region but beyond the city's borders.[88] They, overwhelmingly, were suburban dwellers.

Their most salient characteristic was their geographical dispersal. The leading suburbs inhabited by people in the study population were, in rank order, Scarsdale; Bronxville; Montclair, New Jersey; Greenwich, Connecticut; New Rochelle; Garden City; and Rye. But while Scarsdale was the favorite, less than 4 percent of the people in the project lived there, and taken as a whole, the top ten suburbs comprised just 15 percent of the entire study population. In total, the 2,458 people in the study resided in more than sixty-five different suburbs.

This geographical dispersal had a conspicuous regional pattern. Although elites were concentrated in three different corners of the metropolitan region—Westchester County and Fairfield County in the north; New Jersey in the west; and Long Island in the east—they showed a marked preference for the northern and the close-in Jersey suburbs. Garden City was the only Long Island community in the top ten, and there were only three Long Island suburbs among the top twenty-five (see map 4).[89]

As of the 1940s, relatively more land had been made available for suburban development north and west of New York City than east of it. In the 1940s upper-class estates still occupied many parts of Nassau County that were most suitable for suburbanization, and Long Island was thus weighted toward old money and blue blood rather than toward corporate elites. Of the fifteen communities in Nassau and Suffolk counties that people

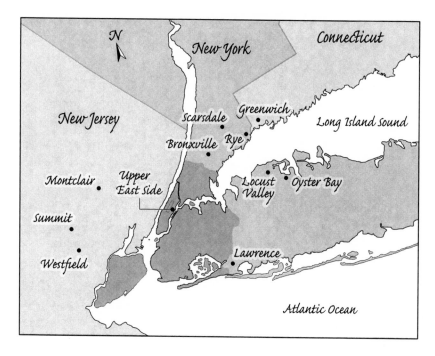

MAP 4 Upper-class areas in the New York region in 1940.

in the study population most favored, nine were "old-money suburbs" like Lawrence, Oyster Bay, and Locust Valley.[90] There were old-money suburbs elsewhere in the region—Morristown in New Jersey and Greenwich and New Canaan in Connecticut—but they existed in tandem with numerous upper-middle-class and middle-class suburbs.

The development of these elite suburbs coincided with the emergence of the Upper East Side of Manhattan, which by the 1920s had supplanted Murray Hill as the premier upper-class neighborhood in New York City. The Upper East Side extended from about Sixtieth Street to Ninety-Sixth Street between Fifth Avenue and Park Avenue. It rose after the electrification of the New York Central Railroad eliminated the open cut that had marred Park Avenue above Forty-Second Street. Unlike earlier upper-class neighborhoods that had not survived for very long, the Upper East Side has become a permanent part of the urban landscape, largely because the emergence of Harlem as an African American quarter to its north capped further expansion uptown.[91]

An analysis of the 1949 *Social Register* shows that the people listed there had a different residential geography than the economic elites in the study group.[92] The preferred area of residence for the *Social Register* crowd was overwhelmingly the Upper East Side, accounting for one-third of all residential addresses.[93] By contrast, only 13 percent of economic elites in the study group lived on the Upper East Side.[94] In moving to the suburbs, corporate elites literally distanced themselves from social elites.

An upper class that at the turn of the century had emphasized its cohesiveness and its interconnections had by the 1940s dispersed geographically. Since the mid-nineteenth century there had been divergent social and cultural ways of being a part of the city's upper class, and to this was now added greater physical and social distance. This diffusion enlarged the social space available to corporate elites and let them foster their own ways of life and their own communities, and that, in turn, bent the vertical structure of the Gilded Age upper class toward the horizontal.

While the concurrent development of a new uptown upper-class neighborhood and new elite suburbs was not entirely unique to New York City, the geographical scope and the wealth of this phenomenon was nonetheless extraordinary.[95] The Upper East Side became the single largest and richest upper-class urban neighborhood in the United States, and combined with the new elite suburbs, this upper-class geography is a striking testament to the tremendous wealth, size, and internal diversity of the New York City upper class.[96]

SCARSDALE

The quintessential elite suburb of the 1940s was Scarsdale, located some twenty miles north of midtown Manhattan in central Westchester County. When the tracks of the Harlem Railroad first reached the village in 1844, wealthy New Yorkers started to build country estates there where they could go for the summers or on weekends. Scarsdale was not yet urban, but its social ties to New York City put its country landscape inside the metropolitan shadow. In 1853, for instance, Lewis G. Morris, whose main residence was in the Morris Heights section that is named for his family in what is now the Bronx, consolidated several farms into a 440-acre estate he christened Herdsdale Farms.[97] Other upper-class New Yorkers made the village their primary home, including a branch of the Bleecker line. A member of the Bleecker family who was born in Scarsdale in 1860 recalled having grown up in "the country" at a time when orchards and pastures were commonplace and could remember the Bronx River as a clean, pretty stream where she went ice-skating.[98]

These pastoral scenes ceased to exist after around 1890, when realtors started to purchase farmland and turn it into residential subdivisions. Scarsdale continued to be in the shadow of New York City, but now it transitioned from being part of the metropolitan countryside to a residential suburb.[99] Between 1890 and 1915 the number of its residents increased from 633 to 2,712 and the number of its farms dropped from about 35 to 12.[100] By 1940 the village had nearly 13,000 inhabitants. Annual sales of commutation tickets at the Scarsdale station on the Harlem line of the New York Central Railroad tripled between 1919 and 1927. After a lull during the Great Depression, commuter rail traffic surged again during World War II.[101] People also drove, of course, but the railroad was the real lifeline with New York City.

In his 1954 history of Scarsdale, Harry Hansen described the throngs of men and women of "the business and professional class" who converged on Grand Central Terminal after 5 o'clock on weekday afternoons for a roughly thirty-five-minute commute to the "green landscapes" of affluent Westchester County.[102] Exiting the train station in the village center, these commuters beheld what Hansen called "a rural landscape unlike any seen in a modern American town."[103]

Here, bordered by sycamores and elms, the Bronx River flows into a wide pool, then tumbles over a stone milldam and breaks into foam on the rocky bed below. Here wildfowl, interrupting their flight, dive into the waters or preen their feathers along the banks. Beyond the river runs the concrete highway, and behind that rises a steep hill that gives the whole landscape a verdant background.[104]

This lovely park-like spot was an example of "second nature," a phrase that environmentalists apply to settings that have been altered to suit specific human needs.[105] Like the rest of Scarsdale, it was lush, orderly, and harmonious, and it was tightly controlled to exclude annoying people and land uses.

From this idyllic gateway, some commuters entered residential terrain that had been devised to be similarly alluring—"the area," Hansen said of elegant subdivisions like Heathcote and Murray Hill, "of winding roads with few sidewalks, landscaped grounds that lie in deep shade, and the white two-storied houses that are characteristic of Scarsdale."[106] (See figure 7.2.) A civil engineer who had moved to Scarsdale as part of its pre–World War I population influx and built a house in the Greenacres section was disturbed when he realized that the residents of more exclusive neighborhoods looked down their noses at him. Scarsdale, he had discovered, was not socially monolithic. Rather, it consisted of discrete subdivisions that had their own identities and income and status levels. At the bottom were places like Arthur Manor, whose residents included policemen, clerks, butchers, and plumbers and where many house lots replicated the standard Manhattan lot size of twenty-five feet by one hundred feet. At the upper end were the subdivisions, notably Murray Hill, where the size of individual lots ranged up to five acres, and Heathcote, the most luxurious neighborhood, where lots ran from about an acre and a half to sixteen acres.[107]

Carol A. O'Connor has determined that the men who inhabited these posh subdivisions differed from other male residents of Scarsdale "less in their fields of endeavor than in the degree of success they had attained."[108] There were, O'Connor tells us, business executives, doctors, lawyers, and engineers living in every subdivision, but those with Heathcote, Fox Meadow, and Murray Hill addresses had advanced further and earned higher incomes. For instance, Everit J. Sadler, a graduate of the U.S. Naval Academy, entered the oil business after completing his obligatory military service and soon went to work for Standard Oil of New Jersey, specializing in its foreign

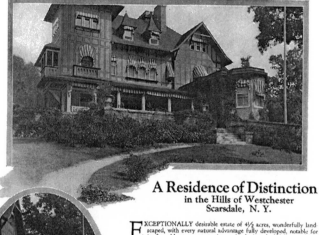

A Residence of Distinction
in the Hills of Westchester
Scarsdale, N. Y.

EXCEPTIONALLY desirable estate of 4½ acres, wonderfully land-scaped, with every natural advantage fully developed, notable for its fine old trees, outcropping rock, sloping shaded lawns, choice shrubbery, attractive gardens and charming vistas. A rare Home in a perfect setting.

Elizabethan Mansion of stucco and timber construction, with spacious, well proportioned rooms, high ceilings, and beautifully furnished throughout with especially designed furniture and fabrics.

On first floor: entrance hall, large living room, music room, library, card room, dining room, breakfast room, sewing room, pantry and kitchen. Second floor: 8 master rooms, 4 baths, 2 sleeping porches. Third floor: 2 double rooms, 2 single rooms, bath. House in perfect condition throughout.

Garage for 4 cars with chauffeur's quarters overhead. Excellent tennis court.

For sale furnished and ready for occupancy at a price representing an excellent value.

PRINCE & RIPLEY	FISH & MARVIN	CHAUNCEY B. GRIFFIN
342 Madison Ave.	527 Fifth Ave.	18 E. 41st St.
Murray Hill 0555	Murray Hill 6526	Murray Hill 9336

FIGURE 7.2 An advertisement from *House & Garden* magazine in the early 1920s for the sale of a spacious suburban estate in a country setting in Scarsdale, New York. Along with many other amenities of the mansion and the grounds, the ad notes that the estate has a four-car garage that has living quarters for a chauffeur. (Author's collection.)

operations in places like Romania and Mexico. By 1930 Sadler had become vice president in charge of production and a company director, and six years later he earned a salary of $90,883 (the equivalent of $1.43 million today). In 1940 Sadler resided with his wife and sister-in-law in a house in Heathcote that had been valued at $110,000 at the time of the 1930 federal census, or about $1.44 million in current dollars. A further gauge of the Sadlers' privileged circumstances is that they had five servants living with them—a chauffeur, a maid, a waitress, a cook, and a gardener, along with the gardener's wife and child. The Sadlers' neighbors on Morris Lane consisted of a vice president of the Mutual Life Insurance Company, a real estate broker, and a stockbroker. They employed from one to four servants apiece.[109]

Murray Hill was a notch or two below Heathcote. Kenneth C. Hogate, an Indiana native who was president and later chairman of the board of Dow Jones & Company, the publisher of the *Wall Street Journal*, lived with his wife and three teenage daughters in Murray Hill and had two live-in servants, an African American couple who worked as chauffer and cook. The heads of nearby households included an insurance executive, the president of a sausage company, and a mining engineer. Most had one or two domestics.[110]

Overall, Scarsdale scored extremely high on indices of economic and educational achievement. In 1950 it had a median household income of $9,516, the highest of any municipality in the metropolitan region and well above that of other affluent Westchester County suburbs such as Larchmont ($5,115), Bronxville ($5,096), and Rye ($4,472). More than half of its residents who were in the labor force were categorized as managers, officials, and proprietors or as professional and technical workers. Males twenty-one years of age or older had completed sixteen years of school, on average, and females, almost thirteen years, both tops in the New York region.[111]

Residents of the elite suburbs replicated many social institutions that existed in New York City. By the early 1950s, there were chapters of the Junior League in Scarsdale and in five other Westchester County communities; of the Daughters of the British Empire and of the New England Society in Bronxville; and of the Daughters of the American Revolution in Scarsdale, Bronxville, and Larchmont. Bryn Mawr, Princeton, Mount Holyoke, and Barnard had alumni clubs in Westchester County, while the

Westchester County Cotillion had been founded in 1939 to provide a local venue where young women could be introduced to society.

Women led most of these institutions. With their husbands away for much of the day in their Manhattan offices, suburban women used non-profit organizations like the Junior League to raise money for the Red Cross, medical clinics, and college scholarships and to sponsor musical concerts, authors' luncheons, and flower shows that enlivened the local civic calendar. In so doing, they carved out their own space where they could exercise leadership responsibilities away from male control.[112]

Elite suburbanization completed the fracturing of the single, all-encompassing standard of social quality that had prevailed in the Gilded Age. Lucy Kavaler, a journalist who in 1960 wrote a discerning popular history of high society, caught this dynamic in quoting the explanation that one young woman gave for why she and her husband were leaving Manhattan: "I'm tired of being a nobody in the city. In the suburbs I'll be able to break into society."[113] Kavaler thought that this young woman, while being perhaps "a trifle optimistic" about her social prospects in suburbia, was "not indulging in idle dreams":[114]

> The base of society is broader in the suburbs than it is in the city. Family background is less important. . . . Income stretches further—in society terms. A family can keep up with the suburban Astors on a bank account that would not make even possible outer-circle life in the city. People are not automatically rejected because of an income based on salary, rather than capital, because of a single part-time maid instead of a retinue of servants.[115]

Life in Manhattan might be richer and more dazzling than in the upscale suburbs, but people in elite suburbs could shift back and forth between their local spheres and events in New York City when they chose. Thus, many debutantes opted to be presented at both the Westchester County Cotillion and at New York City galas like the Debutantes New Year's Ball, where a contingent from Westchester sat together at the same table. Or elite suburbanites could elect to remain on their own turf and develop close personal relationships in a more neighborly setting, even as they sustained lives of privilege and nourished feelings of superiority undiminished by comparisons to Manhattan blue bloods. Elite social space in the suburbs had broadened and blurred to the point that, as Kavaler grasped, it had become harder to delineate what was upper class from what was middle class. That let people define the sources of their distinction on their own terms; they felt more special rubbing shoulders with "suburban Astors" than with the real thing.[116]

Unlike corporate elites in the intermediate zone, the top-ranking and best-paid executives usually lived in Manhattan rather than in the suburbs.[117] Of the ninety-nine corporate leaders serving on the nine nonprofit boards explored earlier in this chapter who could be identified as having primary home addresses somewhere in the metropolitan region, 62 percent were situated in New York City, overwhelmingly on the Upper East Side.[118] The same was true of the New York foreign policy elite: James V. Forrestal, John Foster Dulles, his brother Allen W. Dulles, and John J. McCloy all lived on the Upper East Side.[119]

Corporate elites in the top zone had homes that differed markedly in their cost and aesthetics from the homes of those in the intermediate zone. This disparity was particularly evident when it came to the country houses that some eminent corporate leaders had in the metropolitan region. Magazine publisher Henry Luce and his wife Clare Boothe Luce, a former U.S. representative, owned an eleven-room apartment in River House, one of finest buildings on the Upper East Side, and a 7,200-acre plantation in South Carolina. In 1947 they bought an estate in Ridgefield, Connecticut, that included a twenty-eight-room house, tennis courts, a swimming pool, and stables. The property was situated in a glaciated landscape of rocky outcroppings, wooded hills, and streams and lay along a narrow and twisting rural road, a topography that gave the estate a rough and unfinished country feel while also protecting their privacy. A few years later, Arthur Hays and Iphigene Sulzberger, the publisher of the *New York Times* and his wife, bought an estate in Stamford, Connecticut, that had similar terrain—glaciated, rocky, wooded, with very narrow and winding roads that had no sidewalks. They named it Hillandale. A rock-strewn knoll and trees screened the compound from the road, and even today only a corner of a single building is visible from that vantage point. The estate centered on a sprawling sixteen-room, New England–style house that overlooked a stone patio and a small lake, to which the Sulzbergers added a six-car garage, a swimming pool and pool house, new roads, and footpaths. The Sulzbergers eventually expanded Hillandale to three hundred acres and, except for a belt around the dwellings that was landscaped, preserved most of it as forest.[120]

It took hardly any time to drive from the Luce or Sulzberger dwellings to Rye or Scarsdale, but nobody would have confused the aesthetic of their imposing country estates with that of the suburban residences owned by members of the corporate elite in the intermediate zone. Marvin and Pauline Pierce resided in a Georgian Colonial Revival house in the Indian Village subdivision of Rye, which had a rectilinear street grid to which the building lots and houses conformed. Houses fronted the street; driveways were short and straight; the streets had sidewalks; and plantings set off the houses rather than shielded them. Similarly, Arthur C. Gwynne's American Four-Square house, also in Rye, had been sited to correspond with the street plan and to be visible to the rest of the neighborhood. In Scarsdale, Everit J. Sadler owned a big, Mediterranean-style house with white stucco walls and a red tile roof that also adhered to the street grid. The Sadler property had been landscaped with trees, shrubs, and lawn to call attention to the house rather than to mask it.[121]

These houses in Rye and Scarsdale were large and attractive, but aesthetically they were a far cry from the upper-class estates.

COUNTRY CLUBS

Five days before Christmas 1941, sixteen-year-old Barbara Pierce, then a student at a finishing school in South Carolina, debuted at the Westchester Assembly dance that took place at the Scarsdale Country Club. A short while later she went to a dance at the Round Hill Country Club in Greenwich, Connecticut, where almost everyone in attendance was a student at a private school and most of the young women were debutantes, and a mutual friend introduced her to George H. W. Bush, a senior at Phillips Andover Academy. They met again the following night at a dance at the Apawamis Club in Rye, her family's country club, and began dating. Three years later, in January 1945, Barbara and George Bush held their wedding reception at Apawamis. Country clubs were the venue where this young couple entered a new stage of their lives.

Two decades earlier, a novelist had described the monumental clubhouse of a country club in an unnamed midwestern city as a "gray stucco symbol of the city's growing prosperity" and said that for its well-heeled members "this country club means success. It means leisure."[122] Like militias and men's clubs in the nineteenth century, country clubs gave elites a place to organize their lives, form a community, and legitimate themselves. Marvin Pierce won the member-guest invitational golf tournament of the Apawamis Club several times and Pauline Pierce represented it in county-wide golf tournaments. The Pierces regularly attended dances, cocktail parties, and dinners at Apawamis, and it was where Pauline Pierce hosted golf luncheons and garden club affairs for women in their set. Their children came of age there.[123]

Early country clubs were far different from the country clubs of the 1940s and 1950s that the Pierces knew. Country clubs arose in the 1880s and 1890s as part of the back-to-nature movement of upper- and upper-middle-class Americans who sought moral and emotional regeneration in the open air. These proto–country clubs were rural analogues to the men's clubs that constituted Club World; that is, they were socially exclusive places where the wealthy emulated the English landed gentry by adopting its outdoors sports such as fox hunting, golf, polo, tennis, cricket, and equestrianism. Golf was not yet paramount. Some were dedicated to golf (New Jersey's Essex County Country Club), but others to fox hunting and steeplechasing (like Long Island's Rockaway Hunt Club) and still others to hunting and polo (Long Island's Meadowbrook Hunt Club).[124]

The Tuxedo Club and the Baltusrol Golf Club are good examples of these proto–country clubs. Shortly after developing Tuxedo Park as a rural resort for high society in the Ramapo Mountains to the northwest of

New York City, Pierre Lorillard IV, in 1886, organized the Tuxedo Club to be a "woodland wilderness" where blue bloods could hunt, fish, ride, drive coaches, play tennis, hike, boat, and swim.[125] Hunting and fishing were initially the preferred activities, and Lorillard did not get around to constructing a golf course until six years later. Most of the "privileged few" who joined the Tuxedo Club at the outset belonged to the Union Club, as Lorillard himself did, and its membership also overlapped with the Four Hundred.[126] Most resided in Manhattan, and Lorillard built luxurious cottages where they could stay during their mountain interludes.[127]

In 1895 Louis Keller, the publisher of the *Social Register*, founded the Baltusrol Golf Club on property that he owned near Short Hills, New Jersey. Baltusrol drew from the cream of the *Social Register*: it included Beekmans, Bayards, De Forests, Schermerhorns, and Livingstons. Similar to the Tuxedo Club, Baltusrol was a bucolic resort that offered fine dining and formal dances as well as outdoor sports such as golf, squash, and tennis, and there were bungalows that members could rent on an annual basis.[128]

Between 1900 and 1920 country clubs evolved from being rural retreats of the urban upper class to become—like the Pierces' Apawamis—idiosyncratic suburban institutions that centered on golf and on the family. This transformation happened for two reasons. One was a golf craze. Golf first became popular in United States in the mid-1890s with social elites, but soon caught on with the general public and became the primary recreational activity of upper-middle-class and upper-class American men. In 1915 the *New York Times* estimated that somewhere between 2.5 and 3.5 million Americans had taken up the sport and that there were 112 courses located within fifty miles of New York City.[129] The second factor was that suburbanization gave country clubs a target population that was larger, more year-round, and more varied in income and status than the social elites who had frequented Tuxedo and Baltusrol. In 1924 there were 2,500 country clubs in the United States, including roughly 250 in the New York region.[130]

Country clubs became symbols of suburban affluence and conventionality, and their proliferation inspired both Sinclair Lewis and Booth Tarkington in their 1920s novels that satirized the provincial smugness of bourgeois American society.[131] However, like nineteenth-century elite militias and men's clubs, country clubs accommodated a broad range of class and ethnoreligious groups, running the gamut from highly exclusive clubs like Baltusrol to less selective and more modestly priced ones that served middle- and even working-class clienteles. As private institutions that borrowed their admissions procedures from elite men's clubs and that accepted new applicants only on the recommendation and approval of current members, country clubs replicated existing social groups. In Westchester County, Apawamis and Bonnie Briar were Protestant bastions; Century, Old Oaks, and Sunningdale were German Jewish; and Winged Foot, Irish American.[132]

Unlike the city clubs, country clubs were not all male. Men dominated their governance, and women and children were typically barred from golf courses and other athletic facilities at peak times, but country clubs catered to women and children as well as to men and, out of concern for institutional growth, took pains to build amenities like swimming pools, beach houses, tennis courts, and skating ponds that appealed to every member of the family. Men, women, and children could enjoy their own activities part of the time and come together at other times.[133]

Country clubs hosted civic events like women's clubs meetings, college alumni gatherings, corporate excursions, and golf tournaments, and social rituals such as debutante balls, vacation dances, and wedding receptions.[134] That, and their family-centeredness, made them important sites of community building, particularly for people on the boundary between the upper class and the middle class. Lucy Kavaler observed:

> The country club—and practically every suburb has one—provides a nucleus around which the top social group is formed. Its membership gives a ready-made list of the local elite, to be used by service leagues, community charities, dancing classes for children, debutante cotillions, and subscription dances for grownups.[135]

The key to the social geography of the forty to fifty first-tier country clubs in the metropolitan region was their multiplicity and localization.

Thus, while the Union Club, the Union League Club, and the Metropolitan Club had shared the same Manhattan neighborhood, country clubs were widely dispersed across the region. The decentralized physical geography of country clubs made for social ambiguity. Country clubs did compete with one another, especially if they were close to one another and recruited members from the same demographic pool, but their rivalries were diffused, and the regional dispersal of elite suburbs contributed to the segmentation of corporate elites into localized communities.[136]

Very few country clubs possessed enormous prestige that set them apart from the rest of the top tier. Two of the most fashionable in the region were the Piping Rock and the Creek Club, both situated in the old-money suburb of Locust Valley on the north shore of Long Island. Their grounds were unostentatious but their membership was decidedly posh.[137] A West Coast newspaper once declared Piping Rock to be among "the favorite haunts of the idle rich," while an insider's history of high society pronounced it one of the most "conspicuously fashionable country clubs" in America.[138] The roster of Piping Rock contained Old New Yorkers from the Astor, Delano, Goelet, Havemeyer, and Whitney families, along with a smattering of people from the top zone of the corporate elite, like Juan Trippe, chairman of the board of Pan American Airways, and corporate lawyers Paul D. Cravath, John Foster Dulles, and Allen Dulles. Like the best city clubs, the Piping Rock and the Creek kept their memberships small to preserve their intimacy and exclusivity.[139]

The membership of the Apawamis Club was decidedly more upper-middle class than upper class, and Marvin Pierce and Arthur C. Gwynne, both in the intermediate zone of the corporate elite, were typical of it.[140] Like the Creek and Piping Rock, however, the guiding spirit of the Apawamis Club was a kind of aggressive modesty. Its clubhouse resembled a rambling country house rather than an imposing structure, and members expressed pride in its lack of affectation and in having one of the oldest golf courses in the United States. An institutional history published in 1940 used phrases like "old and famous" (to illustrate members' opinions of the club) and "not pretentious, but comfortable and ample for our needs" (to describe the original golf course and clubhouse;

see figure 7.3).[141] In truth, these representations were more myth than reality: Apawamis had continually lengthened and improved its links until they bore little resemblance to the initial layout, and it substantially renovated and modernized the clubhouse in the late 1940s. With its squash courts, stables, tennis courts, a skating pond, and, after 1934, a beach house on Long Island Sound, Apawamis was among the most luxurious country clubs in the New York region.[142]

But Apawamis's members had their belief system, and they knew what they liked and what they disliked. As it happened, everything they disdained was embodied by the adjoining Westchester Country Club. It was largely a question of taste that determined whether people went to Apawamis or Westchester. If Apawamis embodied old-money values in its predilection for restraint and simplicity, the Westchester Country Club (figure 7.4) exemplified nouveau riche extravagance and flamboyance. Created in 1921 as a profit-making venture by a corporation that operated hotels around the world, its centerpiece was a huge eight-story,

FIGURE 7.3 A postcard of the "homey and unpretentious" clubhouse of the Apawamis Club, in Rye, New York, postmarked in 1911. (Author's collection.)

VIEW OF MAIN CLUB HOUSE TAKEN FROM NUMBER ONE FAIRWAY   WESTCHESTER COUNTRY CLUB, RYE, N. Y.

FIGURE 7.4 The large and ostentatious main clubhouse of the Westchester Country Club, as seen in this postcard from the 1920s. (Author's collection.)

four hundred–room main building that was modeled on resort hotels in Florida and the Caribbean. Ostentation was its watchword: the Westchester had two eighteen-hole golf courses, a dozen tennis courts, a polo field, a range for trap shooting, bridle paths, stables, and an ice-skating lake. The putting green was so large that a hundred people could practice at the same time, and the dining rooms seated 1,200. Boating and bathing facilities on nearby Long Island Sound included eight hundred bathhouses, a man-made lagoon for swimming and canoeing, a casino with a dance floor, and parking for seven hundred cars.

The Westchester Country Club was precisely what the Apawamis Club did not want to be: flashy, commercialized, and impersonal. In the late 1920s the Westchester Country Club had initiation fees of $1,000 (the equivalent of $12,700 today) for resident members and annual dues of $350 ($4,460 in current dollars). By contrast, in 1926 the Rumson Country Club in New Jersey had a $100 entrance fee and annual dues that started at $175 for members who were between twenty-one and thirty years of age and then increased to $250 for those over forty. In 1934 Apawamis charged resident members a $500 initiation fee and annual dues of $250, while years later Piping Rock had an initiation fee of $300 and annual dues of $350 for regular members. The Westchester Country Club was also very large: it had 1,904 regular members and a membership ceiling of 2,000 in 1929. In comparison, both Apawamis and Piping Rock allowed a maximum of 700 regular members, and the Rumson Country Club and the Pelham Country Club each had 250 regular members and 100 associate members. Rejecting the resort model that guided the Westchester, these country clubs opted for smaller sizes that would be conducive to close personal bonds and community spirit.[143]

Few people who belonged to Apawamis had the social stature to gain admission to the Creek or Piping Rock, but the established upper class was nevertheless the source of their taste for settings and behaviors that were modest and restrained and that downplayed materialism. Apawamis members were trying very hard indeed to appear as refined and prestigious as the Creek or Piping Rock members.

PREP SCHOOLS

By the 1940s the centrality of higher education to the modern economy of corporations and of professional and business services had made private schools important pipelines to select colleges and universities and training grounds of acceptable conduct. Prep schools significantly expanded their enrollments and improved their physical plants in the first half of the twentieth century.[144]

The *1940 Alumni Directory* of the Phillips Exeter Academy contained the names of more than one thousand current residents of the New York metropolitan area, including many from the elite suburbs.[145] These alumni represented a wide swath of upper-middle-class and upper-class society, and nearly all belonged in our second zone.[146]

Yet prominent prep schools had a distinct upper-class aura. A 1937 history of high society commended prep schools for nurturing "social Anglophilia"—meaning the customs and beliefs that upper-class Americans took from the English landed gentry to legitimate themselves and strengthen their claims to wealth, prestige, and power.[147] That association with the English landed gentry also increased their appeal for corporate elites, who, mimicking the social elite, sent their children to prestigious private schools in order to separate themselves from the ordinary middle class.

For their part, private school leaders insisted that college preparation was simply a by-product of a more fundamental mission, the inculcation of the prime Victorian virtue of character. In 1913, the *Bulletin of the Phillips Exeter Academy* explained that the school sought "to fit boys for life, whether in or out of college" and that its classrooms "place character above knowledge."[148]

The idea of character had strong religious and nationalistic underpinnings. Most of the earliest boy's boarding schools, such as St. Paul's and Phillips Exeter, were founded by men from old New England families who wanted to preserve the values of their Puritan heritage in a society that seemed to be becoming dangerously heterogeneous and commercial. Leaders of these schools associated moral corruption with cities and immigrants, and through daily chapels, tight schedules, stern discipline, athletics, and other means, they employed Protestant teachings to encourage their boys to develop self-control and denial.[149]

As part of the resurgence of nativism in the 1920s, leading universities invented a new admissions regime to enable them to accept the "right" students and exclude the "wrong" ones. Because the prevailing admissions system stressed academic achievement and employed entrance examinations that measured the knowledge and intellectual proficiency of the applicants, university leaders feared this system was no longer flexible enough for their needs. According to Jerome Karabel in *The Chosen: The Hidden History of Admission and Exclusion at Harvard, Yale, and Princeton*, "the top administrators of the Big Three (and of other leading private colleges, such as Columbia and Dartmouth) recognized that relying solely on any one factor—especially one that could be measured, like academic excellence—would deny them control over the composition of the freshman class."[150] Karabel tells us that these administrators wanted the freedom to admit the dull sons of important donors and alumni and to reject "the brilliant but unpolished children of immigrants, whose very presence prompted privileged young Anglo Saxon men—the probable leaders and donors of the future—to seek their education elsewhere."[151] That is where the idea of character came in; its great advantage was that it was subjective and easily manipulated. "To the gentlemen who ran Harvard, Yale, and Princeton," Karabel continues, and he might well have said, to the leaders of private schools that fed students to the Big Three, "'character' was shorthand for an entire ethos and way of being" that centered on the upper class.[152] The notion of character was thus saturated with class and ethnoracial prejudices.

Making character the fulcrum of a new admissions regime, college and university officials implemented procedures that permitted them to assess the social backgrounds of candidates and weed out undesirables, supplementing standardized tests with the use of personal interviews and recommendations and generating admissions forms that probed the national origins of applicants and inquired whether any members of their families had ever changed their surnames. Interviews and recommendations have become so embedded in American college admissions that by now almost nobody remembers the source of those mechanisms of exclusion: but Karabel reminds us that universities took them from private men's clubs.[153]

For boys, character entailed manliness, athleticism, leadership, resourcefulness, and personality, qualities that upper-class young men were thought to exemplify and immigrants to lack, especially the Eastern European Jews who were beginning to ace the college entrance exams. The classic expression of this masculine ideal is Owen Johnson's 1912 novel *Stover at Yale*, recounting the experiences of Dink Stover during his freshman year in New Haven. Although Stover had captained the football team and been the big man on campus his senior year at the Lawrenceville School, initially he has trouble adjusting to Yale because he does comprehend its social scene and falters in its intense rivalries. Eventually his prowess at football and wrestling helps him mature and become campus leader, and the recognition of his merit comes when he is tapped for Skull and Bones.[154]

Dink Stover is the quintessential all-American man who thrives on competition, but the competition is always athletic and social and never intellectual or academic. For males, athleticism loomed large in this belief system. A fourteen-year-old New Yorker who entered the prestigious Phillips Andover Academy in Massachusetts in 1935 soon realized that he lacked the attributes that mattered to his fellow students. "Most of the wealthier students valued social standing and money, which translated as being upper middle class and WASP; appearance, which included proper clothing and a handsome visage; and athletic prowess."[155] This student fell far short of the Stover ideal: he was Jewish, small in size, had little hand-to-eye coordination, a sparse wardrobe, and almost no money.

Plus he was a good student. *Stover at Yale* has only one extended reference to academics, and that involves Stover's befriending a studious freshman said to be "the shadow of a grind" who is physically small and bespectacled, has no friends, and—in case some dim reader could not divine the point the author was trying to make—wears pink pajamas. Their interactions have a powerful homoerotic undercurrent, with the effeminacy of the drudge setting off the rugged masculinity of the hero. Thus *Stover at Yale* disparages the very intelligence and academic tenacity that contributed to the career accomplishments of the corporate elites who were sending their sons to prep schools like Lawrenceville.[156]

Character figured as prominently in the education of upper-class girls. One exclusive Manhattan school pledged that its goal was "to send out young women who are well-educated, well-mannered and have well-developed characters."[157] For girls, character meant the Victorian ideals of poise and grace and led to curricula and activities heavy on art, elocution, music, home economics, and foreign languages.[158] A fashionable New York City day school told the parents of prospective students that it would instill in their daughters "elegancies of thought and manner" that would sandpaper away their juvenile "awkwardness and carelessness" and leave the "graceful smoothness, unobtrusive melody, and noble harmony of expression" that constituted "true womanhood."[159]

A few fashionable girls' schools, such as Rosemary Hall, in Connecticut, and Brearley, on the Upper East Side, had robust academic programs and took pains to shepherd their best graduates to demanding colleges like Vassar and Bryn Mawr. Yet most girls' schools in this period were little more than finishing schools.[160] A 1922 handbook of private schools accordingly praised Miss Chapin's School for having "won a clientele among the best families of the city, and [having achieved] a position of the highest social prestige."[161] Miss Chapin's drew its students from the likes of the Auchinclosses, Haights, Hoyts, and De Peysters.

The conventions of upper-class womanhood remained largely unchanged at the middle of the twentieth century. A 1936 alumnae register of 278 graduates of the Chapin School listed one movie star (Jane Wyatt), three physicians, two school teachers, a lawyer, a law student, and a medical student. Yet full-time occupations were the exception, and in their personal notes for the alumnae register the vast majority of Chapin graduates put highest priority on their marriages and whether they had borne children, and only then went on to mention personal interests like painting and traveling and volunteer work for the Junior League or the Red Cross. The old norm still held that you did not work for a living or support yourself if you were an upper-class woman.[162]

These prep schools perpetuated the Victorian value system that was used to legitimate upper-class ascendancy, but large numbers of their students came from families in the intermediate zone.

By the end of the 1940s, corporate elites were in a quandary. Their leadership of these massive organizations gave them income, status, and meaning, and they had constructed social spaces where they created their own way of life and their own communities. They were a distinctly American elite, insofar as their work ethic and dedication to moneymaking detached them from the European aristocratic model that had so influenced previous American upper classes. But their emergence also blurred the lines between the upper and middle classes. The social markers that hybrid elites used to distinguish themselves from the middle class were borrowed largely from the Gilded Age upper class and thus conveyed its disdain for career, individual achievement, and moneymaking, undermining their own legitimacy and identity.

Even more than their own spaces, corporate elites needed their own ideology.

8

THE ANTIELITIST ELITE

The 1970s and Beyond

FROM VICTORIAN TO MODERNIST CULTURE

C arolyn Estes, salutatorian of the Rye High School class of 1970, caught the magnitude of the cultural upheaval that was then occurring by proclaiming in her commencement address: "A glacier of tradition is breaking up. All the old certainties—organized religion, family life, patriotism—are being questioned."[1]

Glaciers do not dissolve overnight. The turmoil of the 1960s and 1970s constituted the point of maximum impact of a collision that had been in progress for decades, as a result of a shift from the entrenched Victorian belief system to a new modernist culture. As a rebellion against Victorian strictures, modernism had begun to emerge decades earlier, in the late nineteenth and early twentieth century, when Victorianism was at its height. Two early manifestations of it were the jazz craze of the 1910s and 1920s and the hipster persona of 1940s, both of which drew on the African American experience to test styles of emotional expressiveness and sexuality that flouted Victorianism. As early as the 1930s, modernism had become the dominant culture in the arts and in most intellectual circles. As the progressive reforms of John Dewey spread, it increasingly took over American education. In the 1940s and 1950s novelists William Burroughs and Jack Kerouac defied the established culture by advocating the liberating effects of spontaneity and raw experience.[2] The force of this conflict intensified once the new value system exploded into mass culture in the 1960s, when, according to Estes, youths from the "well-educated, well-informed part of society" who had been aroused by the civil rights and anti-war movements joined the revolt "against the old traditional values and institutions" and helped decimate the last remnants of that Victorian glacier.[3] Estes, whose father was senior vice president and general counsel for General Electric and whose family resided in one of the choicest neighborhoods in Rye and belonged to the Apawamis Club, declared that customary ways of being and feeling had come to seem dated and unacceptable.[4]

Modernist culture represented the antithesis of Victorianism. Where the Victorians had built barriers to protect upper- and middle-class society against people and behaviors they considered to be primitive, animalistic, carnal, or disreputable, modernists regarded almost all obstacles erected on the basis of social categories like race, ethnicity, and gender to be intolerable. They sought instead to integrate social groups and they extolled difference and diversity. Where the Victorians had trumpeted the importance of politeness, self-control, and bodily reserve, modernists admired the senses and the imagination, exhorting people to release themselves from artificial constraints and achieve their maximum fulfillment through personal experimentation and emotional liberation.[5] If innocence had been crucial for Victorianism, the new preference for experience led, among other departures, to sexual freedoms that were exemplified by the publication of Hugh M. Hefner's *Playboy* magazine, starting in 1953; the groundbreaking research in the physiology of human sexual response that William H. Masters and Virginia E. Johnson began in the late 1950s; and the appearance of the landmark *Our Bodies, Ourselves* about female health and sexuality in 1973.[6]

Scholars have long recognized that these cultural transformations encouraged African Americans, women, gays, the disabled, and others to use its meanings to demand fairer social arrangements. What has been less well understood is that these changes also had a profound effect on members of the upper class. For elites, the most important components of the shift in the conventional belief system were the growing mistrust of social divisions and the embrace of socially disadvantaged groups. The Victorian predilection for establishing hierarchies and for segregating the uncouth had coincided with the desire of the upper class to create barriers and impose social codes that confirmed its own exclusivity. By the 1970s the notion that some individuals or groups were inherently superior by dint of their greater wealth and breeding and hence deserving of special status and rewards had become abhorrent. That idea, of course, had been at the core of the Victorian upper class.[7]

The upper and middle classes thus went from being seen as the wellspring of social virtue in Victorian culture to being perceived as repressed, stuffy, and out of touch. Increasingly, many eager to challenge the status quo looked to marginal groups such as African Americans and workers for their inspiration. In the 1920s and 1930s jazz became the first art form from the American lower classes to be adopted by the white upper class. With its roots in poor African American society in the South, its emphasis on improvisation, and its associations with sexual abandon and emotional release, jazz appealed to upper- and middle-class whites who had grown dissatisfied with the formality and exactitude of the classical music tradition of the nineteenth century.[8] In 1929 a magazine lampooned the upper-class New Yorkers who frequented night clubs in Harlem to dance and hear jazz by remarking, "Society's latest fad is the negro."[9] Rock music would vastly increase the influence of lower-class music in the 1950s and 1960s for young people from privileged backgrounds.[10]

Grace Elizabeth Hale observes that a "romance of the outsider" began after World War II when middle-class whites came to believe that people on the periphery of American society possessed cultural and emotional capital that they felt was missing from their own lives.[11] Citing folk music, films like *The Wild One* (1953) and *Rebel Without a Cause* (1955), and the fiction of Jack Kerouac, Hale demonstrates that middle-class whites identified with outcasts as a way to free themselves from their own histories and achieve greater authenticity.[12] So, too, did many upper-class people.

Edward D. Berkowitz concludes that "a genuine rights revolution" swept the United States during the 1970s.[13] Inspired by the African American civil rights movement, women, gays, Native Americans, and people with disabilities viewed their own circumstances with fresh eyes, founding liberation movements that critiqued postwar society and demanding the right to participate fully in American life.[14] The rights revolution had a pronounced effect on elites in metropolitan New York. The public schools in the wealthy suburbs of Rye and Scarsdale added courses on race relations and on the environment and, at the urging of leaders of the local women's liberation movement, reviewed their curricula and programs to provide greater opportunities for female students.[15] On the Upper East Side, upper-class socialites held a charity gala at the town house of W. Averell Harriman that raised money for social programs for Native Americans, Eskimos, and Aleuts. In Midtown, a new private club that rejected the customs of Club World took shape. While it intended that its initiation fees and dues would match those of the best traditional men's clubs and planned to recruit its members from high corporate circles, it pledged to make civic responsibility and a youthful outlook its maxims and to include African Americans, Jews, members of other ethnic and racial minorities, and women.[16]

The pivot for the emergence of this new moral framework was the African American struggle (figure 8.1). In 1970, Rye's Christ Church, an affluent Episcopal congregation, sponsored a seminar on racism in suburbia that became the setting for a tense encounter between upper- and upper-middle-class whites from Rye and African Americans from poor Westchester County communities like Mount Vernon. The climax came when several African Americans charged that the wealth and power of Rye impeded the realization of racial equality and when a Black Panther advocated the use of "any means necessary" to obtain racial justice, even from the "barrel of a gun."[17] That this confrontation, in an exclusive suburb where the African American presence largely comprised domestic servants, happened at all was extraordinary.

There were other signs that social codes were changing. A week after Martin Luther King Jr. was assassinated in April 1968, a memorial service was held in his honor in Rye. As church bells tolled, more than three hundred clergymen, city officials, and others marched to the Rye Presbyterian Church, where Reverend William Guy, the pastor of a nearby Baptist church and the president of the local National Association for the Advancement of Colored People chapter, told the capacity crowd that the time had come for them to act. "Don't be purged by these services of tribute," Guy said. "Only in actively working can we make his message of

FIGURE 8.1 Martin Luther King Jr. speaking during an antiwar demonstration in New York City, 1967. (Library of Congress.)

life and non-violence a reality in our land."[18] Guy was telling these elites that they must look in the mirror and decide how they knew themselves, what they valued, and who they were. If they did not like what they saw in that mirror, he was directing them to make the required readjustments.

Guy's powerful message was reinforced in the years ahead. That fall, Julian Bond, a founding member and the longtime communications director of the Student Nonviolent Coordinating Committee, spoke at Scarsdale High School. The following spring, Harris Wofford, a friend and adviser of King's who had been an attorney for the U.S. Commission on Civil Rights in the 1950s, delivered the commencement address at Scarsdale High. Lectures and exhibits about African and African American art and concerts of African folk music occurred in Scarsdale and Rye and at nearby Sarah Lawrence College. About one hundred Scarsdale residents volunteered for a project that operated a tutoring program in Harlem and summer camps for underprivileged youths, while the Scarsdale Congregational Church organized high school students who taught reading to schoolchildren in East Harlem.[19]

A similar metamorphosis took place in upper-class sections of Manhattan. With Martin Luther King Jr.'s murder occurring just three days before Palm Sunday, a number of clergymen from upper-class congregations used their sermons to tie the martyrdom of the civil rights leader to the "unremitting toil and acceptance of suffering" of Jesus Christ on the cross, with the senior minister at the Madison Avenue Presbyterian Church hailing King as "a man in whom millions . . . could recognize the presence of Christ in our generation."[20] Madison Avenue and two other prestigious houses of worship on the Upper East Side donated their Good Friday offerings to the Southern Christian Leadership Conference. Temple Emanu-El, one of the most influential synagogues in the nation, held a half-hour memorial service in King's honor.

Some interactions across class and racial divides were farcical. In a famous 1970 *New York* magazine article, Tom Wolfe mocked a cocktail party that Leonard and Felicia Bernstein had thrown at their Park Avenue duplex to raise support and money for the legal defense of members of the Black Panther Party who were in attendance. Wolfe derided as "radical chic" this propensity of elite New Yorkers to socialize with militant radicals. Already Carter and Amanda Burden, heirs to the Vanderbilt and Standard Oil fortunes, respectively, had sponsored an event for Cesar Chavez and his United Farm Workers Union at their River House duplex, and benefits honoring grape workers and Native Americans activists had taken place in Southampton. The presence on these occasions of members of the Phipps, Rockefeller, Whitney, Harriman, and Ford families demonstrated the prominence of these social causes in the upper class.[21]

The 1960s and 1970s were a period of unusual alliances, reversals, and outcomes. Few elites entirely comprehended, far less accepted, the critiques of the more militant civil rights and other activists, but neither were they unmoved or unaffected by them. From lording it over commoners in the eighteenth century, to loathing the dangerous classes in the nineteenth century, many elite New Yorkers had come around to romanticizing African Americans and marginalized groups as exemplars of human spirit and social justice.[22] And elites had their own agenda. In espousing civil rights causes and tackling discrimination and poverty, in exposing the falseness and superficiality of genteel society, upper-class New Yorkers were creating performances of feeling and understanding that established their own heightened sensitivity as antielitists and attested to their legitimacy amid the social upheavals of the period. Their reinvention of themselves was in most cases genuine and heartfelt, but they did so above all to further their own pursuit of social prestige and moral authority.

This purge of entrenched values could be painful and confusing. During the 1974–1975 school year, a student who attended the posh Brearley School on the Upper East Side was pushed around and harassed by several students from a nearby public school. In an effort to confront the situation, an entire class met to discuss the matter and settle on a response. They agreed that placing guards on the street or having police officers walk the Brearley girls to their school would only breed more resentment on the part of African American students at Julia Richman, but they also worried that anyone who ran from further harassment would be scorned as a coward. Almost everyone in attendance at the meeting felt that the best course of action would be to open "some sort of communication with the students at Julia Richman" that would bring members of the two institutions together in the promotion of mutual harmony, perhaps through shared classes or after-school activities.[23] Whether or not anything came of this optimistic formula is unclear, but the misgivings that these Brearley students had about crossing class and racial lines and their defensiveness about their reputations for being "nice young ladies" from a "competitive, upper-middle class school" are palpable.[24]

Conflicts also arose inside Brearley between its white and African American students. An African American junior named Lynne Green wrote an article for the school newspaper in 1978 signaling her frustration with white liberals who claimed expertise on the black condition just because they had an African American friend, had read some books on the topic, or volunteered for antipoverty programs. She declared, "I am Black [and] you are White," and:

> You have an invincible wall erected against any black thought, any black plea, any black feeling. But you are masters of deceit and trickery. You have perfected this art to such an extent that you not only succeed in fooling yourself, but often you have succeeded in fooling us, too.[25]

Green told these white students to face the truth:

> It all comes back to the same thing anyway. The fault is yours. Yes, yours, the fault of every white person in America today, from the most obvious racist to the pretending liberal. Because you see, the system is WHITE. White constructed and white administered. If you will not do anything about it then the blacks must, in whatever way they can. So when the time comes, do not expect any sympathy, you will get exactly what you deserve. Black people have taken just about all they can take and they are not being fooled any more by your logical liberal lies.[26]

In an earlier article, Green had assailed the financial and social privileges of the majority of Brearley students: "Many black people hate you, and for very good reason . . . because of your position, your money, your ignorance of them."[27] Much as Reverend William Guy had done in his 1968 eulogy, though at an angrier pitch, Green was instructing her schoolmates to take a hard look at themselves: "I advise you to wake up, evaluate yourselves, and try to feel something for a change."[28]

This abrupt reorientation to promoting social justice and ensuring that everybody achieved their potential created a dilemma for elites who were guardians and beneficiaries of a status quo that was now found wanting. This new mind-set was already responsible for producing a vogue for sociological works that posited the existence of a cohesive and dominant ruling class that subverted democracy and oppressed other Americans. C. Wright Mills's *The Power Elite* (1956) and G. William Domhoff's *Who Rules America?* (1967) and *The Higher Circles* (1970) became standard college reading in this period and stimulated debate in newspapers and on television.

More tellingly, opposition to elite prerogatives also infiltrated the upper-class spaces of *Town & Country* magazine, the Junior League, and select preparatory schools and colleges, as many upper-class Americans began to question the extent of their privileges and the sources of their legitimacy.[29] How, some of them asked, could economic and social elites justify their wealth and power in a country that professed to be democratic and egalitarian, especially at a time of mounting concern about poverty and inequality? Could elites find sources of distinction and legitimacy that were more egalitarian? Were institutions like prep schools, Ivy League universities, and country clubs simply engines of prejudice and discrimination that facilitated upper-class control? Did elites contribute anything to the general welfare, or were they parasites who exploited the lower classes? Could elites and antielitism coexist?

To be sure, some upper-class New Yorkers rejected the new cultural meanings and actively defended institutions like private men's clubs and the *Social Register*. Their primary response consisted of erecting walls to shield themselves and their institutions from external scrutiny and of classifying condemnations of their practices as ill-mannered; thus, an upper class that over the course of the twentieth century had increasingly secluded itself wound up becoming all the more private. Yet other elites, especially corporate executives and professionals who were either on the periphery of or altogether outside the social elite, crafted a distinctive identity for themselves. In the last chapter we saw that executives and professionals were growing in numbers and wealth and establishing a way of life that was separate from that of social elites but that they had not yet forged their own identity or ideology. Now, drawing on modernist values, they started to define themselves as an assortment of individuals from diverse social backgrounds who had obtained their wealth and status through fair and open competition and as a reward for their hard work and accomplishments.

This understanding perpetuated the traditional civic and economic leadership of elites. It also built on the Horatio Alger myth of social mobility that corporate elites had come to stress in the wake of the Great Depression. But the weight it put on "privilege with responsibility" involved two new components that responded to the heightened need for legitimacy that had recently arisen.[30] First, these elites recast merit by applying it to individuals rather than to groups and by accentuating educational and professional achievements rather than inherent qualities like birth and breeding. Second, they positioned themselves as guarantors of fair and equitable treatment for members of disadvantaged groups, including women, African Americans, Latinos, and others. Later in this chapter we will see that ideas of individual merit and social diversity were malleable and would ultimately enable elites to better confirm their own standing and to pass it on to their offspring. Indeed, social reproduction—that is, the ability to transfer one's accumulated advantages on to one's children and grandchildren—would become a leading concern of corporate elites. Yet there is no question that these ideas were advanced by many in the 1960s and 1970s with genuine democratic zeal. Disassociating themselves from the legacy of the Gilded Age upper class, they would be an antielitist elite that would combat discrimination and suffering, span racial and gender divisions, and flatten status hierarchies, while also respecting cultural differences. Many upper- and upper-middle-class Americans wanted to hear that people who adopted antielitist values could remain or become elites, enjoy wealth, luxury, and position, and still be fair and equitable. It was crucial to their whole identity.

The priority that antielitists attached to merit was central to this shift. Achievement as calculated through educational and career accomplishments acquired enormous prestige in the financial and service economy that began to flourish in the mid-1980s and lost much of its antimaterialist taint. Unlike prior upper classes, members of the antielitist elite did not disdain moneymaking and saw wealth as a reward for merit.

The importance that the antielitist elite gave to achievement was closely related to a second tenet, its commitment to an ideal of class-lessness. From its origins in the early nineteenth century, a fundamental characteristic of the American middle class has been the belief that classes ought not to exist in the United States: class can be transcended and no one is locked into a certain class. This particular belief in a kind of classlessness, ironically, became a defining feature of this emerging new upper class. A conviction that they comprised a near-perfect meritocracy enabled professionals, corporate officials, and others to conceive of themselves as being a collection of disparate individuals who had attained their positions through their own efforts rather than as members of a coherent and self-conscious social group that used its cumulative advantages of wealth, status, and networks to reproduce itself.[31]

There was obviously something deeply incongruous about elites who subscribed to antielitism and denied the permanent reality of social classes, but these values accorded with American notions of democracy, equality, individualism, and social mobility. The values of the antielitist elite were also characteristically American in their professed belief in equality. Corporate elites were an economic elite that became an emerging new upper class. Their use of antielitism provided them with an ideology based on democratic and egalitarian values that they employed to legitimate themselves. They also had an idiosyncratic relationship to the middle class. Adopting a middle-class outlook as their basic identity, members of the antielitist elite became hybrids who were adept at moving back and forth between upper- and middle-class worlds, accommodating diversity and putting others at their ease in some instances, while at other times indulging in exclusive activities beyond the material reach of ordinary people.[32]

The formation of this hybrid elite hinged on a shift of the urban economy from manufacturing and commerce to finance and services. This transformation, which was initially poorly understood, involved wrenching economic and social changes that led many New Yorkers to suppose that their city was declining.

ON THE DECLINE?

After more than a century, the period of rapid population growth of New York City came to an end after World War II. The size of the urban population first steadied and then decreased as its suburbs enlarged and its manufacturing atrophied, and in the 1950s the population of the city fell 1.3 percent. Between 1970 and 1980 the number of its inhabitants dropped 10 percent.[33]

This development disconcerted New Yorkers who had long prided themselves on the economic and demographic expansion of their city. Many New Yorkers believed that their city was on the decline. In the late 1970s Edward Costikyan, an influential New York City politician, confided to U.S. Senator Daniel Patrick Moynihan that "the future looks grim" for the city and wrote a *New York Times* op-ed piece entitled "Gotham's Shrinking."[34] Scholars and journalists debated the causes of this degeneration, with conservatives typically blaming it on the liberal Wagner and Lindsay administrations for placating racial minorities with excessive transfer payments that drove up its debt, and with liberals and leftists faulting financial and real estate elites for displacing manufacturing industries and inflating property values. But although these experts disagreed about the sources of decline, almost nobody doubted that New York City was fading.[35]

A critical factor in the branding of New York City as an urban failure was the 1975 fiscal crisis, when the municipal government was unable to pay for its ballooning short-term debt and came close to defaulting on its bonds and entering bankruptcy. The federal government alone had the resources to avert a municipal bankruptcy, but President Gerald R. Ford had served nearly twenty-five years as a Congressman from Michigan and, harboring a deep-seated midwestern resentment of the metropolis, initially refused to provide federal funds for the municipality or guarantee its loans. Ford and his aides upbraided a spendthrift municipal government for expanding its social services beyond a sustainable level. As Republicans, they also had nothing to gain from rescuing a Democratic city and its Democratic officeholders.[36] In late November 1975, however, the federal government relented and extended a temporary line of credit to the State of New York that enabled it to supply seasonal financing to New York City, protecting short-term bondholders from loss and ending the threat of bankruptcy. Yet months of front-page newspaper stories and television broadcasts had rammed home the notion that profligate New York City was out of step with the American mainstream.[37]

Another crisis was that corporate headquarters were abandoning Manhattan. Major corporations could more easily relocate to suburban locations that offered larger and more economical accommodations, lower taxes, more stable workforces, less crime, and shorter commutes. Some corporations had begun to transfer their home offices to the periphery of the New York region, and by the end of the 1970s New York City's share of Fortune 500 headquarters slipped from 138 to fewer than 80.[38]

There were other reasons to think that New York City's best days lay in the past. The "Son of Sam" serial killer stalked the outer boroughs and terrified people there for more than a year in the mid-1970s, while in July 1977 a major blackout precipitated lootings and arson. In October 1977, President Jimmy Carter publicized his commitment to cities by traveling to the South Bronx and walking through empty lots covered with rubble from apartment buildings that had burned down. One site that Carter visited, Charlotte Street, became a national symbol of urban decline.[39] A week after Carter visited the South Bronx, ABC television cameras

THE ANTIELITIST ELITE | 313

broadcasting the second game of the 1977 World Series zoomed in on a vacant school building that was burning out of control about a dozen blocks from Yankee Stadium, and sportscaster Howard Cosell announced, "There it is, ladies and gentlemen, the Bronx is burning."[40]

Once celebrated as the preeminent U.S. seaport, financial center, and corporate headquarters, New York City had now become notorious for its high crime, concentrations of poverty, decaying neighborhoods, and dilapidated infrastructure, an understanding that received corroboration from popular movies such as *Fort Apache the Bronx* (1981) and *Escape from New York* (1981). To the long-standing idea that New York City was matchless for its wealth, grandeur, and refinement had been added a new belief that it was the prime urban disaster zone.[41]

However, amid the deterioration, New York City was undergoing two fundamental economic changes. In 1940 New York City had been the country's foremost manufacturer and its largest port as well as its financial center, but a transition from manufacturing and commerce to finance and services that had been underway for years solidified in subsequent decades.[42] After peaking at one million jobs in 1947, employment in manufacturing plummeted, until by 2000 the city had half the number of manufacturing jobs that it had had a century earlier. The port also deteriorated. From having been the busiest port (in terms of cargo tonnage) in the world in 1940, the port of New York and New Jersey fell to twenty-first place by 2007.[43]

But although New York City stagnated for several decades, its large and diversified economy experienced a surge in finance and in services that altered the distribution of employment and ultimately caused renewed prosperity. Total employment rose barely 2 percent from 1970 to 1990, yet in that interval the number of jobs in professional services increased by 54 percent; in business services by 24 percent; and in finance, insurance, and real estate by 18 percent. A milestone occurred in 1982 when the number of jobs in finance, insurance, and real estate exceeded those in manufacturing.[44]

There were fewer jobs in finance than there had been in manufacturing, but they were higher paying and had a larger multiplier effect. Closely related to finance were two other expanding sectors: professional services (accountants, lawyers, management consultants, etc.) and business services (employment agencies, travel planners, solid waste haulers, etc.). With these three sectors driving its economy forward, New York became more of a white-collar city. For elites, this restructuring was notable for making finance, in the past the most volatile and the most reviled part of the urban economy, the principal source of their wealth and power. As the national and urban economies boomed in the 1980s and 1990s, employment on Wall Street surged.[45]

Compensation for top businesspeople and professionals skyrocketed. In the late 1980s, the two best-paid chief executive officers in the metropolitan area—Richard L. Gelb of Bristol-Myers and Stephen J. Ross of Warner Communications—received total annual compensation (salary, bonus, stock options) of $14.1 million and $11.6 million, respectively. The twenty-five best-paid chief executives in the region took home an average of $3.6 million (the equivalent of $6.9 million today) that same year. In the 1980s and 1990s the starting salaries that major corporate law firms paid their first-year associates became a barometer for measuring corporate compensation generally. Cravath, Swaine & Moore was the trendsetter in the mid-1980s, raising its starting salaries 10 percent to $71,000 (equal to $148,000 in current dollars) in one year alone. Associates who made partner could expect to pull down $1.5 million or more.[46]

The second transformation involved changes to the American urban system. The ascendancy of the northeastern region of the United States ended in the second half of the twentieth century, as manufacturing centers like Pittsburgh and Detroit withered and as cities in other regions such as Atlanta, Houston, Phoenix, and San Diego surged, becoming hubs of information technology, aerospace, the military, and leisure activities. By 1990 only four of the ten largest cities—and none of the fastest-growing ones—were located in the northeast.[47]

New York City remained the primary economic center of the nation, but decentralization brought new urban rivalries. Because New York comprised a decreasing share of the U.S. population and was remote from the fastest-growing regions of the country, its manufacturers and retailers were at a disadvantage in serving national markets. And while the damage to the New York City corporate headquarters complex slowed after the 1970s, the enlargement of southern and western cities offered corporations more alternatives to Manhattan for their home office sites.[48]

Great wealth became more broadly dispersed. When *Forbes* magazine published its initial list of the four hundred wealthiest Americans in 1982, 21 percent of them lived in New York City.[49] By 2009, New York City's share had fallen to 14 percent. There were more people on the 2009 list from New York City than from any other single location, but the other leading places of residence were Dallas (4.2 percent), San Francisco (3.7 percent), Los Angeles (2.7 percent), and Fort Worth (2 percent).[50]

Some of the multimillionaire inhabitants of these flourishing Western and Southern cities had made their money in new industries like computer technology that had arisen in the Sunbelt, while others had achieved success in mature sectors such as retailing and investing that no longer had to be conducted from Manhattan. Unlike Carnegie, Rockefeller, and Frick, these moguls did not need to relocate to New York City to manage their businesses or lead cultured lives. Of the five richest people on the 2009 *Forbes* list, Bill Gates (Microsoft) could be found outside Seattle; Warren Buffett (Berkshire Hathaway investments) in Omaha; Lawrence Ellison (Oracle software) on the San Francisco peninsula; and Christy Walton and Jim C. Walton, beneficiaries of the Wal-Mart fortune, in Jackson, Wyoming, and Bentonville, Arkansas, respectively.[51]

Although the Forbes 400 still includes many extremely wealthy New Yorkers, New York City is no longer synonymous with vast individual wealth to the degree that it had been from the era of John Jacob Astor to the postwar period.[52] This wealth dispersal had one unexpected benefit: in an antielitist epoch, it let elite New Yorkers all more readily distance themselves from the Gilded Age heritage and think of themselves as middle class.[53]

In addition to this economic restructuring, the new social and cultural patterns of urban elites also reflected their embrace of antielitist values.

THE ANTIELITIST TURN

In the 1970s *Town & Country* magazine printed many articles faulting the upper class for its materialism and disparaging practices like debutante cotillions as old-fashioned and pretentious. *Town & Country* was an unlikely bomb-thrower. For more than a century, it had supplied stories about high society, fashion, the arts, and travel to an upper- and upper-middle-class readership. Moreover, *Town & Country* was published by the Hearst Corporation and closely controlled by the wealthy Hearst family. And yet at no other time in U.S. history has an upscale organ questioned the moral authority of the upper class to the extent that *Town & Country* did in the 1970s, a sure sign that the prevailing belief system was fragmenting.

Town & Country journalists like Cornelia K. Wyatt believed that cultural shifts had left upper-class people confused and frustrated. In 1970 Wyatt wrote that an upper class that venerated refinement, sophistication, and civility found itself at odds with a mass culture that craved experimentation and novelty. "While we claim for ourselves a highly refined sensibility, we find simultaneously that our world has become too gross, too confusing, and not in tune with these sensibilities" and feel trapped, as if "enveloped in a powerful, invisible wrapping."[54] Tired of Victorian codes that decreed circumspection and decorum, upper-class Americans, Wyatt contended, yearned for something "new, *in*, and capable of providing kicks."[55]

In another article Wyatt claimed that the current social turbulence had made wealthy Americans feel ashamed of themselves and said, "Let us characterize this era by its prevailing neurosis: guilt."[56] Even though upper-class Americans were "succeeding spectacularly in breaking out of [their] prison of old morality and endless Victorian worries about propriety," they had developed qualms about the extent of their wealth and privilege, the barrenness of their lives, and the wrongs committed against African Americans, Native Americans, and women.[57] Playing on the renowned depiction by Charles Dudley Warner and Mark Twain of the post–Civil War as the "Gilded Age," *Town & Country* titled Wyatt's piece "The 'Guilted' Age."

Psychologists told Wyatt that privileged people who had encountered little personal hardship were more susceptible to guilty feelings because they had never learned how to handle adversity. The unnamed director of a mental health clinic informed her that "those who have a real and nagging doubt about the nature of the comforts they've enjoyed in life" were predisposed to feeling remorseful.[58]

Wyatt stopped short of asking if the rich and wellborn felt guilty because they really *were* guilty. *Town & Country* had its limits, even in the 1970s, and was not prepared to contemplate the possibility that upper-class people were suffering remorse because they had finally awoken to the hardships they had inflicted on those not of their class. Instead, employing popular psychology to define guilt as a neurosis that caused mild personal distress but did not entail unacceptable or offensive behavior, Wyatt informed her readers that guilty feelings were irrational fantasies that had no basis in everyday reality. She deflected the new belief system even as she absorbed it.[59]

Town & Country writers were extremely critical of other rituals of the American upper class. A 1975 piece on genealogical societies deplored the snobbishness of patriotic hereditary organizations such as the Daughters of the American Revolution and the General Society of Mayflower Descendants, accusing elites who harbored "a too heady ancestral consciousness" of bigotry. The magazine voiced approval of just one ancestral society, the Descendants of the Illegitimate Sons and Daughters of the Kings of Britain, whose members cheekily called themselves the Royal Bastards.[60] When a spokesman explained that the Royal Bastards sought "to emphasize that what a man makes of himself is more important than who his parents or his remote ancestry may be," an approving *Town & Country* exclaimed, "Three cheers for the Royal Bastards!"[61]

Town & Country took the same line with respect to debutante balls. "I can't relate to debuts," seventeen-year-old Margaret Erhart, an Upper East Side resident who was descended from the founder of W. R. Grace & Company, told a *New York Times* reporter in 1970. "I don't even know anybody who's coming out."[62] Her family had been listed in the *Social Register* for decades and her grandmother, mother, and older sister had debuted, but Erhart, who planned to work on the Rosebud Indian Mission in South Dakota that summer, refused to do so. Many of her friends from socially prominent families felt the same way. Far from lamenting the declining attendance at debutante cotillions, a *Town & Country* journalist voiced admiration for young women like Erhart who were entering adulthood on their own terms, writing:

> They yearn to discover, connect, separate, and to control what there is to learn unimpeded by artificial timetables as to when they come of age and unbridled by gamelike rules and *comme il fauts* set down by perpetuators of convention from an elite society the young no longer feel the necessity to grace.[63]

Similarly, the magazine commended the New York chapter of the Junior League for attempting to shed its "prim and proper" reputation of being "nice young ladies doing nice things—from a safe distance."[64] As part of a new obligation for meaningful public service, prospective chapter members were now expected to take a five-month training course that dealt with welfare rights, methadone clinics, and court reform and featured field trips to rape crisis centers and police stations.

Further compounding the predicament of the upper class was the emergence of the idea, beginning in the 1940s, that the beliefs and behaviors of "average" Americans defined normality. This notion had multiple origins. The introduction of opinion polls had saturated the populace with information about the preferences of ordinary people, which then went from being descriptive of social reality to becoming an ideal that Americans tried to match. Consumerism's channeling of human desires into those that could be commodified also spawned greater cultural uniformity.[65] One historian has observed that the widespread availability of paperbacks, phonograph records, and television shows put postwar Americans in the incongruous position "of becoming more alike in the midst of a greater variety of cultural forms."[66]

Paradoxically, this rising sameness may have helped render the cultural goal of diversity more acceptable, by making people who were "different" seem less different. Yet normality also became a proscriptive category that people used to evaluate their behavior and that of others. This equation of "average" with "normal" significantly reduced the realm of behaviors and lifestyles deemed acceptable. Although this narrowing of social space affected Americans in general, the middle class had the huge advantage of being in step with the national democratic creed, while the upper class was by definition unusual, due to its small numbers and its wealth and the meanings its members attached to their own distinctiveness.[67]

The fullest expression of this sense of abnormality is a set of memoirs written by upper-class people who understand their way of life in terms of social pathologies.[68] Most of these memoirs were created in the 1990s or later, an indication that the antielitism that arose in the 1960s and 1970s had become embedded. Their prevalent theme of family deterioration is encapsulated by one book title—*Dead End Gene Pool* (2010).[69] Its author is Wendy Burden, the great-great-great-great granddaughter of Cornelius Vanderbilt. Rather than celebrating a privileged lifestyle, Burden exposes ugly truths that she believes lay concealed beneath the elegant and refined surface of the upper class. In particular, she describes episodes of "rich people behaving badly" because they had the money and influence to indulge their vices without having to worry about the consequences.[70] Ultimately, their extravagance did have costs: the death of Cornelius Vanderbilt from syphilis and the nervous breakdown and premature demise of her great-great-grandfather. Burden adds that her grandfather was an alcoholic and a drug addict; her father, a manic-depressive who killed himself; and her mother, a cold and distant woman who drank too much, became a compulsive adulterer, and neglected her children. Cut adrift after her father died and her mother rejected her, Burden recounts being foisted on her grandparents, shuffled to other relatives for lengthy periods, and sexually abused by two servants.[71]

Accounts of mental illness loom large in these memoirs. Philip Van Rensselaer carried an old and storied New York City surname, and although his branch of the family no longer had money, that was enough for him to move back and forth from the upper-class world of a deluxe suite in the Pierre Hotel, summers in Oyster Bay, and admission to

St. Paul's School to the jet-set whirl of the French Riviera. Yet in his family biography *Rich Was Better*, Van Rensselaer blames his unchecked hedonism and distorted upper-class values for causing him to attempt suicide and be committed to a mental hospital due to his alcoholism and bipolar disorder.[72]

Eve Pell's family owned much of what is now the Bronx and Westchester County in the seventeenth century, belonged to the Four Hundred in the late nineteenth century, and remain socially prominent today. In her 2009 memoir, Pell asserts that their dynastic wealth and privilege "brought with it a very close-minded ethos."[73] "We grew up feeling entitled and more deserving than others," an attitude that she now regards as "curiously un-American."[74]

> We took for granted a system antithetical to the American dream: instead of sons outdoing fathers through better education and diligent endeavor, fathers lived better than their children. Instead of ascending steadily into wealth and status, families like ours gently declined. Once-huge fortunes were divided among offspring who had progressively less money, fewer servants, smaller houses, and, by the time my generation came along, not even their own trust funds—we had to depend on our parents for handouts.[75]

Pell and the other upper-class memoirists regard moral and financial declension as family norms. When upper-class people who had burned through their inheritances proved incapable of competing academically and professionally with their more achievement-oriented contemporaries, the result could be downward mobility. Alexandra Aldrich, a direct descendant of the Astor dynasty, wrote in her own memoir that once the money was gone, the only thing left for members of her generation was their identity: "We live off the remains of our ancestral grandeur."[76]

Eve Pell acknowledges that she developed into "a snobbish foxhunting debutante who went to private schools, had maids to make my bed and do my laundry."[77] Over time, though, "the silver spoon to which I was born began to taste bad," and she discovered "that privilege can have corrosive effects on human relations" and that the "collateral damage" it caused her family included alcoholism and suicide.[78] Like the other memoirists, Pell rails against "the emotional walls behind which my social class lived its lives" and sees the severe emotional maladies of her relatives as the price her family has paid for its skewed values and snobbishness.[79]

Living in San Francisco in the late 1960s and early 1970s, Pell rebelled against her birthright by joining first the counterculture (she says that hearing the Grateful Dead perform at Golden Gate Park in 1967 was a decisive influence for her) and then leftist revolutionary circles. She had an affair, wrote for an underground newspaper, and befriended Black Panther leaders. Yet her activism left her leading a "double life," pulled in one direction by family comforts and relationships while simultaneously being repelled by the pomposity and bigotry of the upper class and enticed by the freedoms that were obtainable in the larger world.[80] She regards her confusion and ambivalence as a consequence of her anomalous place in the world.[81]

These memoirists identify the upper class with inauthenticity, emotional barrenness, and self-destructiveness, and several of them yearn for what they view as the normality of the middle class.[82] Their frank admissions of ruined lives and false values let the authors redeem themselves for their elitist sins, while allowing their readers to experience *Schadenfreude*.

RESPONDING TO ANTIELITISM

Institutions were not as malleable as individuals, and some that had their roots in the Victorian age had difficulty adjusting to these cultural transformations.

An example of an organization that has encountered tremendous friction is the Knickerbocker Greys, a military society that was established in 1881 to imbue boys with manly character through close-order drill and army discipline. The likes of the Harrimans, Rockefellers, Roosevelts, and Pells enlisted their sons in the corps, and as late as 1967 the Knickerbocker

Greys easily filled its complement of two hundred cadets and had a lengthy waiting list. However, after the Greys became a target of protests against the Vietnam War, its enrollments fell, and by 1979 it had only eighty-five members. When the Greys responded to this drop-off by recruiting from families on the margin of or outside the social elite, it lost its cachet. By 2007 the Greys were down to twenty-one cadets.[83]

Another vestige of the Gilded Age upper class that ran counter to modern America was the *Social Register*. From the start, of course, the *Social Register*'s very raison d'être had been to include and exclude. What happened in the 1960s and 1970s was that the grounds for some of these exclusions became intolerable, a verdict that the mainstream media delivered by putting the Social Register Association in the spotlight for actions judged to be prejudicial. In 1979, for instance, the *New York Times* pointed out that even though the two most common surnames in the Manhattan telephone directory were Smith and Cohen, there were more than six hundred Smiths and just one Cohen in the New York *Social Register*.

Rumors had spread in late 1962 that Robert L. Pierson, an Episcopalian priest, and his wife, Ann Clark Rockefeller Pierson, a daughter of Governor Nelson A. Rockefeller, were being dropped from the *Social Register* to punish Pierson for his arrest as a Freedom Rider in Mississippi. These rumors proved to be false: in reality, the couple had discontinued their own memberships after having fallen out of sympathy with the association. Yet the story of their banishment made sense in light of the snooty reputation of the *Social Register* and it stuck.

Besides, many such accounts were true. In 1969 newspapers reported that the *Social Register* had omitted Beryl G. Slocum, a former debutante who could trace her lineage back to Miles Standish and Roger Williams, from its next edition because of her recent marriage to Adam Clayton Powell III, a son and namesake of the African American congressman. Around this time, the *Social Register* also cut three other young women for marrying, respectively, a dentist, a state trooper, and a ski instructor. Their removal barely registered on the public antennae. Exclusion per se was not objectionable, but rather exclusions that clashed with basic modernist principles.

The Social Register Association reacted by insisting that it was a private organization that was answerable only to its members. In other words, it sought to erect a wall of privacy to shield its decisions and the lives of its members from scrutiny. Summoning its understanding of proper etiquette, it also treated breaches of its wall as rude and ill-mannered. That strategy has largely succeeded. Even in the 1970s, relatively few people appear to have cancelled their memberships, and by the mid-1980s denunciations of the *Social Register* were being made less frequently and less forcefully and had acquired a ritualistic air. Although the Social Register Association has been careful to maintain a low public profile, it has survived and indeed prospered because it provides a service that is in great demand. If the Knickerbocker Greys seem archaic nowadays, there are plenty of New Yorkers who covet the capacity of the *Social Register* to confer social capital on them.[84]

In 1984 the City of New York passed a law prohibiting discrimination on the basis of sex, race, religion, or national origin by private clubs that regularly received income from the rental of their facilities. The law aimed to force elite men's clubs to admit women as members. A few historically all-male clubs had already ended their exclusionary practices, including the Harvard, Yale, and Princeton Clubs, which did so because their parent universities went coeducational, and the Metropolitan Club, which was in financial trouble and needed the revenues that more members would bring. Most of the rest of the clubs loathed the new law and fought to overturn it in the state and federal courts, but in 1988 the Supreme Court of the United States affirmed the constitutionality of the measure, giving the municipal government the leverage it needed to compel changes in admissions practices. The Union League Club, the University Club, the New York Athletic Club, and the Century Association soon agreed to accept female members. To this day, however, the wealthiest and most exclusive clubs, including the Brook, Union, Knickerbocker, and Racquet and Tennis, remain all male. Their superior resources have let them forgo the facility rentals that would define them as public accommodations under the terms of the municipal law. Like the *Social Register*, they reacted to their altered environment by stressing the private dimension and fortifying their boundaries.[85]

The boards of trustees of Columbia University and New York University once bore a close resemblance to private men's clubs. The two boards have long been dominated by heavyweights in finance, corporate law, and manufacturing and represent amalgamations of immense economic and social power. In 1965 Columbia's twenty-four-person board embodied clubby Old New York, an all-male and mostly WASP bastion that had only three Jews and two Catholics. The NYU board of trustees was significantly more varied. In 1965 it had three women: Brooke Astor, the principal heir to the Astor family fortune; Mary W. Lasker, a philanthropist in the field of medical research; and Ruth L. Farkas, the wife of the owner of Alexander's department stores. Nearly a third of the thirty-nine NYU trustees were Jews, including the heads of the Lehman Brothers; Kuhn, Loeb; Lazard Frères; and Loeb, Rhoades investment banks. Aware that Jewish leaders were grossly underrepresented on the boards of almost every other major New York City nonprofit, NYU administrators seem to have tapped upper-class Jewish networks as a growth strategy that aided its subsequent resurgence.[86]

Because the two universities had civic missions and because their boards were a key part of their public faces, both boards augmented their social diversity. By 1980 half of NYU's trustees were Jewish. In 1980 Columbia's twenty-three-person board contained two women and at least seven Jews and six Catholics, a marked improvement over 1965. Each board included a single African American in 1980. The numbers of women and particularly African Americans remained small, but some members of the newly included groups were blue-chip businesspeople (and major donors) who were in a position to make their presence felt rather than simply be symbols. More to the point, the old social homogeneity had been fractured.[87]

Both the scope and the limitations of institutional adjustments to antielitism are acutely evident in the case of the Foxcroft School, a boarding school for girls from grades nine to twelve that is located forty miles west of Washington, D.C., in the heart of the Virginia fox-hunting country. Founded in 1914, by the late 1920s it enjoyed a reputation as the most fashionable girls' school in the United States. It was part of the social orbit of upper-class northerners.[88] Extraordinarily rich families—Rockefellers and Whitneys from New York, du Ponts from Delaware, Mellons from Pittsburgh, Firestones from Akron, McCormicks and Pattersons from Chicago—sent their daughters there to be "finished."[89]

Finishing schools like Foxcroft and its counterparts, Miss Porter's School and Miss Hall's School, sought to educate the "whole student" by providing instruction in the social graces and high culture and by instilling Victorian traits of character, integrity, and high moral purpose. Academics were not a priority, and many pupils pursued a course of study in arts and letters meant to prepare them for marriage. These girls either did not intend to go to college or else had their eyes on an exclusive women's junior college, like Pine Manor near Boston, where the goal was said to be "a ring by spring."[90]

Equestrian activities and fox hunting were also crucial to Foxcroft and its conception of itself. The sport fostered Anglophilia and linked it to qualities of the English gentry that upper-class Americans wished to emulate, notably the predilection for the countryside, the breeding and training of horses and hounds, the hunting of wild animals, the emphasis on ritual and competition, and the elaborate hierarchy of hunt officials. Although the European aristocracy had lost most of its allure for rich Americans after World War II, some upper-class people resisted this trend. Hanging onto a dying aristocratic world let them personify a social code whose very eclipse demonstrated its superiority to the vulgarity of everyday American life.

An archetypal Anglophile patrician was Paul Mellon, the scion of a Pittsburgh banking family who had studied at Oxford while his father, Andrew W. Mellon, served as U.S. ambassador to the Court of St. James. Paul Mellon had his clothes custom-made in London, was proud of being named honorary knight commander of the Order of the British Empire, and donated a center on British art to Yale University. He and his wife Bunny owned an estate ten miles from Foxcroft where they pursued the English pastimes of fox hunting and trail riding and filled their house with English paintings and French provincial furniture. Members of the du Pont family and Joan Irvine Smith of Irvine Ranch in California had mansions in the area, and Jackie Kennedy leased a four hundred–acre estate near Middleburg when she was in the White House so that she could go fox hunting.[91]

Mainstream modern American culture had come to revile virtually everything that Foxcroft embodied, and by the late 1960s the school had come to seem as out of touch as the Knickerbocker Greys. However, Foxcroft was in little danger of failing, since many wealthy families took a continued interest in "finishing" their daughters. In addition, the school had the newfound potential to become a genuine feeder for demanding colleges and universities now that higher education had become a priority for so many more young women.

Even so, it needed to adapt to the new climate of opinion if it was to thrive. In 1967, the board of trustees hired a new head of school, the first male to be named to that position, who proceeded to strengthen its academic program; abolish a tradition of military marching and drilling that had been thought to imbue the girls with discipline, team spirit, and good posture; and lessen the importance of horseback riding.[92]

Foxcroft administrators welcomed a *Town & Country* journalist to campus as a way to communicate their new direction to a magazine readership that overlapped with its recruitment pool. "Foxcroft has changed," Kathryn Livingston dutifully reported in her 1973 article. "Recent social and cultural upheavals have left their marks."[93] Aware that Foxcroft was "vulnerably image conscious" and that its "students and administration wince at words like *privileged, society,* [and] *finishing school*," she commended it for having gone "from emphasizing tea-pouring niceties to [offering] some beefy college preparatory courses such as calculus, honors English, [and] advanced history of art."[94]

"There's definite talk of careers here," said a student who had applied to Duke, Mount Holyoke, and William & Mary and was thinking of going on to law school. "Not too many of us are planning to be housewives."[95] But old traditions die hard, and the students Livingston interviewed had been selected to convey that aspiration and were atypical of the whole student body. Fifty-five of the fifty-nine members of the class of 1972 did pursue postsecondary education, but more matriculated at Pine Manor Junior College than at any one four-year institution, and the two favorite four-year colleges—the University of Denver and Rollins College—were known as party schools.[96] That pattern remains unchanged today.[97] At best, Foxcroft's attempt to rebrand itself is incomplete.

While Foxcroft has broken with the past with respect to the admission of African American and later Latina students, the consequences of its limited endowment and costly tuition are that the student body remains overwhelmingly well-off, socially exclusive, and white.[98] What changed during the antielitist turn is that understanding of what it meant to be part of the elite came to include academic and professional achievement and openness to social diversity. That has left Foxcroft performing a high-wire act, trying to adhere to meritocratic ideals that are authentically felt while continuing to serve many families that still admire the school's legacy of association with the landed gentry.[99]

Among private girls' schools, Brearley occupies the opposite end of the spectrum of academic rigor from Foxcroft. From its founding in 1884, Brearley set high academic standards, channeled many of its graduates to top colleges, and took pride in producing high achievers like Virginia Gildersleeve, a longtime dean of Barnard College, and Dorothy Schiff, the publisher of the *New York Post*.[100] During the 1970s it experienced strains over the changing role of women. In 1971 a graduate wrote the alumnae bulletin to lament that:

> Too often, reading the Alumnae Notes in the [Brearley] Bulletin, I find a sad progression from what *I'm* doing to what *my husband* is doing to what my *children* are doing to what my *grandchildren* are doing. Is it modesty or lack of self that prompts a woman to say "my husband's a lawyer at such-and-such firm, doing so-and so-, and I'm an architect?" Even if you're not doing as much as your husband and children, it's *you* I'm curious about: after all, I knew you, why should I care about them?[101]

In the 1970s Brearley introduced courses in African American, African, and Asian history, greatly strengthened its math and science offerings, and increased minority enrollments, while speakers at its student assemblies dealt with women's lives, New York City history, and social diversity.

Brearley would later solidify its antielitist position during the late 1990s, as alumnae of African American and Latina descent who had become doctors, lawyers, and businesswomen started getting together every year to reminisce about their experiences and to mentor current parents and students of color.[102]

A distinguishing feature of the antielitist elite has been its support of women's changing roles. Supporting the women's movement enabled upper-class women to take themselves seriously and to be taken seriously by others. It was a similar desire that had inspired their early twentieth-century counterparts to volunteer for the Junior League and the YWCA, but the opening of graduate schools and professional and corporate careers gave upper-class women greater control of their lives. Almost all of the memoirs about upper-class social pathologies discussed earlier in this chapter were written by women, and much of their discontent sprang from their pained awareness that girls had not mattered as much as boys had to their families and that they had been raised to be subservient, please men, and supply social embellishment. Several had experienced sexual abuse, which they attributed to the indifference with which their families regarded them.[103]

Second, favoring women's rights put elites on the good side of the rights revolution and enabled them to deflect accusations of being elitist even as they aided members of their own group. The African American civil rights movement may have constituted the moral core of antielitism, but hardly any African Americans belonged to the upper class, while the elimination of sex discrimination would benefit upper-class women directly and, in view of the cumulative advantages afforded by family wealth and social networks, disproportionately. That upper-class women increasingly eschewed the social sphere for the working world was another factor in the creation of the hybrid upper class.

Following the rash of antielitist articles that *Town & Country* published in the early 1970s, the magazine turned in the mid-1970s, with almost an audible sigh of relief, to celebrating the new educational and career possibilities for elite women. One article identified "A Law Career" as "The Road to Prestige, Riches & Power" and asked, "Should Your Daughter Go

to Law School?"[104] *Town & Country* also heralded the movement of privileged women from the "cushy 'social whirl'" of throwing parties and sitting
on nonprofit boards to pursuing well-compensated, full-time careers.[105]
Beyond the obvious appeal of having elite wives and daughters join elite
sons in achieving educational and career distinction and earning big salaries, the prospect of women's overcoming unfair barriers, being rewarded
for their accomplishments, and augmenting social diversity contributed to
ideals of classlessness and merit that were central to antielitism.[106]

For women and men alike, the main gateway into the hybrid upper
class was higher education. The experiences of the members of three generations of Zacharias family—John E. Zacharias, his son Tom, and his
two grandchildren, Clelia D. and John L.—demonstrate how prestigious
universities generate that mobility.

HIGHER EDUCATION AND THE ACCUMULATION
OF ADVANTAGE: ONE FAMILY'S STORY

In September 1932, seventeen-year-old John E. Zacharias entered
Princeton University as one of 673 members of the class of 1936. Zacharias came from more modest origins than most of his classmates. His
father, Johannes, was a native of Germany who had attended a technical college in Saxony before immigrating to the United States in 1900.
Three decades later, Johannes Zacharias was a supervisor of a New Jersey
worsted mill and his wife, also a German American, taught school. The
couple lived in Clifton, New Jersey, a middle-class suburb of industrial
Paterson, less than twenty miles outside of New York City, and John,
their only child, attended Clifton High School before transferring to
the private Newark Academy.[107]

With fewer families able to afford its tuition and fees during the
Great Depression and the admissions office having to reach deeper into
its recruitment pool than usual, Princeton officials in the 1930s worried
about the mediocre intellectual quality of admitted students. There is no

question that the class of 1936 was, as a whole, socially privileged. Eighty-one percent had gone to private schools. More than half of the freshmen who matriculated between 1928 and 1935 were the sons of bankers, brokers, lawyers, doctors, and business executives, and there were as many sons of U.S. senators and congressmen as there were of machinists and night watchmen.[108]

The member of Princeton class of 1936 who most personified the *Stover at Yale* paradigm of the all-American male who excelled athletically and socially was William Pepper Constable Jr. The Constables were a prominent Maryland family of judges and lawyers, and Pepper Constable's father was the founding senior partner of a major Baltimore law firm. At Princeton, Pepper Constable served as president of his class for his first three years, captained the undefeated football team as a senior, and won the highest award that a Princeton undergraduate can receive, the Pyne Honor Prize, for being the senior who best manifested the qualities of academic excellence, manly character, and leadership. As if that were not enough, his classmates voted him the most thorough gentleman, the best all-around man, the most respected, the most popular, and the handsomest.[109]

Pepper Constable also belonged to one of the "big four" eating clubs around which social life at Princeton revolved. Eating clubs were places where most upperclassmen took their meals and socialized. Princeton had eighteen eating clubs in the mid-1930s, but the big four—Constable's Cap & Gown Club as well as the Ivy Club (figure 8.2), the University Cottage Club, and Tiger Inn—were renowned for their exclusive memberships and fashionable buildings. Like the men's clubs of New York City and the final clubs of Harvard University, the Princeton club system was an instrument of social stratification and power that reified social hierarchies, bestowed marks of distinction upon the favored, and provided entrée into influential business and social networks. Clubs chose their new members during a student's sophomore year through an elaborate but murky selection process called "bicker" that comprised calls by club members on prospective invitees, interviews, secret rankings of the candidates, and finally bids. Club members would go to the dorm room of

FIGURE 8.2 A postcard of the Ivy Club, Princeton University, c. 1907. John L. Zacharias, who graduated from Princeton in 2011, served as president of the Ivy Club, the oldest and most prestigious of the university's eating clubs. (Author's collection.)

a prospective member and talk with him. Afterward, all of the members would meet to review the candidates and make their decisions. The *Daily Princetonian*, the student newspaper, then published a list that disclosed which students had been admitted to which clubs, making the identities of the winners and losers known to everyone.[110]

Unlike Pepper Constable, John E. Zacharias was not Princeton royalty. He majored in economics, never made the honor roll, managed the swimming team, and worked at a student sandwich shop to earn pocket money. His eating club, Dial Lodge, had a so-so reputation. The student newspaper mentioned his name fourteen times during his four years at Princeton, compared with more than 275 mentions for Pepper Constable.

Yet Zacharias made a mark of his own. After studying at the School of Business and the Law School of New York University and serving with the U.S. Navy (and winning two Bronze Stars) during World War II, he worked as an executive for a series of pharmaceutical companies, eventually becoming a vice president in charge of a major operating unit at McKesson & Robbins. In 1946 Zacharias married a young woman from an industrious German American family much like his own. Muriel Eckes's father had earned enough money as a partner in a small accounting firm in lower Manhattan to move his family from gritty Weehawken and West Hoboken to suburban West Orange, New Jersey, and to send his daughter to Smith College.[111] She later graduated from Yale Law School and practiced law in Connecticut, becoming "a real pioneer" and a mentor to younger women attorneys.[112]

John and Muriel Zacharias raised their two children in Wilton, Connecticut, an affluent suburb of New York City. Princeton had altered greatly by the time that their son Tom started his freshman year there in September 1972. Of the 8,488 students who sought admission to the class of 1976, Princeton accepted 1,991 (23 percent), a much higher degree of selectivity than in the era of Tom's father. Legacies like Tom Zacharias comprised 10 percent of all admitted students, also down markedly from the class of 1936, and prep school students accounted for just 36 percent of admitted students, compared with 81 percent for his father's class.

The most conspicuous change was that Princeton had gone coeducational three years earlier and women accounted for one of every three applicants accepted for admission in 1972. The student body was also more ethnically and racially diverse. In 1972, 11 percent of admitted students were African American, 3.7 percent were Asian American, and 2.3 percent were Puerto Rican or Cuban, while the abolition of anti-Semitic quotas had enlarged the Jewish student population. Although Princeton had become much more diverse, there were also some 1,100 people in Tom Zacharias's entering freshman class, making it nearly 40 percent larger than his father's had been.[113]

The 1970s were a volatile time at Princeton. Increased enrollments of women and minorities generated disputes over their representation in the student government and newspaper; the tenuring of female, African American, and Hispanic faculty; and invitations to outside speakers who were antagonistic toward the new student populations.[114] One of Tom Zacharias's classmates was a Puerto Rican woman from the Bronx who subsequently recalled that "this uneasy climate" had made minority students like her hyperconscious of how different they were "from the generations of Princetonians who had walked through Nassau Gate before us."[115] Sonia Sotomayor would graduate summa cum laude and Phi Beta Kappa and receive the same Pyne Honor Prize that Pepper Constable had won forty years earlier, and in 2009 would become the first Hispanic person to be appointed to the U.S. Supreme Court. Initially, however, she had struggled academically because she came from a poor family that had not supplied her with the cultural, social, and economic capital that other students enjoyed. Fortunately, Sotomayor realized early on that "many of the gaps in my knowledge and understanding were simply limits of class and cultural background, not lack of aptitude or application, as I'd feared" and persevered.[116]

A "battle over bicker" erupted in the 1970s, with accusations that the club system was racist and sexist and a formula for social homogeneity being met with equally fervent defenses that it promoted strong friendships and intellectual seriousness. The number of sophomores taking part in bicker fell to 33 percent in Tom Zacharias and Sonia Sotomayor's freshman year of 1972–1973, and there were seven fewer clubs in existence in the 1970s than there had been in the 1930s. Four of the eleven survivors had become nonselective, which meant that they chose their members via lottery. The single most divisive issue confronting the clubs involved coeducation and demands that they accept women. In 1990 a federal judge ended a fight over a sexual discrimination suit that had been brought eleven years earlier by ordering the last two all-male eating clubs, the Ivy Club and the Tiger Inn, to admit women.[117]

For his part, Tom Zacharias compiled a strong academic record, graduating magna cum laude in architecture and urban planning. He took an MBA from the Yale School of Management in 1979. Six years later, he married Clelia LeBoutillier, a vice president of a high-end beauty and fragrance corporation who was an alumna of the Madeira School in northern Virginia and of the University of Pennsylvania.

Clelia LeBoutillier brought enormous social capital to their marriage: she had been a debutante in New York City; her father had been the president of Paine, Webber; and her grandfather had been the president of the Bank of America and a founder of a respected Wall Street stockbrokerage firm. She had her own connection to Princeton in the person of her stepfather, Cheston Carey Jr., the president of a family-owned machine and supply company in Baltimore. At Princeton, Carey played on a national championship lacrosse team as an All-American defender, won election to Phi Beta Kappa, and belonged to the exclusive Ivy Club.[118]

Cheston Carey Jr. and his wife and her daughter were also in the *Social Register*. Nobody in the Zacharias family had ever belonged to it, but his marriage to Clelia LeBoutillier provided entrée, and the couple has been listed in the *Social Register* ever since.[119]

Russell Edwards, a society editor for the *New York Times* who was the longtime arbiter of its wedding section, observed around this time that "importance" was the criterion the newspaper employed to determine which engagement and marriage announcements it would publish from the hundreds it received.[120] And what qualified someone as important? Edwards explained that "importance" meant the education and professional achievements of the bride and the groom, the careers of their parents and grandparents, and the social prominence of their families.[121] Tom Zacharias and Clelia LeBoutillier possessed daunting educational, professional, and society credentials that easily met this standard, and the *New York Times* accordingly published their engagement and wedding announcements.[122]

Wedding notices have always touted the distinction of the couples being married and the families being joined, but the characteristics that are esteemed have changed over time. In an earlier chapter, we observed that the upper class of the late nineteenth and early twentieth centuries was preoccupied with its social credentials and boundaries, and wedding announcements of the period spoke to those concerns. Notices highlighted the pedigrees of the families and friends of the couple and whenever possible associated them with VIPs like the Astors, Vanderbilts, Rhinelanders, and Van Rensselaers.[123]

Turn-of-the-twentieth-century announcements devalued employment and education. Occasionally they supplied the occupations of the participants, but usually little or nothing was said about work or business. Notices generally did not reveal where (or if) the betrothed had gone to college, and when they did supply that intelligence it was to place the bride or groom within a small circle of eminent friends and acquaintances.[124]

By the 1940s notices had come to identify couples' parents and grandparents, where they grew up, where they went to prep school and college, where the bride had debuted, where they planned to live, and so forth. Virtually every notice detailed the colleges (and often the prep schools) that the bride and groom had attended, but while there was enormous prestige attached to going to Yale, Harvard, Vassar, and Smith, the stress was on the school's cachet rather than on a person's course of study or academic accomplishments.[125]

Many announcements from the 1940s said nothing at all about work, and those that mentioned it did so off-handedly, as if to signal that these were sophisticated individuals who did not need to prove their bona fides and were not consumed by their jobs. The stature of a father who was "with the Title Guarantee and Trust Company" and of a groom who was "a partner in the New York Stock Exchange firm of Smith & Gallatin" was assumed.[126] The old standard held that you truly belonged to the aristocracy *only* if you did not need to work or earn money. You could do those things, if you so chose, but you needed everyone to understand that you did not *have* to.[127]

However, by the time that the Zachariases married, wedding and engagement notices were packed with information about the professional and academic achievements of the betrothed and their families. Here, from 1981, is the *New York Times*'s announcement of the engagement of Harriet Lynn Myers of Madison, Connecticut, to William Henniger Brooks of Wayne, New Jersey:

> Miss Myers, who is known as Holly, is with the legal department of the Children's Defense Fund in Washington. She expects to receive a master's degree in social-service administration next month from Case Western Reserve University, where she graduated from the Law School. She is an alumna also of Smith College and studied during her junior

year at the University of London. Her father is president of Quantum Inc., a Wallingford, Conn. manufacturer of composite structures for the aerospace industry.

Mr. Brooks is managing partner of Hyatt Legal Services, a multistate law firm with offices in Kansas City, Mo., and vice president and treasurer of the Block Management Company, a subsidiary of H&R Block, the tax specialist concern, also of Kansas City. He graduated from Dartmouth College and its Amos Tuck School of Business Administration and from the University of Michigan Law School. He was formerly an associate with Shanley & Fisher, a Newark law concern. His father is a retired vice president of the New York Life Insurance Company in New York.[128]

Notices frequently referred to the groom and bride's profession or business in their headlines:

"Bruce Lynn, a Financial Analyst, to Wed Ann Elizabeth Kantor."[129]

"Martha B. Gerson, a Lawyer, to Marry Charles F. Lufkin, Investment Banker"[130]

"Dr. Anne Allan to Wed Dr. S. N. Wilson."[131]

In short, wedding announcements had become résumés. Descriptions of a family's ancestry or a bride's debut and references to a distant relative's high public office or military rank did not disappear, but they lessened as the *Times* and other newspapers concentrated on the educational, professional, and business matters that elites in the New York region (and elsewhere) had come to esteem.[132] Thus, the *Times* reported that a 1985 bride was a product of Princeton Day School, Williams College, and the Amos Tuck School of Business Administration at Dartmouth College and worked at Morgan Stanley and that her husband, an associate with First Boston, had graduated from Phillips Academy, the University of Pennsylvania, and Amos Tuck.[133]

The prestigious schools and imposing professional and business positions of the hybrid upper class attested to their personal superiority, which in turn underscored the extent to which they warranted their material comforts and social status. With the importance that these announcements placed on individual attainments akin to résumés bristling with honors and awards, they conveyed the impression that this hybrid upper class was almost entirely self-replicating. If nobody succeeded who did not deserve to succeed and if their success rested on family endeavors, then wedding notices could provide little evidence of social mobility. People resorted to ambiguous wording (one father was said to be "with the Postal Service in Jamaica, Queens") and euphemistic job titles (like "marketing consultant") that prettified modest occupations in order to create a fiction of solid multigenerational achievement.[134] Such artfulness kept the boundaries between the upper-middle class and the upper-class fluid, and the revelation that the father of one bridegroom was a telephone repairman and that the father of another bride ran a cocktail lounge were like small, forlorn islands adrift in a sea of prosperity.[135]

The Zachariases, on the other hand, epitomized hereditary meritocracy. Prior to his marriage, Tom Zacharias had begun a career in New York City's financial sector. The reinvigorated and restructured metropolitan economy functioned like an elevator in lifting people to new heights, yet few people had the acumen to ride it as high as Tom Zacharias did. Early on, Zacharias became a specialist in real estate finance and investment, rising from a long stint as a senior officer at a real estate–investment concern to become a principal at a global real estate–investment management company and then a senior vice president of a real estate–investment unit of Morgan Stanley. In 2002 he moved to a real estate–investment firm in midtown Manhattan that has more than $10 billion in assets, and three years later he became its chief operating officer. His total annual compensation can exceed $2 million.[136] Zacharias achieved this success through his intelligence, leadership skills, and, above all, hard work. "We spend more time in the office than any other place in our lives—at least some of us do," he once said.[137] That level of professional and business commitment was characteristic of the hybrid upper class.

Tom and Clelia Zacharias's residencies reflect their ascendancy into some of the traditional sites of the upper class: they live on Fifth Avenue and have a summer house in Southampton and a penthouse on the waterfront in West Palm Beach. They entered high society through her family history, his involvement in the governance of the Museum of Modern Art and the Whitney Museum, and their presence at benefits for Memorial Sloan-Kettering and the Southampton Garden Club. They belonged to Southampton's select Meadow Club. Tom Zacharias has been a director of the National Academy of Design and a trustee of the Groton School, which his children, Clelia D. and John L., both attended before following him and their grandfather and step-grandfather to Princeton.[138]

Like her grandfather, Clelia Zacharias majored in economics at Princeton. She took a job in Manhattan in the financial industry after her graduation in 2008, as did her brother three years later. At Princeton, John L. Zacharias rowed on the men's heavyweight crew and won a prize for writing the best senior thesis in the politics department. He was also the president of the Ivy Club, the oldest, most patrician, and costliest eating club and the same one that his step-grandfather had joined. John L. Zacharias accomplished academic, athletic, and social mastery and was a campus star. He may have borne his grandfather's name, but in effect he had become Pepper Constable. This is a perfect example of how social and economic capital accrue over time and how social power is exercised in the hereditary meritocracy.[139]

In three generations, making the most of their admirable work ethic, intelligence, and family bonds and leveraging their wealth and networks, the Zachariases had reached New York City's economic and social elite. Princeton had enabled John E. Zacharias to join the upper-middle class, his son to rise to the highest echelon of the New York City business world, and his grandchildren to replicate their parents' station and perhaps in time to better it. Princeton was where their advantages accumulated, where they made important social and business connections, and where they trained for professional school and the financial industry. It was the point of entry for the Zacharias family into a hybrid upper class that differentiates itself from its late nineteenth and early twentieth-century predecessor above all through the meaning it attaches to career.

Leading colleges and universities had acquired a new primary function as vehicles of social mobility and social reproduction, channeling their students into graduate schools and business, a process that involved competition at almost every step along the way. In a memoir published posthumously in 2010, Louis Auchincloss expressed amazement at how competitive the college experience had become. Born in 1917 into a wealthy old New York family, Auchincloss had studied at a private boy's school on Fifth Avenue and at Groton before entering Yale in 1935. Auchincloss recalled that:

> It was not until law school that the concept of competition entered my life. Admission to Yale had been easy and in those days cost my parents little. Like most of my friends I took the whole college business for granted. None of us really went to work until professional school or a first job. Then we did.[140]

Actually, Auchincloss, his friends, relatives, and acquaintances *had* vied in the social and athletic realms; indeed, their popularity or unpopularity with their peers had reflected their social and athletic prowess.[141] What astounded Auchincloss was that the hybrid upper class also competed over college admissions, grades, academic honors, internships, and so forth.

A notable symptom of this heightened academic competitiveness is the so-called kindergarten madness that New York City families undergo in trying to enroll their young children in the most prestigious private schools.[142] That decisions about the admission of four- to six-year-olds should be a source of parental anxiety may seem bizarre, but it has an awful logic: because kindergarten is the entry point for independent schools that have primary and secondary grades, getting your child into the right institution for kindergarten means that he or she will be there when the time comes to apply to Harvard and Princeton. Well-to-do parents groom their four-year-olds for the all-important standardized admissions test via preparations like tutoring, weekend camps, and workbooks that can total more than $1,000, far beyond the means of middle-class families. Because this coaching takes place more or less sub rosa, the reliance on standardized tests creates the illusion that admissions decisions are being made solely on the basis of cognitive merit, whereas family wealth is the decisive factor. We have observed that members of previous upper classes also attached great significance to social reproduction and manipulated markers such as gentility, networks, and genealogy to achieve the desired results. Yet the tremendous weight that the emergent professional and service economy put on career gave social reproduction new urgency beginning in the 1970s: efforts to skew the outcome of standardized tests (and similar measures) occurred because admission to the best colleges and entry into the most prestigious firms had become vital and was difficult to control.[143]

Today colleges and universities serve both as conduits to lucrative positions in professions and business and as teachers of social values. To the extent that they reproduce established elites, they cannot serve as agents of class mobility, and here the weight that antielitist elites put on achievement conflicts with their other goal of advancing social diversity. As Jerome Karabel recounts in *The Chosen*, the student bodies of the Big Three universities have undergone a dramatic demographic transformation since the 1960s and 1970s and are no longer the near-exclusive preserve of white, Anglo-Saxon, Protestant, and mostly upper-class men from New England and the Middle Atlantic states. In 2000 nonwhites constituted a third of the first-year class at Harvard, with Asian Americans making up half of that number, and women made up almost half of the students at Harvard. A century earlier, Jews had accounted for 7 percent of the freshman class at Harvard; by 2000 they represented more than 20 percent.[144]

"The transformation of Harvard, Yale, and Princeton from enclaves of the Protestant upper class," Karabel writes, "into institutions with a striking degree of racial, ethnic, and religious diversity was by any means historic."[145] That is not the whole story, however. "Yet," he elaborates, "beneath this dramatic and highly visible change in the physiognomy of the student body was a surprising degree of stability in one crucial regard—the privileged class origins of students in the Big Three."[146] At all three universities, a majority of undergraduates managed to pay their tuition and fees without financial aid—"compelling testimony that, more than thirty years after the introduction of need-blind admissions, the Big Three continued to draw most of their students from the most affluent segments of American society."[147]

Social scientists have discovered that the gap between the educational achievements of children of high-income families and those of middle- and low-income families has widened appreciably in the last few decades. The children of the rich have always performed better academically than the children of poor families, but that differential—as gauged by scores on SAT-type tests, rates of college completion, admission to selective colleges, participation in sports and extracurricular activities, and so forth—has grown since the 1970s and now exceeds the gap between whites and blacks. One sociologist concludes that:

> Before 1980, affluent students had little advantage over middle-class students in academic performance; most of the socioeconomic disparity in academics was between the middle class and the poor. But the rich now outperform the middle class by as much as the middle class outperform the poor.[148]

Most scholars attribute this crucial development mainly to wealthy parents investing more of their money, time, knowledge, and connections in the cognitive development and educational accomplishments of their children. While the incomes of the affluent have increased faster than those of the middle class, these scholars report that the key is not that the rich have more money to spend but instead that they are using their resources differently than their predecessors did. Wealthy parents today invest in the educational success of their children—via prekindergarten tutoring, language camps, internships, and preparation for the SATs—to improve their offspring's chances of entering the best universities and securing jobs that have a status and an earning potential that are similar to theirs.[149]

The experience of the Zacharias family demonstrates why cognitive development has become a coveted form of cultural capital; their investments in it has had handsome yields.

SOCIAL MARKERS OF THE HYBRID UPPER CLASS

In recent decades the distribution of wealth and income has grown increasingly unequal in New York City as well as in the nation as a whole. Members of the hybrid upper class are producers and beneficiaries of this development.

A study by the Federal Reserve Bank of Minneapolis reveals "a large and steady increase in wage inequality between 1967 and 2006" that has created rising disparities of consumption and wealth.[150] Economist Edward N. Wolff concludes that from 1983 to 2007 the top 1 percent of the U.S. population (in terms of wealth) received 35 percent of the expansion of net worth and 44 percent of the expansion of income, and that the top 20 percent pocketed 89 percent of the gains in net worth and 87 percent of those in income.[151] According to Joseph E. Stiglitz, the gap between the compensation of chief executive officers and that of the typical worker stood at 243 to 1 in 2010. A quarter-century earlier, it had been 30 to 1.[152]

The reality of this rising inequality must also be seen in light of the meanings and uses that the hybrid upper class gave it. By the 1970s and 1980s the withering of the European aristocracy and its code of gentility had eradicated the old taboo against moneymaking, a development that allowed the hybrid upper class to employ money as its principal means for distinguishing itself from the middle class. Hybrids could utilize their money to buy luxurious goods and services and form a distinctive way of life for themselves, while continuing to think of and present themselves as culturally middle class. Because they viewed wealth chiefly as a reward for their superior individual professional and business achievements, these uses were acceptable under antielitist tenets. Money was also important because it let people present themselves in some settings and situations as middle class and in other settings as elites, a behavioral trait that was essential to their hybridity.[153]

The problem with wealth was no longer its possession but rather its use. You could use your wealth to obtain greater ease and comfort for yourself and your family and to enhance the development of your children. However, you should not wield it to establish your superiority through displays of family ancestry or other elitist behaviors and above all you must not use it to deprive others of justice and dignity. Instead, you ought to employ it to build a better society, either through entrepreneurialism, creative expression, or community service. Old-style charities were now thought to be paternalistic and hierarchical and to inhibit the realization of social justice, but riches spent to empower people by letting them improve the quality of their own lives performed an invaluable public service. John W. Kluge, founder of Metromedia, donated almost a half billion dollars to Columbia University, mainly for scholarships for needy and minority students, while Joseph H. Flom, a specialist in mergers and acquisitions and a named partner at Skadden, Arps, Slate, Meagher & Flom, pledged to cover the college tuition for a class of Harlem sixth graders and established a fellowship program to support recent law school graduates doing public interest law. Corporations have increasingly taken a direct hand in philanthropy: Goldman Sachs recently contributed $2 million to a community college in Queens.[154]

As with previous upper classes, hybrids put great emphasis on their houses. As the metropolitan economy recovered, housing markets that had been in the doldrums for more than a decade began to improve, with apartments on the Upper East Side, single-family homes in wealthy suburbs, and summer houses in the Hamptons sustaining notably high increases.[155] The hybrid upper class had a specific residential aesthetic. They spearheaded the gentrification of brownstone neighborhoods (figure 8.3) that had once been solidly middle class but that then had fallen out of favor and deteriorated, like the Upper West Side of Manhattan and Brooklyn Heights and Park Slope in Brooklyn, and of formerly industrial areas like SoHo and Tribeca in lower Manhattan. Real estate in these areas was generally cheaper than on the Upper

FIGURE 8.3 A brownstone at 236 St. John's Place, in the Park Slope district of Brooklyn, photographed in the mid-1980s. (New York City Municipal Archives.)

East Side, plus it had a gritty street appeal that was highly desirable in modern New York City.[156] The historian of brownstone Brooklyn credits the young white-collar professionals who led this movement for undertaking a cultural revolt against what they regarded as the sameness and bureaucracy of conventional American cities and suburbs and for thinking that the old age and social diversity of run-down neighborhoods harbored an authenticity and a community spirit that the rest of the city lacked. However, the gentrifiers often encountered racial and class conflicts with the working-class residents of these neighborhoods, and their insistence on the universality of liberal values and their championing of increased spending for public schools and the importance of mixed land uses could be paternalistic and elitist.[157]

As wealth and income gaps widened, other cultural tastes became purchasable commodities. In the mid-1990s, premium fitness clubs that saved their clients the time and aggravation of having to compete with other people for machines charged about $1,200 to join, plus annual fees that ranged from $700 to $1,200 and extra for services like massages and personal training.[158] Custom-made men's suits from the best tailors went for $3,000, while Beau Brummel, a high-end men's store, offered fashion-forward ready-to-wear suits for about $1,500, almost double the price of an ordinary Brooks Brothers sack suit.[159]

Insight into the significance of wealth to New York City's hybrids can be obtained by considering the experiences of Susan Aurelia Gitelson, a native New Yorker who graduated from Barnard College in 1963, received a PhD in international affairs from Columbia University, and became the proprietor of a company that manufactured housewares. In 1981 Gitelson began to record her thoughts and feelings in a multivolume journal that is the most extensive unpublished diary to be kept by an affluent New Yorker during the 1980s and 1990s and made available to researchers.

Wealth is a critical element in Gitelson's understanding of success. "I am enjoying the upper middle class life my father did—& led me to expect," she wrote in a 1983 entry. "If an opportunity arises to enter the upper classes, I shall not mind—but I cannot expect this."[160] Her use of the plural "upper classes" is telling. In part because she was primarily oriented to academic and business accomplishment and in part because she was Jewish and upper-middle class and detached from the *Social Register* crowd, Gitelson took no interest in the social elite. She lived on the Upper East Side but neither belonged to the *Social Register* nor paid any attention to it.[161] As with nineteenth-century New York City elites, the social elite and the hybrid elite shared and competed, interacted and separated. Gitelson believed that wealth would suffice to catapult her into the elite, and her phrase the "upper classes" signified her confidence that space up there would be available to her if she could earn enough money. "I used to imagine life at the top . . . but [without] know[ing] how to get there," she wrote. "Now intermediate steps are clearer."[162] By the time that her annual income had reached $50,000 in 1984, Gitelson expressed pride that "in contemporary terms I have reached 'success.'"[163] By 2000 her total annual income from salary and stocks exceeded $450,000 and she was worth $2 million.[164]

Although Gitelson sought wealth openly and avidly, wealth was not all she wanted and she did not seek it unconditionally. If she were to become very rich, she fantasized that she might be elected a trustee of Columbia University, the New York Public Library, or the Metropolitan Museum; be named to the Council on Foreign Relations; or become a patron of the opera and the ballet. In other words, wealth would confer great social and cultural capital, and the opportunities it would provide for civic leadership, philanthropy, and international travel were what she most cared about. By her own estimation, Gitelson never realized her goal of entering the upper classes. She had worked hard to accrue higher social capital but failed to get it because she did not make enough money. While Gitelson certainly had a comfortable lifestyle, she had not attained real wealth, and in the end, her resources fell short of what she needed to enter the new upper class.[165]

As we have found, members of previous upper classes wielded their pocketbooks and their families' prestige to establish greater ease and comfort and more control of their lives. However, unlike their predecessors who had minimized the importance of work, hybrids sought relief from the grueling demands of their high-pressure jobs and the everyday tensions of New York City. The venues and practices that hybrids created in their quest to achieve greater ease and command also acted to distinguish them from the middle class. Many middle-class New Yorkers had the same predilection for fitness clubs, fine foods, and gentrified neighborhoods that hybrids did, and where tastes were shared, money was what could generate the desired separation.[166]

A new type of elite private club has emerged in the metropolitan region to serve these functions. Opened in 2005, Core Club has about six hundred members who have paid an initiation fee of $50,000 and have annual dues of $5,000.[167] Membership is by invitation only and is restricted to leading figures from business, fashion, sports, art, and politics, including chief executive officer William P. Lauder of Estée Lauder, financier Nathaniel Rothschild, philanthropist Beth Rudin DeWoody, and ex-athletes John McEnroe and Dan Marino. Its membership, then, is drawn from successful, high-powered people and is based on achievement without regard to family ties or social pedigree.

Its sleek modern design sets Core Club apart from the stuffy, traditional men's clubs, as does its inclusion of both men and women. Another signal departure is its inconspicuousness on the urban landscape: Core Club is located behind an unmarked door in a condominium building on East Fifty-Fifth Street.[168] Thousands of people regularly pass this spot without being aware of the existence of Core Club, a far cry from the iconic buildings that house the traditional clubs. Yet its fundamental purpose, to provide like-minded people with a site of refuge and comfort, is similar to that of the old private men's clubs: it makes available a dining room, bar, spa, exercise facility, screening room, library, and personal shoppers. One of the architects explained, "Jennie [Saunders, its founder and chief executive officer] insisted it be like a home. She wanted it to feel like the house you like best from your collection of houses."[169]

Not long after Core Club started, a Miami Beach hotel and resort called the Setai Club inaugurated a branch near the New York Stock Exchange in lower Manhattan, giving moneyed Wall Streeters access to a restaurant, bar, health club, spa, and concierge facilities. Annual dues were $5,000 and membership was limited to five hundred. Some of this new breed of private city club, like Soho House New York and the Norwood Club, are less expensive and less exclusive than Core Club and Setai Club, but they, too, are for-profit enterprises that have gender-neutral admissions policies, chic designs, and low urban profiles and that also recruit their members from the ranks of highly successful businesspeople and professionals.[170]

Luxury boxes as we now know them originated in 1965 with the completion of the Astrodome in Houston, the first domed and air-conditioned stadium in the world.[171] Along with other novelties, the Astrodome had

348 | THE ANTIELITIST ELITE

fifty-three individually designed and decorated suites that were furnished with couches and wall-to-wall carpeting and that had their own bars, televisions, and restrooms. A standard thirty-four-seat suite rented for $18,000 (which amounts to $131,000 today) for the baseball season, with many of them leased to corporations that used them to entertain customers.[172] They were an immediate hit with rich Houstonians. From this beginning, luxury boxes spread across the country and became increasingly opulent; they have become another venue that offers ease and comfort and serves as a social marker. The professional football and baseball stadiums that opened in the United States between 1992 and 2012 had a total of more than 5,600 luxury boxes, including 344 in the New York region. Altogether, there are now more than 620 luxury suites in metropolitan New York.[173]

None are more spectacular than the luxury suites at the new Yankee Stadium, each of which hold between twelve and twenty-two people and (in 2009) rented for between $650,000 and $800,000 a year. Occupants of these suites are segregated from regular ticket holders and, apart from the time they spend in the exterior seats, are generally not visible to ordinary fans. A private entrance to the stadium and a private elevator to the suites ensures their seclusion. Although their closest analogue are the opera boxes of opera and symphony halls, these earlier luxury accommodations did not provide concealment. In fact, we have learned that box holders at the Metropolitan Opera House expected to be seen by one another as well as by regular patrons, for the Gilded Age upper class emphasized individual display and group cohesiveness. By contrast, the antielitist elite is less comfortable with social hierarchy and prefers that its spaces be concealed. They object not to the reality of inequality but rather to its flaunting.[174] Many of Yankee Stadium's luxury boxes are leased by corporations such as AT&T, J. P. Morgan, Barclay's, and Fox. In contrast to the illustrious family names of the past, lucrative employment in major corporations now confers great status and privilege.[175]

For hybrids who put in long hours in the office, the ability to move freely around the metropolitan region and avoid the worst congestion and delays was crucial. There are few places in the region that are more time-consuming and irksome to reach than the Hamptons, at the eastern end of Long Island, especially during the summer weekend crunches. A one-way Long Island Rail Road ticket during rush hour cost $10.50 in 1989 and fares on Hampton Jitney buses started at $15. For $69, however, one could catch a commercial flight from LaGuardia Airport to the Hamptons, an option that more and more travelers were choosing as the economy picked up.[176]

According to the general manager of a commuter airline that operated between LaGuardia Airport and the East Hampton Airport, passengers on this route constituted "a unique group" of "business executives, Wall Street brokers, professionals, artists, celebrities" who were "time-conscious people who want to maximize their time."[177] In 1989 Andy Sabin, an Upper East Sider who was the vice chairman of the New York Commodities Exchange and the principal owner of a large precious-metals refiner and recycler, said that he had been flying from the city to his summer place almost every weekend for the past fifteen years. The flight took about thirty minutes, and counting the time it took to go from his office to LaGuardia and then from the East Hampton Airport to his summer house in Amagansett, his entire journey amounted to an hour and a half. That compared favorably to a four-hour drive on the traffic-choked Long Island Expressway, but Sabin noted that the savings involved his frame of mind as well as his time. "There's no tension, no worries about who broke down on the bridge or who's stuck at Exit 39," he said. "I don't have to ruin my time out there worrying about the drive home."[178]

The priority that the hybrid upper class puts on professional and business achievement and on material rewards means that merit must bear all the greater weight as the principal source of its legitimacy.

CONCLUSION

....

The Limits of Antielitism

In June 2010, eighteen-year-old Justin Hudson delivered the graduating speech at Hunter College High School, a public school for the intellectually gifted on the Upper East Side that serves as a gateway to Ivy League colleges and, for some of its students, to the hybrid upper class. In his address, Hudson recalled having been "a fresh-faced, wide-eyed twelve-year old entering the [school's] foreboding, windowless Brick Prison for the first time" and credited its academic rigor and its warm and encouraging faculty and staff for helping him attain a level of academic success that surpassed his initial expectations.[1]

Hudson would matriculate at Columbia University that fall, yet he felt ambivalent about his good fortune. "More than anything else today," he told his classmates, "I feel guilty. I feel guilty because I don't deserve any of this. And neither do you."[2] Hudson used his speech to join a debate about the relationship between achievement and diversity that was convulsing the school. Hunter College High School prided itself on being a meritocracy and was proud that it sent a quarter of its graduates to the Ivy League and had produced luminaries such as Supreme Court Justice Elena Kagan and Bernadine Healy, onetime director of the National Institutes for Health, and that other graduates had gone on to prominent careers on Wall Street and in politics and academia.[3]

Most students gained admission to the high school by passing a test for reading comprehension and mathematical skills that they took in sixth grade. Most, but not all: around fifty high school students were graduates of Hunter Elementary School, to which they had been admitted as prekindergartners on the basis of an IQ test and teacher observations. The sole entry point for Hunter Elementary was kindergarten, and it only accepted children who lived in Manhattan. Elementary school students who made "satisfactory progress" could transfer more or less automatically to the high school in seventh grade without having to take that sixth-grade test. Some high school teachers who argued that the exemption for Hunter Elementary constituted a departure from meritocratic principles wanted to further alter admissions procedures by employing criteria such as interviews and portfolios of student work, but the administrators at Hunter College who oversaw the high school had rejected that idea.[4]

These admissions procedures had become controversial because the number of African American and Latino students enrolled at Hunter College High School had dwindled. In 1995 the incoming seventh-grade class had been 12 percent African American and 6 percent Latino. In 2009 entering seventh graders were 47 percent Asian American, 41 percent white, 8 percent multiracial, 3 percent African American, and 1 percent Latino. At the time, the entire public school system was 70 percent African American and Latino.[5]

Justin Hudson is black and Latino, and his concerns about the low minority enrollment at the high school inspired him to challenge its admissions procedures in his speech. However, instead of criticizing the dearth of African Americans and Latinos or lamenting the growing income gap between the top and bottom strata in New York City, Hudson shrewdly questioned the very idea of merit. The understanding of merit that had solidified in the 1970s rested on the two pillars of achievement and diversity, but the clash over the admissions policy of Hunter College High School showed that achievement and diversity could conflict as well as converge, and Hudson forcefully exposed the tension that had developed between these two ideals:

> We received an outstanding education at no charge based solely on a test we took when we were eleven-year-olds, or four-year-olds. We received superior teachers and additional resources based on our status as "gifted," while kids who naturally needed those resources much more than us wallowed in the mire of a broken [public school] system. And now, we stand on the precipice of our lives, in control of our lives, based purely and simply on luck and circumstances.[6]

Then he assessed the antielitist conception of achievement by tying academic success to the social geography of New York City:

> If you truly believe that the demographics of Hunter represent the distribution of intelligence in this city, then you must believe that the Upper West Side, Bayside, and Flushing are intrinsically more intelligent than the South Bronx, Bedford-Stuyvesant, and Washington Heights, and I refuse to accept that.[7]

Everyone listening to Hudson that day understood the class and ethnic implications of his geographical references: upper- and upper-middle-class whites populated the Upper West Side and Asian Americans predominated in Flushing and increasingly in Bayside, while the South Bronx, Bedford-Stuyvesant, and Washington Heights were largely African American, Latino, and mixed race. He continued:

> It is certainly not Hunter's fault that socioeconomic factors inhibit the educational opportunities of some children from birth, and in some ways I forgive colleges and universities that are forced to review eighteen-year-olds, the end results of a broken system. But, we are talking about eleven-year-olds. Four year-olds. We are deciding children's fates before they even have a chance. We are playing God and we are losing. Kids are losing the opportunity to go to college or obtain a career, because no one

taught them long division or colors. Hunter is perpetuating a system in which children, who contain unbridled and untapped intellect and creativity, are discarded like refuse. And we have the audacity to say they deserved it, because we're smarter than them.

Merit, Hudson insisted, was the central issue:

As students, we throw around platitudes like "deserve" and "earn," most likely because it makes us feel better about ourselves. However, it simply isn't the case. I know for a fact that I did not work as hard as I possibly could have, and I think the same is true for everyone on this stage. Nevertheless, people who work much harder than we ever could imagine will never have the opportunities that lie in front of us.[8]

Hudson believed that everyone in the auditorium, himself included, should feel guilty about their advantaged circumstances, because everyone there was complicit in the prevailing economic and cultural system that promoted egalitarian ideals while in reality restricting opportunities for social mobility (and, he might have noted, social reproduction) to those who benefited from the superior education to which only the privileged had access in the first instance. Arguing that present inequities were intolerable, he said, "I hope that a quality education will not be a privilege for the few in this country. I hope that the Hunter community will descend from its ivory tower made of brick, and distribute its tools evenly to the mass of humanity that is the City of New York."[9]

To his credit Hudson insisted that the entire social landscape—"the mass of humanity that is the City of New York"—must figure in debates about the pursuit of privilege. Contemporary discussions of merit usually focused on providing greater opportunities for the most talented of the poor—like Hudson himself—to enter the best schools and universities but ignored the rest of the "other half" of the city. While improving the lives of even a small number of disadvantaged children was certainly a laudable goal, Hudson understood that merit alone could not remedy the ethnoracialized poverty that afflicted the South Bronx and Bedford-Stuyvesant.

In pinpointing the social and economic basis of hereditary meritocracy, Hudson attacked the legitimacy of the antielitist elite. He unblinkingly identified the central flaw with the present-day understanding of merit by condemning elites for distorting and privileging merit to the point that it reinforced rather than democratized hierarchies. A *New York Times* account of his speech reported that the entire faculty and about half the students gave him a standing ovation and that the high school principal told him, "That was a very good and a very brave speech to make."[10]

It is significant that Hudson spoke at a public school that had a democratic mission to provide equal education rather than at a prestigious independent school that had no such official objective and that depended on contributions from wealthy alumni for much of its advancement. Whether Hudson would have received such a warm response had he been graduating from a private school is doubtful. Still, not everyone at Hunter approved of his speech. According to the *Times*, the president of Hunter College, herself a graduate of the high school, had "looked uncomfortable" on the stage and had not joined in the ovation.[11] In a comment on the Hunter High School website, Alex Liu, another student at the school, expressed his resentment of Hudson's claim that "I didn't deserve an education as outstanding as Hunter's" by pointing out that "I sacrificed countless weekends and summers hunched over workbooks, adding fractions and identifying moods of authors" and that his father, a Chinese immigrant who had survived the Cultural Revolution, had "come to America and eke[d] out a living" to support the aspirations of his children.[12] Family and family sacrifice had indeed become a major buttress for the prevailing conception of merit.

Some of the comments left on the *New York Times* website supported Hudson, with one reader writing, "The test is one of preparedness, not giftedness," and another asking:

I wonder how the kids that passed the exam would do if their parents weren't able to afford the expensive preparation classes, coaches, and tutors to teach them how to pass the test. Just like the SAT, GRE, and the rest of test[s] that are supposed to measure the probability of a student[']s success, this test basically measures if you can pass the test.[13]

However, most of the commentators disagreed with him. A Californian complained, "G-d, I'm tired of hearing about 'diversity.' Whatever happended [sic] to equal opportunity based on individual 'Merit'?," and another reader declared, "Let the intelligence and merits of the applicant dictate the outcome. Period. Let the cards fall where they fall."[14] Most of the comments similarly defined merit in terms of individual accomplishment and denied that it had any social basis other than family.

Like the activists the Reverend William Guy and Lynne Greene in the 1960s and the 1970s, Justin Hudson had held a mirror up to elites and others, imploring them to take an honest look at themselves and make any needed adjustments if their actions did not agree with their own values. However, after forty years, pleas like his had lost their sting, and the responses to Hudson were negative and rehearsed compared with those that had been made a generation ago. Cultural values and social practices that had been new and fluid in the early 1970s had hardened, forming a cultural system that was becoming as inflexible as Victorianism had once been.

The corporate elite was hardly immune to attack. In 2011, the Occupy Wall Street movement arose in New York and in other cities in the United States and abroad, and its slogan "We Are the 99%" galvanized fears and anger that had been building since the 2008 financial crisis over the inequities of corporate capitalism and the mounting concentration of wealth and power in the hands of the few in New York City and elsewhere. Two years later, Bill De Blasio won election as mayor of New York City in a landslide that represented a backlash against the administration of incumbent Mayor Michael R. Bloomberg, a billionaire whose policies were generally seen as favoring corporate and elite interests. However, even though these protests expressed deeply felt grievances, to date they have been proved to be fleeting and episodic and have not achieved the permanence of similar responses to economic and social misery during the Gilded Age and the Great Depression. The pursuit of money and the ideology and privileges of corporate elites had become so well ensconced that popular opposition encountered greater resistance than during the 1890s and 1930s, and the opposition that did arise tended to be less coherent and shorter-lived than before.[15]

Few people in the elite who were listening to Hudson that day in 2010 wanted to scrutinize themselves anymore. They took justifiable pride in their educational and professional accomplishments, they had a keen sense of their prerogatives, and their embrace of antielitism made them feel certain of their own legitimacy.

The final irony is that an ideology that took shape as an egalitarian critique of an earlier upper class has now become the foundation of a new upper class.

ACKNOWLEDGMENTS

....

One of the many pleasures of writing this book has been the opportunity to engage with bright and talented people, and I am happy to recognize their signal contributions to my project.

I owe special thanks to the archivists and librarians who made available the information that I applied to knit this book together. In New York City, I made use of the American Express Archives, American Express Company; the Archives of the Morgan Library & Museum; the AXA Equitable Life Assurance Archives; the Barnard College Archives; the Brearley School Archives; the Brooklyn Historical Society Library; the Century Association Archives Foundation; the Division of Old Records of the New York County Clerk; the Ford Foundation Archives; the Frances Mulhall Achilles Library of the Whitney Museum of American Art; the General Society of Mechanics and Tradesmen Library; the MetLife Archives; the Metropolitan Museum of Art Archives; the Metropolitan Opera Archives; the Municipal Archives of the New York City Department of Records and Information Services; the New-York Historical Society Library; the New York Philharmonic Archives; the New York Public Library, including the General Research Division, the Dorot Jewish Division, the Manuscripts and Archives Division, the Map Division, and the Milstein Division of U.S., Local History and Genealogy, together with the NYPL's Science, Industry, and Business Library; the New York Society Library; the New York Stock Exchange Archives; the New York University Archives; the Rare Book & Manuscript Library and the Columbia University Archives of the Columbia University Libraries; the Records Department of the Surrogate's Court of New York County; and the Trinity Church Archives. Many individuals aided me in the course of my research, and I have to single out Kenneth R. Cobb, assistant commissioner of the New York City Department of Records and Information Services, for his unparalleled generosity and long friendship.

Outside New York City, I thank the archivists and librarians at the American Jewish Archives in Cincinnati, Ohio; the Archives & Special Collections of the Amherst College Library in Amherst, Massachusetts; the Baker Library, Harvard Business School in Boston, Massachusetts; the Baring Archive, ING Barings in London; the Cornell University Library in Ithaca, New York, particularly the Division of Rare and Manuscript Collections at the Carl A. Kroch Library, the John M. Olin Library, and the Library Annex; the Currier Library, Foxcroft School in Middleburg, Virginia; the Family Records Center in London; the Franklin D. Roosevelt Presidential Library and Museum in Hyde Park, New York; the Guildhall Library in London; the Library of Congress in Washington, D.C.; the Rockefeller Archive Center in Sleepy Hollow, New York; the Gerald R. Ford Presidential Library in Ann Arbor, Michigan; the Harry S. Truman Presidential Library and Museum in Independence, Missouri; the Historical Society of Pennsylvania in Philadelphia; the Rothschild Archive in London; the Scarsdale Public Library in Scarsdale, New York; the Seeley G. Mudd Manuscript Library, Princeton University in Princeton, New Jersey; and the Wellesley College Archives in Wellesley, Massachusetts. Closer to home, at the Warren Hunting Smith Library of Hobart and William Smith Colleges, Joseph Chmura, Sara Greenleaf, Michael Hunter, Katie Lamontagne, Dan Mulvey, and Jennifer Nace answered repeated requests for information with good cheer and concrete results.

I proceed by acquiring masses of data and sifting through it to find connections and answers, which I then test and revise over and over again. That is a drawn-out work process, and I depend on critical readings from other scholars to go forward. Although I have presented many parts of this book as papers at historical conferences, the most trenchant criticism that I have received has come in the seminars of my own history department, where my colleagues Joseph R. Avitable, Matthew Crow, Maureen Flynn, Laura Free, Stephen Frug, William Harris, Matthew Kadane, Derek S. Linton, Susanne McNally, Colby Ristow, Daniel J. Singal, Elizabeth Thornberry, and Lisa Yoshikawa have given me the benefit of their time, energy, and ideas. In particular, Dan Singal went above and beyond with his criticism and encouragement, and I greatly appreciate his intellectual and emotional bigheartedness. For reading portions of the manuscript, I express thanks to Stuart Blumin, Lisa Krissoff Boehm, Jodi Dean, Andrew S. Dolkart, Robin L. Einhorn, Courtney N. Good, Richard John, Ann Durkin Keating, Pamela Walker Laird, Karen J. McMullen, Deborah Dash Moore, Jean Neukomm, Mary Beth Norton, Sara Ogger, Joel A. Tarr, and Jenna Weissman-Joselit. The reports of the two anonymous readers for Columbia University Press, particularly the penetrating report of reader two, led to substantial improvements in the final manuscript.

I received research aid from Carl Abbott, Kevin Adams, Kathleen Bartolini-Tuazon, James Borchert, Kenneth R. Bowling, Martha Bond, Christine Brown, Christopher E. Gunn, Grace Helmer, Katarina Hering, Scott G. McKinney, Stanley Mathews, Francesca Morgan, H. Wesley Perkins, Jessica M. Perkins, Steven A. Riess, Mark H. Rose, Umair B. Shames, Donald Spector, Nigel Starck, Harold S. Wechsler, Bill Wheaton, and Jeffrey Zupan. At Hobart and William Smith, my research assistants Susan E. Arena, Megan O. Jordan, Molly M. Rider, Karen J. McMullen, Sara K. Wallace, Jillian C. LaCroix, Meghan A. Paulette, Michele E. Viterise, Julia C. Boyaval, Cassia Ray Horvitz, Anna G. Rusch, Emma Luton, and Courtney N. Good conducted statistical analyses that strengthened my understanding of corporate elites. Judy Mahoney-Benzer, our departmental secretary, helped in more ways than I can count.

I thank my friends for giving me a place to stay during research trips: in New York City, Sara Ogger and Jean Neukomm, Louise B. Williams and Mark Rondeau, Bill Staniford and "901," Ken Cobb, Alan Divack and Amy Zarrow, and Kenneth T. and Barbara Jackson; in Washington, D.C., my uncle, Osborne S. P. Koerner; and in Boston, Ken Winokur and Jane Gillooly. Also, I benefited from research grants from Hobart and William Smith Colleges, the Gilder Lehrman Institute of American History, the Gerald R. Ford Presidential Library, the Harry S. Truman Presidential Library and Museum, and the Rockefeller Archive Center. Parts of this book previously appeared in different form in the *Bulletin of the German Historical Institute* ("Counting Who Counts: Method and Findings of a Statistical Analysis of Elites in the New York Region, 1947," *Bulletin of the German Historical Institute* 55 [Fall 2014]: 57–68), the *Journal of Social History* ("An Unusable Past: Urban Elites, New York City's Evacuation Day, and the Transformations of Memory Culture," *Journal of Social History* 37 [Summer 2004]: 883–913), and the *Journal of Urban History* ("Journeying to 'Old New York': Elite New Yorkers and Their Invention of an Idealized City History in the Late Nineteenth and Early Twentieth Centuries," *Journal of Urban History* 28 [September 2002]: 699–716). I acknowledge and thank their editors for permission to republish here.

My agent, Carol Mann, expertly guided my project through a publishing industry that has been transformed almost beyond recognition by digitalization and found the perfect publisher for it in Columbia University Press. At Columbia, Philip Leventhal figured out how I think and write and how to improve both, and this book is much better for it.

Most of my friends and relatives had no direct involvement with this book, beyond luring me away to go cycling, watch sports, catch a movie, eat and drink, travel, etc. And for that I am more grateful than they can possibly know.

ABBREVIATIONS FOR SELECTED
MANUSCRIPT SOURCES

....

AJA   Jacob Rader Marcus Center of the American Jewish Archives, Cincinnati, Ohio

ALT   American Loyalist Transcripts, Audit Office Records, 1783–1790, Rare Book and Manuscript Reading Room, New York Public Library, New York, N.Y.

AmEx   American Express Corporate Archives, New York, N.Y.

AXAA   AXA Life Assurance Archives, AXA Equitable Life Insurance Company, New York, N.Y.

BHS   Brooklyn Historical Society, Brooklyn, N.Y.

BSA   Brearley School Archives, Brearley School Library, New York, N.Y.

CU   Rare Books and Manuscript Library, Columbia University, New York, N.Y.

COR   Division of Rare and Manuscript Collections, Kroch Library, Cornell University, Ithaca, N.Y.

GRFL   Gerald R. Ford Library, Ann Arbor, Mich.

HBS   Baker Library, Harvard Business School, Harvard University, Boston, Mass.

HSP   Historical Society of Pennsylvania, Philadelphia, Penn.

HSTL   Harry S. Truman Library, Independence, Mo.

MLM   Archives of the Morgan Library and Museum, New York, N.Y.

MMA   Metropolitan Museum of Art Archives, Metropolitan Museum of Art, New York, N.Y.

MO   Metropolitan Opera Archives, New York, N.Y.
N-YHS   Library, New-York Historical Society, New York, N.Y.
NYPL   Manuscripts and Archives Division, New York Public Library, New York, N.Y.
NYSEA   New York Stock Exchange Archives, New York, N.Y.
NYU   New York University Archives, Bobst Library, New York University, New York, N.Y.
PU   Seeley G. Mudd Manuscript Library, Princeton University, Princeton, N.J.
RAC   Rockefeller Archive Center, Sleepy Hollow, N.Y.

NOTES

....

INTRODUCTION

1. L. P. Hartley, *The Go-Between* (London: Hamish Hamilton, 1953; repr., New York: New York Review of Books, 2002), 17.

2. MeasuringWorth.com, accessed July 7, 2015, www.measuringworth.com/uscompare /relativevalue.php. This estimate of current value is based on the standard of living.

3. *Town Topics*, January 26, 1888; *New York Times*, February 7, 11, and 12, 1897; *New York World*, February 11, 12, 14, and 16, 1897; Frederick Townsend Martin, *Things I Remember* (London: Nash, 1913; repr., New York: Arno, 1975), 238–43. See Sven Beckert, *The Monied Metropolis: New York City and the Consolidation of the American Bourgeoisie, 1850–1896* (New York: Cambridge University Press, 2001), 1–2, 334; Eric Homberger, *Mrs. Astor's New York: Money and Social Power in a Gilded Age* (New Haven, Conn.: Yale University Press, 2002), 226; and Justin Kaplan, *When the Astors Owned New York: Blue Bloods and Grand Hotels in a Gilded Age* (New York: Plume, 2007), 106–11.

4. *New York World*, February 14, 1897.

5. Pauline Maier, "Boston and New York in the Eighteenth Century," *Proceedings of the American Antiquarian Society* 41 (1981): 177–95; E. Digby Baltzell, *Puritan Boston and Quaker Philadelphia* (New York: Free Press, 1979; repr., New Brunswick, N.J.: Transaction, 1996), 1–55; Betty G. Farrell, *Elite Families: Class and Power in Nineteenth-Century Boston* (Albany: State University of New York Press, 1993), 1–19; Joseph F. Rishel, *Founding Families of Pittsburgh: The Evolution of a Regional Elite, 1760–1910* (Pittsburgh, Penn.: University of Pittsburgh Press, 1990), 3–13; Kathryn Allamong Jacob, *Capital Elites: High Society in Washington, D.C., After the Civil War* (Washington, D.C.: Smithsonian Institution Press, 1995), 1–13; Frederic Cople Jaher, *The Urban*

Establishment: Upper Strata in Boston, New York, Charleston, Chicago, and Los Angeles (Urbana: University of Illinois Press, 1982), 1–13; David Cannadine, *The Decline and Fall of the British Aristocracy*, rev. ed. (London: Macmillan, 1992), 1–31; David Garrioch, *The Formation of the Parisian Bourgeoisie* (Cambridge, Mass.: Harvard University Press, 1996), 1–14.

6. I frequently employ other descriptors to add variety to the text. "Social elites" and "blue bloods" are used synonymously to describe people who are socially prominent. "Old New Yorkers" belong to families that have long been socially prominent in New York City. "Elites" refers generally to people in high-status groups.

7. This definition borrows from the typology in E. Digby Baltzell, *Philadelphia Gentlemen: The Making of a National Upper Class* (New York: Free Press, 1958; repr., New Brunswick, N.J.: Transaction, 1992), 6–8; *The Protestant Establishment: Aristocracy and Caste in America* (New York: Random House, 1964); vii–xv; *Puritan Boston and Quaker Philadelphia* (New York: Free Press, 1979; repr., New Brunswick, N.J.: Transaction, 1996), 19–30. Sven Beckert has recently conceptualized late-nineteenth-century New York City elites in terms of the "bourgeoisie." In my view, this idea fits the nineteenth century better than it does earlier and later periods. Even there, I see this categorization as being overdetermined by economic factors and insufficiently attentive to the cultural considerations that I consider paramount. See Beckert, *The Monied Metropolis*, 2–14.

8. Thus, Sven Beckert probes the wealthy New York industrialists and merchants who created a new capitalist order; Thomas Kessner looks at New York City as the engine of American industrial might; Eric Homberger writes about the social elites who established an American version of aristocracy; and David Hammack and Keith Revell examine metropolitan decision making: Beckert, *The Monied Metropolis*; Thomas Kessner, *Capital City: New York City and the Men Behind America's Rise to Economic Dominance, 1860–1900* (New York: Simon & Schuster, 2004); Homberger, *Mrs. Astor's New York*; David C. Hammack, *Power and Society: Greater New York at the Turn of the Century* (New York: Columbia University Press, 1987); Keith D. Revell, *Building Gotham: Civic Culture and Public Policy in New York City, 1898–1938* (Baltimore, Md.: Johns Hopkins University Press, 2005). Gilded Age robber barons such as John D. Rockefeller, Andrew Carnegie, and J. Pierpont Morgan are a favorite subject of biographers: Ron Chernow, *Titan: The Life of John D. Rockefeller, Sr.* (New York: Random House, 1998); David Nasaw, *Andrew Carnegie* (New York: Penguin, 2006); David Cannadine, *Mellon: An American Life* (New York: Knopf, 2006); Jean Strouse, *Morgan: American Financier* (New York: Random House, 1999).

9. Pierre Bourdieu, *Distinction: A Social Critique of the Judgment of Taste*, trans. Richard Nice (Cambridge: Harvard University Press, 1984), 1–18, 40–83; *In Other Words: Essays Toward a Reflexive Sociology*, trans. Matthew Adamson (Stanford, Calif.: Stanford University Press, 1990), 9–13, 22, 46–48, 62–63. My discussion relies on Richard Jenkins, *Pierre Bourdieu* (London: Routledge, 1992), 84–99, 128–49.

1. "THE BEST MART ON THE CONTINENT"

1. William Livingston, *A Brief Consideration of New York, with Respect to Its Natural Advantages, Its Superiority in Several Instances, Over Some of the Neighboring Colonies,* ed. Earl Gregg Swem (Metuchen, N.J.: Heartman, 1925), i–v. See also Dorothy Rita Dillon, *The New York Triumvirate: A Study of the Legal and Political Careers of William Livingston, John Morin Scott, William Smith, Jr.* (New York: Columbia University Press, 1949), 16–17, 28–29; Cynthia A. Kierner, *Traders and Gentlefolk: The Livingstons of New York, 1675–1790* (Ithaca, N.Y.: Cornell University Press, 1992), 1–9, 143–47; and Milton M. Klein, *The Politics of Diversity: Essays in the History of Colonial New York* (Port Washington, N.Y.: Kennicat, 1974), 53–95.

2. Livingston, *A Brief Consideration of New York,* 2.

3. Ibid., 3–4.

4. Thomas Pownall, *A Topographical Description of the Dominions of the United States of America,* ed. Louis Mulkearn (Pittsburgh, Penn.: University of Pittsburgh Press, 1949), 42.

5. Livingston, *A Brief Consideration,* 15. On New York harbor, see Robert Greenhalgh Albion, *The Rise of New York Port, 1815–1860* (New York: Scribner's, 1939; repr., Boston: Northeastern University Press, 1984), 16–37.

6. Livingston, *A Brief Consideration,* 15–24.

7. Earl Greg Swem, "Introductory Note," i–v, in Livingston, *A Brief Consideration.*

8. James A. Henretta, *The Origins of American Capitalism: Collected Essays* (Boston: Northeastern University Press, 1991), 121–47; R. C. Nash, "The Organization of Trade and Finance in the British Atlantic Economy, 1600–1830," 95–151, in *The Atlantic Economy During the Seventeenth and Eighteenth Centuries: Organization, Operation, Practice, and Personnel,* ed. Peter A. Coclanis (Columbia, S.C.: University of South Carolina Press, 2005); Cathy Matson, *Merchants & Empire: Trading in Colonial New York* (Baltimore, Md.: Johns Hopkins University Press, 1998), 153–55; W. T. Baxter, *The House of Hancock: Business in Boston, 1724–1775* (New York: Russell & Russell, 1965), 39–61; Christine Leigh Heyrman, *Commerce and Culture: The Maritime Communities of Colonial Massachusetts, 1690–1750* (New York: Norton, 1984), 3–20.

9. "Journal of a French Traveller in the Colonies, 1765, II," *American Historical Review* 27 (October 1921): 82–83; Pownall, *Topographical Description,* 42–45; Andrew Burnaby, *Travels Through the Middle Settlements in North-America in the Years 1759 and 1760, with Observations upon the State of the Colonies,* 2nd ed. (Ithaca, N.Y.: Great Seal, 1960), 75–77; Paul E. Cohen and Robert T. Augustyn, *Manhattan in Maps, 1527–1995* (New York: Rizzoli, 1997), 66–72; and John A. Kouwenhoven, *The Columbia Historical Portrait of New York: An Essay in Graphic History* (New York: Columbia University Press, 1953), 29–68.

10. Thomas J. Davis, "Slavery," in *Encyclopedia of New York City,* 2nd ed., ed. Kenneth T. Jackson (New Haven, Conn.: Yale University Press, 2010), 1191–92; and Ira Berlin and Leslie M. Harris, eds., *Slavery in New York* (New York: New Press, 2005), 3–15.

11. Governor George Clinton to the Board of Trade, May 23, 1749, 511, in *Documents Relative to the Colonial History of the State of New York*, vol. 6, ed. E. B. O'Callaghan (Albany, N.Y.: Weed, Parsons, 1855).

12. Ibid., 507–11; Peter A. Coclanis, "Introduction," xi–xix, in Coclanis, *Atlantic Economy During the Seventeenth and Eighteenth Centuries*.

13. Coclanis, "Introduction"; Bernard Bailyn, *Atlantic History: Concept and Contours* (Cambridge, Mass.: Harvard University Press, 2005), 3–56; David Hancock, "Self-Organized Complexity and the Emergence of an Atlantic Market Economy, 1651–1815," 30–33, in Coclanis, *Atlantic Economy During the Seventeenth and Eighteenth Centuries*; and "Trade in the Atlantic World," ed. John J. McCusker, special issue, *Business History Review* vol. 79 (Winter 2005), esp. John J. McCusker, "Introduction," 697–714.

14. Carl Bridenbaugh, *Cities in Revolt: Urban Life in America, 1743–1776* (New York: Knopf, 1955), 5.

15. Ibid., 5.

16. Gary Nash, *The Urban Crucible: The Northern Seaports and the Origins of the American Revolution* (Cambridge, Mass.: Harvard, 1986), 10–20, 152.

17. John J. McCusker and Russell R. Menard, *The Economy of British America, 1607–1789* (Chapel Hill: University of North Carolina Press, 1985), 189–208; Jacob M. Price, "Economic Function and the Growth of American Port Towns in the Eighteenth Century," 123–86, in *Perspectives in American History*, ed. Donald Fleming and Bernard Bailyn, vol. 8 (Cambridge, Mass.: Charles Warren Center for Studies in American History, 1974); Wim Klooster, *The Dutch in the Americas, 1600–1800* (Providence, R.I.: John Carter Brown Library, 1997), 99–101; and Lester J. Cappon ed., *Atlas of Early American History: The Revolutionary Era, 1760–1790* (Princeton, N.J.: Princeton University Press, 1976), 22–23, 26–29.

18. Oliver A. Rink, *Holland on Hudson: An Economic and Social History of Dutch New York* (Ithaca, N.Y.: Cornell University Press, 1986), 17–23, 69–93; C. R. Boxer, *The Dutch Seaborne Empire, 1600–1800* (London: Hutchinson, 1965; repr., New York: Penguin, 1990), 168–69, 246–48; Klooster, *The Dutch in the Americas*, 53–57; Alice P. Kenny, *Stubborn for Liberty: The Dutch in New York* (Syracuse, N.Y.: Syracuse University Press, 1975), 13–50; Jacob M. Price, "Economic Function and the Growth of American Port Towns," 123–63, in *Perspectives in American History*, vol. 8; and McCusker and Menard, *The Economy of British America*, 189–208.

19. Pownall, *A Topographical Description*, 43–45; *Peter Kalm's Travels in North America: The English Version of 1770*, ed. Adolph B. Benson, vol. 1 (New York: Wilson-Erickson, 1937), 125–36; Burnaby, *Travels Through the Middle Settlements in North-America*, 75–77; and "Journal of a French Traveller in the Colonies, 1765, II," 81–84.

20. Pownall, *A Topographical Description*, 43.

21. Joyce D. Goodfriend, *Before the Melting Pot: Society and Culture in Colonial New York City, 1664–1730* (Princeton, N.J.: Princeton University Press, 1992), 3–21, 217–19.

22. Ibid., 217, 218.

23. Pauline Maier, "Boston and New York in the Eighteenth Century," *Proceedings of the American Antiquarian Society* 41 (1981): 177–95. For scholarship that emphasizes the benefits of Puritanism for economic activity in colonial New England, see Margaret Ellen Newell, *From Dependency to Independence: Economic Revolution in Colonial New England* (Ithaca, N.Y.: Cornell University Press, 1998), 1–35; and John Frederick Martin, *Profits in the Wilderness: Entrepreneurship and the Founding of New England Towns in the Seventeenth Century* (Chapel Hill: University of North Carolina Press, 1991), 1–5.

24. Maier, "Boston and New York," 185.

25. E. Digby Baltzell, *Puritan Boston and Quaker Philadelphia* (New York: Free Press, 1979; repr., New Brunswick, N.J.: Transaction, 1996), 1–55; and Elva Tooker, *Nathan Trotter, Philadelphia Merchant, 1787–1853* (Cambridge, Mass.: Harvard University Press, 1955), 5.

26. Goodfriend, *Before the Melting Pot*, 217–19; Edwin G. Burrows and Mike Wallace, *Gotham: A History of New York City to 1898* (New York: Oxford University Press, 1999), 27–40; and Randall H. Balmer, *A Perfect Babel of Confusion: Dutch Religion and English Culture in the Middle Colonies* (New York: Oxford University Press, 1989), vii–xi.

27. Bridenbaugh, *Cities in Revolt*, 5; and John Robert McNeill, "American Ports and Imperial Trade," 666–69, in *The Atlantic Staple Trade*, vol. 2, *The Economics of Trade*, ed. Susan Socolow (Aldershot, U.K.: Variorum, 1996).

28. *Peter Kalm's Travels*, 1:131.

29. Paul M. Hohenberg and Lynn Hollen Lees, *The Making of Urban Europe, 1000–1950* (Cambridge, Mass.: Harvard University Press, 1985), 227.

30. Brian J. L. Berry, *Theories of Urban Location*, Resource Paper No. 1 (Washington, D.C.: American Association of Geographers, 1968), 5.

31. Joyce Ellis, "Regional and County Centres," 679, in *The Cambridge Urban History of Britain*, vol. 2, *1540–1840*, ed. Peter Clark (Cambridge: Cambridge University Press, 2000). See also John Langton, "Urban Growth and Economic Change: From the Late Seventeenth Century to 1841," 453–90, in *Cambridge Urban History*, vol. 2; Christopher Chalkin, *The Rise of the English Town, 1650–1850* (Cambridge: Cambridge University Press, 2001); P. J. Corfield, *The Impact of English Towns, 1700–1800* (Oxford: Oxford University Press, 1982); Jan De Vries, *European Urbanization, 1500–1800* (Cambridge, Mass.: Harvard University Press, 1984); and Vanessa Harding, "The Population of London, 1550–1700," *London Journal* 15 (1990): 111–28.

32. I base this statement on my examination of every issue of the *London Gazette* from 1665 to 1675.

33. J. R. Jones, *The Anglo-Dutch Wars of the Seventeenth Century* (London: Longman, 1996), 179–225; *London Gazette*, February 26–March 2, March 5–March 9, March 9–March 12, March 16–March 19, 1674.

34. McCusker and Menard, *The Economy of British America*, 189–208; Klooster, *Illicit Riches*, 1–16, 99–103. The phrase "Dutch connection" is McCusker and Menard's (p. 193).

35. P. J. Cain and A. G. Hopkins, *British Imperialism*, vol. 1, *Innovation and Expansion, 1688–1914* (London: Longman, 1993), 22.

36. Cain and Hopkins, *British Imperialism*, 1:1–104; H. V. Bowen, *Elites, Enterprise and the Making of the British Overseas Empire, 1688–1775* (London: Macmillan, 1996), ix–21; and David Hancock, *Citizens of the World: London Merchants and the Integration of the British Atlantic Community, 1735–1785* (Cambridge: Cambridge University Press, 1995), 1–21. For the "military-fiscal state," see John Brewer, *The Sinews of Power: War, Money, and the English State, 1688–1783* (New York: Knopf, 1989), xxi; and Philip Harling and Peter Mandler, "From 'Fiscal-Military' State to Laissez-Faire State, 1760–1850," *Journal of British Studies* 32 (January 1993): 44–70.

37. Matson, *Merchants & Empire*, 1–10, 170–71; Virginia D. Harrington, *The New York Merchant on the Eve of the Revolution* (New York: Columbia University Press, 1935), 11–46; Bruce M. Wilkenfeld, "New York City Neighborhoods, 1730," *New York History* 57 (April 1976): 180; and Klooster, *Illicit Riches*, 99–100.

38. Abigaill Levy Franks to Naphtali Franks, December 16, 1733, 16–18; Abigaill Levy Franks to Naphtali Franks, June 9, 1734, 19–31; Abigaill Levy Franks to Naphtali Franks, December 12, 1735, 44–53, all in Edith B. Gelles, ed., *The Letters of Abigaill Levy Franks, 1733–1748* (New Haven, Conn.: Yale University Press, 2004).

39. Patricia H. Bonomi, *A Factious People: Politics and Society in Colonial New York* (New York: Columbia University Press, 1971), 1–16, 56–75. See also Michael Kammen, *Colonial New York: A History* (New York: Oxford University Press, 1975), 32–34, 44, 55–56, 140; Bernard Bailyn, *The New England Merchants in the Seventeenth Century* (Cambridge, Mass.: Harvard University Press, 1955), 168–197; and Phyllis Whitman Hunter, *Purchasing Identity in the Atlantic World: Massachusetts Merchants, 1670–1780* (Ithaca, N.Y.: Cornell University Press, 2001), 1–13; Darrett B. Rutman, *Winthrop's Boston: A Portrait of a Puritan Town* (New York: Norton, 1965), 274–79; Frederic Cople Jaher, *The Urban Establishment: Upper Strata in Boston, New York, Charleston, Chicago, and Los Angeles* (Urbana: University of Illinois Press), 16–29, 160–84; Bridenbaugh, *Cities in Revolt*, 70–83; Baltzell, *Puritan Boston and Quaker Philadelphia*, 109–74; Gordon S. Wood, *The Americanization of Benjamin Franklin* (New York: Penguin, 2004), 66–83; and Thomas M. Doerflinger, *A Vigorous Spirit of Enterprise: Merchants and Economic Development in Revolutionary Philadelphia* (Chapel Hill: University of North Carolina Press, 1986), 3–69.

40. Stuart M. Blumin, *The Emergence of the Middle Class: Social Experience in the American City, 1760–1900* (Cambridge: Cambridge University Press, 1989), 1–20; Sean Wilentz, *Chants Democratic: New York City & the Rise of the American Working Class, 1788–1850* (New York: Oxford University Press, 1984), 3–19; and Alan Dawley, *Class and Community: The Industrial Revolution in Lynn* (Cambridge, Mass.: Harvard University Press, 1976), 1–10.

41. Jaher, *The Urban Establishment*, 160.

42. Blumin, *Emergence of the Middle Class*, 1–65; Harrington, *New York Merchant*, 11–17; Bonomi, *A Factious People*, 1–16.

43. Maier, "Boston and New York in the Eighteenth Century," 177–95; Bridenbaugh, *Cities in Revolt*, 150–56, 352–58; Nash, *The Urban Crucible*, 23, 137, 202–12; Benjamin W. Labaree, *Patriots and Partisans: The Merchants of Newburyport, 1764–1815* (Cambridge, Mass.: Harvard University Press, 1962), 7–8; Lynne Withy, *Urban Growth in Colonial Rhode Island: Newport and Providence in the Eighteenth Century* (Albany, N.Y.: State University of New York Press, 1984), 13–32; Kenneth A. Lockridge, *The Diary, and Life, of William Byrd II of Virginia, 1674–1744* (Chapel Hill: University of North Carolina Press, 1987), 39–64; Alden Hatch, *The Byrds of Virginia* (New York: Holt, Rinehart and Winston, 1969), 56, 141, 165–67; William Byrd, *The Secret Diary of William Byrd of Westover, 1709–1712*, ed. Louis B. Wright and Marion Tinling (Richmond, Va.: Dietz, 1941), xxi; and William Byrd, *The London Diary (1717–1721) and Other Writings*, ed. Louis B. Wright and Marion Tinling (New York: Oxford, 1958), 50, 71, 73, 83, 121, 122, 124, 127, 128, 135–36, 139, 143, 151, 157, 181. For Philadelphia, see John and Mary Clifford to Thomas Hyam, January 31, 1722, Book 1, Clifford Family Papers, Historical Society of Pennsylvania, Philadelphia, Penn. [hereafter HSP]; Elizabeth Nutt to Thomas Clifford, March 3, 1756, Book 1, Clifford Family Papers, HSP; Henry Drinker to Jones, Campbell & Company, October 12, 1784, Henry Drinker Letterbook, 1772–1785, Henry Drinker Papers, HSP; and John Warder to Parr Bulkeley, June 20, 1777, vol. 2, John Warder Letterbooks, HSP.

44. Naomi Tadmor, *Family and Friends in Eighteenth-Century England: Household, Kinship, and Patronage* (Cambridge: Cambridge University Press, 2001), 11.

45. Max Weber, "Class, Status, Party," 186–88, in *From Max Weber: Essays in Sociology*, ed. H. H. Gerth and C. Wright Mills (New York: Oxford University Press, 1946).

46. Linda Colley, *Britons: Forging the Nation, 1707–1837* (New Haven, Conn.: Yale University Press, 1992), 208–50 and Paul Langford, *A Polite and Commercial People: England, 1727–1783* (New York: Oxford University Press, 1989), 306–29, 578–87.

47. *New York Mercury*, May 3, 1756, October 18, 1756, October 10, 1757, June 5, 1758, November 27, 1758, December 15, 1758, March 17, August 11, and November 17, 1760; *New York Gazette* (Weyman's), November 12, 1759, August 24, 1761; and "Proclamation of Accession of George III by New York Council and Leading Citizens," January 17, 1761, 6–8, in *The Letters and Papers of Cadwallader Colden*, vol. 6, *1761–1764*, *Collections of the New-York Historical Society for the Year 1922* (New York: n.p., 1923).

48. Richard Bushman, *The Refinement of America: Persons, Houses, Cities* (New York: Vintage, 1992), ix–xix; T. H. Breen, *Tobacco Culture: The Mentality of the Great Tidewater Planters on the Eve of the Revolution* (Princeton, N.J.: Princeton University Press, 1985), xi–xxviii, 40–83; and Cain and Hopkins, *British Imperialism*, 1:22–46; Wood, *The Americanization of Benjamin Franklin*, 16–70.

49. *New York Gazette* (Weyman's), August 4, 1760.

50. *New York Mercury*, June 11, 1759, June 20, 1763; *New York Gazette* (Weyman's), January 10, 1763.

51. *New York Mercury*, April 5, 1756, June 20, 1763.

52. *New York Mercury*, May 2, 1757.

53. Ibid.

54. *New York Gazette*, April 21, 1760.

55. *New York Mercury*, October 25, 1756, May 1, 1758. For announcements of weddings, which involved a similar dynamic, see *New York Mercury*, June 5 and November 27, 1758, March 17, 1760, April 26, 1762; and *New York Gazette* (Weyman's), April 9, 1759, July 7 and 14, 1760.

56. *New York Gazette* (Weyman's), October 13, 1760. For the social significance of silver ownership, see Graham Hood, *American Silver: A History of Style, 1650–1900* (New York: Praeger, 1971), 12.

57. *New York Weekly Journal*, February 11, 18, and 25, November 26, and December 3, 1733, May 6, 13, and 20, July 22, August 12 and 19, September 30, 1734; and *New York Evening Post*, October 21 and November 25, 1751, July 27, August 3, October 9, and November 20, 1752.

58. Langford, *A Polite and Commercial People*, 59–121; Bushman, *Refinement of America*, 100–27; and Kevin M. Sweeney, "High-Style Vernacular: Lifestyles of the Colonial Elite," 1–58, in *Of Consuming Interests: The Style of Life in the Eighteenth Century*, ed. Cary Carson, Ronald Hoffman, and Peter J. Albert (Charlottesville: University Press of Virginia, 1994).

59. Esther Singleton, *Social New York Under the Georges: Houses, Streets, and Country Homes, with Chapters on Fashions, Furniture, China, Plate and Manners* (New York: Appleton, 1902), 18–20, 66–69; Thomas Jefferson Wertenbaker, *Father Knickerbocker Rebels: New York City During the Revolution* (New York: Cooper Square, 1969), 15; *New York Mercury*, July 14, 1764; and "Diary of Ezra Styles," 338–39, in *Proceedings of the Massachusetts Historical Society*, 2nd series, vol. 7 (Boston: Massachusetts Historical Society, 1892).

60. Carl Abbott, "The Neighborhoods of New York, 1760–1775," *New York History* 55 (January 1974): 41–49; Singleton, *Social New York*, 15–19; and Burrows and Wallace, *Gotham*, 170–90.

61. *New York Mercury*, June 8, 1761; and *New York Gazette* (Weyman's), June 6, 1762, June 6, 1763.

62. G. D. Scull, ed., "Journals of Capt. John Montresor," 367, 368, in *Collections of the New-York Historical Society for the Year 1881* (New York: New-York Historical Society, 1882).

63. *New York Gazette* (Weyman's), May 26 and June 9, 1766; and *New York Mercury*, May 26 and June 9, 1766.

64. For the idea of the "pedestrian city" or the "walking city," see Sam Bass Warner Jr., *Streetcar Suburbs: The Process of Growth in Boston, 1870–1900* (Cambridge, Mass.: Harvard University Press, 1962), 2, 11–29, 63; and David Ward, *Cities and Immigrants: A Geography of Change in Nineteenth Century America* (New York: Oxford University Press, 1971), 87–89. For criticisms of this idea, see Diane Shaw, *City Building on the Eastern Frontier: Sorting the New Nineteenth-Century City* (Baltimore, Md.: Johns Hopkins University Press, 2004), 1–4, 157. See also James Lemon, *Liberal Dreams and*

Nature's Limits: Great Cities of North America Since 1600 (New York: Oxford University Press, 1996), 78.

65. Elizabeth Blackmar, *Manhattan for Rent, 1785–1850* (Ithaca, N.Y.: Cornell University Press, 1989), 72–108; Blumin, *Emergence of the Middle Class*, 17–28.

66. Adam Arenson, "Libraries in Public Before the Age of Public Libraries: Interpreting the Furnishings and Design of Athenaeums and Other 'Social Libraries,' 1800–1860," 41, in *The Library as Place: History, Community, and Culture*, ed. John E. Buschman and Gloria J. Leckie (Westport, Conn.: Libraries Unlimited, 2006).

67. Ray Oldenburg, *The Great Good Place: Cafés, Coffee Shops, Community Centers, Beauty Parlors, General Stores, Bars, Hangouts, and How They Get You Through the Day* (New York: Paragon House, 1989), 16.

68. Laura Lewison, "Lawn Bowling," 724, in Jackson, *Encyclopedia of New York City*; Steven A. Reiss, "Horse Racing," 611–12, in Jackson, *The Encyclopedia of New York City*; Austin Baxter Keep, *History of the New York Society Library* (New York: De Vinne, 1908), 123–78; Walter Friedman, "Scots," 1160–61, in Jackson, *The Encyclopedia of New York City*; Burrows and Wallace, *Gotham*, 172–75, 248; *New York Gazette* (Weyman's), February 23, 1761, June 6, 1763, November 28, 1763; *New York Mercury*, May 5, 1755; and Singleton, *Social New York*, 40–45.

69. Kevin Lynch, *The Image of the City* (Cambridge, Mass.: MIT Press, 1960), 1–13.

70. Edward T. Hall, *The Hidden Dimension* (Garden City, N.Y.: Anchor, 1969), 44.

71. Toby L. Ditz, "Formative Ventures: Eighteenth-Century Commercial Letters and the Articulation of Experience," 59–78, in *Epistolary Selves: Letters and Letter-Writers, 1600–1945*, ed. Rebecca Earle (Aldershot, U.K.: Ashgate, 1999). See also Charlotte Browne Diary, 1754–1757, Library, New-York Historical Society, New York, N.Y. [hereafter N-YHS].

72. "Diary of Ezra Styles," 339. I have changed Styles's spelling of "Ketteltas" to "Keteltas" in my text in keeping with modern usage.

73. Ibid.

74. Ibid. Styles may have forgotten or may not have registered the musician's name, but it is telling that he remembered and knew the others' names.

75. Elaine G. Breslaw, *Dr. Alexander Hamilton and Provincial America: Expanding the Orbit of Scottish Culture* (Baton Rouge: Louisiana State University Press, 2008), 193–96.

76. Alexander Hamilton, *Gentleman's Progress: The Itinerarium of Dr. Alexander Hamilton, 1744*, ed. Carl Bridenbaugh (Chapel Hill: University of North Carolina Press, 1948), 48.

77. Ibid., 54.

78. "Journal, 1746–1758, of Frances Goelet," entries for January 30 and 31, 1746, March 15, 1747, April 15, 1747, December 21–25, 1750, April 1–July 1, 1751, N-YHS.

79. For war as a catalyst for urban change in the Atlantic world, see McCusker, "Introduction," 699–700; and Thomas Truxes, "Transnational Trade in the Wartime North Atlantic: The Voyage of the Snow *Recovery*," *Business History Review* 79 (Winter 2005): 751–80.

80. Fred Anderson, *Crucible of War: The Seven Years' War and the Fate of Empire in British North America, 1754–1766* (New York: Knopf, 2000), 211–16; Tom Pockock, *Battle for Empire: The Very First World War, 1756–63* (London: O'Mara, 1998), 92–93; Ian K. Steele, *Warpaths: Invasions of North America* (New York: Oxford University Press, 1994), 207–25; and Owen Aubrey Sherrard, *Lord Chatham; Pitt and the Seven Years' War* (London: Bodley Head, 1955), 145–83.

81. Anderson, *Crucible of War*, 258.

82. Ibid., 179–80; Charles Hardy to the Board of Trade, January 16, 1756, 2–7; William Johnson to the Lords of Trade, January 17, 1756, 7–8; John Pownall to William Johnson, March 5, 1756, 40–41; Lords of Trade to Charles Hardy, March 4, 1756, 39–40; Charles Hardy to the Board of Trade, May 10, 1756, 80–83; Sir William Johnson to Board of Trade, May 28, 1756, 86–91; William Pitt to the Governor of New York, December 30, 1757, 339–41; William Pitt to the Governors in America, September 15, 1758, 345–46; William Pitt to the Governors in America, December 9, 1758, 350–52; and William Pitt to Jeffrey Amherst, December 29, 1759, 355–60, all in *Documents Relative to the Colonial History of the State of New York*, vol. 7, ed. E. B. O'Callaghan (Albany, N.Y.: Weed, Parsons, 1856); Daniel K. Richter, *The Ordeal of the Longhouse: The Peoples of the Iroquois League in the Era of European Colonization* (Chapel Hill: University of North Carolina Press, 1992), 255–80; and Kammen, *Colonial New York*, 305–36.

83. *New York Mercury*, November 27 and December 10, 1759, December 1, 1760; and *New York Gazette* (Weyman's), December 1, 1760, January 5, 1761, January 18, 1762.

84. Nash, *The Urban Crucible*, 233.

85. *New York Mercury*, June 21 and 28, 1756, May 8, 1758, November 19, 1759, April 28, June 2 and 9, 1760, November 22, 1762; *New York Gazette* (Weyman's), March 19 and September 10, 1759, October 8, 10 and 16, November 16, 1761, 1761, October 25, 1762, August 1, 1763; Anderson, *Crucible of War*, 250–54, 490; American Loyalist Transcripts, Audit Office Records, 1783–1790, Rare Book and Manuscript Reading Room, New York Public Library, New York, N.Y. [hereafter ALT], vol. 41, *Examinations in London. Memorials, Schedules of Losses, and Evidences*, 523–30; ALT, vol. 17, *Examinations in Nova Scotia, &c. Memorials, Schedules of Losses, Evidences*, 593, 606; ALT, vol. 42, *Examinations in London. Memorials, Schedules of Losses, Evidences*, 89–107; ALT, vol. 45, *Examinations in London. Memorials, Schedules of Losses, Evidences*, 297–301, 495–556; Andrew Elliot to brother, May or June 1755, Andrew Elliot Papers, N-YHS; Matson, *Merchants & Empire*, 270–72; and Jeffrey Amherst to Cadwallader Colden, April 15, 1762, 136–37, in *The Letters and Papers of Cadwallader Colden*, vol. 6.

86. *New York Mercury*, October 30, 1757, August 7 and 10, 1758, February 5 and June 4, 1759, April 28, 1760.

87. *New York Mercury*, March 20 and October 16, 1758, January 22, February 5, April 30, November 27, and December 10 and 17, 1759, May 5 and December 1, 1760, April 6, August 17, and November 23, 1761, June 14 and April 26, 1762, October 24 and 31 and November 21, 1763; and *New York Gazette* (Weyman's), December 1, 1760, January 5, 1761, January 18 and October 25, 1762.

88. *New York Mercury*, July 25, 1763; *New York Gazette* (Weyman's), July 25, 1763.

89. *London Gazette*, January 16 to January 20, 1759.

90. *London Gazette*, Tuesday, October 11–October 15, 1763.

91. *London Gazette*, August 15–August 19, 1758, January 16–January 20, 1759, September 4–September 8, 1759, September 10, 1759, August 15–August 18, 1761, October 11–October 15, 1763, November 8–November 12, 1763; and *New York Mercury*, December 19, 1757, March 20, 1758, October 16, 1758, December 16, 1758, November 19, 1759, December 10, 1759, December 17, 1759, March 3, 1760, December 1, 1760, October 24, 1763, November 21, 1763.

92. *New York Mercury*, January 30, 1764, May 14, 1764; *New York Gazette* (Weyman's), October 20, 1764; Nash, *Urban Crucible*, vi–xv; and Anderson, *Crucible of War*, 591–92.

2. UNCERTAIN ADJUSTMENTS

1. *Rivington's New York Gazette*, November 26, 1783; *The Independent New-York Gazette*, November 29, 1783; Benjamin Tallmadge, *Memoir of Col. Benjamin Tallmadge* (New York: Holman, 1858; repr. New York: Arno, 1968), 62; Committee Appointed to Conduct the Order of Receiving Their Excellencies Governor Clinton and General Washington, untitled broadside, November 24, 1783, American Antiquarian Society, *American Imprints, Evans 4426*; Edwin G. Burrows and Mike Wallace, *Gotham: A History of New York to 1898* (New York: Oxford University Press, 1999), 259–61; Barnet Schecter, *The Battle for New York: The City at the Heart of the American Revolution* (New York: Penguin, 2002), 95–167, 194–97; Douglas Southall Freeman, *George Washington: A Biography*, vol. 5, *Victory with the Help of France* (New York: Scribner's, 1952), 461; and James Thomas Flexner, *George Washington*, vol. 3, *In the American Revolution (1775–1783)* (Boston: Little, Brown, 1967), 522–28.

2. On postrevolutionary ceremony, see David Waldstreicher, *In the Midst of Perpetual Fetes: The Making of American Nationalism, 1776–1820* (Chapel Hill: University of North Carolina Press, 1997); Simon P. Newman, *Parades and the Politics of the Street: Festive Culture in the Early American Republic* (Philadelphia: University of Pennsylvania Press, 1997); Len Travers, *Celebrating the Fourth: Independence Day and the Rites of Nationalism in the Early Republic* (Amherst: University of Massachusetts Press, 1997); and Clifton Hood, "An Unusable Past: Urban Elites, New York City's Evacuation Day, and the Transformation of Memory Culture," *Journal of Social History* 37 (Summer 2004): 883–913.

3. *New York Packet*, January 15, 1784; and *The Independent New-York Gazette*, November 29 and December 6, 1783; *The Independent Journal: or, The General Advertiser*, December 1 and 6, 1783.

4. *The Independent New-York Gazette*, December 6, 1783; and *The Independent Journal: or, The General Advertiser*, December 6, 1783.

5. Robert R. Livingston to John Jay, November 29, 1783, 99, in *The Correspondence and Public Papers of John Jay, 1763–1826*, ed. Henry P. Johnson (New York: Putnam, 1890–93; repr. New York: Da Capo, 1971).

6. *New York Packet*, January 15, 1784; *Independent Journal*, December 1, 1783.

7. *Independent Journal*, December 1, 1783.

8. Tryon to Germain, September 24, 1776, 686–87, in *Documents Relative to the Colonial History of the State of New York*, vol. 8; John Pattison to Mr. Pendleton, November 22, 1779, Stephen Payne Adye to Major Lumm, January 20, 1780, Stephen Payne Adye to Major Lumm, February 7, 1780, Stephen Payne Adye to Lieutenant McNabb, February 8, 1780, Stephen Payne Adye to Lieutenant Symes, February 12, 1780, all in *Official Letters of Major General James Pattison, Collections of the New-York Historical Society for the Year 1875*, vol. 8 (New York: New-York Historical Society, 1876); Edwin G. Burrows, "Prison Ships," in *Encyclopedia of New York City*, 2nd ed., ed. Kenneth T. Jackson (New Haven, Conn.: Yale University Press, 2010), 1039–40; Donald J. Cannon, "Firefighting," in Jackson, *Encyclopedia of New York City*, 449–54; and Burrows and Wallace, *Gotham*, 241–42.

9. Edward Countryman, *A People in Revolution: The American Revolution and Political Society in New York, 1760–1790* (Baltimore, Md.: Johns Hopkins University Press, 1981), 230–79; Burrows and Wallace, *Gotham*, 292–96; and Andrew S. Trees, *The Founding Fathers and the Politics of Character* (Princeton, N.J.: Princeton University Press, 2004), 1–11.

10. *New York Packet*, July 22, 25, and 29 and August 7, 1788.

11. Ibid.

12. Burrows and Wallace, *Gotham*, 295.

13. Ibid., 295.

14. *New York Packet*, July 22, 1788.

15. John Anderson Jr. Diary, entries for July 4, 1794, and November 25, 1795, Library of the New-York Historical Society, New York, N.Y. [hereafter N-YHS]; Alexander Anderson Diary, entry for November 25, 1794, Rare Book and Manuscript Library, Columbia University, New York, N.Y. [hereafter CU].

16. John Anderson Diary, entries for February 19, 1794, February 11, 1795, June 28, 1795, October 9, 1795, July 6, 8, 10, and 18, and August 2, 1796, N-YHS.

17. Paul A. Gilje, *The Road to Mobocracy: Popular Disorder in New York City, 1763–1834* (Chapel Hill: University of North Carolina Press, 1987), 97–112.

18. John Anderson Diary, entries for July 4, 1795, and July 4, 1796, N-YHS.

19. Ibid., entry for July 4, 1795.

20. Ibid., entries for July 17, 1794, August 2, 1795, January 20, October 17, 20, and 26, and November 20, 1797, and May 12, 14, 24, and 28, 1798, N-YHS; and Alexander Anderson Diary, entries for March 17 and September 6, 1793, CU.

21. John Anderson Diary, entries for March 7 and 10, 1794, N-YHS. For the political impact of the French Revolution in New York, see Alfred F. Young, *The Democratic Republicans of New York: The Origins, 1763–1797* (Chapel Hill: University of North Carolina Press, 1967), 345–91.

22. Alexander Anderson Diary, entries for June 11 and August 18, 1793, March 20 and May 18, 1794, CU.

23. Countryman, *A People in Revolution*, 231–45.

24. Joseph S. Tiedemann, *Reluctant Revolutionaries: New York City and the Road to Independence, 1763–1776* (Ithaca, N.Y.: Cornell University Press, 2008), 198–214; Gary Nash, *The Urban Crucible: Social Change, Political Consciousness, and the Origins of the American Revolution* (Cambridge, Mass.: Harvard University Press, 1979), 351–74. Countryman, *A People in Revolution*, 103–30; and Esmond Wright, "The New York Loyalists: A Cross-Section of Colonial Society," 81–84, in *The Loyalist Americans: A Focus on Greater New York*, ed. Robert East and Jacob Judd (Tarrytown, N.Y.: Sleepy Hollow Restorations, 1975).

25. Nash, *The Urban Crucible*, 372.

26. Ibid., 349–74; Tiedemann, *Reluctant Revolutionaries*, 198–214; and Countryman, *A People in Revolution*, 103–30.

27. Cynthia A. Kierner, *Traders and Gentlefolk: The Livingstons of New York, 1675–1790* (Ithaca: Cornell University Press, 1992), 202–19; George Dangerfield, *Chancellor Robert R. Livingston of New York, 1746–1813* (New York: Harcourt, Brace, 1960), 68–105; Judith Van Buskirk, *Generous Enemies: Patriots and Loyalists in Revolutionary New York* (Philadelphia: University of Pennsylvania Press, 2002), 48; and Edward P. Alexander, *A Revolutionary Conservative: James Duane of New York* (New York: Columbia University Press, 1938), 39–51.

28. L. F. S. Upton, *The Loyal Whig: William Smith of New York & Quebec* (Toronto: University of Toronto Press, 1969), 103–19 144–45, 165, 171, 199–223. Kierner, *Traders and Gentlefolk*, 201–42; and Van Buskirk, *Generous Enemies*, 54–68.

29. American Loyalist Transcripts, Audit Office Records, 1783–1790. Rare Book and Manuscript Reading Room, New York Public Library [hereafter abbreviated as ALT], vol. 17, *Examinations in Nova Scotia &c. Memorials, Schedules of Losses, and Evidences*, 604–6; ALT, vol. 41, *Examinations in London. Memorials, Schedules of Losses, and Evidences*, 523–30; ALT, vol. 42, *Examinations in London. Memorials, Schedules of Losses, and Evidences*, 5–13, 177–338; ALT, vol. 43, *Examinations in London. Memorials, Schedules of Losses, and Evidences*, 461–501, 519–43; and Gregory Palmer, *Biographical Sketches of Loyalists of the American Revolution* (Westport, Conn.: Meckler, 1984), 431, 456, 621, 894.

30. *Rivington's Royal Gazette*, October 25, 1777, September 16 and 19, 1778; Palmer, *Biographical Sketches of Loyalists*, 12, 594, 690–91, 772; Eric Robson, *The American Revolution in Its Political and Military Aspects, 1763–1783* (Hamden, Conn.: Archon, 1965), 101; Burrows and Wallace, *Gotham*, 245. For loyalists, see John E. Ferling, *The Loyalist Mind: Joseph Galloway and the American Revolution* (University Park: Pennsylvania State University Press, 1977); William H. Nelson, *The American Tory* (Oxford, U.K.: Clarendon, 1961); Philip Ranlet, *The New York Loyalists* (Knoxville: University of Tennessee Press, 1986); Mary Beth Norton, *The British-American: The Loyalist Exiles in London, 1774–1783* (Boston: Little, Brown, 1972); and Ruma Chopra, *Unnatural Rebellion: Loyalists in New York City During the Revolution* (Charlottesville: University of Virginia Press, 2011), 1–6.

31. Harry B. Yoshpe, *The Disposition of Loyalist Estates in the Southern District of New York* (New York: Columbia University Press, 1939), 18–22, 28–33, 40–43, 46, 50–56.

32. *Rivington's Royal Gazette*, August 7, 1782; Palmer, *Biographical Sketches of Loyalists*, 15–16, 898, 901; Countryman, *A People in Revolution*, 173–74, 215; Maya Jasanoff, *Liberty's Exiles: American Loyalists in the Revolutionary World* (New York: Knopf, 2011), 94; Burrows and Wallace, *Gotham*, 256–59; and Van Buskirk, *Generous Enemies*, 179. For another assessment of the size and composition of the loyalist exodus, see Ranlet, *The New York Loyalists*, 193–94.

33. Palmer, *Biographical Sketches of Loyalists*, 27, 29–30, 77, 254, 308, 422, 473, 593; ALT, vol. 42, *Examinations in London. Memorials, Schedules of Losses, and Evidences*, 91.

34. Ron Chernow, *Alexander Hamilton* (New York: Penguin, 2004), 1–28, 37–82; Robert F. Jones, *"The King of the Alley": William Duer, Politician, Entrepreneur, and Speculator, 1768–1799* (Philadelphia: American Philosophical Society, 1992), vii–x, 1–100.

35. The other groups are the directors of the New York Society for Promoting Agriculture, Arts, and Manufactures from 1789 to 1792; the trustees and members of the New York Society Library in 1793; the members of the Friendly Club in 1795; the directors and subscribers of the American Academy of Fine Arts in 1802; and the trustees and benefactors of the Free School Society in 1805 and 1814. Trinity Church was the city's most prestigious house of worship; Columbia College, also an Episcopalian institution, was where upper-class New Yorkers sent their sons to be educated; the New York Society Library (opened in 1754) and the American Academy of Fine Arts (1802) were civic associations that operated on a subscription basis and fostered an appreciation of learning and the arts; the Manufacturing Society was a booster group that promoted economic growth; the Friendly Club was a small literary discussion circle; and the Hospital Society and the Free School Society were benevolent associations that aided the poor and disadvantaged. These institutions had different missions and were of different sizes and degrees of selectivity, but all were associated with the upper class.

36. I obtained membership lists from the following sources: New York Manufacturing Society, minutes, entries for February 23, March 18, 26, and 31, 1789, New York Manufacturing Society Records, N-YHS; American Academy of Fine Arts, Keeper's Book, vol. 1, American Academy of Fine Arts Records, N-YHS; *A Brief Account of the New-York Hospital* (New York: Collins, 1804), 66–72; *An Account of the Origins of the Free-School Society of New-York* (New York: Collins, 1814), 5–6, 12–13; James E. Cronin, ed., *The Diary of Elihu Hubbard Smith (1771–1798)* (Philadelphia: American Philosophical Society, 1973), 45–46; Columbia University in the City of New York, *Catalogue of Officers and Graduates of Columbia University from the Foundation of King's College in 1754*, 16th ed. (New York: n.p., 1916), 79–88; and *The Charter, Bye-Laws, and Names of the Members of the New-York Society Library, with a Catalog of the Books Belonging to the Said Library* (New York: Swords, 1793), 21–93; Trinity Church Pews Book [2nd Church 1790s and St. Paul's and St. John's], 1–24, Trinity Church Archives, Parish of Trinity Church, New York, N.Y. There were 156 Trinity pew holders; 837 trustees and members of the New York Society Library; 222 officers, governors, senior professional staff, and members of the New York Hospital; 79 directors and subscribers

of the American Academy of Fine Arts and Sciences; 60 trustees and benefactors of the Free School Society; 342 graduates of Colombia College; 16 directors of the New York Manufacturing Society; and 12 members of the Friendly Club. See also William W. Cutler III, "Status, Values and the Education of the Poor: The Trustees of the New York Public School Society, 1805–1853," *American Quarterly* 24 (March 1972): 69–85; M. J. Heale, "From City Fathers to Social Critics: Humanitarianism and Government in New York, 1790–1860," *Journal of American History* 63 (June 1976): 21–41; Raymond A. Mohl, *Poverty in New York, 1783–1825* (New York: Oxford University Press, 1971), 137–58; Conrad Edick Wright, *The Transformation of Charity in Postrevolutionary New England* (Boston: Northeastern University Press, 1992), 49–95. The sources of the occupational data used in this analysis are David Franks, *The New York Directory* (New York: Sheppard Kollack, 1786); *The New York Directory, and Register, for the Year 1789* (New York: Hodge, Allen, and Campbell, 1789); William Duncan, *The New-York Directory, and Register, for the Year 1791* (New York: Swords, 1791); William Duncan, *The New-York Directory, and Register, for the Year 1792* (New York: Swords, 1792); William Duncan, *The New-York Directory, and Register, for the Year 1795* (New York: Swords, 1795); John Low, *The New-York Directory, and Register, for the Year 1796* (New York: Buel, 1796); and *Longworth's American Almanack; New-York Register, and Directory, for the Twenty-Fourth Year of American Independence* (New York: Swords, 1799).

37. A total of 226 men were affiliated with two or more of these eight organizations. This select group included seven members of the Livingston family; four Beekmans, Bownes, and Ludlows; three Phoenixes and Bleeckers; and two De Peysters, Laights, Remsens, and Rhinelanders. Of this 226, a subset of forty-five men belonged to three institutions apiece. This subset included statesmen Alexander Hamilton, Aaron Burr, and De Witt Clinton and great merchants Herman Le Roy, Gilbert Aspinwall, John Atkinson, Peter Goelet, Nicholas Gouverneur, Peter Kemble, and Nicholas Low. Eight men had links to four organizations: John Jay, a president of the Confederation Congress, coauthor of the *Federalist Papers*, a diplomat, the first chief justice of the U.S. Supreme Court, and a governor of New York State; and merchants Matthew Clarkson, Gabriel Ludlow, John R. Murray Sr., his son, John R. Murray Jr., Henry Ten Brook, Gulian Verplanck, and Robert Watts. Four men registered five affiliations apiece: Robert R. Livingston, chancellor of the state of New York and minister to France; great merchant Frederick De Peyster; Henry Rutgers, a wealthy landowner and philanthropist; and John Watts, a great merchant who served in the U.S. Congress and the New York State legislature. Nobody had more than five affiliations apiece.

38. *A Brief Account of the New-York Hospital*, 66; *An Account of the Origins of the Free-School Society*, 6; *The New York Directory, and Register, for the Year 1789*, 94; *The New-York Directory, and Register, for the Year 1790* (New York: Hodge, Allen, and Campbell, 1790), 87; Duncan, *The New-York Directory, and Register, for the Year 1791*, 110, 138; *New York Daily Advertiser*, May 25, 1787. See also Walter Stahr, *John Jay: Founding*

Father (New York: Hambledon & London, 2005), xi–xiv, 1–32; George Dangerfield, *Chancellor Robert R. Livingston of New York, 1746–1813* (New York: Harcourt, Brace, 1960), 183–233; and Herbert Parmet and Marie B. Hecht, *Aaron Burr: Portrait of an Ambitious Man* (New York: Macmillan, 1967), 59–95.

39. The names of officials of the New York State chapter of the Society of the Cincinnati also on our list of the 226 men who belonged to two or more institutions include: Alexander Hamilton, Matthew Clarkson, Ebenezer Stevens, and Brockholst Livingston. William Constable was president of the Saint Patrick's Society; Robert R. Livingston, Alexander Hamilton, and Brockholst Livingston belonged to the Saint Andrew's Society; and Theophylact Bache and Cadwallader D. Colden to the Saint George's Society. Matthew Clarkson was president and John R. Murray Jr. and Brockholst Livingston were vice presidents of the Society for the Prevention of Pauperism. *The New York Directory, and Register, for the Year 1789*, 137; *Rules for the St. Andrew's Society of the State of New-York* (New York: McLean, 1785), 11–14; *The Constitution and By-Laws of the St. George's Society, established in the City of New York, in 1786 for the Purpose of Relieving Their Brethren in Distress* (New York: Grattan, 1830), 21–26; Smith, *The City of New York in the Year of Washington's Inauguration*, 114; and The Society for the Prevention of Pauperism in the City of New-York, *The First Annual Report of the Managers of the Society for the Prevention of Pauperism in the City of New-York, Read and Accepted October 26, 1818* (New York: Seymore, 1818), 27.

40. These five comprised less than 1 percent of the General Society's total membership and only 2 percent of the 226 people who participated in two or more of the eight institutions. The five were Samuel Borrowe, a physician; Francis Childs, a bookseller and stationer; Nathaniel Hawkshurst, a clock and watchmaker; Josiah G. Pierson, a nail manufacturer; and Jacob Sherred, a painter and glazier. They were, at best, on the edge of the upper class. *Register of the General Society of Mechanics and Tradesmen, 1786–*, unpaginated, Library of the General Society of Mechanics and Tradesmen, New York, N.Y. The sources of the occupational data are the city directories citied above.

41. J. P. Brissot De Warville, *New Travels in the United States of America, 1788*, ed. Durand Echeverria, trans. Mara Soceanu Vamos and Durand Echeverria (Cambridge, Mass.: Harvard University Press, 1964), 145.

42. William Strickland, *Journal of a Tour in the United States of America, 1794–1795*, ed. J. E. Strickland (New York: New-York Historical Society, 1971), 44.

43. Robert Greenhalgh Albion, *The Rise of New York Port, 1815–1860* (New York: Scribner's, 1939; repr., Boston: Northeastern University Press, 1984), 1–37; George Rogers Taylor, *The Transportation Revolution, 1815–1860* (New York: Holt, Rinehart and Winston, 1951), 15–103; Gordon C. Bjork, "Foreign Trade," 54–61, in *The Growth of the Seaport Cities, 1790–1825: Proceedings of a Conference Sponsored by the Eleutherian Mills-Hagley Foundation, March 17–19, 1966*, ed. David T. Gilchrist (Charlottesville: University of Virginia Press, 1967); Robert A. Davison, "Comment: New York Foreign

Trade," 68–78, in Gilchrist, *The Growth of the Seaport Cities, 1790–1825*; Nathan A. Miller, *The Enterprise of a Free People: Aspects of Economic Development in New York State During the Canal Period, 1792–1838* (Ithaca, N.Y.: Cornell University Press, 1962), 3–19; and Campbell Gibson, "Population of the 100 Largest Cities and Other Urban Places in the United States: 1790–1990," Population Division Working Paper No. 27 (Washington, D.C.: U.S. Bureau of the Census, Population Division, 1998), tables 2 and 3. New York City had 60,515 inhabitants in 1800. The figures for Philadelphia for 1790 and 1800 are estimates based on adding the populations of Northern Liberties and Southwark Township to those of the city itself to include the main areas that would be part of the consolidation of 1854. This yields 44,000 for 1790 and 61,000 for 1800.

44. Thomas M. Doerflinger, *A Vigorous Spirit of Enterprise: Merchants and Economic Development in Revolutionary Philadelphia* (Chapel Hill: University of North Carolina Press, 1986), 3–7, 283–334, 334–39; Norman Brouwer, "Port of New York," in *Encyclopedia of New York City*, 2nd ed., 1022–26; Richard R. John, *Spreading the News: The American Postal System from Franklin to Morse* (Cambridge, Mass.: Harvard University Press, 1995), 25–63, Bruce W. Bugbee, *Genesis of American Patent and Copyright Law* (Washington, D.C.: Public Affairs Press, 1967), 84–124; and Pauline M. Maier, "The Revolutionary Origins of the American Corporation," *William and Mary Quarterly*, 3rd series, 50 (January 1993): 51–84.

45. *Independent Journal*, March 18, 1786; James W. Darlington, "Agriculture," 28–36, in *Encyclopedia of New York State*, ed. Peter Eisenstadt (Syracuse, N.Y.: Syracuse University Press, 2005).

46. Van Buskirk, *Generous Enemies*, 1–7, 195; Tiedemann, *Reluctant Revolutionaries*, 1–9.

47. Van Buskirk, *Generous Enemies*, 195; Chernow, *Alexander Hamilton*, 194–97; Countryman, *A People in Revolution*, 221–51; Brutus, "To All Adherents to the British Government and Followers of the British Army Commonly Called Tories" (New York: Morton and Horner, 1783), in American Antiquarian Society, *Early American Imprints, Shipton & Mooney 44464*; Civis, "To William Smith, Charles Inglis, Frederick Phillpse, Isaac Low, Hugh and Alexander Wallace, Theophilact Bache, James Rivington, &c. &c. &c." (New York: [Hugh Gaine?], 1783), in American Antiquarian Society, *Early American Imprints, Evans 17871*; and *Independent Journal, or, the General Advertiser*, May 19 and 22, 1784; *New York Packet*, April 8 and May 3, 1784.

48. *Independent Journal*, December 29, 1783.

49. Collin McGregor to James Duncan, January 20, 1784, vol. 1, Collin McGregor Letterbooks, Rare Books and Manuscripts Division, New York Public Library, New York, N.Y. [hereafter NYPL].

50. Collin McGregor to John McKenzie, January 20, 1784, vol. 1, McGregor Letterbooks, NYPL. See also Oscar Zeichner, "The Loyalist Problem in New York After the Revolution," *New York History* 21 (July 1940): 284–302.

51. Frederick Rhinelander to undetermined recipient, April 5, 1774, Letter and Order Book, 1774–1784, Microfilm Edition, Rhinelander Papers, N-YHS.

52. Frederick and Philip Rhinelander to Smithson & Rutgers, January 29, 1778, Letter and Order Book, 1774–1784, Rhinelander Papers, N-YHS; Frederick and Philip Rhinelander to Rawlinson & Chorley, December 28, 1776, Letter and Order Book, 1774–1784, Rhinelander Papers, N-YHS; Frederick and Philip Rhinelander to Rawlinson & Chorley, November 12, 1777, Letter and Order Book, 1774–1784, Rhinelander Papers, N-YHS; Frederick and Philip Rhinelander, Letter and Order Book, 1774–1784, Rhinelander Papers, N-YHS; Frederick and Philip Rhinelander to Rawlinson & Chorley, November 12, 1777, Letter and Order Book, 1774–1784, Rhinelander Papers, N-YHS; Frederick and Philip Rhinelander, Letter and Order Book, 1774–1784, Rhinelander Papers, N-YHS. Frederick Rhinelander to Davis Straghan & Company, May 17, 1779, Rhinelander Letterbook, 1774–1784, Rhinelander Papers N-YHS; and Frederick Rhinelander to Daniel Borden & Son, December 15, 1780, Rhinelander Letterbook, 1774–1784, Rhinelander Papers, N-YHS.

53. Frederick and Philip Rhinelander to Hodgson & Donaldson, February 17, 1783, Frederick and Philip Rhinelander Letterbook, 1774–1784, Rhinelander Papers, N-YHS.

54. Frederick Rhinelander, June 12, 1781, Rhinelander Letterbook, 1774–1784, Rhinelander Papers, N-YHS; Frederick Rhinelander to John Pagan, July 24, 1781, Rhinelander Letterbook, 1774–1784, Rhinelander Papers, N-YHS; Frederick Rhinelander to William Ashton & Company, May 26, 1781, Rhinelander Letterbook, 1774–1784, Rhinelander Papers, N-YHS; George Appleby & Company to George Gibbs, July 20, 1786, William Rhinelander Letterbook, 1795 to 1800 [sic], Rhinelander Papers, N-YHS; George Appelby & Company to Peter Cunningham, August n.d., 1786, William Rhinelander Letterbook, 1795 to 1800 [sic], Rhinelander Papers, N-YHS; George Appleby & Company to Gibbs and Blagge, September 9, 1786, William Rhinelander Letterbook, 1795 to 1800 [sic], Rhinelander Papers, N-YHS; William Rhinelander & Company to Captain Carpenter, January 30, 1793, William Rhinelander Letterbook, 1795 to 1800 [sic], Rhinelander Papers, N-YHS. David C. Francks, *The New York Directory* (New York: Francks, 1787), 31; *The New-York Directory and Register for the Year 1790* (New York: n.p., 1790), 83; and *The New-York Directory and Register for the Year 1791* (New York: Swords, 1791), 105.

55. *Independent Journal, or, The General Advertiser*, January 14, 1786. Bache was one of the 45 men who belonged to three of the eight elite institutions examined earlier.

56. William Constable to Samuel Ward, November 4, 1794, Constable-Pierrepont Papers, NYPL; William Constable to LeRoy, November 30, 1794, Letterbook 4, C-PP; James Phynn to William Constable, January 20, 1788, Box 1, 1788–June 1789 Folder, Constable-Pierrepont Papers, NYPL; William Constable to Messrs. Phynn, Ellice, and Inglis, June 2, 1789, Box 1, 1788–June 1789 Folder, Constable-Pierrepont Papers, NYPL; William Constable to James Phynn, January 1, 1789, Box 1, 1788–June 1789 Folder, Constable-Pierrepont Papers, NYPL; Will of James Phynn, Prob. 11/1351, Folio 291. Will proved in Perogative Court of Canterbury, Microfilm edition, Family Records Centre, P.R.O., 1 Myddleton Street, London EC1R 1UW.

57. Jones, *"The King of the Alley,"* 64.

58. Donald G. Tailby, "Chapters from the Business Career of William Constable: A Merchant of Post-Revolutionary New York," (PhD dissertation, Rutgers University, 1961), 4–76, 109–215; *The Charter, Bye-Laws, and Names of the Members of the New-York Society Library, with a Catalogue of the Books Belonging to the Said Library* (New York: Gaine, 1789), 78; *Independent Journal,* March 11, 1786; and Thomas E. V. Smith, *The City of New York in the Year of Washington's Inauguration* (New York: Randolf, 1889), 114. Constable belonged to three of the eight elite organizations.

59. Bettina Manzo, ed., "A Virginian in New York: The Diary of St. George Tucker, July–August 1786," *New York History* 67 (April 1986): 186.

60. Ibid., 186.

61. Countryman, *A People in Revolution,* 112–13; Sidney I. Pomerantz, *New York: An American City, 1783–1803* (New York: Columbia University Press, 1938; repr. Port Washington, N.Y.: Friedman, 1965), 89–91; and Gibson, "Population of the 100 Largest Cities and Other Urban Places in the United States: 1790–1990," tables 2 and 3.

62. Fluydn Maitand & Company to James Beekman, January 4, 1786, Box 32(a), Folder 1, Beekman Family Papers, NYPL.

63. Ibid.

64. I take the phrase "communities of mutual trust" from David Meyer, *The Roots of American Industrialization* (Baltimore, Md.: Johns Hopkins University Press, 2003), 8. John Inglis to William Constable, February 6, 1790, Box 1, 1780 Letters, Constable-Pierrepont Papers, NYPL; John Inglis to William Constable, February 15, 1791, Box 1, January–June 1791 Folder, Constable-Pierrepont Papers, NYPL; Alexander Macomb to William Constable, April 16, 1794, Box 3, January–May 1794 Folder, Constable-Pierrepont Papers, NYPL; Samuel Ward to William Constable, April 17, 1794, January–May 1794 Folder, Constable-Pierrepont Papers, NYPL; Samuel Ward to William Constable, September 21, 1794, Box 3, September–December 1794 Folder, Constable-Pierrepont Papers, NYPL; John Inglis to William Constable, January 6, 1796, Box 4, January–April 1794 Folder, Constable-Pierrepont Papers, NYPL; John Inglis to William Constable, June 9, 1797, Box 4, June–December 1797 Folder, Constable-Pierrepont Papers, NYPL; John Inglis to William Constable, July 31, 1798, Box 4, July–December 1798 Folder, Constable-Pierrepont Papers, NYPL; and William Constable to Hezekiah Beers Pierrepont, May 4, 1799, Box 18, 1799 Folder, Constable-Pierrepont Papers, NYPL.

65. William Constable to Samuel Ward, November 4, 1794, Letterbook 4, Constable-Pierrepont Papers, NYPL.

66. *Massachusetts Centinel,* August 3, 6, 10, and 13, 1785; *Boston Gazette,* August 8 and 22, 1785; *Universal Daily Register,* October 25, 1785. Britons interpreted this affair as evidence of Boston's anti-British malice. London's *Universal Daily Register* concluded "that a trade with the Massachusetts is not so desirable an object with the British merchants as the Bostonians in their great wisdom may suppose." *Universal Daily Register,* September 21, 1785.

67. *Daily Advertiser,* November 16, 1785. Emphasis in the original.

68. Max M. Edling, *A Revolution in Favor of Government: Origins of the U.S. Constitution and the Making of the American State* (New York: Oxford University Press, 2003), 3–10.

69. Stanley Elkins and Eric McKittrick, *The Age of Federalism: The Early American Republic, 1788–1800* (New York: Oxford University Press, 1993), 186.

70. Manzo, "A Virginian in New York," 185, 191–92; De Warville, *New Travels in the United States of America*, 146; Smith, *The City of New York in the Year of Washington's Inauguration*, 206–8; and Frank Monaghan and Marvin Lowenthal, *This Was New York: The Nation's Capital in 1789* (Garden City, N.Y.: Doubleday, Doran, 1943), 132–34.

71. De Warville, *New Travels in the United States of America*, 142.

72. Ibid., 142.

73. Ibid., 140–41.

74. William Parker Cutler and Julia Perkins Cutler, eds., *Life, Journals and Correspondence of Rev. Manasseh Cutler, LL.D*, vol. 1 (Cincinnati: Clarke, 1888), 228–29. See also William Johnson's Diary, entries for January 13–31, 1785, *Letters of Delegates to Congress*, vol. 22, 110n1.

75. Cutler and Cutler, *Life of Cutler*, 231.

76. Ibid., 241.

77. Ibid., 240.

78. *Independent Journal, or, The General Advertiser*, January 12, 1785.

79. Kenneth R. Bowling, "New York City, Capital of the United States, 1785–1790," 10, in *World of the Founders: New York Communities in the Federal Period*, ed. Stephen L. Schecter and Wendell Tripp (Albany: New York State Commission on the Bicentennial of the United States Constitution, 1990).

80. Bowling, "New York City, Capital of the United States, 1785–1790," 14; *New York Daily Advertiser*, March 3, 4, 5, 9, and 18, April 6 and 21, 1789; *New York Packet*, April 24 and May 28, 1789; William Alexander Duer, *New-York as It Was, During the Latter Part of the Last Century: An Anniversary Address Delivered Before the St. Nicholas Society of the City of New-York, December 1st, 1848* (New York: Stanford and Swords, 1849), 29–31; Smith, *The City of New York in the Year of Washington's Inauguration*, 40–49; and Charlene Bang Bickford and Kenneth R. Bowling, *Birth of the Nation: The First Federal Congress, 1789–1791* (New York and Washington: n.p., 1989), 9–28.

81. *New York Packet*, March 3, 1791; *New York Daily Advertiser*, January 2, July 6, and August 17 and 31, 1790; and Donald Jackson and Dorothy Twohig, eds., *The Diaries of George Washington*, vol. 5, *July 1786–December 1789* (Charlottesville: University Press of Virginia, 1979), 448–53.

82. *New York Packet*, June 11, 1789.

83. For Washington's imagery, see Paul Longmore, *The Invention of George Washington* (Berkeley: University of California Press, 1988); Barry Schwartz, *George Washington: The Making of an American Symbol* (New York: Free Press, 1987); Wendy Wick, *George Washington, an American Icon: The Eighteenth-Century Graphic Portraits* (Baltimore: Smithsonian Institution, 1982); and Marcus Cunliffe, *George Washington: Man and Monument* (Boston: Little, Brown, 1958).

84. Maclay, *Diary of William Maclay*: 136.

85. Ibid., 136.

86. Monaghan and Lowenthal, *This Was New York*: 103–11; Bowling, "New York City, Capital of the United States, 1785–1790," 13–18, in *World of the Founders*; and Rufus Wilmot Griswold, *The Republican Court: Or American Society in the Days of Washington*, vol. 1 (New York: Appleton, 1855), 154–58.

87. Otho Holland Williams to Philip Thomas, June 7, 1789, Otho Holland Williams Papers, Maryland Historical Society, quoted in Bowling, "New York City, Capital of the United States, 1785–1790," 13, 22n; Nathaniel Freeman to John Quincy Adams, June 3, 1789, Adams Family Historical Trust, Massachusetts Historical Society, Boston, Mass. I am grateful to Kenneth R. Bowling for sharing the Freeman quotation with me.

88. Burrows and Wallace, *Gotham*: 175. For references to the "court end" of European capitals, see Thomas Davidson, *An Account of the Surprising Deliverance of the Rev. Mr. John Rogers from a Threatened Imprisonment by Means of a Very Young Lady...* (New York: Hodge and Shober, 1775), 8; George Alexander Stevens, *The Celebrated Lecture on Heads* (Philadelphia: Samuel Dellap, [1775?]), 14; and *Pennsylvania Packet*, August 19, 1785; and *Independent Journal*, July 11, 1787.

89. This advertisement ran in the *New York Journal* on August 2, 9, and 23, 1787. I am grateful to Kathleen Bartolini-Tuazon for this citation.

90. *New York Daily Advertiser*, June 15, 1789. I thank Kathleen Bartoloni-Tuazon for this reference.

91. Ibid. Emphasis in the original.

92. Maclay, *Diary of William Maclay*, 70.

93. Ibid., 19, 21, 29, 46, 71, 74, 80, 83, 112, 122, and 231.

94. For a firsthand account of Washington and his allies' use of displays of social preference as political leverage, see Maclay, *Diary of William Maclay*, 253.

95. Monaghan and Lowenthal, *This Was New York*: 103–11; Donald Jackson and Dorothy Twohig, eds., *The Diaries of George Washington*, vol. 6, *January 1790–December 1799* (Charlottesville: University of Virginia Press, 1979), 2, 12, 17, 24, 30–31, 37, 40, 45, 53–54, 56–59, 71; Bowling, "New York City, Capital of the United States, 1785–1790," 13–17; and Sarah Livingston Jay to John Jay, April 23, 1790, Box 36, Sarah Livingston Jay to John Jay, May 15, 1790, Box 36, John Jay Papers, CU.

96. Abigail Adams to sister, July 12, 1789, in *New Letters of Abigail Adams, 1788–1801*, ed. Stewart Mitchell (Boston: Houghton Mifflin, 1947), 15.

97. For contemporary understandings of political equality in geographic terms, see Rosemarie Zagarri, "Representation and the Removal of State Capitals, 1776–1813," *Journal of American History* 74 (March 1988): 1239–56. See also *New-York Journal, & Patriotic Register*, July 16, 1790; *Gazette of the United States*, July 17, 1790.

98. *Daily Advertiser*, August 31, 1790; Kenneth R. Bowling, "New York City, Capital of the United States, 1785–1790," 1–23; and Kenneth R. Bowling, "New York City, The First Federal Capital," 11–15, in *Well Begun: Chronicles of the Early National Period*, ed.

Stephen L. Schechter and Richard B. Bernstein (Albany: New York State Commission on the Bicentennial of the United States Constitution, 1989).

99. *Cumberland Gazette*, August 30, 1790.

100. *New York Daily Advertiser*, July 1, 3, 17, 18, 25, and 27, and August 21, 1795.

101. For an alternative view that New York City's loss of the national capital damaged the nation and the city, see Elkins and McKitrick, *The Age of Federalism*, 168; and Chernow, *Alexander Hamilton*, 329. The state capital was also removed in the 1790s. Although New York City had been the capital of the province since its founding, the British occupation broke that connection and compelled the revolutionaries to govern the state from elsewhere. After the Revolution ended and the northern and western parts of the state began to be settled, pressure mounted for a permanent seat of government that would be located farther upstate and more accessible to the new areas. In 1797 Albany became the state capital. Stefan Bielinksi, "Albany," 40–44, in Eisenstadt, *Encyclopedia of New York State*.

102. *New York Prices Current*, February 23, 1796; Jones, "*The King of the Alley*," 175–203; *Daily Advertiser*, March 26 and April 18, 1792, April 21, 1794.

103. Burrows and Wallace, *Gotham*, 309–10.

104. Jones, "*The King of the Alley*," 98–106, 114, 128–29, 164–65, 173–86, 202–3; William Duer to the holders of Engagements under the Signature of the Subscriber, March 24, 1792, Microfilm reel 2, William Duer Papers, N-YHS; and William Constable to William Duer, January 22, 1792, Microfilm reel 2, Duer Papers, N-YHS. See also Bruce H. Mann, *Republic of Debtors: Bankruptcy in the Age of American Independence* (Cambridge, Mass.: Harvard University Press, 2002), 106–7, 112–15, 184–96.

105. *New York Journal & Patriotic Register*, March 31, 1792. Emphasis in the original.

106. *New York Journal & Patriotic Register*, April 28, 1792.

107. Ibid. Emphasis in the original.

108. *Daily Advertiser*, January 16, 20, and 21, 1792.

109. *Daily Advertiser*, March 29, 1792.

110. *Daily Advertiser*, February 11, 1792.

3. WEALTH

1. *New York Tribune*, April 2, 1848.

2. *New York Herald*, April 2, 1848; *New York Tribune*, April 1 and 3, 1848; Kenneth Wiggins Porter, *John Jacob Astor, Business Man*, vol. 1 (Cambridge, Mass.: Harvard University Press, 1931), 5; and Axel Madsen, *John Jacob Astor: America's First Millionaire* (New York: Wiley, 2001), 266–68.

3. *New York Herald*, March 31, 1848; *New York Commercial Advertiser*, March 30, 1848.

4. William Armstrong, *The Aristocracy of New York: Who They Are, and What They Were: Being a Social and Business History of the City for Many Years* (New York: New York Publishing, 1848).

5. *New York Herald*, April 2, 1848.

6. *New York Herald*, March 30, 1848.

7. *New York Tribune*, April 2, 1848.

8. Marc A. Weiss, "John Jacob Astor," in *Encyclopedia of New York City*, 2nd ed., ed. Kenneth T. Jackson (New Haven, Conn.: Yale University Press, 2010), 72; Kenneth Wiggins Porter, *John Jacob Astor, Business Man*, vol. 2 (Cambridge, Mass.: Harvard University Press, 1931), 910–52; John D. Haeger, *John Jacob Astor: Business and Finance in the Republic* (Detroit: Wayne State University Press, 1991), 11–93; and Madsen, *John Jacob Astor*, 16–34, 44–59.

9. Porter, *John Jacob Astor*, 2: 1034–44; and "Trinity Church Pews Book [2nd Church 1790s and St. Paul's and St. John's], 23, Trinity Church Archives, Parish of Trinity Church, New York, NY; and Morgan Dix, ed., *A History of the Parish of Trinity Church in the City of New York*, Part 2 (New York: Putnam's, 1901): 132–33, 187–93.

10. *A Great Peace Maker: The Diary of James Gallatin, Secretary to Albert Gallatin, 1813–1827* (New York: Scribner's, 1914), 80.

11. Ibid., 80.

12. Ibid., 167.

13. *New York Commercial Advertiser*, February 26, 1826; Porter, *John Jacob Astor: Business Man*, 2: 876–89.

14. Washington Irving, *Astoria, or Anecdotes of an Enterprise Beyond the Rocky Mountains*, vol. 2 (Philadelphia: Carey, Lea & Blanchard, 1836), 216–18, 260–61. See also Andrew Burstein, *The Original Knickerbocker: The Life of Washington Irving* (New York: Basic, 2007), 276–78; Brian Jones, *Washington Irving: An American Original* (New York: Arcade, 2008), 314–15, 323–34; and Haeger, *John Jacob Astor*, 94–169.

15. *New York Herald*, March 31, 1848.

16. *New York Tribune*, March 30, 1848.

17. Astor gave half of his estate to his son, William B. Astor, and assigned handsome settlements to his other children, donations that allowed the Astor family to become a dynasty and ensured that heritable fortunes became a permanent attribute of the city's upper class. *New York Tribune*, March 30, 1848; William B. Astor, Washington Irving, James Gallatin, Daniel Lord, and John Jacob Astor [Jr.], "Report on Distribution and Appropriation of John Jacob Astor Estate as of June 1, 1849," May 31, 1849, John Jacob Astor Estate, Executors' Report on Distribution and Appropriation as of June 1, 1849 Folder, Box 1, Astor Family Papers, Rare Book and Manuscript Division, New York Public Library [hereafter NYPL]. See also James Parton, *Life of John Jacob Astor, To Which Is Appended a Copy of His Last Will* (New York: American News, 1865).

18. *New York Commercial Advertiser*, March 30, 1848.

19. Horace Mann, *A Few Thoughts for a Young Man: A Lecture, Delivered Before the Boston Mercantile Library, on Its 29th Anniversary* (Syracuse: Hall, 1850), 56.

20. Ibid., 59.

21. Ibid., 64.

22. Charles Astor Bristed, *A Letter to the Hon. Horace Mann* (New York: Kernot, 1850), 23, 21. Emphasis in the original.

23. Ibid., 22.

24. Freeman Hunt, *Lives of American Merchants*, 2 vols. (New York: Office of Hunt's Merchants' Magazine, 1856; repr., New York: Kelley, 1969).

25. Porter, *John Jacob Astor, Businessman*, 2: 910–52; Neil A. Hamilton, *American Business Leaders: From Colonial Times to the Present*, vol. 1 (Santa Barbara, Calif.: ABC-Clio, 1999), 100–01, 274–75; Neil A. Hamilton, *American Business Leaders: From Colonial Times to the Present*, vol. 2 (Santa Barbara, Calif.: ABC-Clio, 1999), 431–32, 547–48; and Robert E. Wright and David J. Cowen, *Financial Founding Fathers: The Men Who Made America Rich* (Chicago: University of Chicago Press, 2006), 114–63.

26. Joseph J. Salvo and Arun Peter Lobo, "Population," in Jackson, *The Encyclopedia of New York City*, 1019.

27. U.S. Department of Commerce, Bureau of the Census, *Historical Statistics of the United States: Colonial Times to 1970*, part 1 (Washington, D.C.: U.S. Government Printing Office, 1975), Series A 195–209, Population of States, by Sex, Race, Urban-Rural Residence, and Age: 1790–1970; U.S. Department of Commerce, Bureau of the Census, *1970 Census of Population*, vol. 1, *Characteristics of the Population*, part A, *Number of Inhabitants*, sect. 1, *United States, Alabama–Mississippi* (Washington, D.C.: U.S. Government Printing Office, 1972), table A, Apportionment and Apportionment Population Based on the 1970 Census; Cynthia A. Kierner, "Livingston Family," 916; Carl L. Westerdahl, "Stephen Van Rensselaer III," 1636; Peter R. Christoph, "Renssaerswijck," 1298–99; and Robert F. Pecorella, "Upstate and Downstate," 1619–22, all in *Encyclopedia of New York State*, ed. Peter Eisenstadt (Syracuse, N.Y.: Syracuse University Press, 2005).

28. This description that follows is based upon *Miller's New York As It Is; Or, Stranger's Guide-Book to the Cities of New York, Brooklyn, and Adjacent Places* (New York: Miller, 1865), 25–26; Lorenzo De Zavala, *Journey to the United States of America*, trans. Wallace Woolsey, ed. John-Michael Rivera (Houston: Arte Pública, 2005), 68–73; Isabella Lucy Bird, *The Englishwoman in America* (London: Murray, 1856; repr., Madison: University of Wisconsin Press, 1966), 334–43; R. Barclay-Allardice, *Agricultural Tour in the United States and Upper Canada, with Miscellaneous Notices* (Edinburgh: Blackwood, 1842), 13; *Journal of a Wanderer; Being A Residence in India, and Six Weeks in North America* (London: Simpkin, Marshall, 1844), 136; *The American Diaries of Richard Cobden*, ed. Elizabeth Hoon Cawley (Princeton, N.J.: Princeton University Press, 1952), 898; Barclay-Allardice, *Agricultural Tour*, 13; and Campbell Gibson, *Population of the 100 Largest Cities and Other Urban Places in the United States: 1790 to 1990*, Population Division Working Paper No. 27, U.S. Bureau of the Census, Population Division (Washington, D.C.: n.p., 1998), table 9.

29. Bird, *The Englishwoman in America*, 334. Emphasis in the original.

30. Tyler Andbinder, *Five Points: The 19th Century New York City Neighborhood That Invented the Tap Dance, Stole Elections, and Became the World's Most Notorious Slum* (New York: Penguin, 2001), 14–140; Herbert Asbury, *The Gangs of New York: An Informal History of the Underworld* (New York: Knopf, 1927; repr., New York: Paragon

House, 1990), 1–20, 105; Joel H. Ross, *What I Saw in New York; Or, a Bird's Eye View of City Life*, 2nd ed. (Auburn, N.Y.: Derby & Miller, 1852), 105; and George C. Foster, *New York Gas-Light and Other Urban Sketches*, ed. Stuart M. Blumin (Berkeley: University of California Press, 1990), 2–57.

31. Ross, *What I Saw in New York*, 164.

32. George Rogers Taylor, *The Transportation Revolution, 1815–1860* (New York: Holt, Rinehart & Winston, 1951), 15–103, 132–52, 243–49, 443; D. W. Meinig, *The Shaping of America: A Geographical Perspective on 500 Years of History*, vol. 2, *Continental America, 1800–1867* (New Haven, Conn.: Yale University Press, 1995), 352–74; Ronald E. Shaw, *Canals for a Nation: The Canal Era in the United States, 1790–1860* (Lexington: University of Kentucky Press, 1990), 30–97; David R. Meyer, *The Roots of American Industrialization* (Baltimore, Md.: Johns Hopkins University Press, 2003), 189–225; and Glenn Porter and Harold Livesay, *Merchants and Manufacturing: Studies in the Changing Structure of Nineteenth-Century Marketing* (Baltimore, Md.: Johns Hopkins University Press, 1971), 1–11.

33. Taylor, *The Transportation Revolution*, 384–97; "Map Illustrating the Mean Center of Population of the United States: 1790 -2000," *United States Census 2000: Centers of Population for 2000*, U.S. Department of Commerce, Census Bureau, accessed March 30, 2007, www.census.gov/geo/www/cenpop/cntpop2k.html (URL no longer active). The U.S. Census Bureau defines the center of population as "the place where an imaginary, flat, weightless and rigid map of the United States would balance perfectly" if all Americans were of identical weight. "Press release: 2000 U.S. Population Centered in Phelps County, Mo," CB01-CN 66, April 2, 2001, U.S. Deaprtment of Commerce, Bureau of the Census, Economics and Statistics Administration, accessed March 24, 2007, www.census.gov/Press-release/www/2001/cb01ca66.html (URL no longer active).

34. If anything, these statistics underestimate New York City's significance as a population center, for they exclude Brooklyn, which in 1860 was the nation's third-largest city. While Brooklyn was still an independent city, it was located just across the East River from Manhattan and had become part of New York City's economic and social orbit. In 1860 New York City and Brooklyn had a combined population of more than one million, nearly twice as large as Philadelphia and five times larger than Baltimore, the country's fourth-largest city. The figure for Philadelphia includes the populations of Northern Liberties and Southwark prior to 1860. Gibson, *Population of the 100 Largest Cities*: tables 4, 5, and 9; Brian J. L. Berry and Allen Pred, *Central Place Studies; A Bibliography of Theory and Applications* (Philadelphia: Regional Science Research Institute, 1965), 3; and Robert Greenhalgh Albion, *The Rise of New York Port, 1815–1860* (New York: Scribner's, 1939; repr., Boston: Northeastern University Press, 1984), 386.

35. Nathan A. Miller, *The Enterprise of a Free People: Aspects of Economic Development in New York State During the Canal Period, 1792–1838* (Ithaca, N.Y.: Cornell University Press, 1962), 3–19; Robert A. Davison, "Comment: New York Foreign Trade," in *The Growth of the Seaport Cities, 1790–1825: Proceedings of a Conference Sponsored by the*

Eleutherian Mills-Hagley Foundation, March 17–19, 1966, ed. David T. Gilchrist (Charlottesville: University of Virginia Press, 1967), 68–78; Albion, *The Rise of New York Port, 1815–1860*, 38–121, 337, 386; Rohit Thomas Aggarwala, "Seat of Empire: New York, Philadelphia, and the Emergence of an American Metropolis, 1776–1837" (PhD dissertation, Columbia University, 2002), 1–48, 253–82; Ronald E. Shaw, *Erie Water West: A History of the Erie Canal, 1792–1854* (Lexington: University of Kentucky Press, 1966), 195–300; Harold D. Woodman, *King Cotton & His Retainers: Financing & Marketing the Cotton Crop of the South, 1800–1925* (Lexington: University of Kentucky Press, 1968), 5–59, 164–75; and Gibson, *Population of the 100 Largest Cities*, tables 3, 5, and 9; Rogers, *The Transportation Revolution*, 32–55, 74–103.

36. *New York As It Is; Or Stranger's Guide-Book to the Cities of New York, Brooklyn, and Adjacent Places* (New York: Miller, 1865), 20; *Phelps' New York City Guide, 1854*: title page, 9; and Frederick Marryat, *Diary in America*, ed. Jules Zanger (Bloomington: Indiana University Press, 1960), 65.

37. Henri Herz, *My Travels in America*, trans. Henry Bertram Hill (Madison: State Historical Society of Wisconsin, 1963), 17.

38. Geert Mak, *Amsterdam*, trans. Philipp Blom (Cambridge, Mass.: Harvard University Press, 2000), 204–24; Geoffrey Cottrell, *Amsterdam: The Life of a City* (Boston: Little, Brown, 1972), 265–77; Charles Withers, "The Demographic History of the City, 1831–1911," in *Glasgow*, vol. 2, *1830–1912*, ed. W. Hamish Fraser and Irene Maver (Manchester, U.K.: Manchester University Press, 1996), 141–62; John Butt, "The Industries of Glasgow," in Fraser and Maver, *Glasgow*, vol. 2, 96–140; Irene Maver, *Glasgow* (Edinburgh, U.K.: Edinburgh University Press, 2000), 37–58; Colin G. Pooley, "Living in Liverpool: The Modern City," in *Liverpool 800: Culture, Character & History*, ed. John Belchem (Liverpool, U.K.: University of Liverpool Press, 2006), 171–255; Graeme J. Milne, *Trade and Traders in Mid-Victorian Liverpool: Mercantile Business and the Making of a World Port* (Liverpool, U.K.: Liverpool University Press, 2000), 46–122; and Richard J. Evans, *Death in Hamburg: Society and Politics in the Cholera Years, 1830–1910* (Oxford: Clarendon Press, 1987), 28–49. Although none of these other four seaports was as populous as New York City, they were big enough to merit a comparison, especially considering the similarities of their economic bases and social structures. In 1850, when New York had a population of 515,547, Liverpool had 422,000 inhabitants; Glasgow, 346,000; Amsterdam, 225,000; and Hamburg, 193,000. Gibson, *Population of the 100 Largest Cities*, table 8; and Paul M. Hohenberg and Lynn Hollen Lees, *The Making of Urban Europe, 1000–1850* (Cambridge, Mass.: Harvard University Press, 1985), 227.

39. A search of the *New York Times* for "business men" yielded 1,108 hits for the 1860s [January 1, 1860–December 31, 1869], 2,349 hits for the 1870s, 4,488 hits for the 1880s, and 7,394 hits for the 1890s. A search for "businessmen" produced 20 hits for the 1860s, 20 for the 1870s, 29 for the 1880s, and 47 for the 1890s.

40. Milne, *Trade and Traders in Mid-Victorian Liverpool*, 95–145; Gordon Jackson and Charles Munn, "Trade, Commerce and Finance," in Fraser and Maver, *Glasgow*,

vol. 2, 52–77; Maver, *Glasgow*, 45–50; Evans, *Death in Hamburg*, 28–44; and Mak, *Amsterdam*, 206, 212.

41. *Classified Mercantile Directory for the Cities of New-York and Brooklyn* (New York: Disturnell, 1837), v–vii, 19–20, 27–31, 45–48, 52–59, 62, 74–79, 84–88, 101–04; Porter and Livesay, *Merchants and Manufacturing*, 1–12, 17–22, 72–78; Diary of Anson G. Phelps, 1842–1853, entry for February 5, 1843, microfilm edition, Microforms Reading Room, NYPL; and Edward N. Tailer Diary, vol. 10, December 26, 1851–December 15, 1852, entry for August 15, 1852, Library of the New-York Historical Society, New York, N.Y. [hereafter N-YHS].

42. Evans, *Death in Hamburg*, 30–31; Butt, "The Industries of Glasgow," 96–140, in Fraser and Maver, *Glasgow*, vol. 2; Richard B. Stott, *Workers in the Metropolis: Class, Ethnicity, and Youth in Antebellum New York City* (Ithaca, N.Y.: Cornell University Press, 1990), 20–21; and Matthew Drennan, "Economy," 394–400, in Jackson, *The Encyclopedia of New York City*.

43. Vincent P. Carosso, *Investment Banking in America: A History* (Cambridge, Mass.: Harvard University Press, 1970), vii–xi, 1–28; Youssef Cassis, *Capitals of Capital: A History of International Financial Centres, 1780–2005* (Cambridge: Cambridge University Press, 2006), 1–6, 37–40, 53–54, 73–74; Robert E. Wright, *The First Wall Street: Chestnut Street, Philadelphia, and the Birth of American Finance* (Chicago: University of Chicago Press, 2005), 1–13, 116–17, 147–63; Charles R. Geist, *Wall Street: A History* (New York: Oxford University Press, 1997), 3–49; and Margaret G. Myers, *The New York Money Market*, vol. 1, *Origins and Development* (New York: Columbia University Press, 1931), 3–102, 162. New York City also became a center of marine insurance as a result of its position as the country's principal seaport.

44. Jackson and Munn, "Trade, Commerce, and Finance," in Fraser and Maver, *Glasgow*, vol. 2, 77–91; Geist, *Wall Street*, 20–43; Myers, *New York Money Market*, 1: 10–42; David Kynaston, *The City of London*, vol. 1, *A World of Its Own, 1815–1890* (London: Pimlico, 1994), 9–27; Prime Ward and King to Barings Brothers, January 23, 1830, HC5.2.15, March 13, 1830, HC5.2.16, Baring Archive, ING Barings, London; Le Roy Bayard & Company to Nathan M. Rothschild, August 6, 1816, IX/112/59C, Rothschild Archive, London; and Nathan M. Rothschild to Messrs. Prime Ward, July 6, 1824, XI/148/17, Rothschild Archive, London.

45. Asa Greene [pseud.], *The Perils of Pearl Street, including a taste of the dangers of Wall Street; by a late merchant* (New York: Betts & Anstice, 1834), 185–86.

46. Frederick Jackson, *A Week in Wall Street By One Who Knows* (New York: n.p., 1841), 135.

47. William Armstrong, *Stocks and Stock-Jobbing in Wall Street: with sketches of the brokers, and fancy stocks; containing a full account of the nature of all kinds of stocks and securities by a reformed stock gambler* (New York: New-York Publishing, 1848), 12.

48. Scott A. Sandage, *Born Losers: A History of Failure in America* (Cambridge, Mass.: Harvard University Press, 2005), 1–43; and Irvin G. Wyllie, *The Self-Made Man in America: The Myth of Rags to Riches* (New York: Free Press, 1954), 8–20.

49. Frederic Cople Jaher, *The Urban Establishment: Upper Strata in Boston, New York, Charleston, Chicago, and Los Angeles* (Urbana: University of Illinois Press, 1982), 1–13, 109–25, 245–81.

50. A similar transformation took place in Glasgow, the fastest-growing city of its size in western Europe in the 1830s. According to Richard H. Trainor, the speed of Glasgow's population growth "was the single most important influence" on its elites and was responsible for "increasing [the] size, diversity, complexity, and external importance of Glasgow's leaders" and for altering their relations with other social groups. Richard H. Trainor, "The Elite," 230, 229, in Fraser and Maver, *Glasgow*, vol. 2. A like phenomenon appears to have occurred in Hamburg and Liverpool. See Evans, *Death in Hamburg*, 28–50, 78–108; and Tony Lane, *Liverpool: City of the Sea* (Liverpool: Liverpool University Press, 1997), 29–56.

51. *New York Journal of Commerce*, March 6 and July 15, 1829, February 17, 1830; *New York Gazette & General Advertiser*, January 15, 1829; *New York Commercial Advertiser*, August 21, 1824, May 5, 1826; *New York Evening Post*, January 3, June 4, and July 30, 1822, April 29, 1825, July 16, August 16 and 22, 1827, May 26, 1830; and Edward Pessen, *Riches, Class, and Power Before the Civil War* (Lexington, Mass.: Heath, 1973), 310–19. See note 1, p. 318 for Pessen's discussion of Beach's misnumbering of his editions. This calculation of the current value of money is made on the basis of the historic standard of living and relies primarily on consumer prices. Moneyworth.com, accessed April 11, 2007, www.measuringworth.com/growth.

52. "Justice to the Rich," *Harper's Weekly* 1 (February 7, 1857), 82.

53. *New York Evening Post*, January 4, 1836.

54. Quoted in the *New York Evening Post*, May 24, 1843.

55. *New York Commercial Advertiser*, May 23, 1843.

56. Ibid.

57. Charles Astor Bristed, *The Upper Ten Thousand: Sketches of American Society* (New York: Stringer & Townsend, 1852), 9.

58. James Dabney McCabe, *The Secrets of the Great City: A Work Descriptive of the Virtues and Vices, the Mysteries, Miseries and Crimes of New York City* (Philadelphia: National Publishing Company, 1868), 79–80.

59. Bristed, *The Upper Ten Thousand*, 8. See also George William Curtis, *The Potiphar Papers* (New York: Harper & Brothers, 1858), 1; and Edward Winslow Martin, *The Secrets of a Great City: A Work Descriptive of the Virtues and Vices, the Mysteries, Miseries and Crimes of New York City* (Philadelphia: National Publishing, 1868), 78.

60. Although Bristed described the upper 10,000 as encompassing American society, he wrote almost entirely about New Yorkers. Bristed, *The Upper Ten Thousand*, 5–11; and Gibson, *Population of the 100 Largest Cities*: table 8.

61. Edward Pessen found that by 1860 the top 1 percent of the population in New York, Philadelphia, Brooklyn, and Boston owned about half of their real and personal property. In all four cities, wealth was distributed more unequally in 1860 than it had been in 1820, and in the cases of New York, Philadelphia, and Boston, more unequally

than in the late eighteenth century. By 1860 the highest 1 percent of the populations of St. Louis and New Orleans controlled about 40 percent of their property. Pessen, *Riches, Class, and Power Before the Civil War*, 22–23, 40–43.

62.　Ibid., 22–23, 40–43; Jaher, *The Urban Establishment*, 159–60, Frederic Cople Jaher, "Style and Status: High Society in Late Nineteenth-Century New York," 258, in *The Rich, the Well Born, and the Powerful: Elites and Upper Classes in History*, ed. Frederic Cople Jaher (Urbana: University of Illinois Press, 1973); Joseph F. Rishel, *Founding Families of Pittsburgh: The Evolution of a Regional Elite, 1760–1910* (Pittsburgh, Pa.: University of Pittsburgh Press, 1990), 184–96; Katharyn Allamong Jacob, *Capital Elites High Society in Washington, D.C., After the Civil War* (Washington, D.C.: Smithsonian Institution Press, 1995), 1–13; Betty G. Farrell, *Elite Families: Class and Power in Nineteenth-Century Boston* (Albany: State University of New York Press, 1993), 1–6; Gary Larson Browne, *Baltimore in the Nation, 1789–1861* (Chapel Hill: University of North Carolina Press, 1980), 3–13, 161–76; and Burton W. Folsom Jr., *Urban Capitalists: Entrepreneurs and City Growth in Pennsylvania's Lackawanna and Lehigh Regions, 1800–1920*, 2nd ed. (Scranton, Pa.: University of Scranton Press, 2001), 3–10.

63.　Manuscript Census, 1850 Federal Census, New York State, New York County, 18th Ward, 147, Ancestry.com, accessed February 11 and March 3, 2006, www.ancestry.com; and Manuscript Census, 1860 Federal Census, New York State, New York County, 1st division of the 15th ward, 18, 317,559, Ancestry.com, accessed March 12, 2006, www .ancestry.com.

64.　Cornelius Rapelye Suydam, Diary Kept During Trip to England, 1830–31, entry for December 5, 1830, N-YHS.

65.　Matthew Kadane, "The Watchful Clothier: The Diary of an Eighteenth Century Protestant-Capitalist" (PhD dissertation, Brown University, 2005), 51–130; Margaret C. Jacob and Matthew Kadane, "Missing, Now Found in the Eighteenth Century: Weber's Protestant Capitalist," *American Historical Review* 108 (February 2003), 20–49; Molly McCarthy, "A Page, A Day: A History of the Daily Diary in America" (PhD dissertation, Brandeis University, 2004), 1–11; Waldron Phoenix Belknap Jr., *The De Peyster Genealogy* (Boston: n.p. 1956), 49–52, 83–85, 97–98; Boyd Hilton, *The Age of Atonement: The Influence of Evangelicalism on Social and Economic Thought, 1795–1865* (Oxford: Clarendon, 1988), 120–25; *Doggett's New York City Directory, Illustrated with Maps of New York and Brooklyn, 1848–1849* (New York: Doggett, 1848), 121; *New York Times*, June 20, 1874; James Ferguson De Peyster Diary, 1841–1852, entries for December 21 and 31, 1841, January 7, 9, 11, 16, 20, and 30, February 20, April 9 and 27, May 2 and 30, and December 11, 1842, February 4 and 27, May 1, 10, 11, 18, and 31, 1843, March 4, May 6, 7, and 28, July 8, August 16, 1845, August 23 and 27, September 19, October 2 and 31, 1846, December 23, 1847, April 16, 1848, April 15 and 25, and June 3, 1849, and February 23, 1852, N-YHS. I am grateful to my colleague Matthew Kadane for helping me conceptualize this section.

66.　De Peyster Diary, entries for April 27 and May 1, 1843, N-YHS.

67. Ibid., entries for August 22 and September 19 1846, November 16 and December 23, 1847, April 16, 1848, and April 15, 1849. Tellingly, De Peyster never felt any corresponding uneasiness over his many charitable activities, and made no attempt to reduce his humanitarian commitments—which were substantial and demanding—in order to devote more time for business. This involvement suggests that, even for De Peyster, there were limits to the pursuit of wealth and that charity was a financial lever that ensured that he did not become overwhelmingly materialistic. Charity also gave him a sphere where he could exercise his family's traditional governance without being challenged or diminished and where he could confirm his high standing.

68. *Constitution, By-Laws and Standing Rules of the Union Club, and a List of the Members* (New York: Ammerman, 1854), 19–27; Chamber of Commerce of the State of New York, *Annual Report of the Chamber of Commerce of the State of New York, for the Year 1858* (New York: Wheeler and Williams, 1859), 340–50. The occupational data are from the following sources: *Trow's New-York City Directory, for 1853–1854* (New York: Trow, 1853); *The New York City Directory, for 1851–1852*, 10th ed. (New York: Doggett & Rode, 1851); *The New-York City Directory, for 1853–1854*, 12th ed. (New York: Rode, 1853); and *Trow's New-York City Directory for 1856–1857* (New York: Trow 1856).

69. Four people had their business addresses but not their occupations listed in the city directories. One reason why so many members' occupations could not be identified—197 altogether—is that many members were not New York City residents.

70. *Constitution, By-Laws and Standing Rules of the Union Club*, 4.

71. An analysis of the overlap of the memberships of eight organizations wholly or partly associated with the upper class is conducive to understanding the relationship of economic and social factions. The groups are: (1) a list of the 294 wealthiest New Yorkers in 1845 compiled from the municipal tax assessment rolls; (2) the graduates of Columbia College between 1815 and 1859; (3) the membership of the Union Club; (4) the membership of the Chamber of Commerce of the State of New York; the memberships of two leading cultural institutions; (5) the New York Society Library and (6) the New-York Historical Society; (7) the trustees and officers of the Public School Society, a voluntary society that operated the public schools by allocating public and private funds into schools for working-class youth; and (8) the members of the New York Association for Improving the Condition of the Poor (AICP). While the AICP had middle-class as well as upper-class benefactors, the other seven were primarily associated with the upper class. The groups varied in size from the AICP's 3,568 beneficiaries to the Public School Society's 86 officers and trustees; they had an aggregate membership of 8,646. The subset of 70 individuals who were affiliated with four or more organizations was a select lot. A number came from distinguished old families, including James Ferguson De Peyster, Cornelius V. S. Roosevelt, and William Laight. Two were well-known attorneys whose fathers had been famous statesmen: John Church Hamilton, the son of Alexander Hamilton, and John Van Buren, the son of President Martin Van Buren. Thirty were among the 294 richest New Yorkers, with two, William B. Astor and James Lennox, being worth

more than $500,000 apiece and seven others having more than $250,000. There were 27 merchants, 18 "gentlemen," 9 lawyers, 5 insurance company executives, 4 bankers, 2 accountants, and no manufacturers. Among the gentlemen were Old New Yorkers William Laight, Thomas Suffern, and Nicholas Low. A few people in this subset, like oil dealer Henry Elsworth, had more middle-class outlooks. There were now different ways of being a part of the upper class. Pessen, *Riches, Class, and Power Before the Civil War*, 323–26, for the list of 294 richest New Yorkers; *List of Persons Holding Rights in the New York Society Library, April 30, 1861* (New York: n.p., 1861), 1–14; New-York Historical Society, *The Charter and By-Laws of the New-York Historical Society* (New York: n.p., 1862), 45–73; *Constitution, By-Laws and Standing Rules of the Union Club*, 19–27; Chamber of Commerce of the State of New York, *Annual Report of the Chamber of Commerce of the State of New York, for the Year 1858*, 340–50; New York Association for Improving the Condition of the Poor, *Twelfth Annual Report of the New York Association for Improving the Condition of the Poor, for the Year 1855; With the By-Laws and a List of Members* (New York: Trow, 1855), 48–63; *Forty-seventh Annual Report of the Trustees of the Public School Society of New York* (New York: Robert, 1853), 15; and Columbia University in the City of New York, *Catalogue of Officers and Graduates of Columbia University from the Foundation of King's College in 1754*, 16th ed. (New York: n.p., 1916), 95–120.

72.   These conclusions revise E. Digby Baltzell's conceptualization of the American upper class. Baltzell's thinking about the upper class was driven by his interest in its internal workings—its structure, values, and institutions—and in its social and political roles rather than in its interactions and boundaries with subordinate groups. He understood that all members of that upper class were not equal and that differences in family background, personal relationships, wealth, and occupational success separated them into distinct social strata. At the core of Baltzell's conceptual model of the higher class position was his idea that it consisted of two overlapping yet antagonistic groups, the *elite* and the *upper class*. The elite was a transitory business elite whose members controlled the economy and achieved personal wealth, while the upper class was a more permanent and well-integrated social elite. According to Baltzell, the *elite* comprised those individuals who achieved the greatest success in their fields. As leaders in their occupations or professions, they became decision makers in the political, cultural, economic, and military spheres, but they remained atomized individuals and did not constitute a community. Over time, however, some elite individuals and their families would begin to associate primarily with one another and develop an outlook and a way of life that differentiated them from the rest of the population, including the business elite. As their personal bonds strengthened, they became more coherent, exclusive, and self-conscious—in short, they formed an upper class. In Baltzell's model, the upper class constituted a group of interconnected families that commanded great social prestige; its members attended the same schools, joined the same clubs, and intermarried. Because of their social prestige, they wielded a generalized class authority, or hegemony. Baltzell's framework helps make sense of

conflicts between parvenus and old money. Yet his conceptualization is rather limited and obscures the messiness of historical reality. His elite and the upper-class classifications exist in opposition to one another and gain coherence and meaning from their antagonism. It is not clear how or when these two elites came into being. Above all, his scheme precludes several lines of inquiry that are pertinent to our analysis of New York's upper class. Baltzell views leading businessmen as atomized individuals who are not part of any groups or communities other than the social upper class that they are presumably seeking to enter, a limited perspective that privileges high society even as it ignores or downplays the business elite's relationships to their own families of origin and their commercial networks. His model is thus not conducive to understanding the relationships between the social and economic elites other than businessmen's supposed emulation of their social betters; it does not take into account people who bridged both elites (through marriage, for instance) or acts of cooperation between the two elites, nor does it consider the social elite's response to the accumulation of wealth on the part of the business elite (as with James Ferguson De Peyster). Baltzell also ignores the middle class and its relations with the upper class. Focusing tightly on the upper class and convinced that it was stable and coherent, Baltzell assumes that the boundaries between the upper and middle classes were clear-cut and impermeable and that the people in these two groups had distinctive ways of life and worldviews. E. Digby Baltzell, *Philadelphia Gentlemen: The Making of a National Upper Class* (New York: Free Press, 1958; repr., New Brunswick, N.J.: Transaction, 1992), 6–8; Baltzell, *The Protestant Establishment: Aristocracy & Caste in America* (New York: Random House, 1964); vii–xv; Baltzell, *Puritan Boston and Quaker Philadelphia* (New York: Free Press, 1979; repr., New Brunswick, N.J.: Transaction, 1996), 19–30.

73. Upward mobility usually receives attention due to the rags-to-riches idea, but studying the upper class of New York City also entails a consideration of three other kinds of social movement: downward mobility (from the upper class to a lower class); sideways mobility (from one elite to another); and stasis (the absence of movement, as when German Jews were excluded from social elites or when wealthy Irish Americans resisted entering that upper class).

74. Stuart M. Blumin, *The Emergence of the Middle Class: Social Experience in the American City, 1760–1900* (Cambridge: Cambridge University Press, 1989), 1–16; Paul E. Johnson, *A Shopkeeper's Millennium: Society and Revivals in Rochester, New York, 1815–1837* (New York: Hill and Wang, 1978), 3–14; and Mary P. Ryan, *Cradle of the Middle Class: The Family in Oneida County, New York, 1790–1865* (Cambridge University Press, 1981), 1–17.

75. Louise L. Stevenson, *The Victorian Homefront: American Thought & Culture, 1860–1880* (Ithaca, N.Y.: Cornell University Press, 2001), xxiv–xxxi; Stana Nenadic, "The Victorian Middle Classes," in Fraser and Maver, *Glasgow*, vol. 2, 265–99; Bristed, *The Upper Ten Thousand*, 5–11, 37–79, 97–126; John A Hadden, Diaries, 1841–1843, entries for January 7 and 21, April 10, May 19, June 27, 1841, January 1, 5, 17, 21, and 24, 1842,

NYPL; and Alfred Janson Bloor Diary, 1848–1857, entry for January 1, 1848, N-YHS. For the emergence of a coherent and self-conscious working class in this period, see Alan Dawley, *Class and Community: The Industrial Revolution in Lynn* (Cambridge, Mass.: Harvard University Press, 1976), 1–10; Bruce Laurie, *Working People of Philadelphia, 1800–1850* (Philadelphia: Temple University Press, 1980), 33–104; Richard B. Stott, *Workers in the Metropolis: Class, Ethnicity, and Youth in Antebellum New York City* (Ithaca, N.Y.: Cornell University Press, 1990), 1–6; and Sean Wilentz, *Chants Democratic: New York City & the Rise of the American Working Class, 1788–1850* (New York: Oxford University Press, 1984), 3–19.

76. John F. Kasson, *Rudeness & Civility: Manners in Nineteenth-Century Urban America* (New York: Hill and Wang, 1990), 43. See also C. Dallett Hemphill, *Bowing to Necessities: A History of Manners in America, 1620–1860* (New York: Oxford University Press, 1999), 129–59.

77. *Perfect Etiquette; Or, How to Behave in Society* (New York: Rideout, n.d.), 4. See also *True Politeness: A Hand-Book* (New York: Manhattan Publishing, n.d.), 5–6, 17–18.

78. *The American Chesterfield, Or, Way to Wealth, Honour, and Distinction* (Philadelphia: Grigg, 1828), 125.

79. *The Habits of Good Society: A Handbook of Ladies and Gentlemen* (New York: Rudd & Carleton, 1860), 13–17, 30–33. See also Elisabeth Celnart, *The Gentleman and Lady's Book of Politeness and Propriety of Deportment* (Philadelphia: Lippincott, Grambo, 1852), vii–xi; and Hemphill, *Bowing to Necessities*, 65–69, 129–36.

80. Wellington Williams, *Appleton's New York City and Vicinity Guide* (New York: Appleton, 1849), 65.

81. Kenneth T. Jackson, *Crabgrass Frontier: The Suburbanization of the United States* (New York: Oxford University Press, 1985), 25–32; Clay Lancaster, *Old Brooklyn Heights* (Rutland, Vt.: Tuttle, 1961), 13–20; "Deeds in Brooklyn," Series III, Box 2, Pierrepont Papers, Brooklyn Historical Society, Brooklyn, N.Y. [hereafter BHS].

82. Samuel Dexter Ward Jr., "Journal of a Tour to New York and other places in the Summer of 1842," entry for August 10, 1842, N-YHS.

83. Jackson, *Crabgrass Frontier*, 30.

84. Bristed, *The Upper Ten Thousand*, 17; and Clifton Hood, *722 Miles: The Building of the Subways and How They Transformed New York* (New York: Simon & Schuster, 1993), 29–55.

85. On this point, see Johnson, *A Shopkeeper's Millennium*, 1–14; and Pessen, *Riches, Class, and Power*, 251–80.

86. Carol Klein, *Gramercy Park: An American Bloomsbury* (Boston: Houghton Mifflin, 1987), 3–58; Kenneth A. Scherzer, *The Unbounded Community: Neighborhood Life and Social Structure in New York City, 1830–1873* (Durham, N.C., 1992), 148–54; and Lisa Keller, "Hudson Square," 627, in Jackson, *Encyclopedia of New York City*.

87. *Phelps' New-York City Guide; Being a Pocket Directory for Strangers and Citizens to the Principal Objects of Interest in the Great Commercial Metropolis and Conductor to Its Environs* (New York: Ensign, Bridgman, & Fanning, 1857), 47.

88. Bristed, *The Upper Ten Thousand*, 23; *Doggett's New York City Directory for 1850–1851* (New York: Doggett, 1850), 29, 49, 137–40, 244, 255, 375; *Trow's New York Directory for the Year Ending May 1, 1860* (New York: Trow, 1859), 415.

89. Manuscript Census, 1850 Federal Census, New York State, Kings County, Brooklyn Ward 1, pp. 1–149, Ancestry.com, accessed November 19–20, 2005, February 11 and March 3, 2006, www.ancestry.com.

90. Manuscript Census, 1850 Federal Census, New York State, New York County, 18th Ward, 1–178.

91. Albion, *The Rise of New York Port*, 241–51; Frederick Henry Wolcott Diary, 1849–1854, vol. 1, entry for December 11, 1849, NYPL; Ellen Fletcher, "A(biel) A(bbot) Low," 768, in Jackson, *The Encyclopedia of New York City*; and Ellen Fletcher Rosebroch, "Abiel Abbot Lowell: A New York Merchant in the China Trade," *Seaport* 14 (Summer 1980): 15.

92. *New York Commercial Advertiser*, May 12, 1846. See also *Brooklyn Eagle*, November 30, 1844, October 31, 1846, December 22, 1847, January 13, February 1, and December 23, 1848, January 29, May 20, and December 23, 1850.

93. *New York Commercial Advertiser*, January 5, 1850; *Brooklyn Eagle*, January 4, 1850; John Faulkner Blake, deposition regarding deed of manumission, February 11, 1860, Series 1, Box 9, Folder 10, Plymouth Church of Pilgrims Collection, BHS; Clifford E. Clark, *Henry Ward Beecher: Spokesman for a Middle-Class America* (Urbana: University of Illinois Press, 1978), 6–28, 76–101; and Richard Wightman Fox, *Trials of Intimacy: Love and Loss in the Beecher-Tilton Scandal* (Chicago: University of Chicago Press, 1999), 1–9. For the importance of Brooklyn's New England culture, see Bertram Wyatt-Brown, *Lewis Tappan and the Evangelical War Against Slavery* (Cleveland: Press of Case Western Reserve University, 1969), 19, 31, 60–73, 107–14, 226, 300, 303; and "Memorandum of Sale on Pierrepont Street to Arthur Tappan, March 12, 1835" and "Arthur Tappan to Hez. Beers Pierrepont, Property Bond, dated March 12, 1835," Folder 2, Box 2, Series 3, Pierrepont Papers, BHS.

94. Manuscript Census, 1850 Federal Census, New York State, New York County, 18th Ward, pp. 13, 20, 26, and 105; *Trow's New York City Directory, for the Year Ending May 1, 1861* (New York: Trow, 1860), 563; and Ralph M. Hower, *History of Macy's of New York, 1858–1919: Chapters in the Evolution of the Department Store* (Cambridge, Mass.: Harvard University Press, 1946), 5–7, 37–48.

95. *Constitution, By-Laws and Standing Rules of the Union Club*, 19–27. The sources for the residential data are *Trow's New-York City Directory, for 1853–1854*; *The New York City Directory, for 1851–1852*, 10th ed.; *The New York City Directory, for 1851–1852*, 12th ed.; and *Trow's New-York City Directory for 1856–1857*.

96. Of the sixty-two people who belonged to four or more of the eight organizations examined above and whose addresses could be learned, fifty-six (90.3 percent) resided in Manhattan, including forty-five (72.5 percent) in the Broadway arc. Just one person lived in Brooklyn. *Trow's New-York City Directory, for 1853–1854*;

The New York City Directory, for 1851–1852, 10th ed.; *The New-York City Directory, for 1853–1854*, 12th ed.; and *Trow's New-York City Directory for 1856–1857.*

97.   The counterexample of Philadelphia underscores this dynamic. Under the influence of the egalitarian and democratic ethos of Quakerism, proper Philadelphians developed a deep-seated privatism that weakened their adhesion to the city, and as early as the 1860s some well-to-do Philadelphia families began to relocate to residential suburbs on the main line of the Pennsylvania Railroad such as Ardmore, Wynnewood, and Bryn Mawr. David R. Contosta, "The Main Line (Philadelphia, Pennsylvania)," 444, in *Encyclopedia of Urban America: The Cities and Suburbs*, ed. Neil Larry Shumsky, vol. 2 (Santa Barbara, Calif.: ABC-Clio, 1998); Baltzell, *Philadelphia Gentlemen*, 5–14, 201–10; and Sam Bass Warner Jr., *The Private City: Philadelphia in Three Periods of Its Growth* (Philadelphia: University of Pennsylvania Press, 1968), ix–xii, 3–21.

98.   *Merchant's House Museum* (New York: n.p., 2006), unpaginated; personal visit to Merchant's House Museum, December 27, 2006; and Moneyworth.com, accessed October 9, 2012, www.measuringworth.com/growth. I use the historic standard of living to measure changes in relative value over time. The Tredwell house, originally numbered 377 Fourth Street, was redesignated as 29 East Fourth Street as part of the renumbering of Manhattan house addresses that began in 1861. Eliza Parker Tredwell, the daughter of a boardinghouse keeper, had decidedly more modest origins than did Seabury Tredwell, but acquired his status and relationships upon their marriage. Mary L. Knapp, *An Old Merchant's House: Life at Home in New York City, 1835–1865* (New York: Girandole, 2012), xiii.

99.   James Kirke Paulding, *The New Mirror for Travellers; and Guide to the Springs* (New York: Carvill, 1828), as excerpted in William S. Tryon, comp. and ed., *A Mirror for Americans: Life and Manners in the United States, 1790–1870, as Recorded by American Traveler*, vol. 1 (Chicago: University of Chicago Press, 1952), 96.

100.   *Merchant's House Museum*; personal visit to Merchant's House Museum, December 27, 2006; and Knapp, *An Old Merchant's House*, 27–49, 83–94.

101.   *Doggett's New York City Directory, 1851* (New York: Doggett, 1851), 177; *Trow's New-York City Directory, for 1853–1854*, 127, 203, 339, 472, 536, 600, 637, 724, 733; *Trow's New-York City Directory, for the Year Ending May 1, 1856* (New York: Trow, 1853), 495, 763; *The New-York City Directory, for 1854–1855*, 13th ed. (New York: Rode, 1854); 1855 New York State Census, City of New York, 15th Ward, 3rd Assembly District: n.p., at New York County Clerk's Division of Old Records, 31 Chambers Street, New York, N.Y.; "Alphabetical List of Persons in Division 3 of Collection District 6 of the State of New York Liable to an Income Tax Under the Excise Laws of the United States, and the Amount thereof assessed by Geo. W. McPherson, Assistant Assessor, and by him returned to the Assessor of Said District, for the Year 1862," 13 and 24, U.S. Tax Assessment Lists, 1862, NARA Series M603, NARA Roll 65, accessed September 20, 2013, www.ancestry.com; and *New York Times*, May 3 and 12, 1936.

102.   Michael and Ariane Batterberry, *On the Town in New York: The Landmark History of Eating, Drinking, and Entertainments from the American Revolution to the Food*

Revolution (New York: Routledge, 1999), 55–109; Celnart, *The Gentleman and Lady's Book of Politeness and Propriety*, 75–81, 59–74; *Perfect Etiquette*, 13–15, 20–26; Kasson, *Rudeness & Civility*, 173–74; Bloor Diary, 1848–1857, entry for January 1, 1848, NYPL; Tailer Diary, vol. 10, December 26, 1851–December 15, 1852, entry for January 1, 1853, N-YHS; Tailer Diary, vol. 13, September 2, 1858–December 31, 1861, entry for January 1, 1860, N-YHS.

103. Julia Kean to Mrs. Looe Baker, December 1832, in Margaret Armstrong, *Five Generations: Life and Letters of an American Family, 1750–1900* (New York: Harper & Brothers, 1930), 210.

104. Ibid., 211.

105. *New York Times*, February 14, March 4, and June 3, 1854, October 11, 1860. Some of the most elaborate balls took place in Newport, R.I., which by the 1850s had already become an upper-class resort that provided a social space for leisure and entertainments that was physically removed from New York City. See *New York Times*, August 26, 1857 and August 16, 1860.

106. Paulding, *The New Mirror for Travellers*, 97.

107. Ibid., 97.

108. *New York Commercial Advertiser*, January 5, 1844.

109. Ibid.

110. Ibid.

111. *Merchant's House Museum*; and Hadden Diaries, 1841–1843, entries for January 7, 9, and 21, April 10, May 19, June 27, 1841, January 1, 5, 17, 21, and 24, 1842, NYPL. See also Paulding, *The New Mirror for Travellers*, 96.

112. Hadden Diaries, entry for December 27, 1841, NYPL. Emphasis in the original.

113. Mary Rech Rockwell, "'Let Deeds Tell': Elite Women in Buffalo, 1880–1910," (PhD dissertation, State University of New York at Buffalo, 1999), 1–36. The classic expression of the operation of upper-class female social power for New York City is Edith Wharton, *The Custom of the Country* (New York: Scribner's, 1913).

114. Hadden Diaries, entries for January 24 and 26, 1842, NYPL; *New York Times*, March 9, 1865, May 2, 1882; and *Merchant's House Museum*.

115. Jackson, *Crabgrass Frontier*, 73–86; Margaret S. Marsh, *Suburban Lives* (New Brunswick, N.J.: Rutgers University Press, 1990), 1–18; *Merchant's House Museum*; 1855 New York State Census, City of New York, 15th Ward, 3rd Assembly District: n.p.; Manuscript census, 1850 Federal Census, New York State, New York County, Eastern Half of the 15th Ward, 329, 380, 411, Ancestry.com, accessed March 12, 2006, www.ancestry.com. Manuscript census, 1850 Federal Census, New York State, 17th Ward, 404, 443, and 450, Ancestry.com, accessed March 12, 2006, www.ancestry.com. Manuscript Census, 1860 Federal Census, New York State, New York County, 3rd division of the 15th ward, 58, Ancestry.com, accessed March 12, 2006, www.ancestry.com. Manuscript Census, 1850 Federal Census, New York State, New York County, 18th Ward, 14; and *Doggett's New York City Directory for 1850–1851*, 331; *Trow's New-York City Directory, for 1853–1854*, 670.

116. The primacy of family (and the absence of estate and income taxes) is evident from a study of the wills of upper-class New Yorkers. Of the twenty-one individuals who were affiliated with five or six of the eight institutions examined above, I was able to locate the wills of fourteen: James Ferguson De Peyster, Eugene Dutilh, David M. Haight, John William Hamersley, Jacob Harsen, William H. Macy, Clement Clark Moore, Edmund H. Pendleton, Cornelius V. S. Roosevelt, Charles H. Russell, Alfred L. Seton, Thomas Suffern, Augustus H. Ward, and Benjamin R. Winthrop. Thirteen of the fourteen left all of their property (excluding payments to executors, who in most cases were relatives) to family members; only Augustus H. Ward made bequests to charities—$3,000 apiece to the American Bible Society, the Bible and Common Prayer Book Society, the Association for Improving the Condition of the Poor, the Orphans Home of the Protestant Episcopal Church, and the Society for Relief of Widows and Orphans—and to his servants. This pattern suggests that John Jacob Astor's charitable bequests, discussed earlier, were, if anything, unusually generous. [De Peyster] Liber 227, Page 89, Proof Date, November 14, 1874; [Dutilh] Liber 537, Page 198, Proof Date, August 20, 1895; [Haight] Liber 236, Page 210, Proof Date, May 13, 1876; [Hamersley] Liber 421, Page 132, Proof Date, June 26, 1889; [Harsen] Liber 74, Page 215, Proof Date, September 15, 1835; [Macy] Liber 389, Page 315, Proof Date, June 16, 1887; [Moore] Liber 149, Page 364, Proof Date, September 22, 1863; [Pendleton] Liber 125, Page 382, Proof Date, October 25, 1858; [Roosevelt] Liber 204, Page 219, Proof Date, August 15, 1871; [Russell] Liber 323, Page 395, Proof Date, March 15, 1884; [Seton] Liber 706, Page 102, Proof Date, March 14, 1903; [Suffern] Liber 180, Page 428, Proof Date, June 17, 1869; [Ward] Liber 186, Page, 35, Proof Date, March 9, 1869; and [Winthrop] Liber 268, Page 136, Proof Date, October 22, 1879. Surrogate's Court, New York State, New York County, Record Room, Surrogate's Courthouse, 31 Chambers Street, New York, N.Y.

117. *Merchant's House Museum*; Tour of Merchants House Museum, including servants' quarters, April 21, 2007; 1855 New York State Census, City of New York, 15th Ward, 3rd Assembly District, n.p; Manuscript Census, 1850, New York County, Eastern Half of the Fifteenth Ward, 487; Manuscript Census, 1860 Federal Census, New York State, New York County, 1st divison of the 15th ward, 317; Manuscript Census, 1860 Federal Census, New York State, New York County, 2nd divison of the 15th ward, 18–25; Ancestry.com, accessed March 12, 2006, www.ancestry.com; Manuscript Census, 1850, Kings County, Brooklyn Ward 1, 1–149; Manuscript Census, 1850 Federal Census, New York County, 18th Ward, 1–178; and Hasia R. Diner, *Erin's Daughters in America: Irish Immigrant Women in the Nineteenth Century* (Baltimore, Md.: Johns Hopkins University Press, 1983), 70–105.

118. *New York Commercial Advertiser*, May 10, 1826.

119. Ibid.

120. *Etiquette for Ladies; with hints on female beauty* (Philadelphia: Carey, Lea & Blanchard, 1838), 93.

121. Ibid., 63–64.

122. "House-servants," *Harper's Weekly* 1 (May 9, 1857), 290.

123. *New York Evening Post*, October 30, 1820, June 10, 1824, July 1 and 4, 1826, December 28, 1826, April 22, 1835, July 17, 1844; *New York Gazette & General Advertiser*, June 26, 1834; *New York Commercial Advertiser*, June 15, 1825, December 23, 1826, August 23 and November 21, 1845, May 28, 1846; *Brooklyn Eagle*, July 6, 1846, July 5, 1851; and Ernest DeW. Mayer, *A Brief History of The Seventh Regiment N.Y.N.G. (107th Infantry)* (New York: n.p., 1931), 1–2. Newspaper accounts often used the terms "company," "corps," and "regiment" interchangeably or ambiguously.

124. This is David Quentin Voight's term for the membership of the Knickerbocker Club, founded in 1845 by a group of young men who enjoyed playing an early variant of baseball and sought to control the sport. David Quentin Voight, *American Baseball: From the Gentlemen's Sport to the Commissioner System* (Norman: University of Oklahoma Press, 1966; repr., University Park: Pennsylvania State University Press, 1983), 8.

125. These ties with the upper class represented a departure from the eighteenth century, when local militias had been known for their poor discipline and resistance to centralized authority, traits that were associated with commoners, while the greater professionalism and orderliness of the regular army, particularly the officer corps, had created a link with national elites. The social meaning of the militia seems to have changed in the 1820s, as nationalism suffused the country following the War of 1812 and as economic development enriched local elites. Mayer, *A Brief History of the Seventh Regiment N.Y.N.G.*, 1–2; *New York Commercial Advertiser*, June 15, 1824, December 23, 1826, August 31, 1835, February 23, 1837; *New York Evening Post*, June 12, 1820, December 28, 1826, July 17, 1844; *New York Gazette & General Advertiser*, November 30, 1824; and Journal of Thomas Hamilton, 1830–1831, entry for November 25, 1830, NYPL.

126. Alfred G. Jones Journals, vol. 4, 1844–1846, entries for January 11 and 18, and April 1, 1845, NYPL; Tailer Diary, vol. 10, December 26, 1851–December 15, 1852, entries for March 23 and June 15, 1852, January 29 and 31, May 18, August 9, 1853, N-YHS; and Moneyworth.com, accessed October 9, 2012, www.measuringworth.com/growth. I use the historic standard of living to measure changes in relative value over time.

127. Tailer Diary, vol. 10, December 26, 1851–December 15, 1852, entry for May 18, 1853, N-YHS.

128. *New York Commercial Advertiser*, May 18, 1820; and Moneyworth.com, accessed October 9, 2012, www.measuringworth.com/growth. Here I employ the historic standard of living to measure changes in relative value over time.

129. *New York Commercial Advertiser*, December 23, 1826, August 23, 1846; and *New York Evening Post*, May 18, 1820, December 28, 1826.

130. John J. Sturtevant, *Recollections of a resident of New York City from 1835–1905*, NYPL, 24.

131. Personnel Roll Book, 1847, unpaginated, series I, subseries 5, Seventh Regiment Papers, N-YHS; Company F Roster, 1819–1900, series 1, subseries 5, Seventh Regiment Records, N-YHS; Roll of Sixth Company, Twenty-Seventh Regiment, First

Brigade of New York State Artillery, undated, Folder 2, Box 22, Seventh Regiment Papers, N-YHS; and *New York City Directory for 1845 and 1846* (New York: Groot and Elston, 1845).

132. *New York Evening Post,* June 12, 1820, December 12, 1826; *New York Commercial Advertiser,* December 23, 1826; Hadden Diaries, entries for January 21 and December 13, 1841, NYPL; and John Ward Jr. Diary, entries for January 9, April 13 and 14, and May 11, 1864, N-YHS. The Sixth Company that Hadden belonged to in the early 1840s was the same elite unit I mentioned above; it was part of the Twenty-Seventh Regiment, which became the Seventh Regiment in 1847. Mayer, *A Brief History of the Seventh Regiment N.Y.N.G.,* 1–2; and Sean Wilentz, *The Rise of American Democracy: Jefferson to Lincoln* (New York: Norton, 2005), 312–455.

133. Alfred G. Jones Journals, vol. 4, 1844–1846, entries for January 11 and April 1, 1845, NYPL; *New York Gazette & General Advertiser,* September 4, 1820; *New York Evening Post,* October 30, 1820, July 17, 1844; *New York Commercial Advertiser,* July 12, 1825, February 23, 1837, July 18 and August 31, 1839, July 18, 1839; and Third Brigade, New York State Militia, "Special Orders, No. 3, May 12, 1849," Box 4, Folder 3, Seventh Regiment Records, N-YHS.

134. Hadden Diary, entries for April 10, May 19, June 2, and July 4 and 22, 1841, NYPL; Ward Diary, entries for November 25, 1859 and November 24, 1865, N-YHS; 27th Regiment, New York State Artillery, Standing Orders, 1831 (New York: n.p., 1831), 1–8; 27th Regiment, New York State Artillery, Standing Orders, 1832 (New York: n.p., 1832), 1–8; New York State Artillery, "Division Orders, June 26, 1824," Box 4, Folder 1, Seventh Regiment Records, N-YHS; *New York Gazette & General Advertiser,* September 20, 1833, June 25, 1834; *New York Commercial Advertiser,* June 25, 1842; *Brooklyn Eagle,* July 3, 1850, July 5, 1851, July 5, 1853, July 5, 1858, July 6, 1858; and Alfred G. Jones Journals, vol. 6, 1849–1850, entries for July 3 and 4, 1848, NYPL.

135. *New York Commercial Advertiser,* February 23, 1837; *New York Gazette & General Advertiser,* December 22, 1828, February 9, 1832; Hadden Diary, entry for March 23, 1841, NYPL; and *New York Evening Post,* August 16, 1836.

136. Trevor N. Dupuy, Curt Johnson, and Grace P. Hayes, *Dictionary of Military Terms: A Guide to the Language of Warfare and Military Institutions* (New York: Wilson, 1986), 88; *New York Commercial Advertiser,* July 1, 1826, February 24, 1831, February 24, 1834, August 23, 1845; *National Trades' Union,* November 28, 1835; *New York Herald,* November 26, 1841, November 26, 1848; *New York Times,* November 27, 1855; Joseph Hamblin, secretary, Board of Officers, May 3, 1853, Box 9, Folder 2, Seventh Regiment Records, N-YHS; Alan Benscholin, memorandum regarding a suitable cap pattern, March 26, 1825, Box 9, Folder 2, Seventh Regiment Records, N-YHS; and Hadden Diary, entries for June 27 and December 13, 1841 and February 12, 1842, NYPL.

137. Hadden Diary, entry for June 27, 1841, NYPL.

138. Hadden Diary, entry for July 21, 1841, NYPL.

139. *New York Commercial Advertiser,* August 31, 1835, July 18, 1839.

140. "Militia-days," *Harper's Weekly* 1 (October 24, 1857), 673.

141. Bertram Wyatt-Brown, *Southern Honor: Ethics and Behavior in the Old South* (New York: Oxford University Press, 1982), 3–14, 20–21, 34, 192; Bertram Wyatt-Brown, *The Shaping of Southern Culture: Honor, Grace, and War, 1760s–1880s* (Chapel Hill: University of North Carolina Press, 2001), ix–xix; Elizabeth Fox-Genovese and Eugene Genovese, *The Mind of the Master Class: History and Faith in the Southern Slaveholders' Worldview* (Cambridge: Cambridge University Press, 2005), 98–111, 118–20, 337–39, 369–62; and George W. Cullum, *Biographical Register of the Officers and Graduates of the U.S. Military Academy at West Point, N.Y.: from its establishment in 1802, to 1890, with the early history of the United States Military Academy*, 3rd rev. and extended ed., vols. 1 and 2 (Boston, Houghton Mifflin, 1891), 1: 244–748, 2: 1–733.

142. Mayer, *A Brief History of the Seventh Regiment*, 2; Alessandro Falassi, "Festival: Definition and Morphology," 10, in *Time Out of Time: Essays on the Festival*, ed. Alessandro Falassi (Albuquerque: University of New Mexico Press, 1987). For the relationship between contests and upper-class virtues such as honor and bravery, see Johan Huizinga, *Homo Ludens: A Study of the Play-Element in Culture*, trans. R. F. C. Hull (London: Routledge and Kegan Paul, 1949), 1–27, 63–71.

143. *New-York Gazette & General Advertiser*, February 25, 1834.

144. John Ward Jr. Diary, entry for November 25, 1859, N-YHS; and Alfred Janson Bloor Diary, 1848–1858, entry for November 25, 1857, N-YHS.

145. *New York Times*, November 26, 1859.

4. ALL FOR THE UNION

1. Caroline Caisson Woolsey, "Resistance to the Draft," in *Noble Women of the North*, comp. and ed. Sylvia G. L. Dannett (New York: Yoseloff, 1959), 264.

2. Allan Nevins and Milton Halsey Thomas, eds., *The Diary of George Templeton Strong*, vol. 3, *The Civil War, 1860–1865* (New York: Macmillan, 1952), 335, 340.

3. Julia Lay, "An Awful Riot Commenced Today," in Dannett, *Noble Women of the North*, 267.

4. Ibid., 267.

5. William Osborn Stoddard, *The Volcano Under the City* (New York: Fords, Howard & Hulbert, 1887), 332.

6. John Ward Jr. Diary, January 1–25, 1864, entry for January 19, 1864, Library, New-York Historical Society, New York, N.Y. [hereafter N-YHS].

7. Ibid.

8. Ibid.

9. Ibid.

10. Ibid., entries for January 8 and 9, 1864; John Ward Jr. Diary, April 1–20, 1864, entries for April 3, 13, and 14, N-YHS; John Ward Jr. Diary, 1865, entries for January 13, May 2 and 4, N-YHS; John Ward Jr. Diary, 1867, entry for January 4, 1867, N-YHS; *New York Times*, July 2, 1861, August 8, 1862, September 2 and 19, 1862, August 16, 1896, February 12, 1911; *New York Herald*, August 10, 1896; *New York Tribune*, August 10, 1896;

Frederick Phisterer, *New York in the War of the Rebellion, 1861 to 1865*, 3rd ed., vol. 1 (Albany, N.Y.: Lyon, 1912), 575–78; *In Memoriam: Alexander Stewart Webb, 1835–1911* (Albany, N.Y.: Lyon, 1916), 11–59, 91–111; and Douglas Southall Freeman, *George Washington: A Biography*, vol. 4, *Leader of the Revolution* (New York: Scribner's, 1951), 101, 292, 391. On Civil War prisoners of war, see Henry P. Riconda, *Prisoners of War in American Conflicts* (Leeham, Md.: Scarecrow, 2003), 103–30. For the impetus that Victorian understandings of duty and masculinity gave to Northerners' decisions to fight, see James M. McPherson, *For Cause and Comrades: Why Men Fought in the Civil War* (New York: Oxford University Press, 1997), 22–29.

11. *New York Times*, February 16, 1917.

12. Thomas A. Chambers, *Memories of War: Visiting Battlegrounds and Bonefields in the Early American Republic* (Ithaca, N.Y.: Cornell University Press, 2012), 1–35. See also Drew Gilpin Faust, *This Republic of Suffering: Death and the American Civil War* (New York: Knopf, 2008), 171–210.

13. Edward N. Tailer Diary, vol. 14, January 1, 1862–August 12, 1866, entry for July 23, 1863, N-YHS.

14. Gregory A. Coco, *A Strange and Blighted Land: Gettysburg, The Aftermath of a Battle* (Gettysburg, Pa.: Thomas, 1995), 7, 64, 303–04.

15. Tailer Diary, vol. 14, entry for July 24, 1863, N-YHS.

16. Ibid.

17. Ibid.

18. Tailer Diary, vol. 14, entry for July 31, 1863, N-YHS.

19. A number of the women who volunteered to serve as nurses for the Union armies came from the upper classes, including upper-class New Yorkers such as Georgeanna Woolsey and Jane Stuart Woolsey. For firsthand accounts of female nurses, see Dannett, *Noble Women of the North*.

20. James M. McPherson has disputed the idea that the Civil War was "a poor man's fight" by arguing that members of the working class were not the only Americans who served in large numbers. McPherson's conclusion may apply to middle- and upper-class men in other Northern communities, but it is not valid for upper-class New York City. James M. McPherson, *Ordeal by Fire: The Civil War and Reconstruction*, 2nd ed. (New York: McGraw-Hill, 1992), 355–57. In challenging the popular notion that the Civil War was "a rich man's war and a poor man's fight," McPherson compares the occupations of Civil War soldiers prior to their enlistment with the occupations of all males in the states from which the soldiers came (Ibid., 355). While acknowledging that the data show that white-collar and professional occupations appear to be underrepresented in the army, McPherson notes that most soldiers were young and that studies of social mobility in nineteenth-century America have shown that a substantial number of young men who began as farm laborers or as farm workers moved into white-collar or professional occupations later in life. "When this is taken into account," McPherson writes, "the Union army appears to have been quite representative of the Northern population" (355). McPherson makes a similar point as

part of a larger argument about the class and ethnic makeup of the Northern soldiery in *Battle Cry of Freedom: The Civil War Era* (New York: Oxford University Press, 1988), 600–08. It is not certain, however, whether that this conclusion is warranted from the evidence at hand. If it can be argued that some proportion of the soldiery would have experienced occupational mobility and would eventually have entered the "professional classes," they still presumably would have been laborers or farmers when they enlisted and served. There is also considerable slippage in the categories of occupation and social class. While occupational status is probably the single best measure of social status, the fluidity and lack of articulation of the mid-nineteenth-century occupational structure makes it difficult to extrapolate social class. Bell I. Wiley, who made some of the statistical studies of soldiers' occupations upon which McPherson drew, did not argue for the soldiery's representativeness. For McPherson's use of Wiley's data, see James M. McPherson, *Ordeal By Fire: The Civil War and Reconstruction*, (New York: Knopf, 1982), 637, 18n. Rather, Wiley cautiously concluded: "The most striking thing about Union soldiers was their diversity. The visitor to a Federal camp at any period of the war would encounter persons of many nationalities, races, creeds, and occupations and observe great variations in dress, habits, temperament, education, wealth, and social status." Bell I. Wiley, *The Life of Billy Yank: The Common Soldier of the Union* (Indianapolis, Ind.: Bobbs-Merrill, 1952), 296; see also pp. 298 and 427, 13n. More to the point, from the standpoint of my study, it seems incontrovertible that soldiers who were laborers or farm laborers prior to their enlistments did not belong to the upper class. Neither McPherson nor Wiley examined the upper class in particular.

21. Richard F. Miller, *Harvard's Civil War: A History of the Twentieth Massachusetts Volunteer Infantry* (Hanover, N.H.: University Press of New England, 2005), 1–9. See also Thomas H. O'Connor, *Civil War Boston: Home Front & Battlefield* (Boston: Northeastern University Press, 1997), 63–70. For the meaning that New York and Boston merchants put on enterprise around the time of the Civil War, see Thomas Kessner, *Capital City: New York City and the Men Behind America's Rise to Economic Dominance, 1860–1900* (New York: Simon & Schuster, 2003), 28–30.

22. Robert A. McCaughey, *Stand, Columbia: A History of Columbia University in the City of New York, 1754–2004* (New York: Columbia University Press, 2003), 141.

23. My interest is in monuments that can be identified with particular people or military units. For a reminder that war memorials take other forms, such as groves of trees, stones, obelisks, flagstaffs, stones, and columns, see Donald Martin Reynolds, *Monuments and Masterpieces: Histories and Views of Public Sculpture in New York City* (New York: Macmillan, 1988), 179–80. *New York Times*, February 12, 1911; *Brooklyn Eagle*, May 31, 1897; *The Shaw Memorial: A Celebration of an American Masterpiece* (Conshohocken, Pa.: Eastern National, 1997), 1–15; Russell Duncan, *Where Hope and Glory Meet: Colonel Robert Gould Shaw and the 54th Massachusetts Infantry* (Athens: University of Georgia Press, 1999), 1–28, 36–42, 52–59, 111–119; and Margot Gayle and Michele Cohen, *The Art Commission and Municipal Art Society Guide to Manhattan's*

Outdoor Sculpture (New York: Prentice Hall, 1988), 47, 72, 96, 103, 105–06, 115, 190–91, 286, 290, 292, 311, 313, and 318. I define as a New Yorker anyone who had a significant connection with New York City prior to the Civil War. I define New York City according to its contemporary boundaries, which are coterminus with Manhattan Island. My definition excludes people like William Tecumseh Sherman, Franz Siegel, and Winfield Scott Hancock who moved to New York City after the war. It also excludes John Ericsson; while his *Monitor* was built in Brooklyn, the peripatetic Ericsson was not closely associated with New York City. By way of further contrast with New York City, proper Bostonians were the subject of many Boston memorials in addition to the Shaw Memorial. See Thomas J. Brown, "Reconstructing Boston: Civic Monuments of the Civil War," 130–55, in *Hope & Glory: Essays on the Legacy of the Fifty-Fourth Massachusetts Regiment*, ed. Martin H. Blatt, Thomas J. Brown, and Donald Yacovone (Amherst, Mass.: University of Massachusetts Press, 2001).

24. For profiles of the Civil War soldiery as a whole, see McPherson, *For Cause and Comrades*, 3–13; and, particularly, McPherson, *Ordeal by Fire*, 2nd ed., 355–57. For Philadelphia, see Gallman, *Mastering Wartime*, 35–53.

25. *New York Tribune*, February 21, 1861. See Jerome Mushkat, *Fernando Wood: A Political Biography* (Kent, Ohio: Kent State University Press, 1990), 75–76, 98–115.

26. *New York Tribune*, February 21, 1861. See also Mushkat, *Fernando Wood*, 98–115; Harold Holzer, "Abraham Lincoln," in *The Encyclopedia of New York City*, 2nd ed., ed. Kenneth T. Jackson (New Haven, Conn.: Yale University Press, 2010), 748–49; and *New York Tribune*, January 14, 1861.

27. *New York Herald*, April 12, 1861.

28. *New York Tribune*, February 18, 1861. On Hammond, see Drew Gilpin Faust, *James Henry Hammond and the Old South: A Design for Mastery* (Baton Rouge: Louisiana State University Press, 1982), 1–4.

29. Frederick H. Wolcott Diary, 1849–1851, entries for January 16, February 12, March 13, 15, and 25, and April 20, 1850, and October 24, 1851, Manuscripts and Archives Division, New York Public Library, New York, N.Y. [hereafter NYPL].

30. "Agencies Ledger No. 2, 1859–65: 2–23," vol. 16, Brown Brothers & Company Records, Manuscripts and Archives Division, NYPL; "Ledger N, 1863–1865: 77–79, 206, 232, 237," vol. 73, Brown Brothers & Company Records; and "Ledger O, 1866," 41 and 77, vol. 74, Brown Brothers & Company Records, NYPL.

31. Moses Taylor to Tomas Terry, June 8, 1861, Letterbook 47, Moses Taylor Papers, Manuscripts and Archives Division, NYPL.

32. Moses Taylor to Messrs. S. & W. Welsh, November 21, 1861, Letterbook 61, Taylor Papers, NYPL; and *New York Herald*, August 4, 1861.

33. *New York Times*, August 31, 1861; *New York Herald*, August 18, 1861; and *New York Tribune*, February 21, 1861.

34. For the effect of the war economy on other Northern cities, see Theodore J. Karamanski, *Rally 'Round the Flag: Chicago and the Civil War* (Chicago: Nelson-Hall, 1993), xi–xiv; J. Matthew Gallman, *Mastering Wartime: A Social History*

of Philadelphia during During the Civil War (Cambridge, Mass.: Cambridge University Press, 1990), 35–53, 251–98; and O'Connor, *Civil War Boston*, 204–05.

35.   Mark R. Wilson, *The Business of the Civil War: Military Mobilization and the State, 1861 – 1865* (Baltimore, Md.: Johns Hopkins University Press, 2006), 1, 122.

36.   Ibid., 74. Edward K. Spann, *Gotham at War: New York City, 1860–1865* (Wilmington, Del.: Scholarly Resources, 2002), 45–55; *New York Times*, November 10, 1861, January 31, February 7, May 13 and October 30, 1863, January 5 and December 17, 1864; *New York Herald*, August 18, 1861, March 30, 1862; *Shipping and Commercial List, and New-York Prices Current*, January 10, 1863; H.A. Wise to Abram S. Hewitt, April 28, 1865, Business Correspondence, 1865 Folder, Box 23, Records of Cooper, Hewitt & Company, Manuscripts Division, Library of Congress, Washington, D.C.; and *New York Tribune*, March 8, 1864. See also Gallman, *Mastering Wartime*, 251–98.

37.   *Shipping and Commercial List, and New-York Prices Current*, April 12, 1862.

38.   *New York Times*, May 20, 1865; J. Matthew Gallman, *The North Fights the Civil War: The Home Front* (Chicago: Dee, 1994), 92–99; Bray Hammond, *Banks and Politics in America: From the Revolution to the Civil War* (Princeton, N.J.: Princeton University Press, 1957), 723–33; Bert W. Rein, *An Analysis and Critique of the Union Financing of the Civil War* (Amherst, Mass.: Amherst College Press, 1962), 7–14, 31–43; and Vincent P. Carosso, *Investment Banking in America: A History* (Cambridge, Mass.: Harvard University Press, 1970), 13–18.

39.   Carosso, *Investment Banking in America*, 13.

40.   *New York Tribune*, November 14, 1862, May 10, 1865; *New York Times*, August 21, 1865, September 17 and 19, 1871; Private Accounts Ledger No. 1, 1864–66, vol. 91: 1–15, Brown Brothers & Company Records, NYPL; Stock Ledger and Dividend Book, 1866–67: 131–33, vol. 116, Brown Brothers & Company Records, NYPL; Open Board of Stock Brokers, Minutes, vol. 1, meetings of December 21, 1863, February 27, 1864, and March 12, 1864, New York Stock Exchange Archives, New York, N.Y.

41.   Melinda Lawson, "Let the Nation Be Your Bank: The Civil War Bond Drives and the Construction of National Patriotism," in *An Uncommon Time: The Civil War and the Northern Home Front*, ed. Paul A. Cimbala and Randall M. Miller (New York: Fordham University Press, 2002), 90–119; Gallman, *The North Fights the Civil War*," 96–97; *New York World*, August 16 and September 5, 1861, December 12, 1863; *New York Tribune*, September 3 and October 9, 1861, October 31, 1863, May 10, 1865; and *New York Times*, May 13, 1865.

42.   David Kynaston, *The City of London*, vol. 1, *A World of Its Own, 1815–1890* (London: Pimlico, 1994), 216, 226; Salmon P. Chase to August Belmont, July 1, 1861, Catalogued Correspondence, Belmont Family Papers, Rare Books and Manuscript Library, Columbia University, New York, N.Y. [hereafter CU]; Salmon P. Chase to August Belmont, September 13, 1861, Catalogued Correspondence, Belmont Family Papers, CU; *New York World*, August 11, 1862; *Shipping and Commercial List, and New-York Prices Current*, April 6 and July 30, 1864; *New York Times*, June 12, 1863; *In Memoriam:*

Jesse Seligman (New York: Cowen, 1894), 5–15; Ross L. Muir and Carl J. White, *Over the Long Term…: The Story of J. & W. Seligman & Co.* (New York: Seligman, 1964), 9, 24–43; and Richard Sylla, "Investment Banking," 654–55, in Jackson, *Encyclopedia of New York City.*

43. Henry W. Bellows, *Historical Sketch of the Union League Club of New York: Its Origins, Organization, and Work, 1863–1879* (New York: Putnam's, 1879), 1–5; Joseph Howard Jr., ed., *The Union League Club: Historical and Biographical, 1863–1890* (New York: Union Historical Association), 3–4; Will Irwin, Earl Chapin May, and Joseph Hotchkiss, *A History of the Union League Club of New York City* (New York: Dodd, Mead, 1952), 7–18; McCaughey, *Stand Columbia!*, 120–30; *New York Times,* February 7, 1913; Nevins and Thomas, *The Diary of George Templeton Strong,* 3: 276, 288, 292–93, 297–98; and *New York Times,* April 19, 1888, June 30, 1892.

44. The founders borrowed the name "Union League Club" from the Union League of Philadelphia, established that December. The Union League of Philadelphia and the Union League Club of New York had the same name as a social movement, known as the union loyalty leagues, that was also inspired by the Sanitary Commission. Union leagues existed as early as 1861, but grew significantly following the 1862 elections. With a membership of upper-middle-class men, local branches of the union leagues emerged in many Northern towns and cities to hold patriotic rallies and fundraising drives, disseminate pamphlets, and back Republican candidates. The members of the more socially exclusive Union League Club of New York would take pains to distance themselves from the leagues. Union League Clubs were founded in Chicago, Brooklyn, and New Haven, appealing to the same elite groups as the New York and Philadelphia clubs but operating independently of one another. *New York Tribune,* January 23, 1861; *New York World,* March 16, 1863; Nevins and Thomas, *The Diary of George Templeton Strong,* 3: 286, 288; *Chronicle of the Union League of Philadelphia, 1862–1902* (Philadelphia: n.p., 1902), 5–11; *Articles of Association and By-Laws of the Union League of Philadelphia, Organized December 27, 1862* (Philadelphia: King & Baird, 1863), 3–4; and Howard Jr., *The Union League Club,* 6. The sources of this occupational and residential data are: *Trow's New York City Directory for the Year Ending July 1, 1860* (New York: Trow, 1859); *Trow's New York City Directory for the Year Ending July 1, 1861* (New York: Trow, 1860); Manuscript Census, 1860 Federal Census, New York State, New York County, 1st division of the 15th ward, 639, Ancestry.com, accessed July 17, 2007, www.ancestry.com; Manuscript Census, 1860 Federal Census, New York State, Richmond County, Township of Castleton, 62, Ancestry.com, accessed July 17, 2007, www.ancestry.com; Manuscript Census, 1870 Federal Census, New York State, New York County, 9th election district of the 19th ward, 108, 303, Ancestry.com, accessed July 17, 2007, www.ancestry.com; Manuscript Census, 1870 Federal Census, New York State, New York County, 16th election district of the 21st ward, 9, Ancestry.com, accessed July 17, 2007, www.ancestry.com; Manuscript Census, 1850 Manuscript Census, New York State, New York County, 1st district of the 8th ward, 292, accessed July 17, 2007, www.ancestry.com.

45. Sven Beckert, *Moneyed Metropolis: New York City and the Consolidation of the American Bourgeoisie, 1850–1896* (New York: Cambridge University Press, 2001), 115–19, 128–32.

46. "Original By-laws of the Club," 169–73, in Irvin, May, and Hotchkiss, *A History of the Union League Club of New York City*.

47. *New York Times*, December 10, 1862, January 27, July 31, and September 10, 1864.

48. Circular letter of January 15, 1863, quoted in Howard Jr., *The Union League Club*, 4.

49. John Jay, *The Political Situation in the United States: A Letter to the Union League Club of New York* (London: Rivingtons, 1866), 2–4; *New York Times*, August 30, November 19, and December 18, 1863, January 11, 26, and 31, February 11, and August 19, 1864.

50. Mushkat, *Fernando Wood*, 24–26, 36–65, 92–115; Amy Bridges, *A City in the Republic: Antebellum New York and the Origins of Machine Politics* (Cambridge: Cambridge University Press, 1984), 1–17, 126–31; Jon C. Teaford, *The Unheralded Triumph: City Government in America, 1870–1900* (Baltimore, Md.: Johns Hopkins University Press, 1984), 1–11.

51. Circular letter of January 15, 1863, quoted in Howard Jr., *The Union League Club*, 4.

52. *New York Tribune*, May 13, 1863.

53. Union League Club of New York, *Report of the Executive Committee, Constitution, By-Laws, and Roll of Members, July 1864* (New York: n.p., 1864), 41–48; Nevins and Thomas, *The Diary of George Templeton Strong*, 3: 321; Junius Henri Browne, *The Great Metropolis: A Mirror of New York* (Hartford, Conn.: American Publishing, 1869), 443. The Union League Club excluded Copperheads such as August Belmont, who would soon combine with other prominent Democrats such as John Van Buren, Fernando Wood, and John T. Hoffman to organize the rival Manhattan Club.

54. *New York Times*, August 30, 1863, November 13, 1864, March 27, April 1, 1868; *New York Tribune*, May 13, 1863; *Brooklyn Eagle*, March 28, 1867; and *Miller's New York As It Is; or, Stranger's Guide-book to the Cities of New York, Brooklyn and Adjacent Places* (New York: Miller, 1869), 81.

55. Jay, *The Political Situation*, 2.

56. Union League Club, *Its Memories of the Past: The President's Address at the Last Meeting in the Old Club House on Union Square, Thursday Evening, March 26, 1868* (New York: n.p., 1868), 4.

57. *New York Times*, August 30, November 19, and December 18, 1863, January 11, 26, and 31, February 11, and August 19, 1864, February 15 and 28, March 27, November 6, December 31, 1868, January 31, 1870; *Brooklyn Eagle*, April 12, 1867; "Additional Articles of Association," 165 and "Charter," 166–67, both in Irwin, May, and Hotchkiss, *A History of the Union League Club*; and Union League Club, *Its Memories of the Past*, 3.

58. Another influence was the sensationalist literature that drew stark contrasts between the "sunshine" and the "shadows" of New York City—between rich and poor, virtue and vice, education and ignorance, and so forth. Authors like George C. Foster castigated the impoverished for their squalid living conditions and their moral depravity, but also blamed the wealthy for retreating into their private realms of luxury and

pleasure instead of carrying out their civic duty to uplift the downtrodden and eliminate the rot before it spread to the rest of city. That perspective corresponded closely to elements of the Union League Club's position. George C. Foster, *New York by Gas-Light and Other Urban Sketches*, ed. Stuart M. Blumin (Berkeley: University of California Press, 1990), 2–57. See also Burton Pike, *The Image of the City in Modern Literature* (Princeton, N.J.: Princeton University Press, 1981).

59. Clifton Hood, "An Unusable Past: Urban Elites, New York City's Evacuation Day, and the Transformations of Memory Culture," *Journal of Social History* 37 (Summer 2004): 883–913; Clifton Hood, "Journeying to 'Old New York': Elite New Yorkers and Their Invention of an Idealized City History in the Late Nineteenth and Early Twentieth Centuries," *Journal of Urban History* 28 (September 2002): 699–716; and Peter Dobkin Hall, "The Empty Tomb: The Making of Dynastic Identity," in George E. Marcus with Peter Dobkin Hall, *Lives in Trust: The Fortunes of Dynastic Families in Late Twentieth-Century America* (Boulder: University of Colorado Press), 255–348.

60. David T. Valentine, *History of the City of New York* (New York: Putnam, 1853); Mary L. Booth, *History of the City of New York from its Earliest Settlement to the Present Time* (New York: Clark, 1859); Junius Henry Browne, *The Great Metropolis, A Mirror of New York: A Complete History of Metropolitan Life and Society, with Sketches of Prominent Places, Persons, and Things in the City, as They Actually Exist* (Hartford: American Publishing, 1869); and Daniel Curry, *New-York: A Historical Sketch of the Rise and Progress of the Metropolitan City of America* (New York: Carlton & Phillips, 1853).

61. Curry, *New-York*, 5, 248–49; and Booth, *History of the City of New York*, dedication page, 8, 10–15.

62. *New York Tribune*, May 13, 1863.

63. Transcription of Oscar Brown 1863 Diary, entry for July 15, 1863. Diary is in the possession of Christine Brown, Montclair, N.J.

64. Iver Bernstein, *The New York City Draft Riots: Their Significance for American Society and Politics in the Age of the Civil War* (New York: Oxford University Press, 1990), 3–14, 259–64; and Barnet Schecter, *The Devil's Own Work: The Civil War Draft Riots and the Fight to Reconstruct America* (New York: Walker, 2005), 1–8, 157–83. See also Bruce, *The Harp and the Eagle*, 190–232; and McPherson, *Ordeal by Fire*, 399. For the importance of urban spatial patterns to riots, see Janet L. Abu-Lughod, *Race, Space, and Riots in Chicago, New York, and Los Angeles* (New York: Oxford University Press, 2007), 3–39.

65. The figure of 105 deaths includes deaths that were directly attributable to the riots and that were confirmed in official documents. This official count is surely too low. The author of a recent narrative history of the draft riots concludes that the "true death toll probably lies somewhere between the documented figure [of 105] and the sober contemporary estimate of 500." Schecter, *The Devil's Own Work*, 252.

66. James D. Gilmore, *Personal Recollections of Abraham Lincoln and the Civil War* (Boston: Page, 1898), 171.

67. A. Hunter Dupree and Leslie H. Fishel Jr., eds., "An Eyewitness Account of the New York Draft Riots, July 1863," *Mississippi Valley Historical Review* 47 (December 1960): 476.

68. The William Steinway Diary, 1861–1893, entry for July 15, 1863, Archives Center, National Museum of American History, Smithsonian Institution, accessed February 19, 2011, http://americanhistory.si.edu/steinwaydiary.

69. Edward N. Tailer Diary, vol. 14, entries for July 14, 15, and 16, 1863, N-YHS.

70. Dupree and Fishel, "An Eyewitness Account," 476.

71. Ibid.

72. Ward Diary, entry for January 8, 1864, N-YHS.

73. Elizabeth Cady Stanton to Nancy Smith, July 20, 1863, North American Women's Letters and Diaries, accessed August 8, 2007, www.alexanderstreet4.com/cgi-bin /aspnawld.

74. Lucy Gibbons Morse, "Personal Recollections of the Draft Riots of 1863," 2, N-YHS. See also Schecter, *The Devil's Own Work*, 192–94, 231–33.

75. Morse, "Personal Recollections of the Draft Riots of 1863," 3.

76. Lucy Gibbons Morse to Anna Hopper, July 17, 1863, North American Women's Letters and Diaries, accessed August 8, 2007, www.alexanderstreet4.com/cgi-bin /aspnawld.

77. Ibid.

78. Morse, "Personal Recollections of the Draft Riots of 1863," 4–5.

79. Ibid., 6.

80. Ibid., 1–6. For a similar emphasis in the newspaper coverage, see *New York Tribune*, July 14 and 15, 1863.

81. "The Health of New York," *Harper's Weekly* 9 (April 1, 1865), 194; *New York Tribune*, July 14, 1863; and William Stone, *History of New York City from the Discovery to the Present Day* (New York: E. Cleave, 1868), 562.

82. *New York Tribune*, July 14, 1863.

83. *New York Times*, August 30, 1863.

84. "The People," *Harper's Weekly* 7 (August 1, 1863), 842. See also "The Late Riot," *Harper's Weekly* 7 (August 22, 1863), 530.

85. "The People," *Harper's Weekly*, 842–43.

86. "Barbarism and Civilization," *Harper's Weekly* 7 (August 1, 1863), 483.

87. *New York Times*, November 20, 1865.

88. "Robespierre and Mr. James Brooks," *Harper's Weekly* 11 (March 23, 1867), 179.

89. Reverend B. Peters, *Discourses on the Late Riots in New York City* (Brooklyn: n.p., 1863), 5.

90. Ibid.

91. Ibid., 5–6.

92. *The Bloody Week: Riot, Murder & Arson, Containing a Full Account of This Wholesale Outrage on Life and Property, Accurately Prepared from Official Sources, by Eye Witnesses, with Portraits of "Andrews," the Leader, and "Rosa," His Eleventh Street Mistress*

(New York: Coutant & Baker, 1863), 1; and David M. Barnes, *The Draft Riots in New York, July, 1863. The Metropolitan Police: Their Services During Riot Week. Their Honorable Record* (New York: Baker & Godwin, 1863), 5–6, 106.

93. Stoddard, *The Volcano Under the City*, 9. See also James B. Fry, *New York and the Conscription of 1863: A Chapter in the History of the Civil War* (New York: Putnam's, 1885), 33.

94. Stoddard, *The Volcano Under the City*, 332–33.

95. Tailer Diary, vol. 14, entry for July 17, 1863, N-YHS.

96. Roger Simon, *Gramsci's Political Thought: An Introduction* (London: Lawrence and Wishart, 1982), 21–28.

97. *New York Times*, September 1, 1854, March 21, 1857, November 25, 1858; and Charles Loring Brace, *The Dangerous Classes of New York and Twenty Years' Work Among Them* (New York: Wynkoop & Hallenbeck, 1872), 25–31.

98. Daniel J. Singal, "Towards a Definition of American Modernism," *American Quarterly* 39 (Spring 1987): 7–26.

99. "How New York Is Misgoverned," *Harper's Weekly* 11 (February 9, 1867): 90; "Home and Foreign Gossip," *Harper's Weekly* 11 (February 23, 1867): 123; "The Riot on St. Patrick's Day," *Harper's Weekly* 11 (April 6, 1867): 209; *Washington Post*, April 21, 1890; E. J. Edwards, "The Rise and Overthrow of the Tweed Ring: Chapters in the History of Tammany," *McClure's Magazine* 5 (July 1895): 132–44; Richard L. Dugdale, "The Origins of Crime in Society," *Atlantic Monthly* 48 (October 1881): 452–61; James R. Gillmore, "The New York 'Tribune' in the Draft Riots: The Story of a Member of the Staff Who Assisted in Arming the 'Tribune' Office," *McClure's Magazine* 5 (October 1895): 445–54; Jacob A. Riis, "The Police Department of New York City," *Outlook* 60 (November 5, 1898): 581–89; Jacob A. Riis, "Will It Last?," *Outlook* 64 (April 21, 1910): 911–13; advertisement for *The Youth's Companion Magazine*, *Outlook* 54 (November 21, 1896) 927; and *New York Times*, January 4, 1891, July 3, 1897.

100. Bailey, "The Fabrication of Deviance," 221–56, in *Protest and Survival: Essays for E.P. Thompson*, ed. John Rule and Robert Malcomson (London: Merlin, 1993); David Taylor, "Beyond the Bounds of Respectable Society: The 'Dangerous Classes' in Victorian and Edwardian England," in *Criminal Conversations: Victorian Crimes, Social Panic, and Moral Outrage*, ed. Judith Rowbotham and Kim Stevenson (Columbus: Ohio State University Press, 2005), 3–22; Ellen Ross, ed., introduction to *Slum Travelers: Ladies and London Poverty, 1860–1920* (Berkeley: University of California Press, 2007), 1–29; and Richard J. Evans, *Death in Hamburg: Society and Politics in the Cholera Years, 1830–1910* (Oxford: Clarendon, 1987), 78–95.

101. Reverend Howard Crosby, "The Dangerous Classes," *North American Review* 136 (April 1883), 345. For similar constructions, see also Brace, *The Dangerous Classes of New York*, 24–31; and *New York Times*, March 19, 1883.

102. Crosby, "The Dangerous Classes," 346. See also *Washington Post*, March 19, 1883.

103. I take this depiction of the "dangerous classes" from Victor Bailey, "The Fabrication of Deviance: 'Dangerous Classes' and 'Criminal Classes' in Victorian England," 222, in Rule and Malcomson, *Protest and Survival*. For accounts of Tammany that express

this perspective, see Rev. Charles H. Parkhurst, *Our Fight with Tammany* (New York: Scribner's, 1895), passim; and Gustavus Myers, *The History of Tammany Hall* (New York: Boni & Liveright, 1917), vii–xi.

104. "The Volcano Under the City," *Army and Navy Journal* 24 (November 27, 1886): 354. I am grateful to Kevin Adams for alerting me to this source.

105. Ibid., 355.

106. Jerry M. Cooper, *The Army and Civil Disorder: Federal Military Intervention in Labor Disputes, 1877–1900* (Westport, Conn.: Greenwood Press, 1980), 3–18; Robert M. Fogelson, *America's Armories: Architecture, Society, and Public Order* (Cambridge, Mass.: Harvard University Press, 1989), 13–47; and Lisa Keller, "Armories," 61–64, in Jackson, *Encyclopedia of New York City*.

107. Simon, *Gramsci's Political Thought*, 22–23.

108. Stoddard, *The Volcano Under the City*, 30, 49, 60–61, 80–81, 92–93, 118, 131, 182–83, 200.

109. Ibid., 69.

110. Ibid., 69.

111. For free labor, see Eric Foner, *Free Soil, Free Labor, Free Men: The Ideology of the Republican Party Before the Civil War* (New York: Oxford University Press, 1970), 9–13.

112. Stoddard, *The Volcano Under the City*, 66.

113. *New York Times*, February 7, 1900; *Washington Post*, November 12, 1902; and Clifton Hood, *722 Miles: The Building of the Subways and How They Transformed New York* (New York: Simon & Schuster, 1993), 56–74.

5. A DYNAMIC BUSINESSMAN'S ARISTOCRACY

1. Francis W. Crowninshield, *Manners for the Metropolis: An Entrance Key to the Fantastic Life of the 400* (New York: Appleton, 1908), 4.

2. *Town Topics and the American Queen*, March 28 and April 11, 1885; *Town Topics*, November 17, 1887; *New York Times*, November 13, 1875, May 28, 1885, January 17, May 26, and April 18, 1887, May 26, 1888, December 5, 1890, May 8 and 29, April 5, and December 30, 1891, December 6, 1896, May 9, 1897; M. F. Sweetser, *How to Know New York City: A Serviceable and Trustworthy Guide, Having Its Starting Point at the Grand Union Hotel* (Boston: Rand, Avery, 1888), 87–89; Paul Porzelt, *The Metropolitan Club of New York* (New York: Rizzoli, 1982), 7–32; Jean Strouse, *Morgan: American Financier* (New York: Random House, 1999), 276–77; and *Officers, Members, Constitution and By-Laws of the Union Club of the City of New York* (New York: n.p., 1894), 13–75.

3. Social Register Association, *Social Register, 1887* (New York: Social Register Association, 1886; facsimile ed., New York: Social Register Association, 1986), 2; and Social Register Association, *Social Register, New York, 1904* (New York: n.p., 1903), 11, 30–31, 74, 122–23, 125, 394, 398, 448, 476–77.

4. Sven Beckert argues that an upper class formed in New York City in the late nineteenth century, an interpretation strongly influenced by scholarship on the formation

of the working and the middle classes. While these two classes were new in the nineteenth century, my view is that a self-conscious and cohesive upper class already existed in the eighteenth and the early nineteenth centuries but underwent major structural and cultural changes beginning in the first half of the nineteenth century and continuing in the Gilded Age. Sven Beckert, *The Monied Metropolis: New York City and the Consolidation of the American Bourgeoisie, 1850–1896* (Cambridge: Cambridge University Press, 2001), 1–14.

5. Examples include Beckert, *The Monied Metropolis*; Thomas Kessner, *Capital City: New York City and the Men Behind America's Rise to Economic Dominance, 1860–1900* (New York: Simon & Schuster, 2004); Eric Homberger, *Mrs. Astor's New York: Money and Social Power in a Gilded Age* (New Haven: Yale University Press, 2004); Ron Chernow, *Titan: The Life of John D. Rockefeller, Sr.* (New York: Random House, 1998); David Nasaw, *Andrew Carnegie* (New York: Penguin, 2006); David Cannadine, *Mellon: An American Life* (New York: Knopf, 2006); and Strouse, *Morgan*.

6. Population figures for New York are for Greater New York, comprising the five boroughs of Manhattan, Brooklyn, the Bronx, Queens, and Staten Island, which came into being with the consolidation of 1898. Joseph J. Salvo and Arun Peter Lobo, "Population," in *The Encyclopedia of New York City*, 2nd ed., ed. Kenneth T. Jackson (New Haven: Yale University Press, 2010), 1018–20; Campbell Gibson, *Population of the 100 Largest Cities and Other Urban Places in the United States: 1790 to 1990*, Population Division Working Paper No. 27, U.S. Bureau of the Census, Population Division (Washington, D.C.: n.p., 1998), table 14, accessed March 23, 2007, www.census.gov /population/www/documentation/twps0027; Paul M. Hohenberg and Lynn Hollen Lees, *The Making of Modern Europe, 1000–1950* (Cambridge, Mass.: Harvard University Press, 1985), 11; Ira Rosenwaike, *Population History of New York City* (Syracuse, N.Y.: Syracuse University Press, 1972), 58; Tertius Chandler, *Four Thousand Years of Urban Growth: An Historical Census* (London: Edwin Mellen, 1987), 492; Tertius Chandler and Gerald Fox, *3000 Years of Urban Growth* (New York: Academic, 1974), 330; and U.S. Census Office, *Twelfth Census of the United States: 1900, Census Reports*, vol. 7, *Manufactures*, part 1, sect. 3, *Urban Manufactures* (Washington, D.C.: Government Printing Office, 1902), ccxxx.

7. "World's Tallest Buildings: Timeline of All Skyscrapers Holding the Title of Tallest Building in the World from 1890 to the Present," web project on Tallest Towers, Skyscraper Museum, New York, N.Y., accessed June 26, 2008, www.skyscraper. org/TALLEST_TOWERS/tallest.htm; "Manhattan Timeformations," web project, Skyscraper Museum, New York, N.Y., accessed June 26, 2008, www.skyscraper. org/timeformations/intro.htm#; U.S. Department of Treasury, Bureau of Statistics, *Foreign Commerce and Navigation of the United States, the Year Ending June 30, 1900* (Washington, D.C.: Government Printing Office, 1900), 50–51; Norman J. Brouwer, "Port of New York," in Jackson, *Encyclopedia of New York City*; and Clifton Hood, *722 Miles: The Building of the Subways and How They Transformed New York* (New York: Simon & Schuster, 1993), 11–18, 1022–26.

8. Western Union Company, *Annual Report, 1892* (New York: Kempster, 1892), 8; Susan B. Carter, editor in chief, *Historical Statistics of the United States: Earliest Times to the Present, Millennial Edition*, vol. 4, *Economic Sectors* (New York: Cambridge University Press, 2006), tables Dg8–21, "Domestic Telegraph Industry, Wire, Offices, Employees, and Finances, 1866–1987."

9. Richard Harding Davis, "Broadway," *Scribner's Magazine* 9 (May 1891): 588.

10. Henry Clews, "Delusions About Wall Street," *North American Review* 145 (October 1887): 412.

11. *Wall Street Journal*, January 2, 1896.

12. Lloyd Wendt, *The Wall Street Journal: The Story of Dow Jones & the Nation's Business Newspaper* (Chicago: Rand McNally, 1982), 30–42, 68; Youssef Cassis, *Capitals of Capital: A History of International Financial Centres, 1780–2005* (New York: Cambridge University Press, 2006), 75–77, 119; George Leland Leffler and Loring C. Farell, *The Stock Market*, 3rd rev. ed. (New York: Ronald, 1968), 91; and *New York Stock Exchange Directory, June 1st, 1889* (New York: Spanzenberg & Bishop, 1889), 7–40, 68–71.

13. Matthew Josephson, *The Robber Barons: The Great American Capitalists, 1861–1901* (New York: Harcourt, Brace, 1934; repr., New York: Harcourt, Brace & World, 1962), vi; Daniel T. Rogers, "In Search of Progressivism," *Reviews in American History* 10 (December 1982): 123–24; Richard R. John, *Network Nation: Inventing American Telecommunications* (Cambridge, Mass.: Harvard University Press, 2010), 156–58; and Richard R. John, "Robber Barons Redux: Antimonopoly Reconsidered," *Enterprise & Society* 13 (March 2012): 1–38.

14. *Adair County News*, January 3, 1900.

15. *Gainesville Star*, October 13, 1903; *Amador Ledger*, August 2, 1903; and *Deseret Evening News*, December 27, 1899.

16. James Bryce, "America Revisited: The Changes of a Quarter-Century: Part I," *Outlook* 80 (March 25, 1905): 734.

17. Ibid., 733.

18. Ibid., 734.

19. Ibid., 734.

20. Arthur Warren, "Philip D. Armour: His Manner of Life, His Immense Enterprises in Trade and Philanthropy," *McClure's Magazine* 2 (February 1894): 260–81; Helen Churchill Candee, "Once Too Often," *Harper's Bazaar* 34 (February 16, 1901): 418–26; Joseph Edgar Chamberlin, "The Sleeplessness of John Colton Dow," *Century* 56 (June 1898): 308–12; Richard Wheatley, "The New York Stock Exchange," *Harper's New Monthly Magazine* 71 (November 1885): 830–53; Richard Wheatley, "The New York Chamber of Commerce," *Harper's New Monthly Magazine* 83 (September 1891): 502–13; Richard Wheatley, "The New York Produce Exchange," *Harper's New Monthly Magazine* 73 (July 1886): 189–218; Samuel Hopkins Adams, "The Realm of Enchantment," *McClure's Magazine* 23 (September 1904): 520–32; and Andrew Carnegie, *The Gospel of Wealth* (Bedford, Mass.: Applewood, 1998), 5–24.

21. "Cornelius Vanderbilt," *Outlook* 63 (September 23, 1899): 192.

22. Ibid., 192.

23. Ibid., 192.

24. *Wall Street Journal*, January 12, 1893.

25. The U.S. Census's categories of "trade and transportation" and "manufacturing and mechanical pursuits" are only approximate equivalents of commerce and manufacturing, respectively. U.S. Department of Commerce and Labor, Bureau of the Census, *Occupations at the Twelfth Census*, sect. 9, *Principal Cities* (Washington, D.C.: Government Printing Office, 1904), 457, 459.

26. U.S. Census Office, *Twelfth Census of the United States: 1900*, vol. 7, *Manufactures: States and Territories*, sect. 3, *Manufactures by States and Territories: Maine–Minnesota*, 388–90; sect. 5, *Manufactures by States and Territories: New York–Ohio*, 620–28; and sect. 6, *Manufactures by States and Territories: Oklahoma–Tennessee*, 792–95. Unlike the aggregate data cited above, these figures are for the five boroughs of Greater New York City.

27. James Bradley, "P. Lorillard and Company," in Jackson, *Encyclopedia of New York City*; Joseph Rishel, *Founding Families of Pittsburgh: The Evolution of a Regional Elite, 1760–1910* (Pittsburgh, Pa.: University of Pittsburgh Press, 1990), 1004; David Nasaw, *Andrew Carnegie* (New York: Penguin, 2006), 117, 70–118; Chernow, *Titan*, 218–23, 578–85; and Leon Stein, *The Triangle Fire* (New York: Carrol & Graf, 1962), 44–46. Manufacturers figure more prominently in Sven Beckert's analysis than in mine, largely because his bourgeoisie category is inclusive, while my upper class and economic elite categories are more exclusive. Beckert, *The Monied Metropolis*, 1–14, 51–55, 60–66, 242–43.

28. Cassis, *Capitals of Capital*, 114.

29. Ibid., 114–24; Mira Wilkins, *The History of Foreign Investment in the United States to 1914* (Cambridge, Mass.: Harvard University Press, 1989), 469–89.

30. Cassis, *Capitals of Capital*, 115–19; Margaret G. Myers, *The New York Money Market*, vol. 1, *Origins and Development* (New York: Columbia University Press, 1931), 234–50; Morton Rothstein, "New York Produce Exchange," in Jackson, *Encyclopedia of New York City*, 928–29; Moses Rothstein, "New York Cotton Exchange," in Jackson, *Encyclopedia of New York City*, 915; George Winslow, "New York Mercantile Exchange," in Jackson, *Encyclopedia of New York City*, 923–24; *Coffee, Sugar & Cocoa Exchanges, Inc., 1882–1982* (New York: n.p. [1982?]), unpaginated; New York Cotton Exchange, *New York Cotton Exchange, 1870–1945* (New York: n.p., 1945), 1–3; New York Produce Exchange, *Ceremony at the Laying of the Cornerstone of the New York Produce Exchange, June 6, 1882* (New York: Vaux and Roper, 1882), 4–11; Vincent P. Carosso, *Investment Banking in America: A History* (Cambridge, Mass.: Harvard University Press, 1970), 18–77; Wilkins, *The History of Foreign Investment in the United States*, 469–89; Ron Chernow, *The House of Morgan: An American Banking Dynasty and the Rise of Modern Finance* (New York: Simon & Schuster, 1990), 70–161; Strouse, *Morgan*, 87–102; and Kathleen Burk, *Morgan Grenfell, 1838–1988: The Biography of a Merchant Bank* (New York: Oxford University Press, 1989), 52–63.

31. New York Stock Exchange Archives, *Records of the New York Stock Exchange, 1817–1869* (New York: n.p., n.d.), 3, 54; George L. Leffler and Loring C. Farwell, *The Stock Market*, 3rd ed. (New York: Ronald, 1963), 91–95; *New York Stock Exchange Directory, 1870* (New York: England, 1870), 5–6, 11–12, 15, 23,–24; and New York Stock Exchange, *Officers, Governing Committees, and Standing Committees, List of Members, with Their Annunciator Numbers and Addresses, Co-Partnerships, Branch Offices, Out-Of-Town Members, and Rules for Delivery* (New York: Searing and Watson, 1900), 8, 16, 18, 19, 25, 28–29.

32. Conservation of Human Resources Project (Columbia University), *The Corporate Headquarters Complex in New York City* (New York: n.p., 1977), 7–38. The figures on headquarters locations are for metropolitan areas, not cities.

33. Here I am indebted to Edwin G. Burrows and Mike Wallace, *Gotham: A History of New York City to 1898* (New York: Oxford, 1999), 1044–50. See also Chernow, *Titan*, 212–24; Kessner, *Capital City*, 234–37; Naomi R. Lamoreaux, *The Great Merger Movement in American Business, 1895–1904* (Cambridge: Cambridge University Press, 1985), 1–13; Conservation of Human Resources Project (Columbia University), *The Corporate Headquarters Complex*, 7–38; Chauncey G. Olinger Jr. and Meghan Lalonde, "Advertising," in Jackson, *Encyclopedia of New York City*, 8–9; Kevin Kenny and Meghan Lalonde, "Lawyers," in Jackson, *Encyclopedia of New York City*, 725–27; Paul J. Miranti Jr., "Accounting," in Jackson, *Encyclopedia of New York City*, 5–6; and Olivier Zunz, *Making America Corporate, 1870–1920* (Chicago: University of Chicago Press, 1990), 1–10.

34. David C. Hammack, *Power and Society: Greater New York at the Turn of the Century* (New York: Russell Sage Foundation, 1982), 3–27; and Beckert, *The Monied Metropolis*, 1–14. See also Emily Rosenberg, *Spreading the American Dream: American Economic and Cultural Expansion, 1890–1945* (New York: Hill and Wang, 1982), 38.

35. Henry Clews, *Twenty-Eight Years in Wall Street* (New York: Irving, 1888), 88.

36. New York Stock Exchange Archives, *Records of the New York Stock Exchange*, 3, 54; Leffler and Farwell, *The Stock Market*, 91–95; *New York Times*, April 19, 22, and 23, 1903; June 10, 1904; *New York Tribune*, April 23, 1903; *Wall Street Journal*, April 23, 1903; and Margot Gayle and Michele Cohen, *The Art Commission and the Municipal Art Society's Guide to Manhattan's Outdoor Sculpture* (New York: Prentice-Hall, 1988), 26.

37. *New York Times*, April 23, 1903.

38. *Owingsville Outlook*, June 13, 1901.

39. Pierpont Morgan's Engagement Diary for 1899, entries for March 24, June 16, 23, and 27, 1899, Archives of the Morgan Library and Museum, New York, N.Y. [hereafter MLM].

40. *John Swinton's Paper*, November 25, 1883.

41. Eugene V. Debs, "The American Movement," in *Debs: His Life, Writings, and Speeches* (Girard, Kans.: Appeal to Reason, 1908), 117.

42. William Jennings Bryan, *The Cross of Gold: Speech Delivered Before the National Democratic Convention at Chicago, July 9, 1896* (Lincoln: University of Nebraska Press, 1996), 28.

43. *New York Times*, August 8, 1896.

44. *Brooklyn Eagle*, August 13, 1896.

45. *Brooklyn Eagle*, August 21, September 25, November 8, 1896; *Columbia Register*, n.d., reprinted in *New York Times*, July 12; *New York Times*, July 12 and 13, September 23, October 23, November 3–9, 1896; *New York Tribune*, August 13, September 24, 1896; and Michael Kazin, *A Godly Hero: The Life of William Jennings Bryan* (New York: Knopf, 2006), 66–67.

46. T. De Witt Talmage, *Social Dynamite; Or, the Wickedness of Modern Society* (Chicago: Chicago Standard, 1887), 113, 123, 132, 144–60, 163, 202, 224, 338–47; May Talmage, comp., *Fifty Short Sermons by T. De Witt Talmage* (New York: Doran, 1923), 28–33; *Washington Post*, April 13, 1902; *New York Tribune*, April 13, 1902; *New York Times*, April 13, 1902; *Brooklyn Eagle*, January 9, 1882, September 15, 1884, November 1, 1886, October 13, 1888; *Berea Citizen*, June 13, 1901; *Owingsville Outlook*, June 13, 1901; *Richmond Dispatch*, February 7, 1902; *Adair County News*, April 17, 1901; and *Salt Lake Herald*, September 30, 1900. Another Protestant cleric who became a critic of corporate capitalism was Washington Gladden, a Congregationalist minister and a leader of the social gospel movement. See *New York Times*, August 27, 1899, March 31 and April 1, 26, and 28, 1905; and Chernow, *Titan*, 499–500.

47. Clews, "Delusions About Wall Street," *North American Review*, 411, 410. See also Clews, *Twenty-eight Years in Wall Street*, 13–18. *New York Times*, February 1, 1923; and *Washington Post*, February 1, 1923. The phrase "dean of Wall Street" is from the *Washington Post* obituary.

48. Clews, "Delusions About Wall Street," *North American Review*, 410.

49. Ibid., 410–21. See also Clews, *The Wall Street Point of View* (New York: Silver, Burdett, 1900), 1–4.

50. *New York Times*, October 9, November 25 and 27, 1883; and *Brooklyn Eagle*, November 26, 1883.

51. Ibid.

52. Ibid.

53. Clifton Hood, "An Unusable Past," *Journal of Social History* 37 (Summer 2004): 883–913; "The Inauguration of Washington," *The Century* 37 (April 1889): 803–33; *Brooklyn Eagle*, November 25–26, 1883; *Souvenir of the Centennial Exhibition of Washington's Inauguration, held in New York City, April 29th and 30th, 1889* (New York: Nicholl & Roy, 1889), 3; "Editor's Easy Chair," *Harper's New Monthly Magazine* 78 (March 1889): 653–55; *Brooklyn Eagle*, April 28–29, and May 1, 1889; *New York Times*, January 12, April 30, and December 8 and 23, 1888, May 1, 1889.

54. *Pictorial New York and Brooklyn: A Guide to the Same and Vicinity* (New York: Smith, Bleakley, 1892), 25. See also Gustav Kobbé, *Kobbé's New York and Its Environs* (New York: Harper, 1891), 80–123; *The Sun's Guide to New York* (Jersey City, NJ: Jersey City Print Company, 1892), 2–12; and Cynthia M. Westover Alden, *Manhattan: Historic and Artistic* (New York: Morse, 1897), 34–45.

55. Kessner, *Capital City*, 238; Chernow, *Titan*, 344; Nasaw, *Andrew Carnegie*, 768; *New York Times*, May 28, 1901, May 26, June 30, and December 22, 1905, April 11, 1907, *Wall Street Journal*, January 3, 1903; and Moneyworth.com, accessed August 14, 2009, www.measuringworth.com/growth. Here I employ the historic standard of living as my measure of changes in relative value over time. Unskilled workers who were employed building the IRT subway earned $2 to $2.25 daily, and skilled workers made $2.50 daily. I base my calculations about their annual wages on the assumption that they put in 6 days a week and 50 weeks a year; obviously, most construction laborers could not count on such regular work. Hood, *722 Miles*, 85.

56. This statement is based on a count of every name in Social Register Association, *Social Register, New York, 1904*, 4–526. See also Social Register Association, *Social Register, 1887*, 2; and *New York Times*, January 2, 1887 and November 24, 1889.

57. Cromwell Childe, *New York: A Guide in Comprehensive Chapters* (New York: Brooklyn Daily Eagle, 1903), 29; *New York Times*, September 13, 1896.

58. *New York Times*, December 7, 1890 and March 8, 1891; *Washington Post*, November 1, 1896; *Wood's Illustrated Hand-Book to New York and Environs: A Guide for the Traveller or Resident* (New York: Carleton, 1873), 76–77; Childe, *New York*, 21; Sweetser, *How to Know New York*, 87–89; Nassau Boat Club of the City of New York, *Constitution, By-laws, Rules, and List of Members, etc.* (New York: n.p., 1892), unpaginated; and *Officers, Members, Constitution and By-Laws of the Union Club*, 88.

59. *Wood's Illustrated Hand-Book*, 76–77; Sweetser, *How to Know New York*, 87–89; *New York Times*, March 9, 1890, April 19 and March 15, 1891; "Personal," *Harper's Bazaar* 30 (June 26, 1897): 535.

60. "Ladies' Clubs," *Harper's Bazaar* 18 (October 17, 1885), 666.

61. Ibid., 666. See also Lillian W. Betts, "The Value of Club Membership to the Individual Member," *Harper's Bazaar* 26 (April 29, 1893): 334–35; and Betts, "Club Loyalty," *Harper's Bazaar* 29 (June 20, 1896): 532.

62. Down-Town Club of Business Men's Republican Association of the City of New York, *Constitution, By-Laws, List of Members, etc.* (New York: n.p., 1889), 31–32; *Constitution, By-Laws, and Rules of the Harvard Club of New York City with List of Officers and Members* (New York: n.p., 1888), 24–27; *Officers, Members, Constitution and By-Laws of the Union Club*, 96–98; Porzelt, *Metropolitan Club*, 57–104; *New York Times*, February 12, 1886, February 13, 1890, September 6, 1891, February 25, 1894, May 9, 1897; Louise L. Stevenson, *The Victorian Homefront: American Thought and Culture, 1860–1880* (Ithaca, N.Y.: Cornell University Press, 1991), xxiii–xxxv; Jane Tompkins, *West of Everything: The Inner Life of the Westerns* (New York: Oxford University Press, 1992), 3–19, 43; and Ray Oldenburg, *The Great Good Place: Cafés, Coffee Shops, Community Centers, Beauty Parlors, General Stores, Bars, Hangouts, and How They Get You Through the Day*, 1st ed. (New York: Paragon, 1989), 16.

63. *New York Times*, June 17 and 18, 1924, March 4, 1928, October 8, 1949; Harper S. Mott Diary, 1886, entries for May 3 and 5, 1886, Library of the New-York Historical Society, New York, N.Y. [hereafter N-YHS]; Mott Diary, 1888, entries for February 3, 7, 18,

and 22, March 1, 2, 7, 12, 14, and 15, 1888, N-YHS; James Norman Whitehouse Diary, 1890, entries for March 8, 15, and 19, April 12, May 26, June 20, 1890, N-YHS; Whitehouse Diary, 1892, entries for February 19 and 22, May 15, 1892, N-YHS; Whitehouse Diary, 1900, entries for August 15 and 17, 1900, N-YHS.

64.   Morgan's Engagement Diary for 1899, entries for March 10, 11, 15, 16, 18, 20, and 25, April 1, May 18, June 16, June 23 and 26, July 20, September 14 and 24, October 7 and 12, November 9, 23, and 28, and December 2, 1899, MLM; Pierpont Morgan's Engagement Diary for 1904, entries for January 16, March 19 and 26, November 17, 19, 25, 26, and 29, December 10, 13, and 20, 1904, MLM.; and Pierpont Morgan's Engagement Diary for 1906, entries for January 6 and 22, 1906, MLM.

65.   *New York Times*, March 15, 1891.

66.   Betts, "The Value of Club Membership," 334–35; "Club Loyalty," 352.

67.   *New York Times*, September 13, 1896.

68.   Ibid.

69.   E. Digby Baltzell, *Puritan Boston and Quaker Philadelphia* (New York: Free Press, 1979; repr., New Brunswick, N.J.: Transaction, 1996), 31–55; Betty G. Farrell, *Elite Families: Class and Power in Nineteenth-Century Boston* (Albany: State University of New York Press, 1993), 1–19; Rishel, *Founding Families of Pittsburgh*, 3–13; Kathryn Allamong Jacob, *Capital Elites: High Society in Washington, D.C., After the Civil War* (Washington, D.C.: Smithsonian Institution Press, 1995), 1–13; and Frederic Cople Jaher, *The Urban Establishment: Upper Strata in Boston, New York, Charleston, Chicago, and Los Angeles* (Urbana: University of Illinois Press, 1982), 1–13.

70.   *Town Topics and the American Queen*, March 28 and April 11, 1885; *Town Topics*, November 17, 1887; *New York Times*, November 13, 1875, May 28, 1885, January 17, May 26, and April 18, 1887, May 26, 1888, December 5, 1890, May 8 and 29, April 5, and December 30, 1891, December 6, 1896, May 9, 1897; Sweetser, *How to Know New York*, 87–89; and *Officers, Members, Constitution and By-Laws of the Union Club*, 13–75. For clubs in other cities, see Alexander W. Williams, *A Social History of the Greater Boston Clubs* ([Boston?]: Barrie, 1970), 16–30; Grace Dwight Potter, "The Social Life of American Cities: Syracuse," *Town & Country* (June 7, 1902): 13–19; Union League Club of Chicago, *The Spirit of the Union League Club, 1879–1926* : (Chicago: The Club, 1926); Clover Club of Philadelphia, *The Clover Club of Philadelphia, 1882–1904 : Souvenir of the 22d Anniversary* (Philadelphia: Burbank, 1904); Metropolitan Club of the City of Washington, *Financial History to January 1, 1897; Report of the Executive Committee* (Washington, D.C.: n.p., 1897); Martha Goode Anderson, "The Social Life of American Cities: Atlanta," *Town & Country* (December 27, 1902): 10–14; and Edwin Fairfax Naulty, "Philadelphia Fox Hunters," *Town & Country* (January 3, 1903): 10–12. See also Robert J. Brugger, *The Maryland Club: A History of Food and Friendship in Baltimore, 1857–1997* (Baltimore: Maryland Club, 1998), 33–63; and Lisa Holton, *For Members Only: A History and Guide to Chicago's Oldest Private Clubs* (Chicago: Lake Claremont, 2008), vii–23.

71.   *New York Times*, March 22, 1891.

72. *Town Topics*, February 2, 1888.

73. *Officers, Members, Constitution and By-Laws of the Union Club*, 85–88, 93–94; *Constitution, By-Laws and Rules of the Harvard Club of New York City, with the List of Officers and Members* (New York: n.p., 1888), 17–18; Down-Town Club of Business Men's Republican Association of the City of New York, *Constitution, By-Laws, List of Members, etc.* (New York: n.p., 1889), 16–17; Nassau Boat Club, *Constitution, By-laws, Rules, and List of Members, etc.*: unpaginated; Porzelt, *Metropolitan Club*, 108.

74. *New York Times*, April 15, 1893, January 7, 1895; and *Town Topics*, April 19, 1888.

75. *Town Topics*, April 19, 1888.

76. Louis Auchincloss, *A Voice from Old New York: A Memoir of My Youth* (Boston: Houghton Mifflin Harcourt, 2010), 6.

77. *New York Times*, April 19, December 6 and 7, 1891, June 5, 1896, March 21, 1897, October 30, 1926.

78. New York Botanical Garden, *Bulletin of the New York Botanical Garden*, 1, no. 1 (April 15, 1896): 8–18; and *New York Times*, July 6, 1911, December 21 and 22, 1938.

79. Maureen E. Montgomery, *Displaying Women: Spectacles of Leisure in Edith Wharton's New York* (New York: Routledge, 1998), 60.

80. *New York Tribune*, January 3, 1904; and Crowinshield, *Manners for the Metropolis*, 29–36, 53.

81. Maud C. Cook, *Social Etiquette; Or, Manners and Customs of Polite Society* (Philadelphia: Keller & Kirkpatrick, 1896), 358.

82. Pauline Robinson Scrapbook, 1894–1912, entries for 1904, N-YHS; and Florence Adele Sloane, *Maverick in Mauve: The Diary of a Romantic Age*, ed. Louis Auchincloss (Garden City, N.Y.: Doubleday, 1983), 22–35, 76–84.

83. *Club Women of New York, 1904* (New York: Mail and Express, c.1904), 47, 55–57, 70–71; Mary I. Wood, *The History of the General Federation of Women's Clubs, for the First Twenty-Two Years of Its Organization* (New York: General Federation of Women's Clubs, 1912), 27–31; *The Junior League for the Promotion of Neighborhood Work, Annual Report 1913* (New York: n.p., 1913), 8–11; *The Young Women's Christian Association of the City of New York, Statement of Work for 1916* (New York: n.p., c. 1916), 5–6; and *New York Times*, February 21, 1905, May 16, 1911, November 30, 1913, September 2, 1916, May 3, 1943, March 20, 1952, February 15, 1954, July 3, 1961.

6. THE WAYS OF MILLIONAIREVILLE

1. Digital Sanborn Maps, 1867–1970, New York City, 1890–1902, vol. 4, 1899, sheets 68, 69, 72, 74, 75, and 77, accessed January 7, 2009, http://sanborn.umi.com; G. W. Bromley & Company, *Atlas of the City of New York, Borough of Manhattan*, sect. 5 (Philadelphia: Bromley, 1898–1899), plates 12, 14, 15, 16, 17, 21, 22, and 27; E. Robinson & R. H. Pidgeon, *Robinson's Atlas of the City of New York* (New York: Robinson, 1885), plates 9, 12, 13, 16, and 18; and "The Invasion of Commerce," *Town & Country* (October 23, 1903), 15.

2. William Dean Howells, *A Hazard of New Fortunes* (New York: Harper, 1890; repr., New York: Penguin, 2001), 272–73.

3. Ibid., 273.

4. Personal interview, Daniel J. Singal, Geneva, N.Y., November 2, 2010.

5. Manuscript Census, 1900 Federal Census, New York State, New York County, enumeration district 7 [hereafter e.d.] 82, sheet 1, 741, sheets 15 and 16, e.d. 776, sheet. 4, e.d. 783, sht. 1, Ancestry.com, accessed November 18, 2009, www.ancestry.com.

6. Digital Sanborn Maps, 1867–1970, New York City, 1890–1902, vol. 4, 1899, sheets 68, 69, 72, 74, 75, and 77, accessed January 7, 2009, http://sanborn.umi.com; Bromley, *Atlas of the City of New York, Borough of Manhattan*, sect. 5, plates 16, 17, 21, and 22; and Robinson, *Robinson's Atlas of the City of New York*, plates 12, 13, 16, and 18.

7. Edith Wharton, "Roman Fever," in *The Collected Short Stores of Edith Wharton*, vol. 2, ed. R. W. B. Lewis (New York: Scribner's, 1968), 835.

8. Edith Wharton, "Autre Temps . . . ," in *The Collected Short Stores of Edith Wharton*, vol. 2, 261.

9. The upper class in New York were not monolithic and reflected a degree of the city's social diversity. For German Catholics and Protestants, see Edwin G. Burrows and Mike Wallace, *Gotham: A History of New York City to 1898* (New York: Oxford University Press, 1999), 1078–79; Richard K. Lieberman, *Steinway & Sons* (New York: Yale University Press, 1995), 73–105. An African American upper class also existed, but it was much closer to the white middle class in terms of its wealth, income, and occupations and did not interact with or seek to join the white upper class. Lawrence Otis Graham, *Our Kind of People: Inside America's Black Upper Class* (New York: HarperCollins, 1999), ix–xviii.

10. Howells, *A Hazard of New Fortunes*, 272; Susie J. Pak, *Gentlemen Bankers: The World of J.P. Morgan* (Cambridge, Mass.: Harvard University Press, 2013), 1–11, 80–106; *American Hebrew*, January 24, 1890, January 8, 1892, January 5, March 2, April 27, and May 4, 1894, January 10, February 21, and April 3 and 24, 1896; *Jewish Messenger*, January 8 and 22 and December 17 and 31, 1886, July 10 and October 24, 1885, February 10 and 17, July 21, and August 11, 1893, November 29, 1895, January 1, 1897; *New York Times*, January 1, 1892, April 22, 1894, January 22 and July 23 and 30, 1897, December 14, 1903, January 11, 1907, April 16, 1912, September 28, 1920, May 4, 1926; Bromley, *Atlas of the City of New York, Borough of Manhattan*, sect. 5, plate 22; Manuscript Census, 1900 Federal Census, New York State, New York County, e.d. 782, sht. 1, e.d. 748, sht.14, e.d. 779, sht. 1, e.d. 782, sht. 1, Ancestry.com, accessed November 18, 2009, www.ancestry.com; Chamber of Commerce of the State of New York, *Thirty-Seventh Annual Report of the Corporation of the Chamber of Commerce for the State of New York for the Year 1894–1895* (New York: Press of the Chamber of Commerce, 1895), 102, 114, 124–26; New York Stock Exchange, *Officers, Governing Committees, and Standing Committees, List of Members, with Their Annunciator Numbers and Addresses, Co-Partnerships, Branch Offices, Out-Of-Town Members, and Rules for Delivery* (New York: Searing and Watson, 1900), 6, 29; Stephen Birmingham, *"Our Crowd": The Great Jewish Families of*

New York (New York: Harper & Row, 1967), 3–13; Irwin Unger and Debbi Unger, *The Guggenheims: A Family History* (New York: HarperCollins, 2005), 48–68; and Naomi W. Cohen, *Jacob H. Schiff: A Study in American Jewish Leadership* (Hanover, N.H.: Brandeis University Press, 1999), 41–81.

11. *New York Times*, June 25, 1880, January 26 and November 26, 1893; Bromley, *Atlas of the City of New York, Borough of Manhattan, From Actual Surveys and Official Plans*, sect. 5, plate 14; Digital Sanborn Maps, 1867–1970, New York City, 1890–1902, vol. 4, 1899, sheets 68 and 69, accessed January 7, 2009, http://sanborn.umi.com; Robinson, *Robinson's Atlas of the City of New York*, plates 12 and 13; Leonard Rimmer, *A History of Old New York Life and the House of the Delmonicos* (New York: n.p., 1898), 13–25; Sophie C. Holt Diary, 1879, entries for January 31, February 12, 17, and 23, 1879, Diaries Collection, Box 5, Manuscripts and Archives Division, New York Public Library, New York, N.Y. [hereafter NYPL]; and Diary of Helen Newel, vol. 3, July 1897–1898, February 21, entries for November 15, 20, 21, 22, 23, 25, and 27, and December 9, 13, 15, and 24, 1897, Library, New-York Historical Society, New York, N.Y. [hereafter N-YHS].

12. *Town & Country* (November 15, 1902): 43; *Town & Country* (March 15, 1902): 47.

13. Cynthia Amneús, *A Separate Sphere: Dressmakers in Cincinnati's Golden Age, 1877–1922* (Lubbock, Tex.: Texas Tech University Press, 2003), 139.

14. *Town & Country* (November 15, 1902): 5; "Evening Costumes," *Town & Country* (December 13, 1902): 52; "Fashion Notes," *Town & Country* (April 19, 1902): 42; and "Autumn Fashions," *Town & Country* (October 24, 1903): 46.

15. Michael C. Kathrens, *Great Houses of New York, 1880–1930* (New York: Acanthus, 2005), 9–20, 26–42, 72–79, 174–82; Sarah Bradford Landau, *George B. Post, Architect: Picturesque Designer and Determined Realist* (New York: Montecelli, 1998), 40–52; *Wood's Illustrated Hand-Book to New York and Environs: A Guide for the Traveller or Resident* (New York: Carleton, 1873), 22; M. F. Sweetser, *How to Know New York City. A Serviceable and Trustworthy Guide, Having Its Starting Point at the Grand Union Hotel* (Boston: Rand, Avery, 1888), 103–11; Cromwell Childe, *New York: A Guide in Comprehensive Chapters* (New York: Brooklyn Daily Eagle, 1903), 23–26; and *New York City (Illustrated) Visitor's Guide and Tourist's Directory of Leading Hotels in New York and Principal Cities* (New York: New York Journal, 1901), 17–20.

16. Kathrens, *Great Houses of New York*, 9.

17. *The Tourist's Hand-Book of New York* (New York: Historical Press, 1905), 23; Childe, *New York*, 23.

18. John D. Hall, *Banner Guide, Excursion Book and Directory of New York City and Vicinity* (New York: n.p., 1905), 9.

19. *New York Times*, February 20, 1886, January 17 and 21, February 24, and April 1, 1890, June 14 and 29, and July 17, 1894, January 19, 1896, September 17, 1897, January 29, 1898.

20. David Nasaw, *Andrew Carnegie* (New York: Penguin, 2006), 119.

21. Ibid., 118.

22. Samuel A. Schreiner Jr., *Henry Clay Frick: The Gospel of Greed* (New York: St. Martin's, 1995), 229–30, 257; David Cannadine, *Mellon: An American Life* (New York: Knopf, 2007), 127–32, 245–74.

23. Grace Eulalie Matthews Ashmore Diary, vol. 1, September 23, 1896–April 17, 1897, entries for October 8, 1896, and March 23 and 29, 1897; vol. 2, April 18, 1897–October 16, 1897, entries for May 24, and June 10 and 14, 1897, Grace Eulalie Matthews Ashmore Papers, NYPL.

24. Article I, section 9 of the U.S. Constitution prohibits the federal government from granting noble titles and forbids anyone who holds public office from accepting titles of nobility from another nation without explicit congressional approval. Intended to protect republicanism against a return to inherited rule or government despotism and to shield the infant republic against threats from foreign monarchs, this proscription of a hereditary aristocracy prevented the formation in the United States of a system of social classification and honor that was commonplace in Europe and other parts of the world. It also contributed to Americans' understandings about egalitarianism and individual social mobility. U.S. Const. art. I, § 9. The drafters of the Constitution adopted these provisions almost verbatim from the Articles of Confederation. Articles of Confederation, art. VI.

25. *New York Times*, May 1, 1885; Clifton Hood, "An Unusable Past," *Journal of Social History* 37 (Summer 2004): 883–913; Wallace Evans Davis, *Patriotism on Parade: The Story of Veterans' and Hereditary Organizations in America, 1783–1900* (Cambridge, Mass.: Harvard University Press, 1955), 44–73; William O. McDowell to William P. Rochester, October 24, 1884, 1870s–1880s Folder, Box 24 Baldwin-McDowell Papers, NYPL; William O. McDowell to Mary McA. T. Tuttle, May 16, 1904, Letterbook April to November 1904, Box 30, Baldwin-McDowell Papers, NYPL; William O. McDowell to Newton L. Collamer, December 14, 1904, Letterbook October 1904–April 1905, Box 32, Baldwin-McDowell Papers, NYPL. Upper-class Americans' admiration for aristocracy was related to other contemporary social practices that venerated family origins and European heritage. For genealogy, see David T. Thackery, *Back to Adam: A Survey of Genealogy in the Western World as Illustrated in the Collections of the Newberry Library, Chicago, Illinois: An Exhibition Catalog* (Chicago: Newberry Library, 1992), 7–24; and John A. Schutz, *The Noble Pursuit: The Sesquicentennial History of the New England Historic Genealogical Society, 1845–1995* (Boston: New England Historic Genealogical Society, 1995), 1–13. For patriotic hereditary societies, see Davis, *Patriotism on Parade*, 44–73.

26. *New York Times*, November 27, 1892.

27. Newel Diary, July 1897–February 21, 1898, entry for July 25, 1897. Diary of Helen Newel, December 18, 1898–March 24, 1900, entries for November 19–27 and December 5, 9, 23, and 25, 1899, N-YHS.

28. Newel Diary, July 1897–February 21, 1898, entry for August 26, 1897, N-YHS; *New York Times*, June 25, 1880, and August 9, 1907.

29. *New York Times*, May 3–8, 16–21, 1887, July 27, 1890, April 5 and 15–16, 1893, October 2, 1895, January 8, April 26, May 8, and September 10, 1899, March 2, 1902, June 30, 1907, December 15, 1908, December 5, 1912, December 15, 1934; and *Town Topics*, September 8, 1887.

30. *Town Topics*, September 1, 1887; Eric Homberger, "Introduction," unpaginated, in Chauncey Depew, *Titled Americans: The Real Heiresses' Guide to Marrying an Aristocrat* (London: n.p., 1890; repr., Oxford: Old House, 2013); Marian Fowler, *In a Gilded Cage: From Heiress to Duchess* (New York: St. Martin's, 1994), xiii–xxvii; Maureen Montgomery, *"Gilded Prostitution": Status, Money, and Transatlantic Marriages, 1870–1914* (New York: Routledge, 1989), 1–13; *New York Times*, February 9, 1890, May 6, 1892, February 19, 1893, May 24, 1894, March 13, 1898, April 26, May 8, June 13, and September 10, 1899, June 29, 1913; and Consuelo Vanderbilt Balsan, *The Glitter and the Gold* (Maidstone, U.K.: Mann, 1973), 23–96. On the Vanderbilt dynasty, see T. J. Stiles, *The First Tycoon: The Epic Life of Cornelius Vanderbilt* (New York: Knopf, 2009), 518–61.

31. Balsan, *The Glitter and the Gold*, 44, 162.

32. Burton J. Hendricks, "The Astor Fortune," *McClure's Magazine* 24 (April 1905): 564; *New York Times*, August 1, 1899; and Justin Kaplan, *When the Astors Owned New York* (New York: Viking, 2006), 53.

33. *Chicago Tribune*, August 2 and 4, 1899; *Boston Globe*, August 3, 1899; *New York Tribune*, August 5, 1899; *New York World*, August 2, 5, 6, and 13, 1899; *New York Times*, August 3 and 7, 1899; *New York Evening Post*, July 19, 1900.

34. *New York Times*, August 7, 1899.

35. Ibid.

36. Ibid.

37. *Washington Post*, January 9, 1892, March 12, 1893, August 31, 1899, October 20, 1919; *Times of London*, October 20, 1919; *New York Times*, March 23, 26, and 28, October 24, 1893, and April 25, 1894, August 2 and 7, 1899, October 20–21, 1919; *New York Evening Post*, July 19, 1900; *San Francisco Call*, July 10, 1910; *New York World*, n.d., cited by *New York Times*, August 3, 1899; and Kaplan, *When the Astors Owned New York*, 112–32.

38. For "aristocratification," see Sven Beckert, *The Monied Metropolis: New York City and the Consolidation of the American Bourgeoisie, 1850–1896* (Cambridge: Cambridge University Press, 2001), 259 fig., 436n.

39. Paul J. Cornell to Ezra Cornell, January n.d., 1861, Folder 14, Box 20, Series 1, Ezra Cornell Papers, Rare and Manuscript Collection, Kroch Library, Cornell University, Ithaca, N.Y. [hereafter COR]; Ezra Cornell to Paul J. Cornell, January 8, 1861, Folder 14, Box 20, Series 1, Cornell Papers, COR; H. D. Hart to Ezra Cornell, February 11, 1864, Folder 5, Box 24, Series 1, Cornell Papers, COR; A. E. Cook to Ezra Cornell, January 22, 1867, Folder 17, Box 28, Series 1 Cornell Papers, COR; Eliza A. Chase to Ezra Cornell, February 18, 1867, Folder 3, Box 29, Series 1, Cornell Papers, COR; and Philip Dorf, *The Builder: A Biography of Ezra Cornell* (New York: Macmillan, 1952), 5–18, 194, 382–83. For the history of genealogy in America, including its institutional organization before the Civil War, see Francesca Morgan, "Lineage as Capital:

Genealogy in Antebellum New England," *New England Quarterly* 83 (June 2010): 250–82; François Weil, *Family Trees: A History of Genealogy in America* (Cambridge, Mass.: Harvard University Press, 2013),1–7, 59–66; and Francesca Morgan, "A Noble Pursuit?: Bourgeois America's Uses of Lineage," in *The American Bourgeoisie: Distinction and Identity in the Nineteenth Century*, ed. Sven Beckert and Julia B. Rosenbaum (New York: Palgrave Macmillan, 2010), 135–51.

40. Thackery, *Back to Adam*, 7–24; Schutz, *The Noble Pursuit*, 1–13; Henry R. Stiles, *A Hand-Book of Practical Suggestions for the Use of Students in Genealogy* (Albany, N.Y.: Munshell's, 1899), 7–16; W. P. W. Phillmore, *How to Write the History of a Family: A Guide for the Genealogist* (London: Stock, 1887), v–vi; *New York Times*, October 22 and 31, 1869.

41. *New York Times*, February 19, 1894, June 7, 1900; *Harper's Bazaar* 31 (October 8, 1898): 862–63; "Editorial Notes," *Outlook* 49 (March 17, 1894): 483.

42. *New York Times*, May 1, 1885; Hood, "An Unusable Past," 883–913; Wallace Evans Davis, *Patriotism on Parade: The Story of Veterans' and Hereditary Organizations in America, 1783–1900* (Cambridge, Mass.: Harvard University Press, 1955), 44–73; William O. McDowell to William P. Rochester, October 24, 1884, 1870s–1880s Folder, Box 24, Baldwin-McDowell Papers, NYPL; William O. McDowell to Mary McA. T. Tuttle, May 16, 1904, Letterbook April to November 1904, Box 30, Baldwin-McDowell Papers, NYPL; and William O. McDowell to Newton L. Collamer, December 14, 1904, Letterbook October 1904–April 1905, Box 32, Baldwin-McDowell Papers, NYPL.

43. *New York Times*, January 4–8, 1887, September 11, 1888; "Personal," *Harper's Bazaar* 29 (June 27, 1896): 547; Ray Stannard Baker, "J. Pierpont Morgan," *McClure's Magazine* 17 (October 1901): 507–16; Hamilton Wright Mabie, "William Shakespeare: Poet, Dramatist, and Man: Part II, Birth and Breeding," *Outlook* 64 (February 3, 1900): 287–97; "Editorial Notes," *Outlook* 49 (March 17, 1894): 502: "Recent Historical Biography," *Atlantic Monthly* 78 (July 1896): 122–38; "The Historical Spirit," *Atlantic Monthly* 73 (March 1894): 409–14: Hamlin Garland, "The Early Life of Ulysses Grant," *McClure's Magazine* 13 (December 1896): 125–29; Ray Stannard Baker, "General Leonard Wood: A Character Sketch," *McClure's Magazine* 14 (February 1900): 368–81; and Frank B. Gessner, "William McKinley," *McClure's Magazine* 2 (December 1893): 22–26. Of Andrew Carnegie, John D. Rockefeller, and Henry Ford, Carnegie came the closest to accepting the rags-to-riches myth when he wrote in his autobiography that the saying "of poor but honest parents" applied to his upbringing. Andrew Carnegie, *The Autobiography of Andrew Carnegie and The Gospel of Wealth* (New York: Signet, 2006), 8. By contrast, Rockefeller more ambiguously described his family as being "people of modest means" but defined modest as not having "plenty of servants to do everything for them," while Ford disputed the popular belief that his parents were "very poor and that the early days were hard ones," saying that "they were not rich, but neither were they poor." John D. Rockefeller, *Random Reminiscences of Men and Events* (New York: Doubleday, Page, 1909), 27; and Henry Ford, *My Life and*

Work: An Autobiography of Henry Ford (Garden City, N.Y.: Garden City Publishing, c.1922), 19.

44. Thackery, *Back to Adam*, 19.

45. John A. Moulton to Henry A. Todd, October 27, 1873, Folder 2, Box 117, Series 6, Allen W. Dulles Papers, Seeley G. Mudd Manuscript Library, Princeton University, Princeton, N.J. [hereafter PU]; Henry A. Todd to Robert B. Todd, October 28, 1873, Folder 2, Box 117, Series 6, Dulles Papers, PU; John E. Todd to Henry A. Todd, February 3, 1874, Folder 3, Box 117, Series 6, Dulles Papers, PU; Henry A. Todd to Robert K. Todd, July 15, 1886, Folder 4, Box 118, Series 6, Dulles Papers, PU; H. Clay Evans to Susan L. Martin, June 23, 1897, Folder 2, Box 119, Series 6, Dulles Papers, PU; F. W. Todd to Henry A. Todd, November 11, 1899, Folder 2, Box 119, Series 6, Dulles Papers, PU; F. W. Todd to Henry A. Todd, September 29, 1900, Folder 2, Box 119, Series, 6, Dulles Papers, PU; Richard Wilberforce to Henry A. Todd, June 30, 1902, Folder 2, Box 119, Series 7, Dulles Papers, PU; John Matthews to Henry A. Todd, September 30, 1903, Folder 3, Box 119, Series 6, Dulles Papers, PU; George B. Blodgett to Henry A. Todd, Folder 3, Box 119, Series 6, Dulles Papers, PU; and Henry A. Todd memorials, 1925–1926, Folder 9, Box 119, Series 6, Dulles Papers, PU.

46. F. W. Todd to Henry A. Todd, June 10, 1874, Folder 3, Box 117, Series 6, Dulles Papers, PU.

47. Susan L. Martin to Henry A. Todd, February 28, 1898, Folder 2, Box 119, Series 6, Dulles Papers, PU.

48. F. W. Todd to Henry A. Todd, March 9, 1874, Folder 3, Box 117, Series 6, Dulles Papers, PU; and Todd to Todd, March 9, 1874, Dulles Papers, PU.

49. Untitled Morton family genealogy, 1–15, n.d., Morton Family History Folder, Box 10, Levin Parsons Morton Papers, NYPL; Joel Andrew Delano, *Genealogy, History and Alliances of the American House of Delano, 1621 to 1899* (New York: n.p., 1899), 20–63.

50. Eric Homberger, *Mrs. Astor's New York: Money and Social Power in a Gilded Age* (New Haven, Conn.: Yale University Press, 2004), 4.

51. *New York Tribune*, March 25, 1888.

52. *New York Times*, March 28, 1886, July 17, 1887, December 10, 1891, February 1–3, 1895; *New York World*, September 9, 1888, February 1 and 3, 1895; *New York Tribune*, February 1, 1895; and *Washington Post*, February 1, 1895.

53. Quoted in *New York Times*, February 1, 1895.

54. *New York Times*, February 1–3, 5, 1895, October 31, 1908; *New York World*, February 1 and 3, 1895; *New York Tribune*, February 1, 1895, October 31, 1908; *Washington Post*, February 1, 1895, October 31, 1908; and Homberger, *Mrs. Astor's New York*, 1–35.

55. Ward MacAllister, *Society as I Have Found It* (New York: Cassell, 1890), 160–61.

56. On sentimentality, see Nina Baym, *Woman's Fiction: A Guide to Novels By and About Women in America, 1820–1870* (Ithaca, N.Y.: Cornell University Press, 1978), 24–25, 56–57, 66–67, 194–95; and Mary Chapman and Glenn Hendler, eds., introduction to *Sentimental Men: Masculinity and the Politics of Affect in American Culture* (Berkeley: University of California Press, 1999), 1–16. See also Stephanie Coontz, *The Social*

Origins of Private Life: A History of American Families, 1600–1900 (New York: Verso, 1988), 263–71.

57. Homberger, *Mrs. Astor's New York*, 1–35, 215; and *New York Times*, January 21, 1885, June 15 and 17, 1888, August 12 and 19, November 22, and December 23, 1888.

58. In fact, McAllister had said that there were "only *about* 400 people" in fashionable society, but contemporaries paid attention to the number he had furnished rather than to his qualification of it, and his initial vagueness did not register with them either. *New York Tribune*, March 25, 1888 (emphasis added).

59. *New York Times*, April 22, 1888.

60. *New York Times*, August 12 and 19, November 22 and 25, and December 23, 1888, February 5 and March 3, 1889.

61. *New York Times*, February 5 and March 3, 1889, March 23 and October 18, 1890, February 13 and 21 and November 27, 1892, April 16 and 30 and June 28 and 30, 1893, March 23 and April 30, 1894.

62. *New York Times*, March 23, 1889, March 23 and October 18, 1890, February 13, 1892, March 23 and April 26, 1894.

63. Henry Whitney McVickar, *The Greatest Show on Earth: Society* (New York: Harper, 1892), unpaginated; and *New York Times*, January 15, 1891, July 5 and 9, 1905.

64. *Town Topics*, August 4, 1882, July 7, August 11, and September 29, 1887, January 12 and 19, 1888,

65. *Town Topics*, January 2, 1890.

66. Ibid.

67. *Town Topics*, December 15, 1887.

68. *New York Times*, December 23, 1888, February 16, 1892, January 1 and 26, 1890, October 31 and November 15, 1908.

69. *New York Tribune*, December 14, 1900.

70. *New York Times*, April 15, 1889, February 1, 1895, April 10, 1897, October 31, 1908; and Homberger, *Mrs. Astor's New York*, 214–19. According to its members, the Patriarch Society disbanded because of a lack of commitment on the part of its membership and a feeling that its entertainments were becoming less successful. *New York Times*, April 10, 1897.

71. Arno J. Mayer, *The Persistence of the Old Regime: Europe to the Great War* (New York: Pantheon, 1981), 79–127.

72. Clifton Hood, *722 Miles: The Building of the Subways and How They Transformed New York* (New York: Simon & Schuster, 1993), 56–74; Keith D. Revell, *Building Gotham: Civic Culture & Public Policy in New York City, 1898–1938* (Baltimore, Md.: Johns Hopkins University Press, 2003), 1–14; Robert Sink, "New York Public Library," in *The Encyclopedia of New York City*, 2nd ed., ed. Kenneth T. Jackson (New Haven, Conn.: Yale University Press, 2010), 929–31; Kurt C. Schlichting, *Grand Central Terminal: Railroads, Engineering, and Architecture in New York City* (Baltimore, Md.: Johns Hopkins University Press, 2001), 1–7; New York Zoological Society, *First Annual Report* (New York: n.p., 1897), 13–22;

and Bernadette G. Callery, "Botanical Gardens," in Jackson, *Encyclopedia of New York City*, 147–48.

73.   New York Botanical Garden, *Bulletin of the New York Botanical Garden*, (Lancasater, Penn.: New Era, 1896), 6–11; New York Zoological Society, *Fourth Annual Report* (New York: n.p., 1900), 6–8; Steven Johnson and Kate Lauber, "Bronx Zoo," in Jackson, *Encyclopedia of New York City*, 167; and Jonathan Peter Spiro, *Defending the Master Race: Conservation, Eugenics, and the Legacy of Madison Grant* (Lebanon, N.H.: University of Vermont Press, 2009), xi–xvi.

74.   For the standard interpretation of the founding of the Metropolitan Opera, see Irving Kolodin, *The Story of the Metropolitan Opera, 1883–1950: A Candid History* (New York: Knopf, 1953), 3–6; Irving Kolodin, *The Metropolitan Opera, 1883–1966: A Candid History* (New York: Knopf, 1967), 3–5; Martin Meyer, *The Met: One Hundred Years of Grand Opera* (New York: Simon & Schuster, 1983), 10–13; John Frederick Cone, *First Rival of the Metropolitan Opera* (New York: Columbia University Press, 1983), 1–3; Paul E. Eisler, *The Metropolitan Opera: The First Twenty-Five Years, 1883–1908* (Croton-on-Hudson, N.Y.: North River, 1984), 4–8; and Charles Affron and Mirella Jona Affron, *Grand Opera: The Story of the Met* (Berkeley: University of California Press, 2014), 1–14.

75.   List of Subscribers to the Metropolitan Opera House Company, April 10, 1880, Metropolitan Opera Minute Books, April 10, 1880–September 1892, Microfilm edition, reel 1, Metropolitan Opera Archives, New York, N.Y. [hereafter MO]; Minutes of the Meeting of the Stockholders of the Metropolitan Opera House Company, April 28, 1880, Metropolitan Opera Minute Books, April 10, 1880–September 1892, Microfilm edition, reel 1, MO; Eisler, *The Metropolitan Opera*, 1–8; and *New York Tribune*, April 11, 1926.

76.   Minutes of the Meeting of the Board of Directors of May 3, 1880, Metropolitan Opera Minute Books, April 10, 1880–September 1892, MO.

77.   Ibid.

78.   *Brooklyn Eagle*, April 9, 1880; and *New York Times*, April 7, 1880.

79.   Minutes of the Meeting of the Board of Directors of March 8, 1882, Metropolitan Opera Minute Books, April 10, 1880–September 1892, MO.

80.   Ibid.

81.   *New York Times*, September 9, 1883. For the comparisons with European houses, see *New York Times*, October 14, 1883.

82.   Montgomery Schuyler, "The Metropolitan Opera-house," *Harper's New Monthly Magazine* 67 (October 1883): 883.

83.   *New York Times*, July 22, August 19, and October 13 and 14, 1883; *New York Tribune*, October 24, 1883, April 11, 1926; Eisler, *Metropolitan Opera*, 16.

84.   Edward C. Stanton, *The Metropolitan Opera House Co. of New York (Limited)*, January 21, 1884: 1, MO.

85.   Minutes of the Meeting of the Board of Directors of May 3, 1880, Metropolitan Opera Minute Books, April 10, 1880–September 1892, MO; William Steinway

Diary, 1861–1893, entry for February 20, 1885, Archives Center, National Museum of American History, Smithsonian Institution, accessed February 19, 2011, http://americanhistory.si.edu/steinwaydiary; William H. Seltsam, comp., *Metropolitan Opera Annals: A Chronicle of Artists and Performances* (New York: Wilson, 1947), 1–4, 9–51; *New York Times*, January 15, February 14 and 16, 1884, November 6, 1886, January 2 and March 3, 1887, October 18, 1896; Stanton, *The Metropolitan Opera House Co. of New York (Limited)*, 1–2; Kolodin, *Story of the Metropolitan Opera*, 7–9; Eisler, *Metropolitan Opera*, 78–171; and Stanley Nadel, "Germans," in Jackson, *Encyclopedia of New York City* 505–07.

86. Calvin Tomkins, *Merchants & Masterpieces: The Story of the Metropolitan Museum of Art*, rev. ed. (New York: Holt, 1989), 15–24; Union League Club, *A Metropolitan Art-museum in the City of New York: Proceedings of a Meeting held at the theatre of the Union League Club, Tuesday evening, November 23, 1869* (New York: n.p., 1869), 8–12.

87. Tomkins, *Merchants & Masterpieces*, 36–60; Metropolitan Museum of Art, *Hand-Book No. 10, General Guide to the Museum Collections, Exclusive of Paintings and Drawings* (New York: Metropolitan Museum of Art, 1888), 3–5; David C. Preyer, *The Art of the Metropolitan Museum of New York* (Boston: Page, 1909), 1–10; Joseph H. Choate to Louis P. di Cesnola, March 6, 1885, Admission–Sunday opening controversy, 1880–83 [*sic*], January–May 1885 Folder, Office of the Secretary Records, Metropolitan Museum of Art Archives, Metropolitan Museum of Art, New York, N.Y. [hereafter MMA]; F. W. Rhinelander to Louis P. di Cesnola, April 27, 1885, Admission–Sunday opening controversy, 1880–85, January–May 1885 Folder, Office of the Secretary Records, MMA; Emily John De Forest Summary Sheet, November 8, 1941, De Forest, Mrs. Robert W. Personal Folder, Office of the Secretary Records, MMA; H. W. Kent to Emily J. De Forest, February 5, 1907, De Forest, Mrs. Robert W. Personal Folder, Office of the Secretary Records, MMA; Emily J. De Forest to H.W. Kent, May 4, 1908, De Forest, Mrs. Robert W. Personal Folder, Office of the Secretary Records, MMA; Emily J. De Forest to H. W. Kent, December 13, 1909, De Forest, Mrs. Robert W. Personal Folder, Office of the Secretary Records, MMA; Emily J. De Forest to H.W. Kent, De Forest, Mrs. Robert W. Personal Folder, Office of the Secretary Records, MMA; H. W. Kent to Emily J. De Forest, October 26, 1920, De Forest, Mrs. Robert W. Personal Folder, Office of the Secretary Records, MMA; De Forest, Robert W. Summary Sheet, undated, De Forest, Robert W. Personal Folder, Office of the Secretary Records, MMA; and *New York Times*, April 26, 1885.

88. *New York Times*, March 31, 1880.

89. James Moske to author, June 17, 2010; *Brooklyn Eagle*, June 14, 1880; *New York Times*, May 10, 1881, June 25 and December 31, 1883, January 6, 1884.

90. Preamble and resolution, passed by the Board of the Commissioners of Public Works, Requesting the Museum of Art and that of Natural History to be open on Sundays to the public, April 23, 1885, Admission–Sunday Opening Controversy, 1880–85, January–May 1885 Folder, Office of the Secretary Records, MMA.

91. "In Common Council," a resolution adopted by the Board of Aldermen, May 18, 1885, and approved by the Mayor May 20, 1885, Admission–Sunday Opening Controversy, 1880–85, January–May 1885 Folder, Office of the Secretary Records, MMA.

92. Joseph H. Choate to Morris K. Jesup, July 10, 1885, Admission–Sunday Opening Controversy, 1880–85, June–July 1885 Folder, Office of the Secretary Records, MMA.

93. S. H. Wales to John Taylor Johnston, February 1, 1885, Admission–Sunday Opening Controversy, 1880–85, January–May 1885 Folder, Office of the Secretary Records, MMA; and Daniel Huntington to Louis P. di Cesnola, January 30, 1880, Admission–Sunday Opening Controversy, 1880–85, January–May 1885 Folder, Office of the Secretary Records, MMA.

94. Minutes of a Meeting of the Conference Committee, held July 2, 1885, Admission–Sunday Opening Controversy, 1880–85, June–July 1885 Folder, Office of the Secretary Records, MMA.

95. New York Times, November 18, 1885. See also Minutes of a Special Meeting of the Conference Committee of the Two Museums, held May 1, 1885, Admission–Sunday Opening Controversy, 1880–85, January–May 1885 Folder, Office of the Secretary Records, MMA.

96. Choate to Jesup, July 10, 1885, MMA.

97. Boston Traveller, n.d., quoted in New York Times, January 6, 1884.

98. Presbytery of New York, resolution adopted opposing Sunday opening, December 13[?], 1885, Admission Sunday Opening Controversy, October–December 1885 Folder, Office of the Secretary Records, MMA; Archbishop Michael A. Corrigan to Louis P. di Cesnola, December 9, 1885, Admission–Sunday Opening Controversy, October–December 1885 Folder, Office of the Secretary, MMA; Petition from the Central Labor Union to the Trustees and Managers of the American Museum of Natural History and the Metropolitan Museum of Art, December 20, 1885, Admission–Sunday Opening Controversy, October–December 1885 Folder, Office of the Secretary, MMA; and New York Times, March 10, 1886.

99. New York Times, March 25, 1893; Robert W. De Forest to Henry G. Marquand, February 25, 1891, Admission–Sunday Opening Controversy, January–April 1891 Folder, Office of the Secretary, MMA; Robert W. De Forest to Henry G. Marquand, May 21, 1891, Admission–Sunday Opening Controversy, May 20–28, 1891 Folder, Office of the Secretary, MMA; Louis P. di Cesnola to Board of Commissioners of the Department of Public Works of the City of New York, May 27, 1891, Admission–Sunday Opening Controversy, May 20–28, 1891 Folder, Office of the Secretary, MMA; Louis P. di Cesnola to William E. Dodge Jr., October 17, 1892, Admission–Sunday Opening Controversy, August 21–December 1892 Folder, Office of the Secretary, MMA; Robert Hoe to Louis P. di Cesnola, May 21, 1891, Admission–Sunday Opening Controversy, May 20–28, 1891 Folder, Office of the Secretary, MMA; and Metropolitan Museum of Art, Twenty-Second Annual Report of the Trustees of the Association for the Metropolitan Museum of Art, Year Ending December 31, 1891 (New York: n.p., 1892), 500.

100. During the first three full calendar years of implementation, from January 1, 1892, until December 31, 1894, Sunday openings accounted for one-third of the museum's total attendance. Metropolitan Museum of Art, *Twenty-Third Annual Report of the Trustees of the Association for the Year Ending December 31, 1892* (New York: n.p., 1893), 537; Metropolitan Museum of Art, *Twenty-Fourth Annual Report of the Trustees of the Association for the Year Ending December 31, 1893* (New York: n.p., 1894), 573; Metropolitan Museum of Art, *Twenty-Fifth Annual Report of the Trustees of the Association for the Year Ending December 31, 1894* (New York: n.p., 1895), 603.

101. *Brooklyn Eagle*, June 1, 1891; and *New York Times*, June 1, 1891.

102. "Report Re Consequences of Sunday Opening to the Trustees of the Metropolitan Museum of Art," November 16, 1891, Admission–Sunday Opening Controversy, June–November 1891 Folder, Office of the Secretary, MMA.

103. Ibid.

104. Ibid.

105. Richard Jenkins, *Pierre Bourdieu* (London: Routledge, 1992), 132–34; Pierre Bourdieu and Alain Darbel, with Dominique Schnapper, *The Love of Art: European Art Museums and Their Public*, trans. Caroline Beattie and Nick Merriman (Cambridge, U.K.: Polity, 1991), 1–4; and Pierre Bourdieu, with Luc Boltanski, *Photography: A Middle-Brow Art*, trans. Shaun Whiteside (Stanford, Calif.: Stanford University Press, 1990), 1–10.

106. Di Cesnola to Dodge, October 17, 1892, MMA; Metropolitan Museum of Art, *Twenty-Second Annual Report*, 500–02; and *New York Times*, December 12, 1882 and June 8, 1895.

107. "Report Re Consequences of Sunday opening," MMA.

108. Thorstein Veblen, *The Theory of the Leisure Class* (New York: Macmillan, 1899; repr., New York: New American Library, 1953), 21, 28.

109. Gustavus Myers, *History of the Great American Fortunes* (Chicago: Kerr, 1909; repr., New York: Modern Library, 1936), 696–712; and Matthew Josephson, *The Robber Barons: The Great American Capitalists, 1861–1901* (New York: Harcourt, Brace, 1934; repr., New York: Harcourt, Brace & World, 1962), 3–31.

110. Beckert, *The Monied Metropolis*, 1–14; Thomas Kessner, *Capital City: New York City and the Men Behind America's Rise to Economic Dominance, 1860–1900* (New York: Simon & Schuster, 2004), xi–xix; David C. Hammack, *Power and Society: Greater New York at the Turn of the Century* (New York: Russell Sage Foundation, 1982), xv–xvi; Jean Strouse, *Morgan: American Financier* (New York: Random House, 1999), ix–xv; Nasaw, *Andrew Carnegie*, ix–xiv; Chernow, *Titan*, xix–xxii.

111. *New York Times*, February 7, 1959. For descriptions of the upper class as the Four Hundred, see *New York Times*, January 16, 1921, December 3, 1930, July 26, 1941, July 10, 1955, January 3, 1960, October 12, 1988, February 1, 1998.

112. Ted Burke, "Parties of the Century," *Town & Country* 128 (December 1974): 149. See also Ted Burke, "The New '400,'" *Town & Country* 121 (May 1967): 88.

113. *New York Times*, October 5, 2008, September 9, 2009; David Patrick Columbia's *New York Social Diary*, accessed November 7, 2010, www.newyorksocialdiary.com /socialdiary/2004/0.

114. Patricia Morrisroe, "The New Snobbery," *New York* 19 (April 7, 1896): 31–42.

115. Museum of the City of New York, "The New York 400," accessed November 7, 2010, www.mcny.org/sidebars/NYC400.html.

7. MAKING SPACES OF THEIR OWN

1. Carol Herselle Krinsky, *Rockefeller Center* (New York: Oxford University Press, 1978), 3–7. See also Daniel Okrent, *Great Fortune: The Epic of Rockefeller Center* (New York: Penguin, 2003), 393–419.

2. "Rockefeller Center: Questions Submitted by the Real Estate Boards of Chicago, St. Louis, and Kansas City—and Answered by Merle Crowell, Director of Public Relations for Rockefeller Center, Inc., at a Meeting of the Chicago Real Estate Board, Wednesday, April 16th, 1941," 1–4, Rockefeller Family Archives, Record Group 2, Office of the Messrs. Rockefeller, Series C, Business Interests, Box 81, Folder 609, Rockefeller Archive Center, Sleepy Hollow, N.Y. [hereafter RAC]; "Rockefeller Center—The Theme," Rockefeller Family Archive, Record Group 2, Office of the Messrs. Rockefeller, Series C, Business Interests, Box 93, Folder 704, RAC; and John Ensor Harr and Peter J. Johnson, *The Rockefeller Century* (New York: Scribner's, 1988), 317–33.

3. New York City Landmarks Preservation Council, *Rockefeller Center Designation Report* (New York: n.p., 1985), 9.

4. Suzanne Loebel, *America's Medicis: The Rockefellers and Their Astonishing Cultural Legacy* (New York: HarperCollins, 2010), xi–xiv. Edward Stettinius Jr. to Harry S. Truman, May 13, 1946, Papers of Harry S. Truman, Confidential File, Box 34, UN Folder, Harry S. Truman Library, Independence, MO [hereafter HSTL]; and Harry S. Truman to Arthur H. Vandenberg, February 6, 1946, Papers of Harry S. Truman, Official File, OF 85, Box 558, 85A–1947 Folder, HSTL.

5. Peter Dobkin Hall, "The Empty Tomb: The Making of Dynastic Identity," 255–348, in *Lives in Trust: The Fortunes of Dynastic Families in Late Twentieth-Century America*, ed. George E. Marcus with Peter Dobkin Hall (Boulder, Colo.: Westview, 1992); Harr and Johnson, *Rockefeller Century*, 431–33; *The Rockefeller Foundation, 1913 to 1988* (New York: Rockefeller Foundation, 1989), 3–30.

6. Duncan Norton-Taylor, "How Top Executives Live," *Fortune* 52 (July 1955): 78.

7. Ibid., 80.

8. Ibid., 78, 80, 82.

9. Ibid., 169; *New York Times*, November 18, 1993; *National Cyclopædia of American Biography*, I (New York: White, 1960), 80; U.S. Department of Commerce and Labor, Bureau of the Census, Thirteenth Census of the United States: 1910, Population, Montclair, Essex County, New Jersey, enumeration district 198 [hereafter e.d.],

p. 15B, accessed August 9, 2012, http://searchancestrylibray.com; U.S Department of Commerce, Bureau of the Census, Fourteenth Census of the United States: 1920, Population, Montclair, Essex County, New Jersey, e.d. 80, p. 8B, accessed August 9, 2012, http://searchancestrylibray.com; and Don G. Mitchell, *Top Man: Reflections of a Chief Executive* (New York: American Management Association, 1970), 11–16.

10.   Quoted in Norton-Taylor, "How Top Executives Live," 169. See also Social Register Association, *Social Register, New York, 1955,* New York: Social Register Association, 1954), 512.

11.   Rakesh Khurana, *From Higher Aims to Hired Hands: The Social Transformation of American Business Schools and the Unfulfilled Promise of Management as a Profession* (Princeton, N.J.: Princeton University Press, 2007), 23; Olivier Zunz, *Making America Corporate, 1870–1920* (Chicago: University of Chicago Press, 1990), 2–10; and Burton J. Bledstein, *The Culture of Professionalism: The Middle Class and The Development of Higher Education in America* (New York: Norton, 1976), 37–38. Following Khurana, I define managers as salaried personnel who stand midway between stock and bond owners, on the one hand, and wage earners, on the other, and who administer business enterprises.

12.   Vincent P. Carroso, *The Morgans: Private International Bankers* (Cambridge, Mass.: Harvard University Press, 1987), 436–38; *New York Times,* January 12, February 20, and March 10, 1912, March 23, 1913; and Zunz, *Making America Corporate, 1870–1920,* 1–10, 103–24.

13.   *New York Times,* September 17, 1953.

14.   Ibid.

15.   Ibid.

16.   *New York Times,* May 25, 1930; Email from Ira Galtman, corporate archivist, American Express Company, to author, January 27, 2010; American Express Company, *Annual Report, 1950* (New York: n.p., 1951), 6; *National Cyclopædia of American Biography,* I: 80; Equitable Life Assurance Society, *Annual Report, 1947* (New York: n.p., 1948), 5; Report by L. W. Carpenter, n.d., accession no. 1984-052, Folder 4, Box 53A, R.G. 4, AXA Life Assurance Archives, AXA Equitable Life Insurance Company, New York City, N.Y. [hereafter AXAA]; Organizational Chart, September 4, 1947, updated to 1948, accession no. 1981-062, organizational charts, 1947–52 file, Box A, R.G. 4, AXAA; R. Carlyle Buley, *The Equitable Life Assurance Society of the United States, 1859–1964,* vol. 1 (New York: n.p. 1967), 366; Buley, *The Equitable Life Assurance Society of the United States, 1859–1964,* vol. 2 (New York: n.p., 1967), 851; and Patricia Conway, "The Equitable Chronicles," *Wharton Real Estate Review* 1 (Spring 1997): 33–49.

17.   "A Model Workshop for Life Insurance," *The Eastern Underwriter* 26 (January 30, 1925): 5.

18.   Ibid., 9. See also Buley, *Equitable Life Assurance Society,* 2: 940–41, 1067.

19.   Real Estate Board of New York, Inc., *1944 Diary and Manual* (New York: Real Estate Board of New York, 1943), 228; and Regina Belz Armstrong, prep., *The Office Industry: Patterns of Growth and Location* (New York: Regional Plan Association, 1972), 1, 15.

20. *New York Times*, February 20, 1912, March 23, 1913, May 25, 1930; Barbara Rizek, Martin Rizek, and Joanne Medvecky, *The Financial District's Lost Neighborhood, 1900–1970* (Portsmouth, N.H.: Arcadia, 2004), 20–21, 40, 46, 105, 119, and 127; E. Belcher Hyde, *Atlas of the Borough of Manhattan, City of New York*, vol. 1, *From the Battery to 23rd Street* (New York: Belcher Hyde, 1907, corrected to 1932), plates 1–5; E. Belcher Hyde, *Atlas of the Borough of Manhattan, City of New York*, vol. 2, *From 23rd Street to 72nd Street* (New York: Belcher Hyde, 1906, corrected to 1932), plates 2–4, 7–9, 12–14, 17–19, and 22–24; and Stanley Buder, "Corporate Headquarters," in *The Encyclopedia of New York City*, 2nd ed., ed. Kenneth T. Jackson (New Haven, Conn.: Yale University Press, 2010), 314–15. See also Conservation of Human Resources Project (Columbia University), *The Corporate Headquarters Complex in New York City* (New York: n.p., 1977), 38; Alison Isenberg, *Downtown America: A History of the Place and the People Who Made It* (Chicago: University of Chicago Press, 2004), 1–12; and Robert M. Fogelson, *Downtown: Its Rise and Fall, 1880–1950* (New Haven, Conn.: Yale University Press, 2001), 1–8.

21. Mira Wilkins, *The History of Foreign Investment in the United States to 1914* (Cambridge, Mass.: Harvard University Press, 1989), ix–xi, 608–25; Margaret G. Myers, *The New York Money Market*, vol. 1, *Origins and Development* (New York: Columbia University Press, 1931), 288–314; Youssef Cassis, *Capitals of Capital: A History of International Financial Centres, 1780–2005* (Cambridge, Mass.: Cambridge University Press, 2006), 115–24, 142–99; David Vogel, "New York City as a National and Global Financial Center," in *Capital of the American Century: The National and International Influence of New York City*, ed. Martin Shefter (New York: Russell Sage Foundation, 1993), 49–94; and David Kynaston, *The City of London*, vol. 3, *Illusions of Gold, 1914–1945* (London: Chatto & Windus, 1999), 10–63, 71, 86, 102, 404, 497.

22. Sloan Wilson, *The Man in the Gray Flannel Suit* (New York: Simon & Schuster, 1955); and William H. Whyte, *The Organization Man* (New York: Simon & Schuster, 1956).

23. Kenneth T. Jackson, "The Capital of Capitalism: The New York Metropolitan Region, 1890–1940," in *Metropolis 1890–1940*, ed. Anthony Sutcliffe (Chicago: University of Chicago Press, 1984), 319–53.

24. N = 160,700 jobs in business headquarters in the New York region, 78,500 in the Chicago region, and 63,500 in the Detroit region. As a proxy for headquarters occupations, this statement uses the occupational category "central administrative and auxiliary employment," an employment grouping of the U.S. Department of Commerce. The metropolitan regions utilized in this measure are standard metropolitan statistical areas and standard consolidated areas, both classifications of the U.S. Census Bureau. Armstrong, *The Office Industry*, 26–29.

25. Table showing office stock in American urban markets, 1955, CBRE Econometric Advisers, email communication from Umair B. Shames to author, July 14, 2014. The other nine cities were Chicago, Boston, Pittsburgh, Philadelphia, San Francisco, Louisville, Milwaukee, Minneapolis, and Detroit. I am grateful to Umair B. Shames and Bill Wheaton for sharing this information.

26. N = 156 headquartered in the New York region, 51 in Chicago, and 25 in Pittsburgh. John Stephens, "City System Behaviour and Corporate Influence: The Headquarters Locations of US Industrial Firms, 1955–75," *Urban Studies* 18 (1981): 296.

27. Three leading works are Sven Beckert, *The Monied Metropolis: New York City and the Consolidation of the American Bourgeoisie, 1850–1896* (New York: Cambridge University Press, 2003); Eric Homberger, *Mrs. Astor's New York: Money and Social Power in a Gilded Age* (New Haven, Conn.: Yale University Press, 2004); and David C. Hammack, *Power and Society: Greater New York at the Turn of the Century* (New York: Columbia University Press, 1987).

28. Ferdinand Pecora, *Wall Street Under Oath: The Study of Our Modern Money Changers* (New York: Simon & Schuster, 1939), 3. On the passage of federal securities legislation, see Anthony J. Badger, *The New Deal: The Depression Years, 1933–40* (New York: Farrar, Straus & Giroux, 1989), 98–102; and Thomas K. McCraw, *American Business Since 1920: How It Worked*, 2nd ed. (Wheeling, Ill.: Harlan Davidson, 2009), 58–63.

29. *New York Times*, May 6, April 27 and 28, and June 7, 1932, January 26, June 24, and March 9, 1933, December 30, 1936.

30. A. Newton Plummer, *The Great American Swindle, Incorporated* (New York: n.p., 1932), 11.

31. Clara E. Laughlin, *So You're Visiting New York City!* (Boston: Houghton, Mifflin, 1939), 5; and Nils Hogner and Guy Scott, *Cartoon Guide of New York City* (New York: Augustin, 1938), 79.

32. John P. Marquand, "Really Simple Fellows, Just Like You and Me," in Marquand, *So Little Time* (Boston: Little, Brown, 1943), 24.

33. Pecora, *Wall Street Under Oath*, x. See also Thomas Gibson, *The Customer and the Stock Broker* (New York: Gibson, 1931), 4.

34. Pecora, *Wall Street Under Oath*, ix.

35. *Fortune* inadvertently undercut its own message by showing Morgan and Harriman to be lightweights and playboys who preferred their hobbies and leisure to business. "Mr. Kuhn and Mr. Loeb," *Fortune* 1 (March 1930): 89–90, 116–18; "The Guggenheims," *Fortune* 1 (July 1930): 71–76; "Lawyers Looking at You," *Fortune* 3 (January 1931): 61–67; "The Most Interesting Line in *Who's Who*," *Fortune* 3 (June 1931): 81, 143–44; and "Mister Morgan," *Fortune* 8 (August 1933): 57–59, 62–63, 76, 78, 81, 84, 86.

36. For representative 1920s profiles, see Francis H. Sisson, "The House of Morgan—Its New Partner," *Forbes* 21 (March 1, 1928): 9–10; and "The du Ponts: Watch Their Growth," *Forbes* 20 (August 15, 1927): 22–23.

37. Felix M. Warburg, untitled diary of world cruise, entries for January 14, May 29, and June 7 and 26, 1927, Folder 2, Box 234, Felix M. Warburg Papers, MS–457, Jacob Rader Marcus Center of the American Jewish Archives, Cincinnati, Ohio.

38. Willard King Bradley, "Greenwich Village at 2 A.M.," *Life* 87 (February 4, 1926): 10; "New York Life: Night Clubs," *Life* 94 (October 18, 1929): 24; Louis Golding, "New York After Midnight," *Vanity Fair* 30 (July 1928): 53, 88–90; John McMullin, "Bright Lights and New York City Nights," *Vogue* 62 (December 15, 1923): 27–30;

Cecil Beaton, "High Lights of the Night-Life of New York," *Vogue* 73 (February 2, 1929): 43–45, 126; Peter H. Kriendler, with Paul Jeffers, *"21:" Every Day Was New Year's Eve: Memoirs of a Saloon Keeper* (Dallas: Taylor, 1999), 125–58. In reality, these were eminently safe adventures: upper-class New Yorkers could cross social barriers and indulge themselves voyeuristically but without having to enter completely uncontrolled environments and situations. Lewis Erenberg, *Steppin' Out: New York Nightlife and the Transformation of American Culture, 1890–1930* (Chicago: University of Chicago Press, 1981), xi–xv, 233–59.

39. F. Scott Fitzgerald, *This Side of Paradise* (New York: Scribner's, 1920); Fitzgerald, *The Beautiful and Damned* (New York: Scribner's, 1922); Fitzgerald, *The Great Gatsby* (New York: Scribner, 1925).

40. *New York Times*, July 23, 1963, and December 6, 1974; and John Brooks, *Once in Golconda: A True Drama of Wall Street 1920–1938* (New York: Norton, 1969), 234–36, 245–54, 271–76.

41. *Wall Street Journal*, October 30 and November 28, 1929.

42. *Wall Street Journal*, October 30 and November 28, 1929, March 29, May 13 and 29, June 11, and October 15 and 16, 1930, January 22 and 28, September 23, October 3 and 17, and November 6, 1931, March 23, July 13, and November 16, 1934; *New York Times*, February 10, 1928, November 28, 1929, July 23, 1963, December 6, 1974; "Statement of Richard Whitney, Made to the Governing Committee and Membership, in Regard to the Investigation of Stock Exchange Practices by the Committee on Banking and Currency of the United States Senate, August 14, 1932" (New York: n.p., 1932), 3–32, Folder 4, Box 3, Record Group 2-2, New York Stock Exchange Archives [hereafter NYSEA]; Richard Whitney, "Public Opinion and the Stock Market," an address to the Boston Chamber of Commerce, January 29, 1931, Folder 1, Box 3, Record Group 2-2, NYSEA; and Richard Whitney, "The Place of the Stock Exchange in American Business," an address delivered to the New York State Bankers Association, Hotel Roosevelt, New York City, January 22, 1931, Folder 1, Box 3, Record Group 2-2, NYSEA.

43. *Wall Street Journal*, April 10, 1935.

44. *New York Times*, April 4 and 29, May 14, June 15 and 26, September 20, 1935, February 2, March 1, and September 26, 1936; *Wall Street Journal*, April 4, 1935, September 26, 1936; and Charles R. Gay, "The Role of Business Leadership in Recovery," an address delivered at a meeting of the Chamber of Commerce of New York State, June 5, 1935, Folder 2, Box 4, Charles R. Gay, R.G. 2.2, Speeches, NYSEA.

45. *New York Times*, March 15, 17, 18, and 19, April 12, May 13, July 1, 1938; and William McC. Martin Jr., "The Stock Exchange, Yesterday, Today, and Tomorrow," an address delivered to the Commonwealth Club, San Francisco, December 5, 1940, Folder 12, Box 5, Martin, William McC. Jr., R.G. 2.2, Speeches, NYSEA. Louis Auchincloss based his novel *The Embezzler* (Boston: Houghton Mifflin, 1966) on the Whitney scandal.

46. Herman E. Krooss, *Executive Opinion: What Business Leaders Said and Thought on Economic Issues 1920s–1950s* (Garden City, N.Y.: Doubleday, 1970), 25; Richard S.

Tedlow, *Keeping the Corporate Image: Public Relations and Business, 1900–1950* (Greenwich, Conn.: JAI, 1979), xiii–xviii, 81–105; Karen S. Miller, *The Voice of Business: Hill & Knowlton and Postwar Public Relations* (Chapel Hill: University of North Carolina Press, 1999), 9–29, 189–94; and William L Bird Jr., *"Better Living," Advertising, Media, and the New Vocabulary of Business Leadership, 1935–1955* (Evanston, Ill.: Northwestern University Press, 1999), 3–9, 11–23, 30–46.

47. Thomas F. Willmore, *The Real Boss of Wall Street* (Detroit: Willmore, 1941), 3; Rudolf L. Weissman, *The New Wall Street* (New York: Harper & Brothers, 1939), ix.

48. H. Wilder Osborne, *Profits Out of Wall Street* (New York: Knopf, 1939), vi.

49. Ibid., ix–x, 261–81; Sidney Rheinstein, *Trade Whims: My Fifty Years on the New York Stock Exchange* (New York: Ronald, 1960), 26–27, 88; John Durand, *Timing: When to Buy and Sell in Today's Markets* (New York: Magazine of Wall Street and Business Analyst, 1938), 1–3; A. T. Miller, *How to Make Money the Next Two Years* (New York: Ticker, 1944), 5–9; Birl E. Shultz, *The Securities Market and How It Works*, 4th ed. (New York: Harper, 1946), vii–ix, 370–83; and Robert Irving Warshow, *Understanding the New Stock Market*, rev. ed. (New York: Blue Ribbon, 1937), vii–10.

50. Khurana, *From Higher Aims to Hired Hands*: 1–20, 195–231.

51. Laurence Bell, "Men of Achievement: Walter S. Gifford," *Forbes* 61 (May 15, 1948): 18–19, 41.

52. Boyden Sparkes, "Men of Achievement: W. Alton Jones," *Forbes* 60 (October 15, 1947): 18.

53. Robert Caro, *The Power Broker: Robert Moses and the Fall of New York* (New York: Random House, 1975), 1–21; and Mason B. Williams, *City of Ambition: FDR, La Guardia, and the Making of Modern New York* (New York: Norton, 2013), 178–201.

54. Matthew P. Drennan, "Economy," in Jackson, *Encyclopedia of New York City*, 394–400; Norman J. Brouwer, "Port of New York," in Jackson, *Encyclopedia of New York City*, 1022–26; Arnold Markoe, "Brooklyn Navy Yard," in Jackson, *Encyclopedia of New York City*, 180–81; *New York Times*, August 30, September 9, and November 25, 1942, March 29 and November 29, 1943, January 30, February 27, and April 4 and 16, 1944, April 29, 1945; Kenneth T. Jackson, "The City Loses the Sword: The Decline of Major Military Activity in the New York Metropolitan Region," in *The Martial Metropolis: U.S. Cities in War and Peace*, ed. Roger W. Lotchin (New York: Praeger, 1984), 153; and Joseph F. Meany Jr., "Brooklyn Army Terminal," in Jackson, *Encyclopedia of New York City*, 274.

55. *New York Times*, June 3, October 12 and 18, and November 11, 1942, May 21, June 16, and September 12, 1943, May 8, July 7, and December 31, 1944; and *Wall Street Journal*, August 27, 1942, June 24, 1943.

56. *New York Times*, November 15, 1942, April 3, 1943, March 26, 2007. New York City also had a significant geographical disadvantage: the proximity of West Coast cities to the Pacific Theater steered federal dollars there. Ann Markusen, Peter Hall, Scott Campbell, and Sabina Deitrick, *The Rise of the Gunbelt: The Military Remapping of Industrial America* (New York: Oxford University Press, 1991), 3–25; and Robert

Lotchin, *Fortress California, 1910–1961: From Warfare to Welfare* (New York: Oxford University Press, 1992), xii–22, 340–43.

57. "Robert L. Clarkson, Former American Express Chairman, Dies in New York," American Express Public Relations Department, press release, March 5, 1969, Clarkson file, Biographical Reference Files, American Express Corporate Archives, New York, N.Y. [hereafter AmEx]; "History of the Board of Directors, American Express Company, 1850–2009," AmEx; *New York Times*, June 30, 1938, December 15, 1942, October 20, 1960, March 5, 1969, July 4, 1970, April 22, 1981, February 8, 1982; New York Central Railroad Company, *Annual Report Together with Statistics and Other Data for the Year 1947* (New York: n.p., 1948), n.p.; and David Rockefeller, *Memoirs* (New York: Random House, 2002), 153, 465.

58. Social Register Association, *Social Register, New York, 1949*, (New York: Social Register Association, 1948), Social Register Association, *Social Register, 1955*, *New York Times*, December 12, 1929, August 4, 1949, February 17 and December 7, 1951, August 19, 1955, September 26, 1957, January 18, 1959, February 25, 1964, May 23, 1966, October 24, 1967, March 4, 1969, September 3, 1976, August 29, 1977, May 10, 1989; untitled news release regarding Thomas I. Parkinson, June 17, 1959, accession no. 1985-047, biographical files, Parkinson file 1, R.G. 12, AXAA; untitled news release regarding Ray D. Murphy, 1964, accession no. 1985-047, biographical files, R.G. 12, AXAA; Profile of Merle Gulick, National Football Foundation's College Football Hall of Fame, accessed January 29, 2010, www.collegefootball.org/famersearch.php?id=20099; U.S. Department of Commerce, Bureau of the Census, Tenth Census of the United States: 1880, Schedule 1-Population, New York City, New York State, e.d. 577, p. 9, Ancestry .com, accessed January 31, 2010, http://ancestry.com [hereafter in this note Ancestry .com]; World War I draft registration card for Maurice H. Mendel, place of registration, New York County, N.Y., roll 1766249, Ancestry.com; U.S. Department of Commerce and Labor, Bureau of the Census, Thirteenth Census of the United States: 1910, Population, New York City, New York State, e.d. 719, p. 19, Ancestry.com; U.S. Department of Commerce, Bureau of Labor, Fifteenth Census of the United States: 1930, Population Schedule, New York City, New York State, e.d. 31–437, p. 21A, Ancestry. com; U.S. Department of Commerce, Bureau of the Census, Twelfth Census of the United States: 1900, Schedule 1-Population, New York City, New York State, e.d. 429, p. 13, Ancestry.com; World War I draft registration card for Henry C. Greaves, place of registration, Kings County, N.Y., roll 1754591, Ancestry.com; U.S. Naturalization Record for Henry C. Greaves, U.S. District Court for the Eastern District of New York, issued May 12, 1904; World War I draft registration card for Alvin B. Dalager, place of registration Mower County, Minn., roll 1675687, Ancestry.com; U.S. Department of Commerce, Bureau of the Census, Twelfth Census of the United States: 1900, Schedule 1-Population, Austin, Mower County, Minn., e.d. 81, p. 9; U.S. Department of Commerce and Labor, Bureau of the Census, Thirteenth Census of the United States: 1910, Population, Austin, Mower County, Minn., e.d. 79, p. 10A and 15A, Ancestry.com; U.S. Department of Commerce, Bureau of the

Census, Fourteenth Census of the United States: 1920, Population, Austin, Mower County, Minn., e.d. 80, p. 12A, Ancestry.com; U.S. Department of Commerce, Bureau of Labor, Fifteenth Census of the United States: 1930, Population Schedule, St. Paul, Ramsey County, Minn., e.d. 62–191, p. 15A, Ancestry.com; World War I draft registration card for William Washington Kingman, place of registration Ramsey County, MN, roll 1682640, Ancestry.com; U.S. Department of Commerce, Bureau of the Census, Fourteenth Census of the United States: 1920, Population, Waynesfield Township, Lucas County, Ohio, e.d. 172, p.12, Ancestry.com; U.S. Department of Commerce, Bureau of the Census, Fifteenth Census of the United States: 1930, Population Schedule, Waynesfield Township, Lucas County, Ohio, e.d. 48–187, p. 16A, Ancestry.com; U.S. Department of Commerce, Bureau of the Census, Twelfth Census of the United States: 1900, Schedule 1-Population, Springfield, Hampden County, Massachusetts, e.d. 581, p. 3, Ancestry.com; U.S. Department of Commerce and Labor, Bureau of the Census, Thirteenth Census of the United States: 1910, Population, Springfield, Hampden County, Massachusetts, e.d. 616, p. 15A, Ancestry.com; U.S. Department of Commerce, Bureau of the Census, Twelfth Census of the United States: 1900, Schedule 1-Population, East Orange, Essex County, New Jersey, e.d. 178, p. 3, Ancestry.com; U.S. Department of Commerce and Labor, Bureau of the Census, Thirteenth Census of the United States: 1910, Population, East Orange, Essex County, New Jersey, e.d. 170, p. 1A, Ancestry.com; World War II draft registration card for Edgar W. Beckwith, place of registration Queens County, N.Y., roll 2370931, Ancestry.com; U.S. Department of Commerce, Bureau of the Census, Fourteenth Census of the United States: 1920, Population, New York City, New York State, e.d. 941, sheet 11, Ancestry.com; World War I draft registration card for Joseph R. Boldt, place of registration Bergen County, N.J., roll 1711911, Ancestry.com; World War II draft registration card for Joseph R. Boldt, place of registration, New York County, N.Y., roll 2283378, Ancestry.com.

59. The representation of corporate elites on these boards ranged from a low of 21 percent for the New York Public Library up to 59 percent for Columbia University and 66 percent for New York University. American Museum of Natural History, *Seventy-Ninth Annual Report, July 1947, Through June 1948* (New York: n.p., 1948), n.p.; *Bulletin of the New York Public Library* 52 (January 1948): 2; *Bulletin of the Museum of Modern Art* 15 (1948): 1–2; New York University, *Reports of the Treasurer for 1948* (New York: New York University, 1948), 5; *The Metropolitan Museum of Art Bulletin*, n.s., 7, *Incorporating the Seventy-Eighth Report of the Trustees for the Year 1947* (Summer 1948): n.p; Metropolitan Opera, *Program for Otello*, November 1948 (New York: Metropolitan Opera, 1948), n.p.; *Program for Carnegie Hall Performance, January 6, 1949* (New York: New York Philharmonic, 1949), n.p. New York Philharmonic Program Collection, New York Philharmonic Archives, New York, N.Y.; *Journal of the New York Botanical Garden*, 49 (December 1948): n.p.; Columbia University in the City of New York, *Columbia Directory Number for the Sessions 1947–1948* (New York: n.p., 1947), unpaginated; *Who's Who in America, 1948–1949*, vol. 25 (Chicago: Marquis, 1948).4;

New York Times;; The National Cyclopædia of American Biography, vol. H (New York: White & Company, 1952), 137–38, *The National Cyclopædia of American Biography*, vol. 44 (New York: White, 1962), 25–27; *The National Cyclopædia of American Biography*, vol. J (New York: White, 1964), 324; *The National Cyclopædia of American Biography*, vol. 29 (New York: White, 1941), 8–9.

60. John J. McCloy Diary, 1942, entries for April 22–23, 1942, Folder 5, Box DY1, Series 2, John J. McCloy Papers, Archives and Special Collections, Amherst College Library, Amherst, Mass.; Memorandum for Files of Telephone Conversation between Dean Acheson and John Foster Dulles, April 5, 1950, Memoranda of Conversations, January–July 1950, April 1950 Folder, Box 66, Acheson Papers, HSTL; Kai Bird, *The Chairman: John J. McCloy—The Making of the American Establishment* (New York: Simon & Schuster, 1992), 57–72; Richard H. Immerman, *John Foster Dulles: Piety, Pragmatism, and Power in U.S. Foreign Policy* (Wilmington, Del.: Scholarly Resources, 1988), 1–21; and Arnold Rogow, *James Forrestal: A Study of Personality, Politics, and Policy* (New York: Macmillan, 1963), 49–66.

61. James R. Kurth, "Between Europe and America: The New York Foreign Policy Elite," 71–94, in Shefter, *Capital of the American Century*.

62. Robert D. Schulzinger, *The Wise Men of Foreign Affairs: The History of the Council on Foreign Relations* (New York: Columbia University Press, 1984), 1–30; Kurth, "Between Europe and America," 74–75; Starr J. Murphy to John D. Rockefeller Jr., March 6, 1919, Folder 29, Box 4, Series Q (World Affairs), Record Group 2, Office of the Messrs. Rockefeller, General Files, Rockefeller Family Archives, RAC; Starr J. Murphy to John D. Rockefeller Jr., April 9, 1919, Folder 29, Box 4, Series Q, Record Group 2, Rockefeller Family Archives, RAC; Walter W. Mallory to Thomas W. Lamont, November 26, 1929, Folder 27, Box 21, Thomas W. Lamont Papers, Baker Library, Harvard Business School, Harvard University, Mass [hereafter HBS]; Hamilton Fish Armstrong to Thomas W. Lamont, January 21, 1935, 1934–1935 Folder, Box 22, Lamont Papers, HBS; and John W. Davis to Thomas W. Lamont, October 14, 1946, Folder 8, Box 22, Lamont Papers, HBS.

63. Augusta Owen Patterson, "A House with a River Terrace," *Town & Country* 87 (October 1, 1932): 32–35; *New York Times*, January 13 and 14, 1930, February 19, 1931, March 2, 8, and 12, 1933; and Townsend Hoopes and Douglas Brinkley, *Driven Patriot: The Life and Times of James Forrestal* (New York: Knopf, 1992), 74–80, 83–87.

64. *New York Times*, December 13, 1971; Thomas J. Watson Jr. and Peter Petre, *Father, Son, & Co.: My Life at IBM and Beyond* (New York: Bantam, 1990), 16–17, 37, 43–44, 76, 210–12, 272–75, 320; Bernard M. Baruch, *Baruch: My Own Story* (New York: Holt, 1957; repr., Cutchogue, N.Y.: Buccaneer, [1996?]), 103, 267–88; U.S. Department of Commerce, Bureau of the Census, Sixteenth Census of the United States: 1940, Population Schedule, New York, New York County, New York State, e.d. 31–1330, p. 1A accessed October 21, 2012, http://searchancestrylibray.com; and William S. Paley, *As It Happened: A Memoir* (Garden City, N.Y.: Doubleday & Company, 1979), 86–88, 92–93, 187–88, 252, 359.

65. *New York Times*, October 29 and November 8, 1899, April 3, 1948, May 3, 1952; and *Wall Street Journal*, July 25 and August 1, 1938, June 22, 1940.

66. Quoted in *New York Times*, April 3, 1948.

67. *New York Times*, November 30, 1883, March 4 and December 30, 1942, September 30, 1949, January 10, 1954, March 1, 1955; and *National Cyclopædia of America Biography* 43 (New York: White, 1961), 164–65.

68. U.S. Department of Commerce, Bureau of the Census, Twelfth Census of the United States: 1900, Schedule No. 1, Population, Harrison, Hamilton County, Ohio, e.d. 297, p. 6, accessed June 20, 2012, http://searchancestrylibrary.com; U.S. Department of Commerce, Bureau of the Census, Twelfth Census of the United States: 1900, Schedule No. 1, Population, City of Dayton, Montgomery County, Ohio, e.d. 73, p. 9B, accessed June 20, 2012, http://searchancestrylibrary.com; U.S. Department of Commerce and Labor, Bureau of the Census, Thirteenth Census of the United States: 1910, Population Schedule, Marysville, Union County, Ohio, e.d. 141, p. 14, accessed June 20, 2012, http://searchancestrylibrary.com; U.S. Department of Commerce, Bureau of the Census, Sixteenth Census of the United States: 1940, Population Schedule, Village of Rye, Westchester County, New York, e.d. 60–329, p. 63A, accessed June 20, 2012, http://searchancestrylibrary.com; McCall Corporation, *Annual Report for the Twenty-Second Year Ending December Thirty-First Nineteen Hundred and Thirty Four* New York: n.p., [1935?]), unpaginated, accessed July 5, 2012, http://search.proquest.com/annual reports; McCall Corporation, *Annual Report for the Twenty-Third Year Ending December Thirty-First Nineteen Hundred and Thirty Five* (New York: n..p., [1936?]), unpaginated, accessed July 5, 2012, http://search.proquest .com/annual reports; *New York Times*, April 14, 1934, April 25, 1935, December 18, 1945, September 24, 1949, July 18, 1969. County, Ohio, e.d. 73, p. 9B, accessed June 20, 2012, http://searchancestrylibrary.com; U.S. Department of Commerce and Labor, Bureau of the Census, Thirteenth Census of the United States: 1910, Population Schedule, Marysville, Union County, Ohio, e.d. 141, p. 14 , accessed June 20, 2012, http://searchancestrylibrary.com; U.S. Department of Commerce, Bureau of the Census, Sixteenth Census of the United States: 1940, Population Schedule, Village of Rye, Westchester County, New York, e.d. 60–329, p. 63A, accessed June 20, 2012, http://searchancestrylibrary.com; McCall Corporation, *Annual Report for the Twenty-Second Year Ending December Thirty-First Nineteen Hundred and Thirty Four* New York: n..p., [1935?]), unpaginated, accessed July 5, 2012, http://search.proquest .com/annual reports; McCall Corporation, *Annual Report for the Twenty-Third Year Ending December Thirty-First Nineteen Hundred and Thirty Five* (New York: n..p., [1936?]), unpaginated, accessed July 5, 2012, http://search.proquest.com/annual reports; and *New York Times*, April 14, 1934, April 25, 1935, December 18, 1945, September 24, 1949, July 18, 1969.

69. Barbara Bush, *Barbara Bush: A Memoir* (New York: Scribner's, 1994), 5; *New York Times*, July 18, 1969; Pamela Kilian, *Barbara Bush: Matriarch of a Dynasty* (New York: St. Martin's, 2002), 13–23; Donnie Radcliffe, *Simply Barbara Bush: A Portrait of*

America's Candid First Lady (New York: Warner, 1989), 73–78; and Myra G. Gutin, *Barbara Bush: Presidential Matriarch* (Lawrence: University Press of Kansas, 2008), 1–13.

70. Bush, *Barbara Bush*, 5–6, 16–17.

71. Ibid., ix. Here Bush is describing her entire life but clearly applies this characterization to her upbringing.

72. Ibid., 1–15; *New York Times*, May 18, 1932, April 7, July 21, and March 21, 1935, August 19 and December 18, 1941, July 18, 1969.

73. None belonged to the *Social Register*. Social Register Association, *Social Register, 1949*.

74. Albert Bigelow Paine, *The Commuters: The Story of a Little Hearth and Garden* (New York: Taylor, 1904); James Forbes, *The Commuters: A Comedy in Four Acts* (New York: French, 1910); Walter B. Hayward, ed., *The Commuter's Garden* (New York: Crowell, 1914); "Herself," *Indiscretions of a Commuter's Wife* (Boston: Little, Brown, 1925); Robert M. Gay, *The Eight Forty-Five: Extracts from the Diary of John Skinner, A Commuter* (Boston: Atlantic Monthly Press, 1925); Eric Hodgins, *Mr. Blandings Builds His Dream House* (New York: Simon & Schuster, 1946); and *New York Times*, March 26, 1948. See also Eileen Panetta, "Westchester: The Suburb in Fiction," 373–409, in *Westchester: the American Suburb*, ed. Roger Panetta (New York: Fordham University Press, 2006); and Stanley J. Solomon, "Images of Suburban Life in American Film," 411–41, in Panetta, *Westchester*.

75. Gay, *The Eight Forty-Five*, 20.

76. George Howe, *Memoirs of a Westchester Realtor: Half A Century of Property Development in Westchester County and Southwestern Connecticut* (New York: Exposition, 1959), 11–19; and *New York Times*, February 26, 1967, January 4, 1998, March 18, 2007.

77. Kurt C. Schlichting, *Grand Central Terminal: Railroads, Engineering, and Architecture in New York City* (Baltimore, Md.: Johns Hopkins University Press 2001), 155–93; Kurt C. Schlichting, *Grand Central's Engineer: William J. Wilgus and the Planning of Modern Manhattan* (Baltimore, Md.: Johns Hopkins University Press, 2012), 72–73; Kathleen LaFrank, "Bronx River Parkway," in *Encyclopedia of New York State*, ed. Peter Eisenstadt (Syracuse, N.Y.: Syracuse University Press, 2005), 217; and Kathleen LaFrank, "Parkways," in Eisenstadt, *Encyclopedia of New York State*, 1181–82.

78. *New York Times*, February 26, 1967.

79. Howe, *Memoirs*, 11.

80. Ibid., 11.

81. Howe, *Memoirs*, 23, 34, 53–57, 65–67; *New York Times*, September 24, 1921, February 5, April 4, October 21, 1928, February 26, 1967.

82. Howe, *Memoirs*, 53, 67–68, 84, 89, 100– 101, 109; *New York Times*, May 19 and June 12, 1950, June 19 and October 7, 1951, January 24, 1953.

83. Keith D. Revell, *Building Gotham: Civic Culture & Public Policy in New York City, 1898–1938* (Baltimore, Md.: Johns Hopkins University Press, 2003), 17–57.

84. Robert D. Yaro and Tony Hiss, *A Region at Risk: The Third Regional Plan for The New York-New Jersey-Connecticut Metropolitan Area* (Washington, D.C.: Island Press, 1996), 1, 19; U.S. Department of Commerce, Bureau of the Census, *Sixteenth Census of the United States: 1940, Population*, vol. 1, *Number of Inhabitants*, section 3, *Alabama–Florida* (Washington, D.C.: U.S. Government Printing Office [hereafter in this chapter USGPO], 1942), 181–82; U.S. Department of Commerce, Bureau of the Census, *Sixteenth Census, Population*, vol. 1, sect. 6, *Minnesota–New Jersey* (Washington, D.C.: USGPO, 1942), 672; U.S. Department of Commerce, Bureau of the Census, *Sixteenth Census, Population*, vol. 1, sect. 7, *New Mexico–New York* (Washington, D.C.: USGPO, 1942), 713; Campbell Gibson, *Population of the 100 Largest Cities and Other Urban Places in the United States: 1790 to 1990*, Population Division Working Paper No. 27 (Washington, D.C.: U.S. Bureau of the Census, Population Division, 1998), table 17, accessed January 13, 2010, www.census.gov/population/www/documentation /twps0027.html; U.S. Department of Commerce, Bureau of the Census, *Sixteenth Census, Population*, vol. 1, sect. 2, *United States Summary* (Washington, D.C.: USGPO, 1942), Map of the United States Showing Population Distribution in 1940.

85. U.S. Department of Commerce, Bureau of the Census, *Thirteenth Census of the United States Taken in the Year 1910*, vol. 2, *Population 1910, Reports by States with Statistics for Counties, Cities and Other Civil Divisions, Alabama–Montana* (Washington, D.C.: USGPO, 1913), table 1; U.S. Department of Commerce, Bureau of the Census, *Thirteenth Census of the United States Taken in the Year 1910*, vol. 3, *Population 1910, Reports by States with Statistics for Counties, Cities and Other Civil Divisions, Nebraska–Wyoming* (Washington, D.C.: USGPO, 1913), tables 1 and 2; U.S. Department of Commerce, Bureau of the Census, *Sixteenth Census of the United States: 1940, Population*, vol. 1, *Number of Inhabitants*, sect. 2, *United States Summary* (Washington, D.C.: Government Printing Office, 1942), tables 14 and 15; U.S. Department of Commerce, Bureau of the Census, *Sixteenth Census of the United States: 1940, Population*, vol. 1, *Number of Inhabitants*, sect. 3, *Alabama–Florida* (Washington, D.C.: USGPO, 1942), table 2; U.S. Department of Commerce, Bureau of the Census, *Sixteenth Census of the United States: 1940, Population*, vol. 1, *Number of Inhabitants*, sect. 6, *Minnesota–New Jersey* (Washington, D.C.: Government Printing Office, 1942), table 2; U.S. Department of Commerce, Bureau of the Census, *Sixteenth Census of the United States: 1940, Population*, vol. 1, *Number of Inhabitants*, sect. 7, *New Mexico–Ohio* (Washington, D.C.: Government Printing Office, 1942), tables 4 and 5; and U.S. Department of Commerce, Bureau of the Census, *Sixteenth Census of the United States: 1940, Population*, vol. 1, *Number of Inhabitants*, sect. 2, *United States Summary* (Washington, D.C.: Government Printing Office, 1942), table 14.

86. Urban historians have recently explored the history of suburbs and of suburbanization, but this new scholarship concentrates on working-class, lower-middle-class, and African American communities. Almost none of it deals with the elite suburbs that this chapter analyzes. Andrew Wiese, *Places of Their Own: African American Suburbanization in the Twentieth Century* (Chicago: University of Chicago Press, 2004);

Becky N. Nicolaides, *My Blue Heaven: Life and Politics in the Working-Class Suburbs of Los Angeles, 1920–1965* (Chicago: University of Chicago Press, 2002); Kevin M. Kruse, *White Flight: Atlanta and the Making of Modern Conservatism* (Princeton, N.J.: Princeton University Press, 2005); and Becky Nicolaides and Andrew Wiese, eds., *The Suburb Reader* (New York: Routledge, 2006). Among the few recent studies to examine upper-class suburbs is a work of cultural geography, James S. Duncan and Nancy G. Duncan's *Landscapes of Privilege: The Politics of the Aesthetic in an American Suburb* (New York: Routledge, 2004).

87. The basis of this analysis is *Who's Who in New York (City and State), 1947*, 11th ed., ed. Winfield Scott Downs (New York: Lewis Historical Publishing, 1947). I will cite my analysis of it as Henry House Elites Project, or HHEP. As its title indicates, this volume contains entries for people from across New York State as well as from metropolitan New York. The first step of this project involved pinpointing individuals who resided in the thirty-one-county New York metropolitan region and discarding the rest. The next step was to demarcate those metropolitan residents who qualified as "elite" and set them aside for further study. That selection was made on the basis of the definition of economic elites utilized in this book, namely, people who made key economic decisions and those who provided support for the decision makers. That determination necessarily centered on job descriptions, since, like most biographical dictionaries, *Who's Who in New York (City and State)* was intended as a reference for business and professional networking and thus supplied particularly detailed information about employment. I supplemented *Who's Who in New York (City and State)* with information from *The National Cyclopædia of American Biography* and Marquis's *Who's Who in America*. The result of this filtering was a cohort of 2,458 men and women. The full population included such well-known figures as Bruce Barton, Prescott Bush, Bernard Baruch, Allen Dulles, John Foster Dulles, Angier Biddle Duke, Walter O'Malley, Eddie Rickenbacker, David Rockefeller, John D. Rockefeller Jr., John D. Rockefeller III, Elmo Burns Roper, Raymond Rubicam, John J. McCloy, David Sarnoff, William Jay Schieffelin, J. C. Penney, Frank Stanton, Robert Moses, Nicholas Murray Butler, Bennett Cerf, Thomas W. Lamont, Thomas S. Lamont, Bradley Martin, Joseph Proskauer, Fiorello H. La Guardia, Arthur Hays Sulzberger, Charles Lewis Tiffany, Oliver Garrision Villard, and Thomas J. Watson. However, there were many more "everyday" elites who may not have been known outside their companies or industries but nevertheless exercised considerable clout as company presidents or vice presidents, or as corporate lawyers, or as publishers and editors. The vital statistics of the full population were entered into a SPSS-based computer program that explored seventy-five variables related to sociological factors such as personal background, education, occupation, place of residence, business affiliations, social associations, and recreational activities. It should be noted that the results of this statistical analysis are not advanced with the view, once commonplace in historical scholarship, that quantification is an infallible method free of the selection bias of qualitative evidence; rather, my belief is that all historical evidence has its

uses and its strengths and weaknesses and should be scrutinized and used in tandem with other evidentiary sources. The findings of an interrogation of this data are consistent with other evidence and confirm that this was indeed a privileged group. Four-fifths were college graduates (N = college graduates, 1,922 [78.2%], not college graduates, 424 [17.2%], unknown, 112 [4.6%], HHEP). About a third had gone to Yale, Harvard, Princeton, or Columbia (N = Yale, 246 [10%], Harvard, 219 [8.9%], Columbia, 186 [7.6%], and Princeton, 132 [5.4%], for a total of 783, or 31.8%, HHEP). Other leading colleges were Cornell, New York University, City College, Williams, Amherst, and UPenn (N = Cornell, 90 [3.7%], NYU 76 [3.1%], CCNY, 47 [1.9%], Williams, 46 [1.9%], Amherst, 35 [1.4%], and UPenn, 33 [1.3%], HHEP). Just under a third identified themselves as lawyers and roughly a tenth as business executives and another tenth as bankers (N = lawyers, 697 [28.4%], executives, 327 [13.3%], bankers, 281 [11.4%], and engineers, 126 [5.1%], HHEP). The top economic sector was business services, which comprised a fifth of the total, followed by banking/brokerage, contracting/engineering, health/medicine, manufacturing, and commerce (N = business services, 556 [22.6%], banking/brokerage, 456 [18.6%], contracting/engineering, 169 [6.9%], health/medicine, 141 [5.7%], manufacturing, 138 [5.6%], and commerce/trade, 114 [4.6%]). The people in the survey worked for 783 different corporations and firms that did business with corporations, with the six leading employers being Milbank, Tweed (15 individuals); Cadwalader, Wickersham, & Taft (15); Chase National Bank (14); Cravath, Swaine & Moore (13); Chadbourne & Parke (11); and Standard Oil (10). Four of the six were corporate law firms (HHEP).

88. N = 2,333 (94.9% of the entire database and 98.5% of those providing information relevant to this question) people reported their office location as being New York City. N = 1,209 (49.2%) who identified their primary residential location as being outside New York City and 1,156 (47.2%) as inside New York City. N = 1,123 (45.7%) residents of the metropolitan region beyond New York City. N = 939 (38.2%) residents of Manhattan, HHEP.

89. N = 87 residents of Scarsdale (3.5%), 60 of Bronxville (2.4%), 55 of Montclair, N.J. (2.2%), 47 of Greenwich, Conn. (1.9%), 30 of New Rochelle (1.2%), 25 of Garden City (1.0%), 24 of Rye (1.0%), 23 of Larchmont (0.9%), 23 of New Canaan, Conn. (0.9%), and 20 of Summit, N.J. (0.8%), HHEP. The three Long Island suburbs that were among the top 25 were Garden City (no. 6), Great Neck (no. 11), and Manhasset (no. 22), HHEP.

90. The top fourteen were, in order, Great Neck, Manhasset, Huntington, Lawrence, Oyster Bay, Locust Valley, Syosset, Hewlett, Port Washington, Old Westbury, Sands Point, Cedarhurst, Glen Head, and Eatons Neck, HHEP. The nine that I have identified as "old-money suburbs" are Lawrence, Oyster Bay, Locust Valley, Syosset, Hewlett, Port Washington, Old Westbury, Sands Point, and Eatons Neck, HHEP. See also Robert Reed Coles and Peter Luyster Van Santvoord, *A History of Glen Cove* (Glen Cove, N.Y.: n.p., 1967), 52–55.

91. Anthony Gronowicz, "Upper East Side," in Jackson, *Encyclopedia of New York City*, 1352.

92. This study consisted of a survey of the listings in the 1949 *Social Register* that was made with a confidence level of 95% and a confidence interval of 4. The sample of 553 cases (of the total 14,500 entries) were selected via a random number generator. I excluded listings of marriages, since they provided the place of the wedding rather than the place of residence. I surveyed home addresses, not individuals, since more than one person usually lived at any given address. I defined the Upper East Side as encompassing the area from Fifth Avenue to Lexington Avenue and from Fifty-Ninth Street to Ninety-Sixth Street, inclusive, plus Sutton Place and Beekman Place. Social Register Association, *Social Register, New York, 1949*, (New York: Social Register Association, 1948).

93. N = 201. Ibid.

94. N = 338, HHEP.

95. This residential pattern of a new uptown neighborhood arising simultaneously with new suburbs was not unique to New York. In Pittsburgh in the 1880s and 1890s, some upper-class families moved from their old quarters downtown and in Allegheny City to new urban neighborhoods in the East End of the city that boasted large houses and mansions positioned closely together on rectilinear blocks. At the same time, others relocated to Sewickley, an upper-class railroad suburb. In Boston, Philadelphia, Cincinnati, Chicago, Buffalo, New Orleans, and Milwaukee, urban upper-class residential districts survived until at least the mid-twentieth century, even as elite suburbs sprouted on the outskirts. That was also the pattern in Brooklyn. James Borchert and Susan Borchert, "Downtown, Uptown, Out of Town: Diverging Patterns of Upper-Class Residential Landscapes in Buffalo, Pittsburgh, and Cleveland, 1885–1935," *Social Science History* 26 (2002): 311–46; James Borchert to author, email, July 11, 2012; and Suleiman Osman, *The Invention of Brownstone Brooklyn: Gentrification and Authenticity in Postwar New York* (New York: Oxford University Press, 2011), 3–51. See also Ann Durkin Keating, *Chicagoland: City and Suburbs in the Railroad Age* (Chicago: University of Chicago Press, 2005); and Michael H. Ebner, *Creating Chicago's North Shore: A Suburban History* (Chicago: University of Chicago Press, 1988).

96. Other sizable social groups in the city have had similarly manifold residential patterns, as with second-generation Eastern European Jews, who by the 1920s had created neighborhoods in the Bronx and Brooklyn that had particular religious and political associations, and with African Americans, who developed major communities in Manhattan and Brooklyn in the same period. See Deborah Dash Moore, *At Home in America: Second Generation New York Jews* (New York: Columbia University Press, 1981), 19–58; Mario A. Charles, "Bedford-Stuyvesant," in Jackson, *Encyclopedia of New York City*, 109–10; and Jeffrey Gurock, Calvin B. Holder, Durahn A. B. Taylor, and Kenneth T. Jackson, "Harlem," in Jackson, *Encyclopedia of New York City*, 573–75.

97. Diana Reische, *Of Colonists and Commuters: A History of Scarsdale* (Scarsdale: Junior League of Scarsdale, 1976), 68–74; and *New York Times*, September 22 and 23, 1900.

98. Emily Olssen Bleecker, *A New York Lady: Memories of Emily Olssen Bleecker*, ed. James Rollinson Boulden (London: n.p., 2007), 61. See also *New York Times*, May 19, 1919, and November 26, 1937.

99. The phrase "metropolitan countryside" is from Adam Zalma.

100. Carol A. O'Connor, *A Sort of Utopia: Scarsdale, 1891–1981* (Albany: State University of New York Press, 1983), 2.

101. *New York Times*, November 18, 1928, March 30, 1943, May 1, 1949, March 5, 1952.

102. Harry Hansen, *Scarsdale: From Colonial Manor to Modern Community* (New York: Harper & Brothers, 1954), 1.

103. Ibid., 2.

104. Ibid., 2.

105. Michael Pollan, *Second Nature: A Gardner's Education* (New York: Grove, 1991), 1–4, 176–80.

106. Hansen, *Scarsdale*, 2.

107. Fred Lavis, *Thirty Years in Scarsdale: New Year's Greetings from Fred Lavis* (New York: n.p., 1946), 7; *New York Times*, November 26, 1950; O'Connor, *A Sort of Utopia*, 1–17, 124; "Scarsdale," in Eisenstadt, *Encyclopedia of New York State*, 1361; and Kenneth T. Jackson, *Crabgrass Frontier: The Suburbanization of the United States* (New York: Oxford University Press, 1985), 94–99.

108. O'Connor, *A Sort of Utopia*, 7.

109. *New York Times*, February 2, 1937, December 8, 1939, October 29, 1947, June 26, 1970; U.S. Department of Commerce, Bureau of the Census, Sixteenth Census of the United States: 1940, Population Schedule, Village of Scarsdale, Westchester County, N.Y., e.d. 60–344, pp. 63A, accessed June 23, 2012, http://searchancestrylibrary.com; MeasuringWorth.com, accessed July 29, 2013, www.measuringworth.com/uscompare /relativevalue.php. My calculations of the current values are based on the consumer price index. On servants, see "A Note on the Servant Problem," *Fortune* 9 (January 1934): 49.

110. U.S. Department of Commerce, Bureau of the Census, Sixteenth Census of the United States: 1940, Population Schedule, Village of Scarsdale, Westchester County, N.Y., e.d. 60–344, p. 7B, accessed June 26, 2012, http://searchancestrylibrary.com. See *New York Times*, February 12, 1947, for Hogate's obituary.

111. O'Connor, *A Sort of Utopia*, 1–15; Jackson, *Crabgrass Frontier*, 94–99; U.S. Department of Commerce, Bureau of the Census, *Seventeenth Decennial Census of the United States: 1950, Census of Population: 1950*, vol. 2, *Characteristics of the Population*, part 32, *New York* (Washington, D.C.: USGPO, 1952), tables 34, 35, 37, and 39; U.S. Department of Commerce, Bureau of the Census, *Seventeenth Decennial Census of the United States: 1950, Census of Housing: 1950*, vol. 1, *General Characteristics*, part 4, *Michigan–New York* (Washington, D.C.: USGPO, 1953), table 17; U.S. Department of Commerce, Bureau of the Census, *Seventeenth Decennial Census of the United States: 1950, Census of Population: 1950*, vol. 2, *Characteristics of the Population*, part 30, *New Jersey* (Washington, D.C.: USGPO, 1952), tables 34, 35, 37, and 39; and U.S. Department of

Commerce, Bureau of the Census, *Seventeenth Decennial Census of the United States: 1950, Census of Population: 1950*, vol. 2, *Characteristics of the Population*, part 7, *Connecticut* (Washington, D.C.: USGPO, 1952), tables 34, 35, 37, and 39. These comparisons exclude Greenwich and Westport, Conn. Instead of reporting data separately for Greenwich and Westport, the Census Bureau amalgamated it into the Stamford–Norwalk Standard Metropolitan Area.

112. *Bronxville Reporter*, May 22, 1946, March 6 and 26, April 17, and May 1, 1947, April 3 and May 6, 1948, October 11, 1949; *Larchmont Times*, April 7, 1938, February 22 and 29, March 7, July 18, and December 19, 1940, September 2 and 9 and December 16, 1943, May 30 and November 14, 1946; *Rye Chronicle*, December 22, 1939, October 4, 1946, September 19, 1947, May 5, 1949; *Bronxville Review-Press*, January 14, 1937, August 5 and 26, 1948; *New York Times*, August 13 and September 9, 1939, October 20, 1942, January 2, 1944, July 19, 1956. The elite working world was overwhelmingly male: 99.2% (N = 2,438) of those included in my study of elites (HHEP) were male and only 0.8% female (N = 20).

113. Quoted in Lucy Kavaler, *The Private World of High Society* (New York: McKay, 1960), 204.

114. Ibid., 204.

115. Ibid., 204. Kavaler observed that social elites in the suburbs could be more selective than was commonly thought. Tellingly, the examples that she cited of this exclusivity were the old-money suburbs on Long Island's North Shore, such as Locust Valley, Glen Cove, and Oyster Bay. Ibid., 210–18.

116. *New York Times*, January 2, 1944.

117. Among the senior staff of the Equitable Life Assurance Society in the late 1940s, Thomas I. Parkinson, the company's president, and Warner H. Mendel (with family money) were Manhattanites, while Merle A. Gulick and Ray D. Murphy resided in Montclair, N.J.; Dr. Edgar W. Beckwith in Bayside, Queens; Alvin B. Dalager in Great Neck, on Long Island; and Henry Greaves in Wilton, Conn. *New York Times*, February 25, 1964, October 24, 1967, March 4, 1969; U.S. Department of Commerce, Bureau of the Census, Sixteenth Census of the United States: 1940, Population Schedule, New York, New York e.d. 31–586, p. 61B, accessed July 30, 2012, http://searchancestrylibray.com; U.S. Department of Commerce, Bureau of the Census, Sixteenth Census of the United States: 1940, Population Schedule, Great Neck, Nassau County, New York State, e.d. 30–220, p. 9A, accessed July 30, 2012, http://searchancestrylibray.com; U.S. Department of Commerce, Bureau of the Census, Sixteenth Census of the United States: 1940, Population Schedule, Great Neck, Nassau County, New York State, e.d. 41–752, p. 1B, accessed July 30, 2012, http://searchancestrylibray.com; Hobart College, *Alumni Directory Number: An Alphabetic, Geographic, and Class Directory of the Alumni* (Geneva, N.Y.: Hobart College, 1940), 29; and Hobart College, *Alumnae Directory Number* (Geneva, N.Y.: Hobart and William Smith Colleges, 1949), 32.

118. N = 61. The sources for this statement are the same as those cited above in the study of the representation of corporate elites on museum boards.

119. U.S. Department of Commerce, Bureau of the Census, Sixteenth Census of the United States: 1940, Population Schedule, New York, New York County, New York State, e.d. 31–1324, p. 5A, accessed October 21, 2012, http://searchancestrylibray.com; U.S. Department of Commerce, Bureau of the Census, Sixteenth Census of the United States: 1940, Population Schedule, New York, New York County, New York State, e.d. 31–1263, p. 10B, accessed October 21, 2012, http://searchancestrylibray.com; and U.S. Department of Commerce, Bureau of the Census, Sixteenth Census of the United States: 1940, Population Schedule, New York, New York County, New York State, e.d. 31–1356, p. 8A, accessed October 21, 2012, http://searchancestrylibray.com.

120. *New York Times*, December 13, 1971; Watson and Petre, *Father, Son, & Co.*, 16–17, 37, 43–44, 76, 210–12, 272–75, 320; Baruch, *Baruch: My Own Story*, 103, 267–88; U.S. Department of Commerce, Bureau of the Census, Sixteenth Census of the United States: 1940, Population Schedule, New York, New York County, New York State, e.d. 31–1330, p. 1A, accessed October 21, 2012, http://searchancestrylibray.com; Paley, *As It Happened*, 86–88, 92–93, 187–88, 252, 359; Alan Brinkley, *The Publisher: Henry Luce and His American Century* (New York: Knopf, 2010), 206–08; Author's tour and photographs of Great Hill Road, Ridgefield, Conn., and Rock Rimmon Road, Stamford, Conn., December 19, 2012; Susan E. Tifft and Alex S. Jones, *The Trust: The Private and Powerful Family Behind the New York Times* (Boston: Little, Brown, 1999), 253–55; Iphigene Ochs Sulzberger, *Iphigene: Memoirs of Iphigene Ochs Sulzberger of the New York Times Family, as Told to Her Granddaughter, Susan W. Dryfoos* (New York: Dodd, Mead, 1981), 237–38.

121. Author's visit and photographs of houses on Morris Lane and Murray Hill Road, Scarsdale, N.Y., December 19, 2012; Author's visits and photographs of houses on Onondaga Street and Ridge Street, Rye, N.Y., December 19, 2012; G. M. Hopkins Company, *Atlas of Westchester County, New York*, vol. 1 (Philadelphia: Hopkins, 1929), sheet 36; Sanborn Map Company, *Insurance Maps of Scarsdale, NY* (New York: Sanborn Map, 1921), sheets 100 and 108; Digital Sanborn Maps, 1867–1970, Summit, N.J., July 1929–January 1950, sheet 37, accessed October 21, 2012, http://sanborn.umi.com/nj/5634; and Google Earth views of sites on Onondaga Street, Ridge Street, and Evergreen Avenue, Rye, N.Y., and Morris Lane, Scarsdale, N.Y., June 28, 2013.

122. Margaret Culkin Banning, *Country Club People* (New York: Doran, 1923), 9, 56.

123. *New York Times*, March 10, 1929, August 7, 1931, August 12, 1932, June 20, 1935, May 18, 1936, May 3, July 21, and December 18, 1941, July 22 and 31, 1946, July 11, 1948; *Rye Chronicle*, December 29, 1944, January 5 and 13, 1945; Radcliffe, *Simply Barbara Bush*, 89–92; Herbert S. Parmet, *George Bush: The Life of a Lone Star Yankee* (New York: Scribner, 1997), 43–44; and Bush, *Barbara Bush*, 16–24.

124. James M. Mayo, *The American Country Club: Its Origins and Development* (New Brunswick, N.J.: Rutgers University Press, 1998), 7–87; Richard J. Moss, *Golf and the American Country Club* (Urbana: University of Illinois Press, 2001), 5–42; Peter J. Schmitt, *Back to Nature: The Arcadian Myth in Urban America* (New York: Oxford

University Press, 1969), xv–xxiii; and Edwin Fairfax Naulty, "Country Clubs in the United States," *Town & Country* 58 (May 30, 1903): 12–14.

125. *Harper's Bazaar* 18 (June 26, 1885): 415.

126. *New York Times*, September 5, 1886, June 1, 1890.

127. Ripley Hitchcock, "Country Club Life," *The Chautaquan* 9 (July 1889): 601; Tuxedo Club, *Officers, Members, Constitution, Rules and History, 1936* (New York: n.p., 1936), 10–13; "The Trap," *Forest and Stream* 31 (November 8, 1888): 314; and *New York Times*, April 5, 1896.

128. *New York Times*, October 28, 1885, October 10 and 20, 1895, April 26 and May 24, 1896, March 28, 1898, August 5, 1903, May 5, 1911, February 19, 1922, March 31, 1925; "Golfing Around New York," *Town & Country* 66 (July 9, 1910): 47; Mayo, *The American Country Club*, 64–87; Ripley Hitchcock, "The Return to the Country, in Two Parts, Part 1," *Christian Union* 39 (June 27, 1889): 816; *Golf Clubs of the MGA: A Centennial History of Golf in the New York Metropolitan Area* (Elmsford, N.Y.: Golf Magazine Properties, 1997), 66; and "Louis Keller and the Social Register," *Town & Country* 59 (October 1, 1904): 17.

129. George B. Kirsch, *Golf in America* (Urbana: University of Illinois Press, 2009), 6; "Popularity of Golf: The Old Scottish Game," *Current Literature* 16 (September 1894): 238; and *A History of the Montclair Golf Club: A Way of Life, 1893–1983* (Montclair, N.J.: Montclair Golf Club, 1983), 49–53.

130. J. Lewis Brown, "The Growth of American Golf," *Outlook* 136 (April 23, 1924): 688. See also Moss, *Golf and the American Country Club*, 6, 1931; and *New York Times*, July 14, 1929.

131. Sinclair Lewis, *Babbitt* (New York: Harcourt, Brace, 1922; repr., New York: Bantam, 1998); Sinclair Lewis, *Main Street* (New York: Grosset & Dunlap, 1920); and Booth Tarkington, *Alice Adams* (Garden City, N.Y.: Doubleday, Page, 1921).

132. Mayo, *The American Country Club*, 192–94; Kirsch, *Golf in America*, 98–103; Peter Levine, "'Our Crowd' at Play: The Elite Jewish Country Club in the 1920s," in *Sports and the American Jew*, ed. Stephen A. Riess (Syracuse: Syracuse University Press, 1998), 160–84; Ebner, *Creating Chicago's North Shore*, 220–24, 236–37; Stephen Hardy, *How Boston Played: Sport, Recreation, and Community, 1865–1915* (Knoxville, Tenn.: University of Tennessee Press, 2003), 139–46; and *Golf Clubs of the MGA*, 249, 256, 276. On Irish American ties to Winged Foot, see *New York Times*, April 29, 1926, October 30, 1935, December 26, 1937, December 25, 1940, April 8 and November 28, 1942, July 16 and August 3, 1947, October 7, 1951, July 1, 1952, February 11, 1954, August 5, 1958. For the cultural predisposition of Irish American elites to resist feelings and displays of social pretension, see Kerby A. Miller, *Emigrants and Exiles: Ireland and the Irish Exodus to North America* (New York: Oxford University Press, 1985), 495–99, 518–20. African American elites had more limited financial resources than white elites, but a pioneering African American country club operated in Scotch Plains, N.J., in the 1920s and 1930s. *Newark Star-Ledger*, February 19, 2009.

133. *Fifty Years of Apawamis* (Rye, N.Y.: n.p., 1940), 15, 45, 82–84, 102–03; Pelham Country Club, *Constitution, Golf Privileges, Rules and Regulations; Officers and Committees, List of Members* (Pelham, N.Y.: n.p., 1930), 16–18; Moss, *Golf and the American Country Club*, 183–92; Margery Wilson, *The New Etiquette: The Modern Code of Social Behavior* (New York: Stokes, 1937), 561; Harold J. Cliffer, *Planning the Golf Clubhouse* (Chicago: National Golf Foundation, 1956), 11–32, 41, 49, 54–55.

134. *Rye Chronicle*, July 7 and December 29, 1939, April 26, 1940, June 27, 1947, August 8, 1948, May 12, 1949; *Larchmont Times*, January 6 and May 16, 1938; *New York Times*, January 26 and 27, February 3, 23, and 24, and September 8, 1946, January 5, September 14, November 30, 1947, May 2, 1948; *Golf Clubs of the MGA*, 50–53, 216–19; Kirsch, *Golf in America*, 85–108; and Moss, *Golf and the American Country Club*, 39–41.

135. Kavaler, *The Private World of High Society*, xii–xiii.

136. Anthony F. Merrill, *The Golf Course Guide* (New York: Crowell, 1950), 42–43, 219–29. See also *Golf Clubs of the MGA.*.

137. Charles W. Kaiser, comp., *Locust Valley: 1776–1976* (New York: Rotary Club of Locust Valley, N.Y., 1976), 87; and Egerton Swartout, "Review of Recent Architectural Magazines," *The American Architect and Architectural Review* 126 (October 24, 1924): 383.

138. *Portland Oregonian*, January 18, 1921; and Dixon Wecter, *The Saga of American Society: A Record of Social Aspiration, 1607–1937* (New York: Scribner's, 1937), 274. See also Charles G. Shaw, "Olives and His Mother Were the Only Things He Loved," *Vanity Fair* 22 (June 1924): 40.

139. *Piping Rock Club* (New York: n.p., 1939), 14–41, 67–71. Trippe, Cravath, and both Dulles brothers were listed in the Social Register. *Social Register, 1949*, 166, 222, 758; H. J. Whigham, "The New Creek Golf Club," *Town & Country* 50 (February 1, 1923): 34–35; "Society Lingers in New York," *Vogue* 59 (June 15, 1922): 38–39; and "The Annual Horse Show at Piping Rock Was Among the Many Outdoor Events That Attracted Smart Society During the Autumn," *Vogue* 64 (December 1, 1924): 71.

140. *Book of the Apawamis Club, Rye, New York: Certificate of Incorporation; Constitution; By-Laws; House Rules; Golf Regulations; Tennis Regulations; Squash Regulations; Officers; List of Members* (Rye, N.Y.: n.p., 1934), 50–62.

141. *Fifty Years of Apawamis*, 1, 40.

142. Ibid., 1–2, 40, 82–83, 102–03, 143; and *Rye Chronicle*, October 18 and 25, 1940, and March 7, 1947.

143. *New York Times*, May 25, June 29, July 2, and August 30, 1929, August 10, 1946. Moneyworth.com, accessed July 12, 2012, www.measuringworth.com/growth. I use the historic standard of living as my measure of changes in relative value over time. *By-laws, House Rules, Officers and Members of the Rumson Country Club 1926* (Rumson, N.J.: n.p., 1926), 17–18; *Book of the Apawamis Club*, 14–15, 24–25; *Piping Rock Club* (New York: n.p., 1939), 67–71; and Pelham Country Club, *Constitution, Golf Privileges, Rules and Regulations; Officers and Committees, List of Members* (Pelham, N.Y.: n.p., 1930), 14–18.

144. Parents could choose from several types of private schools—boarding schools like Phillips Exeter, Lawrenceville, and Foxcroft; country day schools like Riverdale and Horace Mann; and day schools such as Brearley, Spence, and Collegiate—and hundreds of individual schools. Charlotte Johnson Noerdlinger, *And Cheer for the Green and Gold: An Anecdotal History of the Chapin School* (New York: n.p., 2000), 7–9; Jean Parker Waterbury, *A History of Collegiate School, 1638–1968* (New York: n.p., 1965), 123–37; *Browning School: Fiftieth Anniversary, 1888–1938* (New York: n.p., 1938), 7–32; R. A. McCardell, ed., *The Country Day School: History, Curriculum, Philosophy of Horace Mann School* (Dobbs Ferry, N.Y.: Oceana, 1962), 13–44; *The First 125 Years: The Brearley School* (New York: n.p., 2010), 140–63; Roland J. Mulford, *History of the Lawrenceville School, 1810–1935* (Princeton, N.J.: Princeton University Press, 1935), 3, 184–201; Arthur Stanwood Pier, *St. Paul's School, 1855–1954* (New York: Scribner's, 1934), 359–60; Allen Hackett, *Quickened Spirit: A Biography of Frank Sutliff Hackett* (New York: n.p., 1957), 53–57; and *The Handbook of Private Schools: An Annual Descriptive Survey of Independent Education, 2002*, 83rd ed. (Boston: Porter Sargent, 2002).

145. *The Phillips Exeter Academy Alumni Directory: A Catalogue of All Living Graduates and Non-Graduates; Also, the Trustees of the Phillips Exeter Academy, the Officers of the Phillips Exeter Alumni Association and Branch Associations, the Faculty and Other Officers of the School, 1940* (Exeter, NH: n.p., 1940), 200–40.

146. An examination of the 68 graduates who resided in Scarsdale and Rye that year shows that they overwhelmingly belonged to the corporate elite. Of the 53 who could be identified, nine in 10 had jobs that put them in the corporate elite, with their leading fields being manufacturing, investment banking, stock brokering, law, and advertising (N = 48). Although three men who had risen to partnerships in investment banks were clearly wealthy, the highest position that the rest reached was typically vice president—for instance, one retired as executive vice president at the advertising firm BBDO, another as first vice president of Smith Barney, and five others as vice presidents of Chemical Bank, Manufacturers Hanover, Irving Trust, a specialty steel company, and an insurance brokerage (N = 14). My findings are based on an examination of these sources: *New York Times*; U.S. Department of Commerce, Bureau of the Census, Fifteenth Census of the United States: 1930, Population Schedule, New York State, Westchester County, Rye Village, ED 60–340, p 4b, accessed July 13, 2013, http://interactive.ancestrylibrary.com; U.S. Department of Commerce, Bureau of the Census, Fifteenth Census of the United States: 1930, Population Schedule, New York State, Westchester County, Eastchester, ED 60–136, p 26A, accessed July 13, 2013, http://interactive.ancestrylibrary.com; U.S. Department of Commerce, Bureau of the Census, Sixteenth Census of the United States: 1940, Population Schedule, New York State, Westchester County, Rye Village, ED 60–334, Sheet 8a, accessed July 13, 2013, http://interactive.ancestrylibrary.com; U.S. Department of Commerce, Bureau of the Census, Sixteenth Census of the United States: 1940, Population Schedule, New York State, New York County, ED 31–848, Sheet 81a, accessed July 13, 2013, http://interactive.ancestrylibrary.com; U.S. Department of Commerce, Bureau

of the Census, Sixteenth Census of the United States: 1940, Population Schedule, New York State, Westchester County, Rye Village, ED 60–329, Sheet 10a, accessed July 13, 2013, http://interactive.ancestrylibrary.com; U.S. Department of Commerce, Bureau of the Census, Sixteenth Census of the United States: 1940, Population Schedule, New York State, Westchester County, Pelham Manor, ED 60–297, Sheet 12A, accessed July 13, 2013, http://interactive.ancestrylibrary.com; U.S. Department of Commerce, Bureau of the Census, Sixteenth Census of the United States: 1940, Population Schedule, New York State, Westchester County, Scarsdale, ED 60–338, Sheet 10a, accessed July 13, 2013, http://interactive.ancestrylibrary.com; U.S. Department of Commerce, Bureau of the Census, Sixteenth Census of the United States: 1940, Population Schedule, New York State, Westchester County, Scarsdale, ED 60–338, Sheet 12A, accessed July 13, 2013, http://interactive.ancestrylibrary.com. U.S. Department of Commerce, Bureau of the Census, Sixteenth Census of the United States: 1940, Population Schedule, Connecticut, Litchfield County, Washington, ED 3–68, Sheet 11A, , accessed July 13, 2013, http://interactive.ancestrylibrary.com; Connecticut Death Index, 1949–2001, State File 90579, accessed July 13, 2013, http://interactive.ancestrylibrary.com; U.S. Department of Commerce, Bureau of the Census, Sixteenth Census of the United States: 1940, Population Schedule, New York State, Westchester County, Scarsdale, ED 60–345, Sheet 5a, accessed July 13, 2013, http://interactive.ancestrylibrary.com; United Kingdom, Outward Passenger Lists, 1890–1960, for Mauretania, June 4, 1927, at Southampton, accessed July 13, 2013, http://interactive.ancestrylibrary.com; Greenwich, Conn., City Directory, 1941: 315, U.S. City Directories, 1821–1989, accessed July 13, 2013, http://interactive.ancestrylibrary.com; and U.S. Army World War II Enlistment Records, 1938–1946, 20273365, date of enlistment, November 13, 1940, accessed July 13, 2013, http://interactive.ancestrylibrary.com.

147. Wecter, *The Saga of American Society*, 241.

148. "Life at Phillips Exeter," *Bulletin of the Phillips Exeter Academy* 9 (October 1913): 19, 36. See also the Hotchkiss School, *Catalogue, 1932–1933* (Lakeville, Conn.: n.p., 1932), 9.

149. Christopher F. Armstrong, "On the Making of Good Men: Character-Building in the New England Boarding Schools," in Paul W. Kingston and Lionel S. Lewis, eds., *The High Status Track: Studies of Elite Schools and Stratification* (Albany: State University of New York Press, 1990), 3–24. See also Frank D. Ashburn, "The Training of Americans: What Our Educational System Is Doing for Character," in *Education and The Faith of America: Addresses Given During the Centennial Celebration of the Packer Collegiate Institute* (Brooklyn, N.Y.: n.p., 1945), 17.

150. Jerome Karabel, *The Chosen: The Hidden History of Admission and Exclusion at Harvard, Yale, and Princeton* (Boston: Houghton Mifflin, 2005), 2. See also Bledstein, *The Culture of Professionalism*, 129–58; Harold S. Wechsler, *The Qualified Student: A History of Selective College Admission in America* (New York: Wiley, 1977), vii–xii; Marcia Graham Synnott, *The Half-Opened Door: Discrimination and Admissions at Harvard, Yale,*

and Princeton, 1900–1970 (Westport, Conn.: Greenwood, 1979), 3–25; and Dan A. Oren, *Joining the Club: A History of Jews and Yale* (New Haven, Conn.: Yale University Press, 1985), ix–xiv, 41–42, 51–63.

151. Karabel, *The Chosen*, 2.

152. Ibid., 2. See also Richard Hofstadter, *Anti-intellectualism in American Life* (New York: Knopf, 1962), 3–23.

153. Karabel, *The Chosen*, 1–38; 184–97; "Report on the Special Committee on Limitations of Enrollment, Presented to the University Faculty, Monday, March 14, 1921," Folder 2, Box 1, Series 1, Admissions Office Records, Seeley G. Mudd Manuscript Library, Princeton University, Princeton, N.J.; and *Princeton Packet*, November 1, 1972.

154. Owen Johnson, *Stover at Yale* (New York: Grosset & Dunlap, 1912), 1–5, 59–66, 80–85, 110–41, 335–86.

155. John Morton Blum, *A Life with History* (Lawrence: University Press of Kansas, 2004), 4. At Andover, Blum says that Jews were admitted but were "not yet first-class citizens," and there were no Jews and apparently no Catholics on the faculty. Ibid., 4.

156. Johnson, *Stover at Yale*, 295. For a real-life account of this college world, see Louis Auchincloss, *A Voice from Old New York: A Memoir of My Youth* (Boston: Houghton Mifflin Harcourt, 2010), 39–42, 62–80, 95–98.

157. *The Graham School* (New York: n.p., 1914), 3.

158. *Graham School*, 19–23; *A Handbook of American Private Schools: An Annual Survey*, 9th ed. (Boston: Porter Sargent, 1924), 133–41, 217–25; and Gretchen Finletter, *From the Top of the Stairs* (Boston: Little, Brown, 1946), 34–46.

159. *Miss Ann Falconer Perrin's School for Girls, New York City* (New York: n.p., 1891), 4.

160. *Handbook of American Private Schools*, 133–41, 217–25; *Brearley Book*, vol. 10 (New York: Abbey, 1930), 8–29.

161. Chapin School, *The Wheel* 21 (May 1936): 45–72; *Handbook of American Private Schools*, 219.

162. Chapin School, *The Wheel* 21 (May 1936): 45–72. The school changed its name to the Chapin School in 1934. Chapin School website, School History Page, accessed July 10, 2014, www.chapin.edu/page.cfm?p=302.

8. THE ANTIELITIST ELITE

1. Quoted in *Rye Chronicle*, June 25, 1970.

2. Allen J. Matusow, *The Unraveling of America: A History of Liberalism in the 1960s* (New York: Harper & Row, 1984), 275–307.

3. *Rye Chronicle*, June 25, 1970.

4. *Rye Chronicle*, June 25, 1970, July 22, 1971, April 4, 1974, May 22, 1975; *Tarrytown Daily News*, April 13, 1968; and *New York Times*, July 22, 1993.

5. Daniel J. Singal, "Towards a Definition of American Modernism," *American Quarterly* 39 (Spring 1987): 7–26; Lewis Erenberg, *Steppin' Out: New York Nightlife and the Transformation of American Culture, 1890–1930* (Chicago: University of Chicago

Press, 1981), xi–xv. The modernism that I am referencing here as a response to Victorianism should not be confused with the modernist movement in literature and art in the early twentieth century, which involved the tendency of experimental writers and artists to break away from traditional verse forms, narrative techniques, and other conventions to obtain new modes of representation more suitable to an urban-industrial society. Pericles Lewis, *The Cambridge Introduction to Modernism* (Cambridge: Cambridge University Press, 2007), xvii–xviii.

6. Singal, "Towards a Definition of American Modernism," 7–26; Edward D. Berkowitz, *Something Happened: A Political and Cultural Overview of the Seventies* (New York: Columbia University Press, 2006), 133–37; William L. O'Neill, *Coming Apart: An Informal History of America in the 1960's* (Chicago: Quadrangle, 1971), 200–27; *Scarsdale Inquirer*, February 6, 1975; *New York Times*, May 5, 1974, November 18, 1980; Kathy Davis, *The Making of "Our Bodies, Ourselves": How Feminism Travels Across Borders* (Durham, N.C.: Duke University Press, 2007), 1–15; and Thomas Weyr, *Reaching for Paradise: The Playboy Vision of America* (New York: Times Books, 1978), 55–66.

7. Singal, "Towards a Definition of American Modernism," 7–26; Berkowitz, *Something Happened*, 133–37; Bruce J. Schulman, *The Seventies: The Great Shift in American Culture, Society and Politics* (Cambridge, Mass.: Da Capo, 2002), 1–20; Jefferson Cowie, *Stayin' Alive: The 1970s and the Last Days of the Working Class* (New York: New Press, 2010), 1–19.

8. Erenberg, *Steppin' Out*, xi–xv, 233–59; Pitts Sanborn, "Jazz Worship," *The Independent* 112 (May 10, 1924): 262; and Mitzi Kolisch, "Jazz in High Places: Part I," *The Independent* 116 (April 10, 1926): 424. For a first-person account of the allure that jazz had for upper-class New Yorkers before World War I, see Gretchen Finletter, *From the Top of the Stairs* (Boston: Little, Brown, 1946), 73–74. For a first-person account of the upper class's embrace of jazz at a later time, see Peter Duchin, with Charles Michener, *Ghost of a Chance: A Memoir* (New York: Random House, 1996). I owe Marcelle Empey, William Smith class of 2009, for the observation about the upper class and jazz.

9. "New York Life: Local Color," *Life* 94 (July 19, 1929): 22.

10. Duchin, *Ghost of a Chance*, 282–84; Will Hermes, *Love Goes to Buildings on Fire: Five Years in New York That Changed Music Forever* (New York: Faber and Faber, 2011), 134–45.

11. Grace Elizabeth Hale, *A Nation of Outsiders: How the White Middle Class Fell in Love with Rebellion in Postwar America* (New York: Oxford University Press, 2011), 1.

12. Ibid., 1–10, 74–83;

13. Berkowitz, *Something Happened*, 133.

14. Ibid., 133–57.

15. Sandra Stern and Sigrid Brownwood, letter to the editor, *Scarsdale Inquirer*, February 25, 1971; Barbara A. Truex, letter to the editor, *Rye Chronicle*, April 23, 1970; *Rye Chronicle*, February 19 and March 19, 1970; and *Scarsdale Inquirer*, November 14, 1968, May 8, 1969.

16. *New York Times*, May 6, 1971, June 4, 1972.

17. *Rye Chronicle*, September 10, 1970. See also *Rye Chronicle*, May 24, 1969 and April 2, 1970.

18. *Rye Chronicle*, April 11, 1968.

19. *Scarsdale Inquirer*, July 18, September 19 and 26, and November 14, 1968, May 15, 1969, June 11, 1970; *Rye Chronicle*, November 14, 1968.

20. *New York Times*, April 8, 1968.

21. Tom Wolfe, "Radical Chic: That Party at Lenny's," *New York* 2 (June 8, 1970): 26–56; *New York Times*, January 15 and 16 and July 13, 1970, August 14, 1999, October 27, 2007; Felice M. Bernstein, letter to the editor, *New York Times*, January 21, 1968; and Spencer Morgan, "The Mortimer Family," *New York Observer*, December 18, 2006.

22. Martha Biondi, *The Black Revolution on Campus* (Berkeley: University of California Press, 2012): 1–12.

23. Kate Shnayerson, letter to the editor, *The Zephyr* 9 (November–December 1975): 2. See also Zanthe Taylor, "Student Publications," in *The First 125 Years: The Brearley School* (New York: n.p., 2010), 278–85.

24. Unsigned letter to the editor, *The Zephyr* 5 (September 27, 1971): 2.

25. Lynne Green, "Blacks and Whites Clash: To All the Phonies," *The Zephyr* 11 (April 1978): 2.

26. Ibid., 2.

27. Quoted in Sophie Glazer, "Sophie Glazer's Apology," *The Zephyr* 11 (April 1978): 3.

28. Green, "Blacks and Whites Clash," 2.

29. C. Wright Mills, *The Power Elite* (New York: Oxford University Press, 1956); G. William Domhoff, *Who Rules America?* (New York: Englewood Cliffs, N.J.: Prentice-Hall, 1967); Domhoff, *The Higher Circles: The Governing Class in America* (New York: Random House, 1970); *Washington Post*, June 22, 1969, August 17, 1975; *New York Times*, November 21, 1971, May 4 and September 11, 1975 September 6, 1980; Cornelia K. Wyatt, "The 'Guilted' Age," *Town & Country* 125 (April 1971): 61, 113, 119, 134; and "The Junior League: Less Noblesse, More Oblige," *Town & Country* 129 (August 1975): 47–49, 26–27, 100.

30. *Rye Chronicle*, June 25, 1970. In 1970 Rye High School responded to the tumult of social protests by adopting the phrase "privilege with responsibility" as its programmatic theme in 1970.

31. Stuart M. Blumin, *The Emergence of the Middle Class: Social Experience in the American City, 1760–1900* (New York: Cambridge University Press, 1989), 1–16, 285–90; Schulman, *The Seventies*, 68–72; and Joseph F. Kett, *Merit: The History of a Founding Ideal from the American Revolution to the Twenty-First Century* (Ithaca, N.Y.: Cornell University Press, 2013), 1–14.

32. In *Bobos in Paradise*, David Brooks portrays the formation of a new upper class of highly educated professionals who, he says, have a hybrid culture because they have "one foot in the bohemian world of creativity and another foot in the bourgeois realm of ambition and worldly success." David Brooks, *Bobos in Paradise: The New Upper Class and How They Got There* (New York: Simon & Schuster, 2000), 11. Although

I also employ the term "hybrid" to describe a comparable elite group, I am concerned about a different matter than Brooks is, namely, elites' ability to move seamlessly between upper- and middle-class worlds that remain discrete and the uses to which they put that capability.

33. Ira Rosenwaike, *Population History of New York City* (Syracuse, N.Y.: Syracuse University Press, 1972), 131–39; Campbell Gibson, *Population of the 100 Largest Cities and Other Urban Places in the United States: 1790 to 1990*, Population Division Working Paper No. 27 (Washington, D.C.: U.S. Bureau of the Census, Population Division, 1998), tables 16, 17, 20, and 21, accessed April 19, 2010, www.census.gov/population/www/documentation/twps0027.html. "Population of New York Region by Decade in Twentieth Century," a spreadsheet compiled by the Regional Plan Association, email from Jeffrey Zupan to author, April 21, 2010.

34. Edward N. Costikyan to Daniel Patrick Moynihan, June 28, 1977, catalogued correspondence, Edward N. Costikyan Papers, Rare Book and Manuscript Library, Columbia University, New York, NY; and "Gotham's Shrinking," *New York Times*, February 5, 1979.

35. Roger Starr, *The Rise and Fall of New York City* (New York: Basic, 1985), 185–203, 223–41; Charles R. Morris, *The Cost of Good Intentions: New York City and the Liberal Experiment* (New York: Norton, 1980), 11–33; and Robert Fitch, *The Assassination of New York* (London: Verso, 1993), vii–xxi. See also Vincent J. Cannato, *The Ungovernable City: John Lindsay and His Struggle to Save New York City* (New York: Basic, 2001), ix–xv. Scholars commonly understand the concept "urban decline" to involve combined processes of depopulation, deindustrialization, chronic unemployment, social disintegration, building abandonment, and infrastructure decay. Katharine L. Bradbury, Kenneth A. Small, and Anthony Downs, *Urban Decline and the Future of American Cities* (Washington, D.C.: Brookings Institution, 1982), 18–67.

36. Miriam Greenberg, *Branding New York: How a City in Crisis Was Sold to the World* (New York: Routledge, 2008), 3–17; "Press Conference No. 23 of the President of the United States, 7:30 P.M., November 26, 1975," New York City Finances, President's Press Conference, November 26, 1975 Folder, Box 19, Edward C. Schmultz Files, Gerald R. Ford Library, Ann Arbor, Mich. [hereafter GRFL]; Ronald H. Nessen, "News Conference #363," October 31, 1975 (#363) Folder, Box 14, Ronald H. Nessen Files, Ford Library; Ronald H. Nessen, "News Conference #376," November 19, 1975 (#376) Folder, Box 14, Nessen Files, GRFL; NBC News, Transcript of "Meet the Press" broadcast of November 2, 1975, Meet the Press—November 2, 1975 Folder, Box 70, Nessen Files, GRFL; NBC News, Transcript of "Meet the Press," December 7, 1975, Meet the Press—December 7, 1975 Folder, Box 70, Nessen Files, GRFL; CBS News, Transcript of "Face the Nation" broadcast of November 2, 1975, Face the Nation—November 2, 1975 Folder, Box 64, Nessen Papers, GRFL.

37. "Press Conference #23 of the President of the United States, 7:30 P.M., November 26, 1975," New York City Finances, President's Press Conference, November 26, 1975 Folder, Box 19, Edward C. Schmultz Files, GRFL; Statement by the President,

November 26, 1975, New York City—President's Statement, November 26, 1775 Folder, Box 16, Nessen Files, GRFL; *New York Times,* October 10 and 18, and November 14 and 18, 1975; and *Wall Street Journal,* November 28, 1975.

38. *New York Times,* April 6 and May 12, 1977, June 14 and December 22, 1978; Area Consultants, "Corporate Office Migration from New York City," rev. ed., November 11, 1970, 1–6, Corporations Folder, Box 459, Bella S. Abzug Papers, Rare Book and Manuscript Library, Columbia University, New York, N.Y.; and Stanley Buder, "Corporate Headquarters," in *The Encyclopedia of New York City,* 2nd ed., ed. Kenneth T. Jackson (New Haven, Conn.: Yale University Press, 2010), 134–35.

39. *New York Times,* October 6, 1977, March 23, and August 4 and 6, 1980; and *Washington Post,* October 6. 1977.

40. *Washington Post,* October 13, 1977; *New York Times,* March 30, 2005. See also Jonathan Mahler, *Ladies and Gentlemen, the Bronx Is Burning: 1977, Baseball, Politics, and the Battle for the Soul of a City* (New York: Picador, 2006), 330–31.

41. *Washington Post,* February 13, 1981; and *New York Times,* July 10, 1981.

42. Matthew Drennan, "Economy," in Jackson, *Encyclopedia of New York City,* 397–400; Norman J. Brouwer, "Port of New York," in Jackson, *Encyclopedia of New York City,* 1022–26; and U.S. Department of Commerce, Bureau of the Census, *Sixteenth Census of the United States: 1940, Manufactures: 1939,* vol. 3, *Reports for States and Outlying Areas* (Washington, D.C.: U.S. Government Printing Office, 1942), 108, 264, 412, 496, 718, 806, 900, and 904.

43. Drennan, "Economy," in Jackson, *Encyclopedia of New York City,* 362; U.S. Department of Commerce, Census Bureau, *Census 2000, American Factfinder,* Table DP–3, Profile of Selected Economic Characteristics: 2000, Data Set: Census 2000 Summary File 3 (SF 3)—Sample Data, for New York, New York, accessed January 21, 2010, http://factfinder.census.gov/home/saff/main.html?_lang=en; *New York Times,* February 15 and June 15, 1948; Brouwer, "Port of New York," 926–29; and American Association of Port Authorities, "Port Industry Statistics [Online]," table for World Port Rankings—2007 and table for 2008 U.S. Port Cargo Rankings, accessed January 20, 2010, www.aapa-ports.org/Industry/content.cfm?ItemNumber=900&navItem Number=551#Statistics?.

44. Drennan, "Economy," 398–400; and Samuel M. Ehrenhalt, "Some Perspectives on the New York City Economy in a Time of Change," in *New York City's Changing Economic Base,* ed. Benjamin J. Klebaner (New York: Universe, 1981), 6-32.

45. *Wall Street Journal,* January 2, 1980, December 31, 1989, January 2, 1990; *New York Times,* December 23 and 31, 1999, January 3, 8, and 15, 2000; and *Wall Street & Technology,* April 16, 2010, accessed May 27, 2011, www.wallstreetandtech.com/career -management/showArticle.jhtml?articleID=224400491.

46. "The Fortunate 100, *Crain's New York Business* 5 (June 19, 1989): 30–31; "Cravath Swaine Sets Pace with Pay Hikes for Associates," *Crain's New York Business* 3 (November 23, 1987): 16–17; and "New York's Largest Law Firms," *Crain's New York Business* 11 (October 30, 1995): 18–19. Moneyworth.com, accessed June 11, 2015,

www.measuringworth.com/uscompare/relativevalue.php. I use the historic standard of living to measure changes in relative value over time.

47. Gibson, *Population of the 100 Largest Cities and Other Urban Places in the United States: 1790 to 1990*, tables 18 and 22; D. W. Meinig, *The Shaping of America: A Geographical Perspective on 500 Years of History*, vol. 4 *Global America, 1915–2000* (New Haven, Conn.: Yale University Press, 2004), 247–87; and Rosenwaike, *Population History of New York City*, 131–39. See also Carl Abbott, *How Cities Won the West: Four Centuries of Urban Change in Western North America* (Albuquerque: University of New Mexico Press, 2008), 163–85; and David R. Goldfield, *Cotton Fields and Skyscrapers: Southern City and Region, 1607–1980* (Baton Rouge: Louisiana State University Press, 1982), 139–96.

48. *New York Times*, January 1, 1981, May 15 and July 22, 1981, April 25 and 29 and May 14 and 20, 1987; and Buder, "Corporate Headquarters," 134–35.

49. "The Forbes 400," *Forbes* (September 13, 1982): 100–60; and "The Forbes 400 Richest Americans 2009," *Forbes* (September 30, 2009), accessed April 22, 2010, www.forbes .com/lists/2009/54/rich-list-09_The-400-Richest-Americans_Rank_3.html. There were 85 New Yorkers on *Forbes*'s 1982 list and 56 on its 2009 list.

50. "The Forbes 400 Richest Americans 2009," *Forbes*. These listings are for principal residences.

51. This regional shift has had a powerful effect in the realm of high culture. Generous donations from Los Angeles philanthropists have allowed world-class artistic venues such as the Getty Center and the Walt Disney Concert Hall to open and older institutions like the Los Angeles Museum of Contemporary Art to be reconstructed. Multimillionaires have built performance halls and museums in Fort Worth, Dallas, Kansas City, San Diego, and Seattle, while the most improbable legacy of this wealth dispersion may be Crystal Bridges, the $1.2 billion museum of American art that a Wal-Mart heir has unveiled in remote Bentonville, Arkansas. Although these projects have elevated the quality of cultural life in their cities, much of that money would almost certainly have gone into further enhancements of New York City's cultural scene in a previous age when wealth was more tightly concentrated. Meinig, *The Shaping of America*, 4: 247–87; *New York Times*, April 24, 2002, March 31 and May 20, 2004, April 6 and September 26, 2007, June 18, 2011; and *Wall Street Journal*, November 11, 2011.

52. The wealthiest five New Yorkers from *Forbes*'s 2009 list were Michael R. Bloomberg, who attained his wealth in financial news services before becoming mayor in 2001; David R. Koch (petroleum and gas); Carl Icahn (leveraged buyouts); Ronald Perelman (leveraged buyouts); and John Paulson (hedge funds). "The Forbes 400 Richest Americans 2009," *Forbes*. The Upper East Side remains the single wealthiest neighborhood in the country and Greenwich, Purchase, and Bedford Hills are among its wealthiest suburbs. Internal Revenue Service, Statistics of Income, *SOI Tax Stats: Top Wealthholders by State of Residence*, accessed January 13, 2012, www.irs.gov/uac/SOI-Tax-Stats-Top-Wealthholders -by-State-of-Residence.

53. Meinig, *The Shaping of America*, 4: 247–87; *New York Times*, April 24, 2002, March 31 and May 20, 2004, April 6 and September 26, 2007, June 18, 2011; and *Wall Street Journal*, November 11, 2011.

54. Cornelia K. Wyatt, "Boredom: The Year of the Yawn," *Town & Country* 124 (January 1970): 86.

55. Ibid., 86.

56. Wyatt, "The 'Guilted' Age," 61.

57. Ibid., 61.

58. Ibid., 61.

59. Ibid., 113, 119, 134.

60. Dick Miller, "Genealogical Societies: Running Up (and Down) Your Ancestors," *Town & Country* 129 (January 1975): 58.

61. Quoted in ibid., 135.

62. *New York Times*, July 5, 1970.

63. Kathryn Livingston, "To Be or Not to Be a Debutante," *Town & Country* 124 (June 1970): 98.

64. "The Junior League: Less Noblesse, More Oblige," 26–27, 47–49, 100.

65. Sarah E. Igo, *The Averaged American: Surveys, Citizens, and the Making of a Mass Public* (Cambridge, Mass.: Harvard University Press, 2007), 1–22; and Lizabeth Cohen, *A Consumers' Republic: The Politics of Mass Consumption in Postwar America* (New York: Knopf, 2003), 292–344.

66. Degler, *Affluence and Anxiety*, 182.

67. Anna G. Creadick, *Perfectly Average: The Pursuit of Normality in Postwar America* (Amherst: University of Massachusetts Press, 2010), 1–9, 42–68.

68. In his 1990 film *Metropolitan*, Whit Stillman followed a group of young upper-class New Yorkers during the Christmas debutante season. They are caught between the refined standards of their set and the crasser and more competitive mass society, and several of them acknowledge feeling doomed to failure in their lives, an impression that the dark and claustrophobic interiors where much of the action takes place heightens. Although Edith Wharton dwelled on the decay of the old upper class in her fiction earlier in the century, film's status as a popular medium gave this message special poignancy in *Metropolitan*. *Metropolitan* (New Line Cinema, 1990), a film written, produced, and directed by Whit Stillman; and Joseph Aulis, "In Defense of Virtue: Whit Stillman's *Metropolitan*," in *Doomed Bourgeois in Love: Essays on the Films of Whit Stillman*, ed. Mark C. Henrie (Wilmington, Del.: ISI, 2001), 63-83.

69. Wendy Burden, *Dead End Gene Pool: A Memoir* (New York: Gotham, 2010).

70. Ibid., 5.

71. Ibid., 1–8, 95–96, 235–40, 264–79.

72. Philip Van Rensselaer, *Rich Was Better: A Memoir* (New York: Wynwood, 1990), 7–10, 32, 79, 178, 297, and 309.

73. Eve Pell, *We Used to Own the Bronx: Memoirs of a Former Debutante* (Albany: State University of New York Press, 2009), xii.

74. Ibid., xii.

75. Ibid., xiii.

76. Alexandra Aldrich, *The Astor Orphan: A Memoir* (New York: Ecco, 2013), 10. For Aldrich's account of her family's alcoholism and mental illness, see pp. 66–67, 82–83, 114–115, 122–23, and 144. Arthur T. Vanderbilt II has also written about his own family's decline in *Fortune's Children: The Fall of the House of Vanderbilt* (New York: HarperCollins, 1989).

77. Pell, *We Used to Own the Bronx*, xiii.

78. Ibid., xiii.

79. Ibid., 197.

80. Ibid., 145.

81. Ibid., 142–213.

82. Pell, *We Used to Own The Bronx*, 46–53; Tad Friend, *Cheerful Money: Me, My Family, and the Last Days of Wasp Splendor* (New York: Little, Brown, 2009), 9–12, 46–48, 183–84, 203–05; and Aldrich, *The Astor Orphan*, 26–27, 202, 246. For other recent memoirs that similarly emphasize upper-class pathologies, see Millicent Monks, *Songs of Three Islands: A Story of Mental Illness in an Iconic American Family* (New York: Atlas, 2010); Maisie Houghton, *Pitch Uncertain: A Mid-century Middle Daughter Finds Her Voice* (Cambridge, Mass.: TidePool, 2011); and Ivana Lowell, *Why Not Say What Happened?: A Memoir* (New York: Knopf, 2010).

83. "Young Soldiers," *Outlook* 59 (July 30, 1898): 801–02; *New York Times*, April 4, 1901, May 1 and July 2, 1967, February 8, 1969, September 10, 1979, November 18, 1982, March 11, 2007; "The Knickerbocker Greys," accessed January 2, 2012, www.knickerbockergreys.org/The_Knickerbocker_Greys/History.html; and *The Knickerbocker Greys: A Private Drill Class for Boys* (New York: n.p., 1961), unpaginated.

84. "Adam Clayton Powell III, Socialite Wife, Honeymoon in Russia," *Jet* 36 (June 19, 1969): 42–43; *Chicago Tribune*, April 8, 1963; *New York Times*, April 26, May 31, and December 2, 1969, December 5, 1970, February 17, 1971, December 9, 1972, April 7, 1973, October 31, 1977, February 2, 1980, October 19, 1984; *Baltimore Afro American*, January 23, 1971; Social Register Association, *Social Register, New York, 1969* (New York: Social Register Association, 1968), 769; Social Register Association, *Social Register, New York, 1970* (New York: Social Register Association, 1969), 769; Social Register Association, *Social Register, New York, 1972* (New York: Social Register Association, 1971), 671, 765; Social Register Association, *Social Register, New York, 1974* (New York: Social Register Association, 1973), 1066–72; and Social Register Association, *Social Register, New York, 2004* (New York: Social Register Association, 2003), 2–20.

85. *New York Times*, October 25, 1984, February 1 and 2 and April 5, 1987, February 24 and June 21, 1988, July 27, 28, and 29, 1989, April 27, 2010; and Century Association, *The Century Yearbook 2000* (New York: Century Association, c. 2000), 39–258.

86. New York University, *Financial Report 1965–1966*. Duplicate Presidential and Financial Annual Report, 1950–1973. RG 3, Box 1, Folder 2, New York University Archives, Bobst Library, New York University, New York, N.Y. [hereafter NYU]; *Columbia University*

Directory, 1965–1966 (New York: n.p., 1965), iii; *Who's Who in America, 1964–1965,* 33rd ed. (Chicago: Marquis, 1964); *National Cyclopædia of American Biography,* vol. 29 (New York: White, 1941), 257–58; *National Cyclopædia of American Biography,* vol. 55 (Clifton, N.J.: White, 1974), 471; *National Cyclopædia of American Biography,* vol. G (New York: White, 1946), 197–98; *National Cyclopædia of American Biography,* vol. H (New York: White, 1952), 173; *National Cyclopædia of American Biography,* vol. J (New York: White, 1964), 588–89; and *National Cyclopædia of American Biography,* vol. M (Clifton, N.J.: White, 1978), 138–39, 178.

87. These trends have continued: in 2000, there were ten Jews, three women, two Asian Americans, and a Puerto Rican among the twenty-three Columbia trustees. *Columbia University Directory, 1980–81* (New York: n.p., 1980), iii; New York University, *Annual Report 1980–81* (New York: n.p., 1980), Annual Reports (Brademas) 1980–85, 1981–87. RG 3, Box 1, Folder 2. NYU; *Who's Who in America, 1974–1975,* 38th ed., vol. 2 (Chicago: Marquis, 1974); *Who's Who in America, 1980–1981,* 41st ed., vol. 1 (Chicago: Marquis, 1980); *Who's Who in America, 1980–1981,* 41st ed., vol. 2 (Chicago: Marquis' Who's Who, 1980); , *Who's Who in America, 1988–89,* 45th ed., vol. 2 (Chicago: Marquis' Who's Who, 1988); *Who's Who in America, 1990–91,* 46th ed., vol. 1 (Wilmette, IL: Marquis' Who's Who, 1990); *Who's Who Among African Americans, 1996/97,* 9th ed. (New York: Gale Research, 1996); *New York Times,* September 2, 1987, August 4, 1990, October 19, 2002; *Columbia University Officer and Staff Directory, 2000–2001* (New York: n.p., c. 2000), iii–iv.

88. *The Handbook of Private Schools: An Annual Descriptive Survey of Independent Education,* 54th ed. (Boston: Porter Sargent, 1973), 456.

89. Foxcroft had particularly strong ties to New York City that made the school part of the orbit of New York elites. From 1946 through 1949 fully half of its trustees were residents of the New York metropolitan region: Clarence Dillon, senior partner of the Wall Street banking firm of Dillon, Read & Company; Paul H. Nitze, a former vice president of Dillon, Read and a member of the New York foreign policy elite whose wife was the granddaughter of a founder of Standard Oil; Eleanor S. Todd, a leader of the New Jersey Republican party; and two alumnae from socially prominent families, one in New York City and the other in suburban New Jersey. *New York Times,* May 27, 1934, August 22, 1937, April 15, 1979, August 31, 1983, June 29, 1987, February 10, 1989, January 2, 1991; and Foxcroft Alumnae Association, *Gone Away* 13 (1947): 15.

90. "Ten Fashionable Boarding Schools for Girls," *Town & Country* 90 (April 1936): 106–11, 146, 150; Audrey Windsor Bergner, *Old Plantations and Historic Homes Around Middleburg, Virginia and the Families Who Lived and Loved Within Their Walls* (New York: Cornwall, 2001), 28, 44; Middleburg National Bank, *The Story of Middleburg, Virginia, 1787–1958* (Middleburg, Va.: Middleburg National Bank, 1958), 26–31; "Foxcroft's Accolade," *Time* 14 (December 9, 1929), accessed July 20, 2011, www.time.com /time/magazine/article/0,9171,738262,00.html; *New York Times,* December 9, 1979; and *Pittsburgh Post-Gazette,* August 8, 2010.

91. "Foxcroft's Accolade"; MFHA Hunt Map, Masters of the Foxhounds Association & Foundation, accessed July 25, 2011, http://www.mfha.org/hunts-map; Sophy Burnham, *The Landed Gentry* (New York: Putnam's, 1968), 52–61, 259, 267; Burnham, "Memoirs of a Foxcroft Girl," *Town & Country* 127 (June 1973): 80; Caspar W. Whitney, "Fox-Hunting in the United States," in *Hunt Clubs and Country Clubs in America* (Boston: n.p., 1928), 3–37; Alexander Mackay-Smith, *History of the Blue Ridge Hunt* ([Middleburg, Va.?]: n.p., [1958?]), 1–14; "A Cool Mellon," *Vanity Fair* 55 (April 1992): 189–96, 230–38; Paul Mellon, with John Baskett, *Reflections in a Silver Spoon: A Memoir* (New York: William Morrow, 1992), 81–82, 223–24, 227–69, 280–85; and *New York Times*, February 11 and May 19, 1961.

92. "The Prep School Guide: T&C Selects and Rates the Top Fifty," *Town & Country* 126 (August 1972): 55.

93. Kathryn Livingston, "The Foxcroft Girls Speak Out," *Town & Country* 127 (June 1973): 50.

94. Ibid., 50. Emphasis in the original.

95. Quoted in ibid., 52.

96. *The Handbook of Private Schools*, 54th ed., 457.

97. The leading destination in 2008 was the College of Charleston, which, like Denver and Rollins, has a reputation for being party schools. *Handbook of Private Schools: An Annual Descriptive Survey of Independent Education*, 90th ed. (Boston: Alloy Education, 2009), 537.

98. Livingston, "The Foxcroft Girls Speak Out," 51–52. See also "The Prep School Guide," 55; *Handbook of Private Schools*, 90th ed., 537; and "Foxcroft School Facts," accessed July 19, 2011, www.foxcroft.org/about/facts.

99. *Washington Post*, February 25, 2015.

100. Evelyn Janover Halpert, "Mr. Brearley's School," in *The First 125 Years*, 2–17; Evelyn Janover Halpert, "James Greenleaf Croswell," in *The First 125 Years*, 20–37.

101. Jean Goldschmidt Kempton, letter to the editor, *The Brearley Bulletin* 46 (Winter 1971): 14.

102. "To Our Readers," *The Brearley Bulletin* 55 (Fall 1979): 3; "The Present State of Brearley Mathematics," *The Brearley Bulletin* 65 (Spring 1980): 6–7; "Reader Forum: Can Today's Woman Have It All? Balancing the Demands of Career and Family," *The Brearley Bulletin* 68 (Winter 1993): 22–23; "Focus Day 1994: A Special Brearley Self-Government Association Program," *The Brearley Bulletin* 69 (April 1994): 12–13; *Brearley School Catalog 1975–1976* (New York: n.p., 1975), 21–23, Box 5, School Catalogs, 1962/63–1984/85, R. G. Publications, Brearley School Archives, Brearley School Library, New York, N.Y. [hereafter BSA]; *Brearley School Catalog 1984–1985* (New York: n.p., 1984), 19–23, Box 5, School Catalogs, 1962/63–1984/85, R. G. Publications, BSA; Lisa Downing, "A Special Kind of Homecoming," *The Brearley Bulletin* 74 (Spring 2000): 18–19; and Cherise Davis Grant, "Portrait of a Brearley Girl: Cecile Miller Eistrup '58: The School's First Alumna of Color," *The Brearley Bulletin* 74 (Spring 2000): 20–21. See also *New York Times*, March 2 and June 29, 1969, April 7, 1968,

September 5, 1971, December 2, 1979, June 15, 1987, October 26, 1988; and Charlotte Johnson Noerdlinger, *And Cheer for the Green and Gold: An Anecdotal History of the Chapin School* (New York: n.p., 2000): 132–33.

103. Burden, *Dead End Gene Pool*, 10–12; Pell, *We Used to Own the Bronx*, 95–106; Houghton, *Pitch Uncertain*, 5–14, 36–38.

104. Jane Michaels, "A Law Career: The Road to Prestige, Riches & Power: Should Your Daughter Go to Law School?," *Town & Country* 133 (August 1979): 67–68, 152–53. A number of *Town & Country* articles dealt with upper-class girls and women, and the magazine paid close attention to the changes that were happening in the gendering of the family, socializing, education, and work. See Ted Burke, "The New Sexy Ivy League: Coed Yalies & Tigers," *Town & Country* 123 (August 1969): 43, 108, 114; Suzanne Wilding, "Wealthy Working Women (What Are They After?)," *Town & Country* 132 (January 1978): 92–95; and Barbara King, "Marriage at the Top," *Town & Country* 132 (June 1978): 75.

105. Wilding, "Wealthy Working Women," 92.

106. Wyatt, "Boredom: The Year of the Yawn," 86–87; and King, "Marriage at the Top," 75.

107. Manuscript census, 1930 Federal census, State of New Jersey, Passaic County, Clifton City, 3rd ward: 36, Ancestry.com, accessed August 3, 2011, http://search .ancestrylibrary.com/iexec?htx=View&r=5542&dbid=6224&iid=NJT626 _1376-0435&fn=John+E&ln=Zacharias&st=r&ssrc=&pid=21063280; Manuscript census, 1930 Federal Census, State of New Jersey, Hudson County, West Hoboken: 4A; *The Nassau Herald: A Record of the Class of Nineteen Hundred and Thirty-Six of Princeton University* (Princeton: n.p. 1936), 555; and "John E. Zacharias, '36," *Princeton Alumni Weekly*, July 18, 2007, accessed August 2, 2011, http://paw.princeton.edu /memorials/3/18/index.xml.

108. Sixty-three percent were Episcopalian or Presbyterian, compared with only 71 Catholics (10 percent) and 11 Jews (1.6 percent). *The Freshman Herald: Class of Nineteen Hundred Thirty-Six* (Princeton: Department of Personnel, 1932), 27–255; "Confidential Report to the Committee on Admissions: The Quality of the Classes Admitted to Princeton in the Years 1928–1935," (Princeton: n.p., 1935), 3–8, Folder 2, Box 1, Series 1, Admissions Office Records, Seeley G. Mudd Manuscript Library, Princeton University, Princeton, N.J. (hereafter PU); "Analysis of the Freshman Class, September, 1922," (Princeton: n.p., 1922), 1–12, Folder 12, Box 3, Series 4, Admissions Office Records, PU.

109. *The Nassau Herald*, xxiii, 84; Wright, Constable & Skeen, "Firm History: The Constables," accessed August 2, 2011, www.wcslaw.com/about_history_constable.shtml; *Baltimore Sun*, January 29, 2002; and *Daily Princetonian*, February 24, 1936.

110. *Daily Princetonian*, February 27, 1934, November 30, 1939, February 9 and 10, 1940,

111. *Daily Princetonian*, February 27, 1934; "John E. Zacharias, '36"; search of *Daily Princetonian* database for "Zacharias" and "Constable" from August 1932 to June 1936, accessed January 20, 2013, http://libserv23.princeton.edu/princetonperiodicals/cgi-bin /princetonperiodicals?a=q&hs=1&r=1&results=1&dafdq=&dafmq=&dafyq=&datdq

=&datmq=&datyq=&deq=&puq=&tyq=&wofq=&wotq=&yeq=&txf=IN&
txq=&e=————-en-20—1—txt-IN——-; *Putnam County Courier*, June 6, 1946;
U.S. World War II Draft Registration Card, for Peter Albert Eckes, Serial no.
771, 1942, Ancestry.com, accessed August 3, 2011, http://search.ancestrylibrary.com
/iexec?htx=View&r=5542&dbid=1002&iid=2wwii_2371235–1942&fn=Peter
+Albert&ln=Eckes&st=r&ssrc=&pid=7479463; Passenger manifest, Pan American
Airways Flight 131/22, from Bermuda to La Guardia Airport, September 23, 1948,
Ancestry.com, accessed August 2, 2011, http://search.ancestrylibrary.com/iexec?htx
=View&r=5542&dbid=7488&iid=NYT715_7657-0957&fn=Muriel&ln
=Zacharius&st=r&ssrc=&pid=3023972539; *Bridgeport Post*, November 15, 1973 and
May 16, 1974.

112. Louise Parent, quoted in "Women We Love: Louise Parent," *DiversityInc Maga-zine* (May 2010): 33, accessed January 21, 2013, http://diversityinc.com/article/7807 /Louise-Parent-Breaking-Gender-Barriers-for-Women-in-Law.

113. Princeton University, Department of Public Information, press release, April 17, 1972, Folder 1, Box 1, Series 1, Admissions Office Records, PU; *The Freshman Herald, Class of 1976* (Princeton University: n.p., 1972), 89–95; Untitled document. C. 1947, Folder 2, Box 1, Series 1, Admissions Office Records, PU.

114. "Interviews: Shelby Cullom Davis, '30," *Daily Princetonian*, October 4, 1974; T. Harding Jones, "Opinion: The Importance of Seeking Conservatives," *Daily Princetonian*, May 29, 1974; Paul Mogin, "Opinion: Affirmative Action," *Daily Princetonian*, March 12, 1975; Sonia Sotomayor, "Opinion: Anti-Latino Discrimination at Princeton," *Daily Princetonian*, May 10, 1974; Paul Horowitz to the chairman, *Daily Princetonian*, April 14, 1975; Ken Foote to the chairman, *Daily Princetonian*, April 13, 1976; and *Daily Princetonian*, October 16, 1973, February 20 and April 29, 1976.

115. Sonia Sotomayor, *My Beloved World* (New York: Knopf, 2013), 145.

116. Ibid., 135. See also *Daily Princetonian*, March 1, 1976.

117. *New York Times*, September 28, 1990, January 29, 1995, May 16, 1999; Joshua B. Bolten to the chairman, *Daily Princetonian*, February 6, 1976; Thomas S. Bunn III to the chairman, *Daily Princetonian*, February 13, 1976; *Daily Princetonian*, February 8 and 12, 1973, July 25, 1974 (Special Class of 1978 Issue), February 14 and 17, 1975, February 3, 6, and 13, 1976; and Frederic C. Rich, *The First Hundred Years of the Ivy Club, 1879–1979* (Princeton, N.J.: Ivy Club, 1979), 233–61.

118. *Daily Princetonian*, May 30, 1951, October 16, 1974, May 14, 1975; *New York Times*, April 7 and June 23, 1985, February 8, 1990, November 13, 1994, September 14, 1997, October 8, 2002; and "G. Cheston Carey, '51," *Princeton Alumni Weekly*, March 20, 1996, accessed February 9, 2013, http://paw.princeton.edu/memorials/55/68/index.xml.

119. Social Register Association, *Social Register, 1986* (New York: Social Register Associ-ation, 1985), 501; Social Register Association, *Social Register, 1988* (New York: Social Register Association, 1987), 939, 998; Social Register Association, *Social Register, 1990* (New York: Social Register Association, 1989), 910; Social Register Association, *Social Register, 2013* (New York: Social Register Association, 2012), 887.

120. Quoted in Steven Levy, "Getting In," *New York Magazine* 13 (June 30, 1980): 23.

121. Ibid., 23–24.

122. *New York Times*, April 7 and June 23, 1985.

123. *New York Tribune*, May 3, 1903, January 3, 1904; *New York Times*, May 4, 1902; "Town & Country Life," *Town and Country*, 52 (June 14, 1902): 29–35; and "Town & Country Life," *Town and Country*, 52 (June 21, 1902): 22–25.

124. *New York Tribune*, May 3, 1903; *New York Times*, May 4, 1902; and "Town and Country Life," *Town & Country* 52 (June 14, 1902): 29–34.

125. *New York Times*, May 3, 13, 15, and 18, 1947, May 9, 23, and 30, and June 6 and 12, 1948, March 5, 14, 26, and April 7, 1949.

126. *New York Times*, March 3 and April 7, 1949.

127. William R. Taylor, *Cavalier and Yankee: The Old South and American National Character*, 2nd ed. (New York: Oxford University Press, 1993), 15–33.

128. *New York Times*, April 19, 1981.

129. *New York Times*, March 9, 1975.

130. *New York Times*, February 6, 1983.

131. *New York Times*, May 8, 1983.

132. For engagement and wedding announcements in one local paper that served a wealthy suburb, see *Rye Chronicle*, April 23, 1970, May 10, 1973, January 10 and May 2, 1974, January 30, June 19, and September 11, 1975. See also Brooks, *Bobos in Paradise*, 14

133. *New York Times*, June 24, 1983, June 9 and 16, 1985. Significantly, professional and business qualifications now equaled or trumped social qualifications even when it came to blue bloods. When Natalie du Pont wed Frank R. Lyon III in 1974, the *New York Times* communicated the illustrious lineage of the bride by describing her as the granddaughter of a former chairman of the board and president of E.I. du Pont De Nemours & Company and by reporting that the ceremony had occurred at the Long Island estate of her family. Yet it also stressed the position of her father-in-law as "a vice president and director of the Union Carbide Corporation" and that of her husband as "a corporate insurance broker with Marsh & McLennan in New York." *New York Times*, August 26, 1973. Frank and Natalie Lyons seamlessly fused social, educational, business, and financial credentials. BK International Insurance Brokers, profile of Frank R. Lyon, accessed June 26, 2011, www.bkiib.com/Execs/FRL.html. *New York Times*, February 22, 1980, August 31, 2008. "Trustee Frank Lyon '71 and Natalie Lyon Make Major Gift to Support the Elon Academy," *E-News*, March 13, 2008, accessed June 26, 2011, www.elon.edu/e-net/Note.aspx?id=927813. For the Lyons' engagement notice, see *New York Times*, April 8, 1973. For the engagement and wedding announcements in the *Rye Chronicle*, see April 12 and August 30, 1973. Natalie du Pont herself was identified as having graduated from Oldfields School in Glencoe, Md., as having debuted in 1971, and as attending Wheaton College.

134. *New York Times*, March 28, 1976, April 30, 1978, November 4, 1979.

135. *New York Times*, March 28, 1976, September 12 and October 22, 1979. The importance of social diversity to the antielitist elite is also evident from the *New York Times* wedding page. Once a bastion of white Protestants and a trifling number of Jews and Catholics, it did not run its first photograph of an African American bride until 1954. In the 1970s and 1980s, the presence of representative Asian Americans and African Americans became routinized, and in 2002 the *Times* began carrying announcements for same-sex couples. *New York Times*, May 29, 1983, August 18, 2002; and Steven Levy, "Getting In," *New York Magazine* 13 (June 30, 1980): 23–24.

136. *New York Times*, September 14, 1997; W. P. Carey, *2011 Annual Report* (New York: n.p., 2012), 2–5, 9–17; "Profiles: Executive Profile of Thomas E. Zacharias," *Bloomberg Businessweek*, accessed June 26, 2011, http://investing.businessweek.com/research /stocks/people/person.asp?personId=8923450&ticker=WPC:US; Yale School of Management Alumni Profiles, "Profile of Thomas E. Zacharias," accessed June 26, 2011, http://mba.yale.edu/alumni/alumni_profiles/zachariast.shtml; "Profile of Thomas E. Zacharias," Forbes.com, accessed August 5, 2011, http://people.forbes .com/profile/thomas-e-zacharias/87234; and W. P. Carey & Company, press release, "Corporate Property Associates 15 Appoints Thomas E. Zacharias Chief Operating Officer," April 6, 2005, accessed January 21, 2013, www.sec.gov/Archives/edgar /data/1138301/000095012305004155/y07591dexv99w1.txt.

137. Thomas E. Zacharias, comment posted on January 12, 2011, on *Yale Insights: The Yale School of Management's Look at Global Business*, a discussion featuring Dean Joel M. Podolny and Professor Rakesh Khurana about "Can We Make Management a Profession?," April 2007, accessed January 18, 2013, http://qn.som.yale.edu/content /can-we-make-management-profession.

138. *New York Times*, November 13, 1994, October 8, 2002; *New York Social Diary*, entries for June 3, 2003, October 15, 2003, June 3, July 10 and 15, 2008, January 5 and March 15, 2009, January 4, 2010, accessed June 26, 2011, www.newyorksocialdiary.com/nysd /search; "Notes from Southampton," *Southampton Village Crier*, September 16, 2010, accessed August 5, 2011, www.27east.com/news/article.cfm/Southampton/301085 /Notes-from-Southampton-September–16; and *Who's Who in America, 2003*, 57th ed., vol. 2 (New Providence, N.J.: Marquis, 2002), 5841.

139. "John E. Zacharias, '36"; *New York Times*, May 16, 1999; *Daily Princetonian*, April 16, May 7, and October 4, 2010, January 11 and February 7, 2011; Profile of Clelia Zacharias in Princeton University blog "Signac: A Passionate Sailor," c. 2004–05, accessed June 26, 2011, http://blogs.princeton.edu/wri152-3/czachari/archives/001630.html; Alp Invest, News and Publications, accessed August 4, 2011, www.alpinvest.com /leadership/index.asp?viewType=ByRegion&d_Bio_ID=137&Section=7,2,0; "Groton Alums Earn Athletic Distinction," Groton School, accessed August 5, 2011, www.groton.org/contentPage.aspx?pageId=45281&sectionId=403; 2010–2011 Roster of Men's Heavyweight Crew, Princeton University, accessed August 5, 2011,

www.goprincetontigers.com/SportSelect.dbml?SPSID=46844&SPID=4259&DB_
LANG=C&DB_OEM_ID=10600&Q_SEASON=2010; Princeton University, *The
Two Hundred Sixty-Fourth Commencement, May 31, 2011* (Princeton: n.p. 2011), 19, 27;
Profile of John L. Zacharias, BrightScope.com, n.d, accessed January 21, 2013, www
.brightscope.com/financial-planning/advisor/590090/John-L-Zacharias; and Rich,
The First Hundred Years of the Ivy Club, 233–61.

140. Louis Auchincloss, *A Voice from Old New York: A Memoir of My Youth* (Boston:
Houghton Mifflin Harcourt, 2010), 112. See also *New York Times*, January 28, 2010;
and *Washington Post*, January 28, 2010.

141. Auchincloss, *A Voice from Old New York*, 63.

142. Christine Pittel, "Kindergarten Madness," *Town & Country* 154 (November 2000):
244–46.

143. Victoria Goldman, *The Manhattan Directory of Private Nursery Schools*, 6th ed.
(New York: Soho, 2007); Goldman, *The Manhattan Family Guide to Private Schools
and Selective Public Schools*, 6th ed. (New York: Soho, 2010); *New York Times*, July
6 and October 22, 2003, November 14, 2008, July 25, 2010, June 7, 2011, January 27
and April 13, 2012, September 19, 2013; *Wall Street Journal*, September 19, 2013; Kathy
Gogick, "The Price of Admission," *Town & Country* 154 (July 2000): 131; Ben Gose,
"Counselors for Hire," *Town & Country* 154 (July 2000): 128; Joe Queenan, "Getting
Testy," *Town & Country* 158 (November 2004): 240, 242; and Fred Bartels, "Our 1%
Problem: Independent Schools and the Income Gap," *Independent School Magazine*
72 (Fall 2012): n.p.

144. Jerome Karabel, *The Chosen: The Hidden History of Admission and Exclusion at Harvard, Yale, and Princeton* (Boston: Houghton Mifflin, 2005), 536–57. See also Harold S.
Wechsler, *The Qualified Student: A History of Selective College Admission in America*
(New York: Wiley, 1977), vii–xii, 237–58; and Caroline M. Hoxby and Christopher
Avery, *The Missing "One-Offs": The Hidden Supply of High-Achieving, Low Income Students*, NBER Working Paper 18586 (Cambridge, Mass.: National Bureau of Economic Research, 2013), 1–7. An examination of the *Nassau Herald 2008*, the year that
Clelia D. Zacharias graduated, shows that similar demographic changes happened
at Princeton. Princeton University, *Nassau Herald 2008* (Princeton: n.p., 2008), 4–5,
18–21, 154.

145. Karabel, *The Chosen*, 536.

146. Ibid., 536.

147. Ibid., 536–37.

148. Sean F. Reardon, "No Rich Child Left Behind," *New York Times*, April 27, 2013.

149. Ibid.; Sean F. Reardon, "The Widening Academic Achievement Gap Between the
Rich and the Poor: New Evidence and Possible Explanations," in *Whither Opportu-
nity: Rising Inequality, Schools, and Children's Life Chances*, ed. Greg J. Duncan and
Richard J. Murnane (New York: Russell Sage Foundation, 2011), 91–116; Garey Ramey
and Valerie A. Ramey, "The Rug Rat Race," *Brookings Papers on Economic Activity*
(Spring 2010): 129–76; and Greg J. Duncan, Lars Bergman, Kathryn Duckworth,

Katja Kokko, Anna-Lisa Lyyra, Molly Metzger, Lea Pulkkinen, and Sharon Simonton, "The Role of Child Skills and Behaviors in the Intergenerational Transmission of Inequality: A Cross-National Study," n.d, accessed May 6, 2013, www.gse.uci.edu /faculty/profilebridge.php?faculty_id=5614.

150. Jonathan Heathcote, Fabrizio Perri, and Giovanni L. Violante, *Unequal We Stand: An Empirical Analysis of Economic Inequality in the United States, 1967–2006*, Federal Reserve Bank of Minneapolis Research Department Staff Report 436 (October 2009): 42, accessed January 15, 2012, www.minneapolisfed.org/research/sr/sr436.pdf. See also Timothy Noah, *The Great Divergence: America's Growing Inequality Crisis and What We Can Do About It* (New York: Bloomsbury, 2012), 1–9.

151. Edward N. Wolff, "Recent Trends in Household Wealth in the United States: Rising Debt and the Middle-Class Squeeze—An Update to 2007," Working Paper No. 589 (Annandale-on-Hudson, N.Y.: Levy Economics Institute of Bard College, March 2010), 35, 36, and table 3, accessed January 15, 2012, www.levyinstitute.org/pubs /wp_589.pdf.

152. Joseph E. Stiglitz, *The Price of Inequality: How Today's Divided Society Endangers Our Future* (New York: Norton, 2012), 3, 21.

153. Russ Alan Prince and Lewis Schiff, *The Middle-Class Millionaire: The Rise of the New Rich and How They Are Changing America* (New York: Doubleday, 2008).

154. *New York Times*, September 8, 2010, February 23, 2011, March 11, 2015.

155. Peter Hellman, "The Big Boom in Co-Op Apartments," *New York* 10 (May 2, 1977): 39–41; Peter Hellman, "That's Incredible! Those Co-Op Prices," *New York* 14 (April 20, 1981): 26–30; Ralph Gardner Jr., "Class Struggle on Park Avenue," *New York* 32 (June 14, 1999): 22–29; Michael J. McDermott, "Westchester: Best of City and Country Life," *Crain's New York Business* 4 (November 14, 1988): 23; Cara S. Trager, "L.I.: Hard Commute, High Quality of Life," *Crain's New York Business* 4 (November 14, 1988): 21; Gisela Moriarty, "Luxury Homes in Counties Catching Fire," *Crain's New York Business* 12 (August 19, 1996): 24; *New York Times*, October 27, 1996; and Amanda Fung, "High Times for High-End Hampton Homes," *Crain's New York Business* (October 27, 2011), accessed January 15, 2013, www.crainsnewyork.com/article/20111027 /REAL_ESTATE/111029909.

156. Ruth Rejnis, "The Great New York Brownstone Bargains," *New York* 10 (September 26, 1977): 36–39; Barbara Phillips, "Living It Up in Lower Manhattan," *New York* 14 (November 9, 1981): 43–46; Daniel Shaw, "Tribeca," *New York* 20 (May 4, 1987): 96–98; "Hot Spots," *New York* 22 (December 25, 1989–January 1, 1990): 37–41; Eric Pooley, "South-ward-ho: Moving on Down to New Spaces and Places," *New York* 22 (December 25, 1989–January 1, 1990): 82–87; Joyce Gold, "Tribeca," in Jackson, *Encyclopedia of New York City*, 1333; Joyce Gold, "SoHo," in Jackson, *Encyclopedia of New York City*, 1202–03; and Hilda Regier, "Chelsea (i)," in Jackson, *Encyclopedia of New York City*, 234–35.

157. Suleiman Osman, *The Invention of Brownstone Brooklyn: Gentrification and the Search for Authenticity in Postwar New York* (New York: Oxford University Press, 2011), 3–16.

See also "SoHo Loft," *Architectural Digest* 31 (March/April 1974): 91–97; and Marc Kristol, "Raising the Barn," *Dwell* 8 (April 1, 2008): 132.

158. Ylonda Gault, "Health Clubs Reshape Strategy to Boost Profit," *Crain's New York Business* 7 (August 26, 1991): 4; Ylonda Gault, "Survival of the Fittest Among Health Clubs," *Crain's New York Business* 10 (May 9, 1994): 3, 41; and Gault, "Fitness Chains Bulk Up in the City," *Crain's New York Business* 12 (February 26, 1996): 30–31.

159. Phyllis Furman, "Let 'Em Wear Alligator: Shoe Sellers Push Posh," *Crain's New York Business* 4 (October 10, 1988): 3, 37; Furman, "Beau Brummel Looking for More Dandy Spots," *Crain's New York Business* 4 (October 17, 1988): 7; Linda Dyett, "Bespeaking of Suits: Trading Up to Custom," *New York* 21 (February 15, 1988): 52–57; "How Much Things Cost," *New York* 20 (September 7, 1987): 36.

160. Susan Aurelia Gitelson Diary, vol. 3, October 1982–May 1984, entry for March 29, 1983, Box 23, Gitelson Family Papers, MS–178, Jacob Rader Marcus Center of the American Jewish Archives, Cincinnati, Ohio [hereafter AJA].

161. *Manhattan White Pages, 1987–1988* (New York: NYNEX, 1987), 608; and Social Register Association, *Social Register, 1989* (New York: Social Register Association, 1988), 322.

162. Gitelson Diary, vol. 3, entry for September 3, 1983, Box 23, AJA.

163. Gitelson Diary, vol. 4, June 1984–November 1984, entry for September 9, 1984, Box 23, AJA.

164. Gitelson Diary, vol. 22, June 1998–December 1999 [*sic*]. Entry for January 7, 2000, Box 24, AJA.

165. Gitelson Diary, vol. 4, June 1984–November 1984, entry for September 9, 1984, Box 23, AJA; Gitelson Diary, vol. 6, May 1985–February 1986, entries for January 2 and 25, 1986, Box 23; Gitelson Diary, vol. 13, December 1989–November 1990, entry for December 25, 1989, Box 24, AJA; Gitelson Diary, vol. 19, October 1995–July 1996, entries for October 15, 1995 and December 16, 1995, Box 24, AJA; and Bio of Dr. Susan A. Gitelson, Board of Advisers, National Committee on American Foreign Policy, accessed January 14, 2013, http://ncafp.org/2011/experts/dr-susan-aurelia-gitelson.

166. Cynthia Rigg, "Dean & DeLuca: Tops in Culinary Class," *Crain's New York Business* 5 (July 3, 1989): 3, 21; Mimi Sheraton, "A Matter of Taste," *New York* 8 (November 17, 1975): 58–67; Mimi Sheraton, "The Posh Food Guide," *New York* 6 (October 22, 1973): 60–70; and "Un-decorated Look for Darien," *Architectural Digest* 30 (November /December 1973): 34.

167. By contrast, annual membership fees were reportedly $5,000 at the Metropolitan Club and the Union Club and $2,000 at the Century Association. Antonina Jedrzejczak, "New York City's Top Members-Only Clubs for Elite Power Players," *Businessinsider.com*, April 23, 2010, accessed January 16, 2013, www.businessinsider .com/members-only-clubs-2010-4?op=1.

168. Mark Van De Walle, "The Core Club NYC," *Departures* (September 2011), accessed November 23, 2011, www.departures.com/articles/the-core-club-nyc; *New York Times*, August 28, 2005, June 17, 2011; Hitha Prabhakar, "Elite Membership Clubs

Get a Makeover," *Forbes.com*, May 9, 2007, accessed November 23, 2011, www.forbes
.com/2007/05/08/men-clubs-private-forbeslife-cx_hp_07networks_0509clubs.html;
and "The 10 Best Private Clubs," Worth.com, accessed January 16, 2013, www.worth
.com/index.php/component/content/article/911.

169. Quoted in Van De Walle, "The Core Club NYC."

170. *New York Post*, January 18, 2009; Prabhakar, "Elite Membership Clubs Get a Make-
over," 1; "Soho House New York," accessed January 16, 2013, www.sohohouseny.com;
"Norwood Club—House," accessed January 16, 2013, www.norwoodclub.com; and
"The 10 Best Private Clubs."

171. For luxury accommodations and the segregation of the classes in earlier U.S. sports
arenas, see Chad Seifried and Donna Pastore, "The Temporary Home: Analyzing
Baseball Facilities in the United States Pre-1903," *Journal of Sport History* 37 (Sum-
mer 2010): 401–26; and Chad Seifried, "The Evolution of Professional Baseball and
Football Structures in the United States, 1850 to the Present: Toward an Ideal Type,"
Sport History Review 41 (May 2010): 50–80.

172. *New Orleans Times-Picayune*, April 9 and 10, 1965; *New York Times*, December 6, 1964,
April 4, 1965, May 29 and November 15, 1966; Robert C. Trumpbour, *The New Cathedrals:
Politics and Media in the History of Stadium Construction* (Syracuse: Syracuse University Press, 2007), 23–24; and Worth.com, accessed May 30, 2013, www.measuringworth
.com/uscompare/relativevalue.php. I made this calculation on the basis of the standard of living.

173. *New York Times*, June 22, 1972, March 7 and October 20, 1976, June 15, 1983,
April 14, 1986; *Washington Post*, June 23, 1972, May 21, 1995, August 9, 1996; *Los
Angeles Times*, July 2, 1966 and October 23, 1973; Peter Titlebaum and Heather
Lawrence, "The Reinvention of the Luxury Suite in North America," *Journal of
Sponsorship* 4 (March 2011): 124–36; "Beyond the Mini-Burger," *Crain's New York
Business* 23 (July 23, 2007): 19; and Seifried, "Evolution of Professional Baseball
and Football Structures in the United States," 69–71. Seifried's total of 344 luxury suites added in the New York region from 1992 to 2012 includes those at Citi
Field, new Yankee Stadium, and MetLife Stadium. To that total, I added those
at Madison Square Garden and at the Barclay Center. "Barclay Center Suites,"
accessed May 31, 2013, www.nba.com/nets/brooklyn/brooklyn_premium_tickets.
html; and *New York Post*, April 26, 2013. My estimate of the total number of luxury boxes in the New York region pertains only to arenas of major league baseball, the National Football League, the National Basketball Association, and the
National Hockey League. There are also luxury boxes at minor league baseball,
professional soccer, tennis, and other stadiums in the region, but I excluded them
from my estimate.

174. *New York Times*, October 7 and November 29, 2008, January 14 and March 8, 2009;
Wall Street Journal, March 6, 2009; author's interview with Katherine Berlin, Geneva,
N.Y., February 5, 2013; "Yankees Premium: Luxury Suites," accessed May 31, 2013,
http://newyork.yankees.mlb.com/nyy/ticketing/suites_luxury_suites.jsp; "Yankee

Stadium Luxury Suite Tour," uploaded September 16, 2009, YouTube, accessed May 31, 2013, www.youtube.com/watch?v=-bvjezou—0.

175. Providence College Silent Auction, 2014, accessed June 14, 2015, http://alumni .providence.edu/s/1226/social.aspx?pgid=2390&gid=1; Wright Thompson, "Seats of Gold: Yankee Stadium's Legends Suite Was Sparsely Populated at Times This Season—A Sign of What Greed Does to Loyalty," ESPN.com, accessed June 13, 2015, http://sports.espn.go.com/espn/eticket/story?page=091005yankeetickets; and Junior Achievement of New York, Annual Awards Dinner, Tuesday, November 18, 2014, Live Auction of Four VIP Yankees vs. Boston Red Sox Legends Suite Experience—August 4th, 2015, accessed June 13, 2015, www.501auctions.com/janewyork /item/84422.

176. *New York Times*, June 16 and July 30, 1989.

177. Quoted in *New York Times*, July 30, 1989.

178. Quoted in *New York Times*, July 30, 1989; and Manhattan White Pages, 1987–1988, 1343.

CONCLUSION

1. Justin Hudson, "The Brick Tower," June 2010, 2, *New York Times* website, accessed June 26, 2011, www.nytimes.com/packages/pdf/speech.pdf. See also Christopher Hayes, *Twilight of the Elites: America After Meritocracy* (New York: Crown, 2012), 31–34.

2. Hudson, "The Brick Tower," 2.

3. Katharine Davis Fishman, "The Joyful Elite," *New York* 15 (January 18, 1982): 43–48. Hunter College Campus Schools Notable Alumnae/i, accessed July 11, 2015, www .hunterschools.org/notable-alumni.

4. *New York Times*, August 4, 2010. Admissions, General Information and Admissions Procedures, Hunter Elementary School website, accessed August 10, 2011, http:// hces.hunter.cuny.edu/?m1=1&m2=0; Admissions, Hunter College High School website, accessed August 10, 2011, www.hchs.hunter.cuny.edu/index.php/admissions.

5. *New York Times*, August 4, 2010.

6. Hudson, "Brick Tower," 2–3.

7. Ibid., 3.

8. Ibid., 3. See also Joseph F. Kett, *Merit: The History of a Founding Ideal from the American Revolution to the 21st Century* (Ithaca, N.Y.: Cornell University Press, 2013): 1–14, 222–62.

9. Hudson, "Brick Tower," 4.

10. Quoted in *New York Times*, August 4, 2010.

11. Ibid. This observation was based on interviews with high school students and faculty.

12. Alex Lieu, comment posted August 29, 2010, in "Featured, Hunter News, Our Community," *The Hunter Eclectic*, accessed June 26, 2011, www.huntereclectic.com.

13. Tom, comment, August 5, 2010, on "Diversity Debate Convulses High School," *New York Times* website, accessed August 10, 2010, http://community.nytimes.com /comments/www.nytimes.com/2010/08/05/nyregion/05hunter.html; elitewillie, comment, August 5, 2010, on "Diversity Debate."

14. A. smith, comment, August 5, 2010, on "Diversity Debate," DoseOfReality, August 5, 2010, on "Diversity Debate."

15. *New York Times*, October 10 and 29 and November 13, 2011, November 6, 2013.

INDEX

. . . .

Figures are indicated by italicized page numbers.

CPSIA information can be obtained
at www.ICGtesting.com
Printed in the USA
LVOW10*2029230217
525192LV00002B/2/P